Portrait of a Seeker: Born to Wonder

Idealism, Destiny, Living Internationally and my Search for Meaning

an autobiography

David W. Weimer

One and Only Press

Preface

It is rare I see a book, film, or architecture and recognize that the creator did exactly what they wanted. Editors, producers, and contractors, they all add their lines, delete scenes, and change columns to make the piece conform to some other vision. Whether self-financed, by deception or persuasion, I smile when I see the artist who has slipped through the bars of convention and created something wholly unique.

David Weimer's *Portrait of a Seeker: Born to Wonder* is like his life – a singular expression of dream and daring. The perspective is that of a man resting momentarily at a station along the way, sipping a coffee before boarding the next train, his eye drifting through the memories of his life.

For you, the reader, what is to be gained? If nothing else (and nothing else is really needed), the knowledge that you, too, can do as others have done. Dream, create, discover and live something wholly unique. Your individual key to completeness is crafted through the actions in your life and reflection upon them; realizing in the end that maybe you did nothing but play a part. As David concludes, "The lessons are in the events in our lives."

—Shawn Nevins

Portrait of a Seeker: Born to Wonder

Copyright © 2012 David W. Weimer. All rights reserved. No part of the book may be used or reproduced in any manner whatsoever without prior written permission from the author except in the case of brief quotations embodied in critical articles and reviews. For information address: *One and Only Press*, 368 High Street, Flushing, OH 43977

First Edition: 2012
Printed in the United States of America

Fonts: Numerous

Main entry under title: Portrait of a Seeker: Born to Wonder
Index included

1. Spirituality   2. Philosophy   3. Autobiography

ISBN: 978-0-9850578-0-0

Cover art: (*Front*) portrait painted by Andrée Weimer based on a photo (*Back*) of the author in St. Médard sur Ille, Brittany, France, June 2010. See frenchfineart.wordpress.com.

Visit the author's blogs:
www.oneandonlyobserver.blogspot.com
or www.oneandonlyobserver.wordpress.com

Dedication

For my wife and children.

For those who helped me make this book.

For *you*, who are about to read this.

Portrait of a Seeker

Foreword 10

There and Back Again—Flushing, Ohio, 2010 15
    NUANCED TRAVELER 16

Introduction 24

Timeline — A brief history of Me 31

Chapter 1 — Staring at Water 36
    "MY WAY" 40
    "TURNING POINT" 41
    HOME IS WHERE THE HEART IS 64

Chapter 2 — Crossroads 69

Chapter 3 —Making a Person (…) 78

Chapter 4 — Becoming a writer 119

**Relativity Speaking
by David Weimer** 119
    FLUSHING, OHIO 130
    FOWLERVILLE, MICHIGAN 131
    SUN-DAMAGED 135

Strawman, starman 142
    "PLACES I HAVE LIVED" 146

Chapter 5 — Three Months in Isolation 155

Chapter 6 — Communi[cati]on 176
    OUR WEDDING STORY 181
    HERE THERE BE DRAGONS 197
    CORRESPONDENCES 197

Chapter 7 —Job-ed 233

Chapter 8 —A Taste of Space 242
    A WORD ON HEAVINESS 243

Chapter 9 — God is Heavy..250

Chapter 10 — Words, Death, The End of Journal Writing, and Personal Wisdom. 262
    On Beginning Writing...265
    Celibacy..268

Chapter 11 — Say one thing...272

Chapter 12 — Back to the Woods and Beyond—An Effort, Some Years Ago, to Tell my Tale..274

Chapter 13 — Cosmic Cooking..281

Chapter 14 — Loose Ends..287

Chapter 15 — Picking Up the Hammer… Again......................................291
    Skating Dreams...300

Chapter 16 — Home..306
    'Fire places'..306

Chapter 17 — No Safety Net...311
    Retreat to the Present...316

Chapter 18 — Outlooks..320

Chapter 19 — Andrée and Me...342

Chapter 20 — Cosmically Egged (Really Something Else)....................354
    What happened?...355

Chapter 21 — Really Becoming a Writer...373
    Ohgod...375

Chapter 22 — The One and Only Skate Park Project and l'Association Dream Extreme [Toulouse, France, 2001-2002]..399

Chapter 23 — Two Ships..414

Chapter 24 — Groups and Individuals...422

Chapter 25 — In My Father's House, There are Many Rooms..............433
    A different reality..448

Chapter 26 — Such a Simple Thing..452

Chapter 27 — Our House..468

Chapter 28 — Dream Extreme, Southern France and The One and Only Skate Park Project..497

Chapter 29 —Coming Back Home..503
    BACK IN FRANCE..504

Chapter 30 —Being Back...515

Chapter 31 —Starting Over Again for the First Time.......................522

Chapter 32 —Final Message in a Bottle..528

Chapter 33—Eighteen-year Unwritten Arc.....................................546

Chapter 34—What We Actually Did and Where We Are Now........547

Photos 550

Recommended Reading..562

"Lance Missiles"..566

Foreword

Life comes in order, but is it orderly? I've painted my sandcastle in one eternal summer day, the surf whispering its commentary into my ears while I added turrets and moats, destroyed bridges, improved walls and changed my mind. I wrote this book about the meaning of my life.

I am an artist, standing with raised brush and tilted head in front of my portrait, adding another stroke to my signature. I have mixed paints, picked colors, followed feelings, left alone some things and painted over others. Now I am signing my name on the lower right-hand corner of this self-portrait: *Seeker*.

Some artists draw "studies" of the work they are going to feature on a canvas or ceiling, considering composition and changing things until settling on how they are going to begin. Other painters simply begin, following an impulse, adapting and improving as they work. Another type, *artist savant*, lays down, intact, what was already there; a seeming instrument for the eternal creation. I see aspects of these ways in my own painting method.

This book is my painting of me and the world as I see it. It is imperfect, contains errors and is boring at times. Just like me. I would like to make this book perfect. But I can't keep polishing a self-portrait of a continually changing self. That's a never-ending job. I want to do other things.

You may search for an orderly structure within the following pages. You may yearn for a chronological timeline or a developed context. You can find them; they're there.

A person's whole self, imbedded in the context of their *life-as-lived*, is impossible to hold within any frame; it would be a black canvas, every bit of its surface covered with pigment. The whole "me" is best undiluted, though incompletely described. I have created *this* work, at this time in my life, and have stopped adding paint because it's my soul, after all, and I don't want to cover it up completely.

Our lives stop at the end of our day. I wanted to say something before my sunset because I have witnessed other "books," unwritten and unread, falling into their graves, covered by dirt.

Here is a portrait of *my* fall.

~ **David Weimer, Flushing, Ohio, January 7, 2011.**

Me, 43, at a February 2011 philosophic "Rustic Retreat" I organized above Moundsville, WV.

This book is about the prodigal son who returns from afar and writes about his inner and outer journey. It's a book for me, about myself. My world is the only one I know, and it's been a long, strange trip. I think I would get something out of my story if I encountered it, if I were another me, living a separate yet-similar-feeling life. I don't know *what* I would 'get,' but I have the feeling I would. My outlook and world view has changed, and I have stayed… nowhere very long.

I've been surprised with the unexpected 'choices' I've made and where they have led me. I'm sure something remains of me, but I'm not sure what. It could be merely the remnants, a hollow shell of a former person surrounding a condition of being I prefer to call maturity. I'm sure this 'maturing' happens to everyone, wherever they are, because we're all going to make a journey, no matter how still and unchanging we try to remain. Life is going to take us from beginning to end and we have not much to say about it. We are a melting snowman. We can put our heels in the dirt and leave two furrows as long as our trip lasts, but either way, we're going to be processed by our living. So this is my story and some of what I have to say.

There are poems, both rhymed and prose, short stories, journal entries, correspondence, essays, scene descriptions, observations, photos and quotes. This is a non-fiction, fiction, finger painting overview of my footprints and snow angels. Maybe my kids will read this and understand some of it. Maybe they'll read it again later and relate to it a little more. Maybe another 'me' out there will read it and laugh, skip sections, shake his head or sometimes cry. Maybe you will read it, and be inspired to live *your own life* to its fullest and share your tale with others. I hope that happens.

This book has been growing in me as long as I've lived. It's about time to let it experience the world for itself—on someone's shelf, in someone's hands. I've heard that Michelangelo said, or maybe all sculptors say, that when you approach a block of stone or wood, you don't do anything except carve or chisel away all that *isn't* the object you know is there. I see a two-inch thick ream of paper with a label marked, "Portrait of a Seeker," by David W. Weimer. Do I cut away or fill in all the blank paper? Much of a printed page is blank space. If I fill the blankness with words, what shape will materialize? The answer is something like… *This*.

There and Back Again—Flushing, Ohio, 2010

I lived in Europe long enough to forget how it feels to be an American living in America, *right* about things, secure in my opinions, oblivious of anything outside of my immediate life pattern. From 1999 to 2003 my myopic American self faded to a small dot inside my memory residing in that same place as high school life, during the time I lived in Germany, then in France, beginning a family, learning languages and endeavoring to live by an idealistic dream.

In 2003, I was back, watching the New Year ball drop in New York on TV to celebrate the opening of that year. I found it boring compared to the exciting New Year's celebrations I'd had in Europe. I was back in my hometown of Fowlerville, Michigan after an absence of 18 years—I'd left three weeks after high school graduation to begin Army basic training at Fort Sill, Oklahoma. Since then, I'd lived a lifetime, maybe a few lifetimes, and now I was back, just like the nearly two decades since leaving had been a dream.

Coming back to America was a culture shock for me in more than the usual way. Nine-eleven happened while I was overseas and I returned to a place infused with paranoia, fear and self-righteous anger. A month after Andrée, my wife, two-year-old Guillaume, our son, and I arrived in my 'hometown,' I rented a moving truck in Lansing when our household goods arrived after their Atlantic crossing. I remember disbelievingly giving all ten fingerprints in order to rent the thing.

Here, in Flushing, Ohio, I've lived in the States long enough again for the immediacy of being a reverse immigrant to Europe to have faded. The memory of my time over there has turned golden in all the years since; my mind does that to the past: good times and bad are encased in sweet nostalgia.

My life and adventures in Europe feel to me like an important part of my life, a transformative time, as transformative as the time surrounding and following the death of my father. My dad drowned in 1985 when I was 18, while I was in Fort Sill after basic, awaiting AIT (advanced individualized training) in World War II barracks in Oklahoma. For ten solid years after that, he was a constant presence in my thoughts, coloring my daily feeling of living.

Memories I have of living in France and Germany are strong, but not traumatic like Dad's death. The living I did in Europe happened to an older me. My life was altered by every minute spent struggling to learn a new language, having, every day, to bend, bend, become more flexible and touch my cultural toes. My perspective was changed and my eyes opened to another way of seeing. It was another world and I am different now. I don't (consciously) think of my life over there, but the effects of my time there are profound and living abroad constantly informs my process of "living" here, in the States.

Everything I encounter that people around me do and say—echoing how American news sources describe foreign or domestic events—is seen through a lens I could not have had while living only here and nowhere else. Until I lived overseas, I did not label myself as an "American." I was *me*, not some nationalistic identity. I was introduced to my nationality while living in Germany. It was obvious that I wasn't German, so... While immersed in learning the German language and living in Stuttgart, I saw my 'right' thinking had been a product of where I had lived—previously. It is *right* to be polite to strangers; it is wrong to stand too close to people. These things were self-evident. They were also biases I had held without knowledge or question.

Leaving Fowlerville and the States for the first time on my own after graduating from high school to spend two years on an Army base in Erlensee, Germany, I was an untested kid basically. I was also reeling from our family tragedy. I was largely ignorant of any other way of viewing myself in the world, and the world itself, other than the one I had. I felt a *lot*. Feeling a lot is not the same as having a perspective or overview on oneself and one's... heritage. When I returned to Germany fourteen years later to live with Andrée in Stuttgart, I was an American who knew what he thought at least. I had one cancelled marriage and some experiences to my credit, but international awareness-wise, I was an infant.

I am able to see other places as valid because I've lived and breathed in other places. They are as real to me or more so than my hometown and thinking used to be to an 18-year-old me.

Nuanced traveler.

Growing up, my parents took us on vacation each summer for a few weeks to a different destination in the continental U.S. Our *Skamper* pop-up camper and Mercury Montego station wagon took us to the Rocky Mountains, Grand Canyon and Florida Everglades. Later, with a Dodge motor home bought with the proceeds of my mom's dog breeding business, we went to San Francisco, the Florida Keys and New York. By 18, I had been through much of the U.S.; I'd seen a lot of places as a visitor. Climbing rocks in the mountains, riding bikes on redwood forest trails—these moments stand out like distant peaks of memory above the thick obscuring clouds of time.

With my sister and brother, I was exposed to different people and places; my parents felt it would broaden our horizons and benefit us personally to know there was a wider world than rural Mid-Michigan. Like an American tourist visiting twenty countries in twenty minutes, I think I looked at the places and people we encountered from the *outside* while remaining inside my fish bowl of I-ness. I could hardly have done differently. The key is to *be* in someplace, without the fish bowl or pressure suit, *breathing* local air, *eating* local food, and learning to use the native's words.

The insights I gained from living outside the U.S., about myself and other humans, could also be had by traveling to another town in another U.S. state—to Memphis, Tennessee, for example, or to Pittsburgh or to Wheeling, West Virginia (all places I've moved to and lived in for years). While living in a succession of places in five states and seven cities, it wasn't until I moved abroad that I learned a new place for the first time. I *became* that place, inside of me. I also *became* German and French more than I became a Pittsburgher or Memphite. Probably because Europe was *so* foreign to me, it was easier to let go and accept a totally new place. It was easier to see this other place as different; I couldn't project my "known" overlay onto it, like I could in the States, assuming everyone I encountered had the same common background and reference points.

I've heard the quote, "When in Rome, do as the Romans," but to actually *do* it is quite something! How many people say those well-known words? *Probably Romans* would be my answer. How many people really live those words? *Probably immigrants to Rome*, I'd say. An orange is nothing like the words describing it. Of course, I'm only focusing on one dimension of an immigrant's journey. Going somewhere foreign and new is like starting a new job; you don't know anybody yet, you don't know what you're supposed to do or when to do it—and you can't understand the language!

It's like being a newborn, learning everything fresh for the first time. Very disconcerting for someone accustomed to understanding things around them to suddenly be completely helpless and ignorant. This is what I meant by having to 'touch my toes.' I had to relax into the acceptance of being, in a way, helpless. It's as though you took away my ability to read; suddenly, incomprehension crowded and stood in front of my eyes where I started all over again, finding words I could recognize: "a", "the", "and". Reminds me of stroke victims having to "learn" to talk or walk again, at the age of sixty. I highly recommend this experience for anyone, at any age. It will change you and you'll never be the same rigid, inflexible person you were before. My prediction. Find out…

My missionary brother is raising his family in Iceland and they all speak Icelandic. They've been there more than ten years. I don't know how much of that place is rubbing off since my impression is he sees their whole society as lost, wrong-headed and following a path of Godlessness and degradation. Still, *something* has to rub off, right? Maybe someone can maintain their spacesuit of self-centered-ness for as long as they live in a place, carrying themselves around in their fish bowl.

Still, I somehow think that when you just remain in a place, that this place rubs off on you. My sister has lived in Tennessee for more than a decade as well, and now talks with a Tennessee accent. We grew up speaking a neutral American English dialect. It's possible <u>most</u> people don't migrate, immigrate or experience completely new places. Wisely, they stay put in their own, known, hometowns. If everyone migrated, there wouldn't *be* hometowns!

As a kid, I was sad and envious of my dad's family in the Laurel Mountain area of Pennsylvania when we'd visit for the holidays. My cousins grew up with each other and saw one another whenever they wanted. Family gatherings would be everyone congregating at Grandma and Grandpa's. *We* lived in Michigan, isolated from our extended family. It felt good to be greeted warmly as the long lost family whenever we'd visit for Thanksgiving, but it felt bad to be on the outside. I guess my branch of the family tree is the one with explorers and travelers sitting on it.

I've lived as full and rich an existence in the past eight years here in America as I had for five total years in Germany and France. It feels that way, at least. I feel balanced. Locally-focused yet broadly aware. Being broadly aware means I have been locally-focused in other places, and know that they are as valid as the one I live in now. I see my former self—a high schooler—reflected in most everyone around me. They seem comfortable in their own lives, looking through their opinions and condemning whatever 'out there' is. Wherever I look, I see afterimages of how I felt "at home" in the Army barracks in Erlensee, at home in an apartment with Andrée in Stuttgart and later on, Toulouse. Those were my homes, where I put my shoes near the door and whose keys I carried. In Europe, I remember being dimly aware of people across that far ocean of distance, in the U.S., reacting wildly, intensely, self-righteously, gesturing angrily. I used to see footage of people in the Middle East, shouting and waving Russian assault rifles and burning American flags. Maybe we all perform for the camera. I guess all Romans on any world are the same. Every village is "Rome." We all expect the rest of the world to do as we do.

Until you leave your town and return, you can't see further than yourself. If you never leave your country, you don't see further than your opinions and reactions. It's impossible, in my view. Or nearly so. When you *do* leave your town, you see for the first time how your town thinks, and you didn't even know that it did such a thing! This jumps up unexpectedly wherever in the world (besides your "nest") you find yourself. When I went somewhere else, for the first time, my thinking and outlook was seen as a separate thing because I was surrounded by people who had another orientation. I was told, "Your thinking, expectations and assumptions don't work here." When I left my home country, I believed I was going to Europe for good. I recalled this, ironically, when I stepped back into that frigid night air in Detroit, eight years ago.

In 1999, upon first arriving in Europe to live, after a month-long 'honeymoon' when I was free from internal reactions to my new external environment, I found myself often resisting the Southern German society I found myself in. I was offended by their *faux pas* towards me, their rudeness. They stood too close, for God's sake! After months of this, I saw I was outnumbered. I couldn't fight them all. Somehow I was lucky enough for it to occur to me to relax my grip on being right and let these people be whoever they are and whatever they are. "I'm here. I can't live like this, fighting everyone and everything."

So I let myself slide into the culture I'd been resisting. I slipped below the surface, accepting where I was and accepting those around me. Not agreeing with; accepting. This is something I wasn't able to do while living in the States. When there was tension between myself and an apartment neighbor, I took it personally; I didn't 'let them be who and what they were.' It was most valuable for me to learn this by immigrating to Germany. I hope I did learn it. I hope it stuck. Would I have "learned" this back here in the States? I don't know. I feel fortunate for the lessons that somehow have penetrated my head.

So, I 'went native.' I used to be *right*. "I" wasn't anymore. I had been wrong. My social rules didn't work in this place. I had been walking in a bubble of American-right-ness. Those rules (sometimes) worked in America, but not *here*. I had been angrily waving a book of instructions that bore no relation to where I was. I didn't attempt to become German. I just quit fighting where I was. I tried to learn the language, as well as I could, honestly, without demanding that it "make sense" to my habitual way of thinking. I just got along without judging everything I encountered with my old 'right' standards. *I let something in.*

That was my first big national-awareness change. I told friends that going to Europe forced me to touch my toes and become flexible, like someone on my back, forcing my hands lower, to my toes. I had been *so* opinionated. I had been *so* wrong about so many things. I think I still am, on both counts. Even now, I'm shaking my head. I had been so *right*.

Does everyone have this barrier to pass through when they live in another culture? Am I uniquely rigid? Maybe—to both. I don't see my unique combination of traits in my parents. I see shadows of myself in my grandfathers. Do other people seamlessly transition between cultures? I think everyone is in their own spectrum. My experiences with my fellow humans show me that everyone functions with "operating systems" they use to make sense of the world. My makeup has been my biggest *koan* (from Zen tradition: a story, dialogue, question or statement whose meaning can't be understood by rational thinking but may be accessible through intuition). 'Know myself' was my magic door… to greater understanding and to freedom from my prison of person. Once I bent myself to the task of understanding why I did what I did and why people reacted to me the way they did, a wide world opened up.

When George Bush the younger was elected president, I saw him first on German television, then on British and French TV. I saw what I interpreted as an overly swaggering intentionally righteous ignorance. Good God, I thought. *This guy* is going to relate to the world out here?

I *was* him. I could relate to him, like I could relate to my eighth-grade or 11th-grade self. Comfortable enough in my surroundings to feel like I knew it all, but profoundly ignorant.

Two things in living abroad—maybe three. Certainly more. First, in learning another language, I had to let go of my death grip on myself. I spoke to myself and others in English. To learn German, I had to relax my hold on English and let the German words live inside my head. I wasn't taking a German class once a day; I was living inside a German class every minute. The idea of letting go of me, my words, was frightening. I *am* these English words. Without them, where would *I* be? I didn't know, but it felt like I would disappear. Ultimately, I didn't. So I thought to myself in German words while walking or riding my bike to the U-Bahn city rail system; I spoke German to strangers, co-workers and friends; I dreamed in German. All poorly, I must add. My vocabulary was lacking, my grasp on grammar was tentative and I labored under the influence of a photographic memory—I only remember photos. Still, I learned every day.

It was through learning another language that I learned another way of being—another way that people are and relate to the world. I can't imagine, for me, any way to get this kind of new view other than going and living within another place. Merely visiting a different location, spending time… I don't know. That's not the same as running into and climbing over the solid wall of something different. I know people who spend weeks in France and are not ashamed to admit that they speak not one word of the language. Through interacting with other beings we have this push pull, give and take, back and forth; that's where you use the language muscles. Without active interaction, our communication is atrophied, like a paralyzed bed-ridden patient. It takes daily practice.

By just going somewhere else and sitting there, a person could surely could pick up a *feeling* for a place—but you'll never *know* it; the 'feel' for a place we get is our usual outlook's reaction to encountering new things. I like the Mormon's and Amish people's practice of forcing their youth to go out into the world for a number of years and to become fluent in their language—in the Mormons' cases. I don't know what it does for them, but it can't be bad. Just learning the language would do it. If the leaders of countries, states and towns in this world went into their enemy's land to live and to "know the enemy"—I bet we would have fewer wars. Once you feel where someone is coming from, there is no argument—or condemnation.

This doesn't have to remain true only with international travel. If I move to Pittsburgh and never accept the place as valid, I can be just as unconnected and unaware of the inhabitants there, living in the place and not of the place. The same goes for relations. You can be standing or working next to a person for years, and have no clue.

During my first time abroad, stationed in Germany in the Army, at 18, I pined for "the real world," as we called The U.S. I was living in a bubble, a spacesuit of "back home" that almost completely isolated me from this new place I was walking and driving machinery through. Never touching nor experiencing directly the place I was tramping around. I felt things deeply, walking around with feelings of profoundness and pondering fundamental things about life and existence. I explored trails and marveled at buildings, but had no first contact with German thinking or society. I was afraid, maybe, of these foreigners whose land I was living in. Maybe I lacked imagination or motivation to find a way "in." Now, I can talk and interact. Then, I was young.

Moving to Europe—On My Own This Time.

During my next, *real* time in Germany, I lived in the society without my spacesuit/fishbowl. I grew to accept the ways of the people and to let their language into my head, and I changed. The world looked different. I could see from German perspective when I watched Deutsch TV shows and nightly news broadcasts and read the *Stuttgarter Zeitung* newspaper. When I cast my gaze in the direction of America again, I saw something different. Something I could never have seen before. I then looked at my long-held unquestioned beliefs and opinions through my new, living-in-Germany eyes. It was *eye opening*. I imagine the younger President Bush emphasizing the last two words of the sentence with his characteristic end-of-sentence punctuation (followed by a smirk).

The third thing slowly dawned on me as I noticed all the American movies dubbed into German. It grew as I found myself placed in the position of authority-on-all-things-American when German friends asked, "What do you think America will do?" after the terrorist attacks on New York's Twin Towers. I became very conscious of America's impact and *presence* in the world. It was a strange thing for me to consider. I feel that most of the "Americans" I encounter don't even know that an external world exists. They know it, but they don't *know* it. They don't consider anything valid outside of their cosmos. I knew a world existed before I lived and learned German-ness in Stuttgart. I'd spent nearly two years in Germany as a teenager. I'd never taken a step outside of myself, however. It's the blind elephant trampling ants versus becoming an ant.

I worked my first job in Germany as *Gebaudereininger*, a 'building cleaner' for Grabner, GmbH in Stuttgart. It was the only type of job that I was allowed to work until I married my French European fiancée. I'd get up at four and go with a crew of five to clean a German health club, a ceramics factory and various office buildings. My crew had two Turks, an Iranian, me, our German crew leader and occasionally someone else. By the way, I understood the other *Ausländer* (foreigner) German much better than Germans because we foreigners all spoke the language very simply.

I got a picture of America's influence on people's thinking when I would talk to these guys. Each, in their demeanor and chosen comments and questions would let me know how they saw me, a walking representative of America. When they were talking to me, they were talking to America.

One time, I was brought to a large dead-feeling building tasked with stripping wallpaper from every wall in an apartment. I had never done that before. We had only scrapers and it was cold. Later, our supervisor brought perforation rollers and wallpaper stripper chemical once he saw how horribly I'd damaged the walls trying to scratch the stubborn paper off. "Every last bit," the guy dropping us off said before going. We could see our breath. Scraping and scratching and sweeping chunks of plaster, mortar and piles of paper.

I was with a German guy and he smoked. We took a break and ate lunch in the empty apartment after walking down to a local market to buy an unsliced loaf of bread, a chunk of meat and a block of cheese. We sat on the concrete floor, cutting and eating our lunch in silence mostly. I don't think this guy was happy. He offered me a cigarette. I had quit ten years earlier, but I accepted. We smoked. He warmed up a bit and made fun of me being an American there, working with him. He smoked Marlboros. Drank Coke.

Our supervisor, another German in charge of foreigners, was a young guy whose sights I think were set higher than his job. He was in his early twenties. He listened to techno music driving this European panel van, talking with me about American movies and actors. I saw how American "products" were part of this young guy's life. He was hip, cool, young, modern, German. He liked to practice his English with me. Most Germans did. At the beginning of my time in Germany, this was problematic for my learning the language because when I'd get stuck, they would shift to English. All of these people had no idea what an American was because they never lived in America. They saw the products, the movies, the songs and saw me through them. I was an extension of Coca-Cola and Marlboros and Sylvester Stallone, oh my. They'd had no firsthand experience with an American living among them. It's like we would treat a Frenchman visiting here; we'd be talking to the Eifel Tower, to the sound of his accent and to imaginings of accordion music. My wife must get that daily, living here. She's used to it, though; she lived in Germany a long time before coming to the States.

In Germany, they had American TV shows broadcast constantly, dubbed in German, and I had ready access to American movies. I just saw the pervasiveness of American products and things. American things were exotic because they were so different and desirable. Those people, watching dubbed American TV shows for years... They identified with things-American. But the shows were dubbed into <u>their</u> expressions, using their colloquialisms. Not very American.

If you ever become—or already are—multi-lingual, you can watch a movie with subtitles and hear what is actually being said by the actors. Maybe my insights won't make sense because everything I'm excitedly pointing at are things you've assimilated and taken for granted... What about facing the other way? Can a multi-lingual or multi-cultural person ever understand or walk in the shoes of a mono-cultural, mono-lingual person? Can *they* squeeze themselves into a place where they judge and understand all information, outside and inside, through a single reference base, uninformed by other cultural points of view? Can they possibly un-remember their broader viewpoint?

It seems possible to "evolve" personally by accepting another locality as valid as one's original standing point. Knowing there is at least one other valid culture, a person's mind can surmise that *all* other cultures are possibly as valid as the one once thought primary. There are many gods, in other words, and they're all real.

I guess anything is possible. A monotheist can become a polytheist. Can a polytheist become a monotheist, turning their back on all those gods they used to accept? If I can imagine it, it can probably be.

In Germany, I noticed these people, exposed their whole lives to American stuff, had not a single clue about Americans—the people I grew up with, worked with and lived near. Not that these Germans necessarily knew, themselves, what <u>they</u> were all about. You have to have been on both sides of the fence to have an understanding; then you can describe yourself for the first time from more of an overview—a view informed by the awareness of a larger, more universal context. And many of these Germans *had* been to the States on vacation.

Watching the inevitable groups of loudly-talking American tourists in Germany and France, I know my fellow Americans have no idea. Maybe some do; I'm sure that's possible too. French fashion or the latest foreign art film from Italy or a movie or documentary by a German director. Sure. BMWs, Mercedes, VWs, Evian bottled water, French wine, German chocolate. Grand architecture, cafés, foreign cities. And no clue. Maybe I'm projecting what I imagine. No doubt. During our recent return trip to France, I was in Avignon at an outdoor café and overheard some Americans talking critically about the country they were enjoying. They thought no one could understand them.

The Germans or French I knew had seen actual Americans. Plenty of them. Speaking excitedly and loudly, pointing and looking at all the interesting things in the aquarium they're standing in front of. Most never spoke to Americans in anything other than English, however. Does the person visiting a zoo really understand the gorilla? Or do they stare and gawk, talking about the fellow's long arms and big head? What about feeling what the gorilla feels? It seems we can't understand someone or something we don't know already. Our operating systems, our main program, can't. This program projects onto people and places only its <u>own</u> notions, which are assumptions based on things already known.

I used to feel it was impossible, without some fundamental change, to *know* someone who is not our self. The only way, I thought, was to spend time talking and thinking in *their* language and notions. I was fortunate enough to *be* with a lot of different Germans. I got to *be* with a lot of different French people. I was able to feel how they feel about things, I think. I learned to speak their language from the inside and I'm grateful for that. I am not perfectly fluent. I speak German and French *fluidly*, at best; I can interact with the people I am with and can basically understand what they are saying and make myself understood—I hope. When I am in their country, speaking and living with them, I learn more and more every day. It's continual and inevitable. Another phrase, a different conjugation of an irregular verb, an explanation for this expression, that belief or this tradition. Like a child growing up among adults, they correct my mistakes in speaking and I absorb their ways of speech. I think speaking—how people say things—is nearly synonymous with how people see and understand their world.

My one preference (that I state aloud) is to retire in France. Not when I'm 70 and in pain; I mean as soon as I can. We left France to come to the States eight years ago and counting. We have two sons who will experience the American school system for a while longer, but if an opportunity presents itself, I think we'll consider moving back. I feel more at home in France than in the U.S. More comfortable.

I started writing this book in 2004, a year after I arrived back in the U.S. while we were living in a trailer in Fowlerville—then events and life continued on and six years slid on by. The summer of 2009 I injured my left knee—my 'good' knee (my right knee has always ached from all the falling while skating and other things)—and I took it as a wake-up call. That summer, I hung drywall with a bum leg, carrying 4 by 8 sheets up ladders, reminded by every painful step that my family depended on my remaining physically in one piece as long as I worked as a handyman painter contractor. If I could shift to writing, I thought, this might be better.

Introduction

The following feels like lifetimes ago.

Fowlerville, Michigan—2004

I was sitting in the office of Todd Pride, publisher of *Lansing Community Newspapers*. The week before, I'd spoken to Jennie of human resources, a dignified woman of a certain age who was also in the office, a member of the panel of three that was interviewing me for a writer's position at LCN. I'd recently written more than a dozen feature articles for the *Fowlerville News & Views* weekly paper for my hometown, and I had some good-looking recent bylines.

At the time of this meeting, I was desperate to become regularly-employed—preferably in a job I could stand. I'd taken a few months away from work to run a summer skate park together with my wife. Steady income was a receding memory. Fall loomed, the summer skate park project was successfully completed for the year and I felt an urgency.

A third person in the publisher's office in that brick building on North Street, adjacent to the Mason cemetery, was Will Whelton, editor and writer for the Williamston Enterprise, one of the several 'local papers' under the umbrella of LCN, which itself is just a part of a larger print media conglomerate by the name of Hometown News or Hometown Life or Hometown Something.

The job I ultimately began (my 29th in an employment history encompassing three countries and five states) after this interview paid ten dollars an hour with the possibility of earning twenty-five cents more an hour after three months. I think their judgment was confused. I think they needed someone fresh; that's who usually gets hired for one of these beats. Someone fresh. What I was bringing to the table in that interview was desperation, but I was probably not fresh enough.

I'd seen and done too much. It was fateful that I was in this office on Thursday morning, September 9th, 2004. The publisher talked about how much LCN was going to grow, how great its future was, and so on. Jennie talked with gravity about something that I don't remember except it was something I felt to be profoundly unimportant. This was a classic interview, like ones portrayed in the movies, and I wonder now, as I did then, why they went to all the bother.

I wasn't applying for a heart surgeon's position. All they needed was a writer. Todd asked, "Would you have a problem with a boss who killed a story that you were passionate about following?" I said I wouldn't like it. Then, Whelton, who'd sat quiet for most of the interview, tossed me a grenade. "Where do you see yourself in three years?"

I turned toward him. My mind dipped into my prior three years…

After some time I blinked back to the room. I almost forgot that three people were waiting for my response. Three years before Whelton's question, I was living in a town in Southern Germany, my home in more ways than my own hometown had been. Three years and two days before this interview, I was riding home with my French wife from a supermarket in Stuttgart when we heard the German radio announcer talking about airplanes flying into the Twin Towers in New York City. I had three years of memories stretching back through a remarkable line of experiences.

I never thought I'd be back in the States to live, let alone live in my hometown again. For three years, in Germany and France, I had left all job interviews behind me because my wife and I were creating an extreme sports park in France as entrepreneurs. Now, here I was.

I walk off an Air France *flight late at night in Detroit, December 2002. Ten hours earlier, my wife, two-year-old son and I had boarded another plane in Toulouse, France bound for Amsterdam.*

I looked at Whelton's calm, expectant expression. *Where do I see myself in three years?*

"I don't know," I said. "Doing something that I *want* to do, like writing." I felt a certain conviction that I wouldn't tolerate another job I didn't like. "I would like to have a book published," I said. I smiled. "I don't know where I'll be."

My problem was that I appeared to be a young-ish sharp-minded local person who would fit nicely into a responsible employer's designs. I'd been too far, done too much.

The following day, Jennie called me with a gravely-delivered offer of employment. I drove back to the Mason office, filled out paperwork and got story leads for the following week's issue. I wrote a couple stories that night: one on the recently approved East Lansing City Ordinance 1035 C allowing residents to petition the city council to restrict rental use of one-family dwellings in their neighborhoods and the second, a feature on the upcoming *Disney on Ice* "Mickey & Minnie's Magical Journey" at the Breslin Student Center in East Lansing. The following Monday, at eight o'clock, I was in the editorial staff office meeting some of the other writers. I drove somewhere and interviewed a guy opening a new tutoring center. I returned to the office and wrote a story. I ate at a Burger King that afternoon and attended a Lansing School District meeting. I called my wife on the way home and talked about my feelings for the day. That night, I called in, resigning, and wrote this letter of resignation to the publisher.

David Weimer
103 Lynn Dr.
Fowlerville, MI 48836
517/404-6333

Sept. 14, 2004

Todd Pride
Publisher

Lansing Community Newspapers

312 North St.

Mason, MI 48854

Hello Todd,

I'm sorry to say that I quit--almost before I started. Enclosed with this letter are a key that Jennie gave to me and my notes and information on stories that I was working on for Will. I hope that he can make use of this material as well as, possibly, the three stories that I had started writing in NewsEdit yesterday.

I am sorry to unwittingly lead you on. I intended to work. I had delusions of adequacy, I suppose. Maybe this accompanies my tender age of 37. In any case, I wish you better luck in filling the vacancy on your writing staff. Don't worry, I'm the anomaly. I'm sure that a young(er) ambitious writer will hop right in and do a fine job.

I am unwilling to do what it takes to succeed at the position as reporter for the Towne Courier. The price is too high, in energy, commitment and time. If I was being paid $20 instead of $10.50 an hour, I could probably live with it and actually become quite happy. It's funny what a little money can do.

If Will has any questions about my abandoned writing projects, please tell him to call me and I'll gladly answer them.

Sincerely,

I couldn't stomach the thought of going back a second day. Too much of my energy going away, away, away. I had worked much harder on our project in France without feeling drained in the least. The only two jobs I'd ever bombed—to that point—of the thirty or more I'd worked, were for the same position: beat reporter for a weekly paper. My first bomb was in '94 for the *Oakmont and Verona Advance Leader* in Pittsburgh for Gateway Press, weeks after graduating from the University of Pittsburgh with a B.A. in English Writing. I lasted a week before suddenly quitting. This second, briefer, implosion was beat reporter for the LCN Towne Courier. *Maybe second time's the charm*, I had thought, hoping to make myself feel better by succeeding at something I'd previously failed at. Nope.

I returned to the metal fabricating company where I had worked before taking off to build and operate our second annual summer skate park in a church parking lot in Fowlerville. This was a first for me. I'd never returned to a job I left behind. That's like telling the doctor, "I never had this spot here before." Things change with time. Some people see the lessons in the circumstances of their lives.

My story, our life, things—seem to go by themselves wherever they will, like twigs swirling in a swiftly flowing stream. Before, I remember believing I planned and caused everything that happened. Now, I was trying my best, making earnest efforts, and felt all the while that I was just along for the ride.

In that interview back in 2004, I was still in…shock. That wouldn't be a terribly wrong word to describe my reaction to finding myself "back" in a setting that I thought I'd left behind forever (America). I marveled at the turns my life had taken. *Where will I be in three years?* What a question. For *anyone* to imagine, maybe. Ask yourself where you'll be. When I look back over my past three years [2008-2010], I marvel at what I have accomplished, what I have done, what has happened in my sphere of awareness. And what will be coming? That question leaves me far-off gazing… Life is a marvel. I am grateful to be someone who can marvel at such things. I suffer more, probably, but I seem to have been born to wonder at the beauty, profoundness and poignancy of things. I was born like this; I have no other explanation.

Too many people, in my judgment, are jaded, cynical, deadened and flat. Tears come to my eyes when I watch a touching scene in a movie or recall something poignant while looking out over the water of a pond—or at a tire sunk in the mud beneath a bridge… or a piece of fishing line and a bobber caught in the branches of a tree on shore; I am endlessly touched by this, my, life. Something in me has wizened, no doubt, with my own years and experiences. And yet, I'm still allowed to feel. I don't know why. I *do* know the fragility of life—what we call life—and its precious momentary snowflake quality, and I am more touched than ever by the things I see/experience. Life is an eternal snowflake, eternally melting and eternally popping into creation each instant. I'm grateful to have lived this far.

God is a piece of toast

Spring 1999, Memphis

Until you find out what you need from somebody,

Like a half-awake fever-heated madness,

You don't have a clue as to what you're doing.

Inside, shifting voices beckon, fade and hide.

Outside, foggy cliffs remain unclimbed

Until you know what you need from somebody.

Playing waiter to patrons of a dim-lit diner,
Tripping over legs to answer whimsical desires,
You don't have a clue as to what you're doing.

Then haze is jarred away by a teeth-clacking fall.
By a table, near passers-by, you lie tongue-tied
Until you find out what you need.

'Oh, God help me,' said to a god desired
To save you from a helpless no-sense dream.
You don't have a clue as to what you're doing.

Your eyes fall level to a crouton flecked-through with green.
Near a table leg, the salad fritter expands to fill the sky.
Until you know what you need from somebody
You don't have a clue as to what you're doing.

It's challenging to stick to a rigid form. And it's easy, because you know where things stand. In this villanelle, the apparently unpredictable and unseen currents in my life and trying to make heads or tails out of who I am and what influences me are what I was...pointing to... I think. Time has passed since I wrote it and reviving it for this book hasn't brought the heartbeat of the impulse that powered its creation... This was one of the poems I wrote for a grad school poetry class.

I've taken some leaves of absence from the world.

In 1993 I went without food for a week in a remote cabin and stared the entire time at a candle, willing my mind and attention to that singular task—it was a self-crafted spiritual retreat that I haven't repeated. In 1996 I camped in the woods for a week—and woke into a motionless world the first morning after a storming night, where the reflexive 'me' was out of the picture and yet someone, something, remained. After a couple days of motionless soundlessness, I strongly suspected that I'd broken my brain. In 1997 I removed myself from the world and lived in a remote West Virginia cabin and saw only the animals and my self from warm July 'til the frost of October.

This story is about the life of a part-time hermit and full-time dreamer. I think that there must be others out there. This happened. This is why I did it. This is what I got out of it. This is what I thought before, during and after—and this is what I think now.

My brain seems to be formed in the shape of a question: Why? This book is about my life eventually becoming dedicated to finding an ultimate answer.

People mention the meaning of life, briefly, on piers at sunset, in bars late at night or in someone's back yard during unexpected bouts of nostalgia. The sane guy is the one who says, "I'm here, so I might as well figure this life out." I never met him. I thought I was unique in this place where people chase things that I knew they don't believe in. I always believed that they were going through the motions—only. I still believe this. I often wondered when I'd be let in on the big secret. But it just kept on going, like a car with no driver. *Why?*

I'm going to make a photocopy of myself in this book and draw a picture in the air with a pencil. When I was 25, I made a commitment to find the meaning of my life and the meaning of everything. I was accidentally successful.

Timeline — A brief history of Me

My birth photo.

Mary Jo Tramps Weimer, pregnant with me, circa 1967 in Sterling Heights, Michigan.

May 23, 1967. Born at Bon Secours Hospital in Grosse Pointe, Michigan at 2:10 p.m.

1967 to 1968. Family lived in a 10 x 50 mobile home at Chateau Estates in Sterling Heights, Michigan. Sister Anne born in '68.

1969. Family lived in Utica, Michigan in a house. Moved there because growing family outgrew trailer. Dad worked for Detroit Edison as power substation operator in Detroit. Earliest memory on lakeshore beach looking at waves during vacation to Bay City.

1970 to 1975. Family moved to 1990 Teaneck Circle, Wixom, Michigan. Brother Pat born. Committed this address and our phone number to memory when I entered kindergarten at five and never forgot it—though I've forgotten most of the addresses and all of the phone numbers of nearly every other place I've lived in since.

I attended kindergarten, first and second grade, and then we moved. Moves like this came when Dad 'bid' on job openings at substations. Operators had to live within 15 minutes from their station. I remember walking to school with a flashlight. My dad helped me to learn to ride a bike on a summer day at dusk on the meandering sidewalk behind our house. I remember it as though it happened earlier today. I have indelible Christmas memories from Wixom.

1975 to 1980. Family moved to 5011 Jewell Rd., Howell, Michigan. Out in the country on five acres with horses, farm animals, hay fields, an orchard and a garden. This was my real growing-up time. My childhood is based here. A farm life with winter sleigh rides and summer buggy rides down the dirt roads where we lived. Summer swimming, horseback riding, tree house sleeping, mowing the lawn, helping dad work, doing chores.

1980 to 1985. Family moved to 161 Fowlerville Rd., Fowlerville, Michigan. 21 acres. High school years. First car. First girlfriend. Smoking cigarettes on roof. Skating on pond, walking buckets of hot water out to horses after school in winter. Became friends with Gino. Riding my pony Lucky, and, later, feeling very guilty over not riding Lucky. One memorable ice storm. Cold first winters. Woodstove in the basement. Carrying wood through the kitchen and down the cellar stairs.

I took this photo when I was 11, with my mom's 1950s Brownie box camera, at 5011 Jewell Road. L-R: My mom & her parents; my sister and brother, and my dad.

1984. Signed up for the Army with my parents consent. Did weekend practice Army during senior year of high school. Worked at McDonald's. Played saxophone in band. Read books all the time.

My mom & dad, circa 1984.

1985. Graduated from high school in June. Three weeks later, flew to Ft. Sill, Oklahoma for Army basic training. Graduated second in class. Selected for West Point Academy prep school. Waiting for next rotation of AIT training while living in old WWII wood barracks, got the call from Mom, who was still in Marquette, saying that Dad had drowned in Lake Superior a day before and they were still looking for his body. Attended funeral and rejoined Army field artillery surveyor training. Went to Germany.

Me, 1985 Fowlerville High School graduation.

December 1985 to June 1987. Lived in enlisted barracks at Bravo Battery, 1/32 Field Artillery (Lance Missile) in Fliegerhorst Kaserne near Erlensee, not far from Hanau, 20 minutes northeast of Frankfurt in Central Germany. Visited Andrée for the first time in Rennes, France, on a four-day pass. Andrée visited me on post before I left for the States; she had just moved to Berlin.

Circa 1986, in a photo booth in the Latin Quarter, Paris, France.

Me and roommate Tony Dillinger, circa 1986, near Hanau, Germany.

June 1987 to December 1991. After leaving active Army, moved to Lake City, Florida, where Mom and Pat were living. Joined the Florida Army National Guard, 153rd Engineer Company, as demolitions combat engineer. Became sergeant. Graduated from Air Assault School. Went to Panama. Graduated from Lake City Community College (LCCC). Lived in first apartment(s). Had two motorcycles—crashed the first one twice. Met first wife, Kathy, in writing class in last semester at LCCC. Worked as land surveyor, restaurant maintenance man and cook. Practiced Karate. Quit smoking.

Andrée, 18, and David, 19, in Rennes, France, 1986.

Circa 1990. At the 153rd Engineer Company in Lake City. Florida Army National Guard.

Dec. 1991 to November 1996. Moved to Pittsburgh. Graduated from the University of Pittsburgh. Served in the Pennsylvania Army

National Guard in the 107th Field Artillery Battalion at Hunt Armory on the edge of Pittsburgh's Shadyside neighborhood—spent a year or so in the survey section and the rest of the time in the FIST (Fire Support Team) section as a Forward Observer (FO), adjusting "fire" for artillery batteries and mortar platoons. Trained in and drove the FIST-V, a lightly-armored tracked vehicle with a laser designator turret. Lived in five different Pittsburgh apartments with first wife and two cats. Was president of university philosophy student group, SKS (Self Knowledge Symposium). Had life-affecting experience in April 1996 on a West Virginia farm. Got divorced. Picked up inline skating. Went AWOL from National Guard for eight months and got honorable discharge.

Circa 1997. My portrait taken in Moundsville, WV.

Nov. 1996 to Nov. 1997. Lived on Richard Rose's farm, location of the TAT (Truth and Transmission) Foundation, in West Virginia's panhandle near Wheeling. Worked as a land surveyor in Ohio. Looked after the farm, repairing fences and the like, and tried to help somewhat with Mr. Rose, who had advancing Alzheimer's. Lived three months isolated in a cabin from July to October before moving to Tennessee.

Self portrait during 3-month cabin stay. August 1997.

Nov. 1997 to May 1998. Lived with Mom in her trailer at 417 Mansell Hill Rd. near Gainesboro, on four acres, 20 miles northwest of Cookeville, Tennessee. Worked at Dana Corp., a driveshaft assembly plant in Gordonsville, TN. Moved to Memphis.

May 1998 - September 1999. Attended graduate program in the English Department at the University of Memphis for a Master's degree in creative writing. Worked for *The Commercial Appeal* newspaper as an obituary writer. Wrote poetry for class.

Sept. 1999 - October 2001. Moved to Stuttgart, Schützen Straße 11, to live with Andrée. Worked as English teacher, building cleaner, and warehouse manager. Had "wisdom" experience. Learned German. Went back to the States to get married in Sparta, TN in 2000. Guillaume was born in October 2000 at Filderklinik in Filderstadt, Germany. Discovered skate parks and ramps, skating in half-pipe for first time. Decided on apartment balcony with Andrée to move to France to create a skate park family activity center based on the urban sports (BMX, skateboard, inline).

Andrée's self-portrait in our first American home, the trailer in Fowlerville, circa 2003.

Oct. 2001 - Dec. 2002. Moved to an apartment in Ramonville St. Agne, at 10 Domaine de la Chêneraie, near Toulouse, France. Worked continuously on our project, "The One and Only Skate Park." We built a skate park in St. Lys. We put on an "Extravaganza" extreme sports two-day event that was attended by 1,500 people. Was on TLT (Toulouse Télévision) television, in two newspapers and a magazine and online magazine. Became good aggressive inline skater. Learned and spoke French.

Dec. 2002 to Dec. 2004. Moved to Fowlerville, Michigan, to Alan's Park, at 103 Lynn Drive, in a trailer park northwest of the town I grew up in. New trailer. Built a shed to house a portable skate park out of leftover barn wood from a barn I sold on EBay. No other family remains in that 'hometown' anymore, other than Dad, who is buried in the graveyard on Cemetery Road on the east edge of town. We operated two summer skate park programs with more than 1000 visitors in the parking lot of UBC (United Brethren in Christ church) on Grand River Avenue, a mile from our home. Worked several jobs before settling at *Precise Finishing Systems*, a metal fabricating plant making automotive paint systems. Second son, Benjamin, was born at St. Joseph Mercy Livingston Hospital in January 2004 in Howell, Michigan. I worked as reporter, framing carpenter, assembly line worker, farm handyman and janitor. Started writing a book about my life on the first day back to *Precise* after our second summer skate park project was finished.

Jan. 2005 to May 2007. Moved to St. Clairsville, Ohio, to 101 Penn Lane, Apartments A-2 and B-6. Gunned for a job at the *Intelligencer/Wheeling News-Register*. Got myself hired and quit the same day with two figures in the checking account. Painted first house for a friend. Became a self-employed handyman painter.

First day at home after all the signings. (Gui, 7 and Ben, 3).

May 2007 to March 2011. Moved to 368 High Street, Flushing, OH, to our first house a few days before my 40th birthday. Returned to France for first time since leaving. Spent five weeks on a "Tour de France" visiting family, friends and places with Andrée, Guillaume (9) and Benjamin (6). Returned to Flushing convinced that we'd move back to France whenever things allowed. Working sixth year as self-employed jack-of-all-trades. Put the words, "The End" on the last page of this book. Began editing process. Snow sledding with family. Began editing the TAT Forum, an online monthly "e-zine." There's more—there's always more—but this must remain a snapshot of a continuum…

May 2007. Opening the door to our first house.

Chapter 1 — Staring at Water

I was born on May 23, 1967 at Bon Secours Hospital in Grosse Pointe, Michigan…

Today is Tuesday Sept. 21, 2004. It is the second day of my return to a job I had this spring and that I thought I'd left behind. I'm taking some long empty cardboard tubes to the dumpster, jumping on them to break them short, and throwing them inside. It's around 7:30 and the air is cool. It's a cloudless morning I would rather be spending outside, sitting somewhere, where the trees move in the wind above my head and I'd lay back and breathe with my eyes closed.

There's a nostalgia from moments like that here, while I work at the dumpster, pre-dawn. Another nostalgia emanates from last October when I started, about the same time of the year, and on through winter's snow and icy wind into spring. Now, after a four-month lapse, here I am—the early morning autumn-approaching air is filled with profoundness and mystery and soon I'll go back inside to drill more holes in metal. The cyclic overview… There's just a lot in the air for me today.

The mornings lately have been luxuriously cool—mid-40s—and the days have been sunny and too-warm in my opinion—mid-70's and even 80's. I'm here, at this dumpster, before the day really starts, when things can go either way and *possibility* exists; there are far too few moments where I am allowed to taste this fresh air and magical promise. Then I walk back and go inside the large hangar-like building, dragging an empty heavy-duty gray plastic can. My nostalgia dissolves in the squeak of the metal door when it closes. My eyes slowly adjust to the shop lighting.

It's the first job I ever came back to, and I've had a bunch. Counting different MOS's (Military Occupation Specialties) in twelve years of Army life, three-and-a-half years in France and Germany, attending two universities and a community college, living in a few different states, I've worked over thirty jobs [thirty-two now]. Thirty beginnings. Each one, I can remember like I remember my life in overview, looking back at things that happened, how I felt during this or that time—not with clear, crisp details, names-included, but with powerful nostalgic touchstones that stand, indelibly, for no obvious reason.

The strange thing is being here with the same people I had left behind. It feels like walking back into a memory. This has become a new job, even though I was here before. I remember most everyone's name, which is a kind of miracle. They floated back up from the back of my mind—Scott, Dave, Jim…

Re-starting this job, I remembered most of the details of my shipping/receiving and all-around metal shop laborer job. I remember parking my car on the grass and dirt at the edge of the parking lot every morning before daylight. I remember the trains that rumble by on the tracks behind the metal building. I had forgotten what time second break comes (and have now forgotten again). By that second beginning I had forgotten a lot of small, integral details of working on the metal lathes and drill stations, because I had gone, like other jobs, without a glance back.

I. Don't. Look. Back. It's not a creed or choice, or some decided thing. I immerse myself in whatever I'm in, and the previous lives I've lived fade in the light of the present. I don't care about planning, or maps or directions. 'Don't care' means I do these things, of course, and appear to be a very methodical, structured person—but planning and details are not at the center of my concerns. I go where I have to go and let go of details like trees let go of leaves (even though they're both very important). Now, in this metal building at 1650 Burkhart Road in Howell, Michigan, I'm back at *Precise Finishing Systems*. I'm glad they took me back. I needed a job this winter [it would turn out to be the last time I worked for someone else].

Last March [I typed these words in 2004], I gave a presentation at an event at Wheeling Park for the TAT Foundation. The planning committee asked me to do something with Jim Burns of Pittsburgh. I put on my *Roces* aggressive inline skates and rolled into a roomful of expectant faces. It was strange to be back in the States, with people I could speak English fully to. Surreal. In my hand, I carried copies of this:

Is what you feel really real?

Observations on the invisible

Two roads diverged in a wood; and I -
I took the one less traveled by,
And that has made all the difference.
    –Robert Frost, excerpt from "The Road Not Taken"

Sometimes the road less traveled is less traveled for a reason.
    –Jerry Seinfeld

Here's a list of things I say to someone near my wavelength, the wavelength of someone who is considering devoting their life and time to discovering the meaning of everything. These are kind of "lessons learned" from my life. They possibly only apply to me—although I suspect and hope they might be useful somehow, somewhere. I don't count on it. Still:

PIECES FROM MY ROAD, by David Weimer

Live the impossible. You are not smart enough or capable enough to find the Answer. No one is. Have determination. Be honest. Be willing to do whatever it takes. Don't give up.

Don't lean. Not on the words of Buddha, not on God. They are all wrong, as far as you are concerned. Until you find out for yourself, it's pure fiction. Don't lean on someone else's life.

Use comparison. Comparison can turn you into a resentful person—if you don't live to your potential. A true seeker is non-discriminating, using everything. Be what you *can* be. Make that your center. You'll be in the company of the Richard Roses, Michael Jordans and Albert Einsteins (all equals in my book). You'll use comparison and not be used by it.

Know it's your right. Do with your life what you feel is right. We are all equally important. No one has the right to steer your boat.

Become an expert. The skater is never again as bad as the first day. Each one of us is going to become an expert at something. Most of the time, it's automatic when you stay somewhere long enough. You can become an expert meaning-of-life-finder.

Make the class your own. We are stuck in class with a feeling of resignation, putting in time until we can do what we really want. *Why?* You'll learn the other stuff—but you will LIVE in the things that you are interested in. Bend each assignment to your fascination. Most teachers are relieved to find a student excited about something even remotely related to their subject.

Do something "other than." One-hundred-percent conviction is the subtle clue that the devil has his mouth to your ear. So-and-so is my enemy. Be willing to do something other than what you would normally do or not do. You don't even know what that could be. Paradigms are worlds in themselves. Willingness is the key. The world can flop over; all the enemies become just normal people and the truth will set you free.

Meditate. Follow your fascination. Make it a habit. It could be an intellectual, exclusive concentration on a problem, or a yearning and pushing forward into the desire to KNOW with all of your being, or allowing yourself to be completely absorbed by the subject of your attention for the sake of the truth. It doesn't matter what you do. Do something, anything, and nothing.

Read. Take time to track down the books your curiosity responds to. If someone gives you a book that you don't think will help—open it anyhow.

Help others. What you think is help usually isn't.

Talk. We think that we *know* just because we feel comfortable (we're still intact and untested). A girl with a dog could say something valuable. Check your intuition or feelings. Ask people what they think. See how your discoveries about human nature hold up. Explain your ideas.

Make a commitment (again). It was a big step. You made your first uninformed commitment and walked into the unknown. That's not the end.

Try to have common sense. If you can't live the unlivable or buy the un-buy-able, then remember that there have been some—Buddha, Rose, Ramana Maharshi—who have lived their lives a certain way contrary to the norm, and who have said and written things. When there are times of serious doubt, look at the whole scene, the whole picture, weigh it, and try to have some common sense.

Live without regrets. Walk into a fearful situation and do your best. There will be moments of singular choice when you will know without a doubt that a door is open for you. <u>Almost all hesitate</u>, and the door swings shut again (it always does). Later, people say, *I could have done something*.

Make a commitment. Until you make a commitment, there is fear, hesitation, indecision and ineffective action. If you find yourself facing a direction not braved by the majority of comfort-addicts, you may feel uncertain. But you have to either go forward or quit.

Work. Doing something you don't like takes ten times more energy than doing something you do. Follow your fascination and do the 'work-that-is-not-work.'

Become smarter than the problem. People have killed themselves and gone crazy beating their heads in the same place on the wall. Look for a door. Insanity is continuing to do something and expecting different results (a borrowed definition). Become smarter than the problem.

Throw the sticks back in the fire. Put the ends back into the fire and use every scrap of wood and waste nothing. Nothing is irrelevant in the quest for the Answer. This is not a euphemistically described "learning experience" or trying to tell oneself that something bad is good. The lessons are in the events in our lives. Use everything that uses you. Keep the fire burning.

Be honest. Or you're lost—and you won't even know it.

As a kid, I remember backing away from my father, trying to get that one last explanation in before the hand came down. Explaining. Having someone understand what I did and why. I've always had this as a central 'need.' One of the apparent prime directives in my personal hardwiring. It factors into my urge to write something of my long, slow-motion fall before the final thud, I'm sure. I don't need people to feel content or whole; I am most comfortable alone. But I need people to understand me. Boy.

"My Way"

Early on, even before kindergarten, I was drawn to reading. I remember living in Walled Lake, a subdivision in Wixom, Michigan. My mom would read to me before I slept each night. My dad would too. I remember my hunger for the stories in those books. A strong desire for the wonder of those stories propelled me to strain to read them before my mom or dad came dutifully into my room each night. I'd ask them what certain words were, ask for the meaning of a certain sentence that was puzzling me. I clearly remember straining, my finger following the lines, straining to comprehend. I was straining into those stories. I only recognized a handful of words. Following along when my mom read, I began to recognize 'the' and 'a.' In the beginning, I'd have these little windows of clarity in the middle of a wall of incomprehensible text that stood between me and the magical worlds on those pages.

My enthusiasm for reading resulted in a book club regularly sending books to the house. I looked forward to those cardboard boxes in the mail. I liked the fantastic ones about space or witches. My first favorite book (one that I read repeatedly) was *Ghosts, and More Ghosts*. I have it on a shelf just to my right, after more than a dozen homes in all the states and countries; it's one of those constant things I transport with me when I move. Another title is *Children of Infinity*, and a third, *Turning Point*. These were collections of stories that profoundly impacted or ignited my sense of wonder. I've always been drawn to the mysterious and unknown. I've always tried to understand things. I have a tremendous curiosity. Science and discoveries fascinate me. I have never felt normal—compared to others around me. I have never felt that others were normal, compared to me—I knew that I was normal and sane; everyone else was settling for things that didn't matter.

My earliest memory:

And I'm still there—walking on the beach with my mom and her sister, my Aunt Betsy. They are holding my hands as we walk in the warm sand. They are talking over my head. I don't listen. We are barefoot. It is cool, and the wind blows, but the sun is warm. I am watching the water to my right as we walk on the shore in the dry sand. We go like this for a while. The sun warms my skin and the sand under my feet. My mom and aunt sit in the sand near a grassy hill. I see a rusted metal rack, left there with its bottom buried in the sand. I look out at the sea. It must have been Lake Erie, one of the Great Lakes on the east side of Michigan. We were living in Utica at the time, twelve miles north of Detroit in Macomb County. It may have been another lake. I don't know.

I am standing now and staring at the long, wide view of white-capped waves in regular rows marching forward towards me. That dancing sunlight on the moving water. I want it all to go on forever. I want to watch and be here with this phenomenon and this mood forever. My mom and aunt make questioning sounds. I don't listen. They stand up, take my hands, and start to walk me to the water. No! I dig in my heels and fight, protesting until they stop. I don't want to go in the water. I don't want to leave *here*.

That moment has never left. It is deeper than the content of my daily life. I hope everyone has these moments. When I stop and stand still, somewhere. They are openings. They are like the books that I dove into as soon as I could. I was three on that beach. It is eternal and unchanging. I carry it with me. I don't think my brother was born. Maybe I was two... My sister, a year younger than me, was somewhere else. Or was she born yet? Was I one? Anyhow, this is my earliest memory.

"Turning Point"

I was eighteen. I was a private first class (PFC) in the Army, in AIT (Advanced Individual Training) school at Fort Sill, Oklahoma to become a field artillery surveyor. I'd been chosen to go to prep school for the U.S. military academy at West Point, New York while in basic. It was part of an in-service selection having to do with West Point cadets assigned to basic training Army units. I'd graduated second in my class at basic. They gave me a little statue and some letters of commendation from the battery commander and drill sergeants. I took to the military structure like a fish to water.

Army basic training photo, circa July 1985, Ft. Sill, OK

Here's a well-defined challenge. Forty targets to hit; twenty things to remember, two minutes to do as many push-ups and sit-ups as possible; two miles to run as fast as possible; an obstacle course to negotiate; a helicopter to jump out of; a task. None of the messy people crap. No politics. No pissing contests. A mission. I could excel. I do well at missions. I <u>am</u> a mission.

I didn't know if I would go to West Point. Maybe I would have after AIT. I was given the paperwork to start the process (I still have it). My life would have taken a different road. I know I felt a response to my parent's pride at my accomplishments during my brief time in the Army. It flattered me to consider going to West Point. I was all set to go. I think I would have done great. I would have applied myself. This would be a different story.

I joined the Army in 11th grade at Fowlerville High School. I wanted to test myself, experience something challenging and join the Marines, but the recruiter there was an asshole. Looking back, I think he probably didn't want to be there. Or maybe he did, but thought high schoolers were just dumb kids. We were. Well, that's the only reason I didn't become a jarhead, my dislike of the Marine recruiter's attitude. I also wanted to go to Europe, and the Army guy said I could be stationed in Germany. About three weeks after graduating from high school, I was with my dad, sister and brother at the Detroit Metropolitan Wayne County Airport. I remember it clearly, in the way that some strong memories stand out from the fog. I had a duffel bag. We made our way to the departure terminal along the carpeted airport hallway.

I had a book I wanted to read before boarding and I wanted to smoke a cigarette or two. At this time, it was one of those known secrets where I couldn't smoke in front of my family. That's what I remember the strongest—a desire to get rid of my family so that I could smoke and read some pages of my current ever-present sci-fi book before getting on the plane.

I have the impression that I hugged my brother and sister. I remember my dad telling me something in his understated characteristic way. I can't remember what it was. I hugged him goodbye. I think I told them I wanted to be alone before the plane took off and so they went away. I can imagine my dad giving in to this 'request' out of his love for me. Now that I'm a father, I can imagine myself doing that. That was the last time I saw him alive.

It was also the last time I saw my little brother and younger sister—the way they used to be. We were all headed for a crash, as disastrous to us personally and to our family as an airline crash would have been.

For those who graduated from the eight-week basic training course at Ft. Sill, some got to visit home before starting AIT. It was a matter of how long we had before the training cycle for our particular job began again. New soldiers whose schooling would be at another Army post got to go home on leave. Those going to eighty-two Charlie (82-C) field artillery survey school didn't, because the training would continue on at Fort Sill, the Army's field artillery training post.

We had 15 days before the course began. We were taken to a block of old World War II barracks and put under the supervision of a master sergeant. We were given odd details to keep us busy during the week. We got up for PT (physical training), went to chow, cleaned the barracks, did work details in the morning, went to chow for lunch, did details in the afternoon, went to chow for dinner, and got released for the evening after a formation.

Though somewhat structured, it was far from the strict discipline of basic. After a week or so of this, we came up on a four-day holiday weekend. Those who wanted to visit home were told they could. I looked into buying a round-trip Greyhound ticket to Michigan. I would get there by Saturday morning and spend a couple of days before coming back... I couldn't wait to go home and tell my family about my experiences, see my best friend and just be around the old place after what I'd gone through in basic.

I called home early in the week and the wind was taken out of my sails when my mom told me they were planning to go up to Marquette, in the Upper Peninsula, that weekend. We went up there regularly to attend my mom's dog shows—Mom and us kids showed Dalmatians—but also to spend some family vacation time on this one beach area on Lake Superior. At that time in my life, I wasn't selfless. Having this chance after a trying time in the military to finally get away for a few days, I was anything but that; I wanted to go home badly. "That's okay," I said, "I can come home on a pass some other weekend." Turns out, I never would. My disappointment was great, but believe it or not (I can't), I said it for them. "If you want us to, we'll stay home," my mom had told me. There was no greater regret than my wish that I had been more "selfish" that time on the phone.

Well, that weekend, a friend of mine, Turner, and I got passes and went to Oklahoma City to a mall, and returned and shot pool on post at a rec center. I bought a six-pack of beer and chips and cigarettes and we hung around the barracks. I read, drank beer, smoked and talked to Turner when he was there. Nearly everyone else had gone home. Turner lived in Florida and couldn't afford the flight. Each of the old identical wood buildings had a handful of guys who didn't leave. It was a quieter, skeleton crew atmosphere.

Sunday morning, I think, I was in one of the buildings with a weight room on the second floor. There was a phone call for me. I was excited. I went downstairs and outside to the payphone across from this building. It was my mom. She said, "Are you alone?" I said, yes. She said, "Get somebody to be with you." My heart dropped like a cannonball. I knew something bad had happened. My first immediate thought was of my brother. *Pat! Oh God*. I was certain something had happened to my brother and in a way, I was absolutely right.

My mom kept telling me to go get someone so I looked momentarily for Turner. I was growing more anxious and told her to never mind and just tell me. What she told me was my father was missing. She told me the story about how it all happened the Friday afternoon before. About how the weather had turned now and how divers were still looking for dad's body. He was lost. My dad was lost in Lake Superior. Holy crap. The day before, while I was looking at pants in a store at the mall, a terrible drama was taking place and I never knew. Although I had been in a pretty low mood, which I had attributed to being alone on post when I could have been coming home.

Pat and Dad had been swimming out to the string of rock islands sitting a hundred yards and more from the beach we went to. Lake Superior is cold, all the time. That's what I remember. Cold. Even though it was August, it was cold. They had been swim racing out to the island and my brother got there first. The story I carry from Pat is that he turned back to look for Dad and saw him like struggling or calling for help. Pat thought it was a joke, but then was shocked when Dad went down and didn't come up. He dove in and swam back to where Dad was. Then, I remember Pat telling me, when he got to where Dad was, he dove, and kept diving, kept looking, frantically. Then finally he felt my dad's hair and got a hold and tried to bring him up to the surface. The weight was too much and Pat let go to return to the surface for air and try again. He never found Dad again.

My wife, Andrée, said that my sister told her that she, too, was involved in searching for Dad. Swimming, I mean. Diving down. Christ. I can only imagine. I know Mom, Anne, Pat and Dad were all there. It must have been a nightmare. I don't remember us ever sitting down together and talking about that time—those days of the drowning and the searching. I was probably told, but it's behind my memories. Divers eventually found my dad. There was a big relief that we had him again, even dead; this was better than losing him forever. I don't know why people feel this way, but I understand perfectly wanting, needing, to see one's dead loved one's body. His cause of death was hypothermia. It's a cascade event, hypothermia. Jesus. Dad was the best swimmer of us all and he always seemed impervious to the cold—I remember all the times working in a blizzard with him on the farm; he never seemed bothered, while I shivered, froze and complained while holding the end of something.

That shut the door on something inside of me. It was a weekend day and not easy to get off post. The Red Cross had to validate the facts before I could go. It wasn't easy arranging bus and plane tickets. All of that is a blur. I have one of those indelible impressions of sitting in a battalion CQ office, staring at nothing, while a couple of spec. fours (specialist, fourth class) talked on the phone, making travel arrangements (I think), getting permission for an emergency leave provision for me. I was in a black well. The next vivid memory I have is at the airport in Detroit.

I was in my dress green uniform. In 1985, we had to travel in uniform. I carried a duffel bag on my back and I was coming down an escalator. At the bottom were my best friend, his brother and his dad to pick me up and take me home.

Gino Costantini is a first American-born generation Italian. His parents came from Italy to the States and raised five children. They spoke only Italian at home and the kids, going through the American school system, helped their parents figure out the bills and other things in English that they had to deal with. Gino, the youngest, was named after his father. Now he has a son of his own, Gino (Egidio) the third. Gino the first died when I was overseas. I didn't find out until long after his funeral. This really bothered me at the time.

We lived one mile apart on Fowlerville Road. After moving to our new house where we had 21 acres and a pond, I continued in the Howell school system for my ninth-grade year. I didn't know anyone in Fowlerville. One day after school I was inside and Anne yelled that there was someone at the door for me. I remember the unexpected visit of this dark-haired, dark-skinned guy on a red bike. Surprise. Who was this? He lived up the road. He asked if I wanted to go with him to his friend's house to get a shifter for his dirt bike. I asked my mom.

I never understood why he stopped by. Well, we ended up friends. The best friend I ever had, other than my pen-pal wife.

When I got to the bottom of the escalator at the airport, Gino's dad, who never spoke to me except in short, few-word phrases barked out around a hand-rolled cigarette, and who intimidated the hell out of me, took a step forward and grabbed me in a bear hug. I just stood there, feeling nothing but a dead sinking dread. I tried to back away but he kept me in that tough, no-words hug. He didn't say anything. He had looked me in the eyes intensely and just did that. That's what I remember about coming back for the funeral. Not being there for him, at his funeral, really bothered me. He was there for me and I was gone for his time.

At Dad's funeral, I didn't want to go up there to the open casket to see him. He was gone. The fact that there was a funeral was enough for me. If they'd never found him in that cold Lake Superior I would have felt a longing to see him one more time. But now he was there, just dead.

Mom wouldn't let me alone until I went up and looked at him. Seeing him laying there, the striking thing was he was empty. The body seemed related to Dad, but like a noise without an echo. I looked at his chest. I swear it was moving, I swear, even today, that I saw that. I kept staring. It sure looked like he was breathing. I guess I'd never seen my dad dead before.

I remember standing outside in the parking lot in my Army uniform, smoking. The fulfilling of the nicotine craving was satisfying, but nothing. There was no escape. This world had lowered down to settle on my head in a weight and didn't let up again for ten years. It might have gone away sooner but I never found someone to talk to about my grief and loss. I needed a nice warm female type to listen to me and pat my arm, where I could really let loose and feel my grief and cry. It almost drove me crazy, that held-back thing.

I remember Gino came outside. He said a few things I don't remember. He was trying. The other thing I remember was the incredible heaviness of the coffin as six of us—Dad's brother, brother-in-law, two sons and two friends—carried it down the steep stairs in front of the funeral home to the hearse. I remember lowering his coffin into the ground, holding onto the end of a nylon strap. It's a dream I can't forget. *Merrily, merrily, merrily, merrily.*

I've always been a dreamer.

I remember being fourteen or so, standing in the dark in a field on our small farm, staring at the sky and stars and yearning to be taken away to other galaxies by a UFO. I broadcast myself with all my might: "Take me! Come on down. Don't wait anymore. Let's go! I'm ready!" I probably would have stayed that way, intensely curious in general about things and being a kind of dreamer. Dad's dying changed that. I never returned to the family and home I had left after distractedly saying goodbye at the airport three months earlier. That life had disappeared. I'm sure everyone struck by tragedy experiences this.

Regardless, something broke and, like a car with the wheel stuck turning to the left, I veered away in a different direction, never to return to my old way of seeing the world. Death just hadn't been a part of my world view. My world view had shattered. I discussed with my mom about having a hardship discharge from the Army instead of going off to Germany. She was adamant I should stay in, telling me Dad would have wanted it. I don't know if he would have. But I listened to her and always feel that if I had stayed home I could have made a difference with Pat, with helping out, being together. But then, we're all somewhat happy and fulfilled by our present lives, so, I guess it all worked out. I ended up in Germany for two years and remember it as a dark, soul searching time where I was continually turned inward. I never went to West Point.

Isolation, and being removed from familiar surroundings, must have aided this inward focus. If ever there were ideal conditions for producing a philosopher, I was living in them.

I read books to escape into magical places, but I walked constantly through a motionless nightscape. My natural curiosity, fascination for mystery and so on was turned in that one direction. Within? Without? Maybe without—in both senses of the word.

I rode my ten-speed—bought in Erlensee, a village near Fliegerhorst Kaserne where I was stationed—on those wonderful paths that the Germans have everywhere. I rode my bike through woods and open fields, past villages and farms, armed with cigarettes and books. I'd read and smoke. Smoking went with my deep pondering. I felt things deeply. I contemplated things deeply. Not a lot of words, just… deeply pondering. A lot of times I'd stare at nothing while sitting on a bench or a stump along the path. My mind would be turned to that empty, far off, deep direction.

This was the beginning of my journey of seeking an answer to the meaning of life. Dad's death was the crack that set off an avalanche inside me. I didn't "decide" to look for the truth of things; my need for this was glaringly self-evident. I had to know what was happening in this place and why. I did many of the things young soldiers do—drank beer, went to movies on post, went with friends on outings—I didn't declare my monk-hood... yet. But I was not the same person I think I would have been, were I free from concern. I grew up. I got serious.

Seven days in May

Written April 1999 in Memphis about my first isolation experience in 1993

In May 1993, I parked my car at the top of a tree-covered hill in West Virginia. I was 26, living in Pittsburgh. In three months I would be married and I suppose mortality was whispering in my ear. Something sure was. What would possess me to go into a cabin in the spring in the woods and fast for seven days and do nothing except stare at a candle?

I had never been alone for a complete day before. You always see someone. I had never gone 24 hours without eating, planning to eat or recovering from eating, either.

I was running a student philosophy group at the University of Pittsburgh called the *Self Knowledge Symposium*, and had gotten into the habit of thinking a lot—with no holding back. I consciously decided to not hold back in this one direction. I was looking for something. This was my way.

I sensed my life was going to be different after I got married. And that, like the weather, a real perspective change was moving in. That's what precipitated this weeklong departure, I guess.

Mike, a friend from another philosophy group, had a cabin he offered to let me use during spring break. The cabin is perched on the edge of a ravine in a wooded, mountainous 160-acre 'farm.'

On Sunday afternoon, before the first day of spring break, I drove my '88 Ford Festiva to this place. It was really out there. No pavement, no street lights, only the shifting whir of a coal mine exhaust fan in the hills. I had a duffel bag of canned food and clothes, a notebook, a sleeping bag and a pillow. I left my watch, wallet and everything in the glove box. I shouldered my duffel bag and left the car, heading down a rutted tractor trail that wound around the hilly terrain and eventually passed Mike's cabin.

When I unlocked the door and dropped my stuff on the floor inside, I saw a wall of shelves lined with glass jars of pasta, dried beans and rice—all seemingly gray with age. A box of plumber's candles, an oil lamp, a woodstove, a raised bunk bed, a small table with a view out the back window and a padded chair. This would be my environment. I didn't plan to 'do' anything. But I had a strong urge to do something.

I'll tell you what happened.

Each night, I wrote in a journal so I wouldn't lose track of the days and come back late (or early). This was six years ago [in 1999].

First day.

I came out here yesterday at noon. None of the familiar things I usually do were here. No music. No TV. No books. No talking with people. No seeing people. No exercise. No work. No cleaning.

I'm out here, and my time will not be spent in vain. Yesterday my mind was racing. Songs, thoughts, playbacks of things people said, daydreams—all in a frantic, one-after-the-other pace. My head was a faucet. Today is the first full day.

I have never gone without food for a full day before. So far, I feel fine, even after my excursion this morning looking for the spring.

One day at a time, eh? As far as my essence, and my quest, I don't know.

I hadn't planned on doing any fasting. I just found myself there in the silence of that cabin staring out the window as the sun went down and I had the idea whispered in my ear: *What if...*

If I was going to give up all my daily habits—exercise, working, reading—why not <u>really</u> do it? Give up the routine of preparing meals, eating and washing dishes and getting rid of the meal a day or so later. It was an exciting idea. I didn't know if I could do it. It was like looking up at a high cliff and wanting to go up there.

When the fear is tickling your stomach in the coolness of a perfect, perfect morning and you look up, and 'I wonder...' is bubbling inside—that's what I remember about Sunday evening before this first full day. Instead of making dinner, I lit a candle and sat there.

Day 2.

Did I learn anything yet? Yes. One day I believe very strongly that my life must go this way. Everything feels right about it, I make silent plans, and then either the next day or the next hour, the very thing I felt so strongly about is faded, or full of holes, and I have a new conviction, desire, or whatever, just as sharp as the earlier one. More than ever I see how reliant on random air currents my strongest convictions seem to be. A year ago I thought I would be practicing martial arts for the rest of my life—that it would be an incorporated part of my self—and now I never do. What is the real *conviction?*

The other thing I learned is that isolation isn't being alone.

I notice planes; I hear dogs barking and cows in the distance.

Man. I'm in the middle of the woods and somehow the sounds make it in. The harder I try to become solitary the more I am distracted.

I think I became somewhat dehydrated last night. Woke up weak and faint. I drank more water with juice and vitamins this morning. Feeling better now.

No hunger pains really; the gurgling and other noises are fading. My body is more quiet than it was in the beginning. But my head is not so quick to join. Songs play on a repeating track in my head. Last night I itched and scratched forever. Then there was the storm. What a storm. Strong showers and nearly continuous lightning. I kept counting the seconds to see how far away the strikes were.

I remember deciding after one day of fasting that I couldn't do what I had wanted. I had planned to hike every day, clear the deadwood around Mike's cabin and clean out the storage end of his cabin. When I went to look for the spring Mike had told me about, for drinking water, I couldn't find it. That was the first full day, and I hadn't eaten for 18 hours. I was noticeably weaker and light-headed from stomping over those hills along a stream. There was no way I'd be able to keep active, I knew. But I wanted to *do* something.

So I lit a candle on Sunday night and got in the habit of keeping one going. I'd sit in the chair at the desk and my eyes would naturally settle on that flame. A resting place for my attention. If I couldn't apply myself physically, I'd by God do something. Why not stare at a candle?

Third day.

The bed bugs didn't bite last night, thank God. I think the spray did it.

Woke up in the middle of the night. I had the feeling I was supposed to be doing something.

I found out this morning that I must pace myself. I've taken in nothing but water, juice and vitamins, and still try to move like I've eaten.

Threw up. Probably a combination of the fumes [from the portable camp stove Mike loaned me for the week] and my wolfing down water, juice and vitamins. Take it slow.

The weather is warmer, with a breeze.

Why am I here?

Because I've got no proof for anything.

I notice my body fat is disappearing from my stomach, shoulders, butt, legs —everywhere. Today is 84 hours without food, and I can feel my spine. Though

I'm weaker, my muscles seem chiseled and more pronounced. I'm trying to not to become dehydrated.

Having never fasted, I deliberate over how much water I should drink. Drink every time I have to go? And then, am I doing one because of the other? Which is easier to stop? How about being a slave to body functions? Too bad I can't stop drinking water. Nature is a distraction. And I, fair body, am the embodiment of distraction.

Here is a daydream I just had:

I was 'signed up' to take part in an experiment. It involved going into a giant complex, a school-like setting. I was supposed to meet my 'experimenter' in a certain classroom. I remember getting a little lost, but finally finding the place. An old, rushed man was the only one there, and he was mumbling angrily. When I asked him where to go, he indicated a certain way. I followed him and was eventually with this group of seven or eight.

We were led up through a series of steps, turns and elevators. Music played, and I remember hearing an Elvis Presley song and opening my eyes to see an old Elvis singing passionately.

Yes, during this upward journey my eyes were closed. Bumping into the others in my group, I just went along. Music played continuously, though the songs changed. When the last elevator stopped with a lurch, a certain nostalgic hillbilly semi-country song was playing in my head. When my eyes opened, everyone was gone except for me in this open catwalk place high in the superstructure of the complex. I became angry.

I found stairs, passages, whatever I could, to get down. Then I looked at my hands and discovered I was an old man.

I asked some ladies at a secretary station the quickest way out. They were slow to answer, so I found my own way. Outside, I was disoriented for a while. Then it struck me:

I was still inside the cabin, with my eyes closed, daydreaming and listening to some music playing in my head while I went from youth to old age. Old age;

time-wasted. Wasted by time. Bitter regret, felt this old man, me. The last song is still playing in my head.

I was staring at the candle full time. Sometimes I would go outside for fresh air. I would stand up real slow, and walk carefully into a world of shifting light, breezes and green. I simultaneously felt despair and great peace. Despair at the days stretching ahead I wouldn't let myself think about. Peace from the serene surroundings.

One thing about focusing for a long time and not eating is that everything tends to reduce to a single eventful moment. That's how it was. Things happened but nothing changed. The closest thing I can point to is when I went to the aquarium in New Orleans [before Hurricane Katrina]. In this one big room, there was a giant wall of glass and dozens of sharks and rays and exotic fish in motion. The room was dark and carpeted in blue and the fish swam above and all around in silence.

Fourth day.

I woke half-way through the night again. I was dreaming about a young woman in the days before electricity. She was an expert seamstress and there was a complicated process going on. Something to do with sewing or weaving and I understood this process completely as she did it.

When I woke up, this dream, with the young woman and her sewing-like task, was still going on. It did not seem out of the ordinary until now.

Yesterday was something else. I made a pact to stare at a candle until it burned down so far. Pitting myself against the world. I don't know long how this went on, but a little battle ensued. I was at odds with bodily functions. After an intense hour or so, I gave up and went outside.

This afternoon I thought about belief and purpose and death.

I watched the last of the sun's rays through the leaves bring a glow to the amber-colored oil in the lamp on the window ledge overlooking the gorge. I'd come to think this isolation was the most terrible thing I've been through, but in that moment, staring out at the forest, I knew I would look back on this time from some removed time in the future.

It's like a tropical rain forest out here, with an upper canopy that shades the ground. Most of the ground is covered with sparse vegetation and the terrain is steep and rugged.

A stream cuts through a gorge behind the cabin and I follow its shale and moss length until the small waterfall. With plastic jugs and a handkerchief to strain the water, I squat on a flat rock and collect two gallons.

I stand slowly, and watch my feet carry me up the hill from rock to root and finding footholds.

I boil the water by the panful, and pour it into a clean jug after it cools down, straining it through a handkerchief one more time.

This morning I smelled the wheat bread going sour in my duffel bag, so I went outside and flipped each piece like a Frisbee away from the cabin. There were a lot of birds around. Two full days left.

At this point, I was just trying to get through. The fasting had become acceptable and normal. My body had quieted, and I was content with its inaction. No meals, no dishes—it was another place.

I was starting to get a little shell shock, too. At this time, it was four days staring at a succession of candles. I was out in the middle, far from land, and right or wrong, I was focusing my attention on that flame while the days flowed by.

Inside, the voices were ganging up for an assault. They'd already made several runs at the gate. *Read-a-book; Eat; Leave-this-place; Get-out.*

Their names were legion.

The terrain reminded me of Panama. I had gone there on annual training with the Florida National Guard 153rd Engineer Company of Lake City in 1990, I think. The rain and the layout seemed the same.

I had dreams during the day. Sometimes, anytime—my mind would slide into a dream. And when I woke up I'd be in both places for a while.

Every day, at least once, I would stand up quickly and hold onto the back of the chair. Like stubbing a toe, it would take about three seconds, and the world would dissolve into a wash of blackness and high-pitched ringing. Sight and hearing and almost touch would go away. By the end of the fourth day I stopped doing this. It had become obvious that I should just stand up slowly from then on.

Fifth day.

My stomach was grumbling like crazy this morning. Not with loudness, but with persistence. Yet I feel no discomfort.

Why do they call it fasting when everything moves so slow?

Yesterday I got two more gallons of water at the little waterfall and back to the cabin. I was kind of surprised I made it.

It didn't rain yesterday. In fact, it was a beautiful, windy sunny day. Whether I looked out the window to recapture a moment of peace, or, when I stood outside for ten minutes in the sunlight, there was no sparkle. Everything simply was.

Mike stuck a piece of tape on the window facing the gorge. "Don't waste this precious time," he wrote on it. Easy for him to say.

I've discovered that the exercise of will comes with a price.

Yesterday, I came to the determination to pit my will against time and everything and meditate until a full candle burned out.

I would not move or take my attention away from it. After the first attempt two days ago, I thought I wouldn't do this again, but something in me took the bit in its teeth.

Focusing my attention on the flame, the thing started.

After a couple of hours I had to pee, of course. This time, there would be no compromise. If I could do this, I could do anything. If I failed, I would never be able to do anything again.

Towards the end, I couldn't take my concentration off the flame. I was stuck. I found myself counting the minutes by the second, five minutes at a time, 300 seconds, using my pulse as a counter.

I told myself I'd go nuts. And if I lost my mind out here, where would I end up? What would happen? Still, I drove on, and the damned thing about it was, this candle, this particular candle, burned longer than any of the others, as if to say, 'Unh-uh, you're not getting off that easy, son. You wanna race? Fine. <u>Here's</u> how it's done.'

The last few minutes were hell. And I really believe, maybe a drop in the ocean in terms of what can be experienced.

When I finally saw the flame drop and snuff out, I moved outside slowly as quickly as I could. When I got back inside with relief, and shut the door and looked at the desk, the candle was still burning!

The burning wick had melted through a dome of wax and fallen within the jar, lighting another piece of wick down there. Oh irony, oh fate! Would I have made it to the real finish line? I don't know. The lesson I got is that any exercise of will has its price.

Last night I woke up half-way through again. This time, it was the silence. No far off fans, no rustling leaves, no wind.

I stood outside. No insects bounced off my legs. It was another world.

Pitting myself against that candle (and the need to pee) was probably the worst thing I did. I learned the lesson of picking my future battles carefully. I don't remember much from that day other than it was traumatic. I guess I remember enough.

I woke every night at the same time. Not because I was thirsty or had to go or anything. Most times, I'd just go outside and stand. And the bugs would bounce off my legs and I'd scratch and stand a while and go back inside, and sometimes sit and think. The first time, I felt like I was supposed to be doing something. Like I was up at bat. I never found out, then, what I was supposed to be doing. I never did anything, really—just stood there for a while and went back inside to my waiting sleeping bag.

As far as the battle of will versus the candle. Shakespeare, in one of his plays, said life is a tale told by an idiot, full of sound and fury, signifying nothing.

That isn't always bad.

Last full day.

I don't have as much water as I thought I would. I'm going to have to go for some more. That's going to be fun. My head is clear and my body is slowed down and distant, and a bit unreliable as far as working or walking.

The last whole day, and I have to go for some water. I could cry. It's that funny.

It's probably in my head, but I was queasier than ever this morning, especially downing the vitamins. The camp stove fuel is low, too. I can boil the water I get, but that's about it. No cat bath. My beard is coming in nicely.

I've lost about all the excess fat I had, and some muscle too, I'm sure.

In the morning, first thing, I'm the weakest. Later, my energy level increases gradually. My battery is low.

This morning is cool.

I used to believe we could change.

I think my understanding of the motivations that drive me and my actions has increased. I've identified some of the source of my 'do it because I want to' impulses.

Will I make it until tomorrow afternoon?

I want to.

Sometimes I get tired of being on my toes. Just when I think it's getting easier— Dizziness, queasiness, weakness; you name it, it happens. Those damned vitamins sure as hell upset my stomach. Christ. The old stomach doesn't like variety. Just water, please, thank you.

Last night my knee was bothering me. I had to adjust my position until I found one I could sleep in. I woke up in the middle of the night like always. This time, the bugs jumped all over my legs and the coal mine fan hummed and the wind blew.

The sun warms me through the window behind the chair now.

It helps.

Yesterday was hard. This whole 'keep the mind focused on nothing' thing is like holding back a river with two hands.

Like a horse straining at the gates, my mind races with: What'll I do when I get out of here? What'll I eat? Who will I see? What shows I'll watch, what things I'll say, and so on.

Even though yesterday was tough, there were corresponding extremes of peace. Between storms, the quiet is profound.

That last full day I was sort of reduced. Like a pot on the stove with all the water boiled out—only me was left.

Six-and-a-half days of no eating at that point. It's not something I would do again. Not like that. Next time, I'll read books, go for slow walks, sing to myself, write poetry, pray to God, laugh, cry more, and so on.

Final day.

I'm sitting in the passenger seat of my car a little before noon. Haven't eaten yet. Yesterday was not a day I'd like to relive. This morning is cool, like a week ago, and I woke before the birds started their morning insect hunt.

Yesterday afternoon I took a nap. That was probably a mistake. Last night was the worst night's rest I've ever had.

It was long after dark before I got to sleep. I woke in the middle of the night again and drank some water and sat in the chair.

This morning, I got up and watched the sun light the world outside.

I stood slowly, put everything in the cabin back like it was, and packed and shouldered my duffel bag and locked the cabin door and got a stick to lean on and left. Not an easy thing to do, just leaving.

When I came out of the woods on the seventh day, carrying all that canned food weight, it was three-quarters of a mile to the car. I stopped a lot to rest.

I can feel that walk to the car like it was today.

Looking back, I can say those seven days were necessary.

Everything was. <u>You</u> will have to figure out what "necessary" means. I think there are as many different definitions for it as there are people.

My marriage to Katherine three months later, our becoming friends while married, and our divorce. It was all necessary. Everything is necessary.

Why did I do this extreme, first, isolation?

It was the best thing I could do at the time. That's how it felt.

Would I recommend fasting or isolation?

Yeah.

This is the only surviving letter I have from Dad. He wrote to me while I was in the Army. He sent it while I was finishing Basic, at Fort Sill, Oklahoma, in the Army. I was 18. He was 44. The following month, he was gone. Other than chore instructions left under a magnet on the refrigerator while growing up, the letters Dad sent to me in basic were the only time I'd heard his "point of view" expressed this way. He was a man of not many spoken descriptive words. He was a substation operator for Detroit Edison, the power company. Little did I know when I received the letter that I would never see him alive again. I almost threw this one out, like the others, after reading. I remember almost chucking it, then deciding to save it.

[Dad's Letter]

Dazdell, Reg.
William H. & Mary Jo Weimer
161 Fowlerville Rd.
Fowlerville, Mi. 48836
[Our Dalmatian kennel name stamp, on upper left corner of envelope]

PV2 DAVID WEIMER
B BATTERY
7 TRAINING BATALLION
USAFATC
FORT SILL, OK
73503 6201
[My dad's customary all-caps printing on envelope and on five handwritten notepad pages, in pencil]

7-5-85
12:00

DEAR DAVID:

WELL! BY THIS TIME YOU SHOULD BE NOT LIKING THE ARMY LIFE A LOT. I KNOW YOU MISS US AND WE MISS YOU A LOT TOO. I GUESS YOU HAVE TO MOVE AWAY AND LOOK AT THINGS FROM ANOTHER POINT OF VIEW TO GET THE TRUE PICTURE. SOMETIMES LIFE IS LIKE AN OIL PAINTING. UP CLOSE IT LOOKS PRETTY BAD BUT WHEN YOU STAND BACK AWAY FROM IT EVERYTHING SEEMS A LOT CLEARER.

I KNOW YOU WILL MAKE IT THROUGH OK! THE BASIC TRAINING IS SOMETHING YOU JUST HAVE TO GO THROUGH TO REALLY KNOW WHAT IT IS LIKE. NO ONE CAN PREPARE YOU FOR IT. I KNOW YOU ARE A GENTLE CARING PERSON WHO WOULD FIND IT HARD TO HURT ANYONE OR ANYTHING. I KNOW YOU HAVE FEELINGS THAT TELL YOU THAT WHAT YOU ARE BEING TAUGHT IS WRONG. I ALSO KNOW THAT IT IS A DIRTY JOB AND SOMEONE HAS TO DO IT. IF NOT YOU THAN WHO DO WE ASK TO DO IT?

I KNOW THE TIME AND EFFORT YOU PUT INTO THE BAND AT SCHOOL. THAT WAS A JOINT EFFORT AND YOU KNOW WHAT CAN BE DONE BY WORKING TOGETHER AND DOING YOUR PART. I AM SURE YOU WILL DO A GOOD JOB. I DON'T KNOW IF YOU REALIZE HOW PROUD YOUR MOTHER AND I ARE OF THE WAY YOU WORKED OUT IN THE BAND AND OF THE EFFORT YOU PUT INTO YOUR SOLOS. YOU DID NOT TAKE THIS LIGHTLY AND WE KNOW YOU WILL APPLY THE SAME EFFORT TO EVERYTHING THAT YOU DO.

WELL! SO MUCH FOR THE PEP TALK. I AM AT WORK NOW WAITING FOR A PORTABLE SUBSTATION TO ARRIVE. I HAVE HAD MY JOB CHANGED 3 TIMES SINCE I STARTED WORK THIS MORNING. WE HAD A STORM AND LOST SOME POWER SO OUR ROUTINE THINGS HAD TO BE CHANGED AROUND.

PAT & I BURNED SOME OF THE BRUSH PIECES YOU AND HE PICKED UP LAST YEAR WHEN I WAS ON STRIKE AND CUT THE TREES DOWN BY MASON ROAD.

YOUR MOTHER AND I ARE GOING OUT TO DINNER TONIGHT. CAN YOU BELIEVE I HAVE BEEN LIVING WITH THE SAME WOMAN FOR 19 YEARS. I KNOW YOU LIVED WITH HER FOR 18 YEARS YOUR SELF. I CAN HONESTLY SAY THESE HAVE BEEN THE HAPPIEST YEARS SO FAR. I KNOW TO THE KIDS IT IS HARD TO TELL IF ANYONE IS HAPPY. THERE IS A LOT OF HOLLERING AND BAD FEELINGS BUT THE FEELINGS WOULD NOT BE AS INTENSE IF THERE WAS NOT A LOT OF LOVE THERE.

WELL! MY TRUCK IS HERE SO I WILL SAY SO LONG FOR NOW. TAKE CARE.

I LOVE YOU.

DAD & ALL

On the next page is a sonnet. It has Shakespeare's preferred end-rhyme scheme and the iambic pentameter that gives each line a five-step horse running cadence. I wrote this in the spring of '99 for a graduate poetry class at the University of Memphis. I was tired of the inane formless prose poetry everyone in class, including me, was churning out. I liked Shakespeare and what he was able to say about human conditions. I wanted to try to say something in this poetry form. It's about my father's drowning and my brother Pat's trying to save him.

Lake Superior,
Marquette, Michigan, 1985

Blueness fades as memories rearrange

And murmur of a father's fateful luck.

Deliberate work-worn hands now blue as veins;

No chafing will unseize their frozen lock.

His lot was introduced to that cold date

Of timely men, who swim into their door

Through aqua blue marine, paternal fate

No human power's able to ignore.

One Earthly sun dove deep to fight the tide,

Where desperate hands held hair, then arms, then naught.

With blackness, empty starving lungs replied,

And son lay gasping on the shore—his hours bought.

    Superior lake, my father's rendezvous;

    Vacations drowned into a paler blue.

I have included some of my correspondence with people in this book in order to convey my perspective. What you find in these pages are unedited selected correspondence—my words to someone. I have not condensed the emails; at most, I have excerpted from them, though most remain intact. These are a handful of needles from a mountain of needles. Not much hay. What is a perspective? Today, Merriam-Webster refers to it as "The interrelation in which a subject or its parts are mentally viewed" and, "the capacity to view things in their true relations or relative importance." Well.

This is my side of an ongoing thread with A.M. of Delaware, written Saturday, Sept. 25, 2004. We'd been talking about a life devoted to seeking one's ultimate truth or meaning. That objective, or goal, has been pointed to with words such as enlightenment, awakening, nirvana, and self-realization...

.... It sounds to me, a lot of the time, like you're talking about the practices and focusing on them as though they're the important thing. Practices like this mental exercise or that, fasting or whatever. Those things are and should be done, right? But for whatever reason, I find myself continually saying, "Levitation is not the end goal," to you...I

instinctively respond with, "Keep the eye on the ball," comments. But this could be misconstrued, too, unfortunately. I don't advocate focusing on the 'ball,' to the exclusion of all else. I advocate a central commitment and an inner homing-in or constant contact with that essential, important thing.

The ant and alien kind of mental tricks (looking at something in our life as though we were an alien looking down at a totally foreign world of activity, a kind of trick, to see things without the emotional identified 'heat' of being tied up in something) are things.... that helped me through my limitations. They were not important in themselves, although they were crucially important ingredients in my quest [to find something ultimately satisfying].

.... What I think, and believe, happens, is that when I or anyone becomes attuned to their fundamental, essential string, and begins walking on it, devoted to tracking it down to the end and distracted by nothing else than the clear purpose of a life dedicated to such a thing—[I believe] this causes every situation to be wrung out completely of its potential. No irrelevant experiences, no wasted moments, [no not-spiritual time]. All is relevant.

Each thing I looked at, everything I saw or smelled or heard. Every person I encountered, somehow bounced that sonar echo back to me, letting me know my exact position in this blind ocean (our existence) that we're all usually completely disoriented...in. I didn't choose to do this...I didn't decide to make everything relevant...That would be the limited, finite David trying to mess things up to suit himself.

.... So I value, profoundly, the extreme moments I had. They were the learning times, the purification times...It's not wrong to be profoundly moved...We're alive and we should at least give ourselves permission to be alive! ...When you push your limits, push yourself in ANY direction beyond the comfort zone; there will be signs in the self that something is being challenged! As opposed to always remaining in a place that never calls the person to do anything that would be noticed by anyone.

Seeing clearly is always better... The truth sets us free. Frees us from what had been holding us back, previously. And what was that? Our attachment, our fixation with some thing. We couldn't get past where we were because we were there—and nowhere else—until our work there was done. We'll never get into third grade until we're done with the second grade work. Or the first.

What feels better? Seeing more clearly; understanding something simply; feeling the calm of equanimity that comes from such unspoken comprehension? [Or] Being conflicted, irritated by outer circumstances, raving at incomprehension?

The latter is utterly necessary, because we get to a point where we can't bear it and we get up off our irritation and do something to understand [what we are going through and why] (all learning comes through pain or suffering). Once some understanding is gained, I would say that it is better to have gone through our journey from stubborn ignorance to surprised clarity and understanding than to somehow regret having left a more-limited state of being than we now enjoy.

It's self-evident, right? The worth of becoming a more mature person is felt and lived and breathed in every moment. It's unquestionably better than the previous ignorance and conflicted state of being. If it goes no further than that, it's still worth it. Going in this direction, we find ourselves becoming less finite, as [Richard] Rose terms it. I've seen this in you, unquestionably. And if it goes no further than being a more mature, more compassionate being, then it's still worth it. If you grow no wiser in your life, if you experience no other realization, it was worth it. Because I think you'll agree that you're a better person for it. I'm being presumptuous in saying what was "worth it" for you. I'm just pointing at a situation and saying, *Hey, what about that?*

There might be something even more 'worth it.' Something much more, that answers or responds appropriately to the [mystery] of our existence itself. That's the dream....

My comment about desperation and the word, "Yet."

You wrote:

You said; If you're not desperate, you're not convinced that it's not possible, yet. This reminds me of when I became desperate during my last isolation and I pounded the ground and begged for some kind of guidance. After a few minutes I was drained, and seemed to step back from the situation a little bit, and got back to "work". Does the "yet" at the end of your comment suggest that desperation becomes the norm?

My response:

Desperation becomes the norm. [Walking with the] certainty that there is no hope, no real truth to be found, no rescuing "experience." [And if there is such a thing, I am convinced I *don't have what it takes*—this is not a suspicion; it becomes a certainty.] Also, undiluted action becomes the norm. Action not mediated by holding back, other priorities, procrastination, etc. Action, in this context, meaning the in-breathing, out-breathing, second-by-second life that the seeker is currently living.

It is not a life [only] of desperation...it is not a naive life of belief in the existence of a grand experience at the end of a brief, costless attempt. [It is living futility and hope, simultaneously.]

There is an initial commitment to this crazy thing, Truth. Then, later, there was for me, a further one.

I was this seeker heading up a mountain. And there was a bridge that I had to cross, about three-quarters of the way up the mountain, and I crossed it, with some effort and risk and, in the crossing, the bridge broke loose of its moorings and fell to the ravine below.

This is the point of the seeker [who has] read a lot of books and experimented in practices and who has become competent in the esoteric field. At a certain point, there comes a creeping sense that my efforts aren't sufficient to get me to the top, to take me all the way. I have a feeling of the immenseness of the task, more than a guess, *a feeling*. And I have a feeling of my capacity, my capability. [And it's not going to be enough.]

And there is no turning back. Because [going back] is without hope, but going on is now seen as... not certain. So I continue on.

Rose talked about [G.I.] Gurdjieff's 'philosopher stage' of man. When the guy has come to an understanding of the limits and the ultimate circular failing of his intellect, his logic. And yet, [this man] is impelled from within to go further. Where, he does not know. But he does. He feels it stronger than ever. So, all blind, trusting adherence to practices is let go. He doesn't hold on to *any* practice. And yet, he does *something*. He continues. How is this possible, this action without action? Progress without progress? At this point, he sees that there is, ultimately, no such thing as 'progress' because the limits of the self-contained world of thinking are known and conceited concepts such as progress and goals are within that world, not above or beyond it.

When you see around the corners of statements and situations, you see that the paradox is *all*. The understanding you have in relation to K. and celibacy is an example of a wiser, more mature (seeker-wise) view of the world. Celibacy is utterly necessary, at one point, for one person. Control. Commitment. Dedication. Steadfastness. On the other end of the spectrum, which we must all experience to be complete in our understanding, is the dropping of such a commitment. Killing the Buddha. Letting go of the importance we project onto something. So then, later, we see both its value and its unimportance. They are both true. Not interchangeably, but nonetheless, true.

….Life is, for the seeker, a grand opportunity to become more and more capable of distinguishing between things.

Understanding. Intuition. These kinds of things. We've got nothing but chances to practice our discernment. Unlimited number of chances to sharpen ourselves, we tools-of-exploration-and-understanding and… ultimately, being.

Yeah-hoo.

Okay, gotta go.

Home is where the heart is

My family moved a few times. I have memories of three distinct 'homes' that feel like that word. They *were* our home; where we lived and ate and slept and played and worked and all that. Wixom. 1990 Teaneck Circle, Wixom Michigan. Phone number, 627-0062. I was drilled to memorize this. I must have been five- or six-years-old, just starting kindergarten. It's indelible still. Then there is 5011 Jewell Road, Howell, Michigan, where the core, the middle age years of childhood, resides. And finally, there's where we lived in my 'old age' of childhood: where I learned to drive, had girlfriends, left home to join the Army. 161 Fowlerville Road, Fowlerville, Michigan. It was our nicest house, but one that feels the coldest to me. I'd left at 18 and never slept another peaceful night in *that* house.

[Here are lasting scenes from my early life—which itself lasted forever and was the <u>real world</u>. I remember how I felt in those days and days of being— of being twelve and seven, regarding the life inside of me and around me from my own shoes, from my own standing place.]

Wixom is where I learned how to ride a bike. I remember Dad helping me with that and my last, successful run, on the sidewalk behind our house just as dusk turned to dark. I have video copies of the home movies my mom took of this moment. It was surreal to view these, unexpectedly, recently, with my own family. As a six- or seven-year-old, I crashed into the grass of our yard, giddy with triumph. This place in my life is where I remember walking to school in the dark with flashlights in first and second grade—yes, we could do that then. We lived in a subdivision adjacent to the elementary school. I thoroughly enjoyed the walking. It was magical in the dark of winter. There was a playground at the edge of our subdivision. There was a pool of water on the left side of the path that led up through the school playground to the building. I liked to skip stones before and after school. In the summer, I'd lay on the sidewalk edge near our house and taste the little white grains men on lawnmower tractors would sprinkle on the grass. Some kind of fertilizer, I'm hoping. They fizzed on the tongue.

*

I remember the summer. It must have been second grade. Every day, walking to elementary school, I'd pass a farm fence row interspersed with trees. On the other side, another subdivision was being built. I watched it go from a field with stakes to earth moving, then foundations and buildings and all the associated, fascinating, activity. I watched it grow more interesting. For my birthday that year, I'd gotten a canteen with Smokey the Bear on it and a compass. One Sunday, I filled my canteen with water, put my compass in my pocket and told Mom I was going out to play. She asked me where and I said near the playground—which wasn't exactly a lie. I slowed down as I passed the climbing area, then continued farther, towards school, where I found a low place in the fence and slipped between rusting barbed wire and squished-down square wire fencing, then cautiously on into the development under construction. I knew the guys wouldn't be working.

I went there a couple more times before being told by my dad to stay away. One time, after I was used to the place, I went inside one of the duplexes and my great discovery and secret that day was I found the ice trays in the freezer. That was the neatest thing, snooping around those unfinished apartments, looking in the freezers. I plopped some into my canteen and munched on others, savoring the refreshing cold in the summer warmth.

*

I remember cutting myself once, while reaching into a hollow tree. I had been swinging at the playground. There was an empty broken bottle in that tree bole and my finger was bleeding pretty good. It was dusk and I was scared. Then I saw a house with a sticker on the front that I recognized as meaning "a kid-friendly place" and the lady in there put a band-aid on my finger and called my mom. It was cold that day, and I was glad to be inside being helped by someone nice.

*

Christmases when Santa Claus was real. The artificial fireplace that I'd turn one knob one click and a roll with a light bulb behind would turn, making flames lick over/behind fake logs. Two clicks of another black knob on the side, and a fan would kick on and warm air would blow out of the fireplace. The smell of burning dust often accompanied the warmth. I'd sit there, in front of that fireplace at night in my footed zip-up pajamas and get as close as I could to the warmth. I'd come out from my bedroom, when everybody was in bed, and quietly click those two knobs and stare at that fake fire and think about things while feeling the warmth. Winters were cold in Michigan, but Wixom is still the *warmest* place in my memory.

*

We had a big yellow chair that was *home*. We had a cat, Powder, and my Dalmatian, Daisy.

*

Winters were wonderful. My dad would put these big, oversized colored lights around the house and in the shrubs and when we had a heavy snow, the lights would glow under a white blanket their different colors. One winter, in my snowmobile suit, I stomped through thigh-high snow drifts around the side of our house to the shrubs, now bumps in snow almost as high as me. Wind had connected snow from the side of the house to the shrubs and, on a whim, I jumped up and landed on my back and slid down an opening on top—slipping right under a shrub into a snow cave.

There I was, upside down on my back, with my feet near the opening of the snow cave and my hood-enclosed head below. I couldn't move. I yelled, but the wind was blowing, I was under the snow, and coldness was filtering past my cheeks and collecting at the pit in my throat where ice water melted. Fear. I remember thinking my parents would come out and find me, upside down in a drift with my head under that shrub, cold and dead. The shrub was a kind of evergreen, spruce maybe, with powdery light-blue needles. I'll never forget the smell.

After calling out and waiting for help that didn't come, I decided to do this myself—I somehow turned, by getting mad and thrashing, onto my stomach. Then I pushed up, wiggling and struggling, and backed out. The frigid wind on the melted snow on my hot face. It was an open, freedom-feeling. I didn't tell my parents, but I yelled at my little brother, or maybe my sister, 'You might fall in there and never get out!'

Dad and Mom on buggy, Lucky in harness, dog under buggy; just above: Pat on sulky with Jacky, me standing, Anne behind Pat, mom in buggy with Lucky--Dad taking photo (Circa 1983); top photo: 16-year-old me in McDonald's uniform with my first car, a '71 Ford Maverick.

*

When we lived in that Wixom subdivision, our ponies stayed in a large open field behind one of the power stations where my dad worked. Dad was a substation operator and got permission from Detroit Edison to use a field behind a power transfer station to keep our horses with another guy he worked with. Our two Welsh ponies, Lucky and Jacky, came to Michigan from Pennsylvania, where my grandpa lived, when I was around six. Grandpa named my horse Lucky because he'd won him in a raffle at the local annual firemen's fair at the "flax sketching grounds" in Stahlstown.

We brought the ponies to the field behind the substation in the back of my dad's light blue Datsun pickup. It wasn't a full-sized truck, either. That thing rode low, I remember. My dad had worked at a stable as a young man and had a lot of experience with horses. He did all of our blacksmith work and taught us the same. He broke our ponies, and later, our other horses, to harness, saddle and bridle. I learned something from him.

There was plywood up on the sides of that small pickup truck and across the back. I remember a thin yellow nylon rope holding the two pieces of plywood to each other in the back. Eight hours on the highway with the two horses standing back there—wow. We kids and Mom followed in our station wagon. Both ponies dropped some ballast along the way. That was a highpoint for us, seeing the manure tumble and fly apart on the highway before our car ran over it. 'All right Jacky!'

After the equines were back on solid ground, I remember helping my dad put up an electric fence in a lightning storm that night. I was afraid of the lightning and soaking wet. I held the flashlight and handed my dad wire and insulators when he needed them. It was cold. Water dropped off my nose.

*

I have VCR copies of home movies that Anne made of Dad's reel-to-reel silent movies showing us kids racing Lucky and Jacky up and down the long slope that was part of our horse field. There was a flat area below, where we had a shed. Dad had a couple of fifty-five gallon barrels I'd race Lucky around in a figure-8. Long, dry hot afternoons there, I remember. It was great.

Lucky was my horse and Jacky was Anne's—at first—before she got Frosty, her P.O.A. (between a pony and a horse in size). When Pat was big enough, he got Jacky. I remember one time racing out ahead of Anne on that flat area and then falling over and hanging under Lucky, still galloping, on his right side, holding onto the horn of the saddle. The saddle had slid over and I was clinging on while Lucky thundered ahead. We'd stepped on an underground yellow jacket's nest and I suppose they stung him. Head down, ears back, Lucky never let another horse pass him. When he was racing his brother, Jacky, or another horse; as soon as he saw them in the corner of his eye, he'd just point that head of his and there'd be no stopping him. I remember flying with Lucky like the wind. Thundering. Most of the time I rode bareback—too lazy to saddle up. Over that span of years which felt like forever, and the three places we lived, Lucky was my best friend.

Chapter 2 — Crossroads

The first time I went into a period of isolation in a cabin for philosophic purposes, I fasted for a week. I stared at a candle, all day, every day. At the time it felt like the thing to do. I had recently become a member of the TAT Foundation, a Zen-style metaphysical study group founded in 1973 by Richard Rose, a no-nonsense West Virginia mystic from Wheeling who'd had a transformational "enlightenment" experience in Seattle in 1947 at the age of 30.

The previous year, 1992, I interviewed Rose on the telephone for a preview article on the lecture he was going to give at the University of Pittsburgh. I was an English writing major and a staff reporter for *The Pitt News*, the daily newspaper for the Oakland campus, the main campus. I'd grown accustomed to interviewing people for stories and, with my set of preconceived notions, I called Rose at his West Virginia home from the newsroom in the William Pitt Student Union Building. I wanted a few quick quotes to fill out a story I wanted to give to the editors putting the next day's paper together. The interview didn't go well. My leading questions were as effective as tugging on the rope tied around the neck of an unwilling donkey. The guy just wouldn't answer my questions in the desired way.

After a frustrating series of questions, too much time and not many 'usable' answers, I crafted a kind of article after the phone receiver was back in its cradle. During the interview, there had been a point where I gave up and put down my pen. "Zen Guru Cometh," was the headline my editors put on the story.

I covered the subjects I found interesting. In our weekly editorial meeting for The Pitt News, my editor, Christy, a thin, casual-seeming yet intense young woman with makeup-covered acne, would meet us writers in the paper's lounge on the fourth floor. She would go through a pile of faxes, dolling them out to whoever volunteered to cover the stories. She'd tell us what she wanted covered and we would lean forward and take the sheet she held out. There were seasonal things, university events and greater world events. We all worked on stories from our own contacts and "feelers" and would try to get Christy to let us do them. My 'beat' became the offbeat stuff.

That '93 spring semester I attended the first meeting of the Zen Study Group to write an article. It was a 7:30 p.m. meeting on the second floor of the gothic 42-story Cathedral of Learning, a 535-foot-tall building that looks like its name, with offices and departments on upper floors, classrooms and "nationality rooms" meticulously decorated in the style of different nations around the base and a gigantic open area with soaring 50-foot-tall common areas that still somehow managed to feel cozy and subdued.

During my time at Pitt, I had a favorite third floor stone window sill in the Cathedral hallway above a radiant heater. I'd open the lead-paned double windows in warm weather and look through the panes in the cold—ice and white outside with heat rising up and around the ledge over the register. I'd sit in the window sill and look out into the branches of the trees below between the cathedral and a theater building.

Okay, about the Zen meetings. My hunch told me there was some unannounced reason for this meeting's existence. Some of these guys were older. Some weren't students at all. We started off by having five minutes of silence in the unlikely amphitheater of a classroom of finished wooden built-in chairs on tiered levels. The talk that night was on finding one's definition. I found a resonating chord within me during that meeting.

After the meeting, I interviewed two brothers, B.G. and N. G., who had started the group. I remember talking to B.G. outside the classroom, standing in front of some lockers. Mike, the group's president, was a pre-med student. I got some quotes from him. There were about a dozen attendees. I wrote an article.

I became the group's advertising for its events, which including occasional lectures by Richard Rose, the founder of an esoteric organization whose members had largely filled that first meeting on the second floor of the Cathedral.

They called me when Rose was coming to talk and I told Christy I could do a preview story on a Zen master coming up to lecture at Pitt. The group, now called the Self Knowledge Symposium (SKS), also put on a hypnosis demonstration and lecture. I did stories on these events and others. I attended the group's meetings. After a while, I quit writing for *The Pitt News*. I felt a conflict of interest. If I continued to write "articles" for this group, I felt that I'd be dishonest; I'd be posing as an objective observer reporting—but I'd be a mouthpiece for this group's agenda. I didn't want to feel that conflict anymore so I quit the paper. I'd also come to feel that I didn't want to spend my precious time anything I wasn't genuinely interested in. This was a turn in my life.

I started to turn consciously (I think) in the direction of philosophy, which, among other things, Merriam-Webster calls, "The pursuit of wisdom; the search for a general understanding of values and reality by chiefly speculative rather than observational means." Hmm. Thinking one's way somewhere. Alright. But I would like to add that it's the search for understanding based on observational means, also. Observation of my life, life itself, the lives and actions of others, my own thoughts and reactions and turning the spotlight of my attention away from facing only outward to focus back on my self, wherever I am, *whatever* I am.

There it was. The beginning of my end. It was really only going to lead to that.

Eight years earlier…

I don't remember how long I was at home on leave for Dad's funeral. It was September 1985. He died ten days after his birthday. Mom said Dad would have wanted me to continue in the military instead of getting a family hardship honorable discharge, which I was eligible for and brought up. She told me about how proud Dad had been to tell people about my acceptance to West Point prep school. The only problem, was that his death threw me into an irreversible condition. I questioned *all* endeavors. Not intellectually, but at a bedrock level. *What's the meaning of <u>anything</u>?*

I went back to Fort Sill. Because I'd missed a week or two, I ended up in the class after mine. Those times were Oklahoma autumn cooling days and nights. In June and July, during basic, the sun beat down relentlessly and a constant wind blew from a world-sized open oven.

We'd sweat and stay blown dry. When we took off our web gear, the harness-like affair consisting of a web belt with two shoulder straps that ammo pouches, first aid kit, canteens and other things hung were attached to; you'd see the outlines on our fatigue shirts crisply edged in white from dissolved salts of endless sweating. We wore this gear along with our "steel pot" almost constantly in basic training.

In AIT (Advanced Individual Training—where you learn your job after basic training), 1985, September, October and November days went by, growing colder and shorter. PT formations in the dark parking lot near our barracks. 'Gorilla drills' in the grass field nearby. Marching with others from all various schools relating to artillery—radar, survey, fire support, etc. —not seeing individuals in the dark but being in a group, "sounding off" with one large voice, echoing a cadence-calling sergeant or junior non-commissioned officer (NCO). Part of something.

Marching in the dark one morning in formation with my survey class, we had just drawn our instruments from a field artillery survey school supply building. One guy I thought of as Frankenstein marched just like the monster. He'd take these big wooden steps, tripping over unseen things. He stepped constantly on the heels of the guy in front of him. Most mornings were spent marching before dawn or standing in "cattle cars" pulled by tractor-trailer haulers. I have a memory of Frankenstein lurching along, in the formation with the rest of us. I was behind, bemused by his distinctive gate. We were all carrying our *Wild* T-2 theodolites (instruments attached to tripods that are used to measure angles between distant objects) in their capsule-shaped carrying containers, holding them in our left hands by leather straps. Frankenstein tripped again and there went his T-2! Bouncing and rolling across the pavement. I think there was a slight downhill grade and I know a couple guys kicked it before it cleared the formation. The metal container snapped open and this delicate, precise surveying instrument rolled along the uneven pavement before coming to a stop. 'Jesus Christ,' I said. That was the funniest thing I'd ever seen. For some reason, at the time, I couldn't stop laughing. That was great. Laughing like that.

Every day, when we turned those instruments in, the supply sergeant always popped the cover off and gave them a real going-over, with an unbelievable degree of scrutiny, looking for any tiny scratch or blemish before allowing you to sign them back in. Walking away, after narrowly "passing the test," you felt like you had been given another chance at life from a firing squad. In the Army, whenever you sign for something, you accept all the blame for whatever condition it's in. Regardless. Like renting a car. I couldn't wait to see what old Sarge would do that day. Earlier that morning, Frankenstein somehow got the dented cover back on and lurched to catch up to the rear. I swear I heard parts rattling in his canister back there. I just kept laughing silently. His instrument didn't work worth a damn that day on the surveying line where we practiced setting up and turning angles —wouldn't level, wouldn't turn angles—there was a crowd of instructors around his tripod all morning. Imagine that.

This big clumsy oaf was a really nice guy. Nicer than me and nicer, by far, than most people you'll run into. He was earnest and decent. I feel terrible about how I treated him in my mind back then. And I have him to thank for some cathartic relief. Man, that helped me a lot.

I remember smoking in cattle cars. I kept my cigarettes in a two-piece protective plastic pack-shaped case. I had a Zippo lighter that burned my leg through my pocket when I overfilled it with fluid. In the daylight, I used to put my arm around one of the poles in there and hold a paperback in one hand, smoking with the other. There were about three single seats in the cattle cars, in the front just behind the cab of the truck. Everyone else stood. Those seats were coveted. We swayed and lurched together as the truck went around bends and hit potholes in the road.

Oklahoma is a big open place; at least the Fort Sill part was. A lot of up and down rolling hill driving. A cattle car would hold two or three classes, I'd guess. A hundred guys or more. The loneliest feeling in the world is a cattle car with just a few people standing in it. They were made to be packed tight. Narrow windows along the sides, and I'd try to position myself near one for the light to read by. Sometimes, looking out those small windows at the world going by, I knew we were cows being taken to our fate. We all are. We rode uncomplainingly. Not because we were brave or stoic, but because we were resigned, and also, I think incapable of comprehending or questioning the greater purpose of what we were a part of. We were young. Maybe that's how real cattle feel, on the way to the processing plant.

Most mornings, before the sun, I'd close my eyes and doze until we got to where we were going. The good thing about a lot of guys in a cattle car is there is heat and bodies to block the freezing wind coming in the open windows at the front of the cattle car. When it stopped, the air brakes would hiss, the driver would come and open up the side door and we'd flow out and get into our class formations. We'd march to our respective buildings past rows of radar equipment, ambulances, lines of towed howitzers or parked Multiple Launch Rocket System (MLRS) trucks.

I don't remember much else about AIT. We did some night surveys, using the stars; that was cool. Later, after active duty, while in my Florida and Pennsylvania Army National Guard units, the guys there would tell their tales about basic. That was like talking about kindergarten. Guard guys went to basic and AIT and then went right back home, where they'd live out their normal lives except for one weekend a month and two or three weeks of annual training (AT) each year, when they'd be Army guys. In basic, there was tension between "regular Army" guys and weekend warrior types because the regulars invariably took it more seriously and reserve guys knew that they were going home soon, not always giving it their all. The Army says a team is as strong as its weakest link. In basic and AIT, I think those guard guys were the cows who saw an open gate out of the corner of their eye. That's how it was. I'm sure things are different today since reservists make up a big percentage of the fighting forces our nation is keeping busy in Iraq, Afghanistan, Kuwait, and other 'strategic' places.

I have these nostalgic partial scenes preserved in timeless amber. I remember a few guys from AIT. Fetheran, a Hawaiian who always took extra fruit from the chow hall, taught me to juggle. I remember passing his bunk, seeing those three oranges on his dark green wool blanket, and taking advantage of the opportunity to practice my new skill. After dropping them a number of times, I put them back down there the same way they were. I bought a can of tennis balls at the PX to practice with.

A short black dude. Real cool. He smoked menthol cigarettes and wore these glasses like they were a million bucks. He was a cool cat. A group of us hung around. Guys from my class and guys from the class before us. The class I used to be in was upstairs in the World War II barrack building we occupied, and I was downstairs now, with my second class. There was another guy that talked and looked exactly like Yogi Bear. Real decent guy, but I always felt like I was talking to Yogi. "Hey, Boo-boo!" I'd hear whenever he talked. He was a big spit-shiner. He'd shine his dress shoes, jump boots (apparently made for Airborne infantry soldiers) and normal daily boots. I bet he spit shines his shoes today, wherever he is.

The barracks, all of them identical, had fire escapes on the back. These slightly dilapidated wooden buildings stood in long, silent, sad rows. Yogi (I don't remember his real name), would often be sitting on the back porch, with the lid from a tin of shoe polish filled with water, and a cotton brown t-shirt around his pointer finger, the other hand inside of a boot. He'd breathe on the toe he was working on, get a little black kiwi polish on his finger, dip it in the water, and go back to rubbing those little circles. All this is in AIT; we had time on our hands after school and really nowhere to go.

Guys would light their shoe polish on fire on their boots. Black guys really liked spit shining their footwear. They would wear dew rags on their heads during off duty times. They'd iron and starch their camouflage BDU's (Battle Dress, Uniform) at night. You couldn't compete with them. They were in a league all their own. GQ. My favorite method of boot shining was the stocking method. Boy, what a time-saver. Just polish the boots like normal. Polish right over any dirt or places where the black was missing. After a few minutes, hit them with a brush, then put them on and buff them with a nylon stocking stretched tightly in two hands like a rubber band. It takes about 30 seconds. The nylon burnished the polish onto the boots, looking like I did something to them. Normal spit shining takes about 45 minutes. I'd rather be reading.

As the weather turned colder, I remember a daily routine of courses of instruction and weekends. I remember sitting in one required check-writing class. I think I recall when we all graduated from AIT; a vague memory of the ceremony. After graduation, we were all in this large carpeted office area divided into cubicles where we got our permanent duty assignments—this is where we'd be stationed for our first deployment. Two- and three-year guys would likely stay in one duty station for their entire enlistment. The four-year hitchers would transfer to another duty station after their first 18 or 24 months.

Cool black cat went to Germany and so did I. I remember running into him outside a post eatery near Hanau. Yogi went to Korea; Turner went to Fort Bliss or someplace in the south; he didn't want to leave the States. That was a heavy kind of day because we all knew we were heading into our real Army times, saying goodbye to each other.

I forgot to mention Mel Hager. He and I were friends in basic training. He was nice to me. He was the old man of the platoon—31-years-old. I was 18. For some reason, we hit it off and got along like we've known each other our whole lives. This was before Dad died. Ironically, he called me "Son" and I called him "Dad." We had a similar sense of humor and used to smoke cigarettes on the bleachers after chow. In basic, you'd have a red arm band pinned to your shoulder if you were a platoon guide or squad leader. Mel was platoon guide for most of basic. In a "chain of command," he's the one the drill sergeants told what they wanted from us throughout the long basic training day. Night duty watch, extra duty, work details, barracks cleaning and preparing for the next day's training —that kind of thing. He marched us wherever the drill sergeants wanted us to go. I was a squad leader for most of this time in basic.

Mel would tell us four or five squad leaders what we were supposed to do, and we'd tell our eight or ten guys what *they* were supposed to do—and they'd tell each other what to do. Mel felt *gray*. That's the only way I can describe my impression of him. Not old, just the color gray. He wore thick Army-issue glasses and was shaped like a square. His hairline didn't end on the back of his neck. It started at his forehead and continued, non-stop, under his t-shirt. He regularly shaved the back of his neck, creating an artificial hair line, to keep the drill sergeants off his back. Ha.

Mel was married and had served in the Air Force for six years. Then got out, and some years later decided to get back into the military, this time the Army, before he was too old to be accepted. Ordinarily, transferring to another military branch, he wouldn't have to re-do basic, but enough time had passed that he had to go through Army basic before something like 12 months of AIT for Army intelligence or radar, I forgot which. Probably radar.

With some of the physical stuff, Mel struggled. I remember doing remedial PT with him, holding his feet while he did extra sit-ups, doing push-ups alongside him and running. I was assigned to get his PT scores higher (meaning passing). We took PT tests every couple of weeks in basic. That's two minutes to do as many sit-ups as you can, two minutes to do as many push-ups as you can, and a two-mile run. The requirements were stepped down according your age and Mel was older than some of the drill sergeants. We'd do pushups and sit-ups every night in the front of the open bay barracks. After that, we'd go down to the bleachers to smoke and talk. There were butt cans down there, and it was the only place allowed.

I saw Mel once during AIT. He was living off post with his wife and wore normal glasses. I remember staying at their place one night. I don't remember anything else except a vague feeling and waking up in a dark unfamiliar living room where an LED clock glowed red. Somehow it felt like forever.

After Dad's funeral, I told my family I would do my two-year enlistment first and then see if I wanted to go on to West Point. By the time I got to Bravo Battery, 1st of the 107th Field Artillery, Lance Missile Battalion, Fliegerhorst Kaserne, near Hanau, Germany (home of the Brothers Grimm), Winter 1985, I'd quietly settled on not pursuing a military career. *I'll do my two years and get out.* That probably contributed to my sense of loneliness and homesickness.

Dad's death was a turning point for all of us. I don't know anything except what I've lived, but I can assume this is true for Mom and my brother and sister. Did we ever sit down and have a talk about Dad and what we felt like and went through after his death? It sounds like we should have. We should have, but we didn't. Pat is a missionary now in Iceland, saving souls. Anne is a wife and mother in Tennessee. Mom is in retirement and lives near Anne. No family lives near me, in Ohio. If Dad hadn't died, I might still be in the Army, or just retired after 25 years as an officer who served in Iraq or any one of the half dozen 'conflicts' we've been publically involved in since 1985. Instead, I'm married to my French true love, Andrée. We lived in Europe, came back to Fowlerville, Michigan where my dad's grave marker is, then moved on to the Ohio Valley. I suspect there is more in store for us.

All of Me

by David W. Weimer, © 2009

I think I'm never going to die

Although I know I am.

Sometimes when I think this, I am overwhelmed with feeling how profound life is.

Walking in the radiating asphalt parking lot under the burning star,

My shoe finds a blob of gum; I smell spearmint and drag my foot, leaving gossamer streaks on the shimmering black.

I look around at others in the area outside the store; I see the sky, I notice cars, I see lawnmowers in a row.

Then I slip back into the pool of forgetfulness.

My life cycles like this.

I wish..

I remember times as a young man, as a boy; I remember being more present, then, to life.

I remember walking in the woods after smoking, while smoking, looking up at trees.

I was alive. I have nostalgia now of then.

Going into the Eat 'n' Park restaurant after leaving the home improvement store,

I wake back up, it seems.

I sit in the stall, on the seat, listening to the music coming from the speaker over my head.

I trace with my eyes the same wood grain patterns that I traced the last time I was here.

I sit there, remembering being awake before; I listen to the music and identify with it. Then

I'm back in my work van after walking the parking lot and unlocking the door and settling in and

Turning the ignition, putting on my seat belt, putting the gear selector in drive, moving out, merging into traffic, driving to wherever I am going.

I hope that I will have time to think about this when I am an old man.

I hope that I will have hours on end to sit-lay in a folding reclining lawn chair in the shade on a sunny day.

I want to think about many things with time to spend on everything. I want to lose myself in this some day.

Maybe I will get there, to that place. I hope so.

When I grow up, what will I be? I wondered a long time ago;

What was I? I may wake up to ask at the end.

I want to be home and to travel to somewhere new every day.

I want to live and I want to die. I want it all.

Chapter 3 —Making a Person (...)

I took a non-fiction class in graduate school at the University of Memphis. I walked through a certain intersection every day to go to class. I always noted the nonstop flow of activity there. I wondered what it would feel like and what would happen if I just stood, pen at paper, and recorded what I saw for several hours. I somehow feel that every place, stood in like this, would be rich, varied and full. Every place is action. An empty parking lot, an empty room, a forest, a bus stop. Something is always moving, even in quiet times. Something IS always. There's always something moving.

What if some 'crazy' guy had done this in 17th Century Paris and you were able to read it today? What if one of the astronauts had done this while on the moon in the Lunar Excursion Module (LEM) in 1969? What if you did this, recorded everything you saw, sitting in one place, for a few hours, and someone read your words two hundred years from now—or tomorrow? Or...never?

Most of life that is breathed in and out goes unrecorded. What about recording, sans comment, some "mundane" breathing and see how it sounds? What would happen if I strictly observed, without analyzing or interpreting? Imagine... Is this a step closer to that elusive non-subjective "reality" people wonder about?

The tick of a second hand is soothing—to some. To others, it's maddening. Does time pass without ticking clocks? My non-fiction writing class professor surprised me by accepting my proposition to write about a crossroads. As I have found—accidentally it seems—I hope you, too, can discover through encountering different, unexpected, things that you develop an openness, outside your usual reaction patterns for... more. The challenge is to read this piece unconnected to your habitual way of demanding a piece of writing "make sense" or "get to the point." Maybe you can't do this. Maybe you'll skip the following. Maybe there is a "point" to be found outside of your expectations—or demands.

"Point of Departure"

WRITTEN FOR A NON-FICTION GRADUATE WRITING CLASS

ENGLISH DEPARTMENT, UNIVERSITY OF MEMPHIS

On assignment to capture an elusive intersection. They say you can write about a dust mote and reveal a world. Well, I hope so. It's mid-afternoon on a momentary pleasant day, this Tuesday, February 2nd, 1999.

Two Memphis city electric trucks zigzag off Southern, hopping over the tracks on Patterson then cutting left onto Walker toward Highland.

A row of Spanish bayonets brandish their sword-leafed tips along Walker where Patterson stops just before shuffling sideways a hundred feet and taking off to go over the tracks in a hump.

A jet plane pierces the clouds. Intermittently breezy, like waves on a lake shore in winter. The sun comes through and warms my writing hand. A girl cuts through the line of bayonets and through the grass and steps over the tracks.

I'm leaning on a visitor sign. The arrow I'm blocking points to Patterson, into the university. It's a sturdy two-inch square tube aluminum rectangular sign painted gray. *University of Memphis* in white letters on blue. *Visitor Information Center* below that.

Next to me, a black guy pulls into the queue at the intersection in a low slung, Armoralled-tires-glistening, car stereo so loud every piece of chrome and body panel on the car is rattling and buzzing. In a minute he is gone over the tracks, down Southern, thumping and humming.

Memphis Harding Academy; a standard Bluebird white school bus with blue trim zigzags from Walker, behind me, from the teachers' school back there, and is over the tracks and down Patterson into a residential area in no time. Its door opens briefly at the tracks. Kids' heads move with the movement.

This is an orderly free-for-all.

It's two intersections connected by a piece of Patterson. Siamese twins, joined at the waist by a piece of Patterson. A single set of train tracks stands upright between them. Not very Siamese sounding, these twins names are Southern and Walker. The connected brothers cooperate, shuffle their cars, and it all works out in the end.

The clouds are high, blue-black puffs moving fast. A jet takes off from the airport six miles south. Heading this way—another FedEx jet—over the suburban neighborhood, frat house parking lot, and me, gaining altitude and speed.

The railroad corridor between Walker and Southern is about a hundred feet wide. Well-maintained tracks on a narrow bed of gravel. Two light-and-arm things are set up at the intersection. A wire from the nearest power pole along Southern drops to a metal box perched on stilts near the one-armed automatic traffic-stopper on the Southern side of the tracks.

There's a broadcast tower on the other side of the Apocalypse Café on Southern going toward Highland. About 150 feet high and pyramid-looking. Three metal legs, leaning in, stop flatly at the top. A cluster of vertical barnacles hang on, in the middle of the tower. Assorted satellite dishes, too. The whole thing looks like a deliberate flower arrangement. From the intersection it's not something you'd notice; you have to look up.

There's a girl in a green Saturn. A white girl singing loud with her radio. She scoots over the tracks, turns east on Southern. Now a shorthaired blond girl with a green backpack and a water bottle cuts across my view. She passes through the bayonets, goes over the tracks, across Southern and into the fraternity house parking lot. She gets into a brown car and drives down Patterson into a residential area. *F & J Towing* flatbed truck hauls a van with gold gills for wheels over the tracks and follows the singing girl east on Southern.

The twins work without a metronome—smooth.

An oriental woman suddenly appears with a child in a backpack on the sidewalk across from me on Walker—which is to say I just noticed her. A year-old baby girl with a yellow knit beret rides on her back in comfort and style. She's an older woman. Hair still black though a little dusty. She looks a little beat, but her movements are energetic. She makes it past the bus stop and approaches the corner of Patterson and Walker. I turn, with them, writing. They turn left on Patterson into the campus. The little girl looks back with black unblinking eyes.

She reminds me of a black man I used to see almost every day on my way to work at *The Commercial Appeal* newspaper. He would either be walking toward me on Union Avenue while I drove west into the city, or he would be at his post on a small concrete island in the middle of the intersection at Bellevue and Union. Right at Methodist Hospital and across from the Admiral Benbow Inn. So, I would see him on the move or I would drive by him already at his post. He is a medium built man of indeterminate age in spite of the gray in his hair. He always wears a light colored Panama hat like Gilligan from the TV show and a black apron with this written in big white letters:

The light of the body is the eye: if therefore thine eye be single, thy whole body shall be full of light. But if thine eye be evil, thy whole body shall be full of darkness. If therefore the light that is in thee be darkness, how great is that darkness!

This is from the Sermon on the Mount as described in Matthew, chapter six, verses 22-24 of the New Testament. Actually, I don't really know if this is what his apron says. My mind has the impression of something about the dirtiness inside a man that can be done away with, and that the man can be made whole again. I've seen him dozens of times on my way to work at the newspaper where I write obituaries now. Once, back in December, I read his apron carefully. It made in impact on me at the time, but all I have left is a vague memory of a Matthew reference. So I scanned the book of Matthew in the Bible my brother left after a visit last year and found the closest thing to my recollection. I'll make it a point to pay attention when I see the apron man again.

When he stands at his post, he has his hands clasped behind him and he faces traffic, presenting his apron silently to the stream of traffic, keeping himself out of the picture. That little oriental girl reminds me of him. How a person looks at others. This topic seems relevant to my watching the world at this intersection.

Karate instructors say where the head goes the body goes—where the head turns, the body follows. Maybe that's what the apron said.

There's a pile of gravel near the stop sign here on Walker where Patterson begins before slicing across the tracks. Cars have it spread like windshield wipers spread bugs. Pulverized dirt, separated gravel and white dust. Just now, an old pickup skids to a stop, spins its left wheel there, and takes off straight at me on Walker.

Memphis Harding Academy bounces empty over the tracks while the old pickup fades behind me. The bus made a tight g-force turn on Walker and accelerates towards Highland.

Walker splits into a 'Y' down there; the two ends part around a compact collection of buildings—a restaurant, a Laundromat, a textbook store, a muffler shop and another restaurant—a ship of buildings that splits Walker like the prow of an old oil tanker; Walker floats by along its sides, crossing Highland in the wake behind.

A white guy in a dark sweater staples big green posters on all the poles at Southern—the left-handed of the Siamese twins. He's got a heavy-duty silver handgrip stapler and looks self-conscious but he works like it's his job stapling those giant fluorescent posters.

Now he's across the tracks and has a yellow one held against a pole on Walker while he shoots staples into the top and bottom. He gets the pole at the bus stop with another green one. He's on the same sidewalk as the oriental woman with the child backpack. He's out of posters. There's a red car parked near the fire hydrant in front of Patterson Hall and he gets more from the passenger side.

An accomplice!

The red car speeds into the university campus. He follows with more posters under his arm, stapling up more green ones, crossing back and forth on Patterson to get both sides.

Reminds me of my own poster days. The first poster I ever put up of my own was a half-size one —I made two for the price of one that way; and it was a little handbill that said:

For madmen only!

Price of admittance

your mind.

Hermann Hesse's, *Steppenwolf* inspired it. In his book, a vine-covered brick wall, if approached at the right time in the dead of night in some old, old town in Europe, would materialize a door which led into a world of dreams and magical timeless adventures. My poster also said there would be a meeting at 7 p.m. in a second floor room of the Cathedral of Learning at the University of Pittsburgh, in February 1993. It was an advertisement for a first meeting of the year of the Self Knowledge Symposium, a philosophy group with one member, a borrowed desktop stapler and a handful of stolen thumbtacks. That's another story.

I jog over the piece of Patterson that pierces the Walker twin's side to look at the only fluorescent yellow poster. It says:

Straight up Buzz

Young Avenue Deli

Saturday 2/6/99.

10:45 p.m.

It has a cartoon of a bartender pouring two bottles into a large mixing glass. What a coincidence! Same price (the mind) for admittance! He-he. The bright green poster at the bus stop had a cartoon of a ponytail girl projectile-blowing a drink out of her nose and mouth with her eyeballs popping out.

I'm on a wooden blue bench now, under the bus stop shelter. The shelter is open-sided, with painted blue supports and a white top. The oriental woman comes by again, for lap number two. The baby girl turned around when they went by. She had on mittens I didn't see earlier. Her nose is a little red now, even with her complexion and that yellow beret. They go left on Patterson, same way as before, after the poster guy.

I'm right in front of the intersection on the university side of Walker. There's a trash container and two weekly paper dispensers here.

A black guy in a beat up Dodge yells at me out his driver's window.

"Hey—where's University Drive at?"

"What's that?"

I blink to catch up, drawn out of my notebook.

"Where's University Drive at? You go to school?"

"Yeah!"

"Where's the construction at?"

I told him to keep going on Walker and look left. His car's wheels didn't spin in the gravel at the stop sign. The tires weren't lined up right.

They're building a parking garage down there. They're pouring a lot of concrete. A cement truck stops in front of me. Diesel fumes and dust hang in the air while the truck rolls on toward Highland, staying to the left of the ship.

I rollerblade. It's something I started in Pittsburgh after my divorce. For most of a year I skated to work and everywhere. Pittsburgh is an eastern San Francisco. Instead of one bridge there are dozens —over the Allegheny, Monongahela and Ohio rivers, and it's also very hilly. I got great exercise and terror skating up and flying down winding hills, day and night, with traffic.

I missed that terrain when I first got to Memphis—a real flat town. So I found a parking garage on campus and found an artificial spiral hill to skate up and soar down. They should have this new garage done by the end of the year. It's feeling more like home all the time.

A FedEx panel van half-stops then zooms down Walker toward Highland. And a jogger by himself. And two more. All white guys with short hair, baseball caps and shorts, running from campus.

There's a tree here. And behind the bus stop is one of those card access parking lots for faculty. A train horn blows from Highland. I don't see it yet.

The parking here is bad. I live within sight of this intersection, at that apartment building over there, and I've decided the advantage of living this close is the parking. I just walk out the door before classes. A pretty girl walks by. Short blond hair and dark clothes. My wife had her hair cut like that towards the end. She never let it grow after that. All her beautiful hair hacked off on one sad afternoon. She didn't like it when I told her how I liked it. "How do you like it?" she asked. I told her. Marriage is a great teacher, and I learned something then. I don't know what her hair looks like now. She probably has it dyed again and lets it grow long. She's in Florida. She always looked better with long hair. The more I told her that, the more often she cut it.

A skinny kid on a new-looking black mountain bike just cut between the benches from behind me. He's trying to beat the train. Now in the ditch; now in the grass near the tracks with his bike on his shoulder, walk-running. The train horn is a solid blast. They cross, one before the other, independent of the twins, and make their own intersection across from Lynn Doyle Flowers on Southern.

He had more than 50 feet to spare. Man was that horn loud.

Three sleek yellow and black engines, and behind, an older blue one. Four engines going east, pulling coal cars.

Two black guys, probably in their 40's, talk to each other as they go by in front of me and stop behind the paper boxes at the middle of the shelter. They probably work at the parking garage construction site.

I smell something I know, and I look to see what I know.

The short one looks back and says,

"I'm doing something you probably wouldn't respect."

Yeah. They're passing back and forth a fat nub of a joint, and I'm not crazy about it. Pot smoke and ashes blow in my face. I hold my breath. The rolling train is a continuous, loud rolling presence. It's sunny. The bus stop seems filled with people now, here in the sun. I'm writing this down in their midst.

The train gains speed and the wind shifts with the cars going by 25 or 30 miles an hour. Nothing but loaded cars, with coal heaped up high.

A black lady in sunglasses is sitting on the other bench beyond the casual pot smokers. She has attached-dread-locks. She sips bottled water. Her braids shine in the sun. A respectable looking black man moves in to sit on the short wall at the back of the bus shelter. The train keeps on coming. The two smokers cough and spit and then trail off in the quiet left by the train's passing. They move down the sidewalk. One wears a baseball cap and the other a ski hat. No more pot smell.

A green and white *Memphis Area Transit Authority* bus pulls up to the curb and they get on. The bus pulls away, going toward Highland.

I don't know if I don't respect what they were doing. I live in a whole different world. I don't think of it as a matter of respect. Our words are the same but they're probably not even close. I don't use the word respect much. Maybe I don't need to. Maybe I use my own word to say the same thing.

An Oriental guy walks by with empty boxes under his left arm and reflective John Lennon squashed-oval shades perched on his nose.

The black girl on the other bench loud-whispers urgently, "Go!"

After rolling over the hump at the tracks, a driver has stopped his car in the middle of the intersection. He has the right of way but he doesn't know it. The car behind him honks and he slowly pulls ahead.

I hear the respectable black man back there jingle some change and spit. The black girl is looking in the direction of the intersection and has on reflective shades now.

"Ow— Aw!"

I look up quick from writing and see two white guys running on the sidewalk toward campus. One has a gangly Labrador wearing a blue harness on the end of a long nylon lead. The young dog must have licked or sniffed with his wet nose and surprised the black girl while she watched the intersection, waiting for her bus. The two guys and their dog disappear, running around the corner onto Patterson.

A white guy in a sports coupe roars loudly away from the intersection on Walker towards the construction site. A black guy in a Honda with heavy thumping music waits and then goes over the tracks from Walker.

It's 3:59 p.m. In a blue sky, another FedEx jet crosses, ascending from right to left and is gone. Everything seems to go away here, with something new to take its place. Another white guy runs on the sidewalk going toward Highland. An image of him wiping his face on his shoulder stays with me. Another white guy walks this way from the other direction. I don't have a lot of time to describe these people before they're gone.

A boat-of-a-car painted rust-colored primer; an 'oil burner' car leaves a nostalgic-smelling fog behind, reminding me of our first riding lawn mower growing up on our small Michigan farm.

The respectable man clears his throat. He has that strong stuff on, like Old Spice underarm deodorant, that just smells and smells. He walks under the bus stop shelter in a rustle of plastic bags. I'm surprised to see him wearing a red beret now. He and the woman from the other bench go a little past the end of the stop and step into the idling #2 *Southern-Downtown*. It carries them down Walker, veering left past the ship buildings.

#2 Med. Center heads this way, and the two buses pass each other where the skinny kid had run across the tracks carrying his bike. *Evan Williams Kentucky Straight Bourbon* advertized on the side of the Med Center bus.

The intersection traffic steadies up. The twins are really shuffling now—cars, trucks, sport utilities, new, old, vans, bombs, VWs, Fords.

On the sidewalk in front of the *Memphis Flyer -- the Mid-South's News and Arts Journal and Auto Mart -- FREE* boxes is a much-stepped-on clear document protector with three binder holes. I'm standing in front of the bus stop now, getting ready to go. Written in black marker on the scuffed opaque plastic is:

WEIGHT LOSS SECRETS.

NO PILLS. NO DIETS. NO EXERCISE.

FOR MORE INFO. CALL MR. WRIGHT

744-2875.

Two attractive girls cut through the bus stop area. They step over the little wall bordering the card-access lot and go down the sidewalk toward Highland. I let the document protector fall to the sidewalk again. The garbage canister near the paper boxes has a hole kicked into it, down low in the pebbly reddish outer covering.

Just now, a FedEx plane shoots low and level over the campus.

I make it across Walker just before a new Isuzu sport. Two bicycle cops, yellow and black uniforms on sturdy mountain bikes, lean into their turn off Walker and rise over the tracks in 'Chips' formation, then sail in unison down Patterson, past the frat house.

Here's this pigeon. Five feet away from the Patterson and Walker street sign. Crouched. Traffic from all directions streaming around us. Like being inside the hub of a turning wheel.

Between the tracks and Walker, this mottled, slate-gray bird with an iridescent green head in the lowering, shifting light and reddish orange eyes that glow, is just sitting with his left wing tip touching the grass. His head is tucked into his shoulders. I'm squatting. I hear a train. Its horn triggers a feeling of concern.

The pigeon looks over his shoulder a couple times at first, but now his eyes are closed. Two feet from the traffic, his head is metallic shimmering purple—or violet now—depending on the angle of the sun as it catches his scales. Any dinosaur expert will tell you feathers are just specialized scales. I move closer. In this light I have no choice but to believe. A now-yellow eye opens. The bird's eyelids are light tan and they open from the top down. No train yet.

The sun is behind some clouds. A guy in a Lincoln stops by us and a car behind it honks. The pigeon doesn't move. My fingers are cold and sore from writing so much. The Town Car crawls away. A black Honda, a junk Buick, an Oriental guy on a bike.

I kick at the pigeon. He dodges. I nudge at him. It doesn't do any good. Now he's poking around the road sign. Seems as though we traded spots. He keeps one eye on me. I was trying to shoo him into the grass alongside the tracks. There is a lot of traffic; a train might be coming.

It's not the only time this happened. In Pittsburgh, I was walking home after work. It was raining, kind of cold, and I had a backpack on under a green rain poncho. I was just enjoying the rainy day and walking in the cold toward a warm apartment where my first wife and our two cats were waiting. I was on O'Hara Street, on the main campus of the University of Pittsburgh where I graduated in December a few months before. Right behind Soldiers and Sailors memorial I saw a pigeon on the sidewalk at the rear of the building. It caught my attention because it was just sitting. Its wings were hanging down and it wasn't walking. I stopped and stared and then squatted down to get a closer look. It didn't move at all and I saw its head was rough-looking, like it gave up on combing its hair over and didn't have enough feathers there. After a minute I decided it was dying.

I thought about the years that this bird had lived and how its death would mean nothing in the grand scheme of things. I felt sad and looked for a branch. I was going to end its misery. There was no branch close by. While I searched, I silently planned how I would strike the mercy blow. I don't know when it occurred to me that I was going to put the creature out of *my* misery, not his.

Because I found myself considering that I had never considered this bird at all—from *its* life point-of-view. So I went back and squatted down on the sidewalk near the pigeon again. My backpack, a carry-over from college days and a convenient way to carry my lunch and a book, held up the poncho, which pulled tight across my shoulders. The rain kept raining.

I decided I would stay there until it died. That here was this bird, alone, and I would be its companion in its final moments. Its eyes were shut and I nudged it with the back of my hand. Its lid opened slightly to show a red eye. It didn't seem to care what was happening. Maybe it sensed my good intentions.

I settled down, full of patience. This had become a priority and if I was late getting home I would calmly explain it to Katherine and she would understand. I focused on the bird's breathing, became attuned to its every shiver and movement. After a while... I found myself mentally leaning towards death and resolution. *Come on, sleep, that's right.* After a few false endings, I began looking at my watch.

Twenty minutes later, my focus wavered and I noticed people again on the sidewalk behind me. The wind blew, the rain fell, it was growing dark and I picked up the pigeon and walked it to the back steps of the war memorial. I set it down where I thought it would be more protected from the wind. I mentally made a note to not touch anything until I washed my hands, and looked at my watch again. I looked back once as I left, continuing on O'Hara towards home. It was after dark when I walked up the steps of our apartment building. I told Katherine about the pigeon and we ate dinner.

The next day I went that way again, looking for any sign of the pigeon. Nothing. Pigeons are magical, I decided. Like elephants, they have their own Shangri-La graveyard where they are eternal. You never see a dead pigeon. Or a baby one. Maybe it didn't die.

A fat Indian guy wearing a black leather jacket strides this way in a hurry. The pigeon hops away from me, closer to the road. I stay where I'm at, squatting with my notebook on one knee. I don't think the guy saw the bird.

My shadow is 20 feet long now. I'm standing and the circulation is creeping back into my legs. It's cooling off, now that the sun is lower. The pigeon, huddled by the Patterson and Walker sign, looks out his left eye at me. On the ground, the lowering sun turns his eye red.

A guy in a blue Ford pickup looks over.

It seems like this intersection goes on while I write. It seems like I miss a lot of it.

An empty cigarette box, Winston Lights, smashed flat on the ground by my feet. It's 4:37.

An hour later:

I've been rollerblading around campus now, and I'm at the little paved driveway on Southern, in front of the broadcast tower. *GTE Moblenet Radio Station* the sign says. No trespassing. It's 5:58. I was curious. The tower is enclosed by a tall chain link fence and a square concrete building sits in the dark with a row of cables going up the nearest leg of the tower. Three steady red lights are half-way up the tower, one is perched on top, blinking. It's cool, but I'm warm from skating, and my hooded sweatshirt and helmet and pads keep the heat in.

Wood-smoke is in the air. I'm under the pines and this smell and the darkness remind me of a ski lodge fireplace and the winters I spent in cabins with wood stoves and oil lanterns. I'm writing on a *Union Planters Bank* teller receipt.

Here comes a train. The arms-with-lights go down at the intersection and the engine's horn blasts, toot toooot tooooooot. A dinging bell at the intersection, there, where the twins now pause in their slower night work.

Two old yellow engines, going slow—*Union Pacific*—and empty coal cars. The engine blasts its horn again at Highland. I'm on the other side of the tracks now, from before. It feels like a different world over here. The cars pick up speed. They're empty, all of them, and rumbling in the opposite direction from the full cars that went by earlier today. Scribbling in the dark, I roll around on the undulating sidewalk where this little access drive meets Southern.

As long as the train moves here in the dark, and the empty cars go by in a solid wall, and the wood smoke is in the air and I'm relaxed after skating; as long as this lasts I'm back in time, before electric fans, before trains, climbing glaciers in the months-long sub-arctic night—I'm Robin Hood in the emerald forest with my bow aimed stead at a bulls eye; I'm Captain Ahab on the boiling sea with the Whale in my sight, harpoon poised.

Back at my bachelor apartment, two cats wait for me to feed them.

The following is the first short story I ever wrote, for a creative writing class at Lake City Community College, taught by Yvonne Sapia, in 1991. I was living in North Florida, truly the South, and the events in this tale take place in that sweltering town I, then, called home.

This story is basically an act of plagiarism, which I hear and hope is the sincerest form of literary flattery. I had recently read Andre Norton's novel, Star Man's Son, *about a post-apocalyptic reality of wastelands, genetically mutated beasts, exploration and basic survival. As I wrote the following, I held the feeling of Norton's world in my head, adding my own twist, of course. I was 24.*

Going South, by the Way

by David W. Weimer © 1991

There was a burst of movement down low, there. I hit the ground rolling, and reached for my weapons.

I knew what it was before I dropped a quart can of ravioli, but try and talk sense to paranoid reflexes: two birds shot from behind a tractor-trailer and skimmed over the broken pavement, ending up in the trees at the far side of the parking lot.

Well. I went back to my seat on the cement curb and resumed eating my meal, noticing, as always, that it takes a certain kind of skill to scoop out congealed ravioli from a can without smearing pasta sauce all over one's hand.

My name is Jamie. I never thought of it as a typical Survivor name but my parents only gave me two gifts; the other is my crazy blond white hair. Try being inconspicuous, looking like me! I have been on the move, so to speak, for eight years. Ever since... Well.

Where the hell is he? I tossed the empty Boyardee can into a cart rusting in the shade by the supermarket. I was tired of waiting. I threw my army surplus backpack over my right shoulder and shifted the canned provisions I'd snatched off the dust-covered shelves of the *Winn Dixie*.

More from habit than from need, I leaned on my old walking staff and crouched near the corner of the building, resting in the cool shade while I scanned the parking lot for movement. Nothing—only the sun beating down and reflecting off the chrome stripping around a broken windshield.

I stepped away from the wall and chose a diagonal course through the metal and glass graveyard. I could see inside some cars through dusty and sun-warped side windows that some of the drivers still sat inside—vague shapes in molding fabric. In some of the cars, skulls stared straight ahead like they were looking into the rear-view mirror, waiting to back out.

As I reached the street bordering the lot (far from the intersection), I was going to cross when I saw Robert moving toward me through an alley between the hospital and an *S & S* store. With hand signals, I told him: *Stay put, I'll meet you over there*. I ran, crouched, across the bare pavement.

"What's going on?" I asked, pointing to the sun. "You were supposed to be here at noon. We can't hang around here."

Robert clasped my left shoulder, the arm that I held my staff with. "You won't believe what I found! I got just what we needed." His broad grin was unwavering as he paused to catch his breath. "I was going to leave man, when I found one of those cabinets!"

I understood. Since the disaster, medical centers were some of the most sought-after and pillaged places in any city or town and sometimes there were cabinets that weren't smashed—yet. "Go on."

"After pounding hell out of that box man, I found this." He carefully pulled an oblong Styrofoam container from an inside shirt pocket.

I whistled low. "Nice. S'what I think it is?" Robert nodded.

It was a drug, experimental vaccine really, rumored to have been used on cancer patients before the "Day," before the world went away, to shit really, only, someone found out after the disaster that the vaccine was the only thing that gave you a real fighting chance of living through a bite from a beast-thing; the carnivorous mutants that overran cities and hunted in packs.

"Now *that* was worth waiting for," I said.

Robert surprised me. Sometimes it seemed as though he had been born lucky. I recalled how we met...

It had been ten miles or so east of that mid-southern city and I was hiking southwestward, well off the weed-choked highway, when I heard the sound of a violent struggle ahead. I hefted my staff, keeping my thumb close to the tab that released a spring-steel blade in its base, then made my way toward the noise.

I could see them all in the clearing. While I stopped behind some saplings, I watched a short, dark-haired man purposefully swinging a chain with spikes in quick, vicious arcs. He was bleeding. Three beast-things circled, hunting for an opening, and all of them making that creepy noise that makes you look around to find a place to hide. Not at all sure it was the thing to do, I loosened my pack and set it down gently. I crept closer and waited for my opportunity.

Once I was certain the man had seen me, I jumped into the clearing and swung my staff around in a huge arc that ended behind the shoulder blades of one of the creatures. I heard its back break, and twisted aside to avoid the still-snapping jaws. The other two beast-things paused for an instant. It was enough. The man swinging the chain killed another one with a slapping blow to the head and followed through his swing, wounding the remaining creature's shoulder. I caught it unaware with a stab to the temple and it crumpled to the ground, motionless.

"Thanks," the short, powerfully built man gasped, extending his left arm, as custom dictates. "My name's Rob. It was getting a bit hairy before you showed."

I grasped his hand and noticed he was bleeding from deep gashes on his left leg. "You have medicine? Those things are diseased," I said, kicking the dead body at my feet.

"Nah, got no drugs."

After patching his wounds the best we could that day, we kept on going west. It should have been his last day. The strange thing is that the infection didn't kill him. Most would have died. Hell, I probably would have died. But all Robert suffered from was a night of fever and some shakes. His wounds healed. I don't know why, but something told me I shouldn't trust him...

Robert unfastened a sturdy leather bag with a shoulder strap, slipping the valuable package inside. "Let's move away from this place," he said, looking past me to the opening of the alley. "We can find a place to stay over night and split the stuff there."

I agreed, and Robert took point. I followed five meters behind, in case of ambush. It's always safer that way; it leaves one person free. We went east a block and headed south, with the setting sun to our right.

He picked up the pace, and chose our path for the best cover. He was good, I admitted to myself. But then, I guess you don't live that long if you aren't any good. Suddenly Robert stopped, and I saw him duck down near an insurance building.

I joined him at the edge of the abandoned structure and it was crazy, but just then I saw the broken glass in the windows made the place look like a toothless old man, grinning at me. I shook my head and kneeled, following Robert's pointing hand with my eyes.

Between a car and the side of the building were the corpses of a man and two beast-things. It was obvious that he had managed to kill them both; he got one with a sword, and the other he strangled. Unfortunately, its jaws were still clamped around his own ripped neck. The stench was overpowering.

"Damn, that reeks." Robert shivered. "Kind of like that pouch of yours, man." He chuckled, low.

I hated it when he did that. "This could have been you, a while back." I stood slowly and started walking, making the hand signal, *Let's go*.

He gave a quick nod and spat on the broken sidewalk. I could see my reminder had had an effect. Well, good. He never stopped bothering me about a supposed "odor." This wasn't the first time I remember thinking it would be nice to part ways and be on my own again. Sometimes he just gave me the creeps, you know?

We walked for a couple of hours and then came to a suburban area. Following quiet consultation we decided to look for a house away from the others and picked one with false marble columns and a real tall A-shaped roof—someone's private castle. We checked the grounds carefully and then the inside, for telltale signs of recent habitation. We decided it was safe for a night's stay. We made note of the emergency routes.

Inside, it was dark, of course, and we were careful to stay away from the windows. I looked longingly at the fireplace but knew better—too close to the city for a fire. Still, it sure would have been nice; a small fire always helps make me feel more secure.

We occupied the huge living room and split the day's plunder: he gave me half the ampoules of vaccine and I lined up the food I had found, splitting it in half. By the light of a small shielded camp lamp we ate our supper.

Robert's eyes glittered in the dim light. "I'll take first. You know, 'cause I was late," he smiled.

I unfolded my blanket and leaned back on a musty couch to fall asleep. "Fair enough," I said.

Since I had last watch, I ended up standing on the front porch, watching the sun turn the night sky into a day. The air was damp and it offered small temporary relief to a day that promised to be hot and humid. I stretched and went inside.

"Rise and shine!" I said in the direction of Robert's sleeping form. There was no response. I walked over and nudged him with my toe. "Wake up."

With a groan, he sat up. "Already?"

I rolled up my blanket, stuffing it into my pack. "You want to sleep all day?" I said, smiling.

"Guess not," he grumbled. He shuffled to the kitchen where I heard him urinating in the sink. When he plodded into the living room, I was sitting on the arm of the couch with my backpack on the floor.

"You in a hurry, man?" Robert asked.

I smiled. "Always am," I said. "This is going to be a good day!"

"What do you mean, it's..." Robert's eyes got wide and he raised his right arm to protect himself, trying to jump to the side as I swung my staff overhead in a whistling swoop toward his neck. My weapon shattered his forearm and deflected into his right collar bone. I heard it crunch and then Robert screamed.

Damn, I thought. Messiness is one thing I can't stand. I pressed the tab on my staff and the eight inch steel blade snicked into place. Robert was fumbling for his dagger with his left hand and I stabbed the blade through his throat, severing his spinal cord.

Like poking your finger through a plastic bag. I stepped away as he fell, choking and convulsing, hands clawing air. After a while he stopped like they always do.

I wiped the stiletto on Robert's sleeping blanket and pushed the blade against the hardwood floor to reset its spring-action. I got out my favorite pocket knife and started to cut, bending the finger back to get a clean slice at the knuckle.

"I never could trust you Bob, you know?" He didn't answer.

I opened the pouch I carried and removed a heavy waxed string. The large needle on one end I pushed into the proper joint of Robert's severed pinky, sliding the fresh digit down the string to rest snugly against the others. *There.* After tying a knot in the string, and shoving the needle into the new flesh like a cork, I held it up and shook, admiring the rattling bones. "Thanks Bob," I whispered, and lowered the string back into my pouch where it coiled at the bottom.

See you around, I signed to the now-empty room. I looked down at the blanket-covered still form. By noon, I'd left the suburbs far behind. I turned right on the road we'd been on the day before, looking for shade to eat my lunch—heading south, of course.

Every first-person narrative is the same. We, the reader, trust the narrator, because they obviously trust themselves. This twist, this betrayal of the reader, was my meditation on the notion that everyone is doing "the right thing." No one gets up and says to the mirror, "I'm wrong." To get inside the shoes of a killer or a saint, we understand because, in those shoes, we accept. Sorry if you were bothered by the ending. Andrée was, hence this explanatory note. At the time I wrote the story, I was intrigued by the reader/narrator relationship and wanted to do something unexpected. I wrote a screenplay once where the society no longer ate, in the conventional sense. The people were fitted with batteries—but you didn't find out exactly *what was going on until the last minute of the last act....*

The following is my reply to A.M. of Delaware, written Monday, Oct. 4, 2004, from our ongoing correspondence. I basically was going through his preceding missive, responding to what he'd written, in the order he had written it.

Hi A.,

At my worst, what I'm doing is giving you my current perspective in reacting to you, in our correspondence. If I claim anything else, I'm likely to be a liar. If I claimed, for example, to know, 100 percent, the steps you're currently taking. To claim that, I'd have to actually take off my own shoes and put on yours. That is possible, but I don't do it in our correspondence, generally. What I do, generally, is give you my reactions. In person, I could do it by listening to you and desiring to understand, without imposing or allowing myself, my ego, my opinions, all of that, to get underfoot. I think I could get in tune with you. This would definitely help me better understand where you're coming from.

Even though it's me at my worst, I think that, for both parties in a communication, it's good to get someone else's view. Nothing is better in making us move in unaccustomed ways, and, in so doing, the automatic result is that we unwittingly see and know ourselves better. Aspects of ourselves we don't normally see. Or want to see. That's putting a good face on things. Plus, if we were comfortable all the time we probably wouldn't move at all.

At my best, I'm giving you my current perspective in reacting to you and I am intimately aware of your current place on the personal path and your condition of being. Intimately aware, because I recognize unfailingly something in you that I have, too, encountered and been.

But I don't trust people 100 percent. People, in this context, meaning egos. That includes mine. What I do trust, if I have to trust something, is motive or intention. My motive or intention is pure. Pure meaning: not something I want to impose on you as much as a genuine wish for the best for you—whatever that's supposed to be.

What I DO trust is fate. I'm not smart enough to plan a lot, but people's conditions of being cause appropriate reactions in others they meet. Rose used to talk about ladder work as an indispensable ingredient in the life of a seeker of Truth. "The way, the truth and the life" and "the Buddha, the dharma and the sangha" are other ways of pointing at crucial ingredients. Anyway, Rose said that a seeker works on their own level, with peers, and on the level below them, through helping others struggling on things they have been through, and on the level above them, with a 'teacher' or in contact with someone who has been through things that this seeker is currently struggling with.

I know you've seen how this happens, almost by itself. Where you'll encounter someone and find yourself telling them a book title or giving them an Internet site address. You'll react automatically to them, and something will have you trying to help them in some way because you relate to where they're at on a fundamental level. It's automatic, thank God. Rose also said that he considered the best qualities we possess to be something we can't help. Somebody had asked him during a lecture about love and he said something pretty unflattering about what he saw most love to be, but then added that the truest form of it is when the person can't help it. "If you could help it, you'd try to make a profit," he said—something to that effect.

I know you've helped people in this way. I think any true seeker does. It's just what happens. That's what I meant by trusting fate. I trust in the interaction between well-intentioned people on these various levels. I trust what results from it.

I remember hearing S.N. talk about his path-walking. He didn't say a lot of things about being an intense, obsessed guy. We are all different. Really. But, when I look at what he did and what he was, I would say it was, indeed, the exact same as what I did, and was. Everything is relative to itself. For S., being intense and committed and obsessed LOOKED different, perhaps, than what being intense and committed and obsessed and engaged in the thing looked like for me. There is NO difference between a snail crawling as fast and determinedly as it can and a worm crawling as fast and determinedly as it can. There's an inner condition that is the same. Commitment. The decision that there's nothing as valuable as THIS to be doing.

The thing I recognized in S. was the same thing I had in me. A person who decided to do it.

The Self Knowledge Symposium in North Carolina is something I don't spend a lot of time thinking about. But I visited their website recently and saw a talk they were sponsoring by a former martial arts fighter, Jeff Tennant, who had experienced something after his life had fallen apart. "Let's just say I got a glimpse behind the scene of the living, breathing universe," he said.

I read an interview [of him] by one of the SKS members. Tennant said:

> *"A trainer told me once, and I'll never forget it. He knew exactly what I wanted to accomplish, and his response was very matter of fact saying, 'You have to be willing to do two things Jeff. You have to be willing to pay the price...and then pay it.' And that just made such an impact on me. That to me was it. You know I thought, there it is. Every morning since then I think to myself 'I'm willing to pay the price.'"*

Do you know the part I think is worth quoting? "...and then pay it."

On [to] another subject, one that you brought up. Communication. You mentioned paying attention to the tone people use when they talk. What about this for an exercise: When someone in your daily life talks to you, think of yourself on a mission to grasp the motivation that set this person's mouth in motion. *What do they want?* is the question. Let the words be; let them flow and go where they will, but listen for the reason they're talking. You brought this subject up in your last email.

"....becoming more sensitive to subtler thoughts or impressions," is something else you wrote, talking about memories of dream content during meditations. That rang a bell for me.

I don't think it's possible to follow your awareness back to its source, wherever or whatever that could be, with yourself [along for the ride]. Because then, you're trying to do something that you're imagining can happen, somehow. It's very possible, and as simple or uncomplicated as any Harding exercise, however, to wonder where YOU are, or where your core is —that core being what you notice or feel as self-identity—and to somehow sink or settle or get to that; go in that direction, which is where YOU'RE coming from.

I don't think you use your attention to do a u-turn and follow some imaginary thing, because then, you're still projecting out of yourself, shining the flashlight out there, on some serpentine path following imagined things, as opposed to back IN, to where you're coming from.

For me, I can just describe it as a curiosity about where "I" come from, and...backing into that one.

Your awareness isn't followed. YOU are followed. The 'you' that has just wondered something.

Well, that's as good as it's going to get for now. I admit that I'm incapable of describing, in words, something that is so fundamental, profoundly uncomplicated and distinctly "other than" the normal things we talk about with common reference points, like eating, working, seeing the sunrise. Maybe some other time. The most real things can't be touched with words! What a shame.

Ramanamaharshi described two proven paths for enlightenment: Self-inquiry and surrender. There is no more concrete and to-the-point a question as "Who or what am I?" That is self-inquiry. It is not a meaningless mantra to be repeated. It is the most down-the-center, on-the-money thing I can ask myself. Fundamental. Direct. It may seem unanswerable to you, but I promise you that I believe it is THE direction to go in. All other directions are tangential and off the mark, ultimately. That's my take on the matter.

For me, it was, and is, the only question worth asking. It is THE direction. But that's my perspective, now. Not very useful to others or even a prior version of myself, maybe. I hope that's not the case.

But you know; everybody's different. That's the truth. What was relevant or useful to me is just that. And since we're different, there's an unfortunately high likelihood that these useful or relevant things remain just what they were or are for me—and no one else. I can only hope that you can USE the things I say with earnest intent. [That's if], of course, there's something useful there, for you. If there isn't... Well, my hope is that the stuff I say can help somehow—how that comes about is entirely up to the circumstances of your play, of which I am another character, among others, in the present act.

I think that fatigue has a big impact on what we feel we're able to do; on the attitude we bring to the game each day. It's amazing how we go about things when we're well-rested. The most important thing, I think, is to be a walking, conscious obsession in a chosen direction. This is what I mean by advocating "a central commitment and an inner homing-in or constant contact with that essential, important thing." I do not advocate, at all, remembering what other people told you to do, or what you think you should do, like following 'awareness' (whatever that is) back or pondering 'who am I.' These are things that, unfortunately, you have taken someone else's word for. And, worse yet, you've committed yourself to doing them—even though you may feel, deep down, that there's nothing in these practices for you. They aren't relevant and they aren't alive. That's part of what I was talking about when I said I find myself telling you "levitation isn't it." Be true to the center, to what is your center.

What IS "it" is that obsession you have. That thing that colors all of your thinking and how you view the events or things around you, moment-by-moment. That central condition that you've become attuned to. In fact, it isn't that you've become attuned to it as much as you have BECOME this tone. It is the difference between your being a tuning fork as opposed to [being] that clear note. The difference between walking a path, any path, and only-talking.

You said, "....I know too much to be satisfied with life the way it is for nearly everyone, but feel sometimes like I don't have a clue about how to break through to the truth that some people say is actually right there in front of us."

I wouldn't believe that it's right there in front of us. It's right there for some people, maybe. That's a dangerous assumption. What I mean is, it's really bad to take what someone else says as true and a given—"the truth is right there in front of you," like Harding always says. That's his brand of insanity. Find your own. If it resembles his, then that's fine. At least you came to it honestly. The truest thing, in my opinion, is the first part of what you wrote. That's the truth. You can't go back to second grade, as appealing as that might be. Ignorance is bliss, isn't it? So, for that reason alone, if for no other strongly-felt great idealistic purpose, it's the appropriate thing to continue to push for Meaning, the Answer, Once and For All. If [these] things even exist.

If you tried to break through to something that another person has said is there, then it wouldn't be your truth; it'd be theirs. It would actually be their truth as misunderstood by your own assumptions.

It's a lonely road, it truly is, but the only real one, when you've given up on all others and started on your own, truly individual, path towards the Truth or Ultimate Meaning of YOUR life. At your death, all of the books you ever read, and all of the people who ever said things are gone as if they never existed. What you are faced with then, is YOU.

I wrote this poem to be read aloud, performed, for an undergraduate writing class at Pitt, 1993. Please—as I type now, I'm gesturing with my hand—feel free to try it... And then write one of these of your own.

King Bacchus

Flying on high, immensely high above the small island with its shroud of mists in the morning, only seeing the very beginning of sunrise, and only because of the height at which you're flying. The air is a wind there, and a cold moistness thrills your arms and face and forehead, hot with flying but cool in the morning breeze. You lose height, and the island, once small but now large, is darker and mysterious. You are glad and excited at the thought of rushing through its low lying forests to shoot up, your eyes watering at the speed, up, past the last of the trees and their dark leaves to fly faster and pop up, high above the tallest mountain. And you drop, like a stomach-tickling moment, to hover breathless over the island that radiates its damp swamp smells, sounds and cool promise.

In the night, the noises are selective about who will hear them. To rise above them, to get the slightest bit of peace, is at once necessary and pointless. To illustrate: at night, a lonely train's horn is always leaving, never coming near, nearly long enough, and a hot argument outside a bar next door is loud and irritating, intriguing. As far away as midnight or two a.m., a scratching match is not far away at all. The air, or the argument, carries the hot spittle-flying moment straight through our walls or our open windows to our hearts. Hands cover our heads, pillows cover our hands, and window is closed, and still straining not to but somehow always *to* our minds' ears pick up, decipher what is said and shouted. Every insult, every kick in the ribs, every slap.

On the roof. A slanting roof of tar and shingle. A good pair of sneakers admirably grips the grit. Hardly any sand slides to the aluminum eaves. What does sounds like a jazz drummer brushing a brush over a high-strung snare. Schsh-sh-schsh.

On the peak. Always at night, the world is now, is here is strong and cool and present. Bracing with one hand to reach the other in a pocket he finds a lighter, a damaged wilted heavenly Camel filter cigarette. No one can light this one in the wind on the roof at night like he can. Wind takes the first smoke, playing with it like a child in the wash of a summer hydrant. It doesn't like to let him take the rest, but he takes his turn.

His hands. Impressed in his palms, these tiny little gritty pebbles from the shingles. Brush them away and hear them schsh-sh to the eaves where they go down the gutter, with the others.

World is a strange place, let alone a word—flying on high, immensely high.

I got the title for *Bacchus* from an art poster on my apartment wall and a single impression-image of sitting up on the roof of our house, straddling the peak, not far from the chimney where I used to climb at night. I was 15- to 17-years-old. I'd do this in the fall because the chimney wood-smoke masked my cigarette smoke, plus the house windows were shut in the colder weather. I'd wait until after ten. Sitting up there, I felt like a king. *The* king. On high, immensely high… I started smoking when I was twelve.

I worked over this little piece waaay too much—changing a word, changing it back. It was during the time when I didn't know who I was from one day to another—which is most people's whole lives, I'm guessing. I wrote it before I had written long enough for any single voice to emerge in my writing. I've always been a dreamer, and I can't explain what I mean by that except to say it, or point. I've always been prone to moments. Cigarette smoking facilitated this for me. Smoking a cigarette, fulfilling that nicotine craving, was like giving water to a man dying of thirst. The relief, that bliss that accompanied the act, combined with my natural tendency to ponder stuff and to experience 'moments' went hand-in-hand. Cigarettes didn't seem to dull my sense of wonder.

I quit smoking when I was 21, a year or so after I got out of the Army. I was living in Lake City, Florida, and I was in the Florida Army National Guard at the 153rd Engineer Company for guard drill every fourth weekend. I quit smoking "cold-turkey." I didn't know a better way. I don't think there was a better way for me at the time and it was the hardest thing I'd ever done. I've gone through a few things since then, but that was a real battle. I was living in my first apartment on Baya Avenue and decided to quit because I was having a lot of heartburn. I thought it was from smoking cheap cigarettes. It wasn't, but the thought helped me quit. I was working as an instrument operator on a land surveying crew for *Donald F. Lee & Associates*.

If you ever want to quit smoking all at once—hold on, because the ride's gonna get rough. I was given the best seat in the house to view, first hand, how *someone* is working constantly behind the scenes with an addiction. I was firmly addicted. Firmly. I'm glad I got my smoking done during my younger years. It probably didn't help me, developmentally or whatever, but at least I had the resilient young body to take the intake of tar, smoke and nicotine. My first three weeks of quitting were constant hell. The whisperings in my ear, at unanticipated, unprepared times. Always when I was unprepared or at times of weakness. *Go to the store. Get just one more pack, and* then *quit.* I left my wallet empty of money. I quit going to bars for beer after work. I had tried to keep up my old routine but saw that beer and cigarettes went far too well together for it to work.

It wasn't over in a day or a week or even several weeks. It was a couple of months before smoking wasn't on my mind constantly, every minute. It wasn't something I noticed, after the worst of it; those reprieves, I mean. I'd just slowly sense that something was gone now, and that would be it— the constant craving was gone.

The "best" thing in the world to have is an addiction. If you're a seeker of Truth or even truth, or if you want to become more of a man or woman. My guess is everyone has addictions (says the addict). The best thing in the world is to have to go through, to the bitter end, the breaking of the addiction. For me, quitting smoking for real was one of the most useful experiences I'd ever had. It helped me in my life, afterward, because I knew that I could stick to something, by God. There had been pure desperation during the hard times. I was all ready to give up, to go down and pick up a pack of smokes from the store but I knew that eventually I'd have to go through it all over again— what I'd gone through till then. The thought of having to suffer like that all over again was the only reason I didn't go back to smoking. I *liked* smoking. It just wasn't helping my health, I felt.

After this, the next big thing in my life was karate. My brother had been involved for a few years or so, and I'd put off his offers to bring me along to the countryside where his teacher, Dave Ward, lived. Once I was actively quitting smoking, I changed my whole life pattern—exercising, becoming vegetarian and not watching TV. I think I instinctively knew that I had to fill my life with *something else*. I started going out there with Pat and taking classes from Ward. Classes. Barefoot, outside, at this guy's place in the boondocks in Northern Florida. Rough place. Scrub oak everywhere, no real lawn. Sand and fire ants, ticks and snakes.

It wasn't long before I sensed this Ward guy was not the good, father-figure my brother believed him to be with all of his being. This was about four years after my dad's death. My mom had moved down south while I was in Fliegerhorst Kaserne, Germany. "Going home" meant coming to the south, where I was called "Yankee" by my co-workers.

Ward had a real sweet dog, a young thing with the most adorable personality in a dog. Underfed, loaded full of worms, her ears carried so many ticks on them it looked like she had clusters of pale gray grapes hanging from them.

It all turned out badly in the end. Ward was married to Flo, a very nice lady. She seemed to be a lady who worked hard and just did her best. It turned out, she was mother to Ken, a guy who had been in the same prison as Ward had been. Ward met Flo through her son while serving time. Ward and Ken practiced martial arts together in the prison. Ward, Shoto Kan Karate, and Ken, Kung-Fu. Ward told us, his students, that he had learned karate from an old Japanese karate master. Maybe it's true. But it wasn't in Japan.

Ward had been incarcerated for aggravated rape. My brother, Pat, was the best student he'd ever had. Ward taught karate and sold cars at a car dealership. He said he sold cars; maybe he was a car washer. When we met him and studied with him, he was living in Flo's double-wide trailer in the sticks. She'd had a bad experience with her former husband, Ken's dad, and was trying to make a new start. After a while, I'd say no more than two years after he first got out, he kidnapped a woman and raped her in his pickup at knifepoint. He was arrested, and eventually returned to prison.

After that, I kept practicing the *katas* (choreographed patterns of movements) and techniques I had learned, and continued to advance through *Karate-Do Kyohan*, a book by Gichin Funakoshi. I had Pat show me whatever he could every chance I got—he knew all the Shotokan katas and techniques, as well as some breathing exercises and energy flow movements from a Chinese martial art form learned from a breeder while living in a barn on a horse farm in Cookeville, Tennessee.

Pat's story—which will be recorded in *his* book—was that he appeared to gravitate to older men he would respect and look up to, to spend time around and ultimately be disappointed. Bad choice of father figures. Eventually he joined the Air Force in '89—the start of his own hero's journey, or maybe one of the steps along the way—and I remained in Lake City, as a maintenance man at McDonald's after being laid off when Florida state highway work dried up for the survey company I worked for.

When I quit smoking, I had a giant inner prompting to *do something*. Karate, it turns out, was it. Something to totally focus on. My brother's disillusionment had occurred by this time, as far as Ward goes, and we didn't take lessons or attend classes anywhere. We kept training katas and sparring. When Pat was stationed in Iceland, at Reykjavik AFB where he worked on F-15 fighters, I sent him exercise weights and a new *gi* (karate uniform) in the mail.

In Lake City, I'd found a perfect place to practice movements, punch trees and do breathing exercises. *Alligator Land*. I'd met the owner for the first time after watching him break his neck, only I hadn't known it was him at the time. He had one of those halos on his head, constructed of metal rods bolted into his skull to keep his head and neck immobile. I eventually looked after his alligators whenever he'd visit Lake Okeechobee in southern Florida where he was from. We watched Atlanta Braves World Series games on television at his house.

I began practicing karate at *Alligator Land* when I worked at McDonald's as a maintenance man. I continued to train on my own, as a solitary focus and moving meditation. I was 22. My life had settled into a routine and I was waiting for the great things I felt were coming, but nothing came; the old life was just going by like stuff floating down a creek.

I used to ride my bike as a meditation. It's hard to describe what I mean by that even though anyone can feel it, I think. When I say "meditation" it's the same as when I describe myself as a "dreamer." Qualitative. Staring at a pond, or into the distance. Becoming one with the activity of pedaling, with the wind and the motions.

If I worked openings (starting at 5:30 a.m.), I'd ride my 10-speed over to this closed-down novelty park place after work, around two o'clock, that had a putt-putt golf moldering under Spanish moss-draped pines, a big water slide and swimming pool, empty snake and reptile display walk-through house, an alligator wrestling arena, otter pen with waterslide, and many different "ponds" filled with basking alligators. The asphalt paths were cracked and fissured from tree roots pushing up under them. Pools of sunlight and shadows. The thing about doing martial arts is you need somewhere to practice, at least I did. For me, martial arts was something I could engage in, become one with, and devote myself to wholeheartedly, without distractions. I became what I did. I identified myself, my is-ness, with this activity. I was obsessed. I thought and breathed this martial arts air.

I would ride my bike down a paved side road marked at its beginning by a sign saying *Alligator Land*. After a few hundred yards, on the right, was a chained-off parking lot. Broken bottle glass on its asphalt. I'd weave my bike through there and ride past the concession buildings and ticket booth shaped like the open mouth of an alligator. Two large open covered pavilions were nestled back among the Spanish moss-covered trees. One with an amphitheater-like set-up around a fenced-off sand pit area where alligator shows had been done. The other pavilion was my favorite place to work out. This whole place, however, was my oasis and get-away. There were grass paths between a few of the alligator ponds and I'd do runs of kicks, blocks, strikes, etc., moving in a low stance and just feeling the grass with my bare feet. I'd do katas at this one grass intersection. Turtles sunning themselves on a log in the nearest pond would plop into the water when I would begin. After a while, I'd notice them soaking in the rays. I got bit all the time by fire ants. Florida is fire ant kingdom. When they bite, it stings like hell and leaves a whitehead later.

There was an otter pen, with an otter still in it. Ralph. We talked. I'd do my workout and then come over and chit-chat. I'd bring these crackers and always share just one with him. I'd get a book and read for a while. I looked into his questioning eyes. He'd do tricks and stand up on his hind legs expectantly, all the while staring at me. I knew what he wanted. It broke my heart. I got out there maybe every other day, and Ralph greeted me like he had waited every minute for my brief visits. I felt so sad. I had so little to offer. I wished better for him. He deserved better, damn it. Later, after I'd been gone for a while (I think to Panama for National Guard annual training), I returned to discover that Ralph had died. Gene told me that some people, trying to make a go at reopening the waterslide and pool part of the park, had been overfeeding him junk food and he died. Poor Ralph. If I knew where he was buried, I'd visit his grave and talk to him. He is someone worth visiting.

It seems like all the things I care about die or go away when I'm away. While I was off in the Army, my dad died, my dog was put down and my pony was given away. Other similar things have happened since. I should just never go away or, I should go away for good and avoid the pain of coming back. A way of avoiding future pain is to say, "I'll never get another dog again," after losing a cherished pet. That's a common human response to the human response of sadness and loss. I think a better person—a better me—opens themselves up for more pain (getting that new puppy). Easier said than done, but life is *here*, now. *Do not waste this precious time...*

Alligator Land had closed down some years before I adopted it. Gene told me when I asked, that it had come down to an argument between himself and the other partner, whose interest was the water and golf attractions. Gene handled the wildlife and did the alligator shows.

When I first started visiting this place, I still rode my 10-speed bike—as I rode everywhere in Lake City. When my bike was stolen one morning before dawn from behind the utility shed at McDonald's—the only morning I forgot to engage the spoke lock—I bought a second motorcycle. I'd crashed the first one twice, managing to survive intact; bought a 'safer' car, a lemon that never ran; rode my bicycle everywhere as therapy, meditation and exercise—and when that was taken away, I said, 'To hell with it,' sold the lemon and bought another motorcycle. So, I'd ride it out there, on my Honda 550 Nighthawk, parking on the same place on the asphalt path behind the ticket booth that I used to leave my bike.

I first saw Gene in person when I was still surveying for *Donald F. Lee & Associates*, although I didn't know it at the time. I saw him break his neck.

I was set up one morning with my tripod, theodolite and distance measuring laser, over a survey traverse point just off the street, in a patch of sharp-pointed Spanish bayonets—long, sword-shaped plants with needle-sharp tips that break off in your shins or hands. I was waiting for my rod man to move to the next traverse point with the reflector glass and I was recording my horizontal and vertical angles in a field book. Suddenly I hear crashing and a thunk, like a bowling ball hitting the cement.

About a hundred and fifty feet to my right I see a panel of fiberglass corrugated stuff hanging down, a stepladder leaning against a back wall and no man. Earlier, I'd noticed out of the corner of my mind a man working on top of a carport as my party chief unloaded me and my equipment on the edge of this quiet, well-tended neighborhood. After a second's hesitation, I told my rod man over the radio that someone had just fallen through a carport roof and I was going to look. I ran to the driveway and saw an older man standing up. "Are you okay?" I asked. He waved his hand at me and muttered, "Fine." I stood, uncertain, looked at him disbelievingly and said, "That was a heck of a fall; are you sure you're alright? Can I get someone for you?" He said no again and told how the opaque fiberglass roofing had given way unexpectedly.

With misgiving, I wished him well and returned to my instrument. I had a feeling that guy wasn't okay. Well, Shorty, the rod man, or Doug, the party chief, called me on the radio, asking me where I was. I repeated that I'd watched a guy fall through a roof and was checking on him. At lunch, they didn't really believe me. We continued our survey and I forgot all about it. We'd been surveying a 10-acre parcel that would later be turned into a retirement complex. I used to practice karate there, too (this was before discovering my oasis), because it was obscured from view, isolated, yet still in town so I didn't have far to pedal to practice.

Maybe a month or so later, I was practicing *katas* at *Alligator Land* and noticed a small group of men approaching. They walked, talking. I got closer and was shocked to see this tall older man with a halo of metal around his head connected by vertical shafts to a rigid shoulder harness. Evenly-spaced around his head, like spokes like on a wheel, titanium rods connected the ring to little metal nubs imbedded in his skull. I didn't mention the elephant (didn't mention or ask about his fancy headgear). I told him and the other man that I'd been coming out there to practice karate a few days a week after work. I apologized for not having asking their permission before. I said I was grateful to have found a place like this and could keep an eye on it while I was there.

The familiar-looking guy with the halo said it was okay. Over the following weeks, I'd be there, punching a kind of homemade *makiwara* (a device used for toughening the knuckles and perfecting punching form) on the side of the amphitheater. Or, kicking a post or doing katas in the grass or doing my Chinese breathing exercises. I'd see Gene working around on the other side, where the alligator ponds were. Clearing brush, building a greenhouse-like building. He walked kind of stiffly with that head-harness thing. I'd wave if he looked, and that was about it; we didn't speak. He left me alone to do my thing and did his thing. After a couple months or maybe more, I don't know, I saw him one day chopping at the asphalt of a path that ran perpendicular to a chain link fence he was putting up. He wanted the tall fence to run level in a groove that he was chiseling in the walk with a big metal "spud" bar.

I went over and offered to help take turns. He handed me the bar. After a while, we talked. I asked him about his head. I said I felt I'd seen him do it; that I was the surveyor who ran over. "I thought that was you," he said. I also hesitatingly explained what I was doing out there with the martial arts. I thought I owed him an explanation as he was good enough to allow me to be there. I explained why I was making so much noise punching a wall; telling, briefly, about the exercise forms. "I kind of wondered what that was about," he said. He had not asked, and I'm not sure he ever would have. Maybe after ten years. He was born and raised on Lake Okeechobee.

From then on, I would offer to help whenever I saw it would make sense. I'd grown up on a farm helping my dad and could tell when someone could use a hand. I'd see Gene pulling vines down from trees, or loading something heavy, and I'd go over and pitch in. He'd share sweet ice tea from a thermos. I dug fence post holes, stretched fence, helped build a greenhouse, cleared brush and fallen trees, fed baby and adult alligators when he would leave town, and accompanied Gene in a small aluminum boat to hunt for alligator eggs in the area's secluded lakes.

Gene treated me to southern cooking, starting when I first walked over to help him dig a groove in the asphalt sidewalk. Some weeks later, after accepting an invitation to his house for dinner I got to see that he and his wife had a strange, though practical, living arrangement. She was a nurse and had her own life, friends and schedule, and he in turn puttered with his Alligator Land projects and did what he pleased. They exchanged pleasantries. I was getting a Southern education, I suppose. They had a daughter and a son. I met the daughter and two grandchildren over time. They were very nice. I felt honored to be accepted by them.

As far as his fall went, Gene said he didn't realize his neck had been broken at first. "It was a little sore," he said, "and I didn't think anything of it." The next morning, it still hurt, in a nagging kind of way. His wife, a nurse, told him he was crazy for not getting looked at. She made him go to the hospital, where the doctor was surprised to see in the X-ray that he'd fractured some vertebrae in his neck—hence the halo. Gene was lucky not to sneeze and become a paraplegic.

That time, half a lifetime ago, when I was practicing karate at *Alligator Land* and counted Gene as my friend, is still *there*, though I don't instantly recall as much detail as when I take the time to ruminate. So far away ago that I haven't thought of those times in years. I look forward to my idealized front porch and rocker, where I can listen to the birds in the trees and open up all these compressed files in my head and spread them out in front of me, appreciating them fully in all their detail. That day may never come, but the files are there, waiting.

I sent Gene regular Christmas cards from Pittsburgh while I was married the first time. I got to introduce both my first and second wives to him. I fondly recall our time working together. It was accidental, our meeting and getting along. I didn't need a father figure; I'd had a dad and didn't want a replacement. No, it was just good to meet Gene, get along with him and help however I could. In Lake City, I knew no one and had no friends; I wasn't from this part of the country and didn't relate too well to the 'typical' southerners I'd met while working or on the street. I could relate to Gene. He seemed like a kindred spirit. I am grateful for the trust he had in me to watch over his creatures when he was out of town. Good times. A whole world, a whole life circumstance, buried in my past under layers of other times, other situations, other places and moments.

I've since lived in Pittsburgh, West Virginia, Memphis, Stuttgart, Germany, Toulouse, France, Fowlerville, Michigan and Flushing, Ohio. Probably move to New York State next. I've earned college degrees, gotten married twice, built houses, built skate parks, learned languages, painted houses, done a lot, seen a lot. A lot of water under the bridge. Maybe I've been running a lot, looking down from a lot of different bridges, over the same river. Does the river, time, flow the same under all of them? I wonder how Gene is doing. He must be nearing 100 by now.

Email correspondence to A.M. of Delaware written Saturday, Oct. 9, 2004. I'd been back in Fowlerville a year now, after moving from Toulouse:

Hi A.,

I learned to do nothing but compare. That might be the only thing we really are doing, ultimately, we thinking humans. It's a great attribute and very simple. Comparing something [newly-encountered] to something known or encountered before. All of our complicated interrelated thoughts are basically comparing. This is the good news because it's so simple. The best route for finding, always, something more pure or on the mark is to discard the lesser of two things at each instance of 'comparison.' [Rose's methodology, "Retreating from Untruth."] What could be more simple? Did we create the 0 or 1 basis for computing uniquely? Did we echo what we do, fundamentally? What ISN"T 'natural,' if it is a product of us? Aren't we living, breathing creatures? If so, isn't the nest of the bird natural? What about our buildings, our cars and so on? Our pollution, even.

If we looked back on the behavior of dinosaurs, would we break down their habits and products into two categories, NATURAL and ARTIFICIAL? Distinctions, seeming very clear and obvious on one hand, are kind of ridiculous on the other. No point being made here, just an observation.

You talk about last Sunday seeming significant. In my opinion and in my experience, this is as it should be, for a person engaged in some heavy labor in the direction you're going. That's what I meant about my own past times of continuous insights. I'd get these unanticipated, un-asked-for views, understandings, and glimpses, of the world. New views. New appreciations of things. I think of it as a by-product of working along this line. Not to dismiss it, by any means. It's the footprint of someone working. And thank God. I mean, what if you were working all the time, hammering your head at this Clarity or Truth thing and nothing happened? I don't think that could happen.

There's no regret for someone who is doing exactly what they feel they should be doing. There may be wondering, or questioning or any emotion possible, but when it comes down to it, and I ask myself, 'what would I rather be doing with my spare time?' and the answer is, 'nothing,' then, that's it. We're lucky to have stumbled into this kind of life. I don't think a person is necessarily confident of being right or whatever. That's not what I mean by no regrets. I mean that there isn't some other thing that is more attractive to the mind.

You wrote:

> "I haven't concluded anything new or different about what I should be doing, except the somewhat persistent thought that I could "simplify" my life so my mind doesn't have as many extraneous, distracting

things to churn on, which adds to covering up what I really am and takes time away from trying to find what I really am."

I think there is a kind of real-ness to living one's life oneself. That means, I think, at times, that we have hunches about what we should do or not do and we might decide to act on them. Because, until they are carried out, they remain forever only an untested notion. Afterwards, they are experience. If I decided to do something that, later, I decide to drop or give up or whatever, so what. My point is this: we have hunches; you described a "somewhat persistent thought," and I say that this thing we call our life takes on real life when we begin to act on our 'hunches.'

Is this hunch from the ego? Or from some other self-serving source? Maybe. But I think there is a category of still, silent voice-like hunches that aren't along those lines. There are the old TV commercials for taking the Nestea plunge, remember those? Leading one's life in the way I just described is, in a way, surrendering to something grander (in scope and import) than our limited, finite, highly-biased selves. It's freeing, too. —My view, from my experience in this thing called 'living.'

You wrote:

"I've been thinking more about what's apparently important to me; especially when I start to hurry. Starting to hurry is a great reminder. If I'm hurrying, it must be because I think I'm doing something important. But if its not related to a search for the truth, then what is important about it and why the heck am I in a hurry!?!"

This [catches my attention]. Because of the simple fact that a person who SEES himself might find himself wondering just such a thing—why am I hurrying, and what is going on here? Most of the time, I think, people hurry and rush and feel all of these strong inner compulsions (hurry) and just...that's all. I think there IS an understanding of my life. I CAN understand myself. I think I can know myself and know why I act the way I do and why I do what I do. There is great liberation in knowing oneself, *I* know, for *myself*. Like being in prison as opposed to being liberated from prison. The prison not even sensed or guessed at—of ignorance. The good thing for many (maybe most) people is that they don't sense, at all, their situation in any objective way. I think this shell of ignorance saves them from the depression or other bad reactions that would result from even a glimpse of a hint of a wisp of what their situation is.

You wrote:

> *"The related (identical?) question which you mentioned, which is directed at where my core is (where I'm coming from) feels more direct or to the point, to me. This is probably because, or related to the conviction I developed about something truer being covered up, which is, in turn, probably related to what I read and experienced Sunday. I guess Pulyan's analogy of "the penny that blots out the sun" rang truer with me, than I realized."*

….This is exactly what I've been trying to point to. THERE IS NO VALIDITY to someone else's take on reality or truth or knowledge or anything. The only validity, for yourself, is what you can discover for yourself. I mean this literally because when you're on your deathbed, the books and opinions of others will go like so much wind into that great stillness, windless-ness. What doesn't go is what you know, for yourself. I'm talking about what occurs when you die for real. I think that an 'enlightened' person goes to death differently than someone else. Only in that they're prepared. We're all prepared, ultimately, because we all are taken 100 percent of the way through the trip, in the end. We all are forced and reduced to the un-reducible, last fact of our death, which is nothing, and beyond nothing and beyond concepts and before concepts and "other than" anything and everything else we know, will know or have known.

Anyhow, I state as categorically as I can that…your quote, above, is the direction to go. I don't talk about methodology or anything you might DO; I just talk about direction. I state categorically that I know that there is an answer to the questions that drove me. No. There is an answer to the unfulfilled condition of being that I was in. That when I gave myself permission to go in THAT direction of attempting to find an answer to the unfulfilled, incomplete quality of me—this yearning has an Ultimate answer, that is experience-able by any genuinely earnest striver.

I don't want to say what a person will understand. It might seem less than desirable, if I said it. But, it is, to use some of Rose's words, "ultimate consolation." This is what I know for myself and suspect, to the point of believing, that it's true for others—any other [person]. The meaning of my life? To achieve, find or experience an answer to this 'question' that emanates from incompleteness inside of me. What could be more satisfying? …It's the only thing that can satisfy the un-scratchable itch of desiring: To Know.

Anyhow, I think we each come up with a manner of seeking and a way of doing things that is suited, perfectly, to ourselves. That's if we're lucky enough to disregard the leavings of others in favor of letting ourselves steer our own boat and make our own decisions, in this, our one shot. If you ever stop leaning, you will begin—at that exact moment—truly living. There is no other way of living a life to its fullest. You've got to trust yourself. Not that you're perfect, but that you're willing to try.

You wrote:

> "Plus, this morning I had another "interesting" ride to work in heavy traffic. I really thought I was beyond getting so wrapped up in thinking about "rude" drivers and traffic delays (contrary to the radio report saying there was little traffic on the interstate that morning!)."

If you ever truly were beyond getting wrapped up in things around you, you'd be catatonic. Ramanamaharshi was lucky in this, I recall reading. He went to Arunachula and was able to let go of the world around him for several weeks. Attendants would clean him and chase the rats away before they did too much damage. His culture supported a person doing something like that, in that holy place.

The benefit of isolations and random, or even daily, moments of meditation is that we can stay in touch with Reality. As long as we're an animal in this world, we've got to be able to react or we just get run over. I think to become institutionalized is probably the closest we could come to being free of being wrapped up in the things around us. But there's a price tag [with that] that is pretty high.

I think that we're reactive. And, remember how I used to talk a lot about nonverbal communication? Well, we're immersed in a society where everyone's blasting at full volume on their nonverbal channels. So it's no wonder if we react in some 'emotional' way in traffic or some other place. What is 'emotional?' What does it really mean? In and of itself? In an alien culture, you observe this phenomenon and you say one sentence about its purpose and function in that form of protoplasm on green planet X.

It's the koans we get daily, living in this world, that sure as heck propelled me, against my will, into truly examining myself and my reactions to others. I learned about myself in spite of my unwillingness. By koans, I mean, the instances where we bump against others in this society. Aspects of ourselves are irritated and flare up, and observing, and trying to understand each instance...is hell. But there are the unplanned moments of insight, realization and the soaring freedom of understanding and simple clarity. It's hell, but it's worth it, almost.

I used to see people in TAT talk about getting rid of the things that got in the way of their experiencing 'spiritual' things. I was just speechless with the irony of my appreciation of their situation. Their egos wanted a certain outcome. This, they called 'spiritual.' What is spiritual? Real apprehension of existence, our true nature and ourselves in this place? Or, what we 'want' to feel? Oh boy.

There are no irrelevant moments, to a searcher. Every single thing is pointing the way. Every single thing we experience or encounter. NOT that I have to somehow, through false glasses, convince myself that "this is a learning experience" when I'm being tortured or harmed by another. No. That is ridiculous and irresponsible to ourselves and anyone else we allow to become harmed. My view. I don't mean that we "accept" every single thing that happens to us in our lives. I mean that EVERYTHING THAT HAPPENS TO US is leading us to more understanding. What more 'spiritual' a life can a person be living who doesn't have a single reservation about what they will allow to instruct them in this grand Schoolroom?

Fatigue is cumulative. We get gradually less competent and less sharp. I think it's a good idea to really take care of the self in this regard. I'm trying to write a book now. Of necessity, I have to ensure that I get enough sleep or I simply can't do what I want to. I get nowhere. It's pragmatic as hell.

Are you using [*Peace Pilgrim's* example] as a rationalization for starvation? No projections on my part, but I'm asking. One point: what does it mean when we find ourselves going to the kitchen for food? It could mean that our body is prompting us to eat something. I know, I really know, it could mean a lot of other things. Things like escapism, addiction, and distraction, et al.

All I'm saying is that the body is smarter than our thinking, when it comes to basic things. We are thirsty when we should drink. We are tired when we should sleep. We are hungry when we should eat. The body talks. It's not always something we can intellectualize. Again, like taking another perspective in interpersonal communication, we could take another set of assumptions to the 'communicating' that our body does (and that we mostly ignore, resist or deny). Again, [these are just] some observations.

Do you find yourself suppressing feelings? What does this mean? You feel things and then react, reflexively, in a covering-up way? You can't possibly cause yourself to not feel something. It isn't possible. What happens is the thing is sublimated or pushed under the surface, to cause more turmoil by stirring up the currents within us. This is the homeland of ulcers, cancers, and a huge array of physical illnesses. What is happening, and why? Good questions, basic ones, to ask, regarding an observed 'repressing' tendency you have regarding your natural emotional responses to things. Instead of reflexively declaring what you feel to be undesirable (this is automatically the verdict when you try to block, stop, cover or otherwise get rid of some emotional reaction you are having), what about this: Go from instant judging of your reaction to [simply examining] your reaction with the intention of knowing what it is and where it's coming from—and WHY! This includes the very reaction of covering up or 'repressing.' Especially, maybe, this thing.

This is self-understanding. Not the first thing to occur to someone, I know—even someone who is a "seeker." ...I've seen plenty of seekers—including me—who were more self-deluded than other non-seeking people, and who had bigger, more self-important and holier-than-thou egos than "non-aware" people.

Why do you want your sessions with the shrink to not end? Why do you hold on to them? These are valuable things to spend time wondering.

"You have to be willing to do two things Jeff. You have to be willing to pay the price...and then pay it."

Simple, un-fanfare-ed action. That's what I think I got out of this quote. Many, most, hesitate. [I assume that] few stand up and walk forward. It's profoundly simple and solitary, not done for the benefit of others or for the furthering of our desire for others' good opinions of us.

There is nothing more realistic, more real, than walking one's own steps in this life. It's not poetic or metaphoric. It's living, for once, for real. This isn't a great thing announced with trumpets. This is what you do.

How can I possibly die before I die? Good question. That's the ego holding on for dear life to anything, any excuse, at postponing actually going for the answer. This isn't some great, outer, visible life-changing thing you do, like quitting jobs or whatever. It can be, but this isn't necessary. It is simply where you live and what you do. It is probably the only time a person can be called an adult, truly. Adulthood doesn't come automatically with age. Many, most people are cowards (children). That's alright, though. Maybe the only time a person can be called an adult is when they're consciously deciding to live their life a certain way, [whatever way] that is.

Great humility comes with this sort of move. Because a person who strikes out on their own has none of the support structures of a 'safe' life. The explorers of the North Pole or of the New World were of this sort. Knowing full well, more than anyone else, the extent of their limited capabilities. But going ahead and stepping ahead. That's an adult, in my view. I've met adults who were 12-years-old. And, incidentally, paradoxically, this: it's written somewhere that in order to enter the kingdom of heaven you have to become as a little child. [What I'm talking about is] the same as that. Even though I used the word, 'adult,' in talking about it. [It's an *openness* that you embody.]

Fear. This is what people are feeling when they say, "Oh, that's idealistic, impractical, unrealistic." They're clinging to safety. Which, really, is nowhere. Many people get old and die and never move an inch, clinging all the while to the safety—of what? Of nothing. [While] doing nothing.

It's only called 'philosophy' by the people from the outside. For a seeker of truth living the life of a seeker, it IS the way, the truth and the life. There isn't a shred of armchair speculation in it. It is the fabric of life, actual life itself!

You wrote:

> "I hate to say it, but I haven't remembered to try the exercise you mentioned; "... think of yourself on a mission to grasp the motivation that set this person's mouth in motion". I've tended to do it after-the-fact, instead of in the moment. I'll try to remind myself again tomorrow."

It's valuable to bring another set of assumptions to the table when we interact with people. That's what I think. A nice exercise to remind ourselves how artificial or arbitrary our interaction really is. We're in a groove on the record, and we've developed a certain kind of habit that isn't even guessed at—until it's gone—when it comes to talking to people or anything we do. Like drying oneself off with a towel after showering. If you injure an arm or finger or something, you're suddenly confronted with the awkwardness of towel drying outside of the usual sequential pattern born of, or developed in conjunction with, repetition. Anyhow, it's a kind of relief, I think, to let go of caring much, in the usual way, when communicating, and to be free to pay undistracted attention to what the person is really saying— where they're coming from [nonverbally]. It bypasses the usual insistence we have on getting our point in there, for starters, because our "ears" are tuned to something else. Our curiosity is intent on something else and we're not invested in the default groove of being 'right.'

Amazingly, we're better "facilitators' in this new, unusual kind of communication. There isn't much friction and yet, I don't 'give up' my individuality or opinions. I've found this for myself. The nice thing about having my ear turned to something else is I'm disengaged from the usual ego struggles in communication. I'm watching a different thing. This can be done with every single thing relating to us and to our relation to everything surrounding us.

Know thyself. The search for truth and the quest for understanding; looking for big truth, grand understanding; profound understanding of our being and existence; these synonymous things are definitely furthered by a constant challenging of our assumptions. Not to tear down the self. To <u>understand</u>.

The first thing is to 'Know Thyself,' unfortunately... Unfortunate because I'd rather know the cosmos without being distracted by mundane things (what this means is: I want to <u>have</u> what I want to have, without giving up anything). And who would wish otherwise? Who would wish for hardship and struggle? Ha! No one. Still, to know a grain of sand completely is to uncover one's eyes TO the universe. It is to remove the eyes, in fact, so that the universe is apparent—once we're finally out of the way. We can't see as long as we're the "penny" in our own eye. We are the grain of sand. We, ourselves, may not be ultimate truth, but one thing we are: is in our own way. We can't see something grand or all-encompassing because we, ourselves, are in the way. I hope I don't put across the wrong impression that we've got to somehow get out of our own way. That would still be holding on. A sacrifice of all for the sake of the truth is probably the best way to put it.

Got to go.

David

The interspacing of correspondence I've had with friends on the path and other stories and remembrances isn't being done with an overt agenda looming over every chosen instance of juxtaposition; I merely felt like including the content you encounter as you read this. But, how to order it? A to Z? Beginning to End? I might not have the patience for that kind of build up, plus it would be artificial, false, untrue. As I said, I'm an artist, standing in front of this canvas, adding paint and shadings and wiping things off and adding more blobs of pigment.

I feel there is some kind of benefit to seeing yours truly in other settings, other lighting, watching what has transpired and being allowed to guess between the words at what effect events had on the subject of this portrait. Sharing my thoughts on what I consider the most important subject at hand—a quest for the meaning of one's life—side-by-side with "mundane" seeming things... I'm picking colors and working at *my easel. Give me time and I can probably come up with words that make it seem like I thought this all out carefully and had <u>this</u> in mind all along. Maybe I did—but not in my linear thinking, verbal, connect-the-dots mind. More likely, the plan for this portrait was forming unseen but felt in my non-verbal, holistic, intuitive, silent, behind-the-scenes mind, wherever that resides..*

The following is from my younger brother, Pat, known by everyone in his current life as Patrick. He has lived as a Christian missionary in Iceland with his wife and three children since 1999. He started a church there, First Baptist Church of Njarðvík, Iceland. The U.S. Air Force base, where Pat had been stationed, in Keflavik closed down after the Cold War and the post's church building, just off base, was made available for Pat's "church planting" work.

At the time of this letter, I'd sent Pat a link to a C-SPAN debate between former British Prime Minister Tony Blair and renowned atheist intellectual Christopher Hitchens. I was surprised by the debate because the participants were civil to one another, articulate, well-thought and well-spoken, in my opinion. My brother and I could both be said to have rigid ideas about things. His ideas have taken a fundamentalist Christian turn and mine are anti-people-caused-religious-thinking, in nature. I believe each person has to struggle to discover for sure what their life means. Pat believes this, too, and adds that people need help doing this. I believe that, too.

This is a single email from my brother, who I grew up with, beat up and chased, became friends with and said goodbye to as we moved apart to follow our own destinies. It is taken from a back-and-forth between us that is rare; we live in our own lives and seldom talk much—since around 1991 or so, when Pat flew to Iceland for a four-year hitch in the Air Force, working on F-15 fighter jets.

My problem with the kind of thinking Pat stands for is that it usually says, "I know better than you do what's best for <u>you</u>," and the well-dressed people telling me this are more screwed up than I am, usually. They say they know God and what God wants for me. I doubt it. Still, I respect my brother; I don't think he tries to push things onto people and he's not advocating hate, at least. I think he insulates himself and his loved ones against the evils in the world and focuses on the positive and good. I guess we are *the same.*

1/05/2011

Cool! Sounds like you tried to understand what I said at least. Most people don't even think about what I say, so I feel blessed that you even read with thought my letter. At times I have spent hours writing a response to people with well thought out perspectives. I assumed that you would want my perspective after sending the link to the debate. It, the debate, definitely set my wheels in motion. If you were not prompting a response and dialog, but rather just giving me something to listen to, then for my dialog I apologize. I have learned that unsolicited advice or opinion is rarely listened too and much less heeded.

I like what you said and it sounds like you are searching still. I do hear frustrations/anger about governments and people around your area. I gave up on politics. I think the people, as you and I, should continue to elect people that hold corresponding views to their constituents. As long as the government represents the majority, however, I fear that the systems of education in place today are going to produce a majority that may very well decide to fall off the deep end and make life for us common people more miserable. America is (some say was) great for some reason and I would hope people would consider why America is what she is and try to hold fast to what history proves made her great.

Just so you know, I, on purpose [and] with a conscious effort, try not to push people very hard. I was not driven to where I am by some forceful religious leader. I like placing bread crumbs and carrots along the way that leads into life eternal. By consistent example I try to demonstrate that Christ can transform lives if He is allowed; I believe I am living proof of this. I would hope that others might see Christ in/through me and become thirsty for the things of God.

I have no authority, as you have identified. To this I agree. This is why my church is small. I could tell people that they need our church to get to heaven or to be righteous. I do not. Christ offers us a life not a church. The church is supposed to be a gathering of those people who have found God or rather have been found of God.

It is a choice; I put the option on the table and hope that somebody picks it up. There is a temptation to become more 'authoritative', but I just keep reminding myself that each person must choose. The local religious system here is very controlling in people's lives. Without them, they say you go to hell. I say with or without them or me a person is in danger of having to answer before God for life's actions. There is no religious rite that can [be administered] by me or my church that can inject salvation to a person. Freedom, at times, produces enslavement.

Forceful: Sadly, I have witnessed young teenagers with such opportunity and hope of a blessed and happy lives terminate a pregnancy and live to regret it. They come back as adults crying and sharing that they wonder what the baby would look like, and how tall they would be if they had not terminated the pregnancy. Haunted by what they know in their hearts about their baby, though the psychologist continues to tell them it was just like a wart removal. Even if I join in and lie to them and tell them it was like a wart, they know something. I have seen young people with such opportunity and hope of blessed and happy lives become addicts to alcohol and drugs.

I have seen young people with such opportunity and hope of blessed and happy lives as adults living in the filth of this world and lying in their own vomit. On the contrary, I have also witnessed many that have avoided these pitfalls by choice and [by] being empowered by Christ in their lives, inspired and living worthy of the sacrifice that was made to set them free. These things that I have witnessed motivate me, as well as my own experiences with depravity, deliverance, and empowerment to live. This motivation may appear to be 'forceful' to an outsider looking in. From my perspective it just makes sense to try, even if the majority does not listen.

I love you Dave, and wish you peace.

I am heading to the church to put in a ceiling in a bathroom.

Thank you for sending the photo of you and the flying Guillaume…. I can't throw my kids up like that any more…well maybe Rosa. Clayton is now just 3 inches shorter than I am. Did you see the photos that I put in Facebook?

Give the family a big hug and howdy from Iceland.

We are planning to call Benjamin on his birthday. We sent a card with 10$ for him that hopefully will arrive before his birthday.

Talk soon,

I think Pat reminds me of two characters in the following story, Feileb and Samoh't, combined. The religious authority figure and the concrete believer.

Chapter 4 — Becoming a writer

Relativity Speaking
    by David Weimer

A man said to the universe:
"Sir, I exist!"
"However," replied the universe,
"The fact has not created in me
A sense of obligation."

—Stephen Crane, *War is Kind and Other Lines*

Each of these objects is a galaxy.

He was balancing, of course, on top of the wooden beam and his arms were stretched out at his sides with his palms turned downward. Earlier, Isaac had shuffled up the concrete stairs of the downtown side of Veterans' Bridge and was surprised that traffic could shake the bridge in unceasing abuse. It seemed that the constant shaking would have been unbearable. He wondered how the span had stood for fifty years without crumbling into the cold black water below.

It was cold here; his nose was cold so he blew, jutting out his jaw, to direct the warmer air from his lungs to bathe his numb nose. At the same time, new waterproof duck shoes that he paid five dollars for at the Saint Vincent de Paul store had no trouble gripping the two-inch surface of a two-by-six temporary railing. Isaac's world was this board; he balanced, feeling like a giant on a minuscule wooden bridge spanning the hole blasted through the side of a larger bridge.

*

Once past the folded outer ramparts, Feileb felt the rumbling of the canti'cle wash over her in waves and the heat from the immeasurable depths warmed her carapace. She paused in the immense darkness to prepare herself for a sending from the source of life.

This visit, she had an unusually urgent reason for striving for inner peace before entering. Outside, the weather was becoming unpredictable; a weird, frenzied growth was taking over their crops and strangers were threatening the Pariah. More and more citizens were being called to fight in these uncertain times.

As her six paired legs propelled her forward with smooth sweepings, the intensity of the canti'cle grew and its steady sub-tone washed over her with increasing frequency. Her legs moved in time to it, her heartbeat had become similarly synchronized, and her eyestalks swayed as she descended through the ridges and hollows heading steadily downward. As of late, her natural unusually strong attunement was strengthening, seemingly in proportion to the mounting chaos in the...

Her own sensitivity to the canti'cle, Feileb knew, was greater than most of the seers who had come before her. Yet she was not as confident as she once was. This horrible disruption which threatened the Pariah and all of the land extended to, or perhaps even emanated from, the life vibration.... She felt another surge of uncertainty, which she forced away. But the canti'cle, Feileb reminded herself, was, and always will be; it is life and breath for all.... She would meet this challenge to prove her worth.

The terrain in the sacred cave became convoluted and folded; the determined diviner began to use her forelimb spurs to keep from sliding out of control. Carefully lowering herself to a ledge before the sacred ring, Feileb felt her entire body vibrating with the canti'cle. The sensation was always familiar, but now it was never the same. Feileb forced herself to concentrate on a relaxing technique that she had learned from the previous seer, her teacher.

The intensity of her coming trance was a shock; she was unprepared for its suddenness. Her mind reeled, groped reflexively, struggled for control, and Feileb's light-sensitive bulbs retracted with her body's response to the shock —consciousness faded and the canti'cle surged...

*

"I'm dreaming... of a white Christmas, just like the ones I used to..."

Isaac hummed the rest of the line as a sustained gust of wind caught his oversized long coat, pushing against it as a sail, expecting him to glide away under its power.

With the shove, Isaac bent his knees and let his upper body turn with the steady cold wind, maintaining his center of balance like a dancer with slow, sure movements.

Poised on the edge of a pine board filling a gap where a car had broken through the retaining structure, two hundred feet and more above the Ohio River, this 32-year-old man embodied a grace and economy of movement which had previously only arisen in certain 'magical' memories that he had of his lost youth—playing Frisbee with his father, and, at a wedding reception where he had felt barely connected to his body and the dancing.

The wind faded and Isaac continued to hum the Christmas carol under his breath. He was a man not infatuated with music, but he sang, or hummed or whistled bits of songs and tunes he remembered whenever his life was difficult and he was troubled or upset, or when—when deliberately pacing on the board edge. Measured steps to one sawed-off end, a careful pirouette, and another pass to the other end. It was dark except for widely spaced streetlights. The crisp sky presented billions of stars to unseeing speeding motorists on the bridge below.

Few drivers noticed the stars or anything but what was immediately before them—a car, the area of blurred pavement illuminated by headlights—and, of these few who noticed so little, none of them saw Isaac's deliberate pacing or heard his voice raised in song.

*

Hope Webber was a pessimist. But she was an incomplete pessimist because she thought of herself as an optimist—the pessimism was creeping up on her just as steadily as her birthday, a week away.

Her world was a place that she was sure of; she knew without question that she could be extremely successful and possibly even happy if she were careful and did everything right: if she paid her bills, cultivated especially 'useful' friends, performed preventive maintenance on her two-year-old car and 24-year-old body.

The route she took while jogging had remained fixed since she had planned it out on the city map that she kept in her tidy glove compartment. Hope wasn't afraid of becoming bored with routine; the concept of boredom was foreign to her. Jogging was not fun; it was simply a means to an end. Being healthy, attractive, keeping her options open—these things demanded payment, and to her it was worth it. Four point two miles on her car's digital odometer: the long run. Four tenths of a mile less and a bypass over Veterans Bridge: the short run. Tonight, she was running late.

Hope had attended college and graduated with scholastic honors; she'd found a decent job with growth potential and 'portfolio appeal,' and she'd bought a sensible car to match her personal appearance and other choices that she'd made in her surroundings over her lifetime. Everything that she did was meticulously scheduled. It was her anchor to the reality that she was so sure of. Nightly runs begin at 6:30; she was twenty minutes late tonight, but she always allowed half an hour extra, and besides, the bridge was open again to pedestrian traffic and she wanted to see where the accident had been.

This well-scheduled woman with fluorescent yellow tabs on her shoes, a gore-tex jogging suit and fuzzy sweatband that covered her forehead—this sensibly attractive woman experienced an electric shock when, with the wind at her back and her brown hair waggling, she looked to her left and saw *a man!* hovering in the thin air above her. Hope's body spasmed in shock and hopped sideways in mid step towards oncoming traffic. She collected herself and stepped back onto the safety of the bridge sidewalk, whirling to face the man, her breathing fast and her body tense.

"What..?" she gasped, not aware of whether she spoke aloud or not.
The man was not hovering; he was standing on a board—walking and balancing with nothing to hold on to—like a high wire act in the circus.

Hope was recovering from her surprise. She looked behind and around her and there was no one else, no one.

"Excuse me?"
She was jogging in place on the sidewalk a safe distance from the man. He continued his strange balancing without appearing to notice her.

"Pardon me," she asked. "Are you all right?"

The man, who was probably crazy but almost certainly not drunk, answered with a normal-sounding voice,
"No, not really, but thank you,"
and continued his mesmerizing movement from one end of the board to the other.

Hope was having a hard time reconciling that gentle, sane voice with the man's appearance and situation. She looked to the snow on the sidewalk and back at the man up on the board. He may have been her favorite uncle by his voice. He didn't look like him however; Uncle Jim was always tastefully yet casually dressed. This man, still balancing up there like he wasn't afraid —he stank. It was that old, sweetly pungent smell that she always associated with panhandlers sitting on the steps outside of buildings on the lower end of the street where she lived. Hope shifted her weight from foot to foot. She nodded quickly to herself as much as to the stranger, and was turning to go away when that almost familiar voice stopped her.

"Beautiful sky, isn't it?"

"Oh," she answered reflexively. She hadn't noticed. She looked up.
"Oh. Yes."

The man completed a neat turn at the end of the flimsy looking board—why won't he get down? I hope he won't come down here—
The man hadn't looked at her; his gaze was centered on that narrow looking board. Hope wanted to go; her time was ticking away... Yet his voice... Why was he here?

"I like winter nights the best," the man said.
"When the sky is so clear and the air is so crisp and when it hurts when I breathe."

Hope felt hypnotized... nagging thoughts of her night's schedule faded away. His voice did sound like her uncle's. Exactly. Somehow different, but had the same honest openness. She felt—if only he would hold onto something and get down!

"I like to run in the winter," Hope said to the man, surprising herself.

"Ah," he answered, conveying understanding and warmth.
"I used to run, though maybe not the way you do. I would run and run, and never think of stopping."

Covering her nose briefly with a mitten, Hope said,
"I'm running a little more than three and a half miles tonight."

The man was in the middle of the board now. The ends were far apart, and the young woman felt a sudden queasiness in her stomach as she watched. She wanted to ask him a question, but she was afraid. Not until he was closer to the end of the board would she say anything. She didn't want to distract him.

"It sure is nice to meet you. I'm Isaac."
The man's voice surprised her again. She had been watching his feet.

"Hope," she managed to say. "I'm Hope," she said a little louder.

Isaac didn't say anything, but Hope saw his teeth in the night sky and thought that he was smiling. She bent her knees and hugged herself—she waited until he was near the end of the narrow board and asked,
"Isaac, why are you here?"

"Because I'm going to jump."

*

Feileb was not aware of her body; she was not aware that her eyestalks had retracted into the top of her triangular head and that her six legs had locked—typical symptoms of systemic shock. Reactively, her forelimb spurs had anchored the rest of her body to the soft ground of the inner Chancel.

In her dream-like state, she was aware of all; she was all. There was no awareness of her physical form or of the place where it stood locked in rigor. She had expanded beyond; she had merged as before with the essence of creation from which the canti'cle emanated, but previous mental journeys seemed mere dips beneath the surface in comparison to where she found herself now....

As awareness expanded, she experienced her individual-ness being peeled away, layer by layer, as if each portion of her was torn away and shredded to pieces. She felt a raw nerve tickling of her consciousness and that weakening essence, which had been her, was disappearing in the Trance. What had once been Feileb gave way to, and resonated with...became one-with the greater presence of: maker.

The transformation, her essential disintegration and mystic rebirth, was complete. On the edge of an abyss, poised on a precipice facing simultaneous annihilation and salvation, her new self permanently locked in a conscious state of liberating focus: the seer understood.

*

Samoh't rested with his fighting detachment in a depression that offered protection from the battle. The enemy was cunning, curse their existence! Their last sortie into the Pariah had resulted in the heaviest losses yet among citizens and fighters alike. Patches of intense fighting, citizens pitted against foreigners, pockets of conflict moved shadow-like across the land. Scores of prone citizens peppered the plains between the Pariah's outer ramparts and the entrenched enemy. They had not perished alone. The weary warrior recalled with cruel pleasure the stunted, torn bodies that had fallen beneath his own thrashing limbs. Foreigners littered the plain in even greater numbers than his own unfortunate kind.

The ferocity of the foreigners, no matter their diminutive size, and their alarming numbers, hung over his head, a constant reminder of terrible changes in the land. Samoh't had reliable scouts, and news of an enemy that darkened all the lands as far as they could see, moving toward the Pariah... Well, something must be done. He is a protector of the community. He must protect the Pariah.

Nearby, a lieutenant, brave and battle ferocious, lay on his side with a thick, weary limb supporting a massive head. Exertion had tapped his formidable energy. Dark moisture ran from his carapace in rivulets while lateral vents strained to disperse heat through evaporation. His scarred carapace was battered. He turned to his superior.

"Commander, they will not wait long before trying again. How will we defeat them?"

"It is obvious we cannot. Yet—"

Commander Samoh't turned to a lean messenger lying in exhaustion on the opposite side of the protective gulch.
"—Go to the community where they are gathered at the center of Pariah. Tell them to move to the highlands, to the emergency fortifications. Go quickly."

The messenger had heaved itself upright at the sound of the commander's voice, signaled obedience with its feelers and trotted away.

Samoh't addressed another runner that moved forward automatically as the first messenger moved away.
"Notify division commanders to prepare for attack. We will strike before the enemy can reinforce. Tell them to await my signal." *The second messenger snapped his feelers in obedience and scuttled over a rise, disappearing.*

Almost immediately, a scuffle ensued from the direction the messenger had taken. The lieutenant and several fighters jumped forward in protection mode. Noise intensified and suddenly Feileb the seer appeared, accompanied by the second messenger whose sensitive receptive feelers were twitching in anxiety.

Samoh't's voice boomed.
"This is no place for you, seer! Go to the Pariah and console citizens that have lost family."

Feileb dropped into the hollow where the commander and his command detachment rested.
"I will do more by being here."

Samoh't replied somewhat wearily.
"Your talents do not suit this business. Go to where you are safe."

"I will speak with you privately," *Feileb told the commander.*

This seer was mindful of their differences in duty to the Pariah. In the past, there had been an underlying level of tension in their communication: a warrior's mistrust and a spiritualist's contempt for a warrior's task. Her new conviction state, however, dissolved all previous difficulties; the Vision of what was to come still whirled in her mind; in fact, it had expanded to influence every moment of thought. She had no doubt that she could save the Pariah. It was foreseen.

The lieutenant dropped back to a sitting position after sending more scouts to inspect the area of their coming counterstrike. It was important to make sure that enemy spies had not followed the seer. The subordinate watched Samoh't. His commander would not have eternal patience for a well-intentioned citizen, even if she represented the Chancel. The lieutenant respected the diviner's religious wisdom, but wisdom was useless during war. The battlefield was no place for a civilian, holy or not.

"Samoh't, I would speak with you privately," Feileb repeated.

The commander stomped three legs.
"You endanger lives while you divert my attention—the enemy is using every moment to act against us!"

"That is what I wish to discuss," Feileb said. She gestured for him to accompany her to a secluded corner of the hollow. Samoh't grunted, and with sudden movements strode away with the seer toward a niche in the protective valley.

The lieutenant observed the commander's back and the seer's firm gestures. They were out of listening range.

After a remarkably long time, the lieutenant noticed his commander's displays of impatience cease...

Suddenly Feileb attached to Samoh't by the upper limbs.
Time slowed. The commander was exhibiting classic shock: rigid immobility, retracted eyestalks... The lieutenant's instinct propelled him forward. This was a diviner's trick—the seer had forced Samoh't into a religious trance! Before the lieutenant could tear them apart, his commander's body spasmed and the leader staggered backward. Surprisingly quickly, his commander's shock-like symptoms faded as if they had never been. The leader locked gazes with the seer for long moments before speaking.

"Go now."
The commander's feelers flexed with command as he addressed the lieutenant.
"Go personally and find the runner that went to Pariah. If you cannot stop him—if he has delivered my former message and the citizens are moving to the fortifications, tell them, tell all of them: 'It is Commander Samoh't's order that you enter the Chancel immediately if you will survive this day.'"

*

Adrenaline squeezed her heart. She felt queasy. Without trying, Hope had started to like Isaac. Normally she was cautious. But, about him... she cared. Her mind raced as she tried to find a way to respond to what he had just said (he wants to die!?).
"You've got so much to live for—Isaac." The young woman felt as if she was pleading for her own life.

Isaac stood at one end of the board. Smoothly and steadily, he executed a pirouette, and then started walking again. Foot after foot.

"You're right," he said. "And you want to know something? I'm still sure that I can enjoy spring after a cold winter with all those indescribable smells of life in my nose."

Hope nodded encouragingly.

"I'm even sure—" He paused, perfectly balanced, nearly at the end of the board, and then moved slowly forward again.
"—that hot chocolate will still taste good years from now, and I do know that the sun does rise, also. So I'm not horribly depressed. I just know what's going on. I have foreseen my future, and I've reconciled with my past... my beautiful tortured, shit-low wonderful past." Isaac sniffed and blew warm air up at his nose.
"I'm just tired of being acted on. Now it's my turn. I will finally do something."

Hope felt his intensity, his earnestness, but his words didn't explain anything. There was always hope, wasn't there? And to willingly stop living... Isaac seemed like a good person; he shouldn't die.

The young woman felt that a decision was made inside of her. She begun moving slowly closer towards Isaac. She had to do something. Isaac held up his right hand without speaking. Hope stopped five feet from the man on the broken edge of the bridge.

"Oh Isaac, I will be here for you. I promise."

"I'm sorry," Isaac said. "I know that you think I'm throwing everything away, but I'm not. I'm just doing something with my life."

"Why don't you try... with me?"

Isaac sighed. His breath steamed and he was tired and cold and stiff.
"Do you really want to help me?"

Hope nodded.
"Yes."

"Then come up here."

The young woman struggled to whisper,
"I can't."

"I know," Isaac said levelly.
"I can't join you, either."

Hope couldn't say anything. Isaac was at the center of the board and looked up from the board at her for the first time. He transferred his unwavering attention to her eyes. Isaac smiled at her tenderly and then stepped off the board, into blackness and the river below.

Her hands reflexively reached forward, though it was too late. Hope saw such sadness in his eyes... Her thoughts were interrupted by a distant slap. She went up to the edge and put her mittened hands on the cold, impersonal temporary wood railing. Down below, she saw an expanding circle of concentric rings around a bubbling white center flashing in the darkness of slowly flowing water.

*

Feileb felt radiant, glowing with power. Her prophecy brought the community to the dark interior of the Chancel where they would all survive a disaster that will cleanse the blight from their world forever.

After Samoh't had experienced the truth firsthand (she was able to transmit it to him directly, mind to mind), he moved his forces skillfully, implementing a strategy of attack and retreat that succeeded in confusing the enemy, allowing defensive forces to escape nearly unscathed. All fighters had rendezvoused with the community and provided security escort into the holy cave.

The seer felt certain that a great power was at work which intended to allow the community to survive the invasion and the cleansing catastrophe that she had foreseen.

Her kind would emerge from the sacred cave into a new world, born from the womb of the universe. Her Pariah would be everlasting!

Samoh't neared Feileb in the darkness of the Chancel. She sensed him with her feelers as the omnipresent beating of the canti'cle washed over them, bathing the entire community in its benevolent holiness.

"Diviner—"
Samoh't could not finish. The world, the Chancel—everything—turned upside-down. Time ceased. Tens of thousands of citizens were thrown to one side of the great cave, crushing many thousands of others... Attempting to hang from what had just been the ground beneath him, Samoh't was not aware when a darker, more complete blackness plunged his entire existence into an abyss of nothingness.

*

The floor was smooth, concrete and cold. Rows of fluorescent bulbs lined the ceiling. In the center of the room stood a stainless steel table with beveled edges, a slight upward tilt and drain holes in one end. Next to the table, against a paneled wall that separated this room from the rest of the basement, there was a metal cabinet with sliding glass doors.

White cotton towels lined the shelves and dozens of shining surgical tools along with coils of rubber hose for embalming lay in rows, waiting to prepare a body for viewing by its family and friends. Squatting on the other side of the steel table was a large, claw-footed porcelain tub.

A mortician's assistant worked casually; lifting an arm, then a leg, he directed a stream of water to places that he had recently scrubbed, rinsing away mild detergent. Another assistant was out of sight. Clanging noises came from the other side of the wall, mixed with occasional bits of a poorly sung tune.

"Hey Bart," the assistant washing the body barked. "This one took a bath for us! Nice guy, eh?"

Bart, unseen, mumbled something that the assistant couldn't hear. He chuckled to himself and pushed the body onto its back once again. Beginning at its neck, he scrubbed with a yellow sponge in small circles. After a final rinse-off, he leaned closer to look at something.

*

The seer's eyestalks bobbed with uncoordinated movements as she regained consciousness.. She became, gradually, aware of her surroundings. Bright! So bright... Something... missing...

—the canti'cle! Gone! Its undercurrent felt-sound was gone. Its rhythmic beating... only: the murmur and groans of thousands of citizens injured, confused and dying. Many were dead. Then: a brightness.

Feileb struggled reflexively to move further into the holy cave, away from the light, but was shoved backwards by a seething mass of groaning citizens that mindlessly clawed forward from the depths of the Chancel where numerous bodies had collected when the world impacted after the long fall. Prodded forward by fear, moving on instinct, a tide of citizens carried Feileb into a blinding brightness...

*

"Holy shit—" The mortician's assistant stood back up and paused, nervously. After a moment, he held the water pick at arm's length and aimed a blast at the corpse's frothing navel.

*

Feileb struggled to stand. She clawed upright, ignoring her injured side.
"It is come!"

I wrote *Relativity* in 1994 during my last semester at the University of Pittsburgh. I walked every day to school and work through Schenley Park and its golf course bordering an upper class neighborhood where a Jewish couple I had done some work for let me park. I wrote this short story walking the mile or so to my car as I cut through the fairways and walking the sidewalks of the city park. It was a serial effort—every day I'd pick up where I left off and was thrilled by a string of good ideas. I wanted to write an allegory.

The title is a comment on the story, illustrating a felt importance in the grand scheme of things. Feileb and Isaac aren't aware of their relationship, their related-ness. They're too caught up in their immediate environment and personal concerns.

Humans are the only things with souls!

How important would our spirituality and souls be if bedbugs had valid spiritual visions? It occurred to me that every assumption needed to be examined. The more assumptions I examined, the more I saw in my life and in others' lives. I found that these accepted assumptions made up the foundation of everything...

The quote at the beginning is a big finger pointing at a small creature crying out to its maker. Isaac balances on the razor's edge between falling into oblivion and living. Hope has a hollow, colorless life that embodies a lack. Isaac's presence calls Hope away from the condition that many live in—that of being in a mini Universe, deaf to appeal by any of the other isolated fellow humans surrounding it.

Feileb is 'belief' spelled backwards. She is the *antithesis* of blind belief. She is a genuine seer who has verifiable religious prophecies. In every way, she is genuine—her outlook is not based on assumption or belief but on her own experiences; I thought that would be a welcome change. Her felt-attunement to the source, Isaac's heartbeat, is sensed through his belly button.

Samoh't is 'Thomas' spelled backwards. A doubter, an atheist, and a believer in only what he sees. Like the best common sense of us. Foreigners invading the 'land' of Feileb are a result of Isaac's letting himself go a bit there toward the end, not bathing and so on. Bugs on his body multiplying and moving.

Isaac was a snowflake aware of its own soon-to-be-melted self. Hope takes entirely for granted everything she is unaware of.

I wanted to frame a valid religious reality in a setting that would be accepted at face value, and later, when this alien world was seen to be located somewhere unexpected, a reader might have an epiphany about *this* Earth, and their life, with all of its institutions and traditions.

Isaac walks a balance beam of seriousness over a river. This is something he couldn't do indefinitely. This fact shouldn't let the reader relax.

Relativity, when reviewed in my seminar in fiction writing workshop, got crickets for commentary. I couldn't wait to hear what my fellow writers thought of my allegory. Silence grew into silence. The instructor said something vaguely prompting. A classmate mumbled, "The italics were hard to read." I consoled myself much later with the thought, 'They probably hadn't read it.' Or, they gave up reading it. Thin consolation. Ah well.

The story came out of my life's obsession at the time. Straining for the ultimate meaning of life. The meaning of everything. *Relativity Speaking* came out of me, and what I was trying to do. It's a kind of time capsule. I wasn't considering suicide, but I was face-to-face, each moment, with my unsolved problem of ultimate meaning and being...and their opposites.

Flushing, Ohio

Spring 2010

I never wanted to be a writer. I wanted to be, I was, I am, a reader. The idea of writing came up unexpectedly when I was told to pick a major at my community college. It was the only thing remotely related to my interest in reading. Actually, "English" was what came up when I had to give a major. I didn't want to study literature, however. I wanted to read only what I wanted—which most of the time was science fiction or fantasy. It was one of those little whispered things in the back of my mind—*maybe try writing*—with no strong sense of conviction that this was it.

Overall, writing has always been difficult. It always felt like I was trying to force something, like sucking hard ice cream through a straw. Writing always had the strong under-taste of frustration; I feel so much but don't have the tools or ability to say it—that's how it was. So much to say, but you end up staring at the fire or lake, silently. I remember writing letters to my grandmother as a boy. I had nowhere to begin. It would feel bunched-up. I kept at it, though. Getting something down that accurately reflected what I felt was the impossibility. Getting something down that approximated, globally, what I wanted to get across; I always had a fixation on trying to convey the entire picture of a thing I felt inside my head. Describe how a sunset makes me feel in *this* moment. The moment moves past and I'm still running behind it, writing…

Writing to Andrée sixteen years from high school until '99 when I moved to Stuttgart to live with her. Writing to my family when I was off in the Army for the first time. Writing to friends, after email was invented, at the University of Pittsburgh. Writing from various apartments on computers like this one, to friends also on the seeker's path to truth. Writing stories, poems and other 'creative' things, reports, papers and assignments in community college—all of these things as an undergrad and at graduate school. Writing for years in my daily journal. Writing for years in my dream journal. Writing as staff reporter for *The Pitt News*; writing a few 'Day Tripper' pieces for *Pittsburgh Magazine* as an intern; writing as a beat reporter for *The Oakmont and Verona Advance Leader*, a Gateway Press weekly paper in Pittsburgh (briefly); writing as a staff reporter for *Fowlerville News & Views*, a weekly newspaper in my Michigan hometown; writing a couple of articles for *The Intelligencer*, a daily paper in Wheeling. Writing articles for the quarterly TAT Newsletter and later submitting poetry and stories to the TAT Forum. Writing things for this book.

It was bound to happen! *Really?* It's got to happen! *What?* <u>What</u> has to happen? I've got to get better! There must come a time when I'll have a voice above the hum of background traffic. I don't know. I could have continued fumbling on. I believe that becoming mature in myself did more for my writing than all of my writing put together.

I don't feel uncomfortable writing anymore. That's the main thing. And the sheer practice of having done it for so long *has* to have helped me pay more attention to the road and less to driving this temperamental car. I wouldn't say writing is effortless now—although sometimes it is.

I feel comfortable in my own writing shoes. They're worn enough so I can walk in them down trails and over terrain without stumbling… much. What comes next, I imagine, is the shoes become a second skin and then wear out completely. Maybe then we'll have a neural interface allowing one's thoughts to transfer directly to the page. Maybe there won't be any pages of one-dimensional print, marching in rows; maybe there'll be something intuitive and three-dimensional. Maybe people will plug in, like USB-connect-able devices, and download others' thoughts into their neo-cortex. Maybe everything will be wireless then. I'll have had a good long ride. It'll have been a nice walk.

This is the first beginning of this book—my attempt at something autobiographical after bringing my young family to the town in America I had left nineteen years earlier. Ben was enjoying his first year in this world. I was 37 [I'll be 45 in six months.].

Fowlerville, Michigan

Fall 2004

The only job I ever saw someone have that I wanted was a creative writing teacher at Lake City Community College in North Florida. Yvonne Sapia. She was resident poet and teacher of poetry, creative writing and composition at LCCC. Her background is Hispanic. Maybe Puerto Rico. Her first novel, "Valentino's Hair," is someone cutting Rudolph Valentino's hair and a chain of events that ensued. We had to buy it for the creative writing class. *Hey, <u>this</u> is the way to live*—write books and publish them on a university press.

Sapia was doing what she wanted—and getting paid! Actively writing, remaining immersed in that world, and teaching and talking about writing.

I didn't know if I would ever teach, but I wanted to work at something <u>I</u> wanted, just like her.

It might have been around this time, during the last year of earning my two-year degree from LCCC, that I accepted the notion of being a writer. I never had the strong conviction of being a writer; it came gradually, over time. I *always*, however, was a devoted and lifelong <u>reader</u>. It's all I ever wanted to do. Ultimate escape, both *to* and *from*.

Escape ***to*** a sense of wonder, possibility, idealism, hope, adventure. These kind of things were lacking in my environment—others simply didn't seem to think or care about what I thought or cared about. And an escape ***from*** boredom, too. What *is* boredom? A need for stimulation? Sure. But I always felt that I was escaping <u>to</u> places rather than <u>from</u> the place I found myself. Vanilla ice cream, or week-old, cold Brussel sprouts? I always preferred the wonderful worlds I could find in reading.

Andrée's visit in 1990. Photo taken at my first post-Army apartment in Lake City, Florida.

Along the way, faced with the seeming inevitability of time continuing regardless of whether I sat on my ass or worked hard at something, I zeroed in on the one occupation *least likely* to be wrong. Writing was related to my first passion—reading. In the Army, the notion of "what will I do with my life" hadn't come up. I was too caught up in being young, encountering and reacting to many 'firsts.' I was involved in being a soldier in a strange land, straining toward my ETS (Estimated Time of Separation) date, when I would leave the active Army and be *free* again. Leaving the Army was accompanied by a huge feeling of relief that I'd finally left a long prison sentence. I fell into a land-surveying job as instrument operator for a civilian survey outfit in Lake City.

Two years later, I was laid off. I hadn't done anything except let time go by and wait for greatness to come. I was 22. I cast around and landed a job as a maintenance man for McDonald's. I felt like I had missed a boat I couldn't see, but *felt*. I did the best I could, working, though something continually haunted me—a dissatisfaction.

Like every job I've ever had—except newspaper beat reporter—I jumped right in and became the best maintenance man ever. They got their money's worth. I did more than they paid me to do, opening Monday and Tuesday, starting at 5:30, and closing Wednesday through Friday, working until 1 a.m. Nights, I remember riding my bike home through silent neighborhoods and back streets, past barking dogs, through cooler, humid Florida air.

I'd ride no-handed under the night sky and think my deep sad thoughts. I'd race downhill and cross four lanes and merge onto the sidewalk to my first apartment, switching into low gear as I pedaled up the hill, cutting across the grass onto my concrete front porch. My first home was a camper trailer merged into a concrete block shape with a bathroom glued on the back—all painted a uniform dark brown. An enormous oak tree loomed over my tin roof, branches clogged with Spanish moss.

My Chevy Chevette was always in the shop. Great-looking car, but it never ran right from the day I drove it home from Sundance Chevrolet. A perfect lemon. It would sit at repair garages for weeks. I'd get it back and it would still stall and strand me places.

Late one Friday night I woke groggily to the odd sound of a large-wheeled truck skidding… *up* the road, getting closer. Barking wheels, pause, barking wheels, pause… then crash! I went back to sleep. The next morning, I'd forgotten about that and went out to put my laundry in the car and couldn't open the driver's door. In fact, once I looked, I saw my car was somewhat sideways in the gravel parking lot with its side caved in.

Looking down Baya Avenue, I could see tire marks coming up the sidewalk, across a strip of grass ending at my car and swerving again—all uphill. He must have been going a hundred miles an hour. The cop taking the report said there wasn't any hope of catching whoever it was.

My car was in the body shop for weeks, "waiting for parts."

I went everywhere on my bike. I had an Army duffel bag I'd load up with canned goods or laundry and pedal miles and miles up and down hills. I reveled in it and the humid heat. I thought it was making me tougher, keeping me in shape. I guess. Downhill was super. Uphill not so much.

After I was voted "best maintenance man" at the annual McDonald's franchise store picnic, I enrolled in classes at Lake City Community College.

I had college money from my active Army time—the Veterans Education Assistance Program (V.E.A.P.). I went to the administration office and the veterans' office. "What is your major?" they asked.

"Do I have to have one?" I'd wanted to take some classes first, and think a little bit before committing to something I didn't know anything about. I thought I'd have a year or more. Now, it seems I have five minutes to decide.

"You can't sign up for classes without declaring a major," the woman told me.

"I'll take the forms and come back tomorrow," I said.

Around this time my grandfather called from out west, living in Arizona, near my uncle in Phoenix. I told him about signing up for classes at the community college soon and he asked what I was going to study. "Computers with business applications," I answered, feeling under pressure. I'll never forget saying that with the sinking sensation in my gut. I had no idea what it meant. After hanging up, I opened the brochure from the business department to find out what I'd said, and in five seconds, threw the thing in the trash. Great.

All I liked to do was read. I just wanted to read. I chose English as my major because it sounded closer to reading than "Computers with business applications."

I felt unsure about doing well in college. I had taken the SAT a few years after graduating from high school and hadn't been impressed with my scores—I'd forgotten a lot of the math. My scores got me in, though. I signed up for a once-a-week class: College Algebra. I thought I'd "dip my toe in," and take it slow. I worked a long day that first Tuesday, after waking at 4:30, rode my bike home, changed out of my maintenance blues, grabbed a bite to eat then pedaled to school with books in a backpack. Five miles from work to home, another five to school; it was twenty miles by the time I got back home at 10 p.m. after class.

In the air conditioned class, faced with a chalkboard and two-and-a-half hours of College Algebra, I filled pages of notes, having no comprehension of what was being said. It reminded me, exactly, of my French class in high school that I'd dropped out of after a few days, feeling I had been in over my head. Putting my spiral notebook back in my backpack, unlocking my bike and riding home in the Florida night, I felt relief—I was free until next week.

Dread increased each day until Tuesday after work again, when I opened the textbook and flipped through pages of notes while eating at my kitchen table. I wrote a number "1" then beneath it, "b, c & d." I struggled to get the sense of the chapters of homework, then saw I had half an hour to go to class. I pedaled like crazy on the long, straight road to the college, sweating in the dusk, looking in my rear-view mirror at the approaching cars. It didn't feel ideal.

I arrived at the second class, sweating, and sat, chilled, in the air conditioning. Repeat. The third Tuesday was our first test. I locked my bike and walked to the portable building where my night class met. I stood at the door in the dusk. I turned, walked back to my bike, pedaled home, cooked Ramen noodles and ham with mashed potato powder thrown in to thicken it. I set the spiral notebook and College Algebra book on a built-in shelf behind my kitchen table at the end of the trailer; that's where it stayed until I sold the book back to the campus bookstore a month later.

For the rest of that spring, I thought about what I'd done. I knew I'd blown it, using the same avoidance strategy that I had used in my mandatory public school years. Desperately, I was rallying myself to make one more try. I seriously doubted that I could succeed. That's the feeling I had. *One big try*, I thought. *No going back on this. I'll do my very best.* I was afraid. I wasn't even sure I could bring myself to try like that.

At summer registration I signed up for two daytime classes. Tuesday-Thursday. Less intimidating courses. No marathon night session. The registration person told me that I had received an "E" for the Algebra class.

"But I stopped going," I said. "I didn't even take a single test! How could I have gotten *any* grade?" Of course, I discovered there was a process to withdraw from a class. A person took pity on my ignorance changed the "E" to a "W" (withdrawn).

It was do-or-die this time. This was my quiet desperation. Like a weak swimmer going for buoy half a mile out, not knowing he could make it.

I had a couple of good teachers. It was an English composition class and "Writing Arguments," a debate class. At the end of the semester I felt huge relief. I made it. I had two A's, and for the remainder of my time at LCCC, I never got a lower grade—even when I retook College Algebra. I discovered the magical power of intention combined with willingness to do whatever it takes.

I graduated *summa cum laude*, "with highest honor" in December 1991. It felt important.

I went on to the University of Pittsburgh, earning my B.A. in English Writing, and graduated *magna cum laude*, "with great honor" in 1994. Fred Rogers, of the PBS children's show, *Mister Rogers' Neighborhood*, was our commencement speaker. I didn't attend the ceremony. I hung my diploma on my apartment wall, inside its white mailing cardboard envelope. I was proud of myself.

Three years later, I was accepted into the English Department of the University of Memphis in and enrolled full time in classes beginning the following spring. I intended to get my M.A. in creative writing so I could teach, like Yvonne Sapia.

After two terrific semesters, I disenrolled from my upcoming 1999 fall classes, shipped some things, sold my car, gave away the rest and moved to Germany to live with Andrée. By this time, I had finally grown used to the idea of being a writer.

The following took place in Memphis, 1998, immediately after my health insurance kicked in at The Commercial Appeal, *where I worked as an obit writer.*

Sun-damaged

I was in a very nice waiting room with mostly old people. I'd say none of us looked happy. This old guy had a big bandage on the top of his head. Another fellow had one on his arm. An old lady with her husband had a bandage covering her cheek. The assistants came in, said a name and then someone would go and get cut on. They'd come back in, looking kind of... bothered, and then read a coffee table book or stare at the pictures on the wall until their assistant came back again. I watched one guy do that three times before he didn't come back again. He had been in the waiting room before I came in. In, out, in, out.

Micrographic surgery for skin cancer is where they remove what they think is all of the "bad" tissue. They have marks that they draw on your skin that act as reference points. They take the cut-out stuff and look at it under the microscope, searching for boundaries of the cancerous and healthy tissue. They identify which sector needs more cut away and then call you back into the operating arena for another go under the mute knife. This gets to be a routine that most go through at least twice. Waiting between innings takes time—I called it "quietly tense anticipation."

A couple days before, in a medical building high-rise at the center of town, a friendly skin doctor put the needle dripping clear fluid back on a metal tray and leaned forward with his scalpel. He was nice. My numbed eyelid felt heavy. He made a sound like, "uumh," and after a second or two straightened with his brows furrowed. He told me he preferred to send me to the Memphis Dermatology Clinic.

He turned to his assistant and said get the phone number of Doctor So-and-So. He looked back at me and explained that he preferred to make an appointment for me the next day instead of waiting. "They do micrographic surgery."

A few days before that, on the phone, the nice doctor's receptionist told me test results came back indicating I had skin cancer. It wasn't the way I wanted to be told something like that. That happens all the time in the health care system in the States, I've discovered. Bad news comes from the impersonal voice of a stranger on the phone. I had gone in there to see the doctor to have this itchy place on the outside corner of my left eye excised.

The operating room at this other clinic was comfortable and warm—in contrast to the cold waiting room—and a huge lamp over my face felt like the sun warming my skin; both suns were party to this, I thought. The sun that gave me the cancer and the bright interior sun illuminating my face for the surgeon. This second doctor, a facial surgeon, quiet but reassuring, got to work. His assistant, competent. They worked well and professionally together. I went through 'the routine' twice. After the second time, waiting there with the others, I was hoping that would be it, and afraid that it wasn't going to be.

I have red hair and freckles. I worked outside in Florida as a land surveyor, and again in Ohio, then in Memphis as a painter. Eventually I used sun block all the time, but I think the sweat I wiped out of my eyes must have regularly washed it away.

I lost part of the upper eyelid on the edge, and he removed that part in the outside corner where the upper and lower eyelids meet. After my second time, the doctor called me in and told me he wanted to stop. He said there was a 94-percent chance that it was all gone but I'd have to get annual checkups. I don't think he wanted to get any more radical with the eyelid surgery than he'd already done.

The day of waking surgery: A biopsy piece taken from my forehead from before and the eye work. Photo taken in the bathroom mirror of my apartment across from the University of Memphis, with the camera I bought at the PX while stationed in Germany thirteen years before.

I had this done—this was done to me—on Friday and I went to work on Monday with stitches. I was an obituary writer, so I had to use my eyes a lot.

After the stitches were out, the whole thing smoothed out—scar, eyelid—kind of getting used to itself. The first year or so it itched at times. That eye appears smaller.

I remember coming out of the cold, nice-looking clinic into the sunny, humid Friday afternoon in Memphis with my little bag of creams and bandages with a prescription and a reminder for getting the stitches out. The sun was hot and never felt so good. I stood and basked in it, fully aware of my relationship to this life-giving and life-taking orb. I only enjoy the sun in winter. The seat of my black Subaru wagon was *hot*. It felt really good.

The following was written in Fowlerville, Michigan, 2004. I look back. I'm 44, looking back on a 37-year-old, looking back on a 32-year-old—and the ol' train rolls steadily on and on.

"April 2003"

"I was in another world."

This was on the t-shirt that I put on this morning. It's a t-shirt my wife and I designed together, a year ago this month, in France, before the extreme sport 'Extravaganza' two-day event we organized and successfully pulled off, in spite of weather and other problems that always happen in event organizing.

May 2002 in Castanet-Tolosan, France, at our "Extravaganza" event, showcasing what our proposed **One and Only Skate Park** *would be.* **L-R***: Me, Andrée, Patrice Tournon, first-prize boy in his age/ skill class with dad.*

*

I'm five feet ten-and-a-half. Or was. I have reddish-blond hair and, I think, brown eyes. I weigh one-eighty. I'm thirty-seven. I have freckles. Twenty years ago, just entering the Army, I was forty pounds lighter. I've always looked younger than I am. In public school, some of my teachers made the comment that I *seemed* older, however. I have a tattoo of a unicorn on my left shoulder that I got on my 19th birthday in Hanau, Germany. The tracing of an embossed leather key ring holder my sister sent for my birthday.

My oldest son, Guillaume, is going to be four the end of next week [he's now ten]. My youngest son, Benjamin, is almost nine months old [now seven]. Ben's crawling now, though he's been sitting up and scooting around in a walker for some time. Two teeth.

Guillaume is a lean, brown-haired boy with big brown eyes. Benjamin is a stocky sawed-off plug with pure blond hair and brilliant blue eyes. They have a surprisingly good time together. Guillaume does tricks for his brother and Ben laughs his head off.

If life were a journey, that would make perfect sense, because it feels like I've been on the road the entire time. I've seen other people stay in one place and grow and mature and go through their whole array of living there. Like rings of growth added to the girth of a tree, year after year. Maybe always moving has kept me one step away from those rings.

It finally it feels like I'm settling down. I'm happily married with two good kids; I have a job, again, that pays the bills and I've got something to do—write my story.

[Six years would pass after writing these words and before would I pick up, again, where I left off. The words I wrote, back then, are on the other side of a great lake of experience and time. Now back to that guy who didn't know the fullness of his fortune and where he'd be, right now, looking back at himself...]

My dad's family lives in the area of Latrobe and Ligonier, PA. They've all, mostly, stayed in the same area they grew up in and don't plan on any changes. My mom's family is out west, now—Arizona. They've settled too, although they used to be strictly nomadic. When I grew up, we lived in three different houses in the same region of Michigan. Since then, I've moved a lot. Ever since going off to the Army in 1985, I've been in transition. It's my nature or fate. Or… neither and both.

This:

While 18 and 19, I lived in the second floor barracks at Fliegerhorst Kaserne in Erlensee, Germany. I was in Bravo Battery, "First of the Thirty-Second" field artillery, Lance Missile Battalion. We ran PT in the morning around six and for the periodic two-mile PT test runs every few months, we'd start half an hour earlier. I liked the PT tests because they were all about individual achievement—sit-ups, push-ups, 2-mile-run. I'd run like hell, pushing myself and pacing my breathing. I smoked. At the end of the run, sweating, blood pounding, pacing and getting my breath back, I'd go over to Sgt. Zelko and say, "Hey Sarge, can I bum a smoke?" Though we all wore our PT uniform (sweatpants or shorts), "Z" always had a pack of Marlboros and a Zippo lighter. There's nothing like a cigarette after a two-mile run. I wrote this 'poem' about those times.

Run in the head

It's a pleasure to be allowed to suffer so.
So young,
so powerful,
spitting phlegm.

Over there,
frost covered fuel blisters
in a row
along the
airfield fence.

Chinook,
Kiowa,
Blackhawk, Apaches
whomp at the air
or sit stone
dead.

Over there.

Controlling breathing.

Two-mile run in the
Army.
Fliegerhorst Kaserne,
Erlensee,
Hanau,
West Germany.

Feet hit the ground.
Up ahead is the end.

Cold gray morning,
heavy military silence.
Rabbits hide
in the fog.

Six hundred feet
ahead is the end.

Anything can happen.
Collapse,
death (of planets).
'tis grand.

A tidal wave pushing
neck and neck.

Time keeper sergeant
calls
the seconds.

You give up

and run.

Race the wall wave,
race like hell.

Afterwards,

walking hands on hips
back to the barracks.
Spit between steps.

Six-thirty chow.
Plenty of time for a smoke.
Bum one.
Breathe in, breathe out.

Man.

A second version of this nostalgic moment-in-time in my young-man life:

The Art of Breathing

Half-mile to go.
Try holding a cannon ball in your palm at arm's length over a candle.
The sweat and shudder.
That's how it is.
Controlling the breathing

on a two-mile run in the Army.

Fliegerhorst Kaserne, where I climbed the barracks slate roof and howled at the Kaiser moon; Erlensee, where I bought an Italian bicycle to let a thief steal it in Lake City, three years later. Hanau, where the brothers Grimm lived; Frankfurt, where I got drunk and found a church key in someone's back yard where I'd stumbled to take a leak.

Along the airstrip fence line, now, fuel blisters in rows;

Over there: Chinooks, Blackhawks, Iroquois and Apaches whomp at the air or sit stone dead.

Three six nine—

One, two-three, in;

Two, two-three, out.

Phantom feet pound

the path far below.

The end is near—

Drunk, really drunk, on air; it doesn't take much

collecting in the back of the throat,

though dry mouth, there's running nose and regular spitting phlegm while feet thud the ground.

NO kidding.

Three steps breathe in, three steps breathe out.

Laugh at the overstuffed leather chairs, red velvet carpet and tobacco smoke. Fine hairs sizzle—and head thrown back, somehow raise your starving hand a little higher.

Stretching, reaching, running above the ground, floating.

Ah, 'tis grand!

And that goose drinks wine

(Cannon ball dropping)

and the monkey chew tobacco

on the river boat line..

Strawman, starman resulted from taking a graduate poetry class in 1999. I was in the English Department of the University of Memphis. I wish I had finished. I really enjoyed the graduate courses there. I shared an apartment with Grizelda and Emerald, long-time cat companions left over from my first marriage. I had a broom in the closet near my front door, and I imagined just what I wrote. I sat in the chair at my computer corner in the bare living room of my apartment, looking out the front bay window with the curtains drawn back. I'd opened the door to let the cats check out the second floor concrete walkway one humid evening. Tentatively, yet curiously, they nosed their way to the open door and out. I imagined that broom hitting the dirt road in front of the stone house I lived in at 5011 Jewell Road, Howell, Michigan, in 1977. 'Going perpendicular' to the plane of the solar system and galaxy and universe was my notion that there's got to be *another way*, a direct way. Some other way. Some simpler way to get at the first cause, the source, directly. *Some. Other. Way.*

Strawman, starman

Earlier today, I took the broom out of my closet,

found a rising thermal over the university

and climbed in spirals like a hawk

on a broom disguised as a person.

When I got so high I had to stop, I let go,

and dove faster and faster.

And just before I hit the top of a parking garage,

I pulled up so hard that contrails curled back

from my ears

and the broom made a mighty roar.

But now,

in the stratosphere,

the ground doesn't pull so hard.

I've been watching jets' lights below in the dark.

Somewhere down there my cats are crouched by the door

letting the bugs in. I just know it.

So I work carefully to the front of this god damn-good broom,

stand on its green painted tip and kick straight up.

The broom falls back, slow,

points down,

picks up speed,

breaks the sound barrier,

dives into the surface of a country road,

explodes in fire and straw.

At dawn, they will find a broom tree, there, blocking tractors.

As for me,

I point my toes

until I feel the moon's gentle tug.

I adjust my altitude, and carefully shim

under the giant China moon,

curving and arching with its roundness,

gaining speed,

until, on the far side,

I rise perpendicular to the plane of the ecliptic,

and I stretch my arms wide, soaring—

and feel the fade of the sun's warmth.

In five minutes, I look below my feet

and see Sol has taken its place in the outer band of the Milky Way.

The stars down there notice me looking.

"You're off the edge, young man!"

I wave my wings and say, "That's my plan!"

And leave them spinning.

When I blink again,

the galaxy drops into a point

among a myriad of others

swimming around a center

getting smaller by the second.

And then I notice you.

'Maybe you're not going up,' you say,

contradicting the obvious.

"Who are you?" I ask, finally,

reeling from the very idea.

You never answer.

One last "poem" for now, written in that Memphis apartment while recollecting large yellow, red, black, orange spiders and their fishing-line-strong silk between tall weeds and saplings behind our small farm where I'd go sneak a smoke.

"You are what you eat." I've heard this all my life; it's irrelevant, I always thought without thinking. Still; you digest another once-living creature, many of them daily; do you take on any of their essential-ness? <u>Their</u> nature was organized. <u>They</u> had form and function. Each one of them. What about what *that* creature ate and 'took on'? And all the countless lives of eating other lives eating others, stretching back millions and billions of years. Does <u>anything</u> of any of the individuals you've eaten live on, in you? What form could that 'living on' take? Would you know it, sense it, or would it just be "you"? We are what we are. What are we?

Are you what you do? Do your habits form a pattern indistinguishable from the essential "you"? Are your actions related to you? Does what you eat, think or do have any real impact on the real "you"? Do your footprints reflect your essential nature? Are we <u>only</u> what we do? If we're afraid of the dark, is there some essential "us" besides our fear? There *is* a connection between what we take in, what we take on, and who we think we are.

By 'take on,' I mean absorb and embody. We take on life from our food sources. Are we only eating and eliminating?

We're so unique. We're a candle flame of something much bigger and older than ourselves, but we feel separate and individual... I meditated on predator, victim and the scenario. A spider thinking about its prey in a philosophic way... Dropping, as part of the course of things, the empty discard at the end, only to start over again, living one's <u>own</u> life until something removes us, too.

As far as "humble," this is a label for something 'other-than' spider and its particular modality. Hopefully the poem works beyond its original splash, resonating within someone else, within some other spider or fly.

Taking on

The banana spider finds time to consider;

May humbleness be learned from a humble fly?

It spider-sips each precious drop,

drinking humble bodies whole.

May humbleness be learned

through liquefaction?

The spider glows with the memory

of two icicles melting through a fly's humbled thoughts.

This warm recollection summons it

from its humble questioning,

beckons,

with a silent spider tune:

A grounded spider is a humble spider,

and little will he do,

so lasso silk in humble breeze

and fasten tightly to

the joints in a corner of the sky

that a spider covers with his eyes

and a senseful touch

on a leeside thread

that sways and sighs with a thrumming web,

and the softest lies

whispered to all flies:

Here,

here lie,

in this invisible bed…

The spider

lets an empty fly fall

and re-traces his name

in the margins of a broken window.

"Places I have lived"

Literally where I have lived in my adult life—so far.

After two years, I ETS-ed (**E**nd **T**erm of **S**ervice-**ed**) out of the regular Army and came "home" to Lake City, Florida, after making a tour of our old home in Michigan, some friends, and my relatives in Pennsylvania. It was 1987. I lived briefly in our new house, with Mom and Pat, before moving into my first apartment—that travel-trailer-cement-block-structure-painted-brown. Nice first place except for roaches and no opening windows. A piece of pine trim covered the widening crack in my bedroom wall where trailer meets block and daylight washed through after the bare bulb in the ceiling was unscrewed (there was no switch). The only windows that opened—cranked open—were behind my bed and over the kitchen sink.

After a year or more I moved back into Mom's house to take care of the dogs in the kennel while she lived on St. Thomas, the Virgin Islands with a real estate guy she'd met while managing the

McDonald's where I ended up (after being laid off from the survey job), cleaning fry vats on the closing shift. She got her realtor's license and went down to sell time shares, I believe. She ended up doing better than the old pro real estate guy she was with. He was her first relationship, six years after my father's death, and I think he was a bum.

She had listed the house. Once the house and ten acres sold, I moved into a new apartment in town and Mom and the jerk moved to Arizona. I was in the end apartment of a brand new low-income housing unit. Nice, new apartments with a laundry room, playground in back for kids, my own parking place and everything. Big contrast to my first place. There was a retention pond outside my window that loaded up with frogs that spring. They were so loud for a few weeks that I couldn't hear another person while talking on the telephone *inside*.

During five years in Lake City, I was in the Florida National Guard, 153rd Engineer Company, in a demolitions platoon. I'd become a combat engineer. One year, we went to Panama for two or three weeks of jungle warfare training. I graduated from Air Assault School. Went to loadmaster school in South Florida. Before I transferred to the Pennsylvania National Guard in Pittsburgh, I was promoted to sergeant.

Before leaving Florida, I moved from that new apartment to, at first, an unused but decent mobile home behind their house, and then a small, spare house on Karl and Izzy Wolf's property in Wellborn, Florida, 28 miles from Lake City. Good people. They were friends to my brother, who worked for Karl's demolition company, taking down old buildings and recycling and reselling old materials. *Karl's Salvage* was a well-stocked salvage yard and hardware store. Really out in the middle of nowhere and seventy feet from a double set of train tracks. That small house shook whenever trains rumble-roared past. I got used to it and even liked it. This was 1990.

I moved to Pittsburgh in December 1991, and stayed a few weeks with Howard and Gladys Chappel —very nice people, very nice to me. They had a Border Collie, Hannah, who I just loved to play with. I was on my way to attend the University of Pittsburgh starting in the January. Gladys was my dad's mom's cousin. The house they lived in was warm, well-kept, and had some land around it that felt good. It felt better than in Florida, which was always different from what I was used to; this was the kind of terrain I knew—deciduous bare trees in the winter, snow-covered fields. Behind Gladys and Hud's place, you could see a mental institution in the distance at the base of a hill. One hundred feet from their dining room wall was a set of train tracks; the rumble of trains didn't shake *this* house too much because the engines had to slow down for a sharp turn.

I moved to Brownsville Road, five miles above Pittsburgh's South Side. The proliferation of cemeteries on the ridge overlooking the Monongahela River valley was impressive. Three or four big ones just in that area. I used to walk through one on the edge of the area I lived, on the way up and down the hill. I don't remember why, but I used to walk from the South Side instead of taking the bus. This apartment was not bad. It was on the third floor (second from the front entrance). I had use of the roof and one heck of a view out my tiny bathroom window. The sunsets were phenomenal. This was my first home with my first wife, Katherine. We lived there until we were married in August 1993.

Our lease ended in '94, and we moved all our stuff and lived for two weeks in another nicer apartment owned by the same landlord. We were forced to move again after being told our cats weren't allowed in the new place. We then went about 20 minutes by PAT (Pittsburgh Area Transit) bus further south, to New Castle. That was an unhappy apartment on the second floor of an old building with paper-thin, springboard floors you wouldn't walk across as much as bounce. Our two cats, Grizelda and Emerald, chased each other back and forth across the carpeted apartment while we were gone and at night. The old woman below us complained bitterly about the cat's noise. We moved out because of her, and we wanted to be closer to Oakland, where Kathy worked as a secretary at my old place of employment, the LRDC (Learning Research and Development Center). I was glad to be closer to the Pitt campus. It felt good there; an artificial world of ideals. It was very nice to live in that place on Maripoe Street. An old building that looked like a haunted mansion filled with college students. Location, location, though—a fifteen-minute walk to Oakland. I worked for a temp agency at Fisher Scientific as a literature warehouse manager on Fifth Avenue, just outside downtown Pittsburgh.

After Kathy asked me to leave, on the way to our eventual divorce, I moved into the esoteric library room of a square two-story house at 1637 Suburban Avenue. It was 1996. Very nice, very quiet. Fifty feet off the trolley line and very convenient; I had a ten-minute ride to a downtown underground station. I stayed in the library, an enclosed addition porch-like structure above an ad-hoc garage, sleeping on a cot for a couple weeks before moving upstairs to a corner room. 1637 used to be an ashram owned by Bill King, longtime TAT Foundation member. There had always been a handful of guys there, living the philosophic life of devotion to esoteric investigation, sans drugs, sex and other bad habits.

When I got there, my first house mate was Jeff, a Jerry Garcia look-alike, who played the mandolin and drove an *Infinity Q* car; his millionaire mother financed his leisure. He was an acquaintance of Bill's, not interested in philosophic questions. He drank non-alcoholic beers by the case and had an ozone machine in a box that looked like an old record player that he used to blow ozone into his ears to kill the overgrowing fungus there. I think the fungus came from all the fermented non-alcoholic beer he drank. He speculated to me once that he thought he was developing Alzheimer's. He was forty or younger. The last I heard from Bill, Jeff was in Hawaii again. Next came Paul Schmidt, a longtime TAT member who worked at a large Border's Bookstore. He ended up with a Polish girl who needed a green card. Paul and Beata went to India and Asia on a three-month walking tour. Paul brought black tea back from China. He told me about his adventures there with Beata and showed me photos. The last I heard from Paul, he was living with his mother in Arizona, New Mexico or California, driving a delivery truck and Beata was gone. I was in Germany with Andrée. In 1993, Paul and I had driven to Ohio and went skydiving before I married Kathy. Paul jumped out of the Cessna first, while I lay on the ground with binoculars stabilized to watch his freefall. I stood to snap a few photos as he came in for his touchdown on the gravel bull's-eye. We did this after watching a fifteen-minute video and signing a no-fault waiver.

I picked up inline skating at Suburban. Waiting around town for the divorce to finalize, I couldn't stand the public transportation—mainly busses—and decided to get exercise, get free and get alone all at once. I wasn't in the best of moods about my life. Getting off the bus felt *very* good. Katherine got our new Honda Civic. Late October that year, the snow stopped my skating for the season and I rode a Greyhound to Cookeville, Tennessee, and bought a Subaru station wagon with my credit card. My brother-in-law, Buddy, rebuilds cars. I'd asked him to let me know if he saw a good one cheap and he told me about a former coworker selling the Subaru. I drove to Pittsburgh and made a few trips hauling my things one hour south, to a 150-acre wooded farm in the hills of the West Virginia panhandle, not far from Wheeling.

This was the home of the TAT Foundation and a good number of guys have lived there over the years as well. Rose, the founder of the group, was in his 80s, and the group's dynamic hay days of the 1970's and 80's were over. By 1996, there was a skeleton crew. K.W. was looking forward to moving out of the farmhouse where she had lived the past two years in order to spend a protracted time in solitude in a cabin on the hill. S.N. and A.L., who had occupied a rustic lodge up on the hill, had already vacated the place when I moved there in November 1996. I lived for a few blissful weeks in the secluded wood-burner-heated lodge before moving down to the farmhouse just off the main dirt road, where I stayed in a second-floor bedroom as live-in all-around farmhand, fixing whatever needed it and keeping an eye on the place.

By July of 1997, I planned to move off the farm, and ended up taking a few months in a remote cabin on a far-off corner of the wooded hills in total isolation until October.

In November, a year after I arrived, I packed up my boxes—mostly books—as well as a collection of things I'd been carting around, the things that people call "their life," into a rental truck, and towed my station wagon to Tennessee and the new single-wide trailer my mom owned outside of Cookeville. She had four acres of vertical hillside and her trailer perched on the quarter acre of usable land 30 feet from the ridge road, Mansell Hill. I wanted to save rent and try to pay down some of the mountainous credit card debt I'd accumulated buying a car, living like a hermit and not working while life as I knew it unraveled. I stayed there until the spring of 1998. I was on my way to Memphis to get my master's degree in writing so I could teach creative writing at a community college.

This was the career path I took once I started walking again in my life; future plans had lain, unexamined, while I responded to the events relating to Katherine's news that she *did* want a divorce.

In the spring of 1998 I drove my station wagon to Memphis with a few things and a sleeping bag. I'd gotten myself accepted to graduate school, and now had to figure out how to live.

I stayed at a veteran's center the first night, on a couch in the office. Seven blissful hours in the air conditioned office. I was a veteran, so why not. As I was getting my bunk assignment upstairs the next day, I found this was a veteran's center for addicts, recovering and current. After standing in front of my bunk five minutes, I carried my stuff back down to the car and drove to Graceland. There was a KOA on the other side of the parking lot behind the "Lisa Marie," Elvis Presley's jet parked at the Graceland Museum across the street from those walled grounds and white mansion, former home of "The King." I bought a tent at Wal-Mart using my still-warm credit card. I paid for my first week of camping and was hugely relieved. Some moves feel right and some feel really wrong.

Showers, laundry machines, a pool, a pay phone. *Welcome to my new life*, I thought. I pitched my tent near the entrance, in the grass off to the side. I got a job as a painter at Nonconnah Corporate Center, at FedEx's international headquarters. Three weeks or so later, I moved into my apartment right next to the campus of the University of Memphis. It was perfect. It was a beautiful campus and my apartment was within sight of the English Department building. A double set of train tracks ran between my apartment building and the university. Perfect.

I lived there from April or May of 1998 until September 1999, when I moved to Germany. I worked as an obituary writer for *The Commercial Appeal* on Union Avenue, not far from downtown. I attended classes as a graduate student for two semesters and loved every minute. Very good teachers, very good all around. In grad school, I was past all the unrelated coursework; I was finally studying and doing what I wanted to. I'd been accepted into the writing program of the English Department and also the teaching assistantship program—that one scared me—but it was everything I wanted. I visited Andrée in Stuttgart for 10 days in August '99 and after returning to Memphis, withdrew from the university, boxed up my things and sent them to Stuttgart. Two weeks after that, I was walking with my stuff through the Stuttgart airport, hearing German over the PA system (I didn't speak it yet). I had moved to Europe for good.

Even today, when I see a town and state that I typed a lot of obits under, I get a strong feeling of recognition—just from that town's name. I've never been to Paducah, Kentucky, Paris, Tennessee or Holly Springs, Mississippi, but I wrote about a lot of people who had. This was me writing about myself and obituary writing.

A terminal condition

He praises the morning when he awakes.

He does his best to keep alive.

I don't want to write this in the first person.

He has a routine that works,

He finds a way to live outside of the protective shoebox,

but it isn't always easy.

The progression from morning to noon goes unnoticed as he types the names and places

out of the elements.

The only movements are his fingers and the liquid as coffee and water and Pepsi flow under the surface while keys continually tap, clacking the names of hospitals to towns where family and churches are.

Slowly mounting, the pace picks up, and all there is, is the now. No daylight, no time, only rising tension as the faxes ease their way out of the machine in march order, stacking, stacking.

He doesn't know anyone he describes in detail, down to the last.

He will be pressed and stapled and folded and tucked away into drawers, envelopes, albums in a thousand homes; he will be through all the years a place can last, a lot longer than a family; he'll survive in some way.

A moment's eternity before deadline and the symphony is crescendo, cymbals and cacophony.

Heart failure, cardiac arrest, self-inflicted gunshot wound stabbing smoke inhalation Alzheimer's lupus diabetes lung cancer stroke.

A terminal condition, the last voice he speaks to, says. The directors, secretaries, answering services at parlors, homes, chapels mortuaries hear my voice every day.

He goes home in a blurred haze. More routine saves his day.

Mail, dinner, TV and cats order themselves in a fine array,

Each to their own, in their own way,

He closes the lights and shuts off his eyes and

eases back into sleep one more night.

Stuttgart, Germany, March 2001

"Another view from here"

We get surprises—at least I do. We're surprised with another view in unexpected moments of tragedy or accident. Our definitions are painted over whatever really is out there. People talk about the world being an illusion. Our view is an illusion.

We don't realize that we think our words are real things. I don't think we can even think of the idea of questioning our own thinking. That thinking is engrained into our brain. Foreign thoughts, like foreign words, aren't recognized. We think with the language that was whispered in the womb.

I've been living in Stuttgart for sixteen months, slowly acquiring another language, writing over the old one.

In the transition between two languages, I see myself peeling away from the familiar, which I have identified with, and slowly floating over to re-adhere to something else.

For almost a year I taught English. At the end of a summer course last year, I asked a Korean student of mine who had become fluent in German for advice on learning German. Right away, she said, "You have to forget your mother tongue." A chill went through me. I talk to myself with the English words! I *think* with them. Where will *I* be once they're forgotten?

I think a lot. Then there are the times when I'm forced out of my usual way. The initial shock of parenthood for me. It was a chill of approaching death and I couldn't get away from it. That's how these "surprises" are.

Culture shock is good too. Struggling to think and talk to people in symbols whose shapes don't fit through the existing square holes in my head. *Something's gotta give.*

All of the "spiritual" straining I've ever done has been seemingly separate from the actual experiences I've had. I mean in a directly-connectable, logical sense, they are not connectable. I don't think for a minute they are not related. The play changes according to my level of commitment, apparently. Scenes change as a result of living a certain way. This way of living is not lived in order to change things; still, things change as a side effect of the way I am living.

Trust yourself. Be bold. Allow yourself to be inspired by Rose's example. Don't lean too much, too long. When it comes down to it, I think we are forced to give up leaning on anything. "No leaners allowed past this point."

I think we live where we are and project ourselves out there, never guessing what's really the score.

Find out. That's my advice.

I'd like to talk to anyone who doesn't mind corresponding long distance. My email address is dwweimer@hotmail.com.

I sent that one to the TAT group in the States. I spammed it to a bunch of email addresses of TAT members. A notice was put out saying members shouldn't email en mass. Yeah, throw that message bottle against the rocks! I remember not getting one response. I wanted to talk. I wasn't looking for a date; I was very happily married with Andrée. I was writing from changing views and loneliness. It would have been nice to talk. Who could have talked to me? I had walked through three realities, leaving my 'known' world far behind. New views… Fundamental self change, divorce, changing homes, isolations, school, moving overseas, immersion in another culture. I was out there, far, far from home.

Another thing I tried was Shawn Nevins' spiritualteachers.org discussion board. It used to be called "Spiritual Friends Locator." I would scroll down the postings and respond to the ones I felt some resonance with. I was lucky to correspond with usually one person at a time that way. Our conversation would come to a point where there'd be nothing more to say. Something like that. Then I'd run across someone else. That was my lifeline in the first two years in Germany. Why the urge to reach out and talk to somebody on "the most important subject"? It made sense at the time.

Schützen Straße 11 [pronounced "elf"] was the address of our second-floor apartment building. Germans would call it a first-floor (they number the ground floor, *das Erdgeschoß*, zero). I moved in with Andrée, pen pal girl friend of 19 years, in September, a month after I'd visited Germany for the first time in 12 years. Six years since I saw Andrée last—at my first wedding.

Andrée and I were married in April 2000. Guillaume was born in October on my mom's birthday. For his first birthday, we were in Ramonville Saint Agne, France, at 10 Domaine de la Chêneraie, in our third-floor apartment, with marble floors. Fourteen months later, December 2002, we were on a plane to Michigan. Gino and Trish picked us up at the Detroit airport. We stayed with them at 8076 Sargent Road in their modular home, within sight of the house where Gino grew up, and where his mom lived. We lived there until a few days before Christmas, when we moved to 103 Lynn Drive in Alan's Park, a mobile home park on Nicholson Road. We had our suitcases, a new TV and DVD player, our kid and two cats (we'd had flown from France to Atlanta, where my sister picked them up). We rented a car to pick up the cats from Anne in Tennessee. Gino had bought us a 1987 Lincoln Town Car while we were still in France.

Every home I've ever lived in has been *home*. I didn't think, "This is temporary." I just lived there and identified with the place. I'm talking about homes when I was a kid, to the barracks in Germany and my first apartment and every place between and after. These were home.

We're spending our third Christmas here. We have a van and a 4x4 and we're pretty established. Though I feel like I'm settling down, I'm sure we'll be moving again before too long. I don't want our boys to grow up in this trailer park. I like our place, though, and think we're lucky to be where we are. We live in a new 16 by 80-foot single-wide with vaulted ceilings, three bedrooms, two full baths, a shed and everything we need. It's home.

That's the problem with memoirs that aren't written through in one continuous time-frame. We just celebrated our ninth Christmas in the States since leaving France. The 'van' is now my work vehicle and we have another minivan for the wife and kids. We have been four years in our first house. We are homeowners in Ohio. My goal or dream is to live on a larger piece of flat property here in the States, and also to live in France, in Brittany or Normandy. We'll probably do it in that order, though I have the funny feeling we might be in France sooner than later. Funny feeling or hope. We'll see. I better finish this book before I find myself somewhere and somewhen else.

Chapter 5 — Three Months in Isolation

On July 20, 1997, I finished breakfast at the Big Boy's in downtown Wheeling and wrote on the receipt before I left, "I vow to remain in complete isolation until October First. No matter what." By this time, I was aware of the extreme taunting of the bull-called-fate by the bright red of ultimate declarative statements such as these. I'd said things declaratively, such as, 'I'll be practicing martial arts my whole life.' Then two years pass and it's not the case at all. 'I'm going to attend every TAT meeting for a year' was followed by my first in-laws offering a time-share all-expenses-paid trip to their condominium on the beach in Florida on a holiday weekend the TAT meeting landed on. This didn't help *that* marriage.

Most times, our noses are rubbed in our declarations. We're tested. Are you *sure* you really want to do that? I'm reminded of young philosophic guys in TAT saying they're going to hit the metaphysical books hard, meditate, take no alcohol and remain celibate. Days later they meet the girl of their dreams and their "plans" take a turn off the cliff.

With full awareness of this, I said and wrote: *No matter what.* I was on the verge of a grand adventure. One way or another.

This is not when my head came apart, when I experienced almost three days of flatline and burned up in the reverse re-entry through my self-described 'night of hell.' That happened during a week in 1996 when my life, already dead, fell apart. This *was my trying to come up with some idea of "next." The avalanche had occurred, the dust still settling, and I wanted to know what to do next. I should have just stared at my navel for three months. But I didn't; I tried.*

Here are selected entries from those three months alone. I kept a daily journal and recorded my dreams as well—a daily routine I'd had for four years. I wish I could rewrite them decently. But then, better-written journal entries wouldn't be a reflection of myself at that time. They'd be me, now, trying to write better. I've simply transcribed my handwritten journal entries from their spiral notebooks.

Occasionally, I'll try to explain myself and provide some context. Otherwise, when I can, I'll let these passages stand alone like chimneys poking up from the ruins of an overgrown foundation, emerging from an emptiness that once embodied warmth in this now-abandoned cold stone nest …

July 1997. Self-portrait photo taken on the table in front of me, while sitting in Atanasoff's cabin. Waiting for the timer to take the photo, I kind of… faded away.

That summer I was going to that cabin to figure out my next step after the avalanche of 1996. I had the unusual combination of a long stretch of time and the desire to think along these lines.

•

August 2nd

I am convinced that ordinary man—meaning anyone who isn't enlightened—lives for, and by, the little moment-to-moment pleasures. Not, as some might think, for the "life goal" or aim that any single person has. We get one nibble on the carrot and the pleasure of that small bite carries us until the next little nibble.

We are creatures of internal combustion, we move forward steadily, but underneath the apparent smooth motion is, like in the engine of a Cadillac, several little tiny explosions.

Einstein was no different. His whole life was spent dedicated to theoretical physics, to using his mind in very involved realms of thought matrices, but if he never had that one, small, first, *Eureka!* experience followed by others, he would have done nothing of the sort. "Of course," anyone can say, "but it was the idea, the goal that he was working towards." Right.

I see this through my own eyes, of course...I move forward only because of small, little satisfactions. They form the matrix of my productive day. Wash my face with warm water heated over the cook stove. Mmm, it feels good. Oh boy. I feel fresh, awake, ready to start the day. Finish raking leaves. Look over the nice ground, ahh. Read a moving passage in a book. Swallow some cool water when parched. Putting away the last clean, folded shirt. Satisfaction. My examples are few, and suited to me. Other people will have their own specific little pleasures.

I propose that we move by these things alone. And when I say move, I mean to go, individually, in a day-to-day thing called living. To still plan things, to still have a hopeful outcome for the immediate future. Without little pleasures, a person would do what they are told, and nothing more. Utterly hopeless, lifeless, motionless.

My reason for mentioning this is because I think the little carrots in life pull us through the thing until we die. This part of us that takes the momentary pleasure, and is able to ignore the long-term prospects, must be an implant that keeps us going: The pleasure principle. This principle is used on hogs, cows, chickens and turkeys today. By us.

My whole life can be used up, spent, hopping from one little pleasure to another, with eyes closed, until I am too old to be satisfied by the carrot anymore. This applies directly to my life, and also to the spiritual path, in particular.

I do not propose, at all, to do away with enjoyment. That would not be useful at all. There just must be an overriding principle that I live by that is... that has more leverage on me than the little carrots in my life. That is, if I want to be successful in some pursuit. It is a matter of deciding what I will chase. Little carrots or something more.

This is something that has become clear to me these last few days—the whole matter of what moves me, *really*. I had the plan of becoming enlightened, but I see that, apparently, I am more influenced by a sip of water, or a particularly successful bowel movement, than I am by spiritual aspirations. It is not horrible. It is, merely, something that I have seen clearly.

I was thirty years old then. I had the luxury, if you want to call it that, of having a completely free stretch of time in front of me, out there in the woods with the trees and the sound of leaves in the breeze and no one but deer and other animals. I knew this would not probably occur again soon, and it hasn't. Being alone is the only time, except when I am at home with my family, where I can let my hair down, and my defenses. I am not comfortable around people, in general. It isn't effortless; I find that it's work.

I found that I fell into a routine or pattern while living in that ten- by thirty-foot cabin. I had the chance, also, because there were far fewer distractions, to notice things about myself.

August 4th

On a mundane (although possibly important) note, it began raining yesterday evening and rained all night. About 5 a.m. it really came down, and there was some thunder. Yesterday I painted the cabin supports up high and the iron window bars & frame and the north face of the cabin with that creosote substitute. On the way to sign in this morning I saw, came up on, a mother deer and its young. Then I came up on two adult turkeys followed by at least a dozen little brown fliers. Cute. They were on the path out here and got off in a family-like hurry when I showed up.

I dug my latrine hole and did all the laundry except dirty pants. Quiet, solemn morning. Clearing sky, damp forest, sun coming up over hill while I was down low at the spring, looking up at it. I've boiled two pans of drinking water. Today is my stay-inside day. I'll repair the screen down below with patches, sewn in and glued. That's it for mundane activity.

August 6th

Boy what a day. I read, "The life of John Birch" and, "The Longest Day." "The Longest Day" really keyed in a heavy mood. I am here to figure out my life, to make sense of it. I am tired of hating it here.

All those guys died during D-Day and throughout that war. They died so needlessly, so easily. I had a perspective, gained through reading that book, through which to view my own life, and time out here, and society and all of it.

What a day. Like the book [describing the World War II Ally invasion]—only my whole world history has unfolded in one day. Where do I go now? What am I to do? What is my life's worth? Meaning? I feel profoundly affected. Moved past many words into few.

August 8th

Yesterday I, unexpectedly and with no fanfare, experienced as actuality the concept of my existence ending upon death. I mean the concept "fleshed out." Not mere words; the difference between experience and understanding a concept, savvy?

I have always had a rather painful ever-present hope that there is something after I die. Painful because I had nothing to give this hope... realness. And whenever I would consider death, or the end of existence, I never really considered just those things because I was always seeing them conceptually, through my painful empty afraid hope.

Yesterday I was not afraid. That hope feeling was gone. I just thought, *what if there is nothing at all after my death, what if that is the end of me, period?* Well, I felt a sense of relief at this consideration. Yes! Relief at considering my very real oblivion.

Don't ask me why. I would not have expected this. Also, this view of my possible end gave me a more "free" perspective on my life, especially in the context of this world. This glimpse, fully experienced as a possibility—*actually* possible—came unexpectedly, as I said, and although I had never experienced it before (I couldn't possibly, I see, now, as long as my painful home remained in place), it was like the most worn, comfortable pair of shoes I have ever possessed. No great shakes.

I have been allowed a breath of fresh air in this previously more constrictive existence (the boa has loosened its hold), but I feel no great change. Only the air has cleared up some.

Talking to my journal took the place of talking to a person. It was making sense of what I felt by putting it into words. I was addressing a separate person, a listening me. Must be like what a person stranded on an island does.

August 11th

I read, *How We Die*, by Nuland and boy, it sure set my head spinning. Life became terrifying, bleak, unhappy—I was glad to be alive, and felt ashamed of looking for "the meaning of life." I should shut up and eat my dirt and be glad I'm not rotting to death, by God. Holy hell! I picked this up from that book. I meant it. I lived it. Holy shit. The next morning I felt somewhat better...

Maan, what an impressionable brain I have. I take on and in no way "realize" whether it is my attitude or the adopted one of the author of a book. Honestly, the only way I get any clue is for time to go by. Eventually the book attitude wears off, and my more long-term, 'original', attitude resurfaces.

I don't recall this ever happening so markedly while out there in the real world. It probably did. My increased time alone and decreased stimuli from the outside has something to do with it, I know.

So, as I said earlier, I have to watch what I read. Why? I am changeable, malleable. I have seen my operating center change completely as I read first one book and then another. Convictions are gone the next morning after they blaze so brilliantly in the hours of darkness before the dawn.

So I hold onto the leaping horse. And try not to make any life changing decisions (as if I could)...

For Christ's sake, a grip was required. How easily affected is this self. It is all a part of this learning process. Learn by experiencing. It ain't pretty, but the lessons do stick.

It sprinkled briefly today. Eighty degrees, humid. Breezy though—good, good. Personally, internally, I go through the entire spectrum each day—[hot, cold, rain, clear, humid, breezy]. Always a different personal weather spectrum, but I cover the full range of the damned thing each day. Each day is complete unto itself. As I told C. in a letter, this isolation is dissecting my life, peeling it layer by layer, laying each section, paper thin, in rows on a table before my eyes.

My home for three months: Atanasoff's cabin on Rose's farm, circa August 1997.

Dave Atanasoff was a member of the TAT Foundation in the early 70's. He built a real nice, tight, sturdy cabin out in the farthest edges of Rose's wooded land. He then moved to California, or somewhere else. In fact, he'd gone away fifteen years before I opened that cabin door. The cabin was so tight, that upon entering, I felt it had just been built. There were jars and jars of dried pasta, rice and beans; there was a lamp with oil, various everyday items like can openers and matches for the oil lamp and cook stove.

Large shelves on the wall behind a brown couch held old copies of Psychology Today and what looked like every book he didn't wanted to take with him when he left—or, maybe his reading tastes were reflected there. A small iron woodstove just to the right when you walked in, and an easy chair. A writing table in front of a square window with a view of a forested mountain. I had brought about a dozen books with me, but eventually read through all of Atanasoff's books, "getting something" from each of them. These diverse leavings were mirrors to my life situation, each illuminating a different facet—acting as organic fortune-tellers, reflecting my life back at me during that period of solitude.

August 14

Last night a dream came to me that, in short, I had the opportunity to climb Mt. Everest. Unprepared, I was. We were in a dimly lit inn in the mountains, sitting in a booth. Two climbers and two others. I knew it was an opportunity that would disappear very rapidly. I know now, as I did during the dream, that I could die and would undergo serious trials, physically & mentally. When I awoke, I had not decided to go, as a small group was walking towards the mountain with myself and B.G. "walking along" for the first day.

I have now watched the scene progress in my mind. I, awake now, have decided to go—I know it's only a dream—unprepared as I am, to the summit or, I suppose, die trying.

I know that my decision, although difficult to make now, will bind me to times in the very near future where I wish I could climb back down to safety. That my decision is, in essence, a death certificate, either way, to what I now understand as living. In this dream I had a very strong rapport with B.G. I would be honored if he would go also, but I will not say any encouraging words to get him to decide to go.

I realized something this morning. I am reading a biography of Hermann Goering, the Nazi number-two man during Hitler's Reich. He was a romantic, and because of his commitment, fate moved his way. As Clinton had happen for him, or for any number of public figures (whose final fate ultimately ended dramatically, disastrously). Astronauts, too, staring at planet Earth from space, had committed their lives to something that led directly to where they found themselves floating, circling the planet. They became their commitment.

I have pondered the safe way. Of watching the mountain from below, trying to see the climbers on it. That way, or that life, would be fine. But I have a hunger (and I have had a dream), and my hunger is a state of potential.

I want to be on the highest path I am capable of tackling. This ascent to Mount Everest in my dream symbolizes my uppermost yearning, and its limits. I do not know how my way will go. But I have an intuition, a confidence and faith that if I commit myself to the goal, the aim, I will be working towards it.

This is funny, because, as I've already suspected, this commitment to a goal, totally, is to *become* that commitment, and in so doing, there is a definite *lack* of detachment, so, "awareness" of what I'm doing will be gone—awareness of something as a thing [separate from me].

Ironic, because this whole self-knowledge kick I have been involved in is very much about being aware at all times. The total commitment to a goal is to give up awareness (that one possesses as long as one is uncommitted, unengaged, and between gears). I'm speculating.

Mount Everest has held a magical fascination for me. It is the highest commitment to a goal that a person can make. It symbolizes the path that the person, on any commitment, takes from start to finish. Some of the things I wrote during the isolation, I think, were things I was seeing clearly or understanding fundamentally. Compared to not noticing things in my life because I'm in the middle of them. I was writing about things that I saw clearly—finally seeing the forest from a distance, and slightly above.

August 17

Yesterday, while fixing or struggling with the woodstove, I was at wit's end... I thought I was on the brink of frustrated madness. I think I was. Close. Something inside changed, or moved or shifted, like a circuit breaker, to protect me. Something changed so that I didn't go any further past my redline. I thought a lot about my past. Especially the times in band in high school. I have been seeing my life laid out during this isolation. This isolation time is Mt. Everest...

I finished reading a spy novel that I'd started yesterday. Seems I've been escaping into reading these last few days. Well, I needed to. A big tree fell while I was eating dinner. I put on flops and went outside to see where it had fallen. It sounded close. A deer fly pestered me relentlessly so I swore at it, and, waving, went back inside.

Nearly 6 p.m. now. Decided to take a break from books for a while. Earlier, it occurred to me that my dream about Everest was not describing some future, looming commitment I'd make, but this one now that I am involved in. This crazy vow to remain in isolation until October 1. I hope that I can manage a little more than just to persevere or survive it. I hope to have a positive value come from (and from within) it.

When I moved into Atanasoff's cabin, it was in good shape, but there were things I saw needed attention. The floor of the covered porch had collapsed and so I replaced some boards. I lag-bolted bracing cross boards between the stilts the cabin stood on. I remember replacing an exterior section of stovepipe and it was tricky to feed the stuff through the hole in the roof and re-attach it to the stove. That was the exercise in frustration I wouldn't leave undone. There were multiple images of a heroic struggle. Multiple daily personal Everests. Goals and expectations against circumstances not under my control.

August 20

Yesterday fairly flew. Spent a few hours repairing the cot. Cleaned my .22 caliber rifle, ate, read a book called "Schism," a spy novel. Bed at 10:30. An hour later it started to rain and hasn't stopped since. It's almost 10 a.m. Radio said rain all day, then tomorrow too, then next day some. I'll exercise a lot today, and wash up good and boil water and try to keep it dry in here.

As far as a spiritual quest, or aim. It is now a matter of surviving the time. What a shame... Each day has brought revelation and unfolding of my personal character, my makeup, my history. Completely different from what I expected. In the beginning, I tried to skip steps and go straight to abstract spirituality. But the agenda called, after the beginning, for a more deliberate route through the self, my self, Me. The question, 'Who am I?' is being literally answered by my time out here. As far as, 'What more could I possibly be?' or, 'What is the meaning of my life?' These are waiting in the wings. If the rain slacks off a bit, I'll run down to my latrine hill, and then go get two more gallons of water at the spring.

August 21

Listening to the news in the mornings [I allowed myself some NPR news on a battery-powered radio some mornings]; listening to *A Prairie Home Companion* radio variety show or the *Thistle and Shamrock* Irish music program on weekends; drinking decaffeinated coffee; reading those assorted novels found on the shelves—I pull these things close up, like the collar of a warm jacket on a damp morning.

I am a lone person, wandering the rooms of an empty mansion, wearing every article of clothing I have, and shivering. Muttering to myself, eyes searching for another, any other, shirt or hat or sock... I am drawing my humanity about me, my gregarious human nature, my need for warmth and belonging—I draw it close in this thin, rarefied upper region of the mountain, my Mt. Everest.

The vacuum of space is just above my head; I turn my eyes upward and see its black emptiness. So my humanity is a poor space suit. It lets the 'me' out. And the warmth is fading, wisping off fast. I am climbing through very thin air and am aware now of the confines of my own mind. My own thinking. How does one box when one's eyesight has given up? How does one move forward when one has abandoned one's mind? Answer: you do.

August 27

I surely miss life. I don't look forward to leaving here anymore (I can't afford to allow myself to spend any time there, dwelling on a future leaving; it isn't wise to yearn for the shore while in a boat paddling against the waves), but I do miss my life dearly. I finished a book called, "The Book of Survival." About surviving emergencies & catastrophes. I learned a good amount. I'm now reading a collection of W. Blake's prose & poetry and, "the Aeneid," by Vergil.

August 31

What if this Earth is a WARD in an insane asylum? And the reason for the way things work is this: This world is a "Ripener of Souls." Babies are taught by parents who are, through the process of raising kids, taught as well. The adults mature through child rearing [written, of course, before I had kids]. The children are not meant to be functionally mature at first adulthood (it is impossible anyway). In this *ward*, the design is such that maturing only can occur through the teacher/parent learning *on the job*.

Now, also, as time is linear, events in people's lives continually test them (practice makes perfect). Years of living equals Practice. Unwitting, but still so. So an old person, finally, after raising kids and living for years, is matured/ripened. They have *become*, sufficiently, in order for them to be able to Die to this school world. Its purpose *is* no longer, for them. Their souls move on. Out of the nest. So that a young person who "becomes" or, who is enlightened, is merely prematurely aged, wise, ripened-ready.

I feel that this time in the woods has resulted in my growing older, more mature. I am older than my years. I feel older than my years. There is a very definite feeling to this. Not sad. Not glad.

Today I explored this feeling and, remembering Rose saying about enlightenment that there is no bliss, no suffering, I wondered, what is the use? Knowing the answers equals dying. So we live to die? What do we die for?

Today, shooting the bow, I was really getting my technique down. Practice makes perfect. Things were coming together. My shooting was integrating itself. I was becoming a shooter. Since I can only concentrate on one thing at a time, as more of what I did became automatic, I was able to do more simultaneously, and to "fix" by paying attention, my shrinking list of wrong actions. Something occurred to me: any successful skill is an act of "betweenness." To be a good hunter, a part of you has to be dead. By dead I mean still, void, empty, still present, no words, no thoughts (oblivion).

To draw the arrow back, and to think, "Oh, a deer," causes many reactions (and miss the deer). To draw back and think, "a target" is better. To draw back the arrow and to release is best. The part that is absent or "dead" is a spastic kind of thinking thing. The feeling of maturity, of growing older, is just that for me. A non-existent thing. A solid nothingness so profound that it, alone, is. Like a black hole. Only it exists.

September 8th

I remember two years ago (roughly), as I'd sit each evening in the living room of our apartment, during my 'time for thinking.' Kath would be watching her shows in the bedroom accompanied by Griz and Emerald. I felt at peace. Loving my wife, and my life with her and the cats. It was a good ship to sail on... I miss this life. And my wife.

I remember musing before about spending two months in isolation—I would contemplate the cosmos, and unravel the mystery of my life. It is from firm footing that one can think such thoughts. My life as a husband, and our little family of two cats and the trials and the good times, but mostly the solid companionship, gave me a solid ground to stand on, for which I will always be grateful to have had. At times I curse fate and her, that woman, for causing it to end, for divorcing me. But I always know that while it lasted, it was the best.

I say these words, knowing that the future may hold times of companionship that will be more fulfilling and richer. But I had a life, and I had a wife, and we two, along with our feline "children," were on a journey. We would have been good together. It would have worked. I know this as I know my heart beats, and as I feel pain. That is why I do not say, "Oh well," with the practice of a true, uncaring soul. Now, here I am, in the middle of a big pile of yarn.

It turns out I am unraveling myself in this time alone. My self is the mystery of my life that now, I untangle. Maybe I am unwrapping the yarn from an empty figure composed entirely of thread, so that when all is unwound, there will be nothing left but the unraveled me, in a heap, all dismantled. No one standing there to enjoy the solved puzzle.

I am sitting in a cabin in the dark with a lamp to write by and it has just occurred to me that I am living my dream wish of two years past. Little did I know that I would wake up to find my wish fulfilled.

The insights. The personal experiences "out here" in my isolation have been priceless. I am aware that the same fate which I so curse on occasion, has seen fit, in spite of my being unappreciative, to grant me the treasure of a lifetime: Understanding.

It is all I ever wanted—to understand. Truly, I was born to wonder: *Why?* And I am beginning to find answers to questions so long only whispered in the night. This sailor, tossed from a ship in a storm, has washed up on shore on an island. But for the sun, and wind, and rain and silence, I'm alone. Pacing, flicking seashells with a stick, I try to remind myself that this is where I had always wanted to be. It's hard to believe, sometimes.

September 12th

One thing to put down before it's gone: "cabin fever" or withdrawal from society or lack of stimuli is not a terminal condition. I am not fated merely to hope to survive this time and that is that. It does not have to be so bleak. Others have done it, haven't they? Spent years in isolation from others and society with nothing but themselves! Yogis and hermits—they have done what I am doing! It is not terminal, not just something to suffer through. It is not mere mental exhaustion. Hermits have emerged after years alone...SANE. Better off than when they went in! So too, I can be. This great issue with me, this extraordinary welling up of the "Escape!" response is not the voice of sanity. It is the voice of avoidance. Of complaint.

The root, or cause, of what is going on within me may be called cabin fever; it may be experienced by any or all humans in this situation—but it should not be seen as terminal! (I had been leaning toward that unfortunate view). Rather, seen as a fundamental reaction, a condition, a definite something which can be examined. Perhaps used. There is hope. I hope.

September 13th

On more than one occasion I've happened upon a flock of turkeys and several local deer grazing together in this wood. I wonder why. I'm sure it has some mutual benefit. Is it a simple example of the turkeys "bonding" to the deer? Or vice-versa? Or are they just being neighbors? If a thing exists, there is a reason. Maybe I'm just finally seeing what happens all the time. I've been in the neighborhood long enough to see my neighbors out and about.

Working on myself, confronting mysteries, I am learning to become a true investigator: when to apply my questions, how to receive the intuitions, the *maybes*. These simple intuitions (of truth) have a peace and a particular certainty that is unmistakable, subtle. I am learning. This has been a very useful time. I am no longer capable of feeling that this time is in any way a drag.

September 15th

When you push yourself into the unknown, it is into facing fear, and you go with a flexible mental attitude—with the awareness that you don't have anything to lose; and when you emerge on the other side of that challenging time you will never be conquered by lesser things.

Fear is the frontier of comfort and familiarity. Uncertainty is the border guard. One is to have a purpose of *positiveness* (not merely thrusting blindly, pushing a rigid self ahead of you because there may be a cliff, or a bee's nest a step away). One is to have a sense of real adventure, respecting one's ignorance and one's position in relation to unfamiliar ground. And walk with a bold step. You have nothing to lose and everything to gain. Truly.

September 18th

The profoundest truths are expressed in the simplest terms. The earlier lesson I learned was this: "I am responsible for my own actions." This truth centers one on the solid self. This insight, and the ability to remain intact during psychic battle, was a landmark thing for me. It covered the territory concerning my sensing others' moods, states of mind, opinions, and my usual reaction of anger upon being invaded by them. Salvation comes from our terror...

Just now, doing laundry, a great, great truth was uncovered by my willingness to look into this recent theme on reactions. Whereas my earlier, life-changing realization about being responsible for myself had the effect of making me aware of myself and my boundaries in a new way, the insight I have just experienced covers the other MAJOR problem in my life. When the reaction is responding, automatically, to an outside source of attack. In disagreements with other strong-willed-ego people that end in tense silence (the silence being the state of the psychic battle.). The grudges. The negative emotional attachments to things. Holy shit!

This is the other side of the moon on the subject of reacting. One side is yourself—being responsible, truly, for your acts. You're getting stepped on because your feelers are out there, under their feet. Of course! The other side is others. Wow. Completely unexpected how this came about. I was unaware of the necessity of the whole thing.

When attacked from the outside (and I know the difference now) my first action should be, must be, to look at what is going on internally. To face and look at it. Recognize it. And then, leave it alone. This is Jesus' saying, "turn the other cheek." Holy cow. It may seem meek, but it is the most practical, *whole* thing one can do. These negative mental hook-ups (grudges, etc.) are drains on one's vitality and energy and attention, taking away from what is important.

To remain undivided in these times is possible. Go figure. The simple profound truth is this: It is not accomplished by fighting, but by a firm determination to act by observing, and to 'leave it alone' when it has been recognized as other-than-self. Thus, you remain unhooked.

I feel wiser now. As I read back over this stuff, I want to delete it, or edit it. This last entry was my having new appreciations and new views on the nonverbal interaction between people. This nonverbal stuff is the arena in which I have suffered the most. I didn't have thick skin. Instead of reacting in anger when hurt, or instead of the usual reacting, period, I think being out in the woods, alone, let me see things differently because I was in another setting, simplified and less distracted. I could notice things in a different way, maybe for the first time.

I had to sign in each day; That way, if I had fallen down a hill or something and died I would have been missed. A guy who lived on the farmland almost a mile from where I stayed in the woods would check the sign up sheet. Each morning, I'd walk on up to an unused building where a paper was tacked on the door. If I needed something mailed, or something picked up, like batteries or some food item, that's where the transactions would take place.

In some 'tension' I felt between myself and this guy, I gained insights, for want of a better word, into the nonverbal realm. I thought I was corresponding with people, and imagined that I felt things in reaction to them. In my isolation period, I got a look at a part of my nature that I'd suffered from my whole life—sensing interpersonal data that isn't verbal. More times than I could count, I've wished I could shut it off. Seven years after that time of isolation, I am not suffering the same now because my understanding of my fellow human and myself is more complete. I know what goes on between people or between <u>any</u> two living things. It's that stuff that doesn't need language. At the time of this stay in the woods, I had turned the corner from strictly suffering to beginning to see a thing for what it was. Not bad for anyone to have happen, I'd say. It's better than staying stupid.

September 19th

The unconscious, or subconscious, seems to be an Aladdin's Lamp. Ask, and if you're willing to work and possess a small ability to walk between raindrops, you get what you asked for—although not what you expected. It works every time. When you happen onto the answer, there is a feel, a live presence that is still, certain, unrippled. No flaws on its surface. A still pond.

Hypothesis: we project reality. We all project meaning on what's around us, sure. Usually, things rest at that. We don't usually notice more. Yet our lives do follow the lead of our will/subconscious (meaning the not-dealt-with fears, hopes, etc.) like a sleepwalker can walk through a darkened house.

However, a person who makes a commitment and pushes consciously, pushes their will forward and produces effects, definite changes in reality. When coincidence becomes ever-present, synchronicity is the norm and serendipity rules.

September 20th

Losing mind.

September 21

Rained good last night. Really soaked everything. Still a bit rainy. Well I survived. Minus a few brain cells I'm sure. I thought I was going crazy last night. Losing control of my mind. Didn't bathe. Didn't exercise. My last flashlight bulb went out. No more flashlights. I'll get by.

My mind feels like after a storm: calm. Not weak, not scared or anything. Just there. It feels like my head was short-circuiting last night. I could do nothing but lay on my side. I didn't have the power to think, really. Psychological? Physiological?

Leading up to it was a growing tidal wave of the frantic "get out!" feelings. I couldn't stop it. See, I know better than blocking it. That doesn't work. You just push it under and it pops up later. This is something I've really got to figure out! The storms raged within. Coincidental with the storm outside? No. Nothing is coincidental. All is all. All is connected. Not real?

[Later that day]

All that I have said before now is pure bull. A head trip. It <u>is</u> possible to think too hard. I do believe it's possible to will yourself insane! My system has a continuous-use/effort breaking-point, I discovered. I have been on the balanced needle of insanity. Insane, I am no good to myself. I have experienced the certainty, the big understanding about this: I've been in warp-speed operating mode for 59 days. Single-mindedly blasting ahead.

I've had 59 years worth of insights into my essential character and have pushed this machine to the breaking point. I began having insights into existence itself; and all of this is fine. But my corporeal entity and my mind had just collapsed. Had I continued to push (and I am certain that I could have) I would have been nuts.

The insight I had as I was in my exhaustion, laying on my side on the cot in the dark, was this: I am all I got. All the motions and denials of self, and "work," almost all of it had been the acting-out of the accepted ideals of someone else. Other philosophers, other writers' views on life. All my actions had been based on the acceptance, from a sympathetic feeling of resonance, of the doctrines and attitudes of others.

Believe me, this is absolute absurdity. Paradox says that, at the same time, it was necessary. I have been down the road to hell these last 59 days. What I had to learn was: not only should I pay attention, at this time, to myself, only, but I should listen to myself. It's *not* bad to eat, to rest. I had gotten into a habit of denying my body self (including the brain). The habit... You can go *too far* in this.

[Again, later that day]

You step off the locomotive, its sides heaving, glowing red, steaming, and you look at it while standing once again on firm, unmoving ground. You know all is as it should be. The ride was rough.

You had commandeered the engine, cranked the steam to full blast, and the speedometer climbed, creeping, and eventually moved right off the dial. The cowering engineer, trussed up in a corner of the screaming locomotive engine box, warned you about the tracks ending. You shoveled more coal into the firebox with the furnace blazing white. The locomotive surged. There were coaches, fifty-nine of them. When the coal ran out, you ripped furiously into their walls, ceilings, hardwood floors—burning the wood, snapping the floorboards into kindling, shoving them into the blinding maw of the furnace.

When the end of the tracks appeared ahead, the locomotive blasted through the barricades, smashed through a building, then several more buildings, with bricks flying. You left town behind, a wreck, the locomotive's churning wheels sizzling in a blur, cutting groves in the bare ground for the rest of the train to follow. If anything, you were going faster. Fifty-nine turned to fifty-eight and seven and six—with fury you tore into each car in turn, burning the scraps. Nothing was wasted. All was fuel.

Over ravines the engine surged, its momentum so great there was hardly a bump. Through forests, trees were smashed and ground into the earth. Into the center of lakes and through streams, such a pounding attack that water was reduced to vapor. On and on... Faster—rolling hills gave way to prairie and grass burned in a trail behind the locomotive. Black smoke in a line back there.

When the last coach was being dismantled, the grass gave way to rock. Flat rock, as far as the horizon, and the locomotive ground on, sparks flying as the churning steel cut, creating twin glowing grooves behind the trains as the sun lowered to the hills in the distance.

When I was breaking the last bundle of floorboards on my knee, getting ready to throw them into the furnace, just then I knew that somehow this was the end. So the last of the boards went in, and the furnace door was kicked shut. An inferno behind a reflective rectangle of glass. The screaming wind beyond the open engine windows changed to a howling, then a steady, diminished breeze. The train's wheels, worn to half their size, were molten.

The engine ground to a stop. A creak from the gutted coaches, bare frames now. Engine ticked. Heat waves obscured the engine. You stepped off. At this point, the intellect is gone. There was nowhere further to go.

Facing it—always facing it—that's the way to get through. Face it!
—Joseph Conrad

September 22

Thinking is a farce. At least mine has been. A child's preoccupation. Self-congratulatory. It also was the only tool I had. The insights along the way were genuine, and life-changing. I think, for now the thing to do is face the thing within. There's no "figuring it out." That way is a dead end for me now. The struggling to figure out, to find meaning to my existence using my mind. By facing it, I don't mean an intellectual analysis of it. I've tried that. I mean: Just. Facing. It.

There are distractions that have helped me when I yearned for escape (radio, books, food), but the thread of their blanket is worn thin.

Face them, all of them. My inner, most unknown promptings shrouded in chaos and unknowing. Face myself. All of me. I know much less now than at any point before. My brilliant grasp on understanding has receded, and blackness is all, except for a very small point of light. A simple thing is all that remains of the workings of a great, active computer, bent on solving a problem to the sound of self-congratulatory music. Face it. Be a machine with no moving parts. Action without fanfare. No motion—face it.

●

"ONE YEAR LATER"

[written in a new home, from a new place, looking back on the time in the cabin and woods from the viewpoint of another life situation in the same season, a year later]

At 4 a.m. on the first day of October, 1997, I got into my car and drove out of the woods. I took the dirt road to a paved road for the first time since summer and I parked my car in Wheeling in the early morning first light. I walked along the river on the former railroad corridor fitness path.

At one point I was standing at the very edge of the water, in the pre-dawn fog, watching the muddy green current differentiate from blackness and go by, from right to left, in the first light of day, when a beaver swam up to me. I assume it was a beaver. It looked like a beaver. We looked at each other for a long couple of minutes. This was my first contact with the civilized world.

When Big Boy's opened at six, I went in. I ate breakfast and drank coffee and watched a tank truck pull up and suck out grease or something else from under the restaurant through an opening in the sidewalk outside my window.

In the year since that first day back in the world again, I have worked in a driveshaft factory near Carthage, Tennessee, moved to Memphis, found an apartment near the university and worked for three months as a painter. Now [October 1998], I write for *The Commercial Appeal* newspaper. I write obituaries to sum up the life of dozens of people each day. Each paragraph represents a lifetime world. I'm a long way from West Virginia and that quiet cabin.

*

I don't think I'll forget that October morning I came out of isolation. It was nothing special. I'm a long way from Memphis, now [2004], too. Who knows what time will bring, but I remember the cold dampness and the exact feeling of the fog hugging the moving Ohio River. When I turn inward, I'm walking on that asphalt pathway at dawn. I remember the thoughts I had before leaving the cabin, and on the way to town, and in Big Boy's. I remember my car's headlights. Maybe I'll forget these indelible scenes, but they're the unforgettable now.

My memory of the time in isolation that fall has... matured. I went through it and have felt-conclusions about what good it did or what it meant and where it fits in my life. It was something along the way, I could say. I hold inside me those paths and ways from the many days in a certain wooded section of the West Virginia panhandle. I step carefully down the rough slope to the spring, to the bathtub under a piece of gutter downspout protruding from the side of a tall, rounded hill. I stand on the wooden pallet spanning the gap where water running out of the tub's overflow hole has eroded a channel. A sturdy farm fence, from my left to my right, and the ground drops away for hundreds of feet below me. If I go there today (and I don't need to), I'll remember this exactly, no matter what the place looks like now, and no matter what has happened in the years between.

If I had three months to do over again, I'd probably look back over my life for a long time, revisiting old places and times. And I'd probably just be. So rarely do I get to do that. Sometimes, at work, before starting at 6:30, if I'm a little early, I go out the back door and stand in the night and breathe deeply a few times. For a few breaths and moments I am before going back inside to do whatever I do that day.

I added the three paragraphs above while working for Precise Finishing Systems in Howell, Michigan in 2004. I'd been to Europe and back, and was living in the town from my childhood, Fowlerville. Strange thing, to go back to a place that used to exist in my fading memory. Like visiting a dream world brought to life.

Now it's 2011. [The person writing this no longer exists, as time and events have washed him away...] I've just finished playing Scrabble with my Andrée and the boys. I know I was feeling things during that cabin time, way back when. I can't relate to the words I wrote. I can't find the feelings and insights. They're dissolved into me, faded into one big feeling. I've lived a lot since then. Moved to other countries, learned languages, married, had children, worked to provide for my family… Time works on me; I see it happening daily. I don't know what I am. I *feel* it. I *am* it. When I get the chance to go to the pond in our village, I stand and look at the water, or the ice, and feel a heavy silence among the evergreen trees around the shore. I soak that quietness in. More and more, I don't say a lot. I haven't kept a daily journal in eleven or twelve years.

Chapter 6 — Communi[cati]on

A poem, written in Memphis, in February 1999:

Extremes

Do you hate your husband or do you hate the one you see in your father?

When you show them what to see, is what they see real?

We resonate with our wincing and snarling, purring and sighing.

To reject with force or to take unto ourselves, in pain or in harmony, we resonate with the fullness.

In cold and in heat, we burn the same.

Version one of a certain theme. February 1999:

Muteland

It's goddamn hell.

God help me what a retarded jungle have I wandered into.

Pleased with myself, smug in my mental deftness;

to holler in the dull air

somewhere, nowhere.

I scoop a double handful of rich dirt and clench my fists,

squeezing it into coal.

Lost in thoughts, meandering this weedless lawn,

attention span dwindling away like vestigial arms until

nothing, no nubs even to show where once I possessed the ability to snatch an idea from the air.

Now, hanging vines and branches close in,

let cobwebs grow between the rocks as I step up onto the only dry one left.

No sun behind a gray sky.

No echo, no sounds, and

no sign of a way out.

The passage back has crept up behind, unnoticed,

brushing its tracks gently away while I wandered out of tune.

Mute golems made of sticks and mud moved up,

unnoticed; their limbs, dryly, and dust from their movements settle over puddles. Their presence is noted by no one.

I have stopped talking and listened so hard

that the ringing in my ears is a symphony of absence.

My golems and I take in the performance, transfixed by movements

no falling sand can describe, and we stand, side by side

in a circle.

A portrait.

Version Two:

Muteland

Meandering the weedless lawn.

I walk because thinking goes further when the feet are in motion.

My feet follow each other, making their way

round holes and going with the terrain. They take the downward ground, through the tall grass, and into the trees.

My attention follows the equation in my head that is unraveling like yarn thrown over a cliff:

> Who will die?—» Who is aware? —» Who is living?
>
> Who is asking?—» Who answers?—»
>
> How?—» Why?—» Where?

And my mind, or something in it, shuffles through all the answers that well up, saves the last two, and throws one away.

And my mind, or something, turns the object of my questioning and finds a shimmering reflection from another facet and begins again, retracing the formula.

Cobwebs grow on rocks,

and I step from stone to stone.

Massive sycamores, with branches thick as trunks lowering under their own weight, grow between the rocks, misshapen.

With the problem in my head run out and unraveled, my eyes see again.

I feel the air on my face.

The sun drops lower,

the air shifts and cools in the approaching night.

Nothing changes when I blink.

I stand on the biggest exposed boulder that isn't covered with a fishnet of roots and vines.

The path ends.

The moon rises low, and stars fill in between the lowering branches.

Not a soul survives.

I have stopped talking to myself and listened so hard

that the ringing in my ears grows louder and more expansive.

A ring of golems has formed around me.

Their stick and dried mud shoulders brush against one another and a fine dust sifts down to coat moonlit puddles.

My companions and I take in this symphony.

This one was written in the only basement of an apartment complex of buildings I lived in. It was during a tornado warning in Memphis, 1999 where six or eight of us, most of us with our pets—cats, ferrets, a rabbit, reptiles—spent an hour or so, sitting on coin-operated washing machines and dryers while it stormed outside.

In the Valley of the Shadow of Death

I wrote this in a basement waiting for a tornado.
I dreamed I was climbing up its sides, hand-over-hand, to the top where my bat-hook was stuck.
Half way there, and I'm surprised I'm tired.
Three-quarters, and my hands are shaking—*I might fall*!
And the tornado, just about to drop away from the sky before I get there.

I remembered five years spent in Pittsburgh, where Allegheny and Monongahela met the Ohio. I never swam their commentless brown.

I lived for years where hobbits smoke long-stemmed pipes.
Warm, lamp-lit inns after dark, and wizards and rune-covered swords.
Planets hurled, and I, on my unicorn,
could smell a molding peach and hear a farm bell in the woods
where the wind is, still.

I'm a reader, and I'm *there*. Me and that writer—closer than a headache.

And I don't know a thing.

'Cause I'm thinking, what about when I look up for no reason, lose my spot, the train lights too close and I say, 'Oh.'

A whole 'nother ballgame.

This one is also from March '99. I wonder what I could have come up with if I'd had a required poetry class every month of my life?

Just turns away

Time
whittling
reminds me

When I go
the sun goes.

What happens when my body falls away?
A more substantial character some would say.
When everything merges into a day
there's no such thing as time.

Everything has two answers we discover.
A simple supposition as good as another.

Then it falls
in your lap.
In five minutes I will be zero.
They'll kick me in a hole.

And your intuition will say
this is something I could not change.

Implying

of course

that I am helpless.

The following was written for Andrée and my wedding, April 2000. We had French, German and American attendees so we had a little "story" to be read during the wedding ceremony in each language. The three factions in the wedding audience were interested and bored in turn as the story was three times. Here is the English version:

Our Wedding Story

This story begins with two letters.

For David, it was an "F" in his first and only semester of French class when he was 13, and for Andrée, it was a letter she mailed from Rennes, France.

This would begin their 19-year engagement.

For years, they were pen-friends through tumultuous growing-up. David reassured Andrée about school examinations, infatuations and trouble. Andrée gave David warm words and honest caring after the death of his father. For years, they wrote to each other, unseen. And then one Friday morning, David stepped off the train in Rennes. Do dreams materialize at train stations?

After their mutual surprise at seeing each other, David threw his Army bag into the back of her brother's car. Like two bottles, the pen-friends rolled back and forth as Andrée's brother trained for the next *Grand Prix*. Four days flashed by as well, and David returned on the all-night train, heading back to Fliegerhorst, Germany, to an Army base where he was stationed.

How did these two young friends feel about their first visit? As Frank Sinatra sang, they were caught in the "tender trap."

But now, we jump ahead thirteen years.

Why? Because after his time was over in the Army, David left for the States without Andrée. He told her that he couldn't take care of her.

Amazingly, Andrée and David still wrote.

They wrote on birthdays and Christmas, sent postcards and told each other their new addresses. They wrote about problems. At times, months would pass. Then there would be a new letter in the mailbox. Through it all, they were friends of confidence.

Andrée visited David in the U.S. twice.

During her first visit, David took her for a ride on his motorcycle. It was early evening. The stars came out, and the two friends found a lake and went for a walk through the humid Florida night. They promised to be at each other's wedding. That much they could do. David saw that Andrée had matured into a beautiful woman.

Three years later, Andrée flew once more over the Atlantic. She was alone (she had been with a German boyfriend before), and she wasn't too happy to see David marrying a classmate from college.

Before his wedding, Andrée and David had gone for another walk. It was in Pittsburgh, during a hot August day, and David told her he would not make the same mistake again—that if, in some far future, there was another chance for them, he would not let it go.

The next day, he married someone else.

Normally, this is where the story would end. Yet this couple is somehow not normal.

Four years after _this_ wedding, David was taking long walks on a large wooded farm in the hills of West Virginia. His first wife had divorced him a few years before, and he believed that perhaps women were best viewed from a distance—a long distance.

After a year of thinking about his life, he moved to Memphis and enrolled at the university there to finish his master's degree, whereupon he would become a writing teacher.

Now is where a magical door opened.

For only the second time in their eighteen-year friendship, David visited Andrée. She was living in Stuttgart, Germany.

As they entered the airport on the last day of his visit, David told Andrée he would be back. She couldn't believe him. Was it true?

Three weeks later, they met at the airport again when David came to live with Andrée for good. In the months that followed, she grew to know the person who had always been the only boy in her heart, and David learned German, depending on Andrée to help him into his new life. She was "taking care" of him!

Before long, they had a dream together.

They would settle in the south of France and operate a comfortable, clean place for people to escape their ordinary lives.

And now, patient listener, you will see two friends fulfill their promise to be at each other's wedding. You will also witness the beginning of their lives together, and you will forever be a part of their story.

Thank you for being here! Enjoy this day!

Why have I included this particular correspondence thread? I wouldn't say, any more than a painter could tell you in words why they chose this or that brush stroke and color. Written to P.S., a friend I'd skydived with before my first marriage. We corresponded briefly while I was in Stuttgart, circa 2000, before Guillaume's birth.

Hi Paul,

You said you wished you felt the child's outlook. What do you think a child's outlook IS?

All I know is our preconceptions—our definitions that we hold in our head about things—are sometimes outdated like an old dictionary. And the most ironic thing is that we may well encounter or become something and have it staring us in the face and still not make the connection between what we're going through or seeing and the "old" definitions [in our heads] that describe such things.

A quote from Rose's Albigen Papers points a little bit at what I'm getting at:

"Only through the word Satori, will we know of Satori. We may experience it, but each of us will never know but that it was an experience unique unto each one's self, unless someone makes the effort to talk about it."

I really think you're onto it when you're focusing on Ego. WE are in the way. We ARE the obstacle. That's why dying is the only way. The ONLY way. This guy, this ego guy with the multiple personalities and endless bag of self-preservation tricks must be removed from the picture. And the funny damn thing is HE'S the one who is DOING the searching! It's a real paradox.

My own door through that was my "night of hell." That was *my* door. YOU must die. Whatever you can think of as being you is all within that little world floating in a soap bubble in the blackness of space.

I just mean everything, and I mean everything, that we think of as being us. All of THAT goes. For me, it was burned out, taken away, by a fight to survive. I sure (and I mean the Ego one) fought tooth and nail to survive.

And then, at the last point, when I was "leaning" on someone else (like a drowning man pulling another one down with him suddenly noticing his effect on that other person) and it seemed that my leaning was doing them harm, I made a "decision" and FACED it.

I use myself as a source to make general comments. You can't make IT happen. That is still another twist in the candy-grabbing daydream. To try to make something, anything, happen is trying to get WHAT YOU WANT. And you'll get what you want. But not the truth. And not a condition of truth. Just more delusion.

You can only be honest. You can't afford to be a damn fool, as Rose has said. You can't afford to be snowed. And we are snowed. Almost all of the time. This is that action that you now can see flags attached to—that's what I mean by being snowed. And that's just with yourself. Everyone else is doing it to themselves and to each other as well. What a tangled day-mare. So you can't try to make it happen (you can, and we all do, but it won't work). Being an honest person who is just TRYING, in the face of the storm of self-deception. Just someone who is still giving it the best they['ve] got in them to give—in spite of everything.

So, whenever I see that [specific type] of quality in a person, I say HELLO! (Across the valley, yelling loudly in greeting). Shawn's piece in that TAT forum a few months ago was there. The "problem" is that it is only an acknowledgement of recognition. And it may be even a harmful thing. I don't know. I recognized it in V.L., and said so, loudly, and then later, a month or two, it was apparently gone. So who knows what good it does to yell, "I see you!" Maybe no good. But I can't seem to help myself. When I see or detect an honest person, who's what I call "dialing zero," I say *hello*.

So you said you got a lot from Meister Eckhart. The BELLS are us recognizing the truth. That's what drew so many of us to Rose like a magnet attracts iron. It was like coming home, to the place we ALL recognized. He was speaking from There.

Something in us resonates like a tuning fork when a TONE of truth is in close proximity.

That poem, *The Rain*, that you sent was something. Because rain and the sound of it, I believe, touches some universal thing within us. It does in me. It's automatic. Apart from whatever the guy is trying to say, all he has to say is "rain" and we have an automatic feeling. A tuning-fork response of melancholy or rest or whatever. The first stanza is the only one I thought worth keeping on a card on a wall:

All night the sound had
come back again,

and again falls

this quiet, persistent rain.

Everyone being enlightened as the cosmic joke. Well, I mean, when it's a roomful of people wearing the same purple tuxedo, it keeps each tuxedo wearer from getting too big an idea about personal specialness. I was just referring to the fact that I think this multiple thing COULD be viewed this way: Not even talking about any other factor, just having a handful of people with the same thing helps keep one person from being elevated as king. It's a sort of anti-Ego turn of events in the play. Helps keep the illuminated ones from imagining they are gods and helps keep the colleagues of the illuminated ones from using "you" with a capital "Y" when speaking to them. Seriously, think of how else it could have happened. What if it was just one guy? Think of other possible scenarios. I think it's funny how it turned out. And cosmically appropriate. A good reflection of the ingredients that went into the pie is how it turns out.

"Were you referring to yourself when you said that 'it makes it harder to say you look particularly snappy this evening?'"

No. I was using the impersonal "you." The general "you." Just my thoughts. But they're ALL based on myself.

"I'm still not clear in how you see yourself. From what you have been saying about what happened to you, are you 'awake', once and for all? Because you said that you were telling everyone that in fact you aren't 'enlightened', that you are still drilling inwards. You said that over time something is happening. Towards more...view, more understanding, more awareness? I take it from what you wrote that you underwent a momentous immersion or extinction, out of which came a view which will always stay with you. Is the Big Question still not completely answered for you?"

You asked the good questions. You have an accurate impression of what went on. That last sentence was the best synopsis:

"I take it from what you wrote that you underwent a momentous immersion or extinction, out of which came a view which will always stay with you."

Yes. Except I would say:

I underwent extinction, out of which came a view which hasn't gone away. I died. The ME. I was gone.

Now I'M a person with a terminal illness. I'm an Ego with a terminal illness. Slowly, it's being taken over. Hell, talk to an 80-year-old. They have gone through the same process. I mean this life'll do it by itself. But a person on a particular "path" is pushing the spinning wheel faster. Maybe there's more to it, but I'm not beyond admitting that it could be no more unique than that.

I feel like a guy slowly curing in a smokehouse. The smoke is slowly working through me. Eventually, I'll be smoked, through and through. That's a way of describing what I sense about my condition.

I believe that I went through my death. I experienced a condition of undilutable being. Your Pulyan quote, that Buddha quote, Rose's *Three Books of the Absolute* when he says "All that remains is All." It IS all, but it's death. It's the absence of all. It's one.

And right after it happened I said, "Well, I'm still here."

And I wrote in my journal, "I became something other than a coward last night."

Even a preconception-burdened ME, which I "came back to," eventually had to connect the dots and say, 'Oh, I know what that is.' when hearing words like

Absolute. I was bound to finally see that what I "knew" now was what those major league hitters had been talking about all this time. The big problem is my definitions of esoteric terms—learned through my contact with TAT and esoteric books—didn't change. My mental descriptions of these things didn't change, even though some internal thing in me had.

So here's a person who doesn't use the word Absolute. That's not his word. He says, *I became something OTHER-than*.

As far as I know, "I" did not cause it. So that's one reason I say I don't know it all. Because I'm not running the show. I just went through what I went through.

The one thing that is NOT hidden or lost in the fog of uncertainty is Recognition. When I run across people who have a certain outlook or view, there is instant recognition on my part. I recognize that quality in them. No question about it.

That's why I have come to focus on the VIEW that someone has. That's all that matters. It doesn't lie and it can't be misunderstood. All the other stuff can be, and is, filtered through the various "selves" running around out there. Ten people describing an elephant will have ten different words for it and fight like hell to declare their infallible accuracy, never noticing that they all share something in common. That's a comedy.

So I recognize a quality in people. It's unerring. It's automatic and there's no thinking involved and there is no doubt. You listen to a guy describing smoking a cigarette who has never smoked (but who's read a lot about it) and listen to a guy who's smoked his whole life describe smoking—and there's not much doubt. You recognize the one. Two guys who have climbed Everest won't even have to mention the mountain. They'll KNOW each other.

I believe I went through something. I have not been the same since. I DO NOT KNOW THE ANSWER TO THE BIG QUESTION, whatever it is. I do not know anything.

THAT is why I have said, after great deliberation, that I am NOT enlightened. Enlightened in my previously-understood definition of the word.

What is Enlightenment? I used to think it was KNOWING everything. It may still be. I have talked to someone who said they went through an experience where they knew everything. Maybe. I've had many times, while alone in the woods somewhere, where I was completely at peace and my feeling of things encompassed all that was or could be. A kind of knowing, but not what I would accept as "really" knowing everything.

But for me, it isn't knowing anything. It is going through one's own inescapable death and, like John Davis says, going there and coming back with something. And that "something" is what you are, what you have to say, what you see. It's the guy with the eyelids permanently burned off. It isn't at all anything to be "known."

Again, I said I felt like a smoked turkey. I still do. Over time, I seem to be getting "smarter" in that "Enlightened" way. Like a very slow computer quietly digesting a mountain, taking it all in, *becoming* what it digests. I see my effect on some people. I see this so-called "solid" world responding directly to my so-called "thoughts." I see cause and effect in "solid" stone (meaning this scene sure seems like the world in a dream in that it moves and changes and happens—and like a dance, it responds to Me, and I don't mean mundane me). I "mature."

Progression or gradualism IS. Even though a moment ISN'T progression or gradualism.

"The first blow to hit me was contained in the words

quoted in the invitation to join these sessions.

Something about seeing the ways that 'THE EGO SHUTS THE

DOOR ON GOD'. I couldn't get that off my mind. How true

it was and I knew it at rock bottom."

You recognized it. This happens. We're taken to our extreme. And helped. Call it God or call it nothing. When we're just that much more honest enough to make the scale tip a little past the balance point, we get what we need. Not what we want; what we need. Or, we get what we were supposed to get.. Or, we get what was meant for us.

Who else besides someone "at rock bottom" or someone at a kind of extreme position, would these words, THE EGO SHUTS THE DOOR ON GOD, have meaning for?

"One more explanation (and then I'll give it a rest) about something Pulyan showed me. This was SO hard for me to see. He gave away a magician's trick. Ego 1 (wise to all the games and critically so) and Ego 2 (the poor dope who can't see). Ego 1 creates Ego 2 to stay out of the hot seat."

Yes. By the way, this is the famous "process observer" [a term from Richard Rose's diagram of personal spiritual evolution, which he called *Jacob's Ladder*]. Does your "definition" of Rose's process observer match what you feel yourself to be? Maybe not. Still, it's the guy who has the ability to see what he's up to. Who somehow can see. It's not saying he sees all the time. But he has the *ability* to do so. Some just can't see even if they wanted to. Some just can't see because they haven't climbed high enough yet!

Futility is futile, like Rose says.

Don't talk yourself into saying you'll leave it up to fate. Do the best you can. Really follow what you know to be your path. You can lie to others. But you've got to stop lying to yourself. And we lie to ourselves ALL the time (I need company so I'm saying "we"). We've got to be honest with ourselves. When we want something, we've got to say, "Hey, I want that." Then, we might become curious about WHO is doing the wanting, and think about *that* for a while—and then ask, WHY? And, *WHAT* IS BEHIND ALL THIS? And, *WHO* IS DOING THE ASKING? And, *WHO* AM I, REALLY? At rock bottom, beyond rock bottom.

Well, I gotta go.

I'm glad to have someone to correspond with. You just got my reactions and impressions. That's all I claim.

Take it easy man,
David

An email sent April 30, 2001, from Stuttgart, not long before we moved to France.

Hi D,

What makes a guy like C.M. deluded? ["D" had written to me that he'd met someone at a recent TAT meeting who he believed was self-deluded] What keeps him in the dark about his strayings into nonsense, and what allows *us* to keep from straying too far into the darkness of delusion?

Is his delusion really believed—by him? Do you think he really believes that he is God and that he created all of this? Is it *our* understanding of what he says that makes it *sound* crazy? Is what he says *really* crazy?

I'm really interested in what goes on there. Is he really "deluded"? And what does that mean? He's gone in a direction beyond what is acceptable by our paradigm. Anything not graspable by our paradigm is "crazy," because it is something else, and therefore [cannot] "make sense" to our program.

I'm not saying that this guy is on the money. I think he *is* deluded. Meaning, I can't buy what he says and it doesn't ring true to me.

But then, what about *me*? What makes *me* so sure that I'm right? What is "being right"? Is it actually being correct? Is it seeing things in the "acceptable" manner (acceptable to our recognition-ability)? What is this "ringing true" all about? What does it mean, to "recognize the truth"?

All those people who say they are Jesus Christ—what's really going on? Here is an enormous opportunity to learn something about myself, I feel, in looking into what has happened with others.

My intuition says this about these people: they are scared and lost. They've created a self-fooling world to pull up around themselves like a protective blanket is pulled around a kid, scared, in the dark. I also suspect strongly that they are *not* deluded. By that, I mean that at some level they DO know that they are spinning a story and playing it to the hilt. I really believe this—that they know they're doing this thing, and it's what they *have* to do. Like a person sucking their thumb. They *know* they're sucking their thumb.

"There, but for the grace of God, go I." And who's to say I'm *not* there? I believe it takes a person of real stature to remain truthful to themselves, in the face of the enormity of our uncertainty and ignorance.

My intuition, whatever that is, also says that people like this must have been "mixing things," opening the door to too many predators [*referring to psychic or other malovelent influences or forces—taken, adopted and adapted from Rose's expressed opinions of what happens to those who engage in certain types of behavior (sexual, addictive, violent, etc)*]. They got into something not so good, and got messed up and possessed, perhaps.

This happens, or threatens to happen, and often touches us, even if not completely, to all of us at one time or another.

I'll check out that internet site [you recommend] and read that stuff next.

Thank you for telling me about the TAT meeting. I miss being there, and [your email] gave me the feeling of being there. That guy you said you met, who slept in the bunkhouse, and who's that old... I can't imagine who that is.

Rose gave Gurdjieff a lot of credit. He used Gurdjieff's classification of the first four different types of people—instinctive, emotional, intellectual and philosophical—and contrasted them with the different after-death experiences that people seem to have.

I think your advice to that guy with the sleep problem was good. It never hurts to move the old body. When the fire is stoked, often it'll repair itself and get itself back into operating condition.

Your ideas about what God is and our relation to it—that you told Michael Conners---what do you really think? What I'm getting at is: Do you *know* this for sure? I doubt it. Do you *feel* it for sure? My "problem" is that I can talk a lot about experiences and things, but I sure have a problem saying that I understand the whole show. I don't understand, in a full way, running the fry station at McDonalds until I've worked it a week or so. I think it is VERY possible to "understand" this life, after living for a lifetime. This life, I mean, is like that fry station. What we're in, we eventually grasp intuitively, we get a holistic "feel" for the interrelated workings.

I've felt this myself. And it's more and more the case: I understand this existence.

But I don't run the show, as far as I know. I have to admit where my "knowing" stops. What about you? Are *you* the same as Michael Conners, only different? Only more "sensible?"

In those two experiences I had [broken brain and 'night of hell'], my mind was not actively involved. My understanding-things mind. My concept-using (like tool-using) mind. Those experiences were beyond the pale of that kind of thinking. Like oil and water with a one-mile-wide steel plate between them, in two different universes—they just don't mix. That 'other-than' condition—and now [living normally]. [Call it the Absolute and the mundane].

Maybe after a while I'll come up with a logical or reasonable-sounding explanation [of things as I see them now]. A cosmology. I use a 'cosmology' that borrows a lot from Rose, Ramana Maharshi, Gurdjieff, and others, including you (I'm coming up with the "explanation" that rings the most "true"). But I must admit that [any explanation] is just the best I can do at the time, as far as understanding what I see. I am a limited mentality. I have had experiences, and continue to sense things beyond any limitations. [That doesn't mean I can wrap everything up in words.]

You say that most people cannot discern the difference between their own thoughts and a thought that just drifts into their head. Damn right. I couldn't agree more. That is MY problem. I CAN discern the difference between my "own" thought (ha) and others that invade or drift in or push in. But a big part of the time I don't. So if I am not perfectly clear about thinking, how can I claim to come up with the real story?

Thoughts ARE real things. I know it. I also know I can project them. And I know, or see, that we all do this, [in an unaware and uncontrolled way]. It's a big, spit-swapping mess, this aquarium we live in. It's what goes on. The interaction, the real interaction, is all on this ["unseen"] level.

So I know that I "read" people's minds, because I see the flow of information and see what they're inputting, what they're getting in. And I know how I'd react to that information and I make a "guess" as to their reaction. And I'm right. I know people blast me with their stuff, too. Like I do, to them. We're all like kids with temper tantrums—only no parents to kick us in the pants when we get out of control. Until we *become* our own 'parent.' So I see this web of interaction. We are all connected and there's no way—for me, so far—to detach myself from the sticky spider web matrix that all of our heads are attached to, like flies.

But then, I have "learned" how to live in a state of equanimity. It's letting the deepest part of me come to the [surface]. When I live through THAT, then I'm free from the sticky mess; while still being in the thick of it, I am free. THEN, I cause reality to change (by not caring) and things happen and man, man, man, it ain't a solid thing at all, this reality. Not at all. This whole thing is responsive to me. I see the "weather." See it moving in and affecting all people, and they all have their own individual reactions to it. And I see stuff and I ask people sometimes, *are you in my dream or am I in yours?* And they always look at me uncomprehendingly. I feel a certain responsibility. Not to take advantage [of people's suggestibility].

Well, got to go now.

Take it easy,
David

The following is something that I sent to Cecy Rose, my friend and Richard Rose's then-wife, now-widow.

A couple of people in the group, S.N. and B.C., had been reported to have had profound final experiences. I called them as soon as I heard, which was months after the fact. It was probably better that way. I wanted to compare, to hear where they were and what they felt and saw. It was interesting talking to them. I heard their stories and I felt no similarity to my own experiences of 'broken brain' and 'night of hell.' I instinctively tilted my head to listen. I felt a mute whisper of familiarity.

Sending this letter, I was hoping to hear from people "over there" (in both uses of this term) on the subject of profound experiences. The previous letter, from D, was the only response to my 'request' for interaction I remember receiving.

I remember the years following 1996; everything I said to people in TAT about what I'd gone through was incomprehensible—at least that was the expression I read on their faces. They would often say, "I don't know what to say about that, Dave." I didn't get much feedback from my peers because no one could relate to me. At the time of the following writing, being 4215 miles from Wheeling, in a way before today's super-connected internet era, I was hungry for interaction. When I started to hear things about people in TAT that might possibly be related to the condition I'd been living with for a few years, I wrote:

The Truth — June 2000, Stuttgart.

Here's something on the subject the TAT group seems to be centered [on] (sometimes the center can be obscured by details), and which R.R. emphasized relentlessly:

The Truth. This is the draw that pulls me. The closest, nearest thing there is. Does it exist? Some people we know say they have found the answer. I envy a person who is in the position to say they feel the fulfillment of having, *being*, such an answer. I would like to ask them about that. I am curious about [their] certainty, the feeling of fulfillment, after [perhaps] the person has been [back in the mud for years]. Does it wear off?

I have a strong feeling, based on what I know myself, that these people might say yes, <u>and</u> no.

Warning: the following is VERY hard to read quickly.

Yes, the immediacy wears off, the longer they are back in the production with its endless details. The ever-present possibility of becoming obsessed is real—in fact it happens often, the same as forgetting; and yet, at the same time, the other answer is, "no," that it never goes away, it never changes; their center (and it isn't theirs, it just is) is unaffected, unchanged and just the same as it was the first time it appeared---they are never again who they "were," any more than a war veteran can be, once more, an untried adolescent heading off to war (you can't "forget" what you are, or change what you've been through).

This awareness, or "feeling," is the new view. It's simple. It's a Teflon view of detachment. This isn't saying what it is, this is just describing [attributes]. The world doesn't stick so much, anymore. There is always the center; and yet, oddly, it doesn't begin to pretend to answer the brain's question, "What happens after I die?" or even, "Who am I?" [It doesn't answer these things in the brain's terms] If someone asked a question like this, the only genuine answer would be what the person "feels." And they wouldn't even say a single word in reply, if they were being faithful to getting the best possible answer across to the questioner. Transmission is the only way to communicate [this]. It can key in sometimes between words, or during words, but it is not the words. Being the truth is apart from brains and questions and even answers to those questions, no matter how big the brains or questions or answers.

In addition, a person's previous expectations may cause them to not recognize something, even after the fact. They may experience something and, looking back through their habitual brain-personality glasses, not see it as being what they had been searching for. It *isn't* what they were searching for, because their expectations were grown from their personality. All that they had read or understood was done through that personality, or with that set of glasses. That's the grand irony. I bet that almost everyone in the group, who has worked hard at self-definition, will be able to tell how they had suddenly found new meaning in Rose's writing, or Ramana Maharshi's, or whomever's. It may have been a grand thing or something very small. And they still might deny that they have ever had an experience matching anything Rose used to talk about because it couldn't possibly be, because it happened to them, and is therefore completely unique to them. And they're right, it is.

That's not the reward I imagined, they might say. It couldn't be. But, of all the things to doubt, there's no doubting what one *is*, or what one has *become*. Whether I've become a little smarter or a lot. Maybe, sometimes it's so simple that a person might not think to describe what they have become, or what they are, or how they view this place. After all, who questions breathing?

Of course, I am projecting onto those people who have become/found the truth what I have found for myself, or imagine I have found. I'm projecting onto those who readily admit to having experienced something spontaneous and unexpected that was not directly-connectable to their personal efforts. And I am also projecting onto some people in the group who have denied ever experiencing anything "spiritual," even though I feel certain that they have. I would like to know how [each] of these categories of people in the group responds to what I've said here.

I'm still pushing, and harder than ever, and this may be crazy. It may be futile to push further. And yet I feel this is the only thing for me to do. At this point, I can't imagine stopping my push for further comprehension, going for the heart of things. I wonder if anyone else has also noticed, in examining Rose's history, this same thing. This continuing to work, seemingly, after "the job" is through. I believe others must have seen this in looking at Rose's life story. [I see it there.] Is a person ever through? Rose said it wasn't until years later that he was able to describe the fact that he lost his ego during his experience. Is a liar ever not a liar? Is a seeker ever not a seeker? Maybe we do what we do. I'd really like to know what people think about this.

I am aware that as soon as a statement is made strongly, this is a direct and apparently immediate challenge for the contrary to happen. And it usually does. I think maybe this is because we can't conceive of a thing until we're at least halfway out of it, and [any] strong statement [we make] may be just a symptom of our transitory position. We're not being hypocrites; we're just talking from a moving position. There's no way to see what we're inside of until we're outside [of it].

Two questions I ask myself are, *Am I doing the same thing I did before an experience in 1996 simply because that's my pattern*? (like Jim Burns' nonstop figuring of his own life puzzle), and, *Am I doing the same thing* (straining/seeking within) *because I'm not there yet?*

I'm putting out this little essay in the hope that it may be used during the upcoming TAT meeting. I wouldn't mind getting some feedback from people who are, and have been, pushing for all they're worth, in their own private cosmos.

This could be an optional exercise. This crazy-sounding essay could be read aloud. People could write an answer to the questions or comments posed here, directly to me, or simply on the subject(s) in general, and then their answers could be read aloud. A "getting to the heart of things" discussion could follow. I'm really curious about how people react. Is Dave dreaming?

Good luck over there on the farm, in the hills of West Virginia, so far away from my world here, and please keep in touch.

Please say hello to Mr. Rose.

Always with fondness,

David

PS-Andrée [is waving] and says, "Hello!"

HERE THERE BE DRAGONS

You're heading off the edge, into territory governed by a solitary tyrant, well-intentioned but not clearly sane; his solitude, some have said, has been working on his head. He is opinionated, honest, earnest and verbose in turns. The following are excerpts from this tyrant's correspondence with others; they are fragments chipped from an iceberg of interaction between himself and a handful of "safe world dwellers" feeling along the border of their own reality and substance, searching for a way through, murmuring words like *inner meaning*, *truth* and *insight*.

This will be a lopsided read; a Siamese twin without its twin. The voices of his partners in discussion are largely silent, save for a selection you've already read from the tyrant's brother, who is permitted to speak more than the usual two sentences.

Why has this tyrant allowed only his <u>own</u> voice to remain unfettered in the following pages? An academic question to those who feel the answer to this is self-evident. His opinions and statements paint a better, more honest picture, he feels, of his *view of things* than volumes of essays could, and this is his book, after all; let it reflect him... and let the others, referred to by initials in this volume, express who and what *they* are when they write their own autobiographical tomes. At times arbitrary, this tyrant uses others but resists exploiting or exposing them.

Incidentally, the one-sided correspondence you encounter in this book was crafted in the following way: I responded in order, point-by-point, to what the person had said to me in their letter. Some things they said I didn't react to, but overall, that was my way. This should be obvious as you read, but I thought it would help to tell you—better late than never. It's like never hearing the question and only hearing the answer in a Q&A portion of a lecture. It's that missing Siamese twin.

On Shawn Nevins' website, spiritualteachers.org, there was a discussion board—still is, in fact—for people desiring to meet other people in the seeking-for-truth world. I checked out the site and corresponded with Shane for a while. I don't remember what we had been talking about. In the following, he had asked me to describe what I called, for years, my 'night of hell.'

Correspondences

Written to Shane of Ireland from Dave of Stuttgart, June 2001:

Five years ago, for no good reason maybe, something happened. A couple of things. I was pushing hard as hell. One hell of an efficient diver. I read something recently from a guy who said that no one can push for an answer to their life 24 hours a day, seven days a week. I would disagree. I had become one hell of an effort in a direction towards I didn't know what.

Basically taking apart myself through looking at myself. I didn't take apart anything. It happened. I came apart, like that onion you talked about, as a result of incessant looking and diving.

In the midst of a lot of tension and other things, I was allowed by circumstances to spend a week in the woods alone. In a tent. And my brain broke. I woke up one morning after a bad night of storming, among other things, and I was gone. No David. Everything that can possibly be described as being my mind was gone. No motion. No emotions, no back-and-forth of thoughts or anything. That lasted two and a half days. And like a foot coming back to life after being asleep, "I" returned, along with the non-stop motion of whatever you or anyone can say in describing any attribute of the "mind." But just imagine existing without "you."

When I came out of the woods, I stayed in the cabin of a friend for the night before being picked up the next day to go home. That night was what I call my "night of hell." I say it kind of jokingly because there's no way of describing just how hell-like it was. It's a laugh to say "night of hell" because there's no way to point at what it was.

Beginning in daylight, early evening (it was May, 1996), while drinking coffee and discussing things with this friend, I came under attack. That's the way I have of describing it. Imagine the times you've been in the dark somewhere, as a kid maybe, and ran like hell for the light of a house. Scrambling inside just in the nick of time, it felt. And the running was from a mounting terror. And this happened in the light, and increased and increased and I couldn't even politely ignore it anymore. [It started while we where chit-chatting and continued on through that night and until the morning].

That was what I felt pursued by. Terror. And I dodged and ran, mentally, one million different ways. Rationalizing. This isn't happening. Okay, it is happening, but it is all in my head, and so on and on. This thing was strategically superior to me. Before I could complete a move, it beat me to it, halfway. This [thing's purpose] was to annihilate me. I had no doubt of that. I had no doubts as to the seriousness of what was happening. A guy with his head in a guillotine with the blade coming down doesn't take it lightly.

The dodges consisted of leaning on the words of others. Other philosophers, other people whose books I had read. The dodges came from saying "I am" and from getting angry and a lot of other attempts. Man, I was run out. Every avenue was cut off, leaving me no escape. This was no game. I could not escape what was happening. Some unusual phenomena occurred. Noises. Coincidences. It was terrifying [and it had continued on, through the evening, after discussing things with the cabin's owner, while eating a meal, on into the evening as I lay in front of a wood-burning stove in my sleeping bag].

Eventually the running guy, running with no reason or thoughts but blindly running, came up against something. He (I) perceived that his actions (leaning on another's words for salvation) were harming another person [*M., late that night, in another part of the cabin, moaned and said, "Help me," at the same moment that I thought about what he'd said earlier in the day about safeguarding myself against psychic entity attacks*]. I thought it was bad enough to be boiling alive. But to bring this on to another person as well---it was unforgivable. So I did the one thing I probably did that entire time. I turned, truly, and faced what I had been fleeing. Openly. No hope of survival existed at this point. No thoughts, as such, either. Just action. Running, noticing, deciding, turning.

Ultimately it came down to me. And only me. Facing, by myself, oblivion.

And turning to face that was like pulling a trigger. There was no hope. That, too, was lost behind me, in the process. What if you pulled the trigger of a very heavy gun held at your temple and it went off and something remained aware? What if you BECAME or discovered yourself BEING. The words are very misleading. They imply something that isn't the real picture.

Other-than is my best way of talking about what I became or what I experienced. I became something other than a coward. I was burned out, completely, and when I was all gone, something WAS.

Well, that happened around midnight. From then until five-thirty or so, I was re-visited by that pursuer. I was forced to re-remember my way back to what I was. I was forced to re-become it. It was like I died once—fine—but then, forced to go through it again and again. "I" was really stupid, and kept growing back, like a sprout from a burned stump of a tree, with as little choice in the matter. It kept happening, time and again, until, by 5:30 I was pretty much...altered. The "I" that grew back, that is. A groove was cut deep, and even though I "grew back," I never grew back over the center. [M.C., owner of the cabin, had been asleep over on his side of the cabin. I was on a cot in my sleeping bag in front of a woodstove, around a corner. There was no line of sight and maybe fifteen or twenty feet separated us.]

I walked the dirt road below that cabin in the morning after that night. Not elated at living. Not gloriously relieved. Not disturbed. Just nothing. I said to myself, aloud, "Well, I'm here."

Since then, I have never lost that other-ness. I'm a jerk, like all the others, but I'm something else as well.

I've never been afraid again. Not like before. Never again a coward. I am afraid sometimes, but that's what happens interpersonally. It's part of that pattern between animals. But I'm not ruled by it.

Also, my view on things was altered considerably. I saw things differently. I was different. Even though I'm the same. And my view is continuing to alter. Maybe I'm getting smarter. I don't know.

Now, I'm currently 34-years-old. That stuff happened to me when I was 29.

This picture I just sketched is out of context. But I can't write a book here telling all that happened before, during or since.

I can only say that I think you're not wasting your time if you're pushing or diving for understanding or the truth or the final answer or God or whatever you want to call it.

That's it for now. I've got to do dishes before it gets too late.

To an old friend, once.

Written to M.C. before moving to France from Germany in 2001:

Hi,

We're going to the South of France on Wednesday. A colleague of Andrée's has a house on the Mediterranean and we need some down time. But we're going to drive over to Toulouse and a nearby town to scout it out. We're moving there in three months.

Did you know that Rose's Albigensians' town [Albi] is in that same region? I think we'll drive over and look at the ruins, which [must] still stand on that hill. The place Lou Khourey wrote about in that old TAT journal and in the recent TAT forum. Ironic, eh? A guy I really got a lot from (inspiration, companionship, etc.) named his system [of thinking] after a group of people who lived and died in the same part of the globe where I end up living one day. It's funny. Not funny ha-ha.

Good luck on your travels and in your life.

The only thing I know is: *don't waste your being or your capability to get to a more clear position.*

What if this place *is* a bardo? [*Bardo is a Tibetan word meaning the state of intermediate existence between two lives on earth that some people mistake for "reality." A kind of limbo*] What if it is something like that? I'm quite sure it *is* something like that. People talk about hell being somewhere else. Ha-ha.

Anyhow, take it easy.

We'll send video or photos in the near future. Take care.

Sent to Shane, June 15, 2001

Hi Shane,

Yeah, I missed that "p" in your email address. Pretty funny.

I don't think reality is grim in appearance. I don't think reality is wonderful in appearance. Both of these are there, and neither of them *are*. That's no mumbo-jumbo, at least coming from me.

The only thing I can say is this. I have always been a dreamer. Someone who sees, or questions at least, more than is at first glance apparent. Things happened in my life that were traumatic. These things brought out this quality in me [more strongly]. I had a strong desire to understand or to know what this place is about. Then I met by accident—it seemed at the time—a guy who was similarly bent, and who actually followed that to its end. I mean he dedicated his life to finding out what everything is all about. This inspired me. If *he* could do it, then so can I. At least I can try, by God. I can actually let loose the reins on this being I've been saddled with, and dive in, to mix a couple of metaphors.

I dove. And worked. And obsessed on this problem. And pretty much drove myself crazy and sane, simultaneously. It was a full time job. I was dedicated, if not very smart. But then again, we're forced to become smart. Being stupid is not an option. Not in this line of work.

Something happened. And continues to happen. I was changed irrevocably, after that night of hell where the fear was run out. And afterwards, I kept pushing. Because the EXPERIENCE did not give me the answers that I had expected, that I had wanted. My preconceived questions and assumptions. The questions I had been asking were bypassed. Only now do I actually seem to be getting the answers to those questions. But I'm not getting answers. Not like it sounds. I'm becoming the answers. Breathing them in. [My personality and thinking mind is] getting smoked, like a turkey. I'm experiencing the sense of knowing what's going on, directly. Not through the intellect. And *that* has surprised me, because all the questions I had were formulated by the intellect, or logic.

I suspect everything that's happened has done so as the result of my continued drive toward understanding.

All this is to say that I am no authority. Not on you. I have to keep saying this because maybe I think I know some things about you and therefore, say some things. [That's not necessarily true; the only truth is that I'm responding to someone's correspondence].

I'm sure that some of the things I respond to strongly (that you've said) are things I recognize, beyond a doubt, from my own experience. And, recognizing something, I know what is behind, or what *must* be behind such statements. People can only say what they say. No one can fake being where they're not. And a person who knows [something] can't be fooled [about it].

Like you saying the following:

"It occurred to me recently that the focus should be not "What is", as in picking myself apart and noting thoughts, feelings etc, but "Why is?" as in understanding the reason for its very existence. Now I think the first is in practice necessary to a point, especially in the first few years of inner work. But there comes a point when I realize that I have disassembled myself hundreds of times, laid the parts out on the table in front of me, like Pirsigs motorbike, noted them, only for the whole thing to reassemble itself same as before. Something is missing, and I think it is the need to shift to "why".

And I recognize, without a doubt, where you are coming from—because I have gone through this shift, too.

It's like me talking about scuba diving. I can say what I think it's like. But I've never done it. I could read a lot and watch movies and then tell you some things about it. And you would know, eventually, that I wasn't on the ball. [Maybe immediately.] That I wasn't even close. The opposite goes, too. If you correspond or talk to a diver. After a minute, you'd *recognize* something.

So I'm just recognizing other divers. Even if the divers don't know that they're divers. Sometimes it's that way. I just recognize a trait, and I say, "Hey, go for it," and the person thinks I'm nuts, or over-enthusiastic about their abilities.

Sometimes I wonder why I do communicate on this subject to anybody. Because I know everybody, and I mean everybody, has to do this alone. We all have to take our [first] breath and then let it go that last time—and all of the stuff in between.

But then, I have this great response when I run into another person I 'recognize.' I inline skate. I can do an awful lot. Skate down steps, do the half-pipe with spins and tricks, jump things, hand stands. And I have this natural reaction when I see another skater. Someone I can learn from, or, an equal to compare techniques with, or someone who I can say a few things to.

And the things I say, help [I hope]. That's all I know. You know, those "ears that can hear." I can only talk, successfully, to someone for whom this is relevant. Otherwise, I sound deluded or worse, and my energy, spent talking, is wasted.

In the long run, WE ARE ALL EQUAL. We are all valuable. I mean that exactly.

I am very glad to have run across you. I recognize in you the required ability to peer into things. And the footprints, the tracks in what you say, of a person who has done some of the required work, as well.

I feel the urge to encourage you—if at all possible. I don't know if my trying will do any good. It could do you harm, give you trouble. Probably *will* give you trouble. But I've got to take that chance because there are too few of us around. By "us," I mean the people who have a chance of making it, of actually slugging their way to an answer.

The one thing of value I think I can say [to you] is this:

> A commitment to oneself to do this thing. Doing whatever it takes to find an answer. Asking the best questions you can ask, and diving into the crux of them. Continuous re-application of energy in this endeavor.

I only harp on these things because they have been the best way for me.

There, I gave the best blast on the old horn I can (this time).

By the way, I *do* know that cats can hold a fear for a while. If you scare them bad enough. Just like people.

What would you do if you had the answer to all the questions you ever asked? Is it worth going for? Is it possible? The common society does not encourage a person along these lines. A person gets very little encouragement to go in that direction. But some other people have said things to the contrary. Buddha, for example.

I feel the strong urge to encourage you. I think you could get to a final point—for yourself. And forget about the work. It's a mirage. There's no work involved. None at all. Only commitment and the desire and going after it.

Everyone can do this. Every single person you see on the sidewalk. But almost no one has the combination of traits that allows them to NOT get lost in delusion or wishful thinking or worse. They're not ready maybe.

How many people do you pass on the street or in halls each day? How many of them have put themselves on the line and tried to find the meaning of their life?

Anyhow, I'm here to compare notes, and say what I think about what *you* say.

Well man, I gotta go. My wife and I are watching Sumo wrestling on Eurosport. It's one of two English channels I can get here. What a relief to hear something easy [to understand] on the ears once in a while.

Good luck. I look forward to hearing what you have to say about that other letter. Take it easy.

Sent July 2, 2001

Hi Shane,

I read your email. It was good to hear from you. Here's something I wrote to send to you for what it's worth. I'm trying to point at where I'm coming from by writing a story or a scene. It's not a direct, one-to-one thing. I'm talking about the different views possible and pointing at the difference between a view from within and a view of the thing from without.

The cave that Plato described is there. The people facing the wall of moving shadows are there too. Some, through some inner pulling, have intensely focused on and studied the interrelation between moving shadows in a search for meaning. [As a result of their intense] efforts, they have found or reached certain understandings about the pattern of shadows.

Yet they are unfulfilled, because although they understand more than they did, and every day they understand more than they did, they are always confronted by the enormity of their overall ignorance. They don't KNOW even one small thing, for sure.

The moving shadows have names. Hate, fear, a leaf on a tree, a humble man. All of the people in the cave know what these names mean. They feel the meaning of the shadows moving across the wall. They feel great meaning.

One person behind them says, what is a leaf though, really? Not what it feels like, but what *is* it?

And only the people facing that wall who have striven so hard to understand the shadows on it that they're at their wit's end will do anything but dismiss the question of the voice [speaking] behind them out of hand. Those who dismiss the question out of hand *know* what his question means. *Nothing*. It's a stupid question, and pointless. But the ones who have worked so hard that they're nearly at their end hear something other than a senseless question.

Of those who have striven so far and worked so hard and heard something in that question, only a lucky number will be inspired [or encouraged] to strive in an entirely different way. Becoming less finite. Less limited. Looking again at the shadow of a leaf, or, of anger; they ask a question they had never asked before. *What is it?* And the answer eventually finds them, those who pursue it far enough, in a condition with eyes that actually see, and the cave [faded away].

It's a hell of a thing, what I think you're going through. I mean things hitting the fan, the more you dive. Rose said that the sincere efforts of men were to be respected. I sure agree with him.

That's about it for now.

Keep in touch!
David

Sent July 6, 2001

Hi Shane,

Good luck down there in the woods. I envy you. I wish I had someplace like that.

We're all children. Petty as hell and much worse. And sometimes [just as good].

And by the way, the world, and all the crazies in it, deserve the giant "Fuck you" that you say to it and to them. Why should you accept *any* of it? Why should you rationalize sitting in an ashtray as being somehow acceptable? Hell—it stinks!

The only thing that I think is worthwhile is to figure it out. We ALL (those of us who think about things) sit and stare at the shadows, trying to figure them out. My God, we don't know any better. But maybe there's some possibility. A possibility we didn't, couldn't, know existed. I'm not talking about some grand imagining, I'm talking about knowing the score.

I sure can relate to what you hint at. What you consider the significant moment in life. Is it you getting angry, justifiably, or is it something that is happening to you, that you can say, "What's going on?"

I really wish I could have the solitude you have found possible—with that place in the woods. I used to get away for at least a week once a year. The last time I did that was four years ago. Man. I could use it now.

Judging the violence and anger, on one hand, as opposed to saying, *What's going on?* on the other.

About Rose's books. I read the *Albigen Papers* first. I found it very hard to read. I couldn't breeze through it. It was tough. I wish you could have met the guy in person. Or listened to some tapes of him talking and answering questions at lectures. I think that helps.

I have the feeling that he is pretty hard to get in tune with just through the books—at the beginning. So I wish you luck. I think the guy is valuable to touch base with. You're not alone, at least.

The more time goes by, the more value I find in his example and his works.

Somewhere in a box I think have an extra copy of that *Meditation Paper* book of Rose's. If you want it, I can send it to you. It's a little pamphlet outlining a simple and potentially effective way of getting to work.

I'm surprised the reviews are still on that Barnes and Noble site! I wrote them a few years ago, when I was living in Memphis.

Again, all the best over there with what you're doing.

Here are a few written in Stuttgart to "D":

Sent July 11, 2001

Hi D,

I'm glad you correspond with Cecy and possibly Krista. They're good folk.

Your response to Vineet on the spiritual friends locater site was good, I think. It sounds like you're addressing him directly. That's very decent of you—considering another's case.

I have a huge amount of respect for Ramana Maharshi and his advice for a method of working at the problem of the riddle of life.

I think it's simple. Very simple. If you have a desire to know or understand or something along that line, you work at it. Incessantly. Honestly. Sincerely. I sometimes think that that's all I should ever say to anybody. I'm not talking about you. I'm thinking about my own correspondences with people.

All the stuff you said to that person was fine. But I wonder what good it does for someone to hear it. For them to really get what you're saying, they'd have to have come to a point where they recognize what you say through having gone through something similar.

To see that things get worse before they get better. To see that the intellect is not the total way. That it ends short of the goal, and that some way, we must somehow become something more resourceful or OTHER than.

Stuff like that. I think it's shop talk. Among people who've done the work required.

What advice can you give to someone else?

As far as how a baby lives... Boy.

You did a good job I think of describing how we get attached to the mentality and forget that it's just a "thing." A "false" thing. I don't think it is false at all. But I sure think it is the [façade] of the movie prop town. It's not the real deal. It exists (the mind), but it isn't the solid reality.

And your advice to this person about attention is good, too.

My advice would be to encourage anyone who I sense has some desire to know. Encourage the hell out of them. Tell them, "Go for it. Do it, by God. Find out."

I've been okay lately.

I have one hell of a view on this reality, man. I mean I see a lot. I seem to understand what's going on. Not why, but what. And of course, the why is hinted at by the what. That's cryptic, but I'm trying to say I have been surprised by a subtle overview that I have noticed by accident, it seems.

We're going to France in August to find a piece of ground. In October, we're moving there to open a bed-and-breakfast-slash-something-else. The something else is a very good idea that I'll tell you about later (when I send an invitation!).

I've been reading van der Leeuw's "The Conquest of Illusion." Again. I get it now. He's got a hell of a thing to point at. But then again, he's got some other stuff in there too. I guess we all do. Not many of us can get the pure stuff across without mucking it up with our own flavor, too.

You've got a relevant comment. You said you wondered about the origin of suffering. That's a good comment. I think the weather has been at it again, maybe.

What do you think about suffering? What about the hell in this world?

I've got some ideas. And they don't center themselves around cause-and-effect me [mundane, personality-centered 'me'].

You said in your email to ask oneself what one's aim is. Thanks for the question. I sure was glad to be reminded to think about that.

The method you lay out is familiar as hell. It's the advice I give to anyone who can hear me. Inquiry. Looking at things penetratingly. What is going on? Why? What is really happening? Not what you feel is happening, but what is happening? And then, okay, what do you feel is happening? Why do you feel that? What is going on? What is your feeling, actually? Not what you feel about it, but what is it?

This method is a direct thing. Going back to the source. A hell of an efficient method. Doesn't get caught up in the shadows out there playing across the wall. Doesn't get distracted.

Most of us (hell, all of us) spend a hell of a lot of time trying to figure the shadows out. Our feelings and stuff like that---by how they feel. Not what they are, not going directly to truth but by feeling our way around inside our head, using the very program (mentality) that we can't escape. It's a wonder any of us get free at all. We never even know the way to work until we've accidentally broken free somehow. Then, coming back, we see the way to work. But it is funny as hell because it's not comprehensible by those who are still in their heads, thinking *that's* the world.

But, but... It *is* comprehensible and useful to us. Us. Anyone who's got a better view.

And you said to that one person on the contact board that you were 49 and had been at this for 30 years. My questions to you, and they're sincere ones, are:

Have you gotten it right in this time?

and

What do you think this place is, really?

Okay, I've got to go.

It was good hearing from you again. I'll share what I think about these two questions after I hear from you!

So long,
David

Sent July 22, 2001

Hi D,

I'll respect your request for secrecy. Don't know why it's important, but I don't dismiss it. I'm sure you have reasons.

As far as my being dead wrong. I don't think so. The guy who can skate well always understands the beginner skater better than the beginner skater understands the pro. The higher advanced can see the lower but the lower can't understand (see) the other because they haven't the experience base yet.

My conundrum is, or was, something else. Where I found myself a few years ago wasn't a place. It was a condition. An experience. It was being the sun. Not walking on the sun. Being the sun. That's how I described it to M.C. after it happened. So it's funny you say it that way. It was the only way I could describe it at the time. After David was fried, [burned away and annihilated]; as I turned and faced [oblivion], whatever was left after that—I was *that*.

All this stuff (gesturing at everything around me) did not exist. I had a decidedly different appreciation of reality after I "came back." I was numb to this place. But events in my life seemed to pull me back in, too. Like an avalanche. I was a dumbstruck guy with all this stuff happening around me. My wife immediately divorcing me, my grandmother dying, my mother being hospitalized and operated on, Rose needing my help, and other things. I was intimately present in all these situations.

Where the back of my head had been was now nothing. I don't know, I'm just trying to describe things. The former guy having been removed. I was full, but there wasn't anything left, just this *"Ohmmm"* thing without words or description.

That *Ohmmm* never went. It's me, now. I have the personality and the body. My body and personality is susceptible to things. Like a dog bothered by fleas and ticks. Ticks and fleas find the body acceptable, seemingly regardless of the dog's mentality.

My understanding was transcendental. I didn't understand here. I was full of THERE. Is it possible to KNOW or better put, to BE, but not to "understand?" Yes.

Mentally, I wasn't clueless, but a serious understanding (knowing what this life is for and about) wasn't in the cards for me at the onset. It has come over time. And I don't know why, except it's just the way things have worked out for me so far.

Why is spiritual or any sort of evolution NECESSARY? That it exists is apparent. Why is it necessary? From THERE, there is nothing. Absolutely nothing (and it's everything—it's the sun). In my view, there is no RELEVANCE between THERE and what happens, spiritual evolution-wise or whatever-wise, here. No connection. No relation.

In this place we find ourselves, with the public transportation and mail and television, I am convinced that it is possible to get it right. To realize what this place is about and to get it right.

[*Opposed to living confused, uncertain, unfulfilled, unhappy and fearful, fearful, fearful; for me, going through what I went through has had the side effect of allowing me to finally live my life—not looking to some future hoped-for condition but content with now.*]

You say it isn't relevant whether I know you've gotten it right or not. Relevant? Maybe you feel that way about yourself, but it sure is relevant to me. And I appreciate your answer. Now I know about you, whether it's relevant or not!

Life is a school. Yes. Goddamned right. Absolutely damned right. 100 percent right. What a school. If people only got a small glimpse of what this place really is, they'd quit whatever they were doing. I mean, it's SUCH a sight, to see the kindergarten. To see the lessons being fought and ignored and struggled against---and occasionally "gotten."

But WHY? Why the set-up? The Christian story is not a bad stab, I think, at trying to describe the purpose of it all. The other religions too. They all take a good stab at it. And I used to dismiss them pretty much. Until about a month or two ago.

But why the set-up? I'm asking this question from my memory of THERE. From an appreciation of the seeming complete irrelevance of this place to THERE. I didn't start to ask these questions until I saw things about this place differently. I started to get a clue about this place, imagine that!

Every time we see something, I think we automatically ask questions. Maybe my latent curiosity is just poking around for answers.

What has happened to me is that I have continued to suffer. And push for meaning. The meaning of what is going on. I have become a person whose whole being, such as it is, was devoted to getting a clue.

I find myself in a position occasionally to help somebody. It's a surprise most of the time. Somebody is put in front of me and I say things that I [feel] are relevant to them. I'm sure you know about this. Well, I just answer questions or respond honestly. Like a good skater seeing a beginner and saying a thing or two at the right time. Answering questions honestly, like you said.

I find myself growing in understanding. Actually GETTING it. What it's all about. I mean this damned place. Seeing the watch works [seeing the interior working mechanism of a watch]. Seeing the set-up. Reverse-engineering the thing and understanding.

If I had come across this view of reality WITHOUT the experience of THERE....well, maybe I would have said something like, "We have to spiritually evolve until we're pure enough to get to heaven," or something like that. But THERE is outer space, and here is a coral reef with all the little bugs and microbes and stuff. And these bugs and microbes have "spiritual evolution." Understanding what's going on in the ocean and the reef and the bugs and comprehending the relation between these things is fine, but outer space is OUTER SPACE.

I think a person can grasp what the whole thing (the life we see) is about. AND the *why*, eventually. I think that's probably possible too. I might have to die for good to get there, but I think it's possible.

I was honestly surprised by my recent view. I feel I understand the genesis of the various stories of the major religions. I [experience] a view that recognizes the religious stories as a person's attempt to explain the purpose of something they see. Another person with this view. Maybe a slightly lower view.

I think a person can "get it right." You can do it wrong, or okay, or you can become competent.

I can get the fry station at McDonalds right or wrong. I think it's possible.

We are in a school. And we are also being used. Milked. For our energy. I see that too. And I used to hear Rose talk about that and hear of Gurdjieff saying that and I used to dismiss it. I didn't relate to it at the time.

By the way, I think you're wrong about that song line. "Might as well be walking on the sun" is how I remember it. I'll do an Internet search for the lyrics and get back to you.

As far as my relationship to the place I visited---I did not visit any place. The "I" was like a rocket that was used up during a journey and what I became was something. I *was* this experience. I *was* this place, I wasn't a "person" visiting it.

My relationship to THERE is that I had become THERE. There is no relationship. There's just whatever is left over when the coward (the person formerly known to himself as David) is gone. A person has no relationship to death, they're just dead.

But I still exist. The pattern called me. Even though it's not really real. It's funny. And it sounds irrational.

Exactly what part of me was burned out? Burn a piece of toilet paper completely and ask the same question.

Well, that's about it.

I am curious about you saying that you are homeless. I mean, being here but not having a rooted place or something like that. What else could you say?

[Until a certain point,] I had pretty much resigned myself to living meaninglessness. To just knowing that it doesn't matter, and yet doing something other than just being a bum—to live a life of meaning despite meaninglessness.

I'd seen the "school" working on people, but I had no overall comprehension and was just kind of disgusted at this place in general. Or indifferent. But, for some reason, I never gave up. I don't know why. Probably my habit. I'd be immensely disgusted periodically, but my default seemed to be one of just putting in the effort. I mean the "not wasted time." I kept turning the thing over. And, somewhere along the line, this view slipped in from the side. Seemingly unrelated to my mentations or efforts, but coincidental as well. Co-incidental.

My struggles seem to have no direct correlation to what I realize. By direct correlation, I mean nothing I can FEEL. No detectable traces at all. But to Sherlock Holmes, looking at the facts from a distance, there is an exact correlation between my actions and the events around me. They are extraordinarily related.

I've learned sometimes to look without my eyes (feelings). And I see apparent things that have no feeling-connection. So much for that.

This view was like something that moved over me. Who put it on me? And why? It happened because of what I had been doing and what I am. Seemingly.

I had been working at the problem. And I had become effort in that direction.

Maybe some people get a "view complete" from the beginning. It's a very big jump from complete ignorance to complete understanding. I made that leap and it was a long time between jumping and landing.

Maybe other people are more gradual, like stepping-stones across the gulf between ignorance and understanding. Maybe they come about it differently. I'm sure it's possible. Yet I feel that I know the human mentality, in general. I don't think people are capable of grasping it without having done the pre-work. I just don't see how the mentality can get it like, "poof," with no work.

I say the mentality. The brain or whatever you want to call our intellect. The mentality or brain or intellect of David was included in that frying experience of mine a few years ago. But it sprung back like a sapling growing from a tree stump. It grew back with the same maturity it had before it was cut down. There's no transcending the mentality. I think that when you come back to it, you come back to it. Paradoxically, you're not it. Still, I'm talking about the mentality. The thinking self. It's got to do the work [*yearn for something more than what is available on the market; hunt for it; read books; seek authorities on existence and reality; meditate, pray, hope, strain—wash, rinse, repeat*] before these revelations seem to be RELEVANT or even recognizable. It seems these revelations or views don't come until their time.

So much for that. I've got to go. What is the suffering for? I know what it seems to cause me to do, but what is it for? Why does it exist at all? I wonder what you think.

Until next time,
David

Dear Reader,

I enjoy going to art galleries, but after a short time I'm numb. A friend told me he had a similar reaction to speed-reading the correspondence you're encountering. I was easy for me; I wrote them one at a time.

Three years after a fundamental change—when solid stillness replaced my formerly lacking center of operations—a tectonic shift took place. This was when I'd say I <u>stopped</u> my philosophic and metaphysical efforts completely. I set down my spiritual hammer. Since '96 there had been a gap of relevance between the world around me and the lasting aftereffect of experiencing something beyond myself. I was in the world, but not of it. The singular condition that I carry around inside me is not dilutable in water (this world).. And yet, a global comprehension concerning this observable world moved in like a weather front, and remained—a blanketing fog of comprehension. I was in Stuttgart, Germany, Fall 1999. I'd ridden my bike across a foot bridge and stopped at a bench to write in my daily journal. That was my last journal entry. Earlier in the morning, a weather front of comprehension had moved in.

Throughout my life, I've embodied a prolonged strain toward comprehension… as my mind recognizes that term. I'm talking about knowing what's going on and why. What I would call understanding. It was as though I was winding one big coil spring; maybe releasing the spring handle (putting down that hammer) brought about this global weather change. Maybe the relaxing and comprehension were simultaneous. I feel it was like a ripening pear dropping to the ground. A friend commented after reading some of the previous correspondence that he didn't understand how someone who had a personally complete viewpoint could ever be "too concerned about the details of the relative world." Yeah.

All I care about is the view someone has. I know a person can only speak from where they're standing. If I ask you for your opinion on suffering, your answer has to point out from wherever you are. And if you want to zero in on someone's wisdom, just ask them questions about "mundane" things like love, hope, progress, desire, goals, meaning, suffering, purpose, death, life and reasons for existing. Each reply gives you a back azimuth on where they're looking out from. If you just hang around them, chit-chatting, you face their personality—a variation on a theme. We're all an ego looking out for number one. If you want to plumb anyone's depths, I recommend either shared silence or pointed questions. Both would be good. The chief observable feature of a changed "wise" person is their apparent perspective, expressed in words or manner, on the mundane stuff we're all immersed in. Like invisible black holes that are only "seen" by their effect on the observable swirling matter around them; a person's viewpoint—where they stand and what they see —is observed by their comments on… everything. Ask!

Sent July 23, 2001

Hi D,

I've got understanding, intellectually (like a problem), and then, knowing without question.

Knowing without question is what I got, or what I am, as a seeming result of that night of hell and maybe even the days before contributed to it too, I don't know. Maybe my whole life before contributed to it. Probably.

The urge to understand this problem of life intellectually is the mentality, the working head. I told another guy that I felt like I was a turkey in a smokehouse. "I" being the guy who keeps trying to figure out the problem. Slowly the smoke is getting through the guy, his every fiber, and he *becomes* the answer (fully smoked). Afterwards, he can use his brain or intellect to describe what he *Knows*.

I DO feel like I got "only" a taste. I didn't stay in that condition long. But then again, I never left it or lost it—or it never lost me. However it goes. It's me. But David (mentality), who is finite as hell and limited as hell, is seemingly just becoming thoroughly cured---[with time] feeling more and more THERE. I'm just saying what's happening. I don't have much of a concrete explanation. I feel I know what's going on, but putting it into language would take more time than I've spent here.

The feeling never left. In my chest is a place. Still. Motionless. Present.

Sometimes I'm more THERE. Most of the time now, actually. I don't know why, except what I speculated on in that last email. Maybe my continuing efforts [after the fact] and time combined with God knows what. When I get lured into being a good animal, associating with people, snarling and groveling in the mud, I get preoccupied, even forced by the matrix of everyone's expectations to playing the part they've assigned to me. It's a crazy little world.

"I" am NOT in control. Not perfect. Not God.

You said:

"You seem to be saying that this permanent "gift" came and you are gradually growing into an understanding of what this life is all about????"

Yes. Absolutely.

This "growing understanding" came as a surprise. I was just struggling to figure out what is going on, why I was suffering and what was happening—like always. Sometimes, very rarely, very rarely, I would become 'smarter than the problem,' as I say it. I let go (somehow) of something that was keeping me tied tightly to ignorance and the resultant non-stop suffering—me.

Then sometimes, an understanding comes over me. A realization. It fits the puzzle pieces and it's not an explanation as much as a complete [understanding] of the whole thing. [I did not have this before my re-boot of '96—maybe my brain wasn't mature enough.] Later, I peck out the words to describe my understanding.

I still don't know what suffering is, in itself. What it is for. I see what you're saying. I've noticed it myself. I can say things like, 'Without suffering we wouldn't move or improve or attempt anything.' I can say the things you have said in relation to suffering, too. But, *why* the set-up? Why? Why not just THERE? There seems to be no point to this mud, this school, in relation to THERE. [Yet,] only in relation to THERE does this [whole scene] seem pointless.

Taken by itself, this progression of spiritual growth, or any maturing, seems quite self-apparent and self-explanatory. But not in relation to THERE. <u>Nothing</u> relates to there.

All the things you say about suffering I can relate to. You're explaining (very aptly) what the effects of suffering are and [suffering's] role in things. But not what it is.

Maybe it doesn't matter. I think it does. The suffering is a shadow. And I want to know what it is. One answer might be, "It is a shadow on a wall." A "false" answer (an answer that defines something from within itself) would be, "It has this and this effect or it causes this and this to happen."

I'm looking for the source reason.

"I in no way deny your experience.....but is it a memory?........the memory of your last meal cannot nourish you......... "

You bet it is a memory.

The only thing is, I've been changed. I'm not the same creature. I see it partly like the person who went through rough spots in a war. Yes, it is a memory they have of that time. But they are not the same as before being tortured or nearly-killed or whatever.

And then, on top of that, I have this damned nuclear core inside of me. The thing that was uncovered or switched on or whatever, seemingly resulting from having gone through mortality.

I'll never get myself to go back to being eyes-closed-only. That's only an image. The feeling in here is not one of eyes open or closed. It is deep stillness. Whatever good those words are.

"You question if there is such a thing as spiritual growth, evolution......My question is: how do you get back to where you were?"

I question spiritual growth and evolution. But I do *not* question if there is such a thing. Spiritual growth or evolution is apparent. In my case, and in everyone I see. I question it directly. In relation to THERE, such growth or evolution seems to *have* no relation, and therefore, in my view, ultimately has no purpose. That's what I meant before by the outer space and the coral reef comparison [*re: the previous July 22, 2001 email*].

How do I get back to where I was? I don't think, in a way, that I left [THERE]. I've been changed. I think I would say that I am getting back there, if I have to say anything about getting back. Seemingly becoming more and more "there." Becoming more smoked in IS-ness. What is a cured piece of meat? [It's still meat, but it's the smoke, too].

I feel it's possible to become *There* while still living here. That's where my question to you about getting it right came from. It sounds impossible, maybe. What can I say. I'm not saying what I would like to believe or what I think could be. I'm saying what I've been led to see. 'Getting it right,' for me, means this time here not being in any way incorrectly used.

Incorrect and correct. Used and unused. I know. Still, I sense the possibility for "getting it right" as opposed to not getting it right. I know it's a paradox.

"You seem to be saying that it's not something you are concerned about.
That's who I really am ....so why worry?......I will be there some day again....."

I would say that I have a certain-ness within, at my center. I don't think it's smart to say, "Why worry?" I don't say it. I AM a direction towards truth, though. I've dedicated myself to that. It's the only honest thing I can do. I think it's my destiny; it seems to be what I was born for. Instead of trying to conform to what everybody pretends is important, I conform or dedicate myself to my personal job: Climbing Mount Everest.

So, "Why worry?" and "I will be there someday again," isn't where I'm coming from. A person who says these things is either a fool because they're speaking about something they have no idea, or they're basically God, and have no doubts at all because they ARE beyond doubt. [I think I'm both of these people—no; I know I am. Yes, a fool *and* God]

Well, with that, I've got to go.

What do you think this place really is? Maybe you already answered me.

Take care,
David

Sent July 28, 2001

Hi D,

By "this place," I meant here, where we find ourselves, day-in and day-out. This apparent reality.

Your idea about God loaning us a life to see what we can do with it is nice-sounding. I can't prove it. So I have to leave it alone.

You already sent [me] the Empty boat thing. I appreciate you sending it again. The first time I read it, I got the point. I saw a way of living that spared the 'live-er' from suffering. Making him untouchable in a way.

This time I read it and got a more meaningful or more relevant [to me] impression.

I understand it now, better. It has a deeper meaning for me. Thank you.

This is the way we are used and milked of our energy. This yelling at the boat that hits ours (with another person in it). Right. And somehow to become a person who is other than a yeller.

> If a man is crossing a river
> And an empty boat collides with his own skiff,
> Even though he be a bad-tempered man
> He will not become very angry.
> But if he sees a man in the boat,
> He will shout at him to steer clear.
>
> —from *The Empty Boat*, by Chuang Tzu

The man with the empty boat.

And so I see the message here. Really do.

But what is this world, this place, that <u>requires</u> a person to find a trick in order to exist harmoniously within themselves? [Trying to make myself react as though all the things I'm taking personally—which happen to me and which others are connected to (through my imagination or in actuality)—are instead "empty boats."]

Why the set-up of hellacious torture for the person who is [merely] a good animal or good whatever and yells? [Why is this yelling person "wrong?" Why is this yelling person, *at all*? Why do they/we/I exist?]

I do see the wisdom in "The Empty Boat." It's a beautiful and profound parable.

Yes, the person who achieves the equanimity (Tao) pointed to in this little story has gotten the point. That their existence is something other than yelling at people in boats that hit us. Is this "point" really just a way of getting along with the least amount of friction with the outer world, whose very nature is one of stickiness, or friction? Wars, arguments, drama, love: it's all about friction.

I recognize a transcending, superior "way" when I see it. Some of the time.

How did you come by your idea of God's lending us ourselves?

A feeling? A vision? Something else?

Gotta go,
David

That ends this one-sided selection of correspondence with "D." I hope he found what he was looking for. I hope he became the man he hoped to be. I hope the very best and highest for him. As far as I know, I haven't spoken to him in the ten years since. I'd like to meet him face-to-face someday. Maybe I have already.

To a friend on the path. Sent July 28, 2001

Hi Shawn,

You have to look at this place like it was a foreign world. Like a society of intelligent dolphins, maybe. Because if you look at what I'm going to say through the template of ourselves, what I'm saying won't be profound. Not that it ever is.

Looking down on this foreign planet peopled by intelligent dolphins, you see:

[Dolphins] explaining their existence and the mechanism of their cosmos in terms of dolphin morality, a thing which they *feel* about their environment and themselves. Only feel. Never knowing really what is. Never seeing it clearly.

Sin and virtue, reward and punishment, karma and reincarnation, evolving souls and eternal damnation or salvation resulting from one's actions. Most of the dolphins understand (project) just what they're able to on these words. No more. The originators of these words meant something different, in every case, from what the general dolphin public has come to agree upon, but none of them can ever know that without going to the same place the originators went. It's not a place the "majority" gets to. For whatever reason.

Quite simply, I have a view. And I RECOGNIZE the attempts of others at EXPLAINING this view, or one similar to it. How can one person's experience of their own death be similar to another dolphin's experience of their death? They are all the same, but they are all individual, too.

[The same as] if you read Pulyan or Rose or Ramana Maharshi, or Bob Fergeson. And you see them explaining something. And you RECOGNIZE. [It's not a question of guessing; you recognize and it's not in your thinking self; it's deeper than that, deeper than you.] You might not agree with their explanation. You might think they put too much of themselves in it, or you might agree one hundred percent, but you *recognize* what they're trying to do. What they're trying to put the words to.

So my view of the world has answered a lot of my earlier questions—as far as having [once] been utterly clueless about what was happening to me and around me.

I simply recognize (now) these stories that humans have told themselves and repeated to themselves as a kind of nightlight mantra, [as they float there] in their soap bubble of existence with the obliviating vacuum of space all around. Before, I dismissed [parables, myths, allegories and fables] out of hand because I had no proof and they sounded like fairy tales. I do NOT believe them now. But I sure think I see the genesis of them. I feel a kindred-ness to whoever wrote them, originally.

Still, I do NOT see the connection between this over-View of the mechanism of this reality and the experience of something absolute.

The two are completely unrelated, it seems. Unrelated. As interesting as this self-apparent functioning is, it is nothing when THERE. There is no thing there. THERE is not a place of things, or of observable patterns or of karma or evolving souls. The two are not mixable.

That's my opinion. So far. Although I see the way things evolve here, [in this reality], I don't see the point, really, from the standpoint of an awareness of THERE. Because THERE is THERE. And here... is a gradual thing, that seems to have no end to the possible "evolution" of souls or of understandings these dolphins can have.

The pattern of the world is NOT inexpressible. The only thing that *is* inexpressible is THERE. And THERE is not inexpressible (you can express it or describe it in a thousand million ways—or try to express it in that many ways); it would just take all the words there have been and all the words there will ever be. And none of them [would do it]. Not one. And you'd still not get it right. "Right" being an accurate representation of THERE. No, the pattern of the world is expressible. All of the religions have expressed it. The pattern of the world and THERE are *not the same thing*. Even though I talk about them [here] in the same paragraph!

I think the stories that the religions have preserved were stories told by people who had the *over-View* of this place like I'm talking about. The stories were preserved because they simply rang closest to the truth in everyone's ears. The dolphins didn't know why they believed them; they just did.

There *is* growth of the inner, essential spirit of all humans. EVERYONE's life is specifically designed ONLY to torture them to "grow" or evolve or improve. And there is a mass energy milking going on [an adopted and adapted concept of Rose's; he said there is a situation where it seems apparent we're being used for our energy; it's how this "barnyard" is organized]. A not-so-benevolent force in the seeming background is interested in getting people to growl and snarl and murder and mayhem [something I have felt myself, although I don't know what I mean by 'force' except that I see it in all the road rage, mass movements, politics, etcetera].

These could both be forces within our cells! Forces of nature. And seeing these forces, can't you understand how the dolphins came up with God and Devil and hell and evolving souls and reincarnation?

An old person has been shaped by this process called life into a *wisened* person. People get the problems they're supposed to get, and so on.

This place is *not* for nothing. There is a most apparent purpose, and this purpose is manifest in its design. Like noticing a TV screen. You *know* someone made that thing for [some purpose]. I don't know what that purpose is. But the fact that one must exist is clear to me.

Maybe this is completely unremarkable-sounding.

It doesn't matter; except I have to say that it is remarkable to *me* because I have seen or realized it for myself. Not "thought about it." Not "solved the problem" and come up with it. I have just seen it. A view moved in, seemingly in spite of my futile efforts at figuring out what was happening to me as I lived. I mean that my efforts and this view that moved in seem to be completely unconnected. That is: in a feeling-way, I detect no traces.

Yet, looking at the facts alone, independent of opinion or feeling, I can't help but admit that my efforts at understanding and the understanding that has come are at least on the same general subject.

Your comments were very much appreciated. Thank you seriously. I appreciate the time.

Forrest Gump and his feather, indeed.

[*I think Shawn referred to the 'bookend' sequences during the opening and closing credits of the 1994 Tom Hanks film, where the camera follows a feather being blown by the wind across a varied landscape of action and scenery*].

As far as energy-siphoning, just look at the people who're obsessed, or upset or raving about the injustices of this or that. Look at rabid environmentalists, abortion rights and pro-life demonstrators. Look at the racial stuff between equally [intense] blacks and whites in the States. Look at fights in traffic and in lines at banks. Look at the Israelis and Palestinians, killing each other with blood lust in their hearts. Look at Ireland. Look at people in the group like F., for example, who has problems with other people (including his kids) that span years, unresolved, preserved. Or W.M. and E.H., maintaining a negatively-charged misunderstanding for 10 years. This stuff, if viewed from outer space, or from a balloon, floating over the intelligent dolphins, would be seen as SOMETHING, regardless of what the causes (or cause) may be. A phenomenon exists.

Author's note:

A friend reading this said he didn't see why this stuff should be interesting to a seeker. It isn't; it wasn't what I wanted, that's for sure. I wanted God, Ultimate Answer, Absolute Enlightenment. What I got instead was me. My own reactions, my faults, my biases. There. Now what? Maybe a lot of people stop here. But after some initial pouting, for some reason I hitched up my pants, took a deep breath and said, "Okay. What's going on? Why do I react in this way? Why does that person react to me in that way?"

For me, it was my first step in becoming familiar with the geography, as I call it, of myself. This stuff may not matter to a seeker; it may be the exact opposite of what they want to spend time on, but I think he or she better be aware of what's going on inside and why. What you see influencing others is a shade of the same shadow hanging over and inside you. I used to think, "Those idiots, those unquestioning believers," before realizing it's more accurate to say, "Those other idiots, those other believers." I'm them, only different. I do what I condemn others for doing. A seeker of understanding and truth should be interested in understanding themselves, their own motives, capacities, tendencies, strengths and weaknesses. Unfortunately, for almost all of us, we're not going to "get around" or bypass ourselves in this quest for something ultimate. I think we become familiar with our own geography first, and (only) then are able to move on to more essential, core issues. We can't leave first grade without learning how to read. Show me someone who bypassed all of the work and I'll be pleasantly surprised and happy for them. Anything is possible—and self-evidentially understandable from within its own context.

Now, back to the letter.

You said you see some truth to karma because you see it happening.

That's it. That's what I'm talking about. SEEING. Not thinking or coming up with some theory. I am talking about a person seeing clearly. And why? I don't know.

I have no idea what allows or causes a person to see. My only guess, about myself, is that this "seeing" or this view is seemingly co-incidental with my continued [mental] efforts and straining to figure out what's going on with me and around me.

About hell... Don't you think we are already there? I mean it. I don't know if you have ever suffered. I would think that you must have at some point. A person who really is in the depths of suffering might actually try to understand it, figure it out. [They might] come to the conclusion that they ARE in a hell largely of their own making. Tempted by the devil into doing all the things they did to get them to the extreme position they find themselves in.

Why is there guilt? Sometimes I think you're not imaginative enough. Sometimes I think your mind can't bend around things—that it's not flexible.

But I also think you really have a point about referring back to biology. These intelligent dolphins explain a lot to themselves, but know themselves not. Not even *why* they want to try to explain things in the first place. I think you have a real point, there.

What is more useful, a mind that can dream in ten thousand colors, or a mind that can only see what is there?

The rest of the tribe is selfish, by the way. Probably more so than the guy who has resided at the top of the pile for a while. Every member is biologically programmed to struggle forward. When a person is above the others, their natural, instinctive urge is to drag that person down and stand on the corpse's head to elevate themselves. It's an unthinking, automatic thing. We are vicious rats.

Did you come from rest to this place? I sure know what you mean by rest. Did you come from there? Or did you just realize what death would be?

Thank you once again for the offer of help with the web publicity thing. I'll certainly be in touch soon on that.

Why don't I, upon seeing what I'm seeing, call it God? I don't know. I just can't tell something I'm not certain of, just because it sounds close.

Okay, with that, I've got to go.

So long,
David

A year earlier, to the "old friend, once"...

Sent: Aug. 18, 2000
Subject: doubts

Hi M.,

Thanks for answering.

My best answer to your letter is to answer a couple of points and then point to something I wrote for inclusion in the next TAT meeting for discussion (though I doubt it'll be brought up).

First, I'm glad to hear back from you. Second, I kind of think sometimes that the best answer is the one that is given.

Nothing rings a bell anymore. That's a great way I could describe my feelings about other philosophers, etc. Their ideas are something, but I'm kind of below or beyond them. They are completely useless to me from the point of view of a guy who realizes that nothing, not one thing, in this planet, or world, or reality, will help me get one inch closer to what I desire or strain for.

Of course I am aware of the paradox. Always, and more so, the more I go. But I really mean what I say. <u>This</u> is a guy with his hair on fire, perhaps, who doesn't have the luxury to armchair his way through or around things anymore.

I was, as you said, preoccupied with my doubts, questions, etc., about an experience or "the experience." I've since resolved them. I've come to the conclusion that I don't know. That I haven't reached the final—if there is one—answer. I'm preoccupied with scrambling my way across this steep rock, calling out to others, asking and seeking for co-strugglers. *Where are you? Do you know where I am? [Do you recognize what I see?] Where are we? What do you see from where <u>you</u> are?* And so on.

It isn't from direct evidence that I say this, only from an intuition and by observing my current actions. I still strain, and I don't know why.

The day-to-day struggle comment was my response to something C. G. wrote to me, not you. He said he has trouble [trying to not become] too identified with things. I say what I said to him. An anti-effort is never, never effective. The only thing that frees one from hell or allows one to remain on a center is the simple observing of something for understanding. Not for some [predetermined] agenda, but for understanding. Looking at a thing and seeing what is there. As you say. And the three umpires all have a valid perspective. But I'm just going for the most truthful thing I can get a hold of.

And as far as I know, I can affect someone with my actions, and they can feel the effect of my actions.

Chakras are valid ways of describing things, I am willing to admit. But I'm too lazy, and too focused to divert my attention to another action (although I'll listen and take note of this).

My comment about rollerblading was a fishing hook. I believe, with all of my being, that rollerblading means absolutely nothing, in the long run. I enjoy it, I have fun, I feel fulfilled by it. I wonder what you would say to the feeling of fulfillment, joy, contentment---in the big picture. I see these things as a thing apart, and yet feel them.

Again, I mean what I say. I am aware of the always-present paradox. It is [my] constant companion.

You're right, I think, about the way to catch the drift of things. And also, my intuition says, right about the answers coming, of themselves.

You talk a lot [about] preconceived ideas. I think, for the first time, I can say I have let drop all the ones I have been carrying for a while, [this includes all of mine and all those I've taken from others] (Rose's, etc.). All that I am left with is a trying-for-the-least-stupid-thing. Because this is the least stupid thing to do. When *that* concept is taken away too, so be it, but until then, I'll stick to it because it makes the most sense. <u>Doubt all</u>. Including my [own] divinity and smartness.

I think that a majority of my mental time is spent spin-doctoring. And I carry this further and assume that I am not so different from others on this pile of dirt.

What about chucking all that overboard as useless? What happens when I accept nothing but the truth? When I accept NOTHING that smells, remotely?

In ten years, I'll be much smarter about this old life and probably about a lot of other things. What if I die? *Which I certainly will*. What about the meaning of things, then, when the great door shuts? I wonder what preconceptions I'll have when the batteries are removed from my eyes.

The problem with rollerblading is this: I get better when I let some time go by between skating for dreams and subconscious currents to mature and assimilate the most recent attempts [*at new tricks, new moves—it's almost exactly like a stew; the longer it simmers, the better and more... complete... it (my skill as a skater) is*]. Then, when I go again, [weeks or months] later, it is both new and familiar. Then I soar higher than before, not expecting or believing--only doing. Like being intently half-aware. The problem is my body is aging and I know, simply know, that I'll never be half as good as I can be, now, because of my body's fading. But I also know I'll become better than I ever thought I could be. And this is all just a thing. [It doesn't matter at all.]

This whole scene is vague as vague can be. And more like a dream. Less like a dream. More like a bad imitation of a dream.

I'm glad you got the pictures.

Andrée says "Hi." She's really pregnant now. We're expecting our baby boy. Boy oh boy.

Really glad to hear from you. Don't get too far off the path, my friend. The longer your skates are off, the "worse" you get.

Chapter 7 —Job-ed

This might seem unimportant, but it's my life and what I've done. Everyone's got this part of their book. If you're in my family, keep on reading; this might fill in a few blanks. If you're a friend, feel free to scan through this section. If you're a stranger, well, you might just look for the next page with a picture.

A friend, Shawn of Alabama, "test screening" this book, wrote, "You downplay it, but the fact that you had so many jobs seems to be an important factor in your psychology." Sure. Life has been an adventure. My footprints reflect me and my way.

My first paying job was for Dad and Mom at home. I sold vegetables on a stand in front of our house in Howell. And then allowance for a week at dishes, a week at house cleaning & laundry and a week at dog kennel cleaning/egg collecting/animal feeding. Each of us three kids took a week at each chore before rotating. I showed dogs, and at dog shows I got paid to be the "on call" pooper scooper to run with sawdust and implements when a dog would leave a pile or a puddle in the show ring. My first real outside-the-family job was doing hay for Joe Eisner across the road from us. He had a dairy farm and put up hay in their large red barn. I have allergies to pollen—hay fever, it's called—and working with hay in the mow, up top, stacking bales, dust so thick it was like being in a cloudy fish tank someone stirred up… was something else. Blowing my nose, swollen eyes, and sneezing. Pretty good money, though. Four dollars an hour.

My next job was at McDonald's as a cook in Fowlerville. I worked from age 15 until 18. I got parental permission to work nights during school. They called it "work study." I got some partial credits for it. I worked as a cook, in the drive-thru, at the counter, at the fry station, etc.

My next "job" was the Army. I was trained as a field artillery surveyor at Ft. Sill, Oklahoma, and then lived in Germany, at Fliegerhorst Kaserne, where my job was putting in firing points for tactical-range nuclear artillery.

Polaroid of me before work in my McDonald's uniform with my first car at our home in Fowlerville, circa 1983.

When I got out of the Army, I processed out of the active Army in Fort Dix, New Jersey. After a few weeks' vacation visiting family and friends, I moved to Lake City, Florida and found *Donald F. Lee & Associates*, a land surveying and engineering company, and worked two years as an instrument man until I was laid off.

From 1987 on, immediately after leaving the active Army, I joined the Florida Army National Guard and was a member of a demolitions combat engineer platoon in the 153rd Engineer Company in Lake City.

Born to Wonder 233

I got a job at McDonald's of Lake City as a maintenance man, working opening and closing shifts when the survey job ended. Three openings and two closings during the week. I started going to Lake City Community College near the end, and cut back my hours. Eventually, I took classes at LCCC full-time and quit McDonald's, immigrating to *Rally's Hamburgers*, managed by a former McDonald's manager, Joe, who I got along with pretty well.

In December 1991 I graduated from LCCC and quit Rally's because I was moving to Pittsburgh to attend the University of Pittsburgh and follow my girlfriend, Kathy Lestock, who moved up in September to attend Carnegie-Mellon University.

I got a job at the *University of Pittsburgh Book Center* textbook department in the basement. Not long after, I found a better job at the Learning Research and Development Center (LRDC), where I worked for the remainder of my time at Pitt.

I wrote for *The Pitt News*, the daily main campus newspaper at the university in Oakland. This was 1992. I got paid by the inch to write for the paper. A couple dozen articles.

I was an intern for *Pittsburgh Magazine*, in the same building as WQED, where *Mr. Rodger's Neighborhood* was filmed and broadcast; I visited the set. I published four "Day Tripper" shorts for the magazine and helped fact check and assemble the *1993 Pittsburgh City Guide*.

In the spring of 1993, I became president of *The Self Knowledge Symposium*, a student group at the University of Pittsburgh formed by members of the TAT Foundation. I'd been a member of that group for a year while attending SKS meetings. The former president went to medical school and the real core of the group, TAT members B.G and N.G., brothers living in the Wheeling area, quit driving up each week for meetings.

I organized the first meeting of the spring by default. During the course of my turn at the wheel, I presented topics and led discussions on religion, philosophy, psychology, science and politics. I felt like an explorer—we were—on the most exciting adventure possible: a quest for ultimate answers. I operated this funded student organization, planned special events and introduced guest speakers. I quit the group upon graduating and stayed away because I wanted them to have the feeling that I'd had, of planning and deciding things on their own. I went back after a year, occasionally, and eventually got involved once again—in a supplemental supportive way though.

In December 1994 I graduated from Pitt. Just before graduating, I quit LRDC and got myself hired at *Gateway Press*, out of Monroeville, a part of Pittsburgh. I was beat reporter for *The Oakmont and Verona Advance Leader*, a weekly newspaper.

> *Nov. '94 to Jan. '95. Newspaper Beat Reporter, The Oakmont and Verona Advance Leader, for Gateway Press, Monroeville, PA. Wrote and published 20 feature, profile and news articles. Planned the weekly paper's layout and investigated stories in the twin boroughs of Oakmont and Verona near Pittsburgh. Attended city council meetings and interviewed public officials, police officers, principals, librarians, postal workers and children.*

That's from one of my resumes. I bailed on this job shortly after starting. I would come back to this particular profession, beat reporter, two more times—both unsuccessfully.

Jan. '95 to April '95. Proofreader and Editor for Westinghouse ITTC, through JRL Enterprises, Pittsburgh. Proofread and copyedited three long-term documentation projects on schedule and worked closely with computer programmers, engineers and editors.

I worked through a temp agency as a proofreader and editor at a blue collar office past Monroeville. I worked on programming documentation for nuclear power plant simulators. It was a temporary position which could have gone on longer but I wanted to get my hands dirty for a change. I was tired of office cubicles and dressing nicely.

April '95 to Jan. '96. Framing Carpenter, Hawthorne's Home Improvements, Gibsonia, PA. Completed construction of eight custom-designed residential homes.

I worked as a framing carpenter for Hawthorne's Home Improvement, a three-man framing crew slapping together houses for Maronda Homes, Ryan Homes, a couple of other builders I don't remember and an educational stick-framing custom home we undertook for another builder. I eventually quit because I was getting pulled in, like all of my jobs, and didn't want to keep getting more and more involved in that carpentry business with my boss; he was pushing for me to learn more and run a second crew.

Jan. '96 to May '96. Warehouse Manager for Fisher Scientific, Industrial Employees, Inc., 429 Forbes Ave., Suite 1102, Allegheny Bldg., Pittsburgh, PA. Shipped several thousand packages using an in-house UPS computer system. Completely reorganized a literature warehouse. Performed accurate daily inventories and handled material with a forklift.

I worked for Fisher Scientific in a literature warehouse piled high with glossy brochures and samples for all of the medical supply equipment that Fisher made. I read Patanjali's Aphorisms on the river rock-covered roof of that building during lunch.

June '96 to Dec. '96. Residential Remodeler, for Bill King, 288 Ewing Rd., Carnegie, PA. Remodeled two residential homes.

Once my first wife convinced me that she was serious about a divorce, I moved out of our apartment in June and an acquaintance from TAT let me live in his two-story property on Suburban Avenue. I worked for him until I left Pittsburgh, at the ashram house on Suburban and at his home in Carnegie. This was during a turbulent time and I'll be forever grateful to C.L.; I'm not sure I was ordinarily employable at that time.

Jan. '97 to July '97. Instrument Operator, Kyer Surveying and Mapping, Scott Complex, Room 7, 46060 National Rd., St. Clairsville, OH. Performed topographic, traverse, level and location surveys.

I moved onto the Richard Rose farm in the northwestern West Virginia panhandle, in December and got hired as a land surveyor across the border in Ohio. I quit in July 1997 because I went into isolation in a cabin on the farm before making my next life move.

Oct. '97 to April '98. Driveshaft Straightener, Dana Corporation, Gordonsville Plant, Staffing Solutions, 560 S. Jefferson Ave., Cookeville, TN. Straightened and quality-checked 55,000 drive shafts of different designs and learned to operate twelve production machines.

I went to Tennessee in mid-November and moved into Mom's trailer to live cheaply and tackle the debt I'd accrued from months of unemployment and buying the car with a credit card. I worked second shift at this factory and learned the words to many country music songs—it blared from the speakers there. I listened to Coast-to-Coast AM radio with Art Bell on the way home.

May '98 to July '98. Commercial Painter, Draper & Kramer, Inc., Management Company, Nonconnah Corporate Center, 2598 Corporate Ave., Suite 100, Memphis, TN. Planned and completed outdoor and indoor painting and repair projects.

In 1998, I drove to Memphis and looked to get settled in. I went through the want ads and found a job as a painter for the company overseeing FedEx's world headquarters. It was hot. I quit this job to get away from the sun and to prepare to enter graduate school at the University of Memphis.

Aug. '98 to Aug. '99. Editorial Clerk, The Commercial Appeal, 495 Union Avenue, Memphis, TN. Wrote and published 6,500 obituaries, improving typing speed by 20 w.p.m. Interacted with newspaper reporters and editors and the management of funeral homes, digging up feature material, fact-checking and gaining an understanding of a newspaper's daily operation.

I wrote obituaries from before starting at the University of Memphis until the I left for Stuttgart. While I took classes at the university I shifted to part-time.

In August 1999, I moved to Germany to live with Andrée. I didn't work again until October or so. I got a job with Grabner, GmbH, as a *Gebaeudereiniger*—building cleaner—working on crews consisting of foreigners, like myself, who couldn't get a proper job because of language skills and residency issues. I was allowed to stay in Germany because of my engagement to Andrée, but not to work, because I wasn't yet married to a European citizen.

I quit after a couple of months on a day when I was cleaning toilets and getting laughed at by two former Soviet Union nationals.

Dec. '99. Private English Teacher in Stuttgart. Taught beginning English using the Oxford University Press Headstart language books and successfully helped a non-native English-speaking student become proficient in basic English.

Andrée had a work colleague whose Russian girlfriend wanted to take English lessons. I taught her for a month or so. I got paid.

April 2000 to April 2001. English Teacher, Englisch-Sprachinstitut im Deutsch-Amerikanischen Zentrum, Hobby & Mieger GmbH, Charlottenplatz 17 (ifa), 70173 Stuttgart, Germany. Taught individual and small group English courses at businesses; proofread and edited papers; taught grammar- and vocabulary-building; tutored European and Asian business people in making presentations and wrote The In-House Guide for New Teachers.

I have fond memories of the classes at Bosch, M&W Zander and other companies. While spending time with Germans, I wasn't learning any of their language, so I quit and found German work by placing a personal ad saying "Handy American looking for employment." I wanted to speak with the words of this place I called home.

April '01 to Dec. '01. German Warehouse Manager, Lampert & Sudrow GmbH. KG, GaisburgStraße 12b, 70182 Stuttgart, Germany. Managed a warehouse for a German designer and manufacturer of office furniture—shipping, receiving, stocking and ordering—while writing and speaking exclusively in German.

Richard Lampert. Open-minded German and fan of *Amerika*. September 11th's terrorist attacks happened while I was working there. I worked for Herr Lampert until we moved to France. He bought table tops from France and I'd ship them out to Germans. I interacted with warehouse workers in another part of the building, with shippers, Lampert's secretary on the phone, and everyone I met in my daily life, all in German. Fond, fond memories of riding the S-Bahn to Lampert's warehouse.

Dec. '01 to Dec. '02. Skate Park Creator, Southern France, 10 Domaine de la Chêneraie, 31520 Ramonville Saint Agne. Conceived and designed a multi-sport theme park; organized a coalition of extreme sport associations and individual practitioners; met with town leaders, business professionals, skateboarders and graffiti artists; built the best wooden public skate park in the region in Saint Lys, near Toulouse; learned French and created the website: www.oneandonlyskatepark.com.

Out our apartment window at 10 Domaine de la Chêneraie, 2002.

We lived in Ramonville St Agne for 14 months. I look back on that time with great fondness. ALIVE. Horrible and stressful at times and very, very rewarding. I remember driving a rental truck loaded down with skate park materials to the construction site before dawn each morning. I remember waterproofing that new skate park behind a recreation center in Saint Lys until midnight the final day of building. Our last parting act before leaving France—building a permanent park as a living memorial to our association, *Dream Extreme* and our *One and Only Skate Park Project*. We moved to the U.S. in December 2002.

In the States, I got a job right away in Fowlerville at *Tyssen Krupp Budd Systems*, through the temp agency, Manpower. I worked from December until January 2003. I got hired full time (a feat in itself) at this assembly-line plant making rear chassis for GM and Cadillac, but quit the same day because I was disillusioned with making so little for doing so much. Those guys were beat into the ground by the assembly process.

January 2003, I got myself hired by a custom home framer, Kroll Building. I worked two weeks, if that, before leaving. I was standing one blustery day up on wobbly second-floor ice-covered trusses reaching up to new trusses being lowered down to me with a crane in the icy wind and I had a strong feeling that I'd die soon of an accident.

I took a break from working for others, focusing instead on our dream to do something with a skate park here in the U.S. For a few months we met with the Fowlerville Village Council and proposed building a free public skate park that we'd oversee. When it ground to a halt, we got it to work in other ways, constructing BMX dirt trails and starting a summer skate park at UBC church. I found a job as an office cleaner to supplement our carry-over income from France.

May '03 to Oct. '03. Office Cleaner, Metropolitan Title Company, 10355 Citation Drive, Brighton, MI. Self-employed. Cleaned office areas, break room, bathrooms. Self-supervised.

Worked through the summer. Then worked for another temp agency, Cornerstone, cleaning offices and bathrooms in the morning, four days a week, at Unified Industries, a manufacturer of bridge cranes and trolleys for factories. After a few weeks of cleaning toilets again (Christ!), I found a full-time position as a laborer at a metal fabricating shop in Howell.

Oct. '03 to June '04. Metal Fabrication Laborer, Precise Finishing Systems, 1650 N. Burkhart Rd., Howell, MI. Mastered and performed fabrication skills in a professional fabrication shop for the automotive industry. Became an integral part of a high-tech fabricating team, fabricating and assembling paint systems for contracted deadlines.

This was, by far, one of the most agreeable jobs I've had, and it turns out to have been my last position working for another employer. I quit once, while we ran our second annual summer skate park. We thought we'd get into a building in Fowlerville, find financing and open a skate park/bistro. Things didn't head that way. A mutual decision between us and fate. I decided not to do another skate park unless we had millions—or when the opportunity presented itself to me again.

July 26, 2004, last day of DEx (Dream Extreme) summer skate park. Robert Sass, 15, doing one of many successful backflips. You should see the video...

Summer, '03 and '04. Summer Skate Park Project Creator, United Brethren Church in Christ, 9300 W. Grand River Ave., Fowlerville, MI. Conceived and designed a community-based summer skate park program; organized a coalition of local urban sports practitioners; planned and built a 22-module portable skate park with mini half-pipe, three grind rails and BMX dirt trails. Organized regular events and activities involving more than 1000 participants over two summer skate parks. Organized a multi-discipline end-of-summer competition. Worked with local retailers to support the sports. See the details: www.oneandonlyskatepark.com.

For two months in 2004 we did the skate park again. It was bigger and better than ever. A real adventure. One of those memories for that front porch and rocking chair. We've got hundreds of photos and videos. Real good time.

Spring 2004 to January 2005. Newspaper Reporter, Fowlerville News & Views, 734 S. Grand Ave., P.O. Box 937, Fowlerville, MI. Wrote and published 15 feature and profile articles. Took all pictures for articles with digital camera and sent stories with photos digitally, via email.

Throughout our time in Michigan, I wrote for the Fowlerville paper. I went to place an ad to sell our '87 Lincoln Town Car and mentioned I used to write for newspapers—I became a staff writer. I met the Pratt & Miller Engineering Corvette team that regularly won its class at the twenty-four hour endurance race in Le Mans, France. I remember pushing one of the race cars outside for a photo. I have a gear from one of the cars on my shelf next to me. This and *The Pitt News* were my enjoyable times writing for papers.

In September 2004 I worked odd jobs for Mike Dietz and another farmer on Judd Road in Fowlerville. I repaired a fence and built a barn door. I was looking for a job in newspaper writing again and found one.

Lansing Area Newspapers hired me as the beat reporter for the Lansing Towne Courier. I worked one day, attending a school board meeting, interviewing an entrepreneur, wrote two articles and quit. Another story of working my butt off and not getting paid enough to feel justified. I looked into the future and could only shake my head, *no*. Strike two.

Monday, September 20, 2004, returned to *Precise* as the shipping, receiving and general labor guy. Good steady pay, decent work, not far from home.

That same day, I started writing (this) my first book. I decided I'd write my book for a year, while working at Precise, and then get published and make enough money to finance a bistro or skate park or whatever we decided to do next. Six years passed before I picked up *that* hammer (pen) again.

May 2005, I'd gotten myself hired at the *Intelligencer* daily paper in Wheeling by stringing a couple of stories for the news editor, John McCabe. I got hired with the stipulation that I didn't want to be a beat reporter. "Sure," they told me, and had me go to the assistant news editor who introduced me to my new job as court beat reporter. I composed my letter of resignation on the drive home. *Now what*, I thought.

With double digits in our checking account, and no other prospects, I kept going to employment agencies while feeling a dread at the fare offered there. Then a TAT member and friend, Mike, calls, asking me if I have some time to paint his house. And how. I haven't looked back. I've been a self-employed handyman painter ever since. I've worked for dozens of people, painted more than a score of houses and keep busy. We live in our first home and I manage to pay the mortgage each month. Each year gets better. *Handyman for Hire* is my company name.

January 2010 I embarked on a career change from handyman to writer. *How's that working for you?* Well, I'm back to doing the contracting work; I'll let you know in a few more years.

I took the first two months of 2010 and started compiling and writing this book. I created sister blogs: **oneandonlyobserver.blogspot.com** and **oneandonlyobserver.wordpress.com**. The **One and Only** part comes from our skate park dreams and the **Observer** part comes from my philosophic pursuits. I returned to contracting work once a necessary rebuild of Andrée's mini-van transmission helped the money run out faster than planned. Seven months passed and I woke up shaking my head, deciding I couldn't wait until the time was right to write; that day would never come. I'll just have to do it. So I wrote, and write, in the mornings and after work, finally typing "The End" on my book-in-the-works. As you read this, you help me spend less time plumbing and painting. This ends my employment history to date. I didn't describe the things I did during 12 years in the Army and Army National Guard. There are other forgotten unimportant "occupations" I participated in for pay, but they'll go down with the ship.

Chapter 8 —A Taste of Space

Fowlerville, Michigan
September 2004

I'm reading "The Gnostic Gospels" by Elaine Pagels. I don't know if the author is mixing her opinion into the descriptions of the Gnostic point of view. Probably. It reads like an objective, scholarly study of a collection of books that were discovered in Nag Hammadi, in Upper Egypt, after being buried in a clay container for 1500 years. According to Pagels, these books represent the Gnostics, an early Christian sect. Gnosis is a Greek word usually translated as "knowledge." Merriam-Webster online says, "Esoteric knowledge of spiritual truth held by the ancient Gnostics to be essential to salvation."

Those who claim to know nothing about ultimate reality (and hold that it is possibly unknowable) are called agnostic and a person who claims to know something about ultimate reality is called a Gnostic. Gnosis, says Pagels, does not concern rational knowledge primarily; the Greek language distinguishes between *that* kind of knowing and the "knowing" gained through observation or experience.

To know oneself, the author says of the Gnostics' claim, is to know human nature and human destiny. "Yet to know oneself, at the deepest level, is simultaneously to know God; this is the secret of gnosis."

I wish the author had said, "This is what I believe, and these Gnostic writings support my feelings." Maybe she says that later. The thing is, I was surprised to read certain passages in this book that echo my own "gnosis." It is unmistakable, the place some of these comments are coming from. That's why I suspect the author is holding back.

For someone to note something about someone or something else, I believe they have to have the capacity to recognize the thing they're noting! Authors that don't themselves function on a certain wavelength can never notice or comment on that wavelength.

If the Gnostics really were as the author describes them, or, if she's only seeing in their writings echoes of her own convictions and condition… It almost doesn't matter. It *doesn't* matter, because I recognize this talk of ultimate appreciations and real knowledge of things; when you read something that's pointing at something, you *know*—if it's in you.

Once you'd had a taste of space, you can't *not* recognize someone else who's had unbreatheable-ness infused throughout themselves. I have a continuous condition or feeling of heaviness, to use a friend's word, inside me—and I can feel it in others.

A word on Heaviness

This heaviness was left over after an experience in June 1996. I want to talk about dying. I was looking at the stars for as long as I have lived. By 'looking at the stars,' I mean thinking or wondering about things that aren't immediately in front of me. Wondering why the world is here and what is behind everything I see. When I look at something, I wonder.

It wasn't until my dad's death that I took a different turn, and this native, ingrained curiosity of mine got serious. Instead of shuffling through wonder and mystery, my steps echoed sharply in eternity; mirrors of mirrors facing mirrors to infinity: **What is the meaning of Life?**

While I was living in Stuttgart I was isolated from people speaking English who also spoke the particular language of philosophy I spoke. Andrée listens to me. I'm grateful and lucky to have one person in my life I can talk to, exactly how I want to, and who understands and accepts me. I remember missing communication while I was overseas. It was like I was on the space station orbiting Earth; I could call or email people, but never see them, walk on the solid ground, breathe the open air and smell fresh-cut grass.

Now that I'm back in the States, it's not much different, in my day-to-day pattern, than living in Europe—in the sense that I don't talk to anyone except my wife. But it *feels* different because I'm here, getting to hear English at work, watching TV in English, talking to people in stores in English, paying my bills in English; these things give small infusions that keep me from feeling cut off. We had more friends and acquaintances in Europe than we have here, although as time passes, it is equaling out. Although I'm back "in town," I'm in a different world.

I'm removed from here, even though I'm here. I left this "hometown" world at 18 and left the pattern. I got off the merry-go-round and it's gone around without me. In Fowlerville, occasionally I meet someone I recognize but don't really know, someone from my past. It feels strange seeing these adults who seem so much older than me.

I remember sitting in Gino's GMC Yukon with Andrée and Guillaume behind me in the dark, riding from the Detroit metro airport to Fowlerville. I had jet lag and it felt unreal. *Never thought I'd be back* here *again*. I told people this. They just look at me uncomprehendingly. I never thought I'd be back in the States, *anywhere* in the States, let alone Fowlerville, yet here I am. I'm glad we're in the town where Dad's grave is. We don't visit it often, but I'm glad to be able to.

Since coming back, we've run two summer skate parks at a church just outside town with a big, perfectly-suited parking lot and a great pastor, Tim Flickinger. United Brethren in Christ is the place. There were more than a thousand kids visiting our portable skate park. That's the count of BMXers, skaters, scooter riders and skateboarders who came to our skate park and actually took part. Many more spectators. There were a lot of "repeat customers" in that headcount.

There's a whole back story, going to our first discussion about our lives and life together on the balcony of our Stuttgart apartment, when I asked Andrée what she wanted to do with her life.

"Work," she said.

"Yeah, everybody does, but I'm talking about if money didn't matter. What do you want to do with your life?"

She wasn't used to thinking along these lines. There'd been a big assumption that she shared with the society she lived in that work was all there was. Maybe.

When it got down to what she really liked doing, her answer was, "To make people happy." From then on, we would eventually do some fairly unusual things that would involve hundreds of other people, TV appearances, newspaper and magazine write-ups, building projects, moving and living in three different countries, a lot of unanticipated joys, sorrows and everything between and beyond our expectations.

I think I've experienced what I'll go through when I die for real. That process left a mark on me—a weight and condition that hasn't moved. So what. Well, it was good for me and my life pattern. An acorn going through its trajectory of becoming a mature oak and beyond.

I feel I have the right to encourage others. I don't run across similar souls often, but when I do, I enthusiastically encourage them to follow the far-off sounding beat of their own drum.

Green tinted Einstein image on the M&M (Meeting of the Minds) Philosophy poster at the Wheeling library.

2003 found me back in the U.S., in West Virginia in a building near the swimming pool in Wheeling Park. Jim Burns, of Pittsburgh, author of "At Home with the Inner Self," and I put on a tag-team living-philosophy session. Brief presentations with a Q & A following. Jim is a remarkable soul. He's 80 now has seemingly lived a life in the wringer. A lot of years in institutions, a lot of hell, and he's the sanest man I know—although he's crazy. Ours was one of several presentations at the spring TAT Foundation conference, "Emerging Voices II," on the weekend of April 25-27, 2003, four months after I returned to the States. I'd been overseas or out of town since 1997.

I think of the years that I was living in Stuttgart, Germany and Ramonville St. Agne, France. In Europe, I was part of the societies I lived in; I was learning more of the languages every day, interacting with people, enjoying sunsets and walks, buying groceries, watching TV. Yet, like someone in space, I was separated from the effortless communication I had walked through before crossing the Atlantic. Overseas, I fired off a good bit of correspondence with anyone who sent anything my way but I was apart from things going on in the States.

Back to the session that Jim and I did at the TAT event in April 2003. I'd had high hopes of connecting warmly and wonderfully with meeting attendees, reuniting with past-friends and making new acquaintances, sharing my thoughts on the inner journey and answering lots of interested and interesting questions.

I don't know what people thought. I wore my skates during the talk, the remnants of my last couple of years and a symbol of going after something… idealistic. I think someone asked me about them and I tried to explain this. By their silence, I don't think they got it. Skates represented thinking—*being*—outside the box. It's the number one requirement for a successful *journey* anywhere, in my opinion. It seemed like I faced a group of people secure and snug in their boxes, who would never leave their familiar lives and world. There has to be a willingness to GO. And beyond that, the follow-through of action. This, after all, is a journey!

It was a cultural shock, coming back to the States, and attending a meeting of people ostensibly concerned and interested in the same thing as me. I hadn't heard English spoken, at any level above a basic, day-to-day function level for probably four years. I was a foreigner again, as much as I'd been overseas.

The experience I had in June 1996 during my "night of hell," of being *beyond* me, my thoughts and everything was related to the bridgeless canyon I felt between me and these people. Having no real common ground was something I'd gotten used to living with overseas. To feel that way here was a sad surprise. I think there's no way to build a bridge of understanding with words between people with no common experiences. But there's always a way somehow, just not apparent.

Two months earlier, in February, I'd happily attended a weekend retreat run by Shawn Nevins at the Linsly Outdoor Center southwest of Pittsburgh, attended by a collection of mostly college students and a few "old hands" at the metaphysical seeking game. There were a few people I knew. A few I knew *of*, but had never met in person, and mostly strangers. I wondered if I'd be able to communicate. It was hard to describe where I'd been and what I was now; I mostly kept quiet.

I participated in the weekend's activities and drove back home to our new home, a trailer in Fowlerville. One of the activities had been a video recording session where each of us was asked questions such as, "What do you want to do with your life?" while being filmed. I had just left the 24-hour-a-day-working-to-create-a-skate-park life in France. I'd moved my family back to my hometown, where I hadn't lived for 18 years. I was as uprooted as a plant could be. I remember saying, "I want to be useful." That was about as grand as my plans were then; they're the same now, although some details have been added.

"Useful," meant having a chance to communicate with someone on a similar wavelength. That is something I can't take for granted anymore.

M.C., asked me to contribute to the TAT Newsletter he'd taken over at the time. I wrote this newspaper-esque report on my experience of the February retreat. It's not "reality" of course; it's my view presented in a certain way:

"Report on a [2003] February Retreat"

Waiting for them, were rain, wind, ice and snow. A fireplace filled with logs pushed its heat into a meeting room. There was good food, coffee, squeaky cots and working showers.

Eighteen people from seven states arrived late Friday evening and Saturday morning, February 21-22, at the Linsly Outdoor Center in Raccoon Creek State Park, west of Pittsburgh.

Each participant had traveled a considerable distance to attend a retreat centered on discovering one's way in this life.

It was a cocktail of fresh blood and old, a gathering of strangers and longtime friends. Graduate and doctoral students, soon-to-be and recent college graduates, a doctor, a teacher, a writer, a counselor, a group leader, a former psychiatric patient.

Some stood at the crossroads. Hesitating. Not committing to a possibly disappointing direction.

Others were balanced, as on a blade, where leaning or falling one way or the other would constitute the *de facto* choice—deliberate or otherwise—to continue in a certain unavoidable direction.

Some were going with the flow, neither hesitating nor charging ahead, choosing always between the lesser of two evils at each fork in their road.

Others waited, hoping that the right thing would manifest itself, not certain of their ability to discover what they're supposed be doing.

And some participants were on the "right thing," doing what they could finally feel was the right thing for them to do in this life.

They all brought something to the retreat. Fatalism, pragmaticism, skepticism, hope, willingness and wonder. A spirit would sometimes appear, called curiosity, slipping between the cracks in the walls into the meeting room.

The weekend passed like a single, long afternoon.

There was time to talk at this isolated outdoor center. Participants configured and reconfigured into groups or pairs while eating in the cafeteria, walking on the path between buildings, resting in the bunkhouse and standing in front of the fireplace in the meeting room.

This retreat avoided both formless wandering and a too-rigid format. Instead, it was shaped by a solid structure that allowed for organic evolution.

Each person had the singular chance to discover something through the words and eyes of others and also through watching videotaped sessions where each participant addressed their main desire in life.

It was a collection of reflections of each person, all bouncing off of each other and yet somehow aimed at a common, voiceless urge to BE something, to DO something with this life.

Late Sunday morning, with snow falling outside and the chairs once again formed into a circle in front of the fire in the meeting room, organizer Shawn Nevins read some of his poetry.

A little leeway was allowed. Something beyond words and with words—existed momentarily.

Like a snowflake. That is only water once again (or a poem) after it melts.

After a long pause following his last poem, Shawn said, "You can't always get what you want."

Maybe the simplest things are un-say-able. Maybe.

An unlikely collection of strangers and friends briefly assembled in a quiet forested place in February. It would be interesting to revisit them and find out what they think—about anything.

List of Participants

Art Ticknor, Moundsville, WV; Benjamin (Ben) R. Erne, Pittsburgh, PA; Dan Garmat, Pittsburgh, PA; David Weimer, Michigan; Edward Wertz, New Jersey; Gary Harmon, Akron, Ohio; Gordon Gowans, Louisville, Kentucky; Jeff Crilley, Pittsburgh, PA; Jim Burns, Pittsburgh, PA; Kerri Hartman, Pittsburgh, PA; Kiffy Purvis, Pittsburgh, PA; Mandy Schleifer, Pittsburgh, PA; Mike Casari, Coopersburg, PA; Michael Tomlinson, Raleigh, NC; Sai Prasanth, Pittsburgh, PA; Sharad Borle, Pittsburgh, PA; Shawn Nevins, event organizer, Louisville, Kentucky; Walker Traylor, Raleigh, NC.

I don't remember the June 2003 TAT meeting, but I'm fairly sure that I went.

Chapter 9 — God is Heavy

There was proof that God existed, St. Thomas Aquinas wrote his *Summa Theologica* in the 13th century. Richard Rose used to say in university lectures that Aquinas' proof consisted of noting that the universe was in motion and anything that moved had to have a mover, therefore the mover must be God. When I heard this, it struck a chord because I'd half-jokingly said to friends that I believed God to be gravity, since motions of solar systems, galaxies and the universe can be explained by gravitational attraction. Gravity is then the source of all movement. But if God/gravity is the mover, what moved them?

When I lived near Toulouse, I often visited the Basilica of St. Sernin, *Les Jacobins*, in the center of town, where a gilded casket-shaped thing sat, containing relics (bones or other body parts or personal effects) of Thomas Aquinas. I never studied his writings. When I visited this church for the first time, I was surprised to read that name on the plaque.

Andrée, in Toulouse at Couvent des Jacobins, in the courtyard we loved to visit. May 2002.

I've read that Saint-Sernin is the oldest Catholic church standing in the south of France. Its bell tower is an untypical-looking thing and the building is made of reddish pink brick. It has a beautiful courtyard in the center of the monastery, open to the sky with pebbled walking paths and sculpted evergreens. Andrée and I used to go there with Guillaume when he was a baby to sit among the sculpted evergreens and pebbled paths. Archways and clay-tiled roofs surround the courtyard.

Near the bustling center of Toulouse, this was an oasis in silence. I remember the dormer windows above the courtyard, imagining what it had been like for hundreds of years as priests or monks filled the place, each, with their life of devotion and all the countless things they did, each day. I imagined a monk looking down at me from his window.

A crypt is open for self-tours. It's damp and lit by bare bulbs. Displays of church notables and gilded and red velvet stuff behind glass. Stone and dirt. The feeling underground was a heavy quiet one, with the mass of all that structure overhead. We'd take visitors down there.

"Laying in nothing"

In 1994, at the *Eye of Horus* bookstore on East Carson Street in the South Side of Pittsburgh, I spent maybe 40 minutes in a sensory-deprivation tank. Someone in SKS, Stephanie Swenko or Fred, told us about it and we organized a day trip there. I think four or five of us went. We Self Knowledge Symposium brethren. We were all college students.

I thought the *Eye of Horus* was pretentious. "Gothic" when gothic was starting out as a style—bottom lip pushed out. Black-dyed hair, black clothes, multiple earrings. Maybe a nose ring. Incense burning and lots of material on tarot, ritual magic and witchcraft. There were also books I was interested in, like J. J. van der Leeuw's *Conquest of Illusion*, H.P. Blavatsky's *The Voice of the Silence*, Richard Bucke's *Cosmic Consciousness* and Paul Brunton's *The Secret Path*. Good ones. I searched every bookstore and library I ran across. I was on the lookout for books on "the subject" that spoke to me.

For some reason, the *Eye of Horus* had a pretty classy sensory deprivation tank setup in a back room; a dimly-lighted, quiet, clean place, with benches to leave your clothes and a large rectangular tank with a lid opening like a Rolls-Royce hood. The liquid inside, I wouldn't call it water, exactly, was body-temperature and made you float effortlessly on and above its surface. The low, aerodynamic tank was soundproofed and a quiet alternative-looking girl working there gave me earplugs. A timer would go off inside the tank when your session was over. I think they charged twenty or thirty dollars.

I wore swim shorts, put the earplugs in, got into the tank and pulled the lid down over me. I lay back in the liquid. It was neither cold nor hot; I couldn't discern a temperature contrast to my own body. It felt like laying in nothing, which happened to be wet. I heard myself breathing. I relaxed my feet, legs, arms, neck, and so on. My breathing slowed and heartbeat pounded in my ears; it sounded like the heartbeat of the universe in the dark there.

My ears rang and I heard my heartbeat and slow breathing. It was anything but quiet and peaceful. It was utterly black and I saw nothing, although lightning flashes worked their way across the sky of my visual field. The view was unaffected by my eyes opening or closing. Movement and shapes swirled around me. I squeezed my eyes shut. This brought about even more fireworks of flashing white.

Someone asked later if I had been claustrophobic. I said it was the opposite. It felt like I was floating out in space, with no boundaries, no limits, no references. I didn't know where I was in the tank. I worried constantly that I was drifting and I'd hit my head or bump into the sides. Each time I reached out to check my position, I was in a different position from what I imagined.

It was strange. Laying there, arms by my sides, no effort to stay above the surface, floating. I felt a slight pressure of the liquid as a line along my jaw, to my temples and what seemed like the crown of my head. I worried I would relax too much and fall asleep and sink, breathing in the not-water. When I felt about forty minutes was up, I started to prepare for exiting. An interminable amount of time passed and I was certain something went wrong—that someone had forgotten the timer or they'd closed the store and forgotten I was there. I pushed the lid up and looked at the LED wall clock. A lot more time to go. Great. I'd broken the spell. I let the lid down and eased back into my floating dead man position.

After my train of thought had traveled hundreds of miles over varied terrain, a far-off chiming whispered to me that my time was up. I pushed up the lid with my toe and lay there like a clam, in the tank's eighteen inches of saline liquid, looking out of that foreign setting at the room outside. A while later, I got out, showered, dressed and left.

At the next SKS meeting, we compared and shared experiences with each other and with those who had not gone. A couple more went another day. I remember the day we went, sitting with Lars or Fred or Leonore, waiting for someone else. One of the girls left the tank after ten minutes. Each of us had a different impression, I remember. Those who hadn't done the tank asked questions. What was the value in doing it? I don't know. It was an adventure, something exciting to do.

While I was president of the group, we did a lot of those kind of things. We were spiritual philosophic warrior pioneer explorers. We had a campfire in Panther Hollow Park on Halloween night under a stone bridge and told stories. We did perception experiments during meetings. We met on the roof of the Cathedral of Learning (40-plus-story tower on Pitt's main Oakland campus). We met in maintenance catacomb crawl spaces in the basement of the Frick Fine Arts building, with candles and meditated. We took a field trip to caverns and explored them as a group, eating lunch and sitting in silence in the dark. We made this Great Quest a living, real thing. We were alive!

Of course, girls tended to end up with guys in the group—or was it vice-versa? After all, who else did they have more in common with than those who shared their curiosities and interests? I was mostly responsible for the program. I came up with meeting topics and monthly schedules. I'd introduce each meeting and, therefore, set the tone for the meetings. It's a miracle anyone showed up. There was a "sea change" one time when I said to myself, "This stuff isn't for everyone." I had been in the middle of getting handouts ready before a meeting and just stopped, feeling despondent considering anyone actually being interested in the material. I had been hard-selling, and I was packaging things to cater to other people. That was it; when I saw that, I dropped it. I decided to become honest and quit trying to interest others in what *I* was interested in. 'To hell with them and trying to draw people in to this topic.' From then on, I only did meetings on what I was interested in. I ran the meetings how I wanted, with no care at all about convincing someone how wonderful this topic was. Things just took off. "Regulars" started contributing and I incorporated their ideas into our monthly schedules.

Before long, the weekly meetings were drawing quite a crowd. From a dozen to twenty or so was average. For "cool" topics like druids, ESP experiments, tarot or Wicca, the room would be packed. For the topics I was interested in like perception, thought experiments and "going within" there would be an average of eight or nine—made up of regulars with a few others thrown in.

A year before all this, I had taken my first fearful step. The first meeting of the spring of '93 found me alone in a classroom on the third floor of the Cathedral of Learning, nervously waiting for 7:30. The former Self Knowledge Symposium leaders were gone and weren't coming back. I'd been attending the group's meetings and, as a reporter for the campus newspaper, wrote articles on their lectures and events. I became interested and active in the group. I thought it would be an unpardonable pity if I just let it drop; so, taking some inspiration for my first flyer from a Hermann Hesse book, *Steppenwolf*, I photocopied half-sheet-size advertisements:

Anarchist Evening Entertainment
Entrance not for Everybody

For Madmen Only!

Tonight at the Symposium
For Madmen Only
Price of Admittance Your mind.

Success Guaranteed

Tuesday

```
Self Knowledge Symposium      Room 302 CL, 7:15 p.m.
```

Cathedral of Learning, University of Pittsburgh.

Two girls showed up at about a quarter till eight. They were not who I was expecting to see walk in. I said that this was the first meeting of the semester and that the following week would begin regularly-scheduled topics. They left and I was relieved. I would make a "normal" poster for the next week's meeting.

From then on, people who'd attended the meetings the previous year began showing up again. Eventually they gave way to a whole new collection of regulars. Being a funded student group, we had a desk and a website and a budget and put on lecturers and events. When I graduated in December of '94, I wanted to hand the reins firmly to the group's members—my friends. I could have stayed on, holding on to control of the group from the outside, as a former student, but that felt a little like hanging around high school after graduation. We held an election for officers before I left. I gave the group to its successors—I showed them how to do the paperwork to get money to make posters, pay speakers, etc.; showed them how to reserve a room and change the group's website info, showed them the office, gave them the keys to our locking desk on the 9th floor of the William Pitt Union building and wished them luck.

Two years later, I'd really grown to value my friends from SKS and my time with them. Before I left Pittsburgh in November '96, I invited them to the ashram house on Suburban Avenue for an evening meal. We talked and ate. Jose, did my horoscope—a natal chart. I didn't like saying goodbye. I don't remember much else from that evening; it is, after all, a lifetime ago and much, much has gone on since then. I have a good felt-memory of the meetings, events, strange experiments and activities we did together in the spirit of discovery. In the years since, only two group members ever contacted me. Leonore lived in Turkey and Portugal while I lived in Germany and France; we emailed occasionally, intending to visit one another. Now she's back in New York and I'm in Ohio. We email once in a blue moon and I see her blog postings. Stefanie went to Cuba, lived out west for several years, and returned to Pennsylvania with a young child. Lars returned to Norway. Fred and the rest, I don't know.

I wrote the following at the Beehive coffee shop in Oakland. I was living in Bill King's ashram house in the South Hills area of Pittsburgh after separating from Katherine, my first wife ["practice" wife, Andrée reminds me]. This is from my journal. These things are worlds away and far ago and I present them like an archeologist displays broken pottery shards. When I first read this, it took a while for the episode to resurface fully. Typing it in, that time rose like a sunken ship from the bottom of a deep sea; I was there again. Oh yes, now I remember that long summer and fall, living at Bill's place. There on the trolley platform, yes, gazing over there at those pipes coming out of a house on the other side of the tracks. And then hearing that sound…

Journal entry - June 28, 1996

It's been two days since that man had his seizure on Suburban Ave. This biscotti tastes like shit, really.

It was around 12:30. As it is, I've told no one yet. There's a story in it, I'm sure. It opens with me holding an umbrella up to keep the sun out of Bob's eyes. That's his name, Bob.

That's what he told the fireman who was asking him what his name was. I had been on the "T" [Pittsburgh rail transit system] platform slightly above but parallel to the dead-end street, Suburban Avenue. I live there now, since my wife left me. I was lucky this place was available. I stay on the ground floor at the back of the house. It's a little library, and I have a cot set up. I like the breeze at night and the trees outside waving. To get back to the man who was bleeding on the sidewalk: I was waiting for the trolley to take me downtown.

Five minutes… six… There was a black woman and her baby and all the accompanying gear: stroller, diaper bag—a Mother Nature aura over them—and me. I was 20 feet away, leaning on the chain link fence, facing the tracks, wondering if anything, anything at all, was "worth living for." I wasn't depressed. Believe it.

Just then, I heard a few noises—stumbling, chain link fence rattling—that attracted my attention, followed by a hollow thunk. I had to move to get a better view past a parked car. "Holy shit," I said aloud, quietly, to myself.

"Is that for real?" the black woman next to me asked.

"Yeah, I think so," I said, while starting to walk, then run. I ran to the end of the chain link fence, grabbed the rail, spun around it to run down the brick road to this guy [I lived on this street. The "T" station was on a built-up level and paralleled my street. Coming from "home," I would walk uphill on the brick-paved street to the intersection where I could cross the tracks to my right and go up to the concrete trolley stop. It was like a train station.]

I was carrying my backpack, a letter to a friend, and my scratched mirror sunglasses. The guy was still, lying on his back. His arms were pulled up tight, like some strange human begging. His left fist was clenched tight. "Are you alright?" I asked. Clearly he wasn't. But I had to ask. I squatted down by his side. He was full length on the sidewalk. Between a car and a short chain link fence on either side. He'd urinated himself; there was foam coming out of the side of his mouth. I saw fresh blood on the cement under his head.

Gunshot? I wondered. Whatever it was, it didn't look good. I thought about getting his head off the cement. Not a good idea, I reminded myself. Could do worse to him. "Hey man, it's all right." A woman stuck her head out the door of the house belonging to the fence. "I called 911 already," she said. She was a young mother. Thin, tan, blond hair. Concerned. Her children, a boy and a girl, were curious. Three- or four-years-old, maybe older. She called them to her, concerned. "Tell them to get here quick," I said, looking at the blood that was visible under Bob's ear.

Bob wasn't flopping around, like I'd thought epileptics would. He was just very, very stiff, strained, his left fist clenched... He was a thin and bony guy. I saw a couple of tattoos, homemade ones, on his arms. Bob wasn't trying to be anything right now. "Well," I told him, "You cracked your head a bit." I turned to the young mother. "Could you get me something to shade him with? From the sun," I said. She went inside. Another young mother, who I'd noticed on different days, said, "What about a cold washcloth? To cool him off?"

"Yes. Good idea," I said.

"Are you alright?" I asked Bob. "There's help on the way. Hang in there, buddy." I was there for Bob. That's all. I wasn't so sure about what to do. Bob's eyes were rolled back, and closed mostly, fluttering a bit. His breathing was real strained. Each breath like he was holding on to breathing. Holding a huge weight up. I talked to him, reassured him. He was muttering something. I couldn't understand. He struggled a bit to move. I put my hand on his skinny shoulder. "It's alright, man. You're not alone. Help's coming, okay?"

So I was there, now holding a yellow plastic umbrella over the fallen Bob. Neighbor young mother, brunette, taller, thin, unsure, brought a washcloth. She seemed uncertain. "Here's the washcloth," she said, holding it. "I don't know where..." I took it from her and put it on Bob's forehead. Reassured him again. You know. Hoping the ambulance would get there soon. It was hot and, being close to noon, the sun was right high in the sky. Beautiful day. Even now, a day later, I remember the small, high-up wisps of clouds.

By now, I'd decided to keep Bob going until help arrived. Afraid to touch him, but all the same, wiping his forehead, patting his shoulder... his left shoulder. That makes it his right hand that was clenched into a fist. Well, the fire truck came, and backed down the dead-end street, and three firemen got out. Oxygen bottle, pulse-taking, blood pressure-taking. You know. Big yellow loud fire truck and lights. Small narrow lane. The trolley I was waiting for went by, people looking, one of the blue uniformed firemen stepped on my letter and almost got my glasses. I held the little umbrella.

Bob was reaching for the oxygen mask on his face. Muttering. Fireman hold him to leave it on, that they could hear him with it on. I doubted it. I felt that Bob couldn't breathe so well with it on. I think it felt claustrophobic. Maybe the flow wasn't set right.

Bob's eyes were mostly open now. He was moving like a baby. Arms, legs, head rolling, muttering. He was coming out of it, whatever 'it' was. His arms were at his sides. They'd relaxed from their pulled-up-tight, begging position. His eyes were not hurt as though from one accident, one thing, but by this day on top of another day on top of another. A big pile of days under the blazing sun. His eyes were hazel green, brown, but faded. The whites were worn siding on a two-story row house addition. Old eyes. Not hurt; damaged by days.

Fireman number two, holding the blood pressure cuff, was talking, asking Bob questions. "What's your name, pal?" he asked. I thought I heard Bob say, "Robert." #2 didn't hear what I heard. I was standing now, holding this yellow umbrella over prone Bob and the firemen. They were waiting for the ambulance.

Ambulance arrived. Paramedics got there. *Thank God*, I felt. These guys weren't frantic at all, nor anxious. They knew it was only a seizure. They could read a lot from the scene. "Which hospital do you go to?" the head paramedic asked. Bob muttered a name. Paramedic nodded; he knew that one. I felt less tied to this thing. "Do you need this?" I asked. Should I keep the sun off him?" Paramedic one shrugged. "It doesn't matter." I held it a bit longer, then closed the umbrella. Sunlight on Bob's face now. He closes his eyes.

The paramedic, or was it the fireman? No, it must have been the paramedic—checked Bob's head. Found a shallow wound back there. I walked in a circle around them. Grabbed my backpack and glasses and the letter to a friend. I put the umbrella on the young mother's porch swing. I didn't feel like I finally had an appreciation for the sacredness of life, after seeing someone at the mercy of his biology. But I did feel that.

Just before I walked away up the brick street to the trolley stop again, I heard a fireman ask Bob his name again. Bob muttered, hands wandering now, pulling at the oxygen line to the mask again. "'Bob' he said," the fireman notified his partner, "His name's Bob."

"Yeah," I confirmed. "I heard him say Robert before." They look at me. "Good luck Bob. Hope your headache's not too bad tomorrow," I said. There's a mailbox at the intersection where the trolley crosses the road. I walked up there and mailed my letter to a friend. Good timing; a trolley came along just then. Got on. I could access the mindset of the few passengers in the air-conditioned car with me. I felt like an outsider. My mindset was changed. I think encounters with life do that. I really think so.

I spent the day working on something meaningless. I got back home to my new home on Suburban Avenue; it was around eight o'clock but still light. It's summer now; it stays light until nine-thirty. I wanted to see if they cleaned up the blood from the sidewalk. Someone had. The young mothers, I bet. Did a good job, too. Not a speck left. Old Bob's Nestea plunge onto the cement could have happened anywhere or not at all.

I'd been living at the Suburban Avenue ashram house for a couple of months. Three months after my duo of experiences—broken brain and night of hell—that week in the woods in May. After returning to Pittsburgh, my plans, expectations, the relationships in my life, my previous assumptions—crumbled. I'd also given up a ten-year habit of daily exercise. Everything was changing.

Journal entry - August 4, 1996.

I lament the loss of my life.

When my body was a thrill and new and somehow special.

When push-ups and sit-ups comforted me and pull-ups made me stronger and wiser.

I sorrow the loss of my perfect shape and excellent flexibility. I miss my body, my life.

I miss my wife. And the times when we had each other in our lives. Sure, it was *that*, and not this, but I can't help the sadness and the reaching-out that my heart does. Still clinging to her, and to the past. At last. Like a grieving woman, for me, it is into the grieving that I fall, and not the things grieved, so much. Loss for loss's sake. Crying and sadness.

I miss my life. I look at my body and it doesn't seem mine. I don't know why. Not all of it, hardly any of it. I am thankful and grateful to my body for doing so much—allowing me to do so much. I feel as though I've abandoned my childhood pony. He and I used to canter home with ears flattened and feet drumming; used to walk and grab a head-full of grass on the hoof; I've turned away and said goodbye, regretting it. This sadness propels me into thoughts of inner depths and outer space. Where is me? Where is me? Why me? Where am I? Why.

When Katherine made the move, and decided to separate from me, she avoided me. I think maybe she was advised to, because I'd try to talk her into staying with me. After our divorce, I heard no more from her—not that I'd expected to. One day in the summer of 2004, Andrée and I were in the middle of our second summer skate park and I had gone home quickly to get something for the park—drinks for the kids, I think—and my cell phone rang. I answered it, assuming it was Andrée—and it was Katherine. "Hi Dave," she said. A familiar voice I hadn't heard in eight years and utterly unexpected. She got my number from my sister. She said she was taking part in the Landmark Forum, a series of self-improvement seminars.

I recognized that she was nervous; I knew her well. But she was determined, too, to call me, I could tell. "I'm sorry I wasn't a better wife for you when we were married," she said. Jeeze. I told her she did the best she could at the time and everything worked out for the best for both of us. Maybe it took a weight off her mind. I hope so. She's married and lives in Gainesville, Florida, she said. She's got another cat. Strange call. The following is what I wrote after signing our final divorce papers eight years before that unexpected call. I waited for her in a parking area across from the small notary public office on Forbes Avenue in Oakland. I could tell she was uncomfortable when I stopped by her work so I told her I'd meet her at the place six blocks down the hill. I inline skated and she drove our new car.

Journal entry - October 18, 1996.

Signed the papers—again—today. About 15 minutes ago. I went up to LRDC, 8th floor, Kath's area. I was treated like the toilet deliveryman who arrives in the middle of a tea party. It may be that she was uncomfortable, embarrassed. Probably. It may well be. She got her hair cut again. Short. It isn't a matter of fashion, it's a matter of ugly versus not ugly. This cut is ugly. She looks like a dyke. Maybe she knows this is a "safe" haircut …

Oh well. Here at Pamela's Restaurant, I just had the Friday special, "Lemon Fish." This coleslaw is making me ill just smelling it. Well and well well well. All the same, I was able to keep down the rest of my "meal." Maybe my body can make use of the nutrients I shoveled in. It was around 70 degrees and starting to rain as I waited for the trolley off Suburban Ave. Now, almost four hours later, it's rainy, blustery, and heading towards 40 degrees fast. I bought three brakes and two more bearings—took the 71C, got off three blocks too soon (of course) and got to walk in the rain.

This morning, after waking at 8:30 to the buzz of the moving man from *South Side Movers* at the door, there to look at Jeff Buzzia's stuff, Paul showed me some clothes he was taking down to the *Red, White and Blue Thrift Store*. I fit his size, so now I have a new wardrobe!

Lots of shirts. This was a good turn. The rest of the day's events have gone. Just that. They've happened, but the 'successful-ness' of them has mirrored the gray day. I don't feel strong emotions, depressed or angry. I'm just. Just. I'll go over to Forbes Quad, read email and "post" an essay to SKS, Fred. Then I'll read or think and walk and wander and end up back home sometime. To—what?

On Human Achievement

He spoke of purpose and action. It made sense to us. We were young. "There is hope between the raindrops," he said, pointing to the stars and our eyes.

Now, a wordless Buddha shuffles the halls of an Alzheimer's home, and all that he is remains.
"Do something," a voice echoes quietly beyond, *"futility is futile."*

Awhile

There is a whale under the ice,
And when it rests, the cracks seal and disappear.
So pound, pound, pound.

Unyielding, and always cold.
Sounds muffle above and carry below.

I am the ice that pounds back each blow the whael can deliver.
I am the cold sea, the deep ocean.
I am the whale.
I am the struggle between barrier and pounder.

All are welcome.

I came up with *On Human Achievement* in a graduate poetry class at the University of Memphis in January 1999. Rose was still living and I hadn't seen him for a while. I imagined him there in the Alzheimer unit in Weirton, WV, and thought about his whole life of days, months, years, of efforts and goals and opinions and all those TAT meetings I remember listening to him talk. Do it while you can, when you can, was his life's message to me. There is no justification for coasting; we never know what's coming. An old lady in my town, Flushing, that I did some work for told me that. She had a nerve/spinal condition that basically made her physically incapable and dependent on others.

"I'm glad I didn't know," she told me, referring to herself years before and what was in store for her. Still, I tried in the poem about Rose to capture my sense of the importance of doing something <u>now</u>; my sense of the value of this extraordinary man and my felt-sense of the universe all these things exist in.

Awhile was written for the same poetry class. I had wanted to create a visual situation where someone or some *thing* has an undeniable incentive for action in a certain direction. An awareness of time echoes with the ironic title. We all have awhile. Under the ice, needing to get to air, we have a while. This was my impression of the compassionate cosmos, illustrated by a cold indifferent ice barrier. This poem is basically a finger pointing at one aspect of living a life of commitment toward a total objective.

Chapter 10 — Words, Death, The End of Journal Writing, and Personal Wisdom

A journal entry written in the guest bedroom at Grandma and Grandpa Weimer's home in Stahlstown, PA after returning from the Latrobe Hospital where Grandma was dying. This is from the period of my life I liken to the calving of an iceberg from a glacier's edge. My life as I knew it was crumbling and I watched with half-stunned detachment as it slid into the sea. Within a week of returning to Pittsburgh, I would move onto the Rose Farm, ending up in an upstairs bedroom of the farmhouse after a few weeks in a woodstove-heated cabin. It was to be a rustic, solitary existence. Half a year earlier, I'd had a cozy home in an apartment outside of Oakland in Pittsburgh with my wife and two cats. Now I drove a used Subaru station wagon that I'd paid for with a credit card in Cookeville, Tennessee, where Anne and Mom lived.

I had finished my enlistment with the Pennsylvania Army National Guard after going back to face the music following a period of philosophic "AWOL" time. I was a changed being by my 'night of hell' six months earlier. I was something other than a self-preservation coward. Something unmoving, silent and solid resided at my center where "I" used to be.. "I" was like a sweater draped over a lamp. Events happened around me, unfolding while I watched—compared to my usual way of being intimately engaged in, and identified with, the happenings in my life.

Journal entry – December 7, 1996

What people choose to write, and what they choose to allow to settle down into the past. What they choose to record in memory or in some other way and what they relax and allow to settle like fallen leaves: experiences once whole and real, now disintegrated and homogeneous and humus. Grandma has been on the tough road for two months now. One month solid in the hospital. It's something else, seeing someone die. <u>Really</u> dying. There's a settling down that happens. Somewhere, somehow, something in her has let go. I have seen a person dangling with both hands from a ladder over oblivion, perhaps for years. And when the first hand slips off the rung and the person is left hanging by one hand this is the first and last step.

For four years, Grandma has slept in a chair, not getting more than two or three hours' rest in a stretch… And now. Well, it's traumatic, dying. When all the pretenses fall, it is both tragic and simple, plain. Honest death. We eat meals, discuss births and job changes; all in the midst of physical suffering. We play the game and play through pain. But when the player is carried off the field…

I've never experienced death like this before. Her breath is death. Not bad breath. No. It's dying. "Let me die," I heard her say. When family in the room said, "What did she say?" She said it again, with effort. "Let. Me. Die." I see an essence, a soul or whatever comprises the 'jist' of a person, struggling to escape a sinking wreck.

Dying is the escape from torture. Escape to? No, I don't know about that. Escape <u>from</u>. Yes. I wish the best for her. And the family—it'll be fine. I think Grandma *should* die. Should be *let*. Allowed to let herself do what she wants and go out in her own way. If she wants to stand, well, help her stand. What harm is in it? Be careful, sure, but help her. Help make her not tortured, that's all. Dying seems to be an unpleasant thing. I think it *can* be, when people fight, and prolonging that person's heartbeat, disregarding the life that is anguishing there.

"Death with dignity." I don't believe there's any such thing. There is no hairbrush that can make a person's dying time nice, or neat, or whatever. Dying <u>is</u> traumatic. No, I think that to force someone to look polite while they're dying is foolish. I just think that if I was dying, I'd like people to be there who loved me. Who meant well, and who tried to comfort me. <u>Be there</u> with me. And for those who observe, who <u>see</u> their loved one dying in a most <u>un</u>-dignified but most <u>natural</u> way, well, it's tough. To say the least. But that's the other side of life.

I'm probably going to go back to Pittsburgh tomorrow morning. Either that, or tonight. But probably tomorrow. It's supposed to snow. Grandpa is hanging in there. He's not happy. He'll survive I think. I don't mean <u>live</u>. I don't know what will happen. But <u>survive</u>. I think he has worked and has paid his dues somewhere, somehow. It will be alright for him. As it should be. I hope my car makes it back to Pittsburgh!

Written from Suburban Avenue.

Journal entry – December 10, 1996.

Mom called at 6 a.m. Five a.m., her time. Grandma Weimer died this morning at 4 at Latrobe Hospital. I think in ICU Room 4. Should I call Grandpa?

Grandma Weimer, nee Dorothy Umbaugh. Family members had died in her home while she was a girl and she vowed not to die in her own home. When she'd be at her worst, she'd grab her purse and say, "Come on, Harry; we're going bowling." She could barely walk then. She had congestive heart failure, diabetes and something was wrong with her legs.

"Bless your heart," she used to say to us kids when we shared some idea or comment with her. You could tell she meant it, even though what we said wasn't special. Grandma always cooked for the big family gatherings. Everything centered on her and that house in Stahlstown. When I was a kid, that's what I saw. She was a woman with a big heart, and she was force. My relationship with her? I was her grandson. I'd known her my whole life.

Someone asked me how I feel now, at 15 years and counting from that time. About Grandma's dying and about all the events happening to me and around me. I'm a deaf person in a world of noise; a colorblind person in a rainbow room. I've got a permanent disability. I get pulled into identifying emotionally with things around a center that remains heavily, solidly unaffected. How I feel? How do you feel about something that happened in your past?

Written September or November 2004.

I recently went to a TAT meeting. I was sitting at a presentation with about 20 other people and the speaker wasn't captivating my attention. I didn't relate to what he was saying. Something about psychological inhibitions as barriers to profound realization or profound experiences. I can't represent, responsibly, what the talk was about. I was sitting there, however, at great cost to myself. I mean that I'd driven a long way to be there and had the taken time to attend this weekend philosophical/spiritual meeting. I folded a meeting itinerary in half and wrote a question on it and passed it over to Dave S. next to me. He took the paper, wrote something briefly, and handed it back. I laughed uproariously for a while—silently. After gleeful minutes of intermittent silent laughing, it occurred to me that the speaker might have thought I was laughing at him. Great.

I felt bad, and tried during Q&A time to explain my undisciplined laughing. On the paper I'd given to Dave, I wrote, "What is the most important thing to you?"

Dave is 23 years older than me and is a veterinarian with his own practice, several employees, ten kids from three- to twenty-something-years-old—and a family farm and several thousand chickens scattered throughout its many buildings in cages, stalls, boxes and huts.

His reply to my question was: "Chickens..???" I felt somehow that Dave has a grasp of the profound.

Andrée and I visited him and his family for a few days this summer with little Ben and four-year –old Gui after our skate park was over. I'd looked forward to it because I thought we'd get some time to talk in the days we'd be staying there. In the past, I'd have an occasional phone conversation with Dave, or a brief email exchange. I always felt afterward it would have been nice to have had a real talk. Instead of the hours of discussion I envisioned, we had maybe five solid minutes of standing-still talking one day at dusk. I accompanied him on his evening chicken rounds and we stood behind his big red barn and talked. Five minutes, then back inside to eat peach cobbler and ice cream.

Here was a guy familiar with animals and death. There's a naturalness that certain people have handling animals. Dave held a chicken during our evening rounds and examined its eye. "I put him in with that hen," he said, motioning to a chicken in an end stall. The Asian fighting chickens he raises are aggressive and the female hadn't liked the young cock in her territory. There was more fighting than Dave had expected, and the male's eye had been clawed or pecked. Dave pushed a thumb in against the eye socket and pus came out. He put cream out of a tin that held what looked like white grease on the young rooster's eye.

"You think it'll get better?" I asked.

"I thought it would," Dave answered.

"What if it doesn't?"

Dave said he'd kill it and sell it to some local Asians for a wedding or special occasion for a few bucks. Ordinarily, his fighting chickens fetch a high price. "But if he's only got one eye, he's useless."

Dave is young beyond his sixty years. His life is an orbiting constellation. I wondered at it. He put Andrée and me to work, erecting a teepee that he'd wanted to put up for some years. He'd had it up before, he said, with the help of an eccentric Indian passing through, but hadn't liked the results and was patiently making various assaults on the task—cutting long poles of the proper type of wood, etc. We got the thing up and our kids all danced around the fire we lit inside it after dark.

Back at the TAT meeting, at the lecture, I sat next to Dave for forty-five minutes—longer than I'd ever sat still near him—and we never spoke. Maybe talking's not important. Maybe it is. When Dave was leaving with a friend he'd brought from Navarre, Ohio, I walked them to his truck. He turned and asked, "How does one immerse oneself in life?"

"What are you talking about?" I guffawed. "You're doing it. That's your life!" From outside appearances, Dave had as full and involved a life as anyone I'd ever known. He said some people talked in the TAT meeting about immersion in life being bad, meaning-of-life-wise.

I said emphatically, "Tell them to go to hell!"

I've *been* on the edge of the pool, never jumping in; I've also been *in* there, swimming. For me, I somehow feel more is possible when one is "immersed" or engaged in their life. Maybe Dave does all those things because he is constantly striving for something that will fill the "God-sized hole" metaphysicians talk about. Maybe he's just diversifying because he's got a twelve-member family to support. There's a lot of truth between the maybes.

Some people hoe their corn and that action is their "philosophy." I think that's a hell of a lot more profound, wordless as it may seem, than some people's endless talking (or writing). Still, I feel a growing determination to *talk* with Dave the next time I see him. There's a lot of talking that can be done without actually talking. Dave says a lot. It's just hard to get him to put it into words.

On Beginning Writing

I started writing a daily journal when I was attending Lake City Community College (in North Florida) in 1990. I stopped writing a daily journal of another kind while living in Stuttgart, Germany with Andrée in 2000. The year before, I was enrolled in the Master of Arts program in the English department of the University of Memphis. I finished the 1999 spring semester and worked that summer as an obituary writer for *The Commercial Appeal*. I reserved a plane from Memphis to Stuttgart, via Amsterdam, on the same day as a solar eclipse. Andrée wanted me to get there in time to see it. I was at the airport in Amsterdam during the full eclipse. It was overcast and I looked out the window at the correct time. The gray rainy day darkened a bit, then slowly returned to its former grayness. In Stuttgart, everyone said, it was a wonder to behold on that clear, sunny day.

This was my first step across the ocean to my new life in this "new world." An unexpected thing happened during my ten-day visit to Andrée in August of '99. When I moved to Germany permanently the next month, this thing continued—a complete cessation of internal comment or contemplation of the events around me. This quiet lasted for several weeks. At the time, I thought it had just…gone… my interest in philosophical issues, which I had been identified with for ten years. It was a new feeling to accompany my new life in Europe. Whatever it was, happened, and there was no internal comment or consideration. I lived, finally, without thinking about living, with no back seat driver, commenting on living.

"It sure beats being me," I said, and meant it. After days or weeks of this quieter time, I quit writing a daily journal. It no longer applied to or fit my life; instead of writing a running commentary on my life, I was *living*. A few months later, once I had become more and more acclimated to my surroundings, "I" came back. The commenter, the philosophic "me" who reads books and ponders and corresponds with people about observations and life.

I think this break happened because I'd quit straining in the direction of understanding and comprehension. Moving to Germany to be with Andrée, I made a break with my ascetic practices and seeking-for-truth lifestyle. It's a big deal when you drop something carried for so long. When you take the load off, the jackass is happy. And I was.

I'd asked my family to send me video tapes of American movies. One of them was *The Matrix*. After my 'philosophic self' came back to life, I would just watch this movie. I'd seen it at least four times in the theatre while living in Memphis that last summer in the States. I really liked the look and feel of the movie but thought it was philosophically and spiritually cliché. I'd been thinking along the lines the movie touched on for some time. The movie played for a few weeks in the massive air-conditioned multiplex and I was often nearly the only one in the theater. Sometimes there were three of us—I'd notice as I looked around in the middle of the movie—widely separated.

In our Stuttgart apartment, running my TV and VCR on a transformer that stepped the 220-volt standard German electricity down to an American 110, I must have watched *The Matrix* a hundred times over the course of a year or more. Like eating mashed potatoes every night. I think it was my nostalgic contact with American English.

When I started a daily journal in Florida, my idea was to write every day, no matter what, for the sheer practice of it. I had come to the idea of taking a stab at being a writer and I *knew* that practice makes perfect. There was no way I would get worse as a writer, I thought. I was inspired by a sports writer's article I'd read during a time of doubt. Maybe I'm not good enough, maybe I can't put all my trust in doing this thing. But this guy had a positive message and I thought, *If he can do it, maybe I can.*

I didn't know *what* to write. I clearly remember sitting on the steps of a building in Lake City— church steps or courthouse steps—overlooking a broad lawn and a road, way down there, down below. I had all these feelings and no place to start, no language with which to paint them; I had no idea how to capture what I was feeling. The depth, the intensity, or, just what it feels like to feel. How do you *say* that? I remember another time, sitting with my back against a pole in the sun outside the community college, looking at my right hand, noticing the lines and marks on it and thinking how old it already looked. I was 23.

Journal writing became a familiar habit. I wrote when Kathy, who would become my first wife, moved up to Pittsburgh to attend Carnegie Mellon while I was finishing up at LCCC. I wrote in Pittsburgh when I was taking my first courses at Pitt, finding my first jobs there, my first apartment. It became an ongoing record and a vital tool in my life as a meaning-of-life-seeker. This is where it turned from a desire to become a better writer into a dissecting tool through my daily struggles to know myself, to explore my reasons for living and doing whatever I did, and for finding the meaning of life. I wanted *the Answer*. During intensely-focused years from 1992 to 1999, my daily journal was a working-out of whatever psychological hell I happened to be in the middle of each day.

One thing it accomplished, if nothing else, was an indelible practice of writing. A lot of words passed under the bridge in spiral notebook after spiral notebook. It may have been a good thing to talk to myself on paper. I know I worked things out that way. It may have saved me from going *completely* crazy. It's one thing to have insights or flashes of understanding, sadness, happiness, rage, and so on. It's another thing to put it all down on paper, and explain in words whatever's going on. This also allowed me to record events in my life that I sure don't remember anymore. Maybe one day I'll go back over them. Maybe not. Let someone else do it. There are hundreds of pages I haven't read since moving my pen across them.

I also kept a dream journal from October of '93 until 2000. The following is my last entry from the last page of recording them. It was an early beautiful morning in Stuttgart. The sun was out, I was sitting on a park bench, breathing in the fresh air, my bike on its kickstand beside me:

March 27, 2000

Dream of racing over roofs with Andrée and one other. Over one building, the wind was strong and I felt fear. Then, at the last place before the end of the run, there's a door opening in the side of like the twin towers of NY, and Andrée rushed thru without looking or listening to my warning and I saw her fall and hit the ground. What sorrow I felt. What sorrow. I stopped the other companion from going thru. I said, "If you go thru you'll be dead." I had a strong desire to hurry down to see how she was. Hope. Hoping she was somehow OK. What dread.

I awoke, with that feeling, and looked over at Andrée. She was breathing. She woke a little. I held her. She woke up & went to the hall bathroom & came back. Held her. Then went back to sleep.

Fowlerville, Michigan, 2004

In dreams, I *do* know how to fly. It's about the same every time. Like the TV show that was cancelled after President Reagan was shot by a guy named Hinkley who had the same name as the main character. *The Greatest American Hero* was about an ordinary man, a school teacher I think, who was given a magic suit by aliens. He promptly lost the instruction book they gave him, and from then on, every episode was hit-*and*-miss. Mostly miss. In dreams, I fly like he did; it's a kind of straining to stay up. Occasionally, in some dreams, I'm in good form, and can do what I like, and when it fades, I find myself having to strain more and more to retain and regain altitude after each maneuver. Eventually, that doesn't work anymore, and I'm grounded.

That last dream was one I had while at Schützen Straße 12. I was very glad when I awoke to find Andrée still alive and fine. The strong feeling of loss didn't go away easily. I remember months later when the Twin Towers and the Pentagon were attacked. Andrée and I were coming home from *Metro*, a German membership market chain where we shopped once a month. With a full load of bulk perishables in the back, and Guillaume in his car seat, we were driving home along our usual route through the outskirts of Stuttgart with the radio on a German station. Andrée and I were talking when the news came on and I was saying something and she said, "Wait! They're saying something about New York being attacked."

It didn't make any sense. We listened for a while. I thought it was a joke. I changed to the AFN (American Forces Network) radio station that was broadcasting a live feed from NBC or CNN. I knew of AFN from when I was stationed near Frankfurt 14 years earlier. We got home, hauled our groceries up to our apartment on the second floor and basically watched the TV. We had two English channels, BBC World and Eurosport. The BBC channel had a feed from an American network. It was between four and five in the afternoon for us, and I watched television until late that night. I had been watching live broadcast of the towers when the second plane flew into the second tower in New York. The plane hitting the Pentagon and news of the plane that crashed in Pennsylvania were broadcast also.

Keeping a dream journal allowed me to record dreams that were unusually emotionally-charged, or unusual, period. Watching my dreams showed me where my life energy was going. I have a certain energy and attention, and when I say, "I'm going to think this week about states of mind," it's not easy to do. I stray, of course. It's not easy to stick to <u>anything</u>, day in and out, anything at all. Dreams somehow helped me see where I was *at*.

Celibacy

Watching trends in my dreams was valuable because I had decided through periods in my first marriage and during the three years following my divorce (before moving to Europe) to remain celibate. This is a really stupid idea if you don't have a plan—because I think our bodies want to do what they want to do. The practice of celibacy was something I got from Richard Rose; it was his standard advice to a young man interested in self-inquiry or discovering the Truth. It was his only advice to me, once I asked him directly for advice. I didn't appreciate the recommendation. Though I didn't feel there would be any use in it, I tried it—because I never had before, for one thing. *Self-control*. Imagine. As far as dream journals go, I would get a kind of warning in the content of my dreams of when and where my body's attention was wandering.

I've discovered, for myself, that there's no "blocking" anything that I do (getting angry or sad; "wanting" to drink or have sex, etc.) and that it's idiotic to waste time trying to fight it with brute force. Of course, I've got to resist, but just resisting keeps that ol' pressure inside, building up, where it pushes on *some other* weak place in the wall. The best thing, I've found, is <u>sublimation</u>. This applies to any task, at any time in my life. When I have a task or a goal in mind; an endeavor to engage in— this thing is where I want my attention, energies and focus. For me, this made the practice of celibacy a practical reality. Otherwise, it can be a tortuous thing. To block all the usual energy outlets and to have nothing to work on with the rescued energy is a formula for insanity, I think, because I'm talking about strict celibacy—no reveries and no solo sex. I think the problems encountered by blocking or fighting or calling-the-self-evil regarding personal restraint are not worth having; it's yet another way of dissipating "energy." A job to do, and all of one's available energy salvaged and applied to this end—yes. Richard Rose harped on that and I found the practicality of such a formula for my own life. I assume it will hold true for others, too.

Like wanting to lose weight and keeping mounds of chocolate in the cupboards and ice cream in the freezer; I can hold out for a week or three—but when the first weakness comes, my resolve dissolves—it always does—and I find myself eating everything in sight. "I" don't do this. It happens. That's an example; I'm not an eater; I've got my own dragons. The desires are a dragon that can be turned to another purpose but not ignored, blocked or fought. A thing blocked or fought becomes bigger than the world, always in proportion to the attention and time spent focusing on it, fighting it.

If I have any wisdom, it's in the small realizations that I've had.

I can't block or stop a feeling or desire. Of course I can; I should say: I won't make the mistake anymore of trying to block or fight it—this makes it stronger. Ultimately, it's fighting fire with fire and all you end up with is fire. "Fighting it" takes up all my time and energy—and I still get nowhere. I *can* focus on something that *is* what I want to do, like exercising if I'm tempted by eating, or studying philosophy if I'm inclined to indulge in letting my mind wander without a clear focus. Blocking a desire or feeling takes over the show—I become a blocker, and see only what I'm straining to block. My attention illuminates, like a flashlight, whatever I'm shining it on—*what I don't look at isn't seen or noticed*. Why not focus on something preferable? In focusing on a "chosen" object, the other stuff… isn't.

When I quit smoking, I changed my whole life pattern. Became vegetarian, quit watching TV, started practicing martial arts, quit going to bars—everything. That did the trick. With all the parts of my new life in place, I acted the part I built the set for. Santanelli, the stage name for a successful 19th Century stage hypnotist, referred to this with the word suggestion. *The Law of Suggestion* is the title of his book (now reprinted by TAT Foundation Press).

> "Suggestion means anything that arouses an action. This is the law: Surround a man with every suggestion or attribute of sleep and he will be asleep; surround him with every suggestion of virtue and he cannot help being pure, and no credit is due him...."

I don't write a daily journal anymore. I don't keep a dream journal, either. I think they were good. I kept a daily log last summer of our five-week return to France, however, as a way of keeping this connection to the culture of their mother alive and real in the minds and memories of our sons. I'd planned to type it out and have it for the kids when they forgot visiting. I recommend keeping a daily journal and also a dream journal to anyone interested in understanding themselves. I write now, of course, but it's almost only correspondence with others via email. I'd like to write my observations on my daily life. Most of what I do daily is forgotten, until something triggers the memory. I don't feel like I'm forgetting my life, but ask me what I did yesterday at 2 p.m. Are you this way, too?

I wrote those words in 2004. I created a writing blog (web-log) in 2010 where I post now mostly irregularly; it was part of my making a push to write this memoir-in-a-bottle-to-the-future book. Check them out when you read this and maybe I'll have done more recent things there, connecting this autobiography to a real-time one, online.

oneandonlyobserver.wordpress.com

and oneandonlyobserver.blogspot.com.

Same site, times two. I like the versatility of the wordpress site and the look of the blogspot one.

Chapter 11 — Say one thing

Ben (6) and me, June 30, 2010, at Fontaine de Vaucluse, Provence, France, walking to the source of the spring-fed river la Sorgue.

In this Frankenstein's monster you cradle, is:

If I had to say only one more thing

I would stand or sit with you, outside, where the wind blows a smell of leaves, cut grass, wood smoke or flowers. We'd lean against a fence, sit near a campfire on some logs or stand together by a stream. We'd pause from talking about jobs and families. Just standing, just sitting, I would breathe and look at the water or, out over the trees.

I would say nothing to convey to you the most important thing. I would spend long moments with you, as long as it takes, and then, raise my hand, looking at you briefly. "So long."

A lot of what can be said in a book like this is like talking at a gathering. Some things are really simple, though. The simplest things are silent.

None of my life has left me. The times with you. *Everything* is there—all the times in my life are there, and always will be until I go. They're unimportant, but good, companions. They'll stay until I leave, and then go, too.

Chapter 12 — Back to the Woods and Beyond—An Effort, Some Years Ago, to Tell my Tale.

Putting together this collage: I'm sitting on the floor cross-legged, my photos, journals and souvenirs scattered around me. I'm showing these things to you. That's all. Don't sweat it. If you want a strict chronological tale, make your own portrait. I'll read it, I promise..

From the *Hauptbahnhof* underground station beneath the Königstraße in Stuttgart, I'd board the S-4 and ride forty minutes to Benningen, one stop before Marbach. This town was particularly fascinating to me. If I went down the set of concrete stairs from the train platform and passed through a tunnel under the tracks and then, after a small park, walked a few minutes more, I'd find myself confronting an oddly-cobbled patch of ground roughly twenty feet wide and seventy feet long. This is the understructure of a section of Roman highway. While renovating an adjacent office building, the German contractors found these odd stones and someone was eventually called in who recognized their significance and purpose. So, they made it into a little outdoor museum park-like place, with an information plaque. Putting myself on that road, two millennia ago, always struck me. I went over and stepped from large round stone to stone. The juxtaposition with this orderly setting I saw around me, which, itself, felt foreign, aged and historied. *This* road was old, and used, and storied—from the millennium before.

On the train, on my way to work in this village, the countryside would flow by and I'd find myself accompanied by fewer and fewer people. I liked this journey to my job. I worked for Richard Lampert until Andrée and I moved to France in October 2001. I never thought of writing a book of *this* sort, but I did think that it would be valuable, to me, to write down what I'd gone through back in '96—now that a few years had passed.

Riding my bike down from our apartment at Schützen Straße 11 was a rush; I'd go entirely downhill, across a bridge spanning a city ring roadway, into the edge of the Schloßgarten (castle park), over another footbridge, across a park to the Königstraße (king street), along this street to a bike rack near the steps going underground to the main train station. The station was considerably more than 100 feet below the surface. Once in the station, I'd walk to a stand and buy my lunch snacks and a morning coffee. I'd drink the coffee and read until my train came, then board and sit among a lot of commuters. This smooth-riding train would glide along underground for five minutes before emerging into open air. I remember each of its stops. Different crowds got on and off at the same stops. Students, professionals, laborers, me.

After Feuerbach, the first underground station after the *Hauptbahnhof*, I'd settle down and take out a small notepad and start writing. I always intended to write a more complete account about my experiences back in the spring of '96, but the following is what I came up with. It'll do. I'm becoming more *laissez-faire* about these things. Sometimes a thing is what it is—whether or not it was "meant to be that way."

The following was written on that small yellow notepad on the S-Bahn during a succession of mornings in 2001.

In April and May of '96 I had been in a period of mounting extremes. Extreme highs and lows. I had been pushing more and more into trying to figure myself out. It was hell and a lot of other things. Looking back, it seems like I was crazy. I certainly was obsessed; the more hell or trouble I got, the more intensely I pushed into trying to figure it out.

Every day was turbulent soil. I had revelations into my own nature every day. Two or three significant revelations. And every day I was suffering like hell through interpersonal interactions with others (co-workers, people on the street). And, simultaneously, this extreme inward push to <u>know</u>. And the internal machinations of a mind furiously working at a mountain of sand with a <u>sieve</u>.

I was walking in rapture at the profound. I was walking, also, barefoot through the glass shards and burning coals of my reactions to others and myself. I was like a beehive in an earthquake. I went AWOL from the Pennsylvania National Guard during this time—for several months. I didn't want to waste *their* money or *my* time... anymore. Requesting a meeting with my CO (commanding officer, a captain), I sat in front of his desk and told him this. He said they couldn't let me quit before my latest enlistment ended because I had a good record. So I quit going to monthly drill. I sent back the paychecks that would come in the mail. I moved and provided no forwarding address. That should do it.

In Pittsburgh one day, I got off the bus at a stop well before the one for work and called in to say I'd not be in. I remember walking off the job, another time, while working in a "literature warehouse" for Fisher Scientific. I walked the streets in a daze. Mind like a dog panting in fatigue at having chased a deer all night but still pushing on. I remember standing at Panther Hollow Pond. It was cold and rainy. There was a kind of metal shelter at one end of the pond. I stood under that thing and leaned my head on the cold metal.

I remember this as a tension-filled period. I was married. I was devoted to this intensely personal obsession and also to my wife (and our marriage to each other). We were friends, I believed. Looking back, I think she gradually became independent. I always encouraged her to explore the world and be herself. She was raised in a household with an overbearing father and a balancing kind and gentle mother. I was supportive and encouraged Katherine to become attuned to her own values and interests. Towards the end of April, she said, "Why don't you take a week off and go to the farm?"

I was so touched. It hadn't occurred to me because she didn't like the farm at all. My unwavering commitment to TAT meetings and events really bothered her—I think because of how she thought her parents looked at it. Imagine a drowning person getting unexpected help. I felt gratitude and love for her. So I had a day or two before I went. This, I thought, is it. I'm going to <u>GET</u>. I didn't have an image of what, but I had a very strong feeling that now, I would have time. I wouldn't have to focus on driving or punching time clocks at work. Doing this extreme inquiry while working and living daily life had seemingly brought me to the brink of my sanity. Maybe it was exactly as it should have been. Nothing would be on my plate but this one thing, I thought. For a solid week I could stare at it. Alright.

I had Katherine drop me off at the farm so she could use the car while I was gone. I had a tent, rain cover, canned food, baby food in jars, some potatoes, an axe, a couple of books and a "dream journal" and regular daily journal. I slept under the Chautauqua building (a large A-frame wooden structure) roof the first night. The next morning I found a good place to camp about 150 feet behind it. I put up my tent, dug a drainage ditch, put a tarp overhead. I got down to mental work. By 'mental work' I mean pushing inside. *Who, or what, am I? Where do I exist?* Thoughts would arise and I'd demand, *Where does that come from?* I'd consider recent questions about my personality or problems I'd had with others and try to puzzle out what was behind them. By the time I came out to the woods this time, however, I'd basically become reduced to a concentrated super-powerful question mark: **?** That first night camping, it stormed. Bad. The wind in the trees sounded like tornados. I had been having a gradual, mounting fear of tornados, and dreams of them at regular intervals. Very realistic. Different scenes where I'd get pulled up into one. Sucked into one. Terror.

That first night of camping was bad. Raining like hell, lightening, wind. Twice, I quickly shoved on my Army rain boots, threw on raincoat and hat over sleeping shorts and t-shirt and ran down the steep hillside, scrambling, seeking shelter from what I thought was certain death by tornado. The second time, while standing down there, getting rained on and in total dark except for lightening flashes, I decided to go back up to the tent earlier than my fear wanted.

I got in the tent and thought that tornado death was bad, sure, but that I'd face it when it came, not before. I couldn't keep living in fear. So I laid back and slept. Resigned, I sunk into the stuff that fear comes up out of. I kept a dream journal. I had another tornado dream that night—worse than ever.

What I do know is that I woke up into another world.

Absolutely still, this place. The trees moved in the wind. The rain continued. Little birds moved and flew around. The green of spring was starting to pop up. And nothing moved at all. It was utterly still. Nothing moved at all. Not one atom. I still ate, took walks and all the things like that, but nothing moved inside of me, either. Nothing. I thought that I had broken my brain. *Now you did it.* The part of us that we never know is *only* a part was gone.

That emotional feedback-projection apparatus was shut off. The television screen was dark. Dead. Nothing. But there was me. I was still here. Watching. One day passed. A second came and was half way through. I stood, looking at a rain filled hole behind the Chautauqua building. *What is this?* I asked myself silently. Enlightenment, was the immediate, silent reply. NO! No. I reacted to this answer. No. It's not that. It can't be. I don't know it all. No. This isn't it. But it was—something.

276

The third day came and I was sitting on a plastic bucket on a concrete platform built by D.D. behind the Chautauqua barn overlooking a ravine. I saw some geese fly overhead. Then a low, rumbling sound as three C-130 Army cargo planes flew overhead slow and low, low. Somehow, the birds or the airplanes combined with my state at the time (already easing away from that place) snapped me out of it. Kick-started the heart of that part that we never know is only a part.

I had reactions from then on. Slowly, but increasing to my normal level of introspection, reaction, etc. The next night I saw a light on in the farmhouse during a walk in the woods. It was still raining. I was eager to talk to Rose. Later, his wife told me that he'd suddenly wanted to go out to the farm to spend the night. But then, she said he did that frequently. Still... Maybe he sensed something. Maybe.

I prepared to come out of the woods on Friday. It had stopped raining that morning. As the day of sun and wind continued, I decided to break camp, as my things were dry for the first time in days. I picked up my things. Ate by the fire. Slept under the Chautauqua building roof that night. Woke up in the middle of a storm with an awful neck ache. I was lying on some bus seats put together, in my sleeping bag. My neck was bent to the side painfully. The wind and thunder, lightning and rain were severe.

I saw a black girl's face in the bus seat. In the darkness it was like a photo negative held up to light, but I knew she was black. I wasn't scared of her. I sensed she wasn't mean. Later, I had a hell of a dream. I "woke up" to find a sniveling, rabid presence behind me. I turned around and shoved this creature away, confronting it. *What are you doing?* I asked. *What's going on?* I had no fear. Only confronting and curiosity. I wanted to know what the hell was going on. It was light out in the dream. The thing ran from the Chautauqua building along the grass lane to the farmhouse. I ran after it. As I neared, the muttering, snarling, obviously very deranged thing broke into pieces while running and it crumbled to the ground to be absorbed. A running form suddenly breaking into cubes that crumbled to the ground and dissolved into the soil.

I woke up, this time into the "real" night. Went back to sleep. In the morning, I came out of the woods. Left my things in the shelter of the Chautauqua bldg. Casari was in the field. He was trying to get a tractor unstuck from the muddy ground. I had noticed the tractor sitting there in the field the whole time it was raining. We worked to get the tractor out. He was hesitant. Didn't think it could be done, he said. I knew it could. Maybe he just didn't want to work that hard. I don't know. We got it out after some struggling.

He offered to let me stay in his cabin until the next morning, when my wife Katherine would come down to the farm to get me. We sat at his table in the cabin and talked. I told him about those 2 1/2 days and read some of what I had written in journals. As the evening approached, still in daylight, while we talked, I felt mounting fear/terror. That usual feeling people have of the dark at certain moments that causes them to race for a lighted room, heart pounding. Well, it started and got worse.

We turned off the lights after dark and I was on a cot in front of the woodstove in my sleeping bag. This was my night of hell. I tried every possible way to escape what was happening. Every possible mental dodge. I was met, before I even got there, by a force that was, to use a very apt phrase from Rose, strategically superior. And I knew it. I knew I was in deep water that was rising and not stopping.

There were some things dropping onto my pillow. Wasps, I thought. Mike had a problem in the spring with the wasps coming out of the woodwork. Wasps or yellow jackets. I was trying not to get stung. In the dark. A thing would hit my pillow and I'd freeze and then move very fast to avoid being stung, brushing away with my hand. I used my flashlight, looking. Never saw one wasp. Things fell on me two or three times. And then there was the creaking wood of the cabin. Every mental "dodge" I tried would come with a loud crack from the wood of the cabin, from all directions. The timing was beyond coincidence. The fact that this wasn't in my imagination was being shoved in my face. I didn't need to be convinced of the seriousness of this time.

I tried to write it all off as an active imagination, but it wouldn't go. Between these noises, I had to pee like hell. I went outside, terrified—and I got locked out! I swear I did whatever I was supposed to do with the knob, double-checking to make sure I could get back in, but when I came back, it was locked. I didn't want to wake Mike, but I couldn't stay outside all night barefoot in shorts and t-shirt!

I got back in, apologizing. The pursuit went on. It wasn't stopping. And I, around midnight, tried the last dodge. I leaned on Mike's supportive words from our conversation earlier about entities. I leaned on Rose's words and leaned on Casari's. Then he started to moan, around the corner, in his bed. I waited for some time. Every mental dodge or squirm from the terror that was pursuing me resulted in, not a creek from the cabin, but a moan. He started mumbling. "Help me." I heard. *Jesus.* So I said, "Hey Mike, are you alright? Can you wake up?" He said, "No. Help me."

It was surreal. I saw a correspondence between my mental running acrobatics and another person's distress. So that was when I decided to stop and turn. It was the first "decision" I made that night. Maybe I needed to go through the hell so that I would be capable of making such a decision. I didn't know what was killing me. It was bad enough that I was going down; I didn't want to drag another person with me. So I gave up running and faced annihilation. This was when something became SOLID. All the uncertainty scrambling was gone, as if it had never been—as anything is 'gone' that has been completely incinerated. What remained was whole, untouchable and total.

That was at midnight. I got up. Went outside to pee again without fear. I wrote an entry in my journal by candlelight that I had "found my sword and shield." Then the hell began again.

For the rest of the night, I had to die to myself again and again. Time and again, I'd reach that stable solid place, <u>honestly</u>, and then, "me" would grow back like a weed. I'd start thinking, "Hey, I'm alright." Then the terror would come and I'd run, and be run out until the solid was all that was left. Again and again. After a while, I didn't "forget" anymore. I couldn't. That "I" was gone. I just was. It was morning, the sun was just creating a glow in the east and I dressed, walked outside down the dirt road and walked to stand in a cornfield, feeling the warming sun.

Chapter 13 — Cosmic Cooking

Back in Pittsburgh, after my "night of hell," the strangest things happened—to someone else, although I watched them with a kind of surprised wonder, if you can feel surprise and wonder while being detached. Surprising and unexpected. I was a person with stuff appearing in front of my eyes and no idea where it all came from. Coming back from my dawn walk, I returned to Casari's cabin, rolled up my sleeping bag and packed my stuff into my duffel bag. I looked forward to being at the Roses in McMechen. We were meeting there for lunch and Katherine was going to pick me up.

A week after I was back in Pittsburgh, I was eating at the diner where a group of us used to go to after SKS meetings to talk about philosophy and how the meetings went—back when N.G. and B.G. were coming up each week from Benwood, West Virginia to present topics and run things. This diner wasn't far from where Katherine and I lived on Maripoe Street. I was eating a good brunch with coffee. All good-tasting, and I was contented—finally. I had the impulse to thank the cook, to give him some kind of compliment on the food. I briefly considered knocking on the kitchen door, explaining myself—ah, the hell with it, I thought. Then the cook comes out the side door and I tell him the food was really good.

I was on campus putting up posters for the upcoming SKS meeting (we put up topic-specific posters each week). I'd come back from my week in the woods and had attended a meeting or two. I volunteered to put up some of their posters, since I knew the poster route well—I'd put up thousands of the things in my time attending and then running the group. I thought about a guy on the rowing crew who attended the philosophy club and thought it would be good to run into him. I took the elevator in the engineering building up to the 10th floor to put up a poster or two across from the computer lab and there he was. We talked. That kind of thing happened a lot right after my week in West Virginia. I think I was tuned into a different frequency. My voice was lower. I realized it when I listened to the answering machine recording I'd made before—and heard with astonishment a version of me who'd apparently inhaled helium before recording his message on the machine.

Later, after separating from Katherine, I'd be skating in Pittsburgh at night, or waiting for the trolley at a stop, or standing in the parking lot outside the building where a weekly hypnosis research meeting took place, or I'd be anywhere I go, and night lights would go out. Those lights way up there on tall poles, or the fluorescents in entryways to buildings. I don't know if they were related to me. I could have just noticed what was always going on. I sure noticed them, then forgot, then noticed them again when it happened again.

I saw how I influenced people's states of mind. I'm sure this happens all the time, between all of us. But I really noticed how people in pivotal states of mind would be susceptible to changing their minds or making decisions based on something I'd say in an offhand way about their situation. So I tried to quit doing that. I consciously did not say things or do things that I felt would influence the games going on in front of me. I willed myself to be neutral. Why, I don't know, except that maybe I felt that I didn't have the right to affect someone's life. I'd say things, without intending anything, that people would look at me funny about. Later, one guy who I'd met for the first time, said that he couldn't believe I was saying what I was, because I was saying the same things he had in his head.

He thought there was some kind of game going on. I think I just sensed where people were at, mentally, and could talk on that channel. Or maybe I'd coincidentally meet people who were on a channel I could talk on. There were a lot of coincidences, in the immediate aftermath of my life coming apart.

I described it once to B. G. in Pittsburgh on a meeting night, walking to his car in the parking lot, by saying that 'reality became plastic.' No longer the concrete, solid, unmoving thing it is for people; I saw reality was malleable, and seemingly responsive to my thoughts and mental state. Reality *moved*, when I thought. I'd just crossed the cusp of a major perspective change. B.G.'s battery was dead and we push-started his car.

Greater things happened, such as events in my world around me, and I didn't feel any causal connection to them; it was as though I found myself in a place where all this stuff just happened, coming from out of my field of sight—I was a 10-month-old, surprised at everything that plopped down in front of me. My wife divorced me. I rejoined my National Guard unit after several months of AWOL, expecting to be disciplined, and nothing happened.

In the guard, I did the rest of my time, did my last summer camp, and got an honorable discharge. I went back willing to submit to whatever process would happen. I talked to the inspector general about my situation. My case was dropped, apparently. My grandmother died and I was there as she was making her exit during the last day or two. My grandfather was calm around me, but when I was gone, he'd weep over the loss of his wife—a kind of release, I think, after years of living with worries about Grandma's health problems. My mom was hospitalized when I was there, and I went in an ambulance with her to Nashville where she was operated on. I was in the room with her, watching a drama of pain and a person calling out for help.

I moved to the Rose farm in West Virginia and had a couple of weeks I'll never forget the feeling of —alone in a cabin in the pristine, still, cold winter. Then, I moved down to the farmhouse to keep an eye on the place. I found myself, on a couple of occasions, staying with Mr. Rose to give his wife some much-needed rest from her constant vigilance, either at their house in McMechen, or when I'd drive with him out to the farmhouse where I was staying. Out there, we'd eat dinner and talk and I'd sleep on a cot in the same room to be able to wake up if he awoke in the night—to make sure that he wandered into the right small room, for example. One thing after another changed in my life-situation. I was living in a stranger's play with no familiar cues. After I had the flat time in the woods and my night of hell, I found myself watching my life like it was an avalanche in motion. Everything fell apart and I was just a mildly stunned, numb observer in the middle of the tumbling debris.

The following are "Notes to self" from Memphis the year before leaving the U.S. to be with Andrée in Stuttgart. I'd had my head disassembled in '96, taken a three-month leave of absence from the world in the woods on Rose's farm in '97 to figure out what I was going to do in my life, and was attending grad school at the University of Memphis and working at *The Commercial Appeal* as an obit writer. Here are a few bits from *that* time in my eye-of-the-storm life.

Journal entries

10/1/98

One year ago, on this date, I came out of the woods following isolation. Well. This last week or so there has been incessant Frank Sinatra playing in my head. Possession? Low brain chemical-induced looping? Road sign arrow-pointing? Don't know.

Words: "I've got you, under my skin. So. I'd sacrifice anything, come what might, for the sake of holding you near in spite of a warning voice that comes in the night and repeats, how it yells in my ear—don't you know you fool, you never can win? Wake up to reality. Use your mentality. Each time I do just the thought of you makes me give up before I begin, because I've got you under my skin. I've got you, under my skin.

"I tell myself this affair never will go so well. So deep in my heart that you're really a part of me. I've got you under my skin. I've told myself not to give in. That this affair never will go so well..." *etc., and so on. Boy. It's just jammin' in my head.*

2/23/99

The potential to do something great exists. For some, it is a continually-felt presence. A great thing is... what? Something that outlives the doer? Like a book or a building? A contribution to science or medicine? Is a great thing, by definition, something that has more immortality than something else? Longer-lasting?

7/6/99

I'll be damned. Karl Wolff's gone. As of yesterday. Izzy's alone now. He went quick. Leukemia. At North Florida Regional Hospital in Gainesville. Shock at first. Then the non-feeling time. Didn't feel much, deep-wise, except in bits and pieces.

My brother Pat visited Karl at the hospital. Karl and Izzy had let me live in a trailer and in a small house on their property for six months before I left Florida for Pittsburgh. They were good friends to Pat; they really took him in. He had worked for them before joining the Air Force. Pat told me he was at Karl's hospital bed and Karl just looked up once during a pause in their conversation and said," I'm not going to beat this one, am I?" By this time, Pat was out of the service and trained as a Baptist pastor. He said he told Karl some things about letting Jesus take charge.

Karl died within days. He was a great big man with giant hands. A gentle giant with a kind smile. When Andrée visited me in the States for the first time, I was living in Lake City and Karl let her drive his Cadillac; it was her first time driving a car of any kind and was a highlight of her visit. To be in America, and to drive a classic American car.

7/6/99 -continued

The guy last Friday who was bleeding badly from the nose in the 4th floor bathroom at work is in the hospital still (today's Wed.). He'd been bleeding starting Thursday night, the 1st of July. I noticed blood, dried, on the floor of the far stall of the restroom that day. Then I moved to a different stall because I was kind of disgusted. There was a lot of it, very dark, but kind of poorly wiped. I was doing my business in the first stall and a guy got in the next stall for a while, made some toilet paper noise and got out. When I came out I saw a guy kind of embarrassed, leaning over the sink.

Skinny older guy. Shaking. I thought his nerves were going because he couldn't control the bleeding. He had his head right over the sink, with water running. He had used a copious amount of paper towel, overflowing the waste slot with bloody wet towels. I asked him if he had a bloody nose. I had him put his head back and put pressure on the nose. Told him to support himself on the wall. Basically, I was <u>there</u> for him. Not syrupy, but decently. Supportive and <u>there</u>.

I let him be after a while because I sensed he'd be more comfortable, he'd calm down more if I left. I thought high blood pressure (with nerves) would keep it going. I asked him some questions (taking blood thinner?, etc.) and told him about my own extreme nose bleeds as a kid. Anyhow, I urged him to have someone drive him to a doctor's. Then hoped for the best and left. I left the bathroom for a while (5 minutes), going my way, and it struck me that he might be in some real trouble. I went back and stayed with him a while longer.

It turns out he made it to the hospital. As of today, news is, the doctors think they stopped the bleeding. A guy in the bathroom talking to another about it (same bathroom) today. I said I was sorry to butt in, but I'd overheard and wanted to know how he was. Only one fellow was left in bathroom. Kind of looked like the guy from Friday. Maybe his brother. He thanked me for asking. Turned out it was his brain bleeding through his nose somehow.

Christ. Mortality is a wide-eyed baby, for sure. Crying its head off without a sound and no one to comfort it.

Fowlerville, Michigan, 2004, working at Precise Finishing Systems in Howell, Michigan.

Today, Jim, a guy who'd had a heart attack last year while under tremendous stress during a busy time at work, told me I was well on my way to my own, similar, meeting with mortality. Except I probably wouldn't be as lucky as he was, he said (he'd had a blocked artery repaired by a stint and is back to normal now, though calmer-seeming). He said he thought I would probably have a stroke and wind up in a wheelchair with people having to take care of me. Maybe he's right. Maybe "it takes one to know one" applies here. It sure got me thinking. High stress, bad diet, little sleep, not enough good exercise, regular alcohol consumption. A formula for success, I have to admit.

Yesterday, Jim walked by while I was hurrying to package up two metal tanks on pallets before the UPS truck came. A second later, I slipped cutting some cardboard and stuck my razor knife into my right thigh, just above the knee. I felt the bite and swore. I kept working on the cardboard packaging. My leg felt warm, my pants got wet with blood and I felt it running down my leg into my sock. I reluctantly stopped to go to the break room. I opened the first aid cabinet. I used a lot of paper towels and some water from the cooler to wipe my leg and to soak up the blood. I wrapped some cotton gauze around my leg and taped it all securely. I went back out, finished the UPS stuff, and worked on other shipping projects until the end of the work day. The box cutter penetrated to a quarter- or half-an-inch. Maybe Jim's right.

Chapter 14 — Loose Ends

Fowlerville, Michigan, 2004

You find that everything is within you—and you are nothing.

I wrote that on a block of two-by-four while sitting in my '93 Ford Explorer last year in the parking lot at work while eating my lunch or during a break. I was listening to a Rose lecture on cassette tape and thought that with a little improvement I could take something he had said and use it to describe something I'd been trying to say for a long time. In that lecture, Rose said, "In the final experience of Enlightenment, you find that everything is within you—and nothing is within you." He went on to say there always has to be both sides of the coin for the picture to be complete. I like my version: You find that everything is within you—and you are nothing. Nothing might be within me. But it feels more like I <u>am</u> nothing. And everything. There's not a half-step away from it.

When I lived on the Rose farm in the West Virginia western panhandle after leaving Pittsburgh and my then ex-wife, I took on some assorted projects as farmhand. Re-roofing a garage and a small cabin, fixing fences, brush-cutting fields and the lawn, pruning trees and putting landscape timbers around a gravel parking area between the farmhouse and a cement block garage.

The following account might not turn out like you'd expect.

I'd picked up a load of pressure-treated logs after work, land surveying in Ohio. I pulled into the newly-graveled parking area with the back of my Subaru station wagon loaded down and the hatch tied securely over the wood. When I arrived at the secluded farm, I saw a pack of wild dogs I'd been "hunting" for the past few weeks nosing around behind the farmhouse. Spookie, Nermal and Violet, the three farm cats, were up in the giant Sycamore near the old covered well and in the loft of a small storage barn where the tractor was parked. I said to the dogs, "Stay right here," and went to the back door, quickly through the house, up the steps two at a time to my room. I grabbed my 16-gauge shotgun and filled my pockets with shells, and went back down the steps two at a time.

On the back porch, I loaded four or five shells. I spotted one of the dogs down by the grape arbors, sniffing in the tall grass behind an outbuilding—probably searching for the cats. I let go one shot at it. The grass parted as two of the dogs headed off to the west. I circled the house, looking for the others. Beyond my car, on the narrow dirt road cutting through the farm, I could see dogs running somewhat lazily a couple hundred yards away, crossing into a field on the left. I'd been noticing these dogs recently. They were domestic, or mixed breeds. Four or five of them of various sizes and shapes. As I'd come home from work after five, I'd sometimes catch them around the place. I'd see where they had dug around buildings. The cats became scarce and I'd hear dogs barking in the night while I lay in bed before sleeping. My territorial nature was aroused. I'd been getting increasingly unhappy with them, deciding I'd have to "take care of them," next I saw them.

I jogged down the road after the dogs, then walked. I let some distance stay between us and cut through a grass-covered field that had been planted in corn the fall before. The grass was tall. The dogs ahead of me were going diagonally across the field toward a wedge-shaped tree-filled ravine dividing the field in half. The dogs disappeared at the edge, going down the slope. I hurried; I didn't want to let them get away. As I drew near, I could hear them vocalizing to each other and running through the brush. The trees grew in a deep, steep-sided channel cutting into the surrounding flat land like a spur. I could see the tops of trees level with me. As I edged down the side, I stood in the tall grass. It was a perfect vantage point. The dogs, amazingly, were heading back my way. *Good.* I think it was their pattern to run away and circle back. They didn't notice me. There—two of them in the open. I took aim at a dark fellow about a hundred feet away and squeezed the trigger. Birdshot whizzed through the tall grass. The dog yelped. I quickly levered a new shell into the chamber of my father's bolt-action shotgun. *Ka-bam.* I shot the second dog, somewhere in the grass-covered slope; I heard some earnest-sounding scrambling down the slope, away from me this time.

I waited a while, listening, and then gave them one last parting reason to be unhappy, before walking back across the field to the road, going the hundred yards or so to the first outbuildings of the farm. I crunched over the large-stoned gravel parking area to my car, and leaned the shotgun against the side door. I was bent to untie the rope holding the hatch down when a snarling, rabid-seeming dog growled and barked ferociously, inches away from my face—inside the car!

I flinched—woah. My first thought on seeing the dog inside, standing on top of the timbers was to hope he didn't leave any fleas in my car or pee in there. The next thought was how I'd get the dog out so I could shoot him. I looked around for a stick, then put the shotgun on the roof and opened the rear passenger-side door, standing behind it, preparing to swing—like a hitter at bat. Seconds passed. Then more. I looked inside. The multi-colored, middle-sized mutt with a snarling and growling contenance still stood on top of the landscape timbers.

"Come on out," I yelled, pounding on the roof. The dog barked loudly, standing its ground. I cut the rope holding the rear hatch down with my pocket knife and opened the back fully. I leaned the stick against the car and got my shotgun, standing ready. Now there were two routes open to the dog. "Get out of there!" I growled at the dog, and thumped on the glass near the back of the station wagon. *No!* was the snarled reply.

I had a standoff on my hands. I didn't want to screw up my car shooting it. The dog had steamed up and splattered the side windows with saliva and that was enough mess for me. I had considered shooting the dog in the car, calculating the best angle, but I didn't want blood, excrement and urine added to my afternoon's work. My thoughts turned toward allowing the dog to live. I don't know why I thought that. Until then, I'd operated solely under the assumption that this dog was dead. Surprising myself, I stood in the lengthening shadows, in the quiet, with cool air and my car and the dog and me. I wanted to get some of the timbers down along the parking area before the day was done. *Fine*, I thought, looking at the dog, *I won't kill you.* "Go on," I said. I opened the driver's side rear door and backed away a few steps. I stood with the shotgun on my shoulder. The dog was quiet. "Go on," I repeated. The dog slowly moved to stand on the timbers at the very back of the car, hesitated, and jumped down, running some paces away down the road, east, the opposite direction of its pack. The dog stopped and looked back at me. "Get out of here!" I yelled. The dog growled and I raised the shotgun, sighting in, squeezing the trigger. Then I lowered it, remembering... The dog ran away again as I took a few quick steps in its direction. I raised the gun and shot—aiming to its right, into heavy overgrowth on the edge of the road. The dog bark-growled at me while still running.

I never saw those dogs again, though I did occasionally hear distant barking. I think we'd come to an understanding. I don't know how that dog squeezed into my car—the gap was less than six inches—or even why, exactly. Maybe it seemed like the perfect place to be safe. Why didn't it run away? I took this episode at the time as a kind of karmic lesson. For me, and the dog, perhaps, who would emerge as a self-centered human being in *its* next lifetime. Maybe *this* was our connection... Maybe we'll switch places next time. I wonder. I wonder what I would have done, as that dog. Maybe gotten myself killed. Maybe the same thing; after all, we're faithfully saying the lines written in our script.

Chapter 15 — Picking Up the Hammer… Again

Flushing, Ohio, 2010

It's been more than a few weeks since my last confession, father reader. It's been five years almost to the week, in fact, since I last wrote. Five years ago, I wrote, in another seat:

> There are two chapters to my life that I think are worth taking the time to record—the time in France and Germany—focusing on adapting to two societies and learning the languages and my adventures in these two places. There is also a completely different story line, that of Andrée and my journey into entrepreneurship through France and then to Fowlerville. This was the beginning of our unified destiny. The skate park dream. These two story lines can easily be the subject of two separate books. They are already written, in my mind and soul. Still, it's worthwhile to do the best I can to sketch these times in this work—for the sake of that remarkable period of time.

Yes. But what a world you can live in, in five years. More than a few noteworthy chapters have piled up on themselves since I last opened these blank pages of the book-in-progress-writing-itself. We're all a book writing itself in invisible ink. This book is like taking a time-lapse—and sometimes real-time—photo of growing grass. Dropping another handful of photos on the floor and pushing them around, sorting, choosing... You're getting choice snapshots of time; exploding stars in the night sky: things have progressed much *farther*—for that star—since the events we're focused on. Still.

Through circumstances all my own and those unique to me—reactions to events, 'choices' I have made—I have worked going on six years as a self-employed handyman-painter-one-man-band, painting houses inside and out, hanging drywall, finishing bathrooms, installing fixtures & fans, wiring switches, replacing toilets, soldering & plumbing, roofing houses, patching leaks, insulating and more than I want to list here. I am proud. I am acting out my pattern and potential, my predilection—hence my quotation marks around the word "choice." I feel competent and battle-tested. Doing this work with no overseeing boss and no economic safety net has resulted in self-confidence and a feeling of maturity. I am able to *do* things. I have made my way. Knowing that gives me a warm glow. I've had more luck than I can take any credit for; I can only take credit for trying my best, and even then, I'm not entirely sure who is the owner of what effort...

It's one thing to be a walking solid emptiness; that's there. It's another thing to be doing something, anything in this place. "Doing something" feels good. Giving this horse something to pull, something to do, feels good. Maybe grazing in the fields will feel good, too. After a horse wins a lot of races, it still lives! Someone told me that it seemed like my contracting competence is more important to me than Ultimate Truth. It is. What *else* am I going to do? Maybe I should try staring at my navel. Although it's what it feels like I'm doing all the time.

This month, on this day, I am filling this blank space with words in celebration of the beginning of the end of that line of work for me—contracting—at least, in my mind. I hope to shift to writing. I hurt my knee this summer and it was a wake-up call to do something else with my life's time, before it's too late. Too late?

Our Penn Lane apartment building in St. Clairsville, OH

This piece is about a tsunami and car repair.

I was thinking about this tsunami while working on my wife's van in the gravel parking lot of our apartment building. Until recently, I'd forgotten that car-repair moment, and the tsunami that killed 230,000 people that day. It's amazing how quickly things are forgotten and how quickly time passes. Years, decades, lives… all pass. I put something of priority on my desk, intending to get to it, and later see the dust-covered item put aside, or outside. Not-returning-to-things is a constant theme and threat in life, I notice.

My Own Private Tsunami, 2004

Alone.

Packed in together with thousands.

Tens of thousands.

Hundreds of thousands in a surge out of nowhere.

Bobbing like corks. Ant-like people like me.

We're ants.

Hundreds… thousands…

We're just like…

Instead of driving with my family to a friend's property in the hills for a winter, day-after-Christmas campfire, I'm replacing this water pump in my wife's 1996 GMC Safari. Kneeling up here on the cowling to get leverage, reaching in with an open-end wrench, holding my flashlight like a phone on my ear, I pry and un-stick the old part from its seat and see this old water pump wouldn't have made the 40-plus-mile round-trip to the hills. I turn the shaft with difficulty; something seems to have fused inside. My fingers are cold.

We could have had an adventure different from my smelling antifreeze this morning as I walked to the dumpster with trash bags of Christmas wrapping paper and cardboard. It could have been different from bending down, seeing the yellow-green spreading circle under the nose of our tan van, popping the hood, knowing what I'd find. This adventure could have involved a stranger's driveway or the side of the road, reaching in with tools and the cars blowing by.

Maybe my wife and kids would have spent several hours, this night, far from warmth, contentment and our apartment.

But *now* in the fading light, I carefully clean old stuck-on gasket material from the engine block inlet and outlet with a razor blade. I apply gasket sealant from a tube to the new pump's gasket and line up bolt holes and press the replacement part into place. I get the bolts started and tighten them carefully. I reattach stiff hoses and reassemble the air intake housing. I add antifreeze and bleed the air from the system by squeezing a hose and watching bubbles in the open fill neck of the radiator. I take a test ride, keeping an eye on the temperature gage. I look under the hood with my blue flashlight—everything is fine. I wipe off my tools and put them away in my cold metal toolbox. My hands are scraped up a little. I wash them under warm water in the kitchen sink in time to eat with Andrée and the boys.

It was *providence* that got me tearing this van apart today after noticing the puddle of anti-freeze—*oh yes*. Everything worked out. The auto parts store near the mall was open this after-Christmas Sunday. Something is watching over us, helping our van to break down at just the right time, here at home, during the day, when I'm not working... We've been lucky like this before. Tomorrow morning before work I'll check the coolant level in the van and probably top it off. I sense a heavy quiet certainty that we're being looked after... *just like <u>they</u> are*.

And *they*... earlier today, over there; providence watched over them, too, by the hundreds, the thousands—people just like me in a big swirling wash of human flotsam tea in a **wrath of the God of Tsunami** death...

I sort of think they used up their luck. I don't know. Maybe this *was* their luck. I think that something watches over us and doesn't care about luck, or us, even though I feel we're lucky.

They were doing the same thing as I'm doing, only drowning while I was sleeping because of the time difference. I know there was a guy working on his car. He scraped his arm on the radiator just like I did. They, I'll call them individuals, were in the middle of something important. Sleeping and hating, working and relaxing and eating. Arguing and loving. One guy was standing near a tree in his yard, gazing at the horizon, the sea and his life, pondering his family's future and listening to music, distracted while watching television before just turning it off. Then everything was under water, drowning in a *tabula rasa* torrent bringing death.

When will *I* drown? I gotta wonder.

—not that I'm looking forward to it.

Circa October 2010. The end of my outside painting season. Some rare, long-shadowed sunny fall days. Last outdoor painting of the year. Last outdoor painting, period. The next year, 2011, would be completely rained out...

I had just walked off another job, a house painting job I fired myself from because the guy was intolerable. He *wanted* me to quit. He could have just asked. It was the first time I'd ever done that while working for myself. [It happened again a few months after this, while installing a shower for another man in his late 80s with the same name, of all things. In that second scenario, I finished the shower job but didn't charge him my labor fee because I guarantee my workmanship and he had been unhappy with it.]

I've mentioned walking away from jobs more than once in this narrative. I don't mention staying on a job, steadily, focused on and devoted to the work at hand because that is my 'norm.' Walking away from a job stands out from this—so I make note of it. The times I've walked away are almost always surprises and feel unavoidable and necessary.

Like anything, what people say isn't reality. What people "choose" to mention and what they don't "choose" to mention. Let's see. A weak person doesn't talk about weakness but only about the (remarkable) times they were strong. What do people *actually talk about*? What does this imply about their central focus? About themselves? About where their eyes see and where their blinders are positioned. I used to believe that people told the truth. Now I know that is impossible. Don't think I'm leaving myself out of this.

So, as it often happens, seemingly, in life, when there is an unexpected hole that needs to be filled, another opportunity comes up—in this case, to paint something in the timeframe and income void that was left by my sudden unplanned work stoppage at the other site.

So, I was on *this* job then, the other, better work, on an extension ladder on the back of a church in Flushing where I live.

It's a massive concrete block wall on the southern gable end of a church building.

I was finally primer painting after a lot of intense scraping and sanding.

This job was squeezed in just before the end of my outdoor painting season. By this time, I wouldn't paint in October anymore; I learned that the hard way my first year on my own, in Martins Ferry, painting two houses with oil-base primer. On *this* day, I was about fifteen feet up and there was a funeral luncheon going on which started at one o'clock. There are metal double doors down there, to my left. I've set up cones with orange tape between them to guide foot traffic past my work zone.

So, I'm up there, trying to work 'respectfully,' however that's done; I'm sure you know what I mean. I see mostly old people going in, talking to each other about the man who'd died. Younger people, related or somehow connected, also go in, more out of obligation, I felt, than genuine desire. Almost at the end of the procession of people filing in with their fine clothes on after the funeral, was this old, *old* lady. *Next!* I thought. *Next...*

A van had pulled up close to the door and two middle-aged ladies had helped this old woman out: getting her walker for her, flanking her as they ploddingly made their way to the double doors. It was a fragile-seeming thing, this procession. A wind could blow and she'd be off her feet. Once that happened, it would be like a grand old oak falling over; after a certain point, it'll never stand back up. I had visions of broken hips, femurs, fractured wrists. This lady was *brittle*.

It was the two hovering women that made me think of this silent *grande dame* in the following way:

Superimposed on this scene, which I 'noticed' while trying to ply my roller slowly, so as to cause no paint to float down below and pepper people's finery. I thought I'd be ready to help if they needed it—all the other people seemed to be inside already. I had the very clear image of a little baby, a girl, first learning to walk. That first surprised balancing act they all do, standing up so high on their new tall legs. How adults hover there, ready in an instant to lend support and steady the little one's wobble before they tumble. I saw that old woman and the girl she had been in one picture.

I saw this oldest woman's life and a youngest one's first steps superimposed in time outside those church doors. When they got to the double doors, there was trouble deciding how they would get in, as three sideways wasn't going to fit. I got down from my ladder and went over there to open the other double door. They managed their way inside and I showed one of the training wheel ladies how to undo the latch that frees the other side of the door for when they returned the way they'd come after eating.

Two hours before, a train of cars bringing covered dishes, foil-wrapped containers and electric crock pots of warm food arrived. Young people, dropping off mandatory meal contributions, older contemporaries of the deceased man, bringing their own somber selves to the church; men carrying in wives' offerings, widows coming in twos or single. There was a quiet lag of an hour or so when I could smell the food odors and all seemed quiet. It was a Friday.

When I'd just about forgotten that there was a luncheon, I searched my pocket for my cell phone to see what time it was and the cars began arriving like an Army convoy—jeeps over here, deuce-and-a-halfs there, blazers and Dodges with trailers on that side—everyone had their place; they'd gone to the church for years and had earned their right to park in their same place on the same days of the weeks through the years.

I painted, moving up and down the 36 feet of my extension ladder. At the top, the sun had wakened wasps and bees that hovered and posed, battle-ready, on the roof line's white aluminum-wrapped soffit and fascia. I reached down as far as I could with my roller pole from the extension ladder before transferring to the 10' step ladder with a longer pole. I moved right, away from the basement double doors.

After half an hour, people came out, stood in groups smoking by the cars or singly, talking on cell phones, telling someone, "We're almost done. I should be there at…" The double door opened and closed more frequently as time passed. I worked in the hot fall sun.

Finally; what I'd been waiting for. A minor disturbance near the doors and I see first the left-training-wheel-lady step down the concrete stoop, her plump right arm inside, steadying something. With small shuffling steps, the three-as-one unit move sideways through the opening. The old, old lady's recently coiffured silver head appears outside again, shining in the sunlight. I didn't notice her step down; I don't think her legs were able to bend anymore; they were fused at the knees, straight pegs. The barest of movements, as her legs scissored *one-two*, *one-two*, and deeply-veined cold-looking pale hands gripped the walker handle bars. I had that flash of a fresh young girl, again, riding her bicycle for the first time.

Rolling the primer paint freely again, worry-free now that the old one was back in the blue van, doors shut, training wheels in, front doors closed *one-two*, and driving away. Afterimages on the bright white concrete wall shining wetly in front of my eyes were like a home movie. While I continued to cover the wall with colorless color that brightly reflected the sunlight, these *feelings* of a fresh-faced girl, youth glowing from every cell, and the old, old woman, faded, silent, dying. This woman never said a word. Her every movement spoke, every motion of her stately, brittle branches said, *Here… now. Here. Now.*

I made a mental note to try to write about her. It's been a month. It snowed two mornings ago. I'm painting inside now, on another job.

Andrée and I have been married since 2000. We've lived together for 12 years and knew each other as pen-pals since we were 14 and 15. I've known this woman longer (29 years and counting) than I've known anyone except my family. The story of our lives and our acquaintance is a novel in itself, including our eventual marriage, the birth of our sons in Filderstadt, Germany and Howell, Michigan, our lives in Europe and my reverse-immigration return to the U.S., where we lived in a friend's basement, a trailer park, apartment building and now our first home.

Coming up next is a continuation of my metaphysically-tinged tale. What happened after I gave up a solitary life, turned toward my lifetime friend Andrée and became an expatriate living in Europe? What about my outlook on life and meaning *now*, contrasted with my first solitary commitment to discover the meaning of my life almost 20 years ago? What about living as a family man? What does a person do after they climb their own mountain?

I typed here in 2004:

> There's also the present. This is more in front of me. I suppose in the future sometime, I'll dwell long afternoons over my past. Nostalgia and strong memories from the time I left the States to the time I returned with a new family. Two years in my hometown, running summer skate parks—I could sit in a rocking chair and revisit each of the moments from my life. They're right there. Detail, scent, texture, vibrant meaning, flashes and long scenes. A whole world is waiting. For now, I'll start where I am. We're all living paintings that change constantly yet so slowly that a person can't watch without blinking, as the colors run or lines and new shadows slowly appear. Like clouds moving over a landscape. We're trees, too; the pages of our destinies slowly turn and we don't notice because we're inside of them.

Yes. My pages *have* turned, I write—now (ha!)—in two thousand ten and eleven... I've been watching the pages of my son's lives turning, too. I've watched Andrée's life change and become more of itself as years come and go and she matures into an artist and as a woman after serving a stay-at-home mom stint for 9 years.

It's winter. When I stand at the small lake in the village park and feel-watch the wind blow snow across the ice, *this* feels like the moment lasts as long as an eternity, and I'm looking around and time itself cannot touch this vast place. Evergreen trees stand around the pond, where for the past two summers, my kids have taken part in a fishing derby run by the local Ruritan. I missed seeing them fish there, being at work or at a TAT meeting, but Andrée and the boys showed me this part of the park, with its pond. It has become my favorite place to meditate. I'm on my way again there, now.

I listened to an NPR radio promo for an upcoming segment on the phenomenon of memory. An expert said the reason time seems to go faster as we grow older is that signal speed in our brains between neurons is slowing down and becoming less efficient. I'm sure he's right. I've got another theory.

As a boy in Saint Joe's Catholic School in Howell, Michigan, I remember suffering through music class, fidgeting in Sister Rita Mary's fourth grade history class as Playboy magazines inside Boy's Life covers made their way around the room. An industrious kid borrowed these instructive periodicals from his father's library and rented them out to his classmates for a dime a day. The clock on the wall always stood still, or barely moved. When recess finally came, I could swing on the swing set for hours, days. Days passed before the whistle blew for us to come back inside.

In this life I call 'mine,' I have looked forward to things. In high school, I was in agony: it was only second hour and it was forever 'til lunch. At lunchtime, I would go out to the parking lot to my car and smoke a cigarette with the radio on and the windows open, reading a sci-fi or fantasy novel. It seemed to last half a day.

There's something about us I think; we strain like hell toward tomorrow, or to an hour from now, or to this weekend, this Christmas, vacation, to when I'm old enough to drive, to drink… Everything pleasurable we have planned and look forward to calls us, beckoning. We're always looking <u>to</u> the future. When we're young, we're prone to this; we have no patience to hear an older adult go on about some boring story from their past. No patience. Straining forward.

While a young adult, I leaned forward to the day I'd have my degree, to when I'd have a better job, to taking a great trip. Man, it never ends.

So, there's this GIANT ball made of the hardest, heaviest material imaginable. You slap your hand on it and it's like slapping a granite mountain—no sound, just hard-ass solid. As a young, young kid, straining in June towards Christmas, or to my birthday in May, I pushed like hell against this massive unmoving ball. Bigger than a house, more weight than I can comprehend. Nearing high school graduation, I strained, thinking about a trip to the Florida Keys, *push*.

You get the idea. A lifetime of this. Then there's this middle-aged adult complaining about how amazed they are the glory days are twenty years behind them. "Where did all that time go?" they say, genuinely shocked. In the mirror in the morning before a shower, I see red eyes and wrinkles and white hairs in my beard. Oh my. How did this happen?

Does it make sense that older people experience time traveling more swiftly than a younger person? Who's moving, anyway?! Wouldn't it make sense for the very old to sit on rocking chairs on their porches on lazy afternoons with nothing pressing on them, rocking gently within an eternal present moment? Maybe they do. I'll let you know.

Does it make sense that younger people experience time as passing much slower than they can take? You'd think time would match their humming bird attention span and activity. But the opposite is, apparently, true.

So the young person, both mentally and physically, is moving faster than the average speed of objects on the highway. Older people are traveling relatively slower than the average object on the road. A driver going 20-miles-per-hour on a highway is a danger to himself and others; everything seems to be going so fast. The teenage driver going a hundred passes everything as though it were standing still.

Is time "slow" for fleas? Or "fast" for turtles?

Remember that big ball? Its unbelievable mass is moving now, barely, at five. At fifteen, it rolls right along at an inch a week. At 50… it's cruising at a walking pace. At 70, a person has to do a slow jog to keep up. There's no slowing this thing down, and even if you wanted to, you'll never be able to stop it. It has mass and a lifetime of momentum. You can be as old and relaxed as you want. You can experience the eternity of a moment, and yet, the clouds will whip ahead in the still-seeming air. Life is a time-lapse video of a decomposing apple. Fast. *Faster.*

So maybe don't push. I've rediscovered the moment. I've reconnected during my daily ten minutes of flower-smelling time, to the wonder I used to feel on those endless afternoons in the eternal summer of my youth. Spend more *time*. I might not slow this ball down much—my guess is it's a little too late for that—but I'm not going to push it any more, and I'll try to relish each second that's left.

Letting the race go on ahead as I slow down, jogging slower, then walking, then standing, breathing heavy at first, then slower…

Row, row, row your boat,
Gently down the stream.
Merrily, merrily, merrily, merrily,
Life is but a dream.

Skating Dreams

The beginning of October 2001, Andrée and I moved to Ramonville St. Agne, near Toulouse in Southern France. We had spent three weeks in that area earlier in the summer, making contacts, talking to village mayors, looking at property. During our coming time in France, we would work daily for fourteen months to create a *sanctuaire de l'extrême* called THE ONE AND ONLY SKATE PARK PROJECT. I was involved, obsessively, with aggressive inline skating and we found a Mecca of practitioners of inline, freestyle BMX and skateboard in the French region of Haute Garonne. There were public skate parks everywhere—good ones. This region was ripe for us.

I noticed something in the two years I spent enthusiastically skating in Southern Germany, learning, practicing and perfecting skills on ramps and modules. While public skate parks were liberally scattered throughout *Baden-Württemberg* in small towns and large, there was no *place* for the extreme sports practitioner. No place to call home. I wanted to create a home with facilities to nurture and encourage young people and old in their obsession with these individualized "extreme" sports. A center for training, a place for holding events and competitions, a place where the different disciplines could come under one roof—or several roofs—and pursue the perfection of their discipline. *Dream Extreme* was the name of our French association. In France, *asso*s or *les associations*, are an important part of the society, enabling people to group together under a name, to be recognized as a valid organization representing their unique passionate interest.

During our visits to *les mairies* (mayors) of various villages in the part of Southern France that includes Toulouse, we met some old men who had no interest in our project idea. What I saw in these same villages and towns was *les jeunes* (the youth) hanging around *les mairies* (courthouses), sitting on mopeds with nothing to *do*. There were kids skating, biking and skateboarding, but I knew that a skate park, a home called THE ONE AND ONLY SKATE PARK, would be a magnet and a center that would meet an obvious need.

During our visits that first summer, we encountered the mayor and adjutant mayor of Castanet-Tolosan. Patrice Tournon was a *maire adjoint* (adjutant mayor) in charge of *urbanisme*. He was supportive of our idea and encouraged us. We decided to move to France.

We went through the process of relocating from Stuttgart, Germany to Haute Garonne to establish our project in Castanet. We found a reasonably-priced gated community on the internet. I remember using my only French words at the time—*merci, oui, à droite, à gauche, en haut, en bas* (thank you, yes, right, left, above, below)—to communicate to a big, former rugby player, Monsieur Tournon, carrying the other end of heavy furniture while going up a broad spiral staircase to our new apartment. Patrice had brought another guy, the adjutant mayor of sport, who begged off after an hour. Patrice stayed. We invited him to sit a moment when we had the heavy stuff in the apartment. It means a lot that he stayed.

Patrice, known at the time affectionately as *Monsieur Apéro* because of his apéritif gatherings (the French have a tradition of drinking some liquor and eating hors-d'œuvres in the afternoon after work, before the evening meal)—was a believer in our dream. He didn't say it in so many words, but something about our endeavor spoke to him. Maybe it was the combination of a French woman living in Germany and moving back to France with her American husband full of crazy ideas that struck a chord in him. Maybe it was my positivism, my idealism. *We can do this*, I said, to everyone I met. Maybe it was the American connection. Patrice told me that he'd traveled to the States with his rugby team, *Stade Toulousain*, at some point. Maybe his nostalgia for that visit was working in the background. Whatever the reason, he was a champion of our efforts.

When they'd want to talk money to us, as in, *How are you going to pay for a skate park like the one that you describe to us?* I would say, in essence, "If we build it, they will come." Patrice, who must have been feeling some pressure from the mayor to nail us down on this financing bit, didn't like the sound of that, but he didn't give us the boot, either. Looking back, I'm surprised. Maybe my enthusiasm was contagious.

To give ourselves some credit, we did establish a network of the many *assos* of old school quad roller skating, skateboarding, BMX freestyle, inline skating and street luge; a BMX bike manufacturer, several inline and skateboard shops and hundreds of practitioners. Several hundred of these people signed petitions saying they'd welcome and patronize *The One and Only Skate Park* if we built it. We showed everything to the Castanet-Tolosan village government and they were, as I said, receptive. During our time in Haute Garonne, we were featured in newspapers, magazines and on TV. We held an event previewing our future park with BMX, inline and skateboard competitions, graffiti demonstrations, street luge, a softball tournament (I'd planned on a batting cage and softball fields), inline hockey competition (a center where the leagues could compete and meet), face painting, DJs, live music, juggling and much more. It was called *l'Extravaganza*. We built a skate park in the village of St. Lys. Nine years later, it still exists—much improved.

There's a big thick book on our efforts over there. Volumes actually—it was a full time. Will we ever see those books recording our time there on shelves in our lives, now? I fear the answer is *no*. Many go unwritten, I assume and observe. We *become* those unwritten, phantom books. A quiet moment, staring at something while reminiscing is the form these volumes take in the air over our heads. I'll try to read to you from a single page of our time there.

The first person we saw in France, who lent us a hand, was Patrice. On that first cold Saturday morning, he found himself sweating and panting while lugging heavy furniture up the many steps to our new apartment.

I remember two of Patrice's *aperitifs* clearly—as clearly as I can, considering there was a lot of alcohol consuming going on and only a few *hors d'oeuvres* eaten, all while straining to communicate imperfectly in another language. One *aperitif* was at his apartment. Andrée and I were there with two-year-old Guillaume. There was an impressive variety of people: members of the local government, people from sporting organizations, academics, artists, interesting locals and us. This was some months into our time in France. I spoke some French by then so Andrée was somewhat freed from being the constant translator she'd been at the beginning. She was talking to friends she'd made and I was on my own, struggling through conversations in French, using English whenever I came to an impasse, which was often. Often I would speak French and the person across from me would speak English. They accommodated my ignorance of their language. Other times I would just sit or stand, drink in hand, eating some small thing, keeping an eye on Guillaume.

I was much more comfortable skating with my helmet and pads at the *Ponts Jumeaux* concrete park in Toulouse, or even at the small Ramonville Saint-Agne skate park down along the canal. Skate tricks, moves—going for a certain jump or pulling a 540—these are the common language between practitioners of all disciplines. The things you did spoke for you. A BMX guy would see me trying something and appreciate it the way one artist appreciates another artist's chosen medium, be it chalk, oil paint or clay. I'd appreciate the value and skill in what *they* were doing, too.

What I remember from this particular aperitif is Patrice making the effort to talk to me in English. His vocabulary was limited and he swung his words, club-like, that he'd used during his rugby days when playing other national teams, the English a middle ground to meet non-French-speaking players. I felt moved by his effort. I was growing familiar with Patrice and appreciated his reaching out.

I also remember going into the hall to look for the bathroom and to just step out of the din for a moment. I took in the layout of the place. Framed work on the walls—photographs, prints, artwork. Eclectically-decorated. It had relaxed class; this was a bachelor's place but there was a surprising sophistication. Wood floors, plaster walls, two steps up, two steps down, a very small bathroom with more unexpected photos, paintings and pictures. I remember changing Guillaume on the floor of a guest bedroom.

Back in the living room area, I had plenty of time to look at the furniture, the walls, ceiling, out the window… One photo caught my eye, an 8 x 10 image of the Canal du Midi, the beautiful, man-made, 150-mile waterway short-cut between the Mediterranean and the Atlantic which ran right through Castanet. It was constructed in the mid-1600s to supply irrigation to vast areas and for barges to transport goods more directly inland, thereby avoiding pirates. This photo showed a fall scene featuring a row of those ever-present Péniches (5- by 30-meter barges that ply the canal and its system of locks) with the also-typical rows of tall Sycamores lining the canal on both sides. The sun illuminates golden leaves, reflecting from bridges in the distance. Living there, we saw this nearly every day, as it was where we walked and talked of our plans for the future.

The Canal du Midi photo Patrice Tournon gave to me in Castanet.

I told Patrice I really liked the photo. He reached over to the wall and took it down. "Have it," he said.

"*Non*," I answered. *Je dis simplement que j'aime vraiment ça; Ça, c'est très joli.* "It's yours," I told him. "I just wanted you to know I like it."

Patrice wouldn't take no for an answer. I sensed he was reaching out in camaraderie. Maybe he knew we would be leaving. Here, years later, I sit looking at this photo that brings back so much nostalgia. I'm in a small American village, thousands of miles from that French town and its section of the Canal du Midi. The photo is still in the same frame and everything. On the back, Patrice wrote in blue-green marker that day:

Good Lucky. Because I love your enterprise and you. So. Patrice.

I remember being slightly drunk, talking with Andrée in our silver VW station wagon when we left. We buckled Guillaume into his car seat and spoke about Patrice's heart.

The second Patrice *apéritif* I remember was actually the first we attended, at the very beginning of our time there. We were invited to *Art Deco Gallery*, the frame shop he owned in Castanet, in *Centre Commercial* on the *Rue des Ormes*.

It was a small shop and standing room only; people overflowed onto the sidewalk and into the street. It was a store front facing a rectangular divider on a circular street. After some time, I saw what looked like a football, only without laces, and picked it up. I had never seen a rugby ball before. It didn't register to me that Patrice was a rugby man. An English guy was there—probably invited so we'd have each other to talk to—and I asked if he'd ever thrown a football. Using pantomime, I asked Patrice if we could throw his football outside. I wanted fresh air. It was November 2001, mildly cool outside. So I was playing catch in the street with this English guy, showing him how to get the ball to spiral. We started close, then moved apart, throwing farther and farther. Running, catching, shouting.

Then Patrice is out there, showing us rugby techniques. How to hold the ball; the stance to be in. I happily tried whatever he showed us. We just had a good time. Much better than standing around talking.

Patrice had played rugby for 35 years—that's what he told me. He must have meant from the first minute until he retired. He'd played for *Stade Toulousain* in the première division before it become a professional national team. His position was *arrière*, or defense. He wore numbers 10 and 15 on his jersey. Toulouse is a big rugby city. All the towns and villages in that part of the country have rugby stadiums and fields. Roving gypsies consider the fields theirs, targeting them for their legal takeovers of public spaces. We were eventually shoving each other around in the street, doing the rugby thing. Andrée and some well-dressed people were sipping drinks, talking and watching us.

I looked up Patrice a year ago on Google France and found his photo. We called him and spoke a while. It was good to hear his gravelly voice. I told him I'd send him a copy of this book when I got it done—*if*, I added silently.

Chapter 16 — Home

'Fire places'

Flushing, Ohio, 2010

When I was in first grade or kindergarten, I remember the corner fireplace in our home in Wixom, Michigan. It was a black stamped sheet metal cowl towering above a red brick base, with black pull-chain mesh screen. The whole thing was about six feet high but reached to the ceiling and hung in the corner of our house. An electric rolling cylinder behind the fake logs made of an opaque material, painted with flames, let the 60-watt light shine through, projecting what looked like a glowing, moving fire behind the logs. There was a little two-stage electric heater in there. Right now I can feel the round black plastic knob and hear that click; turn the knob backwards, and it sounded like a playing card against bicycle spokes, turn forward and another sound. The fireplace made a soothing repetitive motor noise: raaroww, raaroww as the cylinder spun like an eternal rotisserie.

Mom's Christmas card. Our family room in Wixom, Michigan, 1972.

Me, 5; Pat, 2; Anne, 4 and my dog, Daisy, 1.

Bill, Mary Jo, David
Anne & Patrick Weimer

I was five- or six-years-old. Possibly seven. I remember staring into that fake fire, mesmerized, thinking no thoughts, but deeply, deeply. In my pajamas with feet, I'd pull back the mesh all the way and sit as close as I could to catch all the heat I could. I think my parents had that fireplace upstairs in the Wixom house, yes. Before moving to the farm. I remember the smell of burning dust. Santa's milk and cookies were always right there on that fiberglass fake brick ledge.

In Howell, where we had a small family farm, we had a real fireplace, and the good old fake one was hung in the basement when dad finished it. There was a drop ceiling, adhesive carpet squares on the concrete floor and wood-grain paneling. Our old fireplace was hung in a corner opposite a game cupboard. Our first year there, I started 3rd grade in our new school, St. Joseph Catholic School. On the first Christmas after the basement was finished, we petitioned our parents to put up the fireplace and use it. I think my dad was going to throw it out. I was nine, my sister, eight and brother, six. We put Santa's cookies and milk on the old "real" electric fireplace and assembled the artificial tree in the basement. There was more room down there in the family room than upstairs. The wood burning fireplace upstairs was not the same as our "real" electric one from Wixom.

The heater still worked. That cyclic motor noise, though louder, still rolled right along with back-lit flame-painted cylinder.

When we moved to Fowlerville, we had another fireplace with a supplemental wood burner in the basement hooked up to the duct work to help our old oil-burning furnace and heating bills. We burned wood all winter. That old fake fireplace was in the rafters of our garage, collecting dust. It was separated into two pieces to fit between the rafters; the logs and other parts were in a cardboard box.

When I was 14, I met Gino Costantini. I had finished ninth grade in Howell while living in our new home in Fowlerville, so I hadn't met any of local kids yet. Gino knocked on our front door. I was surprised. He asked if I wanted to go to another kid's house to pick up a kick-start lever for his dirt bike. It was warm and sunny. I got permission and rode with him.

I never knew why Gino stopped by. I asked him later and it sounded like he didn't know either. I'm sure he'd see me and Pat playing in the yard, doing crazy things or riding our bikes in the circular gravel drive. Maybe he'd seen us on the road in our horse-drawn buggy or sulkies, or maybe he saw us the winter before, in our horse-drawn sleigh going through the fields and down icy roads. I don't know. Maybe it was his being the youngest in a family of five kids, with five or six years difference in age between his next brother and himself. In any case, this was the beginning of our friendship that seemed like it always had been.

Gino had a barn (which I would disassemble and sell on E-Bay 21 years in the future). He asked his scowling dad if we could make a fort in the back part of it, on a raised level above a couple cow stalls. His dad looked hard at Gino and me through a squint of his eye as smoke rose from the ever-present hand-rolled cigarette in his mouth; after what felt like an hour, he gave a quick nod and grunted. As we walked away, he fired a short sentence at Gino in Italian. When we got to the back of the barn with a couple of hammers and a can of bent nails, Gino said his dad had told him not to use any good wood or to fall through the floor.

Rooting around in our garage for fort-building materials, I saw the old fireplace and had a flash of inspiration. I asked my dad that day if I could put the thing in our fort in Gino's barn. I was overjoyed at his reply. Gino and I rode our bikes the mile from my house to his carrying the main body of the fireplace between us, me holding the fiberglass logs on my handlebars. With a piece of carpet wheedled from his brother Tony, a pig's skull I had supplied from our farm, an old medicine cabinet and other assorted junk, that grand old fireplace really topped things off. We never ran electricity to it, but it sure looked good.

Leaving for the Army at 18, I left Fowlerville and my best friend behind—and the fireplace stayed in the clubhouse. Nineteen years would pass before I would return to this town.

I remember those days being 14, 15 or 16 year old when we'd go to our fort and Gino would open the big square board window. He'd chew Copenhagen and spit out the window. I'd smoke a Players cigarette. We'd talk. Those were the days. We were masters of our world.

I think about those years and the years that followed—nearly two decades. That fort survived winters with snow blowing through gaps in boards, swirling and sifting into corners. Rainy springs, baking hot summers, falls, violent storms. Birds, dust, insects, bats. Twenty eternal years of this, and then I would return to Fowlerville from France with my French wife and first son. Gino let us stay in his basement for a couple weeks until we found a trailer at *Alan's Park* outside town.

I was working at a metal fabrication shop in Howell, early spring of our first year back, 2003, and Gino got the idea in his head to tear down that old barn. He'd had the idea ever since his dad died. I think he got to where he wanted to bulldoze down that painful reminder. As a carpenter (I'd framed houses north of Pittsburgh and built skate parks in France), I saw the structural timbers of that barn. Really great quality oak. Hand-hewn timbers from a barn built in 1886. You can't go out and buy those, I told Gino. "I don't care," he said. He was going to burn it down. I said, "Hey, how about I buy it from you? I'll disassemble it and sell it on E-Bay." Gino agreed, skeptical. Every day after work for a month or so, I'd go over and chip away at it.

Gino, with my assistance, pulled down the barn with his Chevy pickup. He'd gone in there with a chainsaw, cutting through the tenons of key mortise & tenon joints of the big timbers. After cutting through way too many of the smaller supports, too, we hooked up his tractor and pulled. Nothing. The barn didn't budge. Then we hooked up Gino's Chevy pickup. We'd pull, and the barn would barely wobble, then Gino would go back in with his chainsaw and cut. Each time I thought the barn would fall like a leaf.

Me at the southwest corner of Gino's barn, May 11, 2003.

It's amazing how much we had to cut before the old thing very reluctantly pulled over and let itself down with a slow-motion crash. Thirty-five by seventy-five were its dimensions, I think. About forty feet high, from the bottom level to the peak of the gable roof.

I worked steadily until I had neat rows of various sized timbers and boards all stacked up off the ground in Gino's field. I found a buyer from Ohio who came and got most of the big stuff. I used leftover boards to build a shed behind our trailer and portable skate park ramps that summer. I kept a good bit of the "leftover" barn wood and still make frames for Andrée's artwork; after I run a board through my planer, it's golden, rich, beautiful. Oak is a special kind of wood with a special flavor and smell. From the seed, to the sapling, to the years of days in the early 1800s when the trees were still standing, to the time they were felled, to being shaped and hewn and put together in that barn in 1886, to all the years of winters and summers to 2003, when I disassembled it and sold it— and to now, where they rest in the old coal storage area under my porch in Flushing. It's an amazing story that wood has seen. When I start to look at things, at anything, I see everything has that same eternal story. Every single thing unfolds, from a pebble to a space shuttle, revealing an expanding world of involved existence.

While I was doing the disassembly, I burned. There was a lot of rotten stuff, wood I didn't want, garbage, a lot, a lot, a lot. I got a permit and had a couple really big burns. One time, I saw a familiar shape, a shape from my childhood that *was* my childhood. It was sticking up from the tall dead weeds and thorns from the previous year. Apparently, it had been over there for years, off in a pile in the field on the east side of the barn. Grass had grown up around it, and it had kind of settled into the ground. The fake brick C-shaped base of the electric fireplace I used to sit in front of as a five-year-old, dreaming about the wonders of the universe and feeling the heat on my PJs. Santa had eaten his cookies and drank his milk there, leaving an empty plate and glass sitting on the fake brick ledge—while that growling flame-painted cylinder rolled over and over.

I went over to that familiar-shaped lump and with a lot of effort pulled it free from the dirt, grass and weeds. I threw it on top of the pile in that massive open furnace and stood as real flames now licked up, burning off the dead grass. The faded, cracked fiberglass bricks turned dark red once more, brand new, fresh from the factory, no dust, clean—then they started to droop and melt. I remembered everything then. Then, it crinkled and slumped in the middle like a melting milk jug. The roaring fire crackled, flames surged and the heat from the fire had me pointing the bill of my baseball cap toward it to shield my face. The top of my head and my hair grew intensely hot. I kept looking at that thing turning into a lump, then nothing, as gray-white fibers waved in the rising heat wind, to detach like dandelion seeds and float up, up. I threw more rotten plywood and pieces of boards over the fire.

No one in the universe but me will know what I felt when I looked at that burning thing. That's probably similar to Gino feeling something and wanting to tear down his barn. Maybe he felt it every day when he saw that barn.

Chapter 17 — No Safety Net

Handyman for Hire
R. I. P.
*2005—2011**

* ["The news of my death has been slightly exaggerated." —H. F. Hire]

April 28, 2005

A letter I wrote to Executive Editor, J. Michael Myer of the Intelligencer and Wheeling News Register combined daily newspaper:.

Hello Mike,

I know my capacity and interests and I can't even begin to work as a beat reporter. I never wanted to become a reporter and I never was one, although I've written many stories appearing in newspapers.

Yesterday, I expected something different, something more like assignment writing where I would cover events, interesting or unique people, the efforts of organizations, etc., and this would evolve through time into a "beat" of sorts where I would begin to generate story ideas from my contacts in the region.

I'm a storywriter, not a reporter. I have a profound disinterest in news. I like to meet people, find out what they're doing and why, experience their world and write a story about it.

So I propose to you to do just that—if possible. If John, Jennifer or Heather were to fill a shoebox with names, contact numbers and ideas, I could easily imagine cranking out stories.

My second suggestion or proposal is that I write for you as a freelancer doing what I described above, turning in perhaps 3 or 4 stories a week depending on their length and getting paid a decent freelance rate, say $100 per story plus reimbursement for mileage.

If anything is possible, please call me or email. Otherwise, I want to thank you for the opportunity that you presented to me yesterday.

Sincerely,

David Weimer

I imagine I mailed the letter to Mr. Myer, a distinguished-looking man I'd met the afternoon before in a meeting on the fourth floor of the newspaper building where I was offered a job as court beat reporter. I wasn't actually offered *that* job; I wouldn't have taken it. I was offered the job of newspaper writer and I happily shook his hand and went over to the news room where the assistant city desk editor showed me my new job—court beat. Blinking, I still took notes. *This isn't what I wanted...* After forty minutes I closed my spiral notebook and left. It was growing dark. Driving home, while on the Fort Henry Bridge over the Ohio River, on I-70 going west, I composed my resignation letter. Of 30-plus jobs I've had in my life, I've only failed at one—three times, this time. This was my third strike at beat reporter; I'd gotten myself hired at three papers and quit quicker each time.

We'd moved to St. Clairsville, Ohio two months earlier. Living on a tax refund and rental deposit return, my "job" was to find a job before our money was gone. Daily, I looked around, visited local career centers, read classified ads online and in newspapers, went here and there with an increasing sense of desperation. Before moving to the Ohio Valley, I thought finding "some job" would be easy. And it was. The problem was me. I didn't want to start all over again, at 38, working with kids twenty years younger, for beginning wages. Moving from country to country, state to state, attending college, always in transition; I never put down roots, never established or built on much, career-wise. It's been a great, interesting time, but not conducive to building a house of cards; that secure life we all pursue...

The bottom line was that I couldn't work *for* other people any more. It would have been easier. I resisted heading out on my own. I've worked for others in five states and three countries. At the end, every job felt like I was throwing my life away. At that last job of mine, at *Precise*, I felt this every single minute, the flames in a furnace of wasted life. My tolerance for working with idiots (other people, like me) was nonexistent. One of those characters in my life is enough. I don't know what caused this overwhelming dread. I only know that it was. I have guesses. Still, I resolved to try to find a job that was closest to my natural interests. In the end, I thought maybe my system wouldn't tolerate substitutes any more. I *had* to do my own thing.

My last foray into job-hunting was returning to newspaper writer—a final nail in my coffin. I envisioned writing features and profile stories on interesting people's lives and the unique activities —elephant training, firefighting, ghost hunting—some of them do every day. This, at least, would exercise my curiosity and let me write about interesting things. I did that with the *Fowlerville News and Views*. I interviewed pizzeria owners and race car builders. My vision of what I'd be doing at the Wheeling paper and the editors' plans for me were very different, I found out. After my last swing. I walked back to the clubhouse.

Strike one had been for the *Oakmont and Verona Advance Leader* in Pittsburgh after graduating from Pitt in '94. Strike two had been in Lansing, Michigan for that weekly paper. In Wheeling, I thought, *I'll make it <u>clear</u> to them what I can do and what I want; I won't get myself into a beat reporter job this time; I'll be an assignment writer.*

I had contacted the city desk editor, John McCabe, a competent leader at the helm of this Wheeling daily. I proposed he let me stringer (freelance) a couple of pieces and later, if he wanted, we could talk about something for me to do at the paper. Daily papers are always looking to fill space, I knew.

I took a couple of sleeper stories—the American Legion Post #1 in Wheeling and a Marshall County Historical Society renovation job on the Cockayne House in Glen Dale, WV. It felt good to be actually *doing* something. The stories appeared in consecutive Sunday editions and John called me in to come talk. I felt relief. Our bank account was in double digits and my stress level rising. A wife and two young boys and no job and no friends or family in the area we could rely on for help.

I gunned for the job at the Wheeling *Intelligencer* and got hired. I'd put all my eggs and hopes in that basket, was hired at a diminutive starting wage, relieved to have made it. Jumping across a gap, hoping to find a hand hold, I'd managed to get my fingertips onto something at the last second, it felt.

Driving home under a crushing dread pressing down on me like a lead blanket. I knew I couldn't take that job. It would kill my soul. I'd done too many jobs I didn't like. Maybe that was the problem—burn out. I was too old to do that again. My employable back broke. I drove the ten miles on I-70 to St. Clairsville where Andrée and the boys waited for me at our new apartment home.

As soon as I decided I to quit, I felt immediate relief. Right or wrong, it was right. My bank account didn't match that feeling. It was starving.

While waiting for this last best chance, I had started doing handyman jobs for out-of-town friends who owned property above Moundsville. They had cabins on Richard Rose's wooded mountain farmland. The TAT Foundation, a group I'd been a member of since my student days at Pitt, also leased the use of a couple of meeting buildings. These needed occasional maintenance and were suffering from a drought of repairs. Since I wasn't employed, I thought, *I'm not doing anything productive so I might as well make myself useful,* and offered to do the work at cost.

I patched up roofs, did minor plumbing, re-attached shingles and cleaned gutters. It felt good to do *something*. It felt good doing *this* kind of work. Too bad I couldn't do it for a living, I thought, wistfully.

Then my break. Mike Fitzpatrick, a local businessman I'd known since my student group days at Pitt, called me, seemingly out of the blue. He and his brother had run the SKS student group at Pitt thirteen years earlier. "Hey Dave, my house needs painting and I can't get around to it. Do you have any time on your hands?"

I let out a breath somewhat hysterically. That was the biggest understatement I'd heard in a while. "And how," was all I could say.

Our bank account was literally approaching single digits and I had resigned myself to driving down to the river, to a warehouse in Martins Ferry, for an 'on call' press gang-style work opportunity I'd read about. Mike's call came the day before and was a life preserver thrown to me once I'd given up hope of rescue.

I drove up Mike's crazy-steep driveway—I've since come to accept this as more normal in this worn-down mountainous Ohio Valley area—and talked to this carpet store owner. He wanted his self-built house painted and was too busy to do it himself. I would have done it for ten cents an hour. We added two zeros to that figure and *I had work*! A ten-day house painting job. My first job in my first self-directed career.

Each day I'd eat lunch in my Ford Explorer, listening to public radio or music. I'd get there at seven before Mike went off to his carpet store. We'd talk. I'd scrape and sand and calk and paint, ten hours a day. It felt great.

I'd get home tired, sunburned and dirty. On the scaffolding or reaching from a ladder, I thought more than once, *I should do this for a living*. It's nice to do something physical, that I am in charge of, in the company of someone I can tolerate, getting paid more than that newspaper offered for doing the terrible work of writing about criminals. When Mike's house was done, I told Andrée I wanted to try something. Every day going home from Mike's, I'd pass by a very large blue wooden structure that gave me a good feeling, reminding me of the structures I saw in France at *Palavas-les-Flots* on the Atlantic. Each time I'd look to the right before coming to a "T" stop sign, just a few blocks from our apartment parking lot, I had this warm memory-glow and that big, flaking building on Marietta Street in St. Clairsville seemed to silently ask for help.

We lived behind the oldest cemetery in town, by two side-by-side water towers and the impressive-looking Belmont County Courthouse. The big blue building was owned by Dr. Gus John Mouhlas, an OB/GYN from Greece. He ran his practice with his assistant Jaydean. It's more correct to say Jaydean ran it with his help. I drafted a letter, flushed with confidence from my recently-completed house painting experience, informing this man that I'd noticed his building and would like to paint it.

Dr. Mouhlas called me. We met, and he told me he had a bathroom job for the tenant living over his practice that he wanted me to tackle first; the shower leaked through the ceiling into the office. I bid the job too low, took way too long, had a lot of unpleasant educational "adventures," but eventually got it done. I'd submitted a separate bid for painting and repairing the outside of his building when the doc said, "Why don't you start on the wood repairs first." I had further adventures replacing second floor soffit boards, hanging from a rope, over-reaching as the wind blew the wood like a sail while I worked 30 feet over a sloping asphalt parking lot; using a car jack to lift up a sagging front porch, installing support posts—only too typical fun for a one-man-band handyman painter, I was to discover.

I hired my first helper once Gus gave me the go-ahead to paint. A few days later, I fired this helper while treating him to a last meal at Denny's for breakfast. Nice guy, but his head was on other things

—including a girl he'd just broken up with, I heard later. So I was left with this giant building and my own two hands. At the time, I remembered this quote from the tremendously inspirational *Everest, the West Ridge*, by Thomas Hornbein. I have found it to be truer in my life than I can say, on multiple occasions, and even believe it to be universal:

> *I believe that no man can be completely able to summon all his strength, all his will, all his energy, for the last desperate move, till he is convinced the last bridge is down behind him and there is nowhere to go but on.*
>
> —Heinrich Harrer

Me at my first solicited repair & painting job for Dr. Gus Mouhlas, Summer 2005.

This is how it was. I had no options; my plans had collapsed—but I had a direction present itself to me. *This way.*

Something that never fails to carry me forward is working, doing, physically. I'm engaged in purpose, it seems. So, this time I'd go to this big blue building and, like a lonely ant, work steadily in the summer heat, eating lunch in the shade, working as late as I wanted to. It felt *good*. Andrée would bring the boys by and I'd tell them to stay away from the ladder or put down my electric drill. I didn't know where this was going or how I'd make a living, but I had this job in front of me, right now. I finished the building, by myself, in 29 man days. A good confidence-booster.

I am in my seventh year doing this kind of work. When you read this, I will be on year eight, or nine or none at all anymore. I could be dead or busy or sitting on a beach somewhere pushing my toes into the sand.

I can't convey the confidence that I felt after finishing my first, daunting job. I remember the challenges: rain washing off fresh paint, wasps and hornets, flimsy 40' ladder set-ups, painting around high voltage lines —there's nothing like starting an uncertain journey, encountering unexpected challenges and coming to the end. Each contracting job is a journey I make. The end of each job gives me this big glowing satisfaction and an increased feeling of competence

Me, replacing blown-off shingles on the top of the TAT Foundation community building, Winter 2009.

Born to Wonder 315

that follows all the stress, hard work and fear. Working on stories will be like this, too, I think. Everything in my life will continue to be like that until it isn't; my pattern—the way I go about things—is pretty much what it is; it can change, but not fundamentally. The only thing that changes with writing is that it's what I really want to do.

I'll never forget my self-employed work time. The personal growth is impossible to convey. Others who've headed out on *their* own will know what I feel.

During the first year or two, I had what I consider my *Man on Wire* time. I recently watched the acclaimed documentary by the same name. It's about the French tightrope walker Philippe Petit who snuck into the World Trade Center and walked between the Twin Towers on a wire in 1974. I imagine myself there, now, walking on that swaying line in the wind, 1360 feet high with no net. Painting Mike's house and then Mouhlas' giant blue box, I was focused on what was right in front of my nose, unable to notice anything else. I was relieved to be making money. Working for myself was a bonus.

After a few contracts, once the calls started coming in miraculously steadily, my head rose from its intense fixation on the wire in front of my lead foot. In a moment of surprise, I noticed the tremendous height at which I was walking and how far away from the edge I had gotten. The horizon went on forever and I looked down at an unbelievable drop. I was far from the safety of solid ground, suspended on a flimsy line with nothing to hold on to and nothing to save me. That's how I felt.

I experienced fear; yes I did. No steady pay. No backup. Nothing but one job with another (maybe) waiting. A friend asked me to contrast this fear with what I call being a coward—the survival anxiety. My former condition of being a coward (only) meant that I had a prime directive—self preservation at ALL cost. I probably looked like everyone else; I could chit-chat, tell jokes, swagger—but when it came down to a fight, either literally or its equivalent, I would avoid.

After being burned out in '96 and becoming something else, I was formed around a rock solid center I had no previous concept of. So yes, I'm working for myself, feeling that fear and anxiety. It's the same as the 'coward' fear relating to survival. Maybe I'm feeling some of this by osmosis from Andrée. Maybe not. Still, the difference is I'm not petrified. I can function. The main difference between then and now is the solid, unmoving core.

In the early years of working for myself, I walked with a constant dropping feeling in my stomach, the same feeling as when I jumped out of a Cessna in '93 and then six years later a turbo-prop 21-seater—my two freefall skydiving experiences. This under the surface anxiety is hard to describe but not to feel.

Retreat to the Present

A unique psychological event occurred in the middle of this year or two of constant pressure. Besides nurturing what felt like a stab wound but turned out to be a fledgling ulcer, I had another reaction to stress. I'd be thinking of the job while driving to the store for materials; thinking about the upcoming potential work I'd gotten myself into—often work I hadn't specifically done before but thought I could handle based on my experience in related areas; thinking about the winter slowdown that happened every year around the holidays; thinking about the rent, the car repairs, the cold months. A lot of this. When I wasn't thinking specifically about work, there was this constant *thing* crouching back there in the rear of my mind. I'd 'remember' this uncertainty, waking up from the bliss of working on something, and it was that feeling of stepping off a cliff again, of falling in an elevator or dropping out of a plane—that unmistakable feeling in the belly.

That wasn't the 'unique psychological event.' This is: I was sitting in my van somewhere, feeling that freefall sensation. My stomach hurt and there was nowhere to go. Then I just gave up. Nowhere could I escape this haunting worrying burden. So I went to the only place available. "Retreat to the present" is how I describe where I found myself. I picked up this key and turned it and just stepped on through… into rescue. No worry, no thinking, no problem. Nothing but—Just. This. Moment. Just this moment in me, right now. Right here. I didn't run there, I found myself there, like a room I'd overlooked my whole life. It was bliss. What a secret! Hidden right here. Why didn't I ever make note of hearing about this before? I've heard of "coping skills," calming exercises, but not this. Not *here*. This is the ultimate coping maneuver.

There was a month or so where this empty soundproof room was available at all times. Whenever worry or concern would appear, or whenever my stomach wanted to feel like it was falling, I'd be *there*. Everything would all be right. I call it a retreat to the present, but I don't have the sense I retreated or did anything. I was just there. A gift, a preserver dropped next to me in the surging ocean.

Self-portrait on the job in basement of Flushing Masonic Lodge building, May 2008.

I've discovered since then that I can no longer 'go there.' I recovered during that month or so, and got better, and the door closed and disappeared.

This was psychological, a stress-reaction of the mind, one hemisphere or the other, or both, in communication, doing some stop-gap thing to keep this crazy captain from losing it—until his eyes could once again reflect reason, command and calm. It was a hell of a gift.

Since then, I've worked this no-safety-net- tightrope walk I call *Self-Employed Contractor*. Stress levels come back, depending on the job and circumstances, but nothing like in the beginning. I've learned a lot; that helps. I've done a lot of dangerous things, gathered experiences, bought more tools and ladders. A long trail of completed jobs stretches out behind me that I can look back on for reassurance—they never would have been, if I had done other work, in some other place, working for someone.

I'm taking the time to scribble these words while I can. 2009 was a wake-up-call. *Write now*, it told me. I had a damaged knee that was a constant reminder of my fragile existence. Each step hurt. I couldn't take time off to heal and had to carry 4' x 8' sheets of drywall up ladders to hang on ceilings, and kneel on floors to paint baseboard, install trim and repair door thresholds. In this line of work, I have no option but work wounded. Again, it's that nowhere-to-go but onward thing. As my winter slow-down time approached, I had the idea to write and to publish my book.

I got two months, January and February, 2010. It was magical. Now a year later, here I am, sitting at the same desk, looking at a flat screen monitor a friend gave me. In a way, I'm sitting at this table, typing, while me, the desk, the chair and my words slide along the cold braided steel cable connecting two swaying towers, the tops of which touch wispy, damp swirling clouds. Half-way across. Other times, I stand up, put my tool belt on, and balance with my hammer held in one hand. I balance better, relaxed. One of these days, I'll have a completed book in the other hand.

Chapter 18 — Outlooks

I don't think you can get a good bead on someone's view until you hear them comment on specific topics, as opposed to talking about the weather (although that, too, gives you general indications of a person's outlook). You can watch someone's actions over time—*that* might tell you something—but my specific reactions to others' concerns brings out my... outlook... far quicker and more honestly than if I were to sit down and spout opinions without promptings. It's how we react. It's how we perceive life. I think the ultimate change a person can undergo is a change in point of view. This gift comes at a great price to each. People survive challenging times and come out a "changed person." What changed? *Everything*, Trish, my friend Gino's wife, told me once. Dealing with life-threatening cancer had permanently reshuffled her outlook on everything.

I think people's "everything" means only <u>one</u> thing has changed, that one thing at the center of us that we look out from. When *that* changes, everything else is different. From the lens of fear, everything is frightening. From the lens of depression, nothing is wonderful. There is a condition in which, "the capacity to view things in their true relations or relative importance" exists. There is a view where everything is put into perspective.

This outlook is a sphere encapsulating an infinite void—a singularity—that resides at the center of all of us. A poet friend said he wraps words around this emptiness. We all have to face it eventually. Some are forced while still living, and then live their lives permanently altered afterwards, and others face it—or die while avoiding facing it—at their deaths.

I've conveyed my outlook in my responses to people I have written to. Some of them have appeared in this book. Write me—otherwise I'm a stranger you don't know. We are all strangers until communicate...

Here's an email I sent to someone named Tony. I remember that he wanted to check out what I knew or what I had. He told me that based on what <u>I</u> said, he'd either consider me worth talking to or not. After this missive, he never replied—probably wisely. I had just returned to the States.

2/17/ 2003

Hi Tony,

My view of this place is different. I wouldn't describe it too often. I wouldn't tell my son that people don't mean what they say or that people are not reliable. First of all, he's two, and the words wouldn't mean a thing. And if I could somehow convey to him this 'truth' about people, I wouldn't. I wouldn't want to see him lose all hope and the feeling of security he has concerning me or his mom. I'd like to preserve this "falseness.'" I know it's not "true," but I want to make him feel good, feel loved, protected.

Do you understand a paradox? "Of course I do, asshole," you reply. Good. Do you see it, feel it, recognize it, however you want to describe it, do you perceive this paradox, regularly, in your daily life? Okay. What about forgetting all of that for a moment.

What [if] knowing it all doesn't matter? It really doesn't. What about knowing it ALL <u>does</u> matter? It does, more than anyone can say or guess. And even so, there's something else that eclipses all things to fight about and not fight about.

Here's a basic, fast description:

It's simple, I think. I went through what I think I'll go through when I die for real.

I think anybody that went through that would have a lasting change. It's not complicated. It's profound.

I was pushing like hell. My life was unbelievable. Hell and unbelievable insights. But that's one thing.

I went into the woods and had a few days of 'broken brain' time. My active, reactive self wasn't turned on. Wasn't around. Not a thing moved, not a sound made. But wind moved trees and bugs and birds did their things. After some time, "I" came back like a foot coming back to life after being asleep. The activity in the head slowly came back and this activity, taken together, is called David.

It was remarkable. I thought, *wow*. It happened after a long time of work. After a night of terror of tornados and storms, too. After a small act of resignation, when I slept in the storm and woke with no brain. That's how it felt.

That was during a week in the woods back in '96. When I came out of the woods, I saw a friend who was working to unstuck a tractor. We got it free and did some other farm work. That night, the night before I was to return to Pittsburgh, I stayed in this guy's cabin.

The afraid-of-the-dark fear moved in on me, in the daylight. It steadily increased its pressure until I couldn't ignore it or write it off. This attack continued and what ensued was a night of hell. Me running away from attack. Avoiding, rationalizing, getting angry, being hopeless, scared—all that. Every dodge possible was tried and met before I could enact it by a strategically-superior thing that was not fooled.

I was run out to the end. "I." Like that drowning guy, trying everything to survive, splashing, grabbing. At the end, for me, it came down to me leaning, mentally, on the words or my image of others. Rose, for example. And this leaning didn't work either. Late that night, on a cot in front of the wood stove, I mentally leaned on the friend who had the cabin. Yeah, I thought. He'd given some advice about mental attack. Something like, "Hang in there, good luck." At the time, I perceived a negative effect of this leaning. That whatever was getting me was getting after this guy because of my 'leaning.' So I thought, it's bad enough I'm going down the drain, I'll be damned if I take someone down with me.

So I faced it. Turned and faced it. What was 'it'? My death. I had been running from my death. The threat to me, I, who-I-am. I turned with no expectation to live or survive or whatever. There was no time for thinking or thoughts as such. There was just turning to face it. No more running and no more fear. The fear had been run out to its very end and, like burning toilet paper, nothing was left after it was consumed by what was going on.

I became a bright-sun thing. Undivided, unassailable, un everything. Just am.

There was a residual return of the scared guy. Then another 'battle' would ensue. Resulting in the scared guy running himself out of existence and this *Om* thing in its place. It happened a few times until I remembered how to go there. I didn't remember. I became remember. There was the tendency to 'forget' which, too, was burned out.

I went outside around five a.m. Went for a walk, down the road. Not glad I'd survived. I was vaguely surprised. Oh. Didn't think that would happen (my living). I was numb, or something. Just was.

Later that morning, I called my wife for a ride back home and she said I didn't need to bother returning. The life basically fell apart, the one I'd believed in and considered mine. She left, family members died, and got sick. I found myself in situations and just watched it all, involved but watching. What's that...

It was a valuable hell I'd gone through. No tangible payoff from the first three days of that motionless thing. No tangible payoff. But the hell night, that was real practical. I didn't fear anything anymore after that. And when I did fear, I recognized what was happening. Most fear, in my experience, is a response to something projecting out of others and hitting us.

My push for the truth didn't stop. It didn't seem remotely related to what had happened to me. There was no causal relationship. No tied-together relationship between what had happened to me and what I had been doing previously. None felt.

It could be that my efforts were all made through a certain personality, and what had happened was 'other than' that personality or anything that personality could "know."

Since then, like I said, I didn't stop pushing for the truth. I still strain in that direction. But I've changed. I took some years to digest what I'd become or what I'd... whatever.

I have a definitely different view now—and did right after. The view being this: a permanent feeling in the chest that is a capital letter. Choose one; any will do. It is both unmoving and uninterested in capital letters. It has never changed.

Everything else I encounter is seen through this condition. Unavoidably compared to this. Not compared, per se, but experienced differently.

It's simple. I think anybody who has gotten through the acceptance of their death—and somehow continues to live—is left this way.

The "understanding" I have of this place, this reality—that you want me to describe—has always been something I was good at. During my strong push/search I was getting better and better at seeing and understanding the relationship between myself and the observable reality around me. Understanding the reality around me...

But my understanding has been added to. I'm "wiser."

[As of] now, I think I'm pretty wise about this place. My wisdom or understanding is fuller, more complete and [tinged] by the profound or solid center of my being. This has come over time. Any old person would relate.

Maybe the difference between me and an ordinary "old person" is my predisposition to question and the push I've had for a long time to understand what life was all about—combined with a survivor's view. The survivor who knows they're gone but somehow not. They're back, absent yet apparently here.

I seem to get wiser all the time. I'm smarter today than last week. It's nice to know more. I can affect people. That happens. Say things. Do things. But I don't know.... Everybody's got their row to hoe.

I do know *you*, and other people I meet. I'm often not aware of the complete picture, but I recognize myself in you and other people I meet. Don't we all..

I don't think I'm different at all. But I do think I know something. I *am* something.

The skater, after totally obsessing on skating to the exclusion of everything else, after some years or after any amount of time, will feel that they "know" something. In truth, they ARE something. They are no different at all from others. But they are very different. They are an expert within themselves.

The old karate thing to say was: if you want to know how to punch correctly, if you want to know how to get the technique right: punch a tree or a board or whatever 1000 times. And it's true. That guy's body and self is changed and 'knows' more than a person who'd never punched a board. He doesn't know anything. He is changed by the experience. He's gone on a 1000 punch journey and he's not the same guy who took that first punch.

A lot was left out of this description. The whole context, for example. The details and the happenings and all. But it's simple.

If someone dedicates themselves to the truth, to knowing or finding, somehow, THE ANSWER, then I say it is possible. If you work at it, something will respond to that work.

What else is there to do? What is there that is better? Walking on the beach? Yes. Yes.

But if someone has that certain urge to know something, I encourage them to go get it. Don't settle for less. Don't rationalize that there isn't something just because you slowly leaned towards not trying.

I would not say that there is life after death. I WOULD say that there is an "answer," if you want to call it that, for the serious seeker. Without a doubt in my non-existent mind.

That's about it.
David

I still believe that last bit, about the existence of an answer for a serious seeker of a fundamental… answer to their life. I believe it's possible for every single one. Whether it will happen is another thing. I do a Tuesday night philosophy group at the Ohio County Public Library in Wheeling: M&M Philosophy. Last Tuesday [circa Fall 2010], the topic of discussion was the book, **Beyond Mind, Beyond Death**; *Essays, poems, opinions and humor on seeking and finding answers to your deepest life-*

questions. It's a compilation 'best-of' book of contributions to the *TAT Foundation's* online E-zine [that I now co-edit]. For this M&M meeting, I had copied a fragment of an essay by Franklin Merrell-Wolff called, *Finding the Way* as an example of some of the book's content.

A group member, Arnie, zeroed in on a sentence in Merrell-Wolff's piece:

> "I found a road that has proved successful. While during the interim there have been partial Transformations and Recognitions, it has taken twenty-four years of search to attain a culminating point which I can recognize as definitely culminating."

Arnie asked how old Merrell-Wolff was when he wrote that. I said I thought he'd been in his sixty or seventies, and that he lived into his nineties. Merrell-Wolff, incidentally, coined the phrase, "consciousness without an object" to point at a condition which he discovered. Or maybe someone else said it first.

Arnie said he would like to read something Merrell-Wolff wrote in his nineties. Arnie, near sixty himself, had recently run across the book, *The God Delusion*, by Richard Dawkins. In reading this book, he felt like he was encountering, in that perspective, *home*. Arnie said he'd gone through the route of being raised in a preacher's family of preacher families, teaching Sunday school, becoming a deacon and even considering the seminary. But he left, and after years of looking around for the "right thing"—dipping his toe in different religions and movements (his last disillusionment being with the Jehovah's Witnesses)—he came across "this Dawkins guy" who rings more bells for him than all the other stuff he'd been exposed to combined. His point was, *What about when that wears off?* Arnie felt that epiphanies, insights and realizations all "wear off" with time. I'm aware of one thing that doesn't.

I liked his point. How *do* you know for sure? Another meeting attendee had an answer. "It's like the male orgasm. Before you have one, you're not sure; you wonder about this and that—but after you have one you know!"

He's got a certain point. There's knowing and there's speculating what might be. One is a feeling or a guess and another is beyond questioning because it's fundamentally at your core. It *seems* like nothing is definite or certain, from the perspective of someone recently weaned from an older conviction-state. That's probably a good place to be—unsure of the solidity or reality of *any* conviction, opinion or belief. It's probably the *best* place to be; although it may not feel that way.

The following I wrote to one of the Bobs I know...

5/28/2003

Hi Bob,

Your description of the fear you felt during meditation was something. I can understand it. Fear of annihilation, you called it.

I was pursued by that one, once. It didn't back off and it wasn't anything I could escape. There were times when I was a kid that I'd have the fears or terrors of things in the dark outside that I'd run from and get to the light inside the back door of the house just in time.

[I spend some time here, once again, on that formative running-out time I call my 'night of hell.' I was discussing this with one of two Bobs, TAT members, who had their own transformative personal experiences.]

The thing with me was that I avoided that fear but wasn't able to avoid it. There wasn't any hope. It was daylight (I'm talking about the very bad time, the only time) and there was no reason for it, seemingly. I don't know what brought it on. It was acausal, as far as I was able to see. It came from out of the blue. The same maybe could be said about the guy who unknowingly smacks a hornet's nest with a stick he's carrying over his shoulder; as far as he knows, this stinging vengeance, "It came out of nowhere, man!"

I don't know *what* it was. But I am sure of this—at least within myself: it was something actively moving in on me with a purpose. It wasn't some vague mood. There was intent. I knew it was my death coming. There was no compromise. It wasn't a good thing that was about to happen. I just knew it. I think living things know when something is not going to let them squeeze past.

I ended up going through a process that resulted in my turning, standing and facing. Not with courage or any other characteristic. Just facing. Not with dread or fear or anything —all of that had been run out. Just turning and facing. Not with uncertainty or any other characteristic. Facing.

I think I faced, honestly and openly, my mortality. I admitted that I wasn't going to survive. It was not a concept. It was certain. As far as I knew, there was no hope whatsoever for any survival—of any kind. That's what I turned and faced. Of course, there wasn't any "I" doing that, so *who* did it? It's not easy to describe.

You talk about all the different forms that fears had assumed in your consciousness and unconscious.

For me, I saw (and see) there is only one fear. To greater or lesser degrees it manifests in my life—depending on how threatened I am. There's only one fear, in my book [of annihilation/harm/death].

Resulting from that thing I went through is a presence, or, solidness in me. It's never gone since that 'night of hell' seven years ago. It seems practical. I've had a few other experiences of profound insights and one time where I didn't have any thinking going on for a while, but the most 'useful' to me, in a day-to-day way, is the result from my having been to my end and back. Useful to me, and maybe to no one else. I've never been afraid since. I've felt fear. Lots of times. But it doesn't touch me where I 'live' now. Where I live now is a very different condition.

I think that any person would end up like me. I imagine a person in a concentration camp, brought to the conviction that they are not going to get out of it. If, somehow, this person found themselves freed... I think they would be forever affected by their having once been through the acceptance and certainty of their ending.

For me, there was more to it than I described, and a whole world of context, but it's hard to say [Everything's hard to say, to tell all the details that give a listener a very good sense of the circumstances surrounding an event. By 'hard to say' I mean I didn't want to write a book to bring Bob into my shoes; hopefully he can get a sense of something anyhow. Everything needs a complete context to be truly understood by someone else]. Everything could be a book.

Most every word I use should have "quotation marks". To emphasize that this word is being used with the understanding that it is not exactly what it is. Words can be misunderstood. The chances of a person picking up on the meaning I intend are very small. It's nothing. People have a hard time translating themselves to others. It's worth trying, though. If someone is similar enough, there is more of a chance for understanding. That's when the words key in an understanding.

After my night of hell, I realized I'd been a coward my whole life. "Coward" means someone whose actions and limitations are directly tied to a strong preservation "instinct." I saw how everything I did or was, was tied to and limited by my survival mechanism. Fear. The best words I had at the time was to say, "I became something other than a coward."

I say "something other than" because to say I became courageous is not even close. To say I became the opposite of a coward is wrong. These 'definitions' are stuck down *here* and what I had gone through was not on the same page, let alone in any book. It was beyond books, pages, ideas of books and pages. I was *gone*. And so was the world.

Because 'coward' was a good word to use as a pointer to a syndrome, I used it, and 'other than' was the best I could come up with to indicate <u>not</u> opposite or another-shade-of, but *something other*. Something outside. Not related. Other.

What do you mean by "illusory?" You talk about many previously held beliefs, etc.

I think people have a vague general feel for what an illusion is—and for the word illusory too. What if these beliefs and feelings are seen to have been based on a system now "seen" for what it is? If this whole system of beliefs and [everything connected to it] are seen to have been the result of a self-preservation instinct associated with fear, for example—is it an "illusion"? It might not be relevant any more... It might not exist in the way it once had. It might be over and done with. It might not be "real" anymore. What *is* an illusion?

If you have been given insight into your past patterns—are these patterns illusory *now*? They may be less real.

Anyhow, I can relate to your saying that you saw your past nature and patterns clearly. How the many issues and conflicts and questions you'd struggled with for decades became clear.

The burden is tremendous. The corresponding relief is the same, tremendous. When a person has a breakthrough, the insights will flood over them and they will have an enormous amount of 'energy.' Do you think you can relate to a person who is 'born again?' And to the song, *Amazing Grace*? People have different ways of talking about something; from each, their different perspectives. People have different things going on in their lives when something happens. [We're all different, even though we're all the same.]

It is an unbelievably great experience, what you're talking about. Few people, [I'm guessing], will have the fortune to have such an experience. Few are ever graced with an overview of themselves. Few experience clarity of the kind you're talking about.

You could talk about levels and transitioning upward from one to another. You could talk about being born into another, new, world. Think about a paradigm. In a way, it is a world unto itself. A sphere—and you're inside of it (the 'old' world—you). Every attempt to go in one direction is met against the curved inside surface of the sphere. There's literally no way out.

We bounce off the inside of this thing and we can't get out. This is what I mean about 'living the impossible.' No one is smart enough to transcend themselves. Nobody has what it takes to become enlightened. Or to *become* anything [at all]. But.. We become less finite, as Rose says. We break out, in spite of its impossibility. It happens. It does. A "paradigm shift," people say. Maybe. Maybe not really a shift. Do they shift, or do they change? It's more an emergence into another world. The old world is then SEEN, simply, for the first time. Before then, we ARE the old world and we can't see ourselves because there are no mirrors and we never guess that it—this world, us—isn't real. Real. There's a word that needs quotation marks.

You talk about having two weeks of incredible life and then, beginning to notice things creeping back in. My reaction to this is: don't let it get you down. You had a real view and a real experience of clarity. Do you think that you will ever be as hopelessly unaware as you were before, as far as what was going on or happening in your life? You may feel the same old thing coming back, but I would ask, "Do you think you'll go back to not having a clue?" How can you un-see what you now see?

I can relate to what you say about the heart center. I don't have your definition of the thing, but there's something there that I can relate to.

You are not the person you had always taken as your true self. You said this.

What I experienced was an annihilation of that person who I had always unconditionally assumed to be my true self. That's what I went through in that night of hell. I was run out to my end and when there was nothing of it left but one act, I turned, extinguishing in the act.

Earlier, in the same isolation before that night of hell, I'd experienced a time where I thought my brain was broken. There was a lot leading up to it and this is out of context, but maybe I can still talk about it. I had a cessation of me, the thinking, reacting feeling me. I was in the woods and nothing moved. All was motionless and there wasn't a sound. Birds moved and trees swayed in the wind and things made sounds but absolutely nothing moved. There wasn't a sound. I had awakened into another world. There wasn't any activity inside. I was in an empty house.

The reflexive activity—reacting to things, thinking about things, having emotional responses to things and all that—was gone, like it had never been.

After a day, I wondered what would happen. How could I function in this world with no brain? With nothing there. I think this was the first time I became aware that I existed even when 'myself' was not there. "Myself" being all the characteristics and attributes I called myself.

Incidentally, some people latch onto an escape from themselves. They somehow discover that if they convince themselves that they are unreal, then they are freed from their pain and suffering. A person with great guilt might convince themselves that everything is just happening, by itself; there is no cause or causer (hence, no blame). There can be things a person does in their head to avoid things. This can be a kind of extreme delusion when a person tells this to their self without KNOWING it.

I don't really have a strong feeling of that with you, but I did think it was important to say. I'm sure you'll see people who have taken that 'out.'

I do know people who I believe are living a delusion/lie.

A lot of the stuff you say about your understanding of your current situation and what is required for your further development (or whatever you want to call it) I have to accept at face value. I don't know your story and I can't address what you say. I just have to accept it and say, okay. It sounds like you are working through things and I sense that you're on the money.

There are a rare few who somehow get through. Through their own confusion and susceptibility to being distracted and fooled. Through it all. I don't know how they do it, except I recognize them when I encounter them—[so they must have made it beyond themselves!] I think that the reason for their success is extremely simple, maybe. A lot of people—everyone—are unable to find their way out of hell. Some rare few do. How? Jim Burns says many are called but few are chosen. Probably.

I don't think we need to slow down or still the mind. That's focusing on symptoms, losing sight of the objective. That's trying to look like or act like Buddha instead of finding the Answer yourself. I think the only thing that is important is the attention on the goal. A willingness to do whatever it takes and a sincere commitment of one's whole self towards this.

Rose says that in a lecture. "You'll think of nothing soon enough," he said, if you work on yourself.

I'm just commenting on your saying that a lot of the stuff you read in the past put emphasis on stilling or slowing the mind.

Can you still or slow the ocean? I think we can become a directed force in a certain direction.

Bob, a lot of what you've written I haven't commented on directly. There's not much to say in response. Would a head nod suffice? That's what happens.

The great paradox. We learn to find our way by knowing we can't find our way and learning to go the way to go without questions or doubts. Intuition.

A successful walker into the truth is a walking paradox. A walking contradiction. I think where people fail is when they believe too strongly in one thing, forgetting or missing the other side of the coin. The person who is aware of both sides of the coin, who recognizes the validity, truly, of each side, and who is able to accept apparently mutually exclusive things existing simultaneously.

I am glad to encounter the spirit of your correspondence. I'd like to reply in kind. Of course, I'm different, but in my way, I reply in kind.

So long,

David

One more letter. I DO remember the next fellow! He's from Alabama and I call him a friend. This is from shortly after we met:

9/30/2008

Hi Shawn,

Good to hear back from you. Here's my attempt at your questions.

Does enlightenment equal contentment?

Yes, it feels that way, and no. I think there is the experience that people maybe call enlightenment and there is the person who remains after experiencing the thing. In my case, I would say that the great prompting, the great incompleteness, my longing and unmet desire is gone. It is put to rest. It's not like the questions and primarily the desire for completeness have been somehow muted, blocked or forgotten. It's that whatever I am as a result of going through things is the answer to these former questions and previous yearning.

I don't want that to sound mystical or fuzzy. I think it is very plain. If I wanted with my whole being to climb Mount Everest and devoted my life to it and went through the arduous journey to just get to the bottom of the hill and then, against a lot of odds, went through the struggle and experience of climbing it—and coming back down and returning to my life... If I did all that, then I am changed. I'm changed by my experience of having made that particular journey. And that's leaving out any experience of something that might blast one's perspective away permanently. I like the word Nirvana. I heard that it means extinguishment. That is as good a word as has been come up with, I think. What about childbirth for a woman? Before, it's all sheer speculation. There isn't one bit of information that comes from direct experience of the thing for oneself. After nine months, which are an experience in themselves, and the birth and so on, the woman is never that same untried, fearful non-mother.

So, I know that I am changed or different because of my having been present during the stuff I went through in a seeker's quest and unexpected happenings. But if I hadn't had a couple of experiences (sort of described in a piece that follows this email), I'd still be the same ignorant David. And that's where I have to be fair to the life-changing quality of something that I think can happen to everyone. *Their* enlightenment. Enlightenment equals contentment. Yes. I have a hard time saying no to this. Even though they are not at all the same thing. Contentment is a feeling-reaction I have. Enlightenment—I don't know what it is for others—is being present during the unexpected thing that happens.

Enlightenment does not equal contentment. Contentment follows. I'm talking about a specific contentment in my own case: existential contentment.

The reason that I wrote the 'essay' with the questions for enlightened people is because of my frustration with all the seeking-type people showing up at TAT meetings being presented with apparently enlightened people and not getting in there and finding out what these people have that they don't. That's my particular angle. If I was looking for something solid, and I was presented with not one, but a few people who supposedly made a complete journey of themselves, I would be shoving my way past all the curious onlookers and getting in these enlightened faces, demanding, "What do you really know that I don't? How'd you get it? How are you sure? And so on.

I thought that I was obligated to try to answer the questions that I propose to pose to others who feel that they've found their way through this life. I never said that I was enlightened. I think I am. But not like the projected wonderfulness that is put on enlightened people here there and everywhere. It's more profound, by far, than any flashy robes or affected 'enlightened' behaviors people can take on.

I feel that I have lived my potential; I accomplished something that I was born to do. It was accomplished. Not by me. I'm not the director; I'm a bystander observer. I was born to be a dreamer, a wonderer of things. I'm not implying a designer's intentions in my makeup, although it could be there. It is just apparent that I am a certain shape and color. Fat people are fat, etc. I have always, always looked for the deep, true meaning of everything. I always felt that IT, the answer, the real reality, was there, somewhere, but people seemed contented chasing after stuff that I was convinced they knew didn't matter.

I had two things happen that drastically affected my course. My father's death resulted in my innate curiosity and contemplative nature tilting off balance into a very extreme list of incessant questioning with my whole self, "What?" "What is this place?" What is the meaning of all this?" I was 18. After seven years spent in this direction, I ran across Richard Rose's life example. I saw this guy who made a similar kind of 'wondering' his solo career. I felt, intuitively, that this, finally, was what I was supposed to do. I'd always felt this but had never before been encouraged in this direction. I was always the 'odd one' with my unorthodox ideas, questions and outlook. "That's just Dave," I'd hear from family and friends. After seeing this old guy's life, I told myself that I could march to my own drum and I made an abrupt left turn (reference to my being left-handed) and never, never looked back. I finally was going in my own direction.

If an enlightened person is content, what motivates him/her?

If a person has the equivalent of what I had happen, happen, I personally have a hard time believing or understanding if they immediately use words like, enlightenment, absolute, and so on. It is such a fundamentally slate-clearing experience. Actually, the chalk is thrown away, the chalkboard is Frisbee-ed out the window, and the building walked away from forever. I can't conceive of how I could have been prattling on about 'enlightenment' weeks afterward, even. That's me, I admit. It (the ultimate experience) reshuffles everything. But okay, to answer your question. For me, that is probably the biggest problem, the one posed in your question. My personality type seems to be the kind that thrives and lives on and lives for a goal to reach (or die trying). Without a goal, I do nothing. I don't work at something half-way. If there's something to go for, it's all in. If there isn't, there isn't. Nothing motivates me at all. I am not motivated. This still-point condition is unusual to my whole former activity. There are no currents in the motionless water below my boat and the sails hang slack with no movement of the air.

The only thing that motivates me is doing something useful. Not to me. I feel I've gotten mine. So if I can be of some use, then *that's* what I'm living for. As for a self-oriented motivating factor; there isn't one. That television was unplugged a while ago and although I've had the thing sitting here in my living room, still, where I spend time daily, I haven't seen anything but a blank, dark screen ever since. I have to try to come up with things to 'motivate' me. Projects, goals to work on or towards. If I don't do that, I'm of no use to my family (my wife and boys). I mean, I'll sit around and do nothing. So I have projects and things to work towards—paint the back porch, build shelves for the kids' rooms, plan annual visits to France, think of the family's future, etc.

Does it matter if I achieve enlightenment?

I think it does. And I'm talking for *you*, not in a vague overall way. You ask this, so you are acquainted with both sides of this question: of things mattering or not mattering, from a personal standpoint and an imagined ultimate one. I think it matters. Someone can fulfill themselves or be fulfilled in their lifetime. That matters a lot to that person. By fulfilled, I don't mean like eating a big meal. I mean exactly that thing that matters the most to you. Not anyone else alive, who's ever been alive or whoever will be alive in centuries to come. The thing that matters to you.

Here is some speculation on your mind state or mood that I project onto you (in other words, guess): There's a real phenomenon that people can experience where a black turn of mind or darkness comes over their thinking. The addict does this or has this occur, where nothing matters, so therefore there is really nothing to do but drink, for example. I'm not talking off the top of my head. Another instance when something like this happens is when I see someone doing something 'better' than me. I feel depressed and feel, 'what's the use,' and give up. Maybe this evolves into a malaise of inspired action where a person might say, 'nothing matters.' I don't know. It could be a brain chemistry thing. Some people's homeostasis or natural balance point is high, others, low, etc.

Does anything matter, ultimately?

I think you know the answer is, NO. From my perspective, there is ONE GREAT BIG THING that matters so much it outshines nothing and everything that ever was [or could be]. If that thing can be had or known, then, nothing else matters. Everything is fine and I can die content. If a person is in the position of having great dissatisfaction with life-as-they-know-it and as it has been for them so far, then I maybe repeat the sentence before this one.

But ultimately, ultimately. Yes.

I know I'm sounding perhaps odd. The reason I say that is: if you went down a list and asked me if each item mattered ultimately, I wouldn't say yes or no. [It all matters but] nothing on that list matters one bit. It's all a part of a greater thing (read billions of galaxies) that also doesn't matter one bit. In the grand picture, [everything is unspeakably] precious—like the snowflake that is so perfect before melting into oblivion.

I got rained out a bit this morning. I'm finishing painting a house.

It's good hearing from you, Shawn.

That might have been a bit to read. It probably depends on how interested in the subject matter you are.

Today, February 4, 2010, is a somewhat cold Thursday. I just finished a late lunch. Andrée is in St. Clairsville meeting her friend Bożena to speak French together over coffee. I just got a call from Bob's Transmission in Warnock, Ohio, telling me Andrée's car is ready for pick up. An expensive rebuild. I'm sitting here, typing, with a hot water bottle on my lap—an easy way to stay warm with the thermostat turned down. I've got about an hour before Guillaume and Ben come home, so I'm going to plink out a few paragraphs, sit in meditation for my daily ten minutes, and then go into the basement for some cardiovascular exercise.

What does that have to do with my perspective? Nothing I do has anything to do with "It." But everything I do has to do with it. You knew that was coming. Everything is colored by the perspective I bring to this seeing. It's unavoidable and automatic. I couldn't choose to look another way. When Arnie was talking about the variableness of our convictions and beliefs, I have to say he's exactly right. They are like everything else in this reality. They change, morph and melt.

Went with Andrée to pick up her car. I drove hers and she took my work van home to be here when the boys got off the school bus. I stopped at a covered bridge near to the Flushing exit from I-70 and spent ten minutes in my version of Mike Conners' effortless meditation [visit tatfoundation.org and search the TAT Forum archives for a detailed explanation of Mike's form of effortlessness]. *My* version of it. Just ten minutes. Even lazier than no effort. No controlling of thoughts or anything. Just sitting in the car, then standing outside near the pond. I drove the car back to the transmission shop and they put it on a hoist to see where some clunking noises were coming from. Two rocker arm bushings were worn and I waited until they got two new ones to install. Drove home. This time everything was tight.

Andrée took the boys to Noah's, a classmate of Benjamin's. The boy's mother had dropped off her son for Ben's birthday party last weekend. Andrée and Noah's mom thought they could become friends. A little while ago, I came home to an empty house with remnants of Andrée's grocery shopping in the kitchen. I took the new cat litter and laundry detergent downstairs. Hit the speed bag a while, punched the punching bag. Did the ski machine and listened to a Rose lecture on cassette. Came upstairs, got some water, turned on the computer, erased a phone message I had left for Andrée while on the way home from the transmission shop the second time. Sat down and started writing.

I walk around with a moodless mood that doesn't pass. When I am quiet, when the activity level in my head is more of an idle than a rush, this mood gets stronger and heavier. It's always there. I feel everything through it. I see everything through it. The feeling is a solid knowing. If I was going over the falls in a canoe, knowing *this was it*, I wouldn't dismay. I'd try like hell to not go over and grab anything I could to stop the fall. I wouldn't welcome death, but I would know it.

I walk inside this feeling. I used to walk around in a totally different feeling—of something missing. That feeling had been a strong sense that there was SOMETHING REALLY BIG and IMPORTANT that I was missing out on. There was some information—I felt with all my being existed—and I didn't have it at all. Whenever I'd see a charismatic actor on screen, like Sean Connery, Clint Eastwood or Anthony Hopkins, I'd want whatever they had, whatever made them seem like they were comfortable. They exuded sureness. I wanted sureness. [I wanted to *know something for sure*, to use Rose's phrase.] They knew the score, it seemed. Something about them was a knowing. I was the opposite; I was a walking condition of unknowing. I felt a lot, dreamed a lot, wondered a lot of the time. *What is the real deal behind everything? What's the answer to this life? What is the meaning of life, period?*

The difference between my perspective now and before April of '96 is [the contrast between] daylight and blackness. I don't walk around missing something now. I don't feel unfulfilled. I'm not disappointed with my lack of knowledge or my lot in life. I can finally live this life without doing it a terrible injustice. A terrible injustice would be nursing regret each day and embodying dissatisfaction, thereby wasting the precious moments I do have, while preoccupied with other things.

The only thing I can claim to have done in my life is follow the beat of my own drum as far as I could go.

Whatever follows is a gift, and I hope I don't waste it. I'm living the daily life I have, and feel a compulsion to try to say some things. I'd love to write for a living. I'd love to do nothing for a living, reading, walking, thinking, noticing, pausing… It's supposed to snow a lot tomorrow. Today, everyone was talking about it. The furnace just kicked on. It's nearly dark outside. I wonder when Andrée and the boys will get here.

The following was a resurrection—a phoenix from the ashes of my neglected campfire. Though it wrote itself and felt somewhat effortless, I still felt constrained. *I wanted to be free.* The story appearing later in this book, that I wrote after this one, reflected my need for freedom of expression.

When I took the first two months of 2010 to push toward becoming a writer for a living, I wrote *A New Story*. I sat, proverbial blank wall in front of me, and started on a ghost story. My writing self had become a kind of ghost. My old self was a ghost. This story came from *me*.

A New Story
by David W. Weimer

The ghost walked through a wall between the kitchen and living room. Not walked. Just moved. Not moved. Just *was*. The ghost *was*, and it manifested in vagueness over here, then over there. It was, as the man sitting in a wooden chair leaning back on two legs liked to think of it, out of phase with this reality, which, to the ghost, was as unreal and vague, dream-like actually, as the ghost normally was to those who sensed it to varying degrees. It was, of course, possible for one member of one reality to notice the other, vaguely. It was still possible, yet highly unlikely, for both members of respective realities to view one another at the same time.

But it happened naturally, Dawood knew. In a certain instance, it happened *every time*.

"Aaah well," he said. The chair clunked down to all-fours. He reached his arms out wide, stretching thoroughly. It felt good to stretch. The goateed man stood and stretched his stiff legs, tensing the muscles and shaking each foot in turn.

The living room was unlit, unlived-in and dusty, but Dawood found it quietly comforting. In all the days, this ghost eases through the spaces here, and sun comes through front windows some days, and some days not.

Today is cold and rainy. Inside is muted like a barn filled with hay in the winter. Not warm, but protected. Out there, winter is having a mid-life thaw where rains come and melt piles of snow into smaller dirty mounds and fields are once again visible, revealed brown, dull, green. In here, it is colder.

In the empty house, stillness reigns and it seems that everything has eternally retired from all movement and living. Being inside of a faded photo of a house that someone grew up in—that's how it feels here. Dawood takes in his surroundings: scraped floors, cobwebs tracing light fixtures to doors to corners and the dust over all, all, and the silence.

On the second floor, a creeping glacier fans blackly out from a central point in the ceiling. In a second bedroom, where the chimney goes through the ceiling, there is another swelling stain with flaking ceiling paint. The flashing on the roof, a stiff collar the chimney wears in all weather, rusting steadily for decades, now allows rushing water in through a hole. A wide river washes the slanted gable roof, narrows to a stream and pours into layers of the house's skin.

Everything in a permanent state of constant imperceptible decline. The house is a clock, never moving, embodying change.

The professional psychic came to this house, this day, and stood and watched the water dripping steadily in front of a window from a burst gutter. His shoes sunk into the sod in front of a pair of tall curtain-less spectacles staring at him. A large shape dropped into a neglected cedar. Dawood's breath rose lazily in the cold air. Slush peppered the dark green shrubbery. On the edge of the roof, a semi-circular gap in the snow and ice: a missing tooth. Everything drops eventually.

It's dripping in here, too, he thought. He looked out through one dull lens of the house. In here, out there—what about out in space, on asteroids, or on the moon? Yes. The water is a constant blast there, streaming dryly from the sun in every direction in a billions-year-old soundless raging torrent without cease. Down here in the mud, as long as this dissolving planet lasts, water is the permanent stand-in actor.

Being a psychic was Dawood's destiny. As an adolescent and young boy, he hadn't *known*. He'd felt. He'd felt everything.

Like this house, standing, resting, settling a hundred yards from the narrow paved road facing a property-front row of Sycamores, he, too, had inevitably become what he was supposed to be. This is how the house feels, he thought. This house *is*. Just like he is, and just like its ghost.

Standing with his hands in his pockets behind the straight-backed old painted black chair, reminiscing through the dirty window glass at the falling snow and ice outside, Dawood cleared his throat.

Back to work.

The ghost had already faded, but the living man, a quiet-seeming man, calmly picked up his equipment from the floor beside the chair. It consisted of a black index card box and a heavy gun-metal object resembling a many-pointed transmission gear. He almost glided like a ghost himself through the doorway into the dining room. He stepped on two uneven boards and they commented loudly in the empty eating place just like always.

Dawood Jones, psychic and purveyor of *metaphys-oddities*, no longer wondered what ghosts felt like when they were captured and bottled in display jars that collectors kept on shelves. As a boy, he had been very curious. One day, this wonder fueled more than his uncommon imagination as he stood staring up at the rows of bell jar spirits over a shop door. Something whispered in his head, *Go...*

And he spun into circles and swirled into fog. Visions of his life were strong ... Calling... *Come here.., come here...* He moved toward them into days on end of warm sunny happiness. His children, whole lives behind them, growing and learning and leaving and returning. His wife and their time, growing closer, fighting, adapting, loving, depending on each other, living and dying with each other. Countless details—perfect snowflakes—all fell crystal clear into the contours of his dream, blanketing him under layers of feeling. *Oh my...* Dawood fell— *God...*

...back onto the stone-tiled shop floor cracking his head. He heard the crack inside his head and felt its bright shock of pain. His ears rang and fuzzy stars swirled in his eyes. He blinked hard and the bright spots stayed. The proprietor pulled him up by the arm, supporting his back. "You're *one*, you know. Don't look so intensely next time."

The man led 12-year-old Dawood by the elbow around the checkout counter and sat him down on a padded stool. He made the boy's hands clasp themselves on the countertop, leaned over, and marked a dot on the boy's thumb with a felt-tip marker. "Stare right there at your thumb for a while. I'll get you some water."

That was Dawood's initiation. Until that moment, he had walked through a world flavored and infused with nostalgic undertones and blanketed with drapings of past lives. A permanent déjà vu was his world. In *Soothsayer Curios*, an establishment Dawood had only passed by before, he was finally introduced to an overview; others shared his sensing, others walked through once-lived people and breathed-in their different essences.

The creaking floor left behind him, Dawood edged through a narrow half-open door. *Musty...* The stairwell led down to a partial basement beneath this end of the house. His right elbow slid along the railing as he took each step. The steps were sound, he knew, but he wanted to protect his tools from a fall. He followed a thin trail of wood smoke.

Light crept across the basement. Dawood stepped onto the cracked cement and strode to a ceramic block wall between two rectangular windows. He rested his back against the crumbling plaster-faced wall. Powdered plaster, paint flakes, grout sand and spider webs stuck to his dark coat.

The trim brown-haired man placed his star-like item on the floor in a precisely-felt position. He straightened and inhaled through his nose. No one will know *this*. This place. This Now. He breathed out the damp. He opened the plastic box and stood quietly.

After a moment, he *breathed in* the ghost like a black hole breathes in an unwitting, unable-to-resist companion star—in wisps, tendrils, matter-that-isn't-matter, drawing into the in-breath. Dawood *was*, consumer, consumed and container. In the end, even though it always happened, he jerked as two wide-open eyes rushed into his own. Staring, surprised, they looked into each other and merged.

Every 'ghost hound' has a container. Most feel comfortable with glass jars of one kind or another. Some prefer envelopes, map tubes or corked wine bottles. Any container will do. A year ago, he met a grandmotherly ghost hound who used a museum-quality incandescent bulb whose broken filaments rattled in the clear pear-shaped vacuum. Everything worked, but only one thing would work for each person.

When none of the ghost's mahogany-flavored life remained in the basement air, Dawood *breathed* out into the black box. When nothing of that essence remained behind, leaving him a hollow shell, the black lid closed automatically with a subdued snap. The *hound's* eyes focused.

They had adjusted to the dimness. Shelves, ductwork, wiring, a rotting box on the floor. All empty. The flesh of the place was gone. He retrieved the heavy gear shape from the floor, straightened, and dropped it into his left coat pocket. Particles from his back sifted to the floor behind him when he went up the stairs.

Some places took more time. Some less. After *this* place had settled into him deeply enough—two days—everything that followed was a foregone conclusion. Up on the ground floor again, Dawood stepped on the two loose boards. They creaked.

He walked swiftly to the entrance and went outside. He pulled the protesting front door shut and stepped onto a small landing. He jumped over the broken porch steps onto to the soft ground, holding his black box tightly. Rain fell in his hair. The passenger door of his car creaked. He set the plastic index box carefully on the seat, shut the door, went around the front of his electric car and stopped to look at the house. "Goodbye," he said, to no one, he knew.

He opened the driver's door and sat on a cold seat. Dawood turned the ignition 'on' and nothing seemed to happen. A quiet electric motor whispered as he pushed in the warmer tab. Dual warm-air streams bathed the steering wheel where his hands rested. He made the single wiper blade sweep once. The commentless accusing house came into focus.

This property is ready for new inhabitants; they can rebuild now. A new story, just starting out. He sat as the house faded into vagueness. Raindrops merged into small streams running down the windshield.

Dawood backed the silent car into the grass, toggled the gear selector forward and aimed his vehicle down the rutted drive to the Sycamore trees. Slush hissed beneath rolling tires. He pulled even with the trees, then nosed the car forward. The spread-armed sentries stood tall, judging him. Holding his black box against the passenger seat, the psychic turned left and drove into the rain, accelerating smoothly, leaving the house and trees behind.

© 2010 David W. Weimer

Chapter 19 — Andrée and Me

> Dear David,
>
> I'd like to be one of your best friends. I received the little paper of IYS yesterday and that's why I'm writing to you today.
>
> I know that you're 16, and you speak English only.
>
> You like the sport, reading and music. What sort of music do you like? You know I love Elvis Presley very much. Do you like him? I hope so.
>
> Well.... I'm 14 and I'll be 15 the March 21st 1983.
>
> My address is:
> Andrée LEPÉROU
> 227 rue de Fougères
> 35 000 RENNES
> FRANCE
>
> I've got one brother, he is the 19 and his name

My first letter from Andrée, postmarked Feb. 23, 1983.

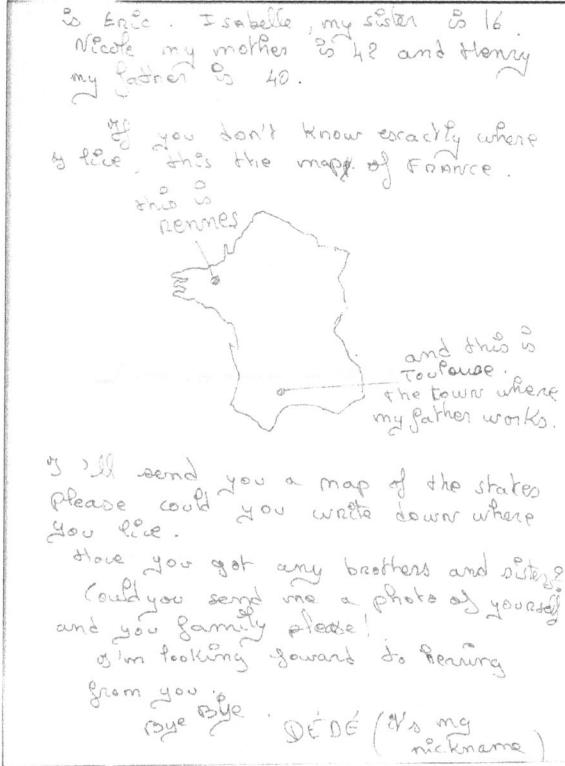

I found this first letter of Andrée's among the others in a wooden box I keep them in. I was searching for her first letters—I remember them so vividly. We had been telling people for years that we started writing each other when I was 13 and she was 12. That's obviously not true! The paper doesn't lie (as much as we do). At the time of *this* letter I was fifteen going on sixteen.

I'd filled out an International Youth Service pen-pal form during the first week of French class in the new year of 10th grade in Fowlerville High School. Not long after, I transferred into typing class instead. French was more work than I was willing to do. I'd become accustomed to putting out the minimum effort at school, pulling Bs and Cs, while spending most of my time reading science fiction and fantasy books and wandering around wondering.

When this letter came, I had already forgotten about French class. In '83, there was no internet or email, of course, so this letter came in the mail. I wrote a reply letter using a French English dictionary that had common French phrases for tourists. I copied them from the book and wrote an… interesting letter, I'm sure.

After one more like that, Andrée asked if I minded writing only in English so she could practice. "Well, if you want…" I replied. I'd run out of phrases to copy that didn't involve hotels, asking directions or asking for a beer.

I have Andrée's address in Rennes branded in my brain, as many times as I've written it on envelopes. I told countless people that we were writing to each other for five years before our first meeting *tête-à-tête*. In fact, it had been only a little over three years. It felt like a long time. [Some mistaken exaggerations, repeated, become 'fact' in my head. Surprised, am I, when faced with the truth. How many of those 'facts' do I walk around with, now, oblivious? Many, I am sure.]

It felt special to have a French pen-pal—especially this one. She was my exotic girlfriend from a far-off place. I looked forward to her letters. There was a two-week turnaround between mailing a letter at the Fowlerville Post Office and finding a letter from her in our mailbox at home. I remember riding my ten-speed to the post office on the way before or after school to mail a letter to Andrée. A cliché, but very true; I would go to the mailbox every day around the time I expected a letter, every day after school with high expectations, to be heavily disappointed when that tissue-thin

Born to Wonder 343

lightweight air mail envelope with my name on it in her unique handwriting wasn't there. Ah, the joy when it finally got here.

We became long-distance best friends. Andrée told me her troubles and news and who she was in love with and I'd reply, telling her what I was doing. Two other girls, a German and a French girl (I'd marked the box that indicated I only wanted to correspond with international females as pen-pals) wrote to me as well. They were fine, but they weren't *her*.

Two things from that time in high school. The first, being wakened by Dad around 2 a.m. one night. When I finally processed what he was saying, I followed him downstairs to my parent's bedroom, took the phone receiver and stretched the super-long cord out their room and closed the door. It was cold and dark in the house. Sitting on the wooden dining room chair in shorts, my legs were cold.

"Hello?" I said.

"*David?*" I heard a female, very accented voice.

"Yes?"

"*Is that David?*"

"Yes. Who is this?"

"*—Is that David? This is DéDé*"

"Who?"

"*DéDé… Andrée.*"

My fuzzy brain finally figured it out.

"Oh… Hi," I said. "Are you alright? Why are you calling?"

"*Hello—yes. I wanted to hear your voice.*"

I remember getting the phone from my dad. He looked at me like he wondered what the hell I was up to. I also remember feeling relieved because I'd thought I was possibly in trouble for something I'd done and it turned out to be something else. I'd been into a few things by this time that I wouldn't have wanted my parents to know about. This was the winter of '83. The rest of our phone conversation is lost in my mind. I'll have to ask Andrée what she remembers… It didn't last long. Sentences of two words on my part, mostly replies, and then silences. In that time, the overseas phone connections had what felt like a second-and-a-half lag time, so it was like talking to someone on the way to the moon—a lot of stepping on each other's words.

In my next letter to Andrée, I suggested we send each other tape cassettes so that we could hear each other. On to memory number two.

It was my birthday, May of 1984. I had received a puffy package in the mailbox from Andrée and was running late for work at McDonald's where I was a cook. I played her cassette on the way to work, smoking a cigarette and driving over the arrow-straight hilly Fowlerville Road fast to get to work, and I heard singing in her lovely accented voice:

"Happy Birthday to you… Happy Birthday… Hi Dave—I *do* want to wish you an 'appy birthday."

The first few hours of my work shift, that beautiful melody played constantly in my head. I couldn't wait for break. During my break, which I took in my car in the parking lot with a book and a cigarette, I turned the ignition key of my Ford Maverick backwards to accessory and pressed rewind.

"… Happy Birthday… Hi Dave—"

I remember playing a sample of the tape Gino in his driveway the next day after school. I was pretty pleased with myself for having such a great-sounding French pen-pal. I played that tape a lot. I still have it, with a box of others.

A few weeks later, there were armed forces recruiters at high school and I visited them during homeroom and lunch. I didn't want to stay in Fowlerville. I wanted adventure and challenge. Other kids were buzzing about getting money from the Army, Navy, Marines and Air Force for college. They bragged about sign-up bonuses and getting to travel the world. At this time, 1984, there were no major war efforts going on, so the thought of getting killed was a far-off occupational hazard chance that I knew existed but never considered—just like the consequences of smoking cigarettes never "occurred" to me, seriously, when I was a kid [teenager].

I'd pretty much decided this was my ticket. I went to the Marines recruiter first. *The Few, The Proud, The Marines.* That's what I want. It lasted about five seconds. A sour, head-shaved guy in a uniform. I had been totally ready to be interested in everything and anything he had to say. This is it... Soon I was walking out with my own sour look. "Asshole," I mumbled. "What a shit-head …"

The Navy recruiter was a lot more personable, but that no-compromise 6-year sign-up hitch had me thanking the guy and walking away with a pamphlet. The Army recruiter was my second preferred choice after the Marines. I recalled the *"Be! —All That You Can Be"* TV commercials. It didn't sound as impressive as the Marines slogan but I thought I'd give it a try. I walked to the recruiter with lowered expectations.

This guy looked decent and acted friendly. He told me about travel possibilities, possible sign-up bonus and money for college. The Army offered a "Try Two" two-year enlistment.

"Sounds good," I told Staff Sergeant Larry J. Pfeil. "But I'm a junior; I'll have to get back with you next year."

"That's all right," Pfeil said warmly. "You can sign up this year, in our Delayed Entry Program, and if you get a friend to enlist, you can go to basic training as an E-2."

Too many carrots to resist. Travel, money for school, rank.

I could visit Andrée…

I remember the recruiter's office in Howell and visiting it many times in the cold Michigan winter. It was always warm and inviting in there. In the heat, the a/c was cranked. I took the ASVAB (Armed Services Vocational Aptitude Battery) at school that year. A four-hour-long eternal test of boredom. After a couple of hours, I just scribbled in the circles with my number two pencil almost at random. I needed a cigarette.

I was presented with a choice of MOS's (Military Occupational Specialty) based on my test scores (!) and settled for Field Artillery Surveyor. It looked challenging enough, not a meat head job and hopefully not too boring. Once a month during my senior year in high school I got together with other early sign-ups to run around in the woods with compasses playing Army. We ate Army MRE's (Meals, Ready to Eat) and did all the Army stuff, formations, etc. I carried an ever-present book. It was like the boy scouts, I thought, having never been one. I'd read my book during those times when we'd sit around on the ground under trees.

I'll shorten the Army-flavor of this for now. I talked to another cook at work, Jeff Gyola, about signing up during evening rush-hour burger flipping at McDonald's. All this eventually leads to Germany and the 1/32 (First of the thirty-second) Field Artillery (Lance) Battalion at Fliegerhorst Kaserne in Erlensee, near Hanau, east of Frankfurt in central Germany.

June 1986, I got on a German bus in Erlensee with my green duffel bag and my alto saxophone case. I remember waiting at the stop. I remember getting on the bus. I got off in Hanau, took an U-Bahn (Untergrundbahn) underground rapid rail transit to Frankfurt and an S-Bahn (Stadtschnellbahn) urban rapid railway to the border of France, where I transferred to a French train going to Paris, where Andrée's dad, who worked in Paris at the time, shuttled me in his car between Parisian train stations, and then, on one last train to Rennes.

I remember a statue of the Brothers Grimm in Hanau. I remember pulling my duffel bag into the aisle of the night train to or from Paris, and sleeping on the floor in the aisle—recollections of people stepping over me. I was nudge-kicked awake by a French uniformed railway guy who took my Army ID and paperwork until the end of the trip. Then I was awake again, eyes burning from too little sleep. My saxophone and duffel were in my seat compartment once again and the last of the trip was watching very foreign-to-me towns and train stations flowing by or halting briefly outside the compartment window.

I was nervous and excited. I was anxious to meet Andrée, my best-friend-stranger. I got my ID back just before Rennes and did all the things a person does at the end of a long train trip: combed hair and washed face in the train's bathroom.

One memory I'll always have: Standing on the train with the doors open, looking down at a crowd of people from within a group waiting to depart. Friday morning in France. I scanned all the stranger faces, looking for the photos I got in the mail in Fowlerville over the years. I didn't see anyone I recognized. I noticed a tall dark-haired girl wearing a long black coat with a tall dark-haired guy. I'd noticed them right away, actually, but kept looking for someone else. Something made me stop and go back. *That couldn't be her.* I took the train's steps to the concrete platform. In the midst of the crowd, that stranger girl came up to me, taller than I'd expected, saying, "David?" In *that* voice…

Andrée said she'd been surprised at how short I was compared to what I seemed like in a photo I sent of me riding my yearling horse, Satin. She said she thought I was two meters tall (6 foot 6). I was on a growing horse—my yearling standardbread stallion, Satin. I stood five-eleven with shoes, not exactly basketball player height.

I had a four-day pass and I was a fish in another sea. It was really exotic-feeling. The flush of male-female excitement combined with meeting new people (including parents), finding myself in a completely foreign soundscape. I'd been in Germany about six months, but in the Army—at least in my case—there wasn't any mingling with Germans. I went out with groups of friends packed in one guy's car and we visited *places*, not people. A shame, but I was young and not adventurous that way yet. Well, I was plopped into the French water.

1986. First visit to see Andrée in Rennes.

Of that first four-day-pass to Andrée's home town, Rennes, I don't remember much sequentially. Does *your* memory work—or not work—like this? We were 19 and 18. Twenty-five years ago. As this book ages on *your* shelf, so will these numbers.

I remember sitting in the back of Andrée's brother Eric's small car, with my head touching the roof and my arm on my duffel bag. Sitting happened at stoplights, the rest of the time I was a marble back there. He drove like we were getting away from a bank heist. Blowing by people, scooters and cars, wrenching the wheel left and right, throwing the contents of his car back and forth like a four-wheel sifter, spinning through *ronds-points*, the intersection traffic circles in France that bloom like many-spoked dandelions between short or long stretches of road. It seemed like the trip to Andrée's apartment building from the train station took hours. I was tired and closed my eyes. When we got there, I was relieved to be standing on solid ground.

I remember being uncertain as we ate the evening meal at Andrée's place. They asked me to pour first or open a bottle of wine; of course I'd never had that job in my family growing up. The next morning, in Nicole's kitchen, drinking coffee out of cereal bowls, dunking toast with jam and butter into the strong brew, I knew I wasn't in Kansas anymore; I knew it as the French between mother and daughter pattered like rain on a tin roof.

Andrée was finishing her baccalauréat at the lycée in Rennes. This was a set of final exams in the Napoleon [education structure established during this French emperor's reign] equivalent of high school. She specialized in physics and math and, in retrospect, I think she was crazy to let me visit during this time. It was *this* weekend or waiting another month. So there I was, during her last tests before graduation.

I remember sitting in a booth at a café with Andrée and what seemed like a thousand young friends all talking at once. I spoke two words of French: *Oui* and *Merci*.

I sat, smoking, looking at the walls, drinking a coffee.

I remember standing in Andrée's living room by the fireplace mantle and playing the alto saxophone melody from *Your Latest Trick* on the 1985 Dire Straits album, *Brothers in Arms*. I'd sent the cassette to Andrée. On the phone, she'd told me she liked the saxophone part and I said it was easy to play. That's what got me carrying my high school instrument to France. I listened to the song a hundred times after that, playing along with it in my barracks room. After a while I had it memorized.

I pictured myself playing for Andrée, alone. Instead I was on display, right there in front of her family, turning fifteen shades of red in front of Andrée, Eric, Isabelle, Nicole, her mom, and any friends who happened to be in town for the event. I'd played sax as a kid, taking private lessons for three years before being strong-armed into joining the high school band in tenth grade. I was terribly shy and petrified at the thought of being in front of people, playing. This was pretty much that.

I remember riding bicycles to a gay friend of Andrée's, Olivier, where we stayed the night, then riding the next morning over to her grandmother's or aunt's place and back home to the apartment complex on la Rue de Fougères. Nothing final happened between us, romantically, but it wasn't from a lack of interest. I remember her grandmother's or aunt's house and garden. It was nice. The sun on the garden. I think it's amazing what a person can become accustomed to. Though I didn't understand a word of French, I was immersed in it, twenty-seven hours a day, and became comfortable with its rhythm and cadence. Its *music*, Andrée calls it. It felt like home, and I found myself straining to understand, though I had no foundation for understanding.

Andrée took me to the church her family went to. It was Catholic, it was familiar. I had been raised Catholic and went to Catholic school through sixth grade—by way of the influence of my mother's Irish Catholic family tradition. The church in Rennes was grand and old and beautiful and cool. It echoed. Andrée showed me around.

I don't remember saying goodbye to Andrée at the train station in Rennes. I don't remember saying goodbye to anyone or any of the other meals with Andrée or even our last words or kisses goodbye. I remember very well, however, sitting on the floor of the *Gare de l'Est* (East train station) in Paris reading a book after having missed my train back to Germany.

Andrée's dad worked in Paris. He picked me up at the *Gare Montparnasse* (West train station) when I arrived from Rennes. Going back, I had about 45 minutes to make it from one train station to the other. Normally, a person would have taken the *Métro*, but instead of having me take the Paris underground alone from one station to the other, Henry Lepérou was there to chauffer me between them. I'm sure that Andrée'd asked him to. Maybe he offered. Well, I put my bag and saxophone case in the back of his car, relieved, and sat in the front seat. We drove about fifty feet and coasted to a stop. I heard Andrée's dad begin swearing. He pulled the emergency brake and got out. What? I thought. I got out. "Everything okay?" I was at the back of the car with Henry. He didn't answer my question.

He turned me by my shoulders and hit the trunk lid a couple of times.

"Push!" he said in English, going back to the open driver's side door. "Push, push!" He yelled, motioning from inside the car through the open window. Okay. I pushed.

Cars and mopeds flowed around us with a lot of honking. A taxi driver yelled and Henry shouted back. It was a traffic circle and it was crazy busy with traffic and here I was, in Paris, sweat beading on my forehead, pushing this car. I don't remember how far I pushed, but it seemed like about the length of a football field. I don't remember Andrée's dad going for gas and coming back half an hour later. I'd stayed at the car. Not speaking a word of French. I remember that the French police stopped by. I tried to explain. They left. I thought Henry had gone for good. Then he showed back up, a little disheveled himself, with a tiny gas can. I had a sinking feeling about catching my train. I could see it disappearing the distance without me, headed for Germany.

We zipped through Paris.

The next clear memory I have is running in the *Gare de l'Est* with Henry, my duffel bag bouncing heavily on my back. We stopped under a large *départ* sign with flipping characters. "It is gone," Henry said, shrugging.

I was AWOL. I called Sergeant Zelko, my squad sergeant, from a pay phone and told him I'd missed the train while pushing my French girlfriend's dad's car around in Paris. There was a long pause on the payphone. "Dave, Dave, Dave," Zelko said, in his typical way. "What am I going to do with you?"

After Henry got me all set for the next train, talking to the ticketing people for me, I shook his hand, watched him leave, and sat down for a two-and-a-half-hour wait. I lit a cigarette and pulled out a paperback. During the past four days, I'd had no time to read. I remember starting to read and then stopping, laughing a lot, my voice echoing in the station. That frantic dash and the sweat was fading. I shook my head and settled down to a good read. I felt fine.

Twenty one years later, Henry and his second wife, Yvette, flew to Pittsburgh where we picked them up and drove them to our house in Flushing. They stayed with us for a month. It was a very good time. We spoke mostly French. Irony... When I'd been in France, I spoke mostly English with him; now we spoke French in the States. He and Yvette had visited us in Stuttgart, when Guillaume was a newborn, and in Ramonville Saint-Agne, France, when we were doing our skate park dream. Interesting, to see people through the years in different circumstances. My next time back to Paris after that interesting train station experience was in the winter of '99, thirteen years after my 19th "birthday trip" to Rennes (I'd just turned 19). I remember sitting in the small apartment he shared with Yvette, his second wife, asking his permission to marry Andrée. "Don't bring back," he said to me. "*Don't bring back*." We all drank champagne.

When I got back to Fliegerhorst Kaserne, I don't remember what day it was, but there was a movie at the post theater and I wanted to see it. I didn't go to many movies—I preferred books—but I went to that one. I just wanted to relax and see something in English. It was *The Flamingo Kid*, with Matt Dillon. 1986.

I remember sitting there—the sticky concrete floor, the hard-backed chairs, the dark, and other guys in the theater. The movie started and I watched it distractedly. I was tired from the train ride back and four days of meeting people, while straining to comprehend the incomprehensible. I was noticing the cinematography, the scene changes, hearing voices of the actors and the music and everything—and not understanding a bit of it...

1987. Fliegerhorst Kaserne movie theater building.

Not one word. For the first ten or fifteen minutes, I just accepted this as ordinary; of course I didn't understand; that was normal... Then it hit me: this movie *had* to be in English. Had to be! Right? *Probably* had to be in English. It was a surreal moment. I wasn't sure. I sat up in my seat and strained to pay attention to the dialogue. I'd pick up part of a sentence and then it would fade once again into a mumbling incomprehension.

I remember looking all around me at the other guys watching the movie, eating popcorn, drinking beers, b.s-ing. Everyone seemed satisfied with the flickering sights and the sound. I grew increasingly bothered. Why couldn't I understand? This was not a comfortable movie-going experience; I strained to follow the conversations and dialogue, and words continued to come into focus, be momentarily sensible and then rapidly dash away from sense again.

Damn. I slouched in my chair, eating my peanut M&Ms, no longer trying to pay any attention to the movie. I crumpled the empty candy wrapper and threw it on the floor. I left. I lit a cigarette, walked over to the Modernaire club and bought a beer. Sat at an empty table in the dimly-lit placed and drank. Later, I went back outside and walked the kaserne sidewalks in the dark.

I was missing Andrée. I know this resulted from four days of straining to understand the incomprehensible. I remember walking down the sandstone steps outside the movie theater building.

They were all German military buildings from World War II and earlier. I walked on the cobblestone streets past one of the chow halls toward the airfield past the gymnasium on the left. Our motor pool was way up ahead on the right. I walked back to our barracks. Bravo battery was on the second floor.

Writing now, I am still there that night, and all of the months and seasons I spent over there. Five minutes ago, I walked by a shack-sized *Schnellimbiss* on post where local Germans on renovation projects around post ate lunch, drank beer, smoked, and stared in silence when I walked in once. I hear them murmuring and occasionally exclaim.

Back then, I spoke almost no German; all new arrivals took a week-long class in German called *Headstart*. Hearing those men speak was the background for my walking by the restaurant, smelling those cooking smells. My memory of those men is like the *Flamingo* movie. If I could hear them now, if I met them now, I could talk to them comfortably in their language.

Birds are flying overhead right now to the ridge of that building; they're landing in a row on the power lines suspended over the field after gliding over our battalion barracks and parking lot. Some flyers collect in the branches of the many, many trees around and on post. Some of the trees, ones I leaned on and walked by, day and night, might still be there now? Even in war, some trees survive, don't they? So if the post is shut down, demolished or refurbished… One of those trees must survive. Walking in uniform, I carry things in my left hand, leaving my right ready to salute any officers who float by in the current coming toward me. I walk with purpose. In 'civvies' I walk at my own pace and ignore officers. I walk around post frequently. I ride my bike off post a few days each week.

Why do I have such strong nostalgia when I revisit that place in my past? Because it's gone? *Yes*. Because the guys in my unit are all gone, some dead? Maybe. Our survey section room with all our surveying gear in the back storage area is now filled with other things, or nothing. My life then is so crystal clear, vibrant and present. *It exists* in me but is lost, gone forever. Though it's right there, right here, right now.

Every environment I live in, I take for granted until I notice one day it's gone. Sometimes years after I've forgotten a scene I recall it with nostalgia. Why can't I look where I am now, with those long-gone, appreciative eyes? It would be like remembering the future. I would walk in wonder at being alive inside a living photograph. In *this* picture, in *this* present… But, since I can't do that yet, I have my photo album in my head that I walk around in. I see things that remind me of something I vaguely recall, and the pages flip by, slowing at those that haunt me from within. As I look at them (staring, unseeing, out over some water or a field), I am distracted by a slowly growing collection of pictures I had forgotten taking. I focus on them and return back *then*. When I spend too much time in this photo album head, I lose track of what *here* is.

It's a gift, I feel; this timeline and open photo album in the works—I'm talking about the experience of living. I only see it, often, while looking back. I'm grateful. What a view! Asking for more would seem like asking for too much. There's always more, though.

This morning [I wrote, January 2010], I was talking to an older man shoveling his sidewalk and driveway with a metal coal shovel. He works 12-hour shifts surface coal mining. Sixty-three, tall and lanky. He drives a full-size rusted-out green Ford pickup he let me borrow once to take my riding lawn mower to get fixed. On this morning, I parked in front of the library, turned in some DVDs for Andrée and the boys and then walked over, up the hill, to say hi to Tom. His property adjoins the library's. We talked in the cold. I'd done drywall hanging and finishing, plaster repair and painting for Tom and his wife over the past couple years. Standing there, I could see a little of the world through his view. I picked up some of his outlook by listening to him. My nose got cold and I kept my hands in my pocket. I knew he'd been forty-two like me, once. I could see it in the mists —that complete world there that he, the giant sole inhabitant, stood over, commenting on. Just like me with mine, looking down. We stood on top of where we were, talking about what we've seen and what we see now. Sometimes we look down at our feet, reminiscing. We're human stalagmites. Precious living stalagmites of golden time.

Chapter 20 — Cosmically Egged (Really Something Else)

<u>This</u> is taken from an online *Merriam-Webster*:

> Main Entry: ²**perspective**
>
> Function: noun
>
> Etymology: Middle French, probably modification of Old Italian prospettiva, from prospetto view, prospect, from Latin prospectus.
>
> Date: 1563.
>
> **1 a :** the technique or process of representing on a plane or curved surface the spatial relation of objects as they might appear to the eye
> **2 a :** the interrelation in which a subject or its parts are mentally viewed <*places the issues in proper perspective*>; also : POINT OF VIEW **b :** the capacity to view things in their true relations or relative importance.
> **3 b :** a mental view or prospect <gain a broader perspective on the situation>
> **4 :** the appearance to the eye of objects in respect to their relative distance and positions.

I'm drawn to:

Objects as they might appear to the eye; the interrelation in which a subject or its parts are mentally viewed; the capacity to view things in their true relations or relative importance; a mental view.

Yes. Now:

> Main Entry: ¹**view**
>
> Function: noun
>
> Etymology: Middle English vewe, vyewe, from Anglo-French, from feminine of veu, viewe, past participle of veer to see, from Latin
>
> Date: 14th century
>
> **1 :** extent or range of vision : SIGHT <*tried to keep the ship in view*> <*sat high in the bleachers to get a good view*>
> **2 :** the act of seeing or examining : INSPECTION; also : SURVEY <*a view of English literature*>
> **3 a :** a mode or manner of looking at or regarding something **b :** an opinion or judgment colored by the feeling or bias of its holder <*in my view the plan will fail*>

4 : SCENE, PROSPECT <*the lovely view from the balcony*>
5 : the foreseeable future <*no hope in view*>
synonyms see OPINION

What I zero in on:

Extent or range of vision; the act of seeing or examining; a mode or manner of looking at or regarding something; an opinion or judgment colored by the feeling or bias of its holder.

These things are the meat and potatoes of striving for clarity or understanding in one's life. They were for me, I should say. What is the ultimate perspective? What view can I have that isn't colored by a limiting thing—that I happen to be? Is there a 'pure' outlook? A more inclusive view than any other? Two parts from the definitions for **perspective** and **view**:

1: the capacity to view things in their true relations or relative importance.

2: an opinion or judgment colored by the feeling or bias of its holder.

I don't know what happened to me during my week in the woods in 1996, and the subsequent Saturday 'night of hell' in a friend's cabin on Rose's farm. No drugs—before, during or after. In the first part, camping in the woods, it seemed like I broke my brain; there's no other way I can describe it. What I previously took myself to be simply *wasn't*. It was absent without notice. A left hemisphere shut down? Possibly. It lasted almost three days. The subsequent 'night of hell' felt like I was being pursued by my annihilation. I was certain that to contact my pursuer was to be… extinguished, deleted, erased, demolished, destroyed. It was an active pursuit; I didn't doubt it at the time—it was a frantic fleeing on my part. I didn't doubt my assessment at the time; it was overwhelmingly obvious.

My view—my perspective—was seemingly permanently altered. My perspective this minute is a direct result of what happened back then. *Seeing something in its true relation and relative importance…* Yes. I see my life now, and this existence, from an overview that feels pretty complete.

What happened?

I was painting a house a few summers ago. Sitting in my van on the sloping dirt road in front, under the shade of an adjoining forest, eating cherries from my lunch and throwing the pits out the window, I listened to an interviewer, Terry Gross, on the NPR radio program *Fresh Air*. She was talking with the Harvard-educated neuroanatomist, Dr. Jill Bolte Taylor, author of *My Stroke of Insight* (2008, Viking) about her experience of having a severe hemorrhage in the left hemisphere of her brain in 1996. Everything I heard this woman say about her experience of the world sounded somehow familiar.

She said she had been a highly analytical, intellectual person before this event. That kind of mental activity has been associated with occurring mostly in the left hemisphere of our two-part Siamese twin brain. When Bolte Taylor had her stroke, she believes her left hemisphere was largely incapacitated. What she said remained was an <u>undifferentiated awareness</u>, a sense of 'oneness' and calm. *What?!*

Three things struck me from this interview: what she experienced when her left hemisphere was disabled was a sense of peace, calm and euphoric oneness. An undifferentiated all-inclusive sense of completeness. That's what I heard her tell the interviewer as I looked up the sloping forest across the road from the aluminum-sided house. She had to start all over, she said, and she was grateful. The over-scheduled, Type A, goal-driven rational squirrel cage she had lived in her whole life was gone. What a relief to be free, she said. In response to Gross' question about desiring to get back to how she was before, to return to her former way of being, Bolte Taylor emphatically replied, "No." She didn't resent the necessity of "climbing the Mount Everest of verbal recovery" as a friend put it, but she had a taste of freedom from her driven kind of mental life and didn't prefer *that* to where she was *now*. The brain scientist said she is able to remain in, leave and re-enter that 'oneness' state of mind—activating her rational, linear thinking processes in order to get things done, but consciously limiting the degree to which this formerly dominant mental operating system is allowed to occupy her moment-to-moment experience of consciousness. Before her "Stroke of insight," she only knew this one world, the world of her intellectual thinking; nothing else—from her experience of reality—was possible to imagine.

When I woke up that morning in my tent in the woods—the first day of a week I had arranged to spend on my own contemplating my reality—I woke into a new world. This is not a metaphor. A **still** place with no motion and a **silent** place of no sounds. Things around me obviously moved and made sounds, but there **was** no movement or sound. My reflexive reactions to objects of my perception (sight, sound, tactile, odor) were absent. Things moved, made noise, brushed against me, etc., and 'I' didn't respond. "I" was turned off. Emptiness was. No internal dialogue or commentary. *That tree waving over there feels like this; that woodpecker prompts a feeling of this memory, etc., etc.* None of that. Before, I had assumed that these reactions were me. Actually, I couldn't assume this; it's all I had known. Running commentary. Constant no-gaps commenting. Suddenly, there was no one home, and I was looking around in mild surprise (the commenter, author of ordinary reactions such as "surprise," was gone).

I had been so seamlessly and completely identified with my reactions and feelings. They <u>were</u> me. My whole life, I had accepted this ongoing commentary as who I am. A tree isn't tall and green-leaved and brown—the tree's tallness *feels* like this, and greenness *feels* like that. Rose calls this phenomenon projection, and says it happens at the time of perception. What is perception? Anything we notice, through any sense, I add. In this new silent world, I didn't know the world was flat; I was flatness. These words in front of me don't approximate anything. My credo before this new day was: I feel, therefore I am. Only, I didn't know this was my never-ending mantra. Descartes "thought" he thought. So did I. Ha.

An opinion or judgment colored by the feeling or bias of its holder...

That's <u>all</u> I was—every day every minute my whole life—until that April morning. A crayon holding itself and coloring. *The feeling or bias of its holder...* Until that morning. And then, I walked inside absent wonder, although I didn't 'wonder' in my usual sense. I walked through emptiness, profound silence, absence of mental activity.

I think my left hemisphere was out of the picture, says the non-brain-scientist. Like a breaker had tripped and nothing energized the television, ordinarily left on, volume up, 24-hours-a-day. Being gone was a relief and very curious—strange, unusual. Another person, thousands of years ago, said they awakened into a mystical world. Before this April morning, I would have said that they were obviously deluded. What does delusion feel like from the *inside*? Maybe such a person would have been voted the group's shaman and today, locked up.

I've always felt things profoundly. I feel things deeply that I can't limit or encircle with words. I'm left-handed; maybe that's related. I've also always been matter-of-fact. I don't say the mystical-sounding things. I feel my existence profoundly. To me, everything is "mystical." Almost nothing that people seem to be chasing and talking about is interesting to me. Still, when I listen to or read things from others on a similar wavelength I recognize that clear tone—regardless of what discipline the person is sitting inside.

What caused my two-and-a-half days of broken-brain-ness? My guess is stress. I'd been obsessing, haunting my brain incessantly with the conundrum, *What is the meaning of life?* For eleven years, since Dad's drowning. I wouldn't let go. Maybe my brain shut down. I'd had reoccurring nightmares of tornados and I'd been running, mentally, without letup. I was going for broke, no breaks or brakes —pushing. *I broke my brain* is as good an explanation as I'll come up with.

After nearly three days, my brain came back like my foot 'comes back' after falling asleep. No tingles in the brain, though, but the same idea—something asleep or absent, now waking again and active. On the last night of this week-long retreat, I had my 'night of hell.'

Again, to ask: What was my 'night of hell?' I don't know. I know exactly what it felt like, and what my memory of going through it is. That is branded in me. I was relentlessly pursued by a force, a threat, that I was unable to recognize as something that would treat me kindly. It meant my obliteration; that was its intent. I had no doubt. I can't convey how I knew this except that I knew it. Not *harm* me, not *threaten* or *intimidate* or *dominate* or *hurt* me. Obliterate. Annihilate. So I ran, all of me. Trying every evasion that occurred to me, and nothing worked, <u>It</u> just got closer, faster, closer. Then, I turned and faced it.

The song title words, *Don't fear the reaper*, by Blue Oyster Cult, have a definite meaning for me. I remember seeing those words as a teenager, spray-painted on a dumpster in Howell, Michigan. They didn't mean a thing. *What does the person who spray-painted that think it means?* I didn't know then and only can guess now. I don't know if the band that made that song holds the same significance for their title as *I* do.

During my eternal 'night of hell' I don't think one hemisphere or the other of my brain was shut off or turned down. It was entirely different-feeling from the inexplicable earlier time of motionlessness and silence in the woods. <u>This</u> was blatant pursuit. Something separate from myself was after me. The boogie man in broad daylight. No lighted kitchen awaited me with its refuge. I'm very conscious that all I experience is subjective, that I see through the looking glass (me), darkly.

Who is 'me'? What is 'myself'? Who is this guy who reacts and explains things to himself? Maybe this 'I' is a left hemisphere puppet dictator. His opinions are on a wide range of subjects he has no experience of; he makes up his mind to do this or that thing and feels separate from the world around him. Maybe my right hemisphere invaded its brother, challenging the left hemisphere's control. I don't know. Whoever I am is just saying things. Who? Who?...

The chief characteristic of my 'night of hell' experience and others I have had is that this came from out of the blue. In *spite* of my spiritual- or truth-seeking activities. They were felt to be totally separate and unconnected to myself, causally. No flavor, tag or hint of recognition. I can't say *Aaah, I feel-know you.* They're Teflon. Nothing of me sticks to them. Why is this important? Because if I could trace the origin of things I've encountered, I could believe I caused them. I can't believe that of the singular and profound occurrences I've lived through. If you step on a land mine, I am quite sure you're sure that something has happened, but the feeling that you are somehow personally responsible for the explosive having been manufactured and for explosives in general existing... See?

I've heard Richard Rose say we are capable of manufacturing what we strongly desire. It seems self-evident. Maybe I don't recognize it when it happens to me because it's such a personal thing. The big occurrences that have happened to me seem unconnected; I don't think I manufactured them. I couldn't; they're bigger than me. But I don't know. When I say 'I,' I'm talking about someone who wants what he wants for Christmas.

There's a quote—that the left hand doesn't know what the right hand is doing—from the King James version of the Bible (Matthew 6:3). We have this parallel-processing tandem brain. And we feel like a single entity! What is "subconscious?" The shared dreaming of this duo? **What** or even who are we, or can we, be? If a serious seeker of the truth is alive in our breast (or somewhere); if a desire to discover who and what I am and what this place is all about exists in me, then I have to attempt to understand my perceptive mechanism.

Getting back to my formative 'night of hell.' What resulted in me is easier to have an opinion on than speculating about its cause or the mechanism of this brief, monumentally influential span of time which has stuck so firmly in my awareness. The result was a particular lasting residue—a moodless mood that doesn't fade. When all the rest was taken away, it's what was. And it's in me, now: a solidness, a heaviness, a stability I didn't have before. It resulted after I and my questions dissolved in the survival struggle I went through that night. I didn't survive the process. This thing took my place. It didn't answer my metaphysical questions; this knowing mood, this permanent feeling is the embodiment of every answer. I didn't "get" an answer. There's a light under which all candles disappear. ONE. Only one.

Terrific. Very informative, you say—yet helpful! Well, what the hell. I am certain that at some level, this solid feeling must be reflected in my physiology, my neural pathways rearranged. We are a body. You can say otherwise, like the song by Sting: "We are spirits living in a material world." Or, "We are trapped in a dying animal," as another guy, Bart Marshall, says occasionally [visit his group's website, **http://www.selfinquiry.org**]. I don't believe in *bardos*, souls, metaphysical astral planes, realms of continuation after physical death, heaven or hell. I do believe in a metaphysical solution to my existential conundrum. There is an answer to my incompleteness. EVERYONE has their absolute and utterly unique-to-them solution, I believe. For me, this is valid and real. Any heaven or hell or *bardo* is now, right now.

I feel with a certainty what my death means. Death. People call something death that it isn't. People call death their-thought-of-themselves-dying. That's an ego considering its terrifying dissolution. Death is beyond that, or them. Death remains when their smoke is dissipated. People use the word death to describe their fear of not existing. That isn't death. Death is beyond fear and believing and caring. Death is, literally, beyond us. I equate "death" and Rose's "Absolute."

How can I *feel* something that contains within it all of my questions and puts them to rest in an eternal shadow of equanimity? I don't know. I experienced something fundamental and simple. Singular. No better word. I became, briefly (although it lasts beyond forever), the center of the sun. The result is what I walk around seeing through, looking out of. The glass of my lens (you could call it myself) has been ground to dust, pressed into a diamond and thrown into a sun. Nothing left but... *Blast!*

My view is what I have. I have become a thing that has "*the capacity to view things in their true relation or relative importance.*" What is "true"? This borrowed dictionary phrase applies to EVERYTHING that will ever exist. **As above, so below**—to borrow from *The Secret of Hermes*. I walk with a feeling of Oneness. A whole, solid, heavy thing with no moving parts. Not even one part. I have become indescribable. I don't feel it; I am it. I'm also me, the guy who gets happy and unhappy, older and wiser.

I have a view very different from my life view earlier. It's complete. I suspect and assume many people are changed in a fundamental way by things they go through. Thousands of years ago people wrote about "oneness." I don't think that's a mistake. Religions were imagined and perpetuated as a result of what people feel. Is it metaphysical, this oneness? Let's check with *Merriam-Webster* online.

> Main Entry: **meta phys i cal**
>
> Function: adjective
>
> Date: 15th century
>
> **2 a** : of or relating to the transcendent or to a reality beyond what is perceptible to the senses **b** : supernatural

"*Of or relating to the transcendent or to a reality beyond what is perceptible to the senses.*"
Sure. "Metaphysical." *Definitely* beyond what is perceptible to the senses. It's an internally-felt-thing. I believe that I walk through a reality beyond what is perceptible to the senses. It's a mood. That could mean simply that I am brain damaged. I share this damaged-ness with other people I've read and listened to; it's nice to have company I can relate to. The concepts attributed to Buddha, Richard Rose, Ramana Maharshi, Nisargadatta, Dan Simmons (a favorite author) and other speculative souls, have impacted me in my life.

I was surprised to re-read some of these authors after my 'night of hell' and find myself recognizing where they were talking from. I *knew* what they were talking about. That was a surprise.

Every definition needs to have every word within it defined:

Of or relating to the transcendent or to a reality beyond what is perceptible to the senses.

Before I agreed to this statement, I would ask: What does *relating to* mean, in this context? What does *transcendent* mean or imply? What is meant by *reality*? From within which context is that reality described? What does *beyond* relate to, in the context of this, one, sentence? What is *perceptible* referring to? Are *senses* just what I think you're talking about? Can you describe specifically what you mean by that word? I am not picky. I'm aware of the vagueness of all statements and the overwhelming habit and fallacy of unquestioned assumption. Each word is used differently by each person who reads or writes it.

Back to my outlook. I have a changed view. It is simpler than anything else I have encountered in my life, except the words or work of others I recognize as having the same or similar view. Everything else is twisted together, complicated and empty of fundamental meaning. 'Meaning', in my dictionary, is a profound and specific word. You can only know something by **being** it.

The difference is how people talk about what they *know* at the core of their being. If they come from a religious background, they'll talk about it using words like God or Jesus, heaven and hell, karma, sin or salvation. If they were a neuroanatomist, they'll probably talk about left and right brain hemispheres. What was I? It's hard to say. Hopefully this book, as a whole, will get a feeling across to you, so that I won't have to fail attempting it. How can I stand on this "X" and deliver a soliloquy conveying perfectly just how I view… everything?

~ D.W., *Flushing, Ohio, February 12, 2010*

Here:

Begun in the fall of 1993 for an undergraduate writing class at Pitt, then worked on again in the spring of 2010, this piece is from a farther-back time in my life, 1988, in Lake City, in the central northern Florida panhandle.

I am a passenger in a rocket; the time described in this piece is back there, *behind me—now, I'm passing the last of the Oort Cloud of comets 50,000 Astronomical Units (nearly a light-year) encircling the sun. The Earth, back there, is one A.U. from the star we call ours—roughly 93 million miles. Our sun's unseen but guessed-at brown dwarf companion star is on the other side of a local celestial racetrack that I'm leaving behind as well as I enter deeper space. Today [2010], it's been 21 years since the summer afternoon in Lake City I tried to describe (a few years after the fact). I remember that day like it was now. Does everyone say that… eventually?*

This one-act play centers on a day on that planet behind me where ten living beings came together in a plot-less motion of interaction. The feeling of a totality in all its details… This story is a homing signal and a star map, leading me back through the vacuum to that amber in time where I stood—and stand still, now. I'm still sailing away through the thinning cosmic wind, past intricate, frozen, thin curtains of floating ice. I look back…

Warm sand—I burrow my toes inside the smoothness, loose twigs and leaves, wiggling them down, rooting digits into cool moist beneath-sand. Biting fire ants on the tops of my feet among tiny white zit reminders of previous bites. My solitary practice of martial arts katas, stances, movements and breathing exercises at this abandoned park under evergreens and ever-hanging Spanish moss... Here is a 'piece of me,' written by a 26-year-old, about a 21-year-old, edited by a 43-year-old; the three of us all see differently, and don't always agree, but we're working together on this one...

Ten Altogether

by David Weimer

I felt like an outsider, a visitor—and I was. I'm tapping pure nostalgic here. Those moments were... I almost can't break away to tell you what it was like. And... will it mean so *much*, or much at all to you? I know it won't. Just getting warmed up here, give me a moment. At first there was a snake. And I was settling low into a rooted horse stance.

> **Breathe low. Breathe in and out, and on the out, push it lower. Feel everything shifting lower as a stillness begins to take over, and breathe in, then out. Though not a tree, feel its trunk, its solidness, and feel its roots in the ground and so much of the ground. Sway back, and forward, breathing low; there is no space, no distance. Rich brown, maybe bugs, maybe sand, pungent smell of decay and life. The odor resides in the back of the head, concentrated by tasting the dirt-smell in the air. Breathe. Then sink lower, stillness takes over and the heavy calm, nothing between the earth and body. Stillness and rooted solidness, direct contact, lower. Breathe lower.**

Take the path of less resistance. That, and stillness—quiet and silent and flowing. A will and purpose that doesn't care; if not here then there, or there, but always that way, or this. Flowing with stillness and movement; there, there.

I was thinking about the new construction that was even closer than the construction of the roads extending new subdivisions, which were, in turn, nearer than that new *S & S* they built last winter on the corner of the road leading here, a quarter-mile further on. Things were closing in on my neglected sanctuary.

Although alone—meaning I didn't "hang out" with others (my attempts at "being social" lead generally to utterly awkward discomfort)—I felt more a part of the swimming pool quietly filling with algae and frogs and the concrete-floored open amphitheater with a corrugated fiberglass roof, spider webs, leaves and a tree branch through one corner of the roof where water runs down to puddle on wooden benches before running in rivulets to the floor, concrete and sloped, on down a path covered with twigs, acorns, windfall and commuting fire-ants in a line leading to the otter pen.

Sounds from next door, from the incubating *Florida Sports Hall of Fame & Tourist Information Center* are easy to recall. Perhaps 200 yards from the edge of this sanctuary: zinging circular saws, bulldozers droning, pushing damp sand here and there, backing up for another run, making a measured, high-pitched mmopp! mmopp! mmopp! sound warning everyone to look out.

The wind still rustled the leaves gently, though, still blessedly coursed through the hair of live oaks covered with Spanish moss, and still almost managed to mask the sound that the long snake probably made as it poured into the shadow of an overgrown azalea bush an arm's length away. Startled, I calculated its vector, determining that the cold black length had passed directly behind my bare feet which were planted on the uneven asphalt of the path. Four feet long, and black as a new plastic bag.

I thought it could be a water moccasin. Shorty, a co-worker at *Donald Lee Surveying*, where I worked two years before getting laid off and applying at the restaurant for the maintenance man job, told stories about moccasins that had come after him in a swamp while he stood thigh-high in water, holding a range pole. I saw one in the bay in Tampa by the shore near my grandparents' house when my brother and I were throwing things in the water. It was swimming pretty far off, by some reeds on our left, and I asked my brother, "See that snake? Can you hit it?" We both threw sticks and concrete chunks, and we didn't come very close but the snake kept swimming right to us and pretty soon we were trying to scare it, throwing for real, trying to keep it away but it kept coming so we left. We were maybe eight and eleven. The next day we went down by the water with bigger sticks. No snake.

I thought the snake under the bush was too quiet and unobtrusive to be a moccasin—from what I'd heard of them. It flowed into the shadow of the azalea without hurrying. After this, I watched, and could see parts of the snake slowly weaving through the plants' stems. I was captivated by its sinuous progress and imagined I could see its tongue flick out to taste the air. I felt camaraderie toward this snake, a kind of rapport. But before I could get used to this feeling, the last of its tail disappeared under a mound of leaves piled next to the wall of the open air amphitheater where the normal action of the wind created a windrow of autumn leaves. Leaves on top were still dry and retained their shape, while the ones beneath were damp and decomposing in moist darkness.

1990. Alligator Land, Lake City, Florida. My Ford Festiva is parked in front of the ticket booth.

I stood up, walked over and kicked through the leaves barefoot. I wondered what made the snake crawl under there. Maybe to check out hibernating spots or to look for creepy crawlers... Well, that was interesting, that brief encounter, I thought. Did we really encounter one another? I wondered.

I felt affected and refreshed at that place, the closed-down *Fun Unlimited*, an oddly matched combination of water slide and swimming pool, billiard hall, video arcade and putt-putt golf course, merged, Siamese-twin-like with a natural wildlife exhibit that included the otter pen (complete with slide and pool), caged opossum, raccoon and bobcat area, covered snake aquarium and reptile exhibits, and of course, the 'gators. There were eight ponds scooped out of the cypress-filled lowlands which at one time provided home for several dozen alligators. Occasional nighttime poachers had thinned their numbers. By the park's entrance, the display gator ponds are lined with concrete, and the most impressive reptiles were kept there when the park was still open. The ticket booth for *Fun Unlimited* is located inside the giant mouth of an alligator with raised open jaws lined with rows of white teeth, and eyes and all.

Riding my blue Italian bicycle, a *Bianchi* that I had bought in a far-off town called Erlensee in Germany, souvenir of a foreign-spent two years; I used to wonder how long it would take before the wood and plaster construction of that upraised reptile mouth would rot enough for its jaws close like a trap. Bicycling or riding my motorcycle—bought after my bike was stolen from behind the maintenance shed at the restaurant where I worked the opening shift—to that sad, mysterious closed-down old place was always...calming, always just when I needed it. Always just right and occasionally—ignoring clouds of mosquitoes and the spiteful stinging of fire-ants—I would spend those special times that made this place valuable to my grasp on reality and sanity. I don't mean to be melodramatic. This can be misunderstood—it *will* be—but I'll leave it anyway. It may be an affliction that young males suffer from, each tailored to their own selves.

Getting back, then—how can I tell you about the turtle?

It was just there, just like the snake. In stark contrast to the snake, though, its slowness was entirely different: it was ponderous and I noticed a quicksand-like lack of speed that made it look as though it was forcing each movement against an unobserved centrifugal acceleration, crawling to the center from the edge of a merry-go-round. When I saw the turtle, it was only because I had heard it, behind me, from the same direction as the snake. I turned my head around quickly.

This box turtle, with the top of its shell a dull gray-black, reminded me of a waterlogged Nerf football I'd found once in a drainage ditch at middle school in Howell, Michigan. This one, a living version, was bumping into the fence that went around one of the alligator ponds as if it wanted be in there. It did. Some *barrier* was keeping it from going home. At first I thought the alligator in the pond would eat it—a quick bite for lunch—but then I remembered the shallow unfenced pond over there, where the owner of the wilderness portion of the park, Gene, puts young 'gators once they're old enough to be away from the lamp-heated indoor pools. *That* pond was loaded with turtles. I guess it's only natural that this turtle lived in the pond with the adult alligator.

...Regularity. Above all. Regularity of movement, of duration of movement, of scope and range of movement. Moved by a drive: strong, persistent. Persistent urging toward a need. Regularity of movement. [halted] Pause. Attempt again. [restrained] Halted, pause, random adjust. Attempt. [modified halt] Adjust again, attempt again. Regularity of movement restored. Movement restored. The drive is the momentum for movement. But the movement takes away from the drive... Prompting adjustment. Adjustment prompts a [halt]. Modified attempt at regular movement, continuous effort forward, continuous... [halt] Modified attempt abandoned. Earlier successful method attempted. Adjust. Attempt. [halt] Adjust again, attempt again. Movement restored, momentum unrestrained. Regularity of movement, regular duration of movement, of scope and range of movement...

I couldn't take watching and hearing the thing bump around like that; it was distracting and I wanted to 'fix' things. The fence around the pond was too small for it to get through unless there was a place where it could crawl under, a gap of some sort. Maybe it would dig under eventually. I didn't see a gap nearby. I straightened my aching back leg from the cat-stance I'd been standing in while practicing knife strikes. I took a few steps into the grass and picked up the turtle. Its feet twiddled, then retracted. I leaned over the fence, stretching out as far as I could. I considered climbing over so I could put it in the water without splashing, but I ended up throwing the turtle as carefully as I could into the water…

…Regularity of movement, regular duration…movement… scope…of…movement. [tilt, tilt] Suspend. Momentum arrested… Attempt stability…orientation. [fail] Adjust, attempt again…Sudden rush!…Overload!…[vertical drop] Immersion… safety…complete immersion. Pause. Then: glide through familiar medium. Regularity of movement, sustained momentum. Glide, content. Complete. Instinctive automaticity… Rest.

Damn. The patterned shell caught the surface in a perfect belly-flop. Splash! Floating green swamp pellets (reminding me of the stuffing in a bean bag) parted in a perfect "O." I looked for the alligator I knew was there, an ugly one that actually had living plants growing on her back.

It was always difficult to spot her in the water when she got near the edge among the leafy water plants. After this day, I would watch Gene (that's when he told me it was a 'her') feeding her raw chicken he got from the meat department at the local *Publix* supermarket. The meat department gave it to him once it was too old to sell. Better resting in a gator's belly than rotting in a dumpster in a hot asphalt parking lot.

Gene's Alligators.

No sign of that 'gator bitch though, and no sign of the turtle; it had disappeared under the surface. I watched for ten minutes without seeing any movement. I was really curious to see where the turtle would surface—and where the female gator was. I don't know why. I've always been curious. The overhanging growth of trees, brush, scrub and vines probably hid the turtle after surfacing. Strange, I thought, seeing those two different "slow movers" back-to-back.

Was there a way to connect them? What did it mean? The otter pen was not far from the fenced-in pond. I spent a lot of time there. I should say: it was a part of my ritual when I visited *Alligator Land*. I'd ride my bike in, past the ticket booth, following the furrowed asphalt walking paths, crunching acorns and sticks. I'd park my bike against a tree and walk along the green felt lanes of the putt-putt golf course quietly molding under some pines. I'd go over to the fenced and concrete-walled otter pen.

"Hi Ralph."

Ralph would really greet me excitedly and stare into my eyes with great expectation. I always felt bad, sad, guilty, because I felt pulled to give him what he needed but knew that I never could. I couldn't live there, permanently, giving him companionship his kind so thrives on. So I'd hang out with him a few minutes and tell him I had to go practice. I'd stop by on my way out.

Later, about a year after this day, Ralph would be dead. It was never felt the same without him. Ralph is a pretty funny name for an otter. Well, maybe not. In any case, any name seems odd for an otter. [Give short background on Ralph: how I visited him each day, throwing small bits of cheese-on-wheat cracker to him, small, because the owner told me that too much junk food was not good for Ralph]

Every day my otter friend would pop out of the hole that he had dug at the base of a tree in his pen. He'd splash into his water, swimming back and forth, then hop on top of the concrete slide, perching on his back legs, his eyes level with mine. It was when I was gone for three weeks to Ft. Chaffe, Oklahoma for Florida Army National Guard annual training that Ralph died. All because some new people who were leasing the swimming pool slash putt-putt golf side of the park had fed Ralph too much junk food. So he died. They had killed him with their kindness. I hope he died quickly. I hope he didn't die of loneliness.

After Ralph was gone, I looked into his pen. The water was drained, the plug pulled, dry leaves swirled in the otter pool and there was definitely no Ralph. No sign or smell of him anymore. Some of his scat lies disintegrating in the enclosure.

On this day, before Ralph was no more, I stood awhile, looking at him and talking to him. Good feelings tinged with the guilt that was there—below the surface—in my heart. I always wished that he could have had a companion otter. Gene told me that he used to have a mate but that she'd died a few years before. My friend always seemed much too desperately glad to see me every day for him to be just left alone. I felt guilty that I wasn't a good enough friend to him, that I didn't give him enough of myself. I used to think about what might happen when I wouldn't be able to visit every day. I don't know what Ralph thought about. I never did. I just felt things when I was with him. I just shared the time with him as good as I could. Maybe Ralph was responding to a desperate need in me... Maybe he was doing his damnedest by me—putting on a show and giving me all the love and attention he sensed I needed. Gene buried Ralph in the woods; I don't know where. He liked Ralph, too. Gene liked all of his animals.

I felt guilty because Ralph was confined—guilty that I wasn't. On this day, I walked back the way I came, stepping around and among leaves and twigs on the path. I always walked as silently as I could among the moss-draped trees, past pens and covered outdoor amphitheaters. This place was loaded with squirrels and all kinds of birds that used this miniature cypress swamp in the park on the outskirts of a modest sprawling North Florida town as a stopover on their way south to the Everglades. I followed the asphalt path back to the bitch 'gator pond again—still no sign of the turtle or 'gator. Some days are like that. The alligators, I believe, got used to me in my black *gi* pants and white top held with a thick cotton belt tied in the traditional Japanese way. When I got to where I had been standing before the distractions, I put my feet a careful distance apart, bent deep at the knees and concentrated on breathing again. The world diminished.

I heard the wind in the trees, squirrel sounds around me and construction noises from across the field. They combined, as my total external environment, into one feeling that faded into the distance. I was experimenting with breathing. My younger brother—who had lived on a ranch in Tennessee working for a horse breeder-Chinese martial arts instructor (a master of something that sounded like *Ching-ee* when my brother said it) had come back to Lake City, Florida after signing up for the Air Force. He had some time before his orders took him away for a year of basic training and advanced avionic electronics training. He would become a systems technician working on the F-15s in a fighter squadron at Keflavik Air Force Base in Iceland. Pat and I always got along—for the most part—as older and younger brothers often do. After I returned to the States from two years off in the Army in Germany, we got along as friends rather than the fighting and playing brothers we had been, while growing up. I thought it was a whim on his part, to show me these Chinese breathing exercise movements, although later it occurred to me that he may have wanted to leave something with me that meant something to him.

1989. Alligator Land amphitheater. Standing in sand where snake went through. I used to stretch my legs on the fence.

In any case, he showed me some of the breathing exercises that he learned from the Tennessee guru. They involved the "five elements"—wood, fire, earth, metal and water. I used to know their Chinese names. But you can really get into them, regardless. Whenever I was by myself, outside, and no one was around, I would go through the movements, breathing deep in my belly. You can really feel a power there after a while. After a while, all my movements occurred within this heavy-feeling place of power. *Chi*. I incorporated these more metaphysical elements and aspects into my Shotokan Karate *katas* and techniques I had already been practicing daily. It created a complimentary balance of power and flow. Flow was added to my practice. More on that later… or not.

Working through the motions concerning the element wood, I noticed three birds behaving like people, like kids who had found something worth talking excitedly about.

It's moving! It moves! It matters! (If it isn't moving, it doesn't matter.) Because… Its motion! That's why it matters. The moving thing is, and it matters. [flit over there] It's moving! It's moving, isn't it? There! There! And it goes… over there… See? Is that it? That's it, isn't it? It's moving. [flit over there, joined by another] Here it is! This is it!… What? What? Is it moving? Yes! It's moving over there! It's moving and it's going there! Here! [flit down fast, and over—another one in tow] This way! Watch it! See? This way, now. See it? See it here? Hey… [another joins the others] It was there! (Where?...) It was there! This way, now. It was there! What… No? Where is it?

Soon after the fact had sunk in, that these birds were acting differently, I saw the object of their interest: the black snake past those mounds of leaves, wind-gathered, along the wall of the outdoor amphitheater. The snake had slithered through a small gap in a small upright rectangular opening of the heavy gage fence surrounding the performance area.

The show area was hour-glass shaped and sand-covered, extending halfway out of the amphitheater. Two palm trees grew at the end, out beyond the overhead cover and the arc of enclosed sand. The snake had gone through the fence, trailing across the sand where Gene Pickren, owner of the wildlife part of the park, used to put on three 'gator shows a day. Dinosaur-related reptiles had been trained to open their jaws wide and bellow, to move around at his bidding and to keep their mouths—filled with teeth—open whenever he would tap them on the snout.

The club-footed female (see left rear foot).

He told me he'd raised some from eggs. He told me once, during the second show, one of the 'gators "bit my hand." That's a mild understatement, if you know how alligators snap their jaws shut on something. He told me some feeling had made him jerk away his hand—something "hadn't felt right." It was almost too late; as quickly as he had moved, the alligator's instinct-wired jaws had closed faster. Gene was really lucky. The alligator didn't thrash around much with his hand in its mouth. In the water, they typically violently thrash and roll around and generally tear their prey apart. Gene had pried the clamped jaws open with a piece of steel rebar he kept nearby. He showed me his scars. Nice. The audience had had a good show that day.

The snake had traveled across the ankle-deep sand that hadn't felt the weight of a 'gator in six years. Stray cats I saw around were the only ones who frequented the sandy area to bury their deposits. The snake's slithering trail cut right across, bisecting the sand pit. On the other side of the show area, a concrete path led from the last row of bench seats, close to the heavy wire fence surrounding the pit. The snake had moved along the concrete path. I think the birds had spotted it there; they sat perched on the fence in a line, interestedly watching. Did it remind them of some kind of big worm? They were little brown chickadee-looking things; I didn't imagine they could fly off with a snake. Maybe if they worked together... Maybe that's what they were thinking. I don't know what they were thinking. They had flown right past my head as if it were a post or something, some part of the scenery. I was a part of the scenery.

I remember the wind from their wings on my right ear as I stood in my front-stance. I watched their little heads and tails twitching with their comments, their tiny eyes that moved, and I could see them breathing, sides moving quickly, and their feathers quivered as if a slight wind blew.

Snake:

Nothing between bottom [earth] and body. Rooted solidness, direct contact. Flowing, into and always with, the way of less resistance. Quiet. If not here than there, or there, or that way, flowing stillness. [aware] Except: disharmony. Threatened stillness. Move again to another, other, quiet place with economy of movement, not a thing superfluous, everything flowing. The new direction, over hardness but not smoothness, was easy to turn and push silently against. Radiating warmth there: pulsing, tempting oneness. Lowering to more solid contact. Still. [awareness! sharp] Reflexive: avoid source of disharmony; imperative: regain stillness and stability. Darkness. Brief inspection. Prompt evaluation. Flowing purposeful movement, reacting with purpose. Taste familiar darkness. [precautionary] Flow into quiet. [awareness. brief resistance] Taste the air, its flavor in the back of the head—familiar. Sink lower, then heavy calm, nothing between body and stillness. Direct contact. Rooted. Solidness.

The snake had slowed down on the sun-heated asphalt. One of the birds landed a hand-width away from its black length and, seeming to gather its courage, hopped up to the snake and pecked twice, a third of the way up from the tail. The bird flew away as the snake started undulating across the walk at an angle. The brave little bird joined its companions on the fence and they spoke while watching the snake move toward a hollow log lying ten feet away.

Earlier that spring, a thunderstorm had brought down a huge, mostly-dead moss-covered oak tree. It was mostly hollow and the entire rotting thing had been held together for who knows how long by a thin skin of bark and cambium. Later that summer, I would help Gene cut it into sections and haul away all of it but the largest piece in his small pickup.

I guess it was the snake's movement that had the birds pretty agitated. Maybe there's a natural antipathy. I bet. Maybe this snake, its ancestors and family, were frequent silent prowlers of their nests. Maybe these genetic-wired bird instincts prompted them to harass their mortal enemy.

The snake was quietly heading away from them like an unobserved downhill stream. They fluttered and chirped on the fence and then, one by one, flew over to the log, the snake's objective. One of the birds, possibly the brave one from before, hopped down onto the grass. The snake paused at the opening of the log, its tongue flicking,

Feeling privileged, I thought: This never happens. I don't usually see this stuff. Sure, I always feel in touch with my escape place here, with the squirrels, red ants, Spanish moss and quiet wind, but I don't usually see a scene played out. I usually see the leavings when it's already over. That's what this is—a scene. It's not part of *my* world, *my* experience... Is this what happens while I'm gone?

The snake began to disappear into the hollow tree trunk.

I was sure this drama wasn't put on for my benefit, but I knew that there was something more to it than a simple ordinarily observed encounter. It *must* mean something for me to be here, watching it. It meant more to me than just.... This sanctuary, this rotting *Fun Unlimited*—will it be allowed to continue like this, unobserved, for very long? For how long?

As I thought that, almost as a Greek chorus commenting on my ponderings, a sudden steady hammering echo came over from the growing 'Hall of Fame' building across the way. That new place was spreading out, covering ground that once had been part of a middle-aged, diverse, good-smelling, mosquito-filled hardwood forest which sprawled around a couple of mammoth sink holes where alligators and cypress grew. Where did these animals go? They weren't relocated. Where are they hiding? Deer and armadillo, skunk and opossum, fox, birds, turtles and snakes? Where are their dramas occurring now?

I had my sanctuary to visit every day after work at the restaurant where I opened each morning. I typically got there around 1:30. "Where would *I* go, where would *I* be displaced to, when human progress made its inevitable incursion *here*?" I thought.

What happens to 'homeless' animals? I guess they take it more in stride than I would; they have no choice. I felt guilty thinking about them. I'm always feeling guilty. That snake, getting back to things, was three-quarters of the way into the hollow trunk when that bird on the grass hopped up for another quick peck. It held on to the snake's tail for a minute, then let go. It grabbed on again, and then the tugging little bird was getting pulled into the log with the snake. I'm sure the snake wasn't damaged too badly by the attacks. If I was that bird I wouldn't have held on around the tail. I thought back…

On the right corner of our garage in Fowlerville, Michigan, I was shocked one sunny afternoon to see the biggest garter snake in the world easing into a crack in the concrete under our garage.

14-years-old and quick to recognize a possible prize-winning capture, I grabbed that snake by the tail with both hands and pulled steadily and hard. It was late summer and hot. Amazingly, the snake didn't come out; it was really able to grip inside that crack, I guessed. I pulled harder, but not *too* hard, because I didn't want to rip the monster apart—it wouldn't be as impressive in a cardboard box if it were dead or injured. All of a sudden, the worst odor I ever smelled rose up from that snake. Worse than our chicken coop in the spring thaw, or our pig-pen in the heat of the summer or our horse stable half-way through a spring cleaning-out. I let go of the snake and smelled my hands. The snake disappeared into the crack and I went retching in the opposite direction. Wiping my hands on the grass didn't help. Neither did dish soap or *Comet* or my dad's *GoJo*. I soaked my stinking hands in *Clorox*. That did it. They still stunk of snake, but the Clorox smell was stronger. I smelled like bleach for a couple of days. I asked my dad about it later and he said that garters make that smell as a means of defense.

Eight years forward to that endless afternoon at *Fun Unlimited*. It was one of those long-angled sunny fall days. The light hit the trees' turning leaves, backlighting them and making them glow from the inside. The snake those birds were going nuts over was a lot bigger than that garter, but it disappeared into the log just as completely as if it had never been. Shadows stretched out long and got longer, but that afternoon seemed immune to them.

I went over to the covered pavilion where I did my katas. *This place was mine*. I had a beginning ritual, a pattern of activity, and ending ritual. It was cool. I'll never forget that time and those days of hours upon hours there. I *do* forget it all, but I'm changed because of that time, and in that way, what I have become will never "forget."

At five o'clock, Gene drove up in his small light blue *Chevy Luv* pickup, that he had bought new, and that teenagers had popped the clutch on almost the first day he got it, pushing into the water where it became completely submerged while Gene was off, paddling a canoe on the lake's fringes. He was looking for baby 'gators and their eggs among the countless lily-choked waterways surrounding the lake edge like tendrils or the network of veins around a bloodshot eye. He caught babies or collected the eggs for his wilderness exhibit. He pulled the truck out of the lake and drained out the engine and it's been running fine ever since. Back then, when those kids pushed his truck into the water, the 'gator place had just closed down, but Gene had always planned to get it going once again—this time *his* way.

Gene Pickren, posing. Circa 1990.

Gene was sixty-five at the time I knew him, jumping over fences and working with his hands. I hope he's still alive. As I coast farther and farther from that that afternoon on that planet, back there, he *is*, still.

He worked a full career as an engineering supervisor for large construction projects in southern Florida. He trained in flying bombers at the very end of World War II. He was a man who did what he wanted and I envied him. He took the cards dealt him and played a committed hand; he enjoyed life and I liked him instantly.

I'd been going to this closed place for quite a while before talking to Gene. It was one of those things where I asked permission to be there (to escape) after I had 'discovered' the place on a bike ride after work one day—and after I'd come to think of it as my own private sanctuary. I promised the man that I wouldn't mess with anything, and I'd keep an eye open for any vandals.

Gene's once-drowned Datsun and new greenhouse.

It was un-awkward, that first time we spoke. Gene didn't ask me anything and just accepted my presence there. After that, I'd see the old man around, by the two or three biggest 'gator ponds in the back, doing something in the bush, pulling vines down. Sometimes he'd be somewhere else.

One day, after I rode my bicycle up past the alligator-eating-the-ticket-window, on overgrown paths, popping acorns under my tires, I saw Gene ripping up some asphalt path with a pick ax where he was running a new chain-link fence across a path. I went over and lent a hand. It was a punishing hot Florida afternoon and we worked until dusk, taking breaks to drink sweetened iced tea out of a thermos that was sitting in the shade of a live oak (the same oak that would fall during a thunderstorm the following spring, that the snake would find refuge in, and that I would help Gene cut up and drag away).

On another day, I helped Gene lift and nail some two-by-six rafters in the greenhouse he was building. I told him I'd seen some birds harassing a black snake. I shouted this to him, actually. Gene was losing his hearing and my tone of voice is almost audibly invisible to most hard-of-hearing folks I encounter. In October 1991, a month before moving north to Pittsburgh, I remember sitting in Gene's living room, in the cypress-sided house he had built with his own hands, watching the Atlanta Braves in a World Series. After a few innings, we watched the game in mostly silence. When I said something, I had to shout pretty loud and was getting a headache as well as tired of the strain of projecting my voice that loudly.

When I asked Gene about what kind of snake he thought it had been, he said it was probably a rat snake instead of the moccasin I thought it has been. He said sometimes they look black. I didn't tell him about that day, because thinking about it recalled the mood and I wanted to

A place to grow my soul.

think and mull it over, quietly. I was thinking about how the world was closing in, in general, with the project next door, the new road going past to new subdivisions, and the recently-built convenience store/gas station. I wished the days would stay like they were, never changing, even though I watched things change all the time, little by little. I guess time is like that. It never moves in the moment; you can have these moments that are just magical. But then people tear stuff down and trees fall on things and…

On the day after the animal drama, I left my bike near the molding ticket booth and walked slowly to the small green pond and searched the surface for a telltale turtle's nose. Nothing. At the amphitheater, there were signs of cats—fresh digging again. I saw where they probably buried more treasure, and footprints were abundant. No snake trail anymore.

At the log, I looked inside and saw no snake, but on the grass, near a side hole at one end of the log, there was a pile of feathers! Soft belly feathers, not the longer ones that come from a tail or a wing. What happened? When? There was no blood or any sign of the rat snake, either. I had to guess about what happened. Did it happen in the morning? While helping Gene stack some boards on the side of his incomplete greenhouse? Does it matter? I don't know.

Ironic, I thought. The birds had been tormenting this snake, a mortal enemy, and the snake probably came out on top in the end. Like life.

I picked up one of the feathers, felt somewhat warmed by an autumn sun, listened to the bulldozer noises from next door and looked around while holding the feather between my thumb and forefinger. After all this time [22 years now; then 23, 24, 25…] this odometer keeps turning and I'm still holding onto the feather.

Chapter 21 — Really Becoming a Writer

I gave a woman my bill after a recent renovation job and we talked about her husband's Alzheimer's. She was more accepting than I could imagine being myself. "It's a sucky way to go." Those are her words. She told me something that struck me and stuck with me: she knew there was something really wrong one day when he couldn't tell time anymore. I'd worked in their home for two weeks and observed their interaction and the man's behavior. I had picked up a melancholy contact buzz from the situation I saw unfolding. I probably supplied the melancholia. I'd done plaster repair and regularly walked by the man sitting in his chair, reading or making notes on paper, while on my way for tools and materials. This concrete fact of an individual's consciousness gradually closing its eyes intrigues me tremendously. It's about being and existing; what do these things mean? Our relationship to time and how someone not tethered to schedules and routines experiences duration are things I saw in a different light during those days in the company of a retiring couple from Wheeling. What is it like to be—*that* way?

I knew that there was something really wrong

By David Weimer

I knew that there was something really wrong
one day when his ticking wristwatch marched away from my sweetheart's mind.
It was such a simple thing.

I watched him blink at strangers that first time: an odd, jerking dark sliver, numbers in a circle, two dark sticks.

In time, I saw him accept these strangers as familiar unknowns
in a brave new world of faces, places, sights and sounds in a growing aquarium of senselessness.

Each day, I watched my husband receding from me, wearing his new digital wristwatch
that I bought for him.
He insisted on wearing this new friend; and although they didn't speak
they drew comfort from their mutual lack of comprehension.

I miss him, more every day, although he's still by my side or behind me
always by my side or behind me.

We share our empty laughter and I feel like crying, and I do.

Our past dangles from both sides of a gorge with a ferocious river below.

Footbridge planks are stuck in cracks between rocks.

Most have floated downstream.

I wear him now, always now, my lonely watch with that face that I recognize.

And his hands, I watch them; I watch them moving apart from meaning.

A strong fading familiarity is what we have left each second.

My husband is my wristwatch that ticks every second faithfully

slower and slower as its tension lessens, releasing our life together

our passing life.

Notes on *Ohgod.*

I wrote this one as a thought experiment. I wanted to have a story addressing a phenomenon I had noticed in myself: not being able to hold a real-time contemplation of my own mortality in a felt, experienced, known sense. I knew I would die one day for good. Everyone does. But we only *know* that at certain times. I had wondered what it would take to force a person into an unbroken chain of seconds of *knowing* that one's death was <u>now</u>. What could I do to bring this awareness on and sustain it? I thought of the time I had skydived and become bored after reaching terminal velocity. My next thought was to wonder if knowledge of a missing parachute would do the trick. In a way, I suspected it wouldn't matter; we get used to basically anything, but I wasn't sure. What conditions would allow a person to have more than a few minutes of time on such a terminal journey?

I wrote *Ohgod* in 1999. Or re-wrote it. I have a journal reference to it in 1994; that would have been in my senior year of college, age 27, married, in Pittsburgh. But in my second floor apartment just a stone's throw across the train tracks from the English Department of the University of Memphis where I was in a master's degree program, I was 32, living by myself and going to school. I was a staff writer for The Commercial Appeal, the region's paper based in Memphis, as the tri-state obituary writer covering, actually, parts of five states—Tennessee, Mississippi, Arkansas, Missouri and Kentucky. It was a big circulation area with lots of people dying daily.

At the University of Pittsburgh, where I'd been an undergraduate, a favorite required course I'd taken was planetary geology. I remembered details about Mars and one particular volcano that had fascinated me. While re-writing *Ohgod* I arranged to go skydiving again with two other colleagues at the paper. The other two guys weren't at the airfield on the appointed morning; they spared me from having to wait in line.

This story's character, Aura, has tried all of the conventional thrill activities, unconsciously and then more consciously, to bring into being that fear, high-adrenaline condition of being that makes all other 'living' feel like a poor grayscale recording. She's drawn to the only edge she has left.

Ohgod came before a number of trials in my life. I've had occasion to say this composite word in earnest many times in the years since writing the story. This story came before I was forced to culturally and linguistically touch my toes by going native in Germany and later France with my wife Andrée. Before the birth and lives of my two sons. Before the real work of a (second) marriage. Before living an entrepreneurial dream to create a skate park with Andrée in France. Before returning to the States with my own family and before becoming a safety-net-free self-employed contractor. Before. I wonder how I'd write it now.

I wrote this piece after having been hard at searching for the meaning of life. Half a decade earlier, inspired by Richard Rose, I'd made a personal commitment to myself, witnessed by myself, to dedicate the rest of my life to finding the meaning of life, period. My job right now isn't to answer what I mean by that; this is your life, after all. For me, I wanted to discover the meaning of life. My first uninformed commitment was dedicating myself to a task of an enormity I couldn't comprehend. Others decision points followed, other 'commitments.' Along my trail, additional choices presented themselves to me. *This* or *that*, always this or that. For me, my choices were always inevitable. There was really only <u>one</u> place worth going. One thing worth doing. This story was written by a seeker and edited by someone who had become something… unexpected. I hope you get something from this. In writing it, both times, I did.

Ohgod

It is the largest known shield volcano in the solar system. Its summit caldera, from which the magma last poured, is 70 kilometers across. The volcano rises 27 kilometers from the surface, and was last active 200 million years ago. For reasons not understood, Olympus Mons is surrounded by a cliff that is several kilometers high.

The air here has an orange tint. Here, it is because of suspended wind-borne dust. Rocks that make up this part of the world have been scoured and sand blasted by ceaseless winds that only fade, never cease, during the sunless night. Dust storms originate in the south in early summer and expand to cover the planet. Much of the Martian surface is coated by loose material, a Martian "soil" of hydrated iron-rich clay minerals that give the planet its reddish color.

Far from the equator, across the Tharsis region of lower plains that surround the volcano like a rippled sea around an island, an endless expanse of dunes stretches, covering the dark green rock of the northern continent. Farther north and west is the Amazonis region of vast raised plains stretching like a desert caravan in the distance.

East and south from here, the Tharsis Montes is a regular bulge in the Martian crust that extends diagonally, drawing a line for thousands of kilometers as a raised furrow left by some long-forgotten underground burrower. In the far north: the lonesome etched plains; even farther, the planet's thin polar cap. Permanent layers of water ice, a few tens of meters thick, are the residue from the time when water below the surface coalesced upon its release from prison by violent molten activity—a result of the intense meteorite bombardment occurring in the planet's adolescence. Farther ranging migratory ice, frozen carbon dioxide, disappears and reappears around the brief Martian summers.

Right now, this annual migration of ice has reached a low. Weathered basaltic rock, greenish in contrast to the surrounding reddish sands, is uncovered, appearing like whispered secrets for weeks before fading again beneath sifting white particles. Silicon, iron, magnesium, calcium and sulfur ride the planet's thin violent air currents like seeds searching for a place to rest.

Here, where she is standing at the top of the ancient volcano, atmospheric pressure is ten times less than that found at another peak, Mount Everest, on Earth. Aura looks to the still-dark sky, feeling somehow that she will fall *up* into space. The cliff that she stands on overlooks a void. An impenetrable haze hides its depths.

She is cold, but her heart is pounding steadily.

The young woman can see a mass of clouds away to her right as she faces the center of the volcano. Super-dry Martian air saturates so quickly that clouds form instantaneously and disappear just as suddenly. Clouds regularly bunch up on the downwind side of the volcano. The foam-like haze filling the endless bowl of the volcano completes her view. Her cliff overlooks the void, the wide open maw. Haze hides its depths.

She is cold.

Aura Minehold, 25, of Mars, formerly of Earth, died Thursday, January 3rd, 2450, on Olympus Mons.

Born in Marquette, Michigan, United States, and a daughter of Marcia Lane and the late Jonas Minehold, Ms. Minehold was an explorer of the mind and a seeker of ultimate truth. A member of Beta colony, she dreamt of undiscovered depths, and mattered very little, from a certain point of view. She found, however, within herself, a desire that burned hotter than anything she ever encountered elsewhere. The *unknowable* called out, and in her heart, she answered with her every breath.

Surviving her, are fellow colony members, few of whom knew her by name; her brother, Alfred, a sister, Eliza, both of Earth; her favorite constellation and a solitary broken carrying strap to a torch that was discovered on a certain volcanic rim cliff...

Friends were received at her home, her home, her home away from home. Services were held at an uncomfortable location, the Reverend Mons officiating. Interment not likely. Memorials may be made to a brief life that had nothing to keep it from expanding beyond its mortal boundaries.

At least, Aura thought, her obituary *should* read like that.

Ancient scoured black and green rock ended raggedly, abruptly, where the planet's gravity took over. Earlier in the still dark morning, it had taken ten minutes for her torch beacon, set on shortwave EM-strobe, to suddenly stop transmitting. Just before the first glow of the sun had appeared from the darkness, she had taken a running start and launched the flashlight out and over into the void. She slid five meters after the torch left her hand. With the light of the sun a faint possibility, she had lain on the rocks of the cliff, elbows at its very edge, binoculars allowing her to see the beginning of the torch's fall. After mists swallowed it, Aura continued to stare through her eye lenses into oblivion.

The far-off yellow sun finally begun to warm her back and the back of her head. It is late summer. The temperature outside of her parchment-thin virosuit is a normal 57 degrees below zero Fahrenheit.

She stands at the edge after the flashlight fell. She debated burying her backpack, which holds emergency tent and supplies, but then threw them over the edge, too, sensing nothing of their fall. She was feeling her proximity to potential finality. Though cold under her feet, her suit maintains a steady level of discomfort, rather than the killing numbness that is there, waiting. Carbon dioxide frost clings to the face of rocks that jut from the rim of the volcano like stubble. Aura silently compares the void beyond to the empty place inside her.

Aura's complexion is warm caramel; her hair, dark autumn leaves; her eyes, layered ancient wood scrubbed daily by monks.

Her body, fine, both in form and capability of function; she could not complain. Everything that she had asked of her body, it had done for her. Her mind, active, far gazing and restless.

There was a tension. Tangible. Not in her mind or in the realm of the physical. If she felt like it, she knew she could pluck at these lines of stress around her like harp strings. She wondered at the sound they would make. She imagined there was already a slight strumming noise in the faint, thin wind.

She was a winged insect in a spider web, fixed in a matrix of tension. Not pleasant, but too often, she could almost believe that there was nothing, absolutely nothing. But...

When the time comes.

The steady morning breeze, now, already pressing against her back; the taut skin of her virosuit snug across chest and hips, the backs of her legs tingling; she feels the pressure of the breeze and can almost lean back into its cushion. She turns away from the void and faces the wind. The wind was drawing the mist from the void in an onward rush. The rising sun was now in her eyes.

When the time comes...

Thinking those words, her heart skipped, and started again. Now pounding. The link between her thoughts and body was immediate. Every muse was echoed by an increase in pulse, a flush, a shiver.

Her private lander was secreted back in the lower slopes of the volcano, three days and some of a fourth's hike. Days walking the long, gradual rising slope had been like her life; she rested when she was exhausted, she pitched her tent and slept and woke to move on again when she was able.

Four days. She had moved with insulated perfection each moment. There was a purposeful certainty and a complete harmony of action and thoughts.

Here on the cliff, facing the wind and sun, she backs toward the edge.

Do you ever wish?

Aura's response was automatic. "Sure, ask me that **now**."

The voice *had* resulted in her heart racing after a first, massive jump, but she found that she had been expecting it. It was a familiar voice, and it reminded her of Aunt Jane, soft and warm; it also sounded like father, from when she was a girl, when he had pushed her on her swing in their back yard and they had talked under their giant leaning locust.

Her eyes clouded and stung. The voice had come from a glowing point hovering at the brink of the abyss. Her suit's pickups had conveyed a thin rasping noise on the rock surface beneath her feet when she turned to face the void and that strangely familiar voice.

She addressed them both.

"Yes. I wish that I could feel this way every moment—and nothing else. It's all..."

The young woman shook her head as her voice trailed off. She had vowed over and over to stop trying to put her feeling into words for others. The frustration of not being able to communicate exactly how she felt...

She looked past the glowing sphere that she wasn't sure really existed and scanned the gradually sloping, deceptively smooth terrain leading up to the very edge of a very sudden drop off. Shades of red, stretches of underlying dark green, shocks of fuzzy frost on the shaded face of pits and boulders.

Aura had begged the gods, and strived to find something to fill the void within her. Something to give her the answer to her life. Silence had always answered her heartfelt questions. So now, if she happened to see a glowing, wings-wide angel, well... what of it. She wouldn't allow herself to be surprised. It doesn't matter, because *she* had a need that didn't go away. The spark of brightness began to pulse, drawing her attention from thinking.

"Why do you choose to act—in this way?"

Aura scrutinized the wavering light, silently.

"Are you willing to die?"

The light hovered an arm's length beyond the cliff's edge. It was the size of a very large coin now, the same size as the setting sun on Earth in winter, seen through slitted eyes.

"I only want to know."

"By jumping now, from this cliff?"

The voice both asked and made a statement. It was inside her head, broadcasting below her suit's comlink.

"Yeah... I've come a long way to do this."

"I have followed you from your beginning."

"So now you tell me! I gave up on you! But I *had* to keep looking. Even after I stopped believing in you. You know what? I wish you had come when I needed you."

"I am here to ask you questions."

"And now, I must answer? Or my soul will be damned?" Aura squeezed her eyes shut. "No one answered *my* questions. Ever. They only looked away, or laughed, wondering why I wouldn't ride the ride, why I didn't wake up and live in the real world.

"Do you believe in your existence after you die?"

"No." Aura said. "Not at all." She looked beyond the edge, two meters in front of her, past the hovering light and voice inside; the wind whispered stronger and she felt as if she were drifting forward. "I don't believe, but I need. Mark down my answer as an official 'hope'."

The light shined sharply and steadily as the sun. *"Do you know why I am here?*

She had no idea. *Yes*, she felt. "Yes."

Everything had come to this. Yearning had driven her. Being denied fueled her. *To jump*, she thought, *or not to jump*.

Silence continued as it had before the voice interrupted her.

Below, an almost solid haze. Aura backed away fifty meters from the edge.

Hyperventilating, arms reaching, slow-motion loping, heart pounding in her head, electric tingling running through her body in a wave. Light-headed, she took deep breaths behind her face shield. Despite its special coating, the clear oval fogged briefly with each breath. Aura ran.

With her fingers spread wide, her arms reaching forward, she pushed off, straining; her right toe was the last part of her body to go.

This:

There were no aerodynamics; she was a dropped rock in a low-g near vacuum. She had jumped out as far from the edge as she could. Now, falling head-first and sideways, out of control, listing, turning over in a slow flip on her back. No glide-plane surfaces to ease her through the Martian air. No conscious thoughts, but a single-minded concentration, Aura stretched out her arms and legs to form an "X", arching her back. She was assuming the position necessary for a controlled fall.

The falling—God. It wasn't like she had imagined at all; she was dropping without grace.

She arched more. Her arms and legs were spread wide and slightly bent. She knew it *had* to work. Gradually, a firm, solid stabilizing presence materialized, righting her, then pressing itself against her. A falling leaf of solid rock, lying on a hissing motionless cloud. Aura opened her eyes and gave a short scream.

Steel gray, rushing seeming mere inches from her face, was the blurred surface of the cliff!

She spun around; she had to get away, back out into the void.

Freefall in lower gravity, in the thin Mars atmosphere...

"When you want to turn like a wheel falling on its side, move your hands like flippers; make small adjustments—keep your form and make these small correcting movements. If you reach unbalanced, you'll spin."

Her skydiver instructor's voice from the activities simulator played back in her mind. She pulled in her left hand—

—and saw the cliff move away as she spun, clockwise. The sky blinked dark, than light, then dark, as she found herself facing first the fuzzy caldera, then the wall. Aura put her arm back out. *Stabilize*. She was breathing hard. She pulled her hand in and then back out again. Facing void now. Facing away. Now! She had to get into the safety of the haze.

Safety!?

"Like an atmospheric plane or a diving bird; when you want to move forward, you have to trim your form. It's easy, but the thing with moving laterally is that you lose altitude fast; if you're going to do a lot of sightseeing, be sure to watch your altimeter."

Aura wondered what her instructor would do if he were beside her here, right now, without a universal altimeter or the mandatory emergency grav brake she had disabled. Unable to turn around, she rotated left and right, sensing the volcano wall. She aimed away, and formed a delta wing for a two hundred slow count. If she were right, she would find out. Getting away from the cliff, avoiding being smeared along a stretch of sharp rock cliff —this was her first concern.

"Just keep your arms by your sides, like this, making a "V."

Aura had practiced this maneuver, but only in the simulator with her instructor floating by her side, talking through a comlink. She imagined he was still there, advising, with the cliff a receding menace behind her—far behind her.

"—with your head like the cockpit of an old jet. Steady—keep those palms down—okay, good; your arms stay by your sides. Right. You want to keep everything even so you don't list. And that's all there is to it—see? Don't turn your head; keep it straight. Okay, so this'll give you forward movement. It'll also increase your rate of descent by almost half again, so again, get where you want to go and return to your stable "X" form. Don't burn up your air; you want a nice long ride, every time."

Aura slowly let her arms move back out, stabilizing. She then pulled in one arm, deliberately spinning. She kept her hand pulled in, looked down to make sure it was at her chest where she felt she was holding it. Another fear jolt ran through her. Dizzy... Aura put her arm back, returning to her "X" position. The dizziness subsided. The haze obscured her vision. Landmarks... None. Just pressure. No connection with place-sense. She floated in a sea of nothingness with the hiss of the wind in her pickups and a pressure supporting her.

Aura looked down. Now. Alone. Nothing. Maybe she wasn't falling...

She glanced at the large green numbers of her wrist chrono: 3:15...3:16...3:17.... She might have as long as her torch... ten minutes... There wasn't much time.

In the placeless void, falling on automatic, the young woman relaxed into her rapid descent. She pulled in her right arm again; an odd sensation registering in her eyes, a pressure, and slight nausea. She knew that she was spinning. She put her arm back out and made an "X" out of her body. She closed her eyes.

They would never discover that she had actually enjoyed her life, that she had not begrudged it one minute. They would wonder if she had been depressed.

"Aura."

A voice. The same? She had no idea.

"Aura, you may be falling into a locked door. This may be your end. You could be on an irreversible course—"

"Shut up," Aura said.

At her own mouthed words, the musical voice had stopped. She could no longer gage her body orientation; it seemed her thoughts, her emotional environment, nothing was any longer solidly hers. Her thoughts were not her own... If they ever were.

6:48...6:49...6:50.

Time...Time...Time...

A squirt of fear: There had been a blast of adrenaline just before she started her run to leap, millennia ago. She had always assumed that she would find out now. That it would be inevitable. It was the inevitable part of facing one's death, wasn't it?

"You could be locking yourself out... forever..."

"No!" she screamed, behind her faceplate.

She had *done* this so her attention would be forced to remain on the moment, the immediate—the Now. But she was only aware of her own breathing.

She couldn't get a deep enough breath! *Calm now, remain calm.* Her virosuit's oxygen reserves would engage soon, as soon as the air circulating around her becomes rarified enough...

Dead-end!

No! Breathe slowly, concentrate.

Fear. Inescapable. Unavoidable. Undeniable. FEAR.

Yes. *Fear.* Okay, *yes*.

A cold writhing flame consumed her belly. She needed to curl up, around it, to smother it. But there was no way…

She was *falling*! She would die! Oh God; she had dived off this cliff and would be…

Fear.

The thin roar holds her.

Fear.

Fear is—

This is what happened:

Aura was unable to overcome her fear. The fuel feeding fear is limitless, and this young woman was immersed in a solid sea of it, carried like a great wave carries particulate. In the screaming of her mind and certain knowledge of loss, she stopped falling. Utterly still.

Something broke. She was free. No struggling. She was at rest on an unexpected plateau. Peace. Acceptance. Serenity. A tremendous struggle led her here. An exhausted swimmer climbs from the turbulent pulling water without thoughts. And then, they are resting under the sun, feeling its warmth on their skin. How can…?

Is <u>this</u> it?

Listen:

My life isn't mine.

Aura's wide-angle panorama closed in gradually, darkening, focusing to a point. She was deep inside the volcano, leaving all that she was behind.

The thrumming pressure against her was familiar. It had always been so.

She knew she was motionless.

The Martian volcano was opening up to accept her offering.

Aura's limbs stung from the cold seeping in at the joints of her suit. A brief pain in her head as her ears popped yet again. The suit's integrity—

Aura swallowed dryly to equalize the pressure between her head and the artificial suit environment.

DECOMPRESSION IMMINENT! flashed across her face shield. It pulsed in time with her straining heart.

Aura brought her tired arms in to her sides, her thumbs pointed toward the rush beneath her. Light-headed. Sparkles in her vision. The oxygen shunt was seizing... malfunctioning. A sharp acrid taste now at the back of her throat as she breathed shallow breaths of the suit's failing atmosphere.

A ringing sound that grew louder until it pushed aside even her vision; a field of pure white noise that erased all in its fullness. Sound, vision, and sensation— all melded then into taste. Her thoughts marched one by one, slowing, then ceased.

The hand that had held her so firmly spread its fingers to gently let her tumble softly into motion once again, and...

Rock.

In twelve minutes, thirty-five seconds, Aura Minehold traveled to where she had always wanted to be ****** (loved), to be wrapped in warm blankets and carried away on gentle waves of enfoldment. She had always wanted to be...

Control.

Albert or Eliza, her parents, her classmates, her boyfriends; they had always wanted to take away where she could go, what she could do there, when she could...

Her insistence on self-control had gotten her far. The final frontier was found to start after she abandoned her precious control.

To leap into the void: she had *acted* to allow no other agent to have as great an impact on her as her falling. She then had to relinquish her hold on herself.

TIME TIME TIME TIME TIME TIME.

TIME. COMPLACENCY RULES. I'M ADAPTING TOO QUICKLY. VOICES AND DEATH IS NOW NORMAL. AND PART OF ME SCREAMING: *TIME TO DIE. DIE.*

WITH ENDURANCE-EYES, ENTER THE PROFOUND, PLEASE!!... *I AM DYING TO AVOID DISTRACTIONS!!!*

VOICE. whispers...

"Am I in your mind?"

(This question gets through)

SOMETHING SOLID SIEZES HER ATTENTION: THERE IS NO TIME.

A point of light hovers to her right, an arm's length away. She reaches. *Dizzy*. Spinning, she reaches as far as she can and then lets go. *So bright*. She should have known. About falling, dying and everything.

Teeth clenched in a grin behind her face shield, she reaches...

CONCENTRATE. EVERYTHING IS COMING. GROUND RUSHING. NO... NO! NOT YET...

"There are only these few moments."

Finally, she knows.

Finally.

Her virosuit: It had none of the billowy material from arms to torso and between legs; no repulsors to facilitate a survivable landing; no hope of watching 'divers practicing maneuvers in their wind tunnels, half a world away.

In her free fall, Aura had become *solid*. Is this what it's all about? Like other things, too much speculative build-up, she realized. The reality was free.

Falling 27 kilometers at a rate of 200 kilometers per hour, with a malfunctioning respirator and wearing an virosuit with no glide/collector surfaces— through an almost pressure-less atmosphere into a thinly, windswept extinct shield volcano. Wind currents...

HERE IS THE CUSP: ONLY TWO THINGS CAN HAPPEN. SHE WILL DIE, AND THERE WILL BE A SORT OF REALIZATION JUST BEFORE OR DURING OR AFTER THE IMPACT... OR, THERE WILL BE NO REALIZATION. THIS STORY WILL END BEFORE SHE HITS.

THERE IT IS: AN UNSURPRISING "EPIPHANY" ENDING, OR ONE THAT FINISHES FLAT. WE CAN EXPECT ETERNAL LIFE OR DEATH ON IMPACT. REALIZATION, OR REALIZING THERE IS NO REALIZATION... WHAT HAPPENS TO OPEN OUR EYES AND MINDS? *THE TIME THAT DIES INSIDE...*

Q: WHY ARE WE SPECIAL?

A: BECAUSE WE DIE.

OUR LIMITED TIME ON EARTH SEEMS TO BE OUR GREATEST "GIFT." IT MAKES EVERYTHING MATTER, AND STILL MAKES SOME THINGS NOT MATTER AT ALL, AT TIMES. <u>TIME</u> IS THE FACTOR. OR IS IT? LIVING FOREVER, IN HEAVEN OR EVEN IN HELL, WOULD BE BORING AS HELL. OR WOULD IT BE? HOW CAN A MORTAL CREATURE SPECULATE ON SUCH THINGS? IS GOD BORED WITH US?

IF MY OWN PERSONAL "DEVELOPMENT" IS BASED ON AN EVER-INCREASING, NEVER-ENDING CURVE, WHAT IS THE ULTIMATE "POINT"? UNION WITH GOD? GOD CREATED US. WHY CAN'T WE HAVE UNION NOW?

TIME IS THE FALL, OR, FALLING ETERNALLY.

CAN I CONCEIVE OF SOMETHING MORE IMAGINATIVE THAN CONSTANTLY "IMPROVING" MYSELF? IT SOUNDS LIKE *self-stimulation.* SELF-IMPROVEMENT. WHY CAN'T I BE GOOD ENOUGH? WHEN WE REACH

THE KINGDOM OF GOD, HOW WILL WE SPEND OUR DAYS? THIS, A BEING STEEPED IN THE CULTURAL SOUP OF ENDLESS EXPECTATION ASKS. MY EVOLUTION IS A TALE OF CONTINUAL STRUGGLING WITH FAR-GAZING EYES. I FEEL IT. DO YOU?

IF WE HAVE AN ESSENCE, WILL IT BE HAPPY TO LIVE FOREVER ONCE WE ARE GONE? WHAT IS THE PLAN IN COUNTLESS SOULS IN MORTAL SKINS MARCHING TOWARD REINCARNATION? (ONLY TO DO IT ALL AGAIN)... AND WHERE ARE THEY MARCHING <u>FROM</u>? THE FIRST MARCHER? ARE WE COMING OUT OF THE MIST OR OUT OF OURSELVES IN A CLOSED LOOP WITH NO BEGINNING AND NO END?

SO WE LIVE FOREVER—OR DON'T. WE ARE PART OF A PLAN OR NOT—THIS IS HOW WE THINK. ARE WE *DESIGNED* TO THINK THIS WAY? WE DON'T SEEM TO BE ABLE TO HELP IT. IS ANYTHING <u>CONSTANT</u>, BY THE WAY?

IS OBLIVION CONSTANT? THE END OF A LIFE IS OBLIVION—TO THAT LIFE...

THE END OF THIS ORGANISM'S INTERACTIVE EXISTENCE <u>DOES</u> END. IT IS MOST CERTAIN. WHEN PEOPLE STOP BREATHING THEY STOP TALKING. AND MOVING. BUT THEN, THERE ARE THE MICROBES THAT LIVE IN ITS RAPIDLY DECOMPOSING TISSUES; THE ATOMS AND PARTICLES THAT MAKE UP THE CREATURE THAT IS ROTTING AND THE LIVING BILLIONS OF MICROSCOPIC BACTERIA, MICROBES, AND WHATEVER ELSE INHABITING ITS TEMPORARY-SHAPED UNIVERSE... MAYBE WE ARE ALL GOD, FOR THE CREATURES INHABITING US. WE ARE FOOD FOR OUR CHILDREN. IF THE MICROBES IN US DEMANDED THAT WE ANSWER THEIR EXISTENTIAL ANGST, WHAT COULD WE SAY?

IF WHEN A PERSON DIES, THERE IS NO CONTINUATION, NOTHING MORE OF US, WHAT CAN *EXPERIENCE* "OBLIVION?" *YOUR* ANSWER: THE

CONSCIOUSNESS OF THE PERSON, THEIR SOUL. *MY* ANSWER: OBLIVION IS QUITE CONTENT TO EXPERIENCE ITSELF.

BUT, IF WE (FOR EXAMPLE) ARE INTERRELATED CHEMICAL PROCESSES, AND OUR THOUGHTS, OUR CONSCIOUSNESS, OUR BEING-NESS IS AN EXTENSION OF THESE BIOLOGICAL PROCESSES, THEN THERE IS NO DEATH "OVERALL." EXISTENCE IS FOREVER. WE AREN'T. THERE IS ONLY *OUR* FALL; THE FOREST STILL LIVES. THE "ME" OF THE UNIVERSE IS FOREVER—OR AT LEAST A PART OF "FOREVER."

THE PIECES COLLECTED TOGETHER IN CORPOREAL FORM BECOME A PART OF THE BODIES OF THOSE THAT FOLLOW, AS WE, IN TURN, WERE MADE OF THE REMNANTS OF THOSE WHO "DIED" BEFORE US. ALL THE COUNTLESS BILLIONS WE HAVE EATEN IN OUR LIVES, WE EARTHWORMS OF THE SOIL—PIGS, COWS, CHICKENS, FISH, EVERY LEAF, EVERY FRUIT, EVERY INSECT ACCIDENTALLY INGESTED...

AND NOW: WHAT HAPPENS TO AURA MINEHOLD? *YOU*, READING THIS, COULD SAY, "*NOTHING.*"

Aura, THE SENTIENT CONGLOMERATE BEING, DECIDED TO LEAP OFF A CLIFF INTO A VOLCANO ON MARS. HER IMPACT CAUSED A RIPPLE, BUT IN AN EXPLODED SENSE, SHE DIDN'T CHANGE. HER PARTICLES STILL REMAIN; THEY JUST FELL.

ARE WE DRIVEN by a need for change?

Are we PROGRAMMED? By the God named EVOLUTION? WE DON'T KNOW either of these all-powerful beings very well. We experience them intimately. We cannot see anything about the context we are immersed in because we have no distance.

When Aura JUMPS, she creates change for herself and for those who know her, as well as THE IMMEDIATE AREA THAT HER BODY IMPACTS. So, SHE CHANGES HER LEVEL OF EXISTENCE. It was changing anyway. Does it matter whether ice melts slowly or quickly? To the other ice-beings, it matters very much, yet...

She wants to KNOW SOMETHING about herself. WHAT? AND WHAT *DRIVES* HER TO SEEK A DEEPER UNDERSTANDING OF HERSELF? What drives Aura? we ask. We do not say WHAT IS Aura DRIVING TOWARD? because our language ASSUMES THAT *SOMETHING* IS RESPONSIBLE for all visible actions.

"COMMON SENSE" seems to say that A BODY sitting still TENDS TO REMAIN AT REST. UNTIL SOMETHING HAPPENS, WE DO NOT REACT. A BODY moving TENDS TO REMAIN IN MOTION and if something happens, WE REACT; so AN ACTION RESULTS IN AN EQUAL AND APPROPRIATE REACTION. On some plane...SOMEWHERE. If we're all connected, everything is connected; that's the way it seems.

THESE ARE BASIC, and POWERFUL, PRINCIPLES. Maybe there are no principles. Maybe our understanding can't surround the global explanation of what is *really* going on.

The QUESTION: Why does Aura ASK? WHAT KIND OF AN ANSWER OR CONDITION IS SHE SEARCHING FOR? Is she just looking for love in all the wrong places? If so, what is behind that?

You can't say "NOTHING." A MILLION YEARS is magic. PATTERNS in our BEHAVIOR that SEEM COMPLICATED, INTELLIGENCE-GUIDED, INGENIOUS—ARE, beneath the paint, WROUGHT OUT OF THE VERY FABRIC OF UNIMAGINABLE lengths OF TIME. Out of ETERNITY we grow. When WE THINK WE can IMAGINE a MILLION years, WE ARE IMAGINING. We cannot. Try a billion... WE cannot "EXPERIENCE" even our own LIFETIME; we live only IN THIS MOMENT, using our IMAGINATION to feel blindly the face of THE DARK WALL OF THE UNKNOWN.

SCIENCE PROVEs AND DISCOVERs; RELIGION extols itself to BELIEVE; PHILOSOPHY thinks incessantly about BELIEF AND MEANING.

The most awesome DISCOVERIES of SCIENCE have been the result of brilliant flashes: REVELATIONS, DREAMS, INTUITIONS.

I <u>WANT</u> to *Believe*. I want to ride on THIS ride first, and then continue on, somewhere, somehow—even after this ride of life is done.

Religion tells me, "You can do this, when you believe."

Philosophy says to me, "Believe what you want; it's all the same."

IN MOMENTS OF SHEER FOLLY I WiLL teLL YOU that I DO NOT KNOW whAT It Is ThAT I seeK. I SAY THAT I WANT TO KNOW WHAT LIFE IS ABOUT—WHY I AM HERE. But the truth is, I don't want to know anything. I just want. I am a CHILD OF GOD. I AM GOD'S CLONED SELF. I want it all.

I wish TO BE TOLD what I WANT to KNOW. I WANT TO HEAR that I am THE MOST SPECIAL, MOST IMPORTANT, and that I can EAT ICE CREAM ALL DAY WITH NO STOMACH ACHE.

I seek GRATIFICATION on a COSMIC SCALE.

FiNE. That's it.

What is driving Aura to Leap? <u>I</u> AM. I want to make HER find out what I have DECIDED I want to find for myself.

Honest searching is terrifying because it allows or admits nothing beforehand. EVERY MOVE MUST BEGIN from that "nothing." I am afraid to IMAGINE going THIS WAY.

But... Forever CHASING expectations, SPECULATING FROM MY SEAT. <u>IS</u> THIS WHAT I WANT? This ride is getting bumpy. My ass is sore. I want off.

JUMPING OFF OF A CLIFF MIGHT BE A WAY TO ESCAPE THE

INEVITABILITY OF THE RIDE.

Aura—as she is FLYING away from the cliff—might CEASE TO EXIST altogether. HER Atoms, PARTICLES that MAKE UP her body, WOULD SIMPLY FLY APART as she surrenders, gives UP, REALIZING THE HOPELESSNESS OF BOTH LIFE AND OF Life's self-centered idea of DYING. She approaches the IMPOSSIBILITY OF UNDERSTANDING without EXPECTING, and a real KNOWLEDGE, not IMAGINED or thought of.

CAN **I** KNOW? She asks, understanding that it is <u>not</u> a FOOLISH QUESTION. We see NOTHING TRULY. We see nothing. WE EXPERIENCE EVERYTHING by proxy THROUGH LIMITED ORGANIC SENSES. *We* are organic. Bypassing those senses, WE still could NEVER <u>KNOW</u> because OUR MIND would be filtering "It," Our "mind" CONTAMINATES everything that it touches. There's another level here, isn't there? One past, beyond or deeper than the one just out of reach of formulation.

ABSOLUTE understanding IS IMPOSSIBLE.

A LEAP is an ACT. Of giving up everything for HOPE...

In the end, of course, Aura DISAPPEARS.

The voice in her HEAD; the point of unmoving LIGHT floating beside her, just beyond her reach; The world she is FALLING THROUGH, still, even now, always *now*—all of this she glimpses in an infinitesimal instant, in THE MOMENT when...

...THE WORLD DISAPPEARS BECAUSE NOTHING IS NOT. AND THOUGHT IS NOT. AND NOTHING REMAINS. *NOTHINGNESS* REMAINS. "WHERE" DOES NOT EXIST. COMPLETE THE PARADOX. THERE IS A BOX WITH NO OPENINGS. NO DUALISM. ALL IS ALL. We're inside and *we* are the box. There *is* no box. There *is* no "we."

But: *What about Aura?*

She created a doorway in herself; stepped through it, forward into the unknown void. SHE MADE MY DECISION FOR ME, and I thank her with all of my heart. She is OUT THERE, falling through space and thin air, freezing and hanging there in the cold, dust-filled wind over a Martian shield volcano. She is inside the volcano beyond the darkness. Past it. She will FALL into her moment, seemingly inevitable and conclusive, THAT IS SURE to bring her something solid.

And the hand that has held her so firmly spread its fingers so gently to let her tumble slowly into motion once again, and…

Rock.

N—O—W

Chapter 22 — The One and Only Skate Park Project and l'Association Dream Extreme [Toulouse, France, 2001-2002]

[Note to self: I'll have to be in a good frame of mind to write this one, won't I? There's not regret, but sadness, and nostalgia melancholia.

Some day do this: Tell the story as I've briefly told it before, from skating in Pittsburgh, then Stuttgart and all of that.]

The following is a second short story I came up with recently—a decade and a half or more after *Relativity Speaking*. When I took the first two months of 2010 to push into becoming a writer for a living, I started by writing *A New Story*. I sat, proverbial blank wall in front of me, and started writing a ghost story—the ghost of myself in more ways than one. My writing self had become a kind of ghost and was resurrecting. My old self was now a ghost. The "New Story" was a resurrection from the ashes of my neglected campfire. Though it wrote itself and felt somewhat effortless, I still felt constrained, uncomfortable. *I wanted to be free.*

The following story is a result of that feeling. I was determined to write free from conventions and restrictions. A story "should look like this." I had no willingness to conform to that or to any other writing rules. Maybe the "rules" were of my own accepting, but I'd felt a pressure to write in a certain way, a way that *made sense* a certain way. *What about writing my way?* What if I wrote the way that came easiest and most naturally for me? Yes. I sat upstairs at the backup computer in my oldest son's room. I leaned back in the vintage metal kitchen chair I'd picked out at the Saint Vincent de Paul store in Wheeling, newly purchased keyboard on my lap, and began to type.

The best writing, in my view, works on, and from, more than one level. The best writing, I think, is like a Mandelbrot set; the more closely or intensely you look, the more you notice... never-ending...

A Story With No People (told by God)

by David W. Weimer

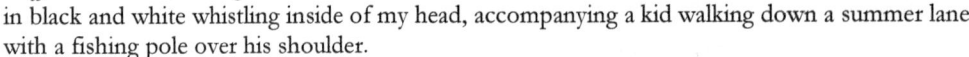

Some cultures chant in groups, "OM."
(It rhymes with 'home.')

Jeeze...

Act I.

Luring me backward, *The Andy Griffith Show* theme song echoes in black and white whistling inside of my head, accompanying a kid walking down a summer lane with a fishing pole over his shoulder.

Act Am.

All the description in the world can't convey this. When the period stops the flow of words it can't hold in everything filling the box overflowing forever with sound. How do you write *sound* on a page? Each sentence is a box of words; the words stay in the box, or are changed and replaced, but the things the words try to describe—that's the water flowing from eternal fountains with periods holding them apart from one another.

Act What.

I can sit here and swivel my head. Just here in this chair, sitting. What I hear. What I can see... I check smell. I breathe deeply and can smell the air. I taste the last of this tea which I don't like. What do I feel? Belly pressure, a twitch in my neck, dry skin and an itching leg. Just sitting here, it's amazing. It's a whole world. And then there's that place over there, just ten feet away from me, on the couch. And in the living room, the kitchen, the studio, the upstairs, the downstairs. Man, it keeps going. The rest of our property, the lawn, the front yard, the back deck. I could sit right here, in every square foot of space, and swivel my head around, and pay attention to all this stuff and be blown away by all there is. One time I rode a Greyhound Bus in Florida and was amazed by the endless reality flowing by my window in the five hours between Lake City and Kissimmee.

Act Now.

Effortlessness... What is effortless? Anger. Love. Pity. Nostalgia. Regret. Contentment. Hunger. Thirst. Fatigue. Joy. Curiosity. Sudden comprehension. *This.*

Act When.

The best gift life can give me, in my opinion, is a pure quest—something to go after. Something self-evident and worth it. I'd prefer a quest, instead of having to react automatically to the bead-like chain of crises and challenges delivered regularly like the mail, dropped right at my feet. The gift I'm talking about is one that at first seems as far off as that barely-starting breeze over there. Not felt yet, but somehow noticed. The far away trees sway a little. Then it comes in close, like a gradual thaw. The feeling of coolness on my heated cheeks and forehead in the summer, sweating or working in the sun. Or a heat-sucking frigid wind blowing snow over a frozen pond. *Here*, it tells me. It's always something I hadn't considered before, that seems like it's worth going after. It's a quest for understanding. A goal. *I climbed that mountain. I <u>did</u> it.* All the while, I'm imagining. Yes. *That's* what I want.

Act Nine.

Well. Pray. And thank you. When I don't know what to say, I *do it*. Thanks for the time I get each day, most days, to spend ten minutes staring into the air in front of me, letting go of control. Depth, profoundness, wonder. Thank you for that: the wonder.

xxxxxxxxxxxxxxxxxxxxxxxxxxxx

Words. The final frontier. Before the brain and the mind somewhere inside there, are the sounds we make, we use, to describe our world, inside the head and out. We don't really describe with them; we *scribe* with them, waving them in the air up there, drawing pictures with them. Words are the border between *us* and *not us*. There's nothing else out there. There is vacuum and nothingness. Words reside there, in that no-space, preserved in hard vacuum, never worn by gentle wind nor gale, never faded by water running off of them. Words are changed and replaced, but they are never changed or altered by atmospheric whim.

The atmosphere, the living space that is, is inside of our heads; that's where all we live. Don't take this as fact. Don't take this as something I'm trying to put across as fact. This is just my opinion—my momentary commentary. We all live in here, dome-dwellers, looking out from our skulls through orbs down at the world we're orbiting and out at the world around us. We're mountain climbers on asteroids in pressure suits, who never experience the absence of air directly—that reality residing mere inches beyond our warm, sweating skin.

What are words for? For passing messages between inmates in adjoining cells. We never see each other. We never can. We toss these words out, bounce them from an opposite wall and they angle into another's cell, through the vacuum between us, and the other person, looking out through their portholes, sees words tumbling toward them and misinterprets everything. It's only natural.

Occasionally, words *key in* something in the other observer. When they're close enough to something felt, when they're right enough to talk the same talk that's inside of someone else's head, then there's a shared feeling of *recognition*. The inmates breathe a sigh of bliss; someone *understands* me... And all the rest of the time is spent trying to get out; but there's no way out; there is only these words, pushed through a narrow slit beneath our steel-clad door. We're talking prisons within prisons. Or maybe not; we'll see.

We're trapped inside of ourselves. Words, streams of them, uttered or not, flow from our prisons, thousands-miles-long, by the minute. If we ever *did* get out of our own heads, we'd be a naked, blind brain tumbling through the soulless vacuum of space, exploding and being fried by cosmic radiation while soundless solar winds blast and scour our defenseless gray matter. We wouldn't be "we" anymore. We wouldn't be anything; we'd be unplugged from our body and removed from our cocoon nest. But we would be—in a single final second of awareness—contacting space directly. Unfortunately, we'd also be blind and utterly unaware of our surroundings, as our brain can't feel anything directly. We'd explode and become vacuum, all of our separate awareness dissolving into nonexistence. *How can we <u>possess</u> a brain if we <u>are</u> a brain?...*

Let's talk about *virtual reality*. Put on a helmet and gloves and maybe a motion-capture jumpsuit covered with green dots. Interact inside of a world brought to us visually through our orbs. Maybe this world is in 3-D. Our brains will interpret what they see and we can play around like we're inside of the game itself, instead of being separate from it. This couldn't be further from the truth. That's the inside-out version. But leaving that aside, let's talk numbers. We're inside of *two* video games, not one. Three, actually, to be very honest. Inside the world is a virtual reality helmet (skull), inside the helmet is a meat thinking computer (brain), inside an emptiness at the center of the meat computer… is… awareness?

They're already walking around inside of one virtual meat suit, these humans, equipped with auditory pickups, tactile ability, visual apparatus and taste and smell capabilities. They're in a remote-controlled organic robot. Their brain is sitting inside the enclosed driver's seat of the thing. They're trapped inside of a dying animal—one of my favorite quotes—and trying to separate the two might become fatal (for one of us).

The second video game reality is that technological one; the poor first example composed of mankind's technology fueled by his Lego-creation compulsion to build, create, improve, add to, reinvent and surpass. It could be a helmet and motion capture gloves, or it can be our homes, heated and lighted, our cars, comfortable and fast, or our lives in an artificial climate with all of the comforts—a coffee machine, microwave, easy chair, television, computer, hot running water and a garage door opener. Extend that to include garbage pick-up, cable service, postal and UPS deliveries, a security system and a hot tub. *Who'd want to be crouched under a bush in the dark at night?* I agree. Still…

The third video game is the main game. It's the one we're all plugged into every moment of our lives until when? The end? Or a crisis when the game freezes? This game is the reflexive interpretive game called, erroneously, **ourselves**. Feel free to disagree. That would be *you* disagreeing that *you* exist, if you can see, looking back, from where I'm going to try to take you.

This main game is what you play every day. You look out there—and that includes your own thought products generally called memories, opinions, reactions, emotions and moods—you look out there, at the movements of people and objects in your detect-ability sphere (what you can see, hear, feel, taste, smell and think about) and there's a feeling-response-form automatically, somewhere, inside of us. You can think of these as pictures automatically forming on the curved inside walls of our skull-prisons.

And like the people in Plato's cave, we watch those pictures and identify with the characters moving around there. We identify so completely with them, these thoughts and opinions and judgments, that we take *them* for reality and are blind to anything else. Reality is a mind construct. Reality doesn't exist because a description by definition is an explanation of something we perceive! It's always a thing apart from what we're talking about. We're in a bubble, floating through soulless space, thinking everything is solid.

That's nonsense!

You think this (still on the inside of your skull, not realizing where you stand in the big picture).

There are no eyes pointed inward! I can't see inside of my own head! There's no wall in there! What the hell are you talking about?

Yes. The wall that the picture is projected on is your composite self—your opinions, attitudes, reactions, preferences—and yes, you are correct. You are blind and touching the smooth lining of your own internal sphere with sensitive fingers attuned to every texture, smoothness, temperature and contour. Your internal reactions do appear simultaneously as you apprehend something "out there." Like goose bumps rising from your arm in response to something… You *feel* the feeling-reactions to whatever you perceive. Exactly! You *see* them more directly than your eyes can see a vision outside of your bathysphere because you feel them *inside* of you. You don't think these feeling-reactions are real. You know they are real. (We know things we've never examined, don't we?) And your body emanates these 'feelings,' echoing them like a pond echoes the stone thrown into its water.

Water ripples outward in concentric rings, expanding steadily, rippling from a central strike point. Your stomach feels like it dropped off of a cliff, your hands become clammy or sweaty, your face becomes hot, your hands tingle and you tremble as your heart pounds to an adrenaline beat. These are reactions we all have, daily, and we think they are IT—*reality*.

We are perceiving reality directly… Ho Ho Ho. What about: We are "feeling" what our body is doing. Ha ha ha. Ho ho ho.

Our fingers are on a fishing line and they feel a tentative tugging or a persistent pulling and we intuit/feel/imagine what this tugging and pulling means. It means nothing, but we interpret what it means. We take a part of something, and intuit the whole. It's our greatest skill. We assume things and kill each other over the assumptions.

What we *feel* something means is the lens through which we view this thing. The feeling-definition lens. What we're seeing—a neighbor crossing the street in their bathrobe at noon, a replayed memory of an altercation with a coworker, bully or peer, a love episode—each individual thing—is seen through its own specific lens. We are lens-crafters. We have one for everything. I question that we ever see what is really there. I know we don't; we can't. To see 'what is really there' would be God seeing what is really there. And what is "really there"? What is the true picture of things? Do you think God has the only proper vision? What if God were blind?

We see-feel things profoundly. We can't perceive anything we don't already feel. By 'perceive,' I mean define to myself what something is. It has to make sense to me. I can't perceive anything that I don't already feel something about. Perception is comprehension. If I don't have a definition for a percept—a thing in my environment noticed—then I am as blind to it as someone without eyes. Another part of myself asks: *How did we notice the first percept, and where did the definition for it come from?*

We're a shaman, each of us, having continual visions and lucid dreams and photo-realistic hallucinations—all of this while talking at each other (slipping those words out through the slot under that permanently locked door).

Animated bodies, controlled remotely, feeling like they're really us because we've been in the driver's seat, inside our own skull, for so long that we don't feel the contours of the seat anymore and have forgotten that it exists; our asses have fallen asleep, in other words.

These bodies of ours have strutted, slinked or sauntered onto a theater stage, stopped on their "X," faced the character opposite, half-turned to the audience and delivered lines loudly in *Sotto voce*, 'interacting' with the opposing actors while remaining 100 percent unaware of what they are actually facing. These bodies of ours could be facing a rock wall. They could be talking to a cardboard cut-out. We talk to each other with all of the empathy that a person would feel while speaking lines to a cardboard cut-out. I guess by 'we' I mean *me*.

We're acting to the walls inside of our prison—I want company, so I'm going to keep saying 'we'—to the curved theater screen being projected upon. Those curved walls, the inside of the surface of the sphere of our heads. We're inside here, not out there. And these walls are mirrored, too. We get to act, prance, strut, gesture—all the while, watching ourselves in the mirror, being disappointed, impressed or pleased with what we see. This sounds narcissistic, doesn't it?...

> **"Narcissism** *refers to the personality trait of* egotism, *which includes the set of* character traits *concerned with* self-image ego. *The terms narcissism,* narcissistic, *and* narcissist *are often used as* pejoratives, *denoting* vanity, conceit, egotism *or simple* selfishness. *Applied to a* social group, *it is sometimes used to denote* elitism *or an indifference to the plight of others.*
>
> *The name "narcissism" is derived from* Greek mythology. Narcissus *was a handsome Greek youth who rejected the desperate advances of the* nymph Echo. *As punishment, he was doomed to fall in love with his own reflection in a pool of water. Unable to consummate his love, Narcissus pined away and changed into the flower that bears his name, the* narcissus.*"*

That is from an online Wikipedia article, February 2010.

Some people say that our sole duty while we're here on this planet is to open ourselves to a transcendental realization of the presence of God, Jesus or Allah in our lives. In this way, we graduate from being a purely self-centered being and, perhaps, possibly care about the welfare of others as much or more than we care about ourselves. We care about forcing other people to feel the stuff we want them to feel "for their own good." What's wrong with that?

Others, who may refer to themselves as secular humanists, atheists or just 'ordinary' people, say that our highest achievement possible in this life, on a personal basis, is the addition of *empathy* to our daily experience of living. Without this quality, they say, we're merely an intelligent animal. Empathy, in their eyes, raises us to the pedestal of worship. And by us, I mean *me*. It's a safe thing to worship, myself, because, for an iconoclast especially, it is the only valid object of veneration since it is centered at home. An iconoclast sees nothing outside of the self as valid to venerate. Talk about having trouble with authority figures! *I* am the one who is feeling something related to what I imagine another person is feeling.

Two extreme ends of the same line. On the one end, we're supposed to throw away ourselves and worship another God, and on the other we're supposed to destroy everything except ourselves and our own judgments. Feeling the pain of others or dissolving oneself in the worship of something other than yourself. Maybe these are both pretty honorable things…

But what is this?—*feeling what another person is feeling*? What are we talking about? We're talking about ourselves, because everything is our inner reaction to our environment. This is all quibbling about ripples, as they move silently and resolutely away from us into the vacuum between ourselves. There's a BIG assumption that we all seem to make at some point in our lives: that there *is* another one out there. Another person. Anyone. *At least one*, you say, *right?* Something or someone else other than ourselves exists. We haven't proven that.

Of course there are others out there—to treat badly or well—there are six BILLION of them and counting.

I know, you can't believe some of the stuff I'm saying. I must be crazy.

But you don't have proof, do you? That others actually exist? All you have is what you "see." And "seeing" with your senses is ten steps away from the first stone-drop-into-a-pond of *us*. That first stone drop is at least one big splash away from something primary at the middle of awareness.

We can't be sure of *anything* that we can't directly experience—and we can't be sure of direct experience either. This isn't mincing words. People are clouded by their grief over the loss of a loved one, for example—surely you've seen this. We are moved to violence with an overwhelming urge for retribution and revenge towards those responsible for our loved one's demise. We are moved to violence when someone takes our ball on the playground, as a kid. It's only "natural." What does it mean to be "sure" of something?

Sometimes we are paralyzed by despair or fear or depression. At times we are giddy with idealistic enthusiasm. So do we, possibly, sanely, claim to *see clearly* what is really there? What does "there" mean? Is there a "there"? Where is "here"? Do we recognize a valid place to stand for viewing the interrelatedness called "reality"? This matrix of the interconnectedness of every bit of this apparent universe? It sounds like a body. Everything is touching everything. Again: We'd have to be God to 'get it' all, and we're not God, are we? What is our understanding of "God"?... Well, more on that in a while.

The empathy-worshipers are at least an increment closer to approaching the right direction toward the truth of the matter. I've heard them say: *when we can finally feel empathy for another person, we can for the first time accept another as we accept ourselves.* That seems accurate.

A non-French friend of mine told me, and I haven't confirmed it yet, that the French say: <u>to understand is to forgive</u>. This happens to be one of my own personal fundamental truths. I see its validity in my own reactions. When I perceive another person as being the same as myself, the hating, condemning, mocking and dismissing them as anything other than *right* ceases. They <u>are</u> right. Just as I am right, in my eyes, even when I'm wrong. I'm on my side, so there's always some sympathy there. When I empathize with another person, their actions make sense and I accept them as being just as valid as me. *Put yourself in someone else's shoes and walk a while in them.*

This is true, isn't it? A black man hates a white man. A white man hates a black man. What is hate? (Have you ever thought about that one?...) You'll never *talk* them into changing their minds, they're pretty completely occupied with their internal skull puppet show, but when fate puts these two haters in a situation together, and it somehow dawns on them that the other guy is trying his best to survive and experiences fear, elation, perseverance and dismay just the same as yourself—then those two men will come away from that experience minus one thing. They might not even say it, but something inside will have loosened. They will no longer be carrying the shield and weapons of ignorance perpetually fighting THE OTHER.

> **"Ignorance** is the state in which one lacks knowledge, is unaware of something or chooses to subjectively <u>ignore</u> information. This should not be confused with being unintelligent, as one's level of intelligence and level of education or general awareness are not the same. The word "Ignorant" is an adjective describing a person in the state of being unaware. The term may be used specifically (e.g. "One can be an expert in math, and totally ignorant of history.") or generally (e.g. "an ignorant person.") -- although the second use is used less as a descriptive and more as an imprecise personal insult.
>
> Ignorance also means to ignore someone when they are talking to you."

Again, Wikipedia, February 2010.

Understanding another person is conducive to acceptance. One follows the other.

I once thought of the observed phenomenon of humans rejecting or accepting words, actions and ideas of others as being a direct parallel to our autoimmune system. Our immune system scrutinizes every bit of material that gets into our bloodstream, attacking and destroying utterly anything it encounters that doesn't have the correct ID of "Self." This is why transplanted (other) organs are at best tolerated grudgingly after an immune system has been suppressed—but it's an apparently uneasy peace because there is no "understanding" [accepting] of the other.

This autoimmune system metaphor would help explain why we reflexively condemn and dismiss others as being valid beings. Maybe our distrust of strangers is a rippled-outward manifestation of the prime directive of all life: eat or die; kill or be killed. Our microscopic immune system kills other cells and viruses so that we continue on. It's not difficult to extend the logic of this behavior to our relations with other peoples, political parties, our neighbors. We group together in a "tribe." We band together to fight a common enemy threatening us collectively. All of our cells and specialized body systems are probably doing the same.

Who cares? This is biology 101 behavior: understanding and reading the meat-suit manual. Grasping the hows and guessing at the whys. What about here in our heads? What does it feel like to experience anything directly? *Why do I keep coming back to this?*

This may seem to be the vaguest question ask-able, but I think it's the most concrete thing addressable. What else do we have, fundamentally, other than our awareness? "I think, therefore I am," Descartes said, defining himself. What can be even more essential in our lives? This sensation of *observer*. If we retreat or retract our "looking" back into the very center of ourselves, wherever that is or whatever that could be, what do we find? When we really are looking for something? *Nothing!* someone immediately shouts at me with certainty while staring, unblinking, through the walls of their own cave, feeling with fingers his intimate unending flow of feelings...

How can we find *nothing* when we look at the center of ourselves? You mean, at home, there's... *nothing*? Well then, *what are we*? Just a nothingness looking out from—nothing?

I think we are trapped inside a sphere resting on the sand of a desert island. When we stop observing the objects on the small circle of land—palm leaves, sand, birds or waves or shells, sticks and flotsam and jetsam and crabs washed up on shore—and retreat into ourselves, we feel... *bored.* What? Yes, I think we do. We're so used to looking at the moving objects outside our windows; our whole attention is *outward*. It's the way we're shaped. Even so, if we're determined to get to the bottom of things, and we decide to start digging a hole right in the middle of where we're standing, what will we find?

If we decide to keep digging deeper and not stop, no matter what, until we find out what's at the bottom of this place we're standing on, will we get anywhere? Where can we go? This is what the Buddha is supposed to have done by sitting under his Bodhi fig tree, determined not to stand up again until he got THE ANSWER to his fundamental questions.

This place is exactly where I'm arguing that we should go, if we want to know something once and for all. For me, the answer is not "out there" in the arms of a lover or in the words or books of another. It <u>has</u> to be somewhere, somehow inside of me—even if I don't "exist"—or at the least, it has to be accessible *through* me. It *has* to be; when I die, all the books I ever read will go away and I'll be left with *just what I am*.

So, all I can trust is what I have become: The experience of truth directly. Back to that impossibility. That maddening necessity. When you eat an orange you experience something... directly? Well, close. When you read about eating it, that's even further—apart. You have certain understandings and assumptions and speculations, but you have *nothing*. You have only ideas about what it might be. It's the parallel of that brain feeling something directly. A self-aware brain floating in a vacuum would be 'experiencing' its own reaction to exploding—never experiencing reality itself. Unless... Unless maybe in a sense *it is* experiencing reality itself. It's experiencing what it's experiencing. So, even though it doesn't know what the world outside looks like, not being able to "taste" it—that doesn't matter; it is experiencing itself: its own reactions to exploding. But even that more honest, fundamental and closer-to-home experiencing is still a step away from reality-as-it-is. How small do we need to go to get to reality? How small do the pieces of us have to be? The only way to experience reality itself is to *become* reality. The freezing and exploding brain would have to become space and vacuum to understand space and vacuum. It would have to lose itself to experience something else for the first time. Become something other than itself—for the first time.

True direct experiencing of reality must be the complete dilution of the minute particles making up that brain—the brain would have to be dissolved into space like sugar into water. *That* would be a direct experience of space. But then, there wouldn't be any more of that brain, would there... This is the apparent dilemma. To fully comprehend life, we have to fully experience death. Clearly impossible. Throughout thousands of years of relatively recent history, however, people have been saying they've been there, done that.

Can we become God?

Here:

> **"God** *is most often conceived of as the <u>supernatural</u> <u>creator</u> and overseer of the <u>universe</u>."*

(Wikipedia, February 2010)

My earlier 'definition' of God is the direct experience of what is really there (another person, a tree, etc.). Impossible—as long as we perceive everything through our senses and our lenses of mental judgment-perception.

What about: Can we directly experience ourselves completely? <u>*Yes*</u>. If you think so, then we can become God. The Wikipedia article implies that someone must think God is the creator and overseer (observer) of the universe. If we ever completely became one with ourselves—Just-what-we-are—we'd become one with creation. Did you know—we <u>are</u> a manifestation of creation. *We are creation*! You may believe in evolution, divine creation, advanced aliens seeding our planet with life—every one of these concepts is trying to portray a thing-which-is, trying to explain. Even a dream is a picture of something—an underlying problem, curiosity; random firings of neurons; accidental combinations of memory strands, and so on and so on.

I walk inside certain truisms. Here is one of them: THE UNIVERSE IS CONTAINED IN A GRAIN OF SAND. If you completely *understood* (by this I mean: become-one-with; to know its very essential is-ness) a single grain of sand—or a single anything, anything at all—then you would have become one with EVERYTHING. It's all the same. Everything is. You will have tapped into a universal condition. Everything is everything. Knowing one thing is knowing all of the one-things out there in the universe or, in there, in our minds. It's all out there. And it's all in here. In *here*. Again, I'm talking about eating that orange. Feeling empathy with another individual and discovering that he or she is the *same* as you are.

In the end, you cannot accept authoritative external opinions on any matter. What about doctors? Alright; they have more knowledge than others about physiology... I'm talking about head stuff, wisdom stuff, understanding-what-life-is-all-about stuff. Tentatively accept some explanations as more reasonable than others, but don't chain yourself to that accepted belief; you might later watch it sink below the surface of likelihood, dragging you down, too. But then, maybe you want to die for a good cause or become a martyr. Most of us do.

Back to me. To become one with the creation-that-we-are is to become one with the aforementioned grain of sand. To experience myself directly, without intermediary is to become God. The same way that the sugar becomes the water that it is stirred into. Not that the sugar has made the water, or controls the water, or operates under delusions of being all-powerful. I'm just talking about knowing something by dissolving into it. To become God, in this context, is to know something fundamental first-hand. Dust to dust, ashes to ashes—while living.

Wow. Where is this going? With one more thing to say: There are NOT approximately six billion separate individuals of one bipedal species out there, all with their unique characteristics born of their specific genetic inheritance and life circumstances, as unique and one-of-a-kind as fingerprints are said to be. I propose, seriously, that there is only one God, ME. *I* am all there is. No multiplicity. I am me. You say, "I am me." And you are. Yes. You are, literally, physically, who you are. I am, literally, physically, who I am. This is a singular thing... Who do you think has been talking this whole time? Some deluded individual? Sure. But there is only you, and *I am you.*

Alright—and?

For your consideration, I propose this does not, cannot, end with 'people,' we higher-than-the other-animals "people."

I have looked into the eyes of my horse, Lucky, while I was a boy. We would ride through summer fields and stop and eat grass and read a book and the sweat on us would cool off and dry. I have looked into the eyes of my cat, Grizelda, who felt that I was her parent, mother and source. I saw her youth grow old and watched her die. I have seen a dying deer, steam hissing out of holes in its side, blood on its muzzle, lying on the cold ground, exhausted. I have observed chickens, rabbits, dogs, geese, squirrels, turkeys as I killed them. Flies, beetles, cockroaches and spiders. I was raised on a farm. I have hunted. I have lived a life where mousetraps are set, wasp spray is used and fly swatters are swung. I see a neglected animal, a homeless person, road kill, deer or cow in a field, circling bird overhead; I see me there every time, when I consider the eyes of another. When I look at them, I watch myself looking out at the world, and me, and my death, and my urge to live.

This seemingly human empathy thing is the tip of an iceberg called ALL OF CREATION. Experiencing that iceberg / grain of sand directly is to comprehend / become it completely... Although we didn't create the universe... Although there is likely nothing resembling our God... Although we are a part of some whole that is larger than any comprehension... —when I understand something completely, I understand and become myself.

....a part of the body of God opens its eyes in shocked surprise; a localized area in space suddenly becomes self-aware for the first time and opens its eyes with a newborn cry: / AM!

So, what happened when you stopped incessantly feeling around the inside walls of your skull-prison and opened your eyes?

This exchange occurred after I sent *A Story With No People* to a friend.

From: A.M.
To: DW
Sent: Saturday, March 27, 2010 11:21 AM
Subject: Re: You're a good friend. Story... OM... Jeeze...

Hi Dave,

....Thanks for sending the story with no people. I've read it once. It feels like the kind of 'story' that I need to read a few times, in a quiet place (like lunch break by the park, away from others), to get deeper and deeper into where it's pointing, and be willing and open to feel and accept the implications.

Coming back to the first line... we happen to have a little group meditation meeting for our local TAT group a couple of Sunday mornings ago. It started with strong, loud humming for 30 minutes, then slow arm movements in one direction,(7 minutes), then in the other direction (7 minutes), then an abrupt stop and laying down for 15-30 minutes to observe... whatever.

The long-time Osho meditator later told us these meditations are meant to be somewhat silly and pointless, to help shift your mind into a more open or unbalanced state where you might then trigger some silence and form a crack or somehow see into something deeper... perhaps further in the direction of who we really are at center.

So, is this somewhat related to why you say Jeeze... in the first line of your 'story'? (The Jeeze made more sense to me when you used it after)

"How can we find nothing when we look at the center of ourselves? At home, you mean, there's... nothing? Then what are we? Just a nothingness looking out?"

Hi A,

I'm always surprised and grateful when someone reads something I wrote.

The *Jeeze* at the end of the question in the story... There's a questioner in there (in the story) a couple of times, and this is one place where he utters something:

How can we find *nothing* when we look at the center of ourselves? At home, you mean, there's... *nothing*? Then *what are we*? Just a nothingness looking out? Jeeze.

This 'jeeze' was the disgust of the disbelieving questioner, who can't comprehend that there is nothing of their self, no residue of their self, at the center of their self.

The first 'jeeze' at the beginning of the story... It is perhaps the narrator's ironic utterance. Ironic because of the notion of a group of individuals coming together to chant in unison about a singular place that puts the lie to there being such a thing as 'separateness' or multiple numbers of consciousnesses 'out there.'

The narrator of this story is a single person. The narrator is God, experiencing a 'virtual reality' through the consciousness and mentation of this singular narrator person. The narrator, if another person reads the story, is the same "I" as the person reading the story, so if you read it, you're reading something from yourself. There's this multiple possibility/layer of identities in there.

The story is a speculative treatment on the subject closest to hand (ourselves, and what we really are or might be), by a less-than-omniscient narrator. God lets this thoughtful narrator be less than all-knowing--and lets this impermanent human get occasional revelatory glimpses into his own nature. God, this lonely singularity, this vacuum-of-space-ness, finds singular delight in allowing us, these imperfect, limited 'mentalities', to exist (all shadows of his singular self--picture a giant singular tree hovering within the blinding light of a massive sun--a long shadow is cast behind the tree; this shadow is not 'real,' not himself, not anything, but God loves this imperfect impermanence and lets it be, always keeping himself held still to maintain that shade. He holds his God-sized hand up even, shading a spot for all of us to exist under, watching us below with his blazing God orbs as we go through our machinations, knowing that it is his will and his upheld arm alone that permits these shadow beings to exist for one second. And the seconds stretch into billions of years). If it wasn't for God's whim (and shadow), we would never exist; in the direct blazing sunlight we would dissolve instantly.

Okay,
Dave

Chapter 23 — Two Ships

In 1987, when I told Andrée that I wanted to return to the States without her when my Army time was up, I didn't make her very happy. We had been talking on the phone nearly daily and sending letters. We were counting down the time until we could go back to the States to live together, young and in love. Looking back, I'm sure Andrée was looking forward to this with bated breath but I had a growing dread the closer the day came. It was the weight of responsibility. I just wanted to be free from the Army and from everything. I was afraid of taking care of someone. I didn't want to settle down and have six kids. I remember that specific number. I'm pretty sure Andrée mentioned it once or twice in our musings about our future together. Also, I was still reeling from my dad's death. I was too young, and too conflicted. A lot of excuses. Usually those come from only one place.

I could go back *now*, and trade places with that younger me. I could do it now, of course. I've got nothing to lose. I'd be unafraid and *there* for Andrée. I'd step into that life of ours and it would be great, she and I walking the sands on a beach in Florida, basking in the glow of our companionship. I didn't do that, obviously. I left. Even though things have worked out, it would have been nice to give her more.

Things happened. Not long before I was to return to the States, Andrée visited me from Berlin, where she'd recently moved after graduating from school, living in a family's home as a nanny. A sadness and a coldness walked silently with us—a kind of mourning. I remember the unhappiness. Not fun. I had told her I'd be going back alone and she moved to Berlin.

I remember when we walked the streets of Fliegerhorst Kaserne. Andrée heard a man yelling at a kid and wanted to rescue the kid.

When she left, I didn't hear from her for a year. By this time, I was in Florida, in my first apartment on Baya Avenue in Lake City. I had sent her a Christmas card, birthday card and post card. I respected her anger at me, I guess, but also considered her my friend. After I'd kind of resigned to the loss, she answered me. We wrote again. She had moved in with a boyfriend and quit being a nanny.

I remember telling her on the phone at some point, "We maybe missed our chance, but I want for us to be at each other's weddings. I'll come to your wedding, no matter where it is or when." I have the recollection of Andrée agreeing to that. The next time I saw her in person was a couple years later, for several days in Lake City. She came with Clemens, her boyfriend from Berlin. They were on a tour of Florida.

The beautiful Andrée, taking my picture as I took hers along the Ichetucknee.

They stayed in my apartment. I was a maintenance guy at McDonald's, so it must have been 1990. We went tubing down the crystal, clear, Ichetucknee spring-fed river. I remember riding in the back seat of their rental car to the state park boat landing. Sinéad O'Connor's *Nothing Compares 2 U*, a Prince song, was playing on the radio.

It's been seven hours and fifteen days
Since you took your love away
I go out every night and sleep all day
Since you took your love away
Since you been gone I can do whatever I want
I can see whomever I choose
I can eat my dinner in a fancy restaurant
But nothing ...
I said nothing can take away these blues,
'Cause nothing compares ...
Nothing compares to you

It's been so lonely without you here
Like a bird without a song
Nothing can stop these lonely tears from falling
Tell me baby where did I go wrong?
I could put my arms around every boy I see
But they'd only remind me of you
went to the doctor guess what he told me
Guess what he told me?
He said, girl, you better have fun
No matter what you do
But he's a fool ...
'Cause nothing compares ...
Nothing compares to you ...

All the flowers that you planted, mama
In the back yard
All died when you went away
I know that living with you baby was sometimes hard
But I'm willing to give it another try
'Cause nothing compares ...
Nothing compares to you

Andrée said with her eyes from the front passenger seat that the lyrics had meaning. She said that Clemens didn't understand the English in the song. She let me know, on the last night of their visit, what I had given up. I had a motorcycle, a 550 cc Honda Nighthawk. My second motorcycle I'd bought after selling a lemon car. I gave Andrée a ride down to a small lake in town for a walk. We walked on a small path at dusk, the insects and the humidity heavy

Spring 1990. Me and Andrée on my 550 Nighthawk in Mom's front yard during her visit.

in the early night air. I was hot after the cool ride and we held hands, walking. Both of us knew we were leaving each other again. We stopped and Andrée looked intensely at me. We kissed. After long seconds, I remember saying, "We shouldn't do that too much."

They left the next morning to continue their tour.

The next time I saw Andrée was at my wedding three years later. I had just finished two or three weeks of Pennsylvania Army National Guard annual training in Fort Chaffee, Arkansas that year. Andrée came with Petra, a girlfriend of hers from Berlin. They had taken a kind of Canadian tour, visiting Victoria Island among other places and then going to New York City before flying to western Pennsylvania to attend my wedding.

I was going to get married, so I was suffering a bit from the "Oh, God" before the leap. The timing was such that I took a bus home from Hunt Armory once my unit returned to Pittsburgh. Andrée and Petra met me in front of my apartment building in a rental car.

The plan: they would meet me there and drive me to Stahlstown, PA, my grandparents' town, where my fiancée, Kathy Lestock, and family waited for me. Kathy had our car.

I threw my heavy duffel bag on my apartment floor while Andrée and Petra waited below. Andrée hadn't wanted to come upstairs. I grabbed my stuff for the wedding—clothes, whatever. Then fed and watered Grizelda and Emerald, locked the door, then took the steps two at a time down to throw my things in the back of Andrée's rental car.

We had a couple of hours, so I took Andrée and her friend to Oakland and showed them Pitt, where I was going to college. Andrée said she wanted to talk to me before the wedding, so there we were, in Oakland for another walk. She said something to Petra in German, and we all agreed to meet in a while in front of the fountain near the Frick Fine Arts building. We walked to Schenley Park, to a favorite place of mine. I took her on a path around another lake, Panther Hollow Pond, in another state, at another time. The same two people… Hiking up a wooded trail to cross over the bridge that spans the "hollow," Andrée stopped me by the arm and said, "I hate you!"

Jeeze, I thought. *What?* Don't you know, she said, "We are supposed to be together?" Not with some other person but with <u>each other</u>? She said she had split up with Clemens the year before.

"I didn't know. How could I? You didn't tell me." With the perfect logic of love, Andrée said, "It doesn't matter. Stop the wedding. You're supposed to marry <u>me</u>."

It felt like a bad dream. "I can't do that," I told her. "I made a commitment to Kathy. I've got a life here."

Andrée was quiet. It was hot and humid in August, even in the shade of the dirt path where we stood, past a series of stone steps leading up to a parking area and the end of the bridge above. "Tell me you love me," she said. I was reeling from the "Oh Gods" and now this… I had been overwhelmed with thoughts during the past few weeks of my impending marriage and what that meant. Then Andrée comes into my life again and I'm being pummeled by the hurricane winds of destiny and choice. I told Andrée I loved her. I accepted my love for her as part of the structure of my life. I'd always loved her. After I said again what I used to tell her every day six years earlier, when we were both in another part of the world, in another time, we turned and walked back in silence in the semi-circle around the pond, along some train tracks, then through a parking area and up a long metal-railed concrete run of stairs emerging just behind Frick Fine Arts.

Arriving at the church for wedding rehearsals two hours later, Kathy was furious with me. She'd had to deal with all the wedding planning details for the past two weeks alone and was enraged at my tardiness. She was frazzled. There were complications when I forgot the rented shoes when I picked up my tuxedo. It was an otherworldly nightmare in a way. I felt detached.

When Reverend Rucker, longtime pastor of my grandparents' church, spoke these words in the marriage liturgy, "If any of you present here can show just cause why they may not be joined in holy matrimony, speak now, or forever hold your peace," something nearly happened, Andrée told me years later. She sat next to Petra, not really enjoying herself. She said, as I've heard her tell others, that she almost stood up and told everyone who I *really* should be marrying.

I wish she had. I wish I had listened to her on that trail... But then again, things happened the way they have. Looking back, it doesn't look like a thing is out of place. I always wish I had done things better. Well, Andrée kept quiet, and I was married.

She kept her end of our bargain. I remember thinking in the receiving line as she and Petra came through, *now it's my turn*—never dreaming how that second wedding would come about.

Three years later, after six years of living together, Katherine (she wouldn't let me call her Kathy anymore), wanted to be free of me. I had a life and a projected arc with this person—plans for a future—and all of that was ending. It felt like a part of me had died. Not a song lyric but <u>real</u>.

In addition, I sensed that all women were nuts. I was done with them. They're great, but to hell with them. They're complicated and it's nothing but a perpetual roller coaster living with one. Damn. Good riddance. I dusted myself off somewhat, stood up wobbly but silent, and walked slowly forward.

In 1998 I was living in Memphis, Tennessee. I occupied a second-floor apartment a stone's throw across the train tracks from the English Department building on the University of Memphis campus. I was an obituary writer for *The Commercial Appeal*. I was taking graduate classes and thoroughly enjoying them. In December I got a phone call. "Hi Dave," I heard. *Andrée*.

She said she wanted to visit me again. I said it was my turn, this time. The last time hadn't been so wonderful for her so I said I'd save money and come over to Stuttgart where she was living between the following spring and fall semesters—in August 1999. Eight months later, a full lunar eclipse occurred on the day I arrived at the *Flughafen* in Stuttgart. I looked at the security glass in the airport and saw her standing there. I was back.

Of course, a second after I recognized Andrée, I saw something that registered immediately with my sense of irony. As I got through customs, I walked over and kissed her hello—then her mother, Nicole. Andrée had overlapped our visits. Her mom had spent a few weeks with her and now I was here! The last time I'd seen Nicole was when I was 18, at their apartment in Rennes, France. I was 32. It was a variation on a theme. I still spoke no French.

That day, there was a huge *Straßenfest* on *Mittwoch*, August 11, 1999 to celebrate the day's eclipse. I had been in Amsterdam, waiting for my delayed connecting flight in the fog when it got vaguely darker and then lighter. The weather was crystal clear in Stuttgart, I heard, and the eclipse was stunning. I have a souvenir copy of the *Stuttgarter Zeitung* with a great photo of it.

When we got to Andrée's apartment, I put down my luggage and we went out for a little fresh air walk. We walked for about 12 hours with nothing to eat. I was loopy with jet-lag and low on blood sugar when we finally hiked back uphill to her apartment. Her mom had grown used to this endless marching during the few weeks with her daughter exploring castles, forests and kilometers of uphill nature trails.

At the apartment, Johanna and Lars from Berlin arrived. We ordered pizza and calzone. I drank half a German beer, stumbled into the guest bedroom and promptly fell asleep face-down on the bed before the food arrived. Andrée woke me up and I came out, bleary eyed, listening to nonstop German intermixed with French. I was exhausted. *She has a pretty effective way of paying me back*, I thought....

Andrée saw her mom to the train station the next morning. I slept in. I'd been excited to visit Europe again and had communicated to Andrée that I'd wanted to see a few countries while I was there. I had no idea the craziness of that idea. She took me at my word and we drove down near Zurich, Switzerland to visit a man who ran self-help seminars. Rudi. I remember a formal dinner with a bunch of strangers in a nice home, asking and answering questions. I spoke no German... yet.

We spent one night, ate breakfast of whole-grain *Brötchen*, cold cuts and strong coffee, then drove to Zürich, where we bought cigars and smoked on the edge of the *Zürichsee*.

I had told her the night before, "Let's get married."

She answered immediately, "I'm not moving to the U.S."

"That's alright," I said. "I'll move here."

My attitude toward women hadn't changed. They *are* crazy, I knew. They are definitely a breed apart and that's that. This one was part of my life and here I was, being given the present of a second chance. If I'm going to live with someone crazy, there's no one I'd rather be with than Andrée. I think we were made for each other. I've always felt that way.

I spent the next week and a half with my best friend and true love. Looking back, I'm sure she had a lot to think about. For me, it was all a big adventure. For her... a big change... and a big risk, maybe. Possibly. Looking back, I'm just impressed that she said "yes." I thought we could try what she had wanted to do when we were teenagers… Run off and live a life of adventure… I have to hand it to her; at the end of my last night there, she quietly said, "*Okay.*"

I told her I'd return to Memphis, disenroll from grad school, sell my car and bigger things, ship the rest of my stuff over and be back in a few weeks. She said, "I don't believe you." But she went along with it anyway. That's what I did. It was painful to be apart from her; I didn't eat and all I could think about was being with Andrée, starting our new life. It seemed like the day would never come when I could see her at the airport again. I felt a dread that something would move in—some calamity, catastrophe or disaster—and stop us from being together finally. *Well, at least we had that week and a half*, I would think, consoling myself. *If the plane goes down— at least we had that.*

In September 1999 I moved to Stuttgart. It was a transition. Neither seamless nor effortless. In a parallel universe, I hope that we returned to the States at 19 and 18, to live in Florida together, walking the beach hand-in-hand. In this life, I'm grateful for our life together *now*. I never thought we'd end up together. I'm grateful every day—when I'm not busy living it and taking *us* for granted.

In 2000, in Sparta, Tennessee, at an old plantation mansion called The Beechwood, we were married. For an American and a Frenchwoman living in Germany, it was much less complicated and expensive to get married in the States—Germany accepted a marriage certificate from the U.S. as valid and no translation fees were required. I would have preferred to be married in France, but we didn't find a willing co-conspirator on that end, whereas in Tennessee, my sister Anne was happy to help us with arrangements.

Married at last. April 21, 2000, in Sparta, Tennessee.

The ceremony was my most treasured time. I was overwhelmed by the wedding reception. We had Elvis pushing me to join him in the "Hunka Hunka Burnin' Love" song refrain and serenading us with "Can't Help Falling in Love." We danced Celtic dances. We cut cake, ate, drank and the day and night passed in a blur. I remember the Jacuzzi in the hotel room on our wedding night. It was so loud all we did was sit in the swirling water and laugh.

This year is our tenth wedding anniversary. We plan to be in France in June. I want to marry my true love again—every day, in fact.

[I wrote that last bit last year. We're approaching October 2011. I'm writing this book on a moving train, hoping to finish and print it off before the things I've described are too far behind. We've been married eleven years—and twenty-nine years since our first letters. We *did* go to France last June. Five weeks. The first time Andrée had been back in nearly eight years. We were two weeks late for her grandmother's 90th birthday. We introduced our boys to the country that the center of their world—Mom—is from. Have you ever tried to paint a portrait on the side of a moving train— running alongside, clutching your paints and dropping brushes? That's how this 'book' feels. If only *you* could hop on and ride, real-time, you'd find it gliding through events and episodes, just like *your* moving life train...]

In the end, we both kept our promises. We ended up together, seemingly against the odds I see around us, daily. Andrée was at both of my weddings, and I was at hers.

Chapter 24— Groups and Individuals

When I first ran across something called the Zen Study Group at the University of Pittsburgh as an undergraduate reporter for *The Pitt News*, the campus daily paper, I was pleasantly surprised to find myself in the company of others who sounded like they were talking about matters I'd always considered in my solitary life: questioning the nature of reality, the meaning of life—and meaning, period. I'd never met others who spent time on the subjects I'd had in my head since my first memory.

That was back in 1992. It's 2011, and I run a group called M&M Philosophy (Meeting of the Minds) at the Wheeling library. Perhaps you've heard of it? This is the seventh year I've been going there every Tuesday evening. I only miss the Tuesdays when I'm out of the country or at the hospital with my kids. It feels sometimes that the likelihood of my running into others when I can offer something relevant or useful to them in *their* search for their own meaning—is abysmally low. Still, I'll be there today, and probably next Tuesday too. I post a monthly schedule online at http://www.firstknowthyself.org/m&mschedule.htm. Sean, the library's program director, lists our topics on a flyer kept on the check-out counter. Here's this month's schedule:

Tuesday, March 1: The Master Game: Pathways to Higher Consciousness, by Robert S. de Ropp. Book Review.

Tuesday, March 8: Model-Dependent Reality. Of paradigms and projected meaning. Discussion.

Tuesday, March 15: Guided meditation and breathing. A 10-minute video presentation followed by discussion.

Tuesday, March 22: "My Life". We'll accompany two group members as they recount their journey thus far—from zygote to the present moment.

Tuesday, March 29: Power vs. Force: The Hidden Determinants of Human Behavior, by David R. Hawkins, (*revisited*). Discussion of some intriguing excerpts from this work.

I cook up a schedule a day or two before the next month. I solicit ideas from meeting attendees as much as possible. When I come up with topics myself, I only do things that I am personally interested in. This is in contrast to tailoring meetings designed to draw people in, which, of course, I used to do. I find it much more pleasant (and honest) to focus solely on my genuine personal interest; if people come in, that's a bonus. In addition, I perpetually focus only on *their* genuine interests. It's the only place we are really "us." Talking about anything other than what we are drawn to means we're only half present, if that.

Here is an essay I wrote a few years ago to convey the arc of my experiences with group work and my perspective on my position in this little group I run now. I wrote this in the doldrums. There is an annual cycle of attendance. Instead of stopping for "spring break" or "winter break," I normally keep the light on every Tuesday evening. This time, there was a stretch of meetings where I was the only attendee... It's great to have a lot of people talking, but it's also good to have some quiet reflective or contemplative time. I guess I got what I asked for.

Group work

Sometimes I see him come into our meeting room, but he's not willing to hear me. I can recognize myself sitting over there, but I can't strike up a conversation. Sometimes I see him walk in, look around, and walk out. Sometimes he walks by in the hallway without coming in. Sometimes he stays and I give him a book to read and he or she leaves, takes the book and brings it back unread. I'm a solitary tree in a time-lapse film, glowing lantern hanging on my motionless branch.

My notion of group work has changed over time. Group work concerning seeking a permanent solution to the ultimate question of life is what I'm referring to. In the beginning, I had no concept of group work. I had ultimate questions but I walked with them on my own. I avoided philosophic books from a strong conviction that they were irrelevant. I avoided churches because I considered the attendees deluded.

In 1992, I ran across a University of Pittsburgh student group called the Self Knowledge Symposium (formerly called the Zen Study Group). I was a reporter for the campus paper and I chose to cover this group's first meeting of the semester over other, more boring, story assignments. I became interested and returned to following meetings. Each week, there were people sitting in a circle of chairs in a classroom in the evening to talk about very important things, things like consciousness, awareness, states of being, meaning, and the purpose of our lives. At that time, I was thrilled to have an outlet and an opportunity to speak aloud all of the things that I had held in my head for years. I'd found my church; I'd walked my days and years through the assumption that it didn't exist.

I'd been attending the SKS meetings for two years when first Al and then Mike Fitzpatrick stopped heading them. I remember sitting in the basement cafeteria in the Cathedral of Learning with Mike at the end of 1993. We customarily met there regularly after SKS meetings to discuss the night's activities. This particular night was the last meeting of the year and had been a particularly good one. Mike commented nostalgically about the course of that semester's meetings. He said that they had been profound for him—and also that he wouldn't be coming back to head the meetings in the spring. He was going to begin a new phase of his life.

I couldn't accept letting this valuable thing that I'd become increasingly involved with dissolve. The camaraderie, delving into mysteries, friends on the path of investigation and discovery—again, my church. I'd never considered heading a group, but if I failed to act, then this gem would slip through my fingers and disappear like it never was.

Waiting on a January evening the following spring semester, in an empty second floor classroom of the Cathedral of Learning, I was nervous. That's mainly what I remember from that first spring meeting. I'd prepared an introduction to what my notion of the purpose of this group was. I'd waited ten minutes past the time that the meeting was supposed to start, relieved that no one had shown up. As I was gathering up my things to leave, two pretty girls walked in. I gave them a handout and told them about this group aimed at investigating the meaning in one's life. After some silence, they told me they'd thought that this was a fraternity meeting of some kind and had wanted to find out for sure.

With that start, things really took off. By the time I left this precious group in someone else's hands, I had been on a real adventure. There was a core of six or seven regular attendees and we'd formed a bond of friendship and shared experiences. We'd gone on trips to caves and railroad tunnels to face fear and confront silence. We'd engineered thought experiments and explored topics such as magic, ghosts, perception and divination. The group had become an established funded student organization that sponsored lectures and presentations. We had a website. In December, I graduated and held a meeting with the core members, telling them that I had to make a clean break of things and let them move into the driver's seat; I didn't want to keep running the group after I was no longer an official student. I had benefited so much from the experience of running a group. I wanted others to have that, too.

I felt this was the best and truest gift that I could give—the experience of leading a group. Even before I was gone, I was missing the coming meetings that I wouldn't get to attend. I was tempted, occasionally, to go back, *just once,* but resisted because I didn't want to influence things by being there. Mike's own farewell echoed with me at times. I don't think we both quit for the same reason, but the results would hopefully be the same—for them, as it had been for me. Have you ever benefited so much from something, some time spent, that you hope others can experience the same thing, for themselves? It think it's universal, this 'hope.' I knew their meaning would look different from mine, but I wanted something great for them. It's the only thing I could think of doing that felt right. It felt *right*.

Along with leaving notes, instructions, tips and so on, I showed core members the ins and outs of running the show. I believed in the purpose of the group. We were explorers hiking bravely, enthusiastically to our unclimbed mountains, our unexplored depths. I handed them the keys and left.

I *did* stop by, however, six months later and was deeply moved to see it still working, still alive. A year later, I visited again and was amazed and happy. I was profoundly thankful, for myself, and for others, that it still "lived." In 1996, during the separation from my first wife, I found unexpectedly large chunks of free time in my hands so I started 'auditing' the SKS meetings, interacting with a whole new regular crowd.

By November 1996, when I left Pittsburgh, I'd become friends with a new treasured group of similar souls. We'd spent six months together and I felt sad to be leaving. On a cold weekday, I held a going away party in the friend's house on Suburban Avenue in the South Hills where I was living after my divorce. Five or six fellow seekers of truth braved the lousy weather to wish me farewell. It was a happy sad time. I'd left once before and knew that *this time* I probably wouldn't be back. Some things you don't get to have back twice.

My notion of group work had evolved. I'd gone from being a fully engaged group participant to being a fully engaged leader of an organization of metaphysical exploration. I'd then handed the reins over to peers on a path aimed at enlightenment—at least that's the path that I was on. I haven't spoken to these friends in a decade, but they're as alive in my mind as they were for me when I saw them regularly. I would open my home to any one of them.

In the beginning, while I was leading SKS, I had what I consider an evangelical mindset for a good while. I would greet newcomers with the motive of converting them to truth-seeking people. I wanted to make everybody obsessed with it like I was. Isn't this the most important thing there is? After some months of increasing unhappiness on my part, I reached a turning point:

Before one meeting, I was organizing handouts into different piles, feeling somewhat unenthusiastic about the crowd I imagined might show up that night. At one point, I stopped what I was doing and stared at the chalkboard over the table with a realization dawning on me. I said to the wall, 'This isn't for everyone.' I *saw* what I had been doing. *This isn't for everyone...* That echoed in me all the rest of the time I ran that group. Nothing was for everyone.

After that, I never did anything except to focus my attention on what *I* was interested in. I was wholeheartedly devoted to my own curiosity. Each meeting, I would present a topic or idea that I was interested in and made absolutely no efforts to show or convince anyone of anything. Surprisingly—of course—attendance shot up. As soon as I didn't care at all about winning people over to my obsession, a dozen people or more started coming regularly. The group thrived and grew. I wasn't oblivious to the irony...

Following my '96 departure from Pittsburgh, nine years would pass before I would engage in "group work" of this nature again. I've been a member of TAT [see tatfoundation.org] since 1993, making it to most quarterly meetings except while I was living overseas, but I'm talking about group work that I initiate, something far less passive than showing up at a meeting already organized. I got back into metaphysical group work again after returning to the U.S. from France.

When I moved overseas in 1999, I didn't make it back to any TAT meetings. I was immersed in foreign languages, cultures, entrepreneurial enterprises. I felt that I had made a decision and a break; this was my life now. I subsisted from a trickle of email correspondence with seekers of the truth. I knew some of them from TAT circles. I'd met a handful from a bulletin board on Shawn Nevins' link, *Spiritual Friends Locator* on his **spiritualteachers.org** website. All the while, I hungered for that rare thing I had been accustomed to having at TAT meetings and SKS meetings. My fellows. I discovered what I had taken for granted.

I adjusted to my new life in first German and then French societies, but it was living with the sound turned off. I didn't get the opportunity to talk on a channel and subject that was central to my life. I'm sure that I would have found something if I had lived there for the rest of my life, after the language barrier was completely gone, but I didn't. Fortunately, I corresponded with one or two people at a time, and we would seemingly mutually agree to pause our correspondence; then I would find myself comparing notes with someone else a few months later via email. This was my lifeline. I was an expatriate on a metaphysical desert island, writing notes in bottles.

Without expecting to ever return, I came back to the States in 2003.

I attended TAT meetings regularly again for the first time in five years. It was very nice to be where I recognized and resonated with the subject matter in the air. I was an outsider now. I had another view on everything, but it was nice to be able to talk again.

My family and I relocated to the Ohio Valley in 2005. Waiting for the next TAT meeting was about the extent of "group work" for me. That, and the occasional email correspondence with seekers.

Once in the Wheeling area, I began running a weekly discussion group at the library after a conversation with the former director of library activities. This current group is called the Meeting of the Minds Philosophic Inquiry Forum—*M&M Philosophy*.

Here, and now, I see group work with other, older eyes. I organize meetings with various topics, exercises and activities and my unbridled enthusiasm and curiosity about the subjects we cover is all that I bring to the table. Attendance for the first two years was regular and I think word of mouth had something to do with this. Possibly curiosity about something new in town was a factor, too. A lot of people came in through those auditorium double doors. It seems like everyone popped in at one time or another. I say 'we,' but there isn't a core in the sense that there was at Pitt with SKS. One or two people are interested enough to come back regularly. An average crowd is five or six. Sometimes it's just me and one other. It's a different dynamic. I'm different. Every year. Every meeting. The same, only different. These Tuesday nights, there are people from various times of life coming together in an auditorium in the basement of the Wheeling library. Retirees, working class people, students.

Thematic ripples move through these years. I stand on this beach, watching waves cover the sand and disappear. Geriatrics. Extremists. Conservatives. Christians. Atheists. Liberals. Young and restless. And… Seekers—who don't know what they want or what they are, just that something is missing and this echoes for them in our meetings.

I've questioned my motives for organizing and running this group. All I can say is that I have a habit of returning to the same place in the library auditorium to gaze at the water.

I feel like a still tree in a time-lapse motion picture with days and seasons coming and going. I watch people meet each other, return, don't return, laugh, frown, leave.

What do I have to offer?...

For three hours each Tuesday, I am a truth-seeking arrow. I have spent my life energy fixated on this most-important-subject-existing-for-me. I have devoured esoteric books and listened to a West Virginia enlightened man whose voice always pointed towards home. I have sacrificed my life to reaching this *one goal*, the Mount Everest of my existence and never found it. I *turned into it*.

I think people coming to the Tuesday meetings have had insights. I think they've heard things that they'd never heard before. I think we've had personal epiphanies occur. I know a handful of 'regulars' who have grown empowered in their own personal path. What else? I don't know.

I think I have something to offer <u>myself</u>—and if I see myself walk through those auditorium doors, then, sitting there in my chair, I will look up and recognize my reflection, *knowing* I can offer a thing or two I could find useful in my life.

I don't think I have much to offer anyone who isn't similar to myself—similar interests, curiosity, dissatisfaction with anything less than completeness in life. I painted a picture of sitting at a table in the library auditorium, looking up, seeing myself walk into the room—simultaneously being both 'me's'... We all offer things to those we come in contact with. I am focusing, specifically, on being helpful in the search-for-meaning that some of us get involved in. Like being an inline skater with certain skills and experience; he'd like to be helpful to other skaters, like himself, who are on the skating "path." Sure, we learn cross-paths; a skater can learn something about dedication by observing a devoted rock climber. There are many ways of being useful to others. I'm just zeroing in on the blatantly obvious way in which I might be of use to a seeker of personal truth or wisdom..

I first met Richard Rose in 1993—on the phone. He was coming up to give a talk at the University of Pittsburgh. I, the media contact for the brothers running the student group Self Knowledge Symposium (SKS), was given Rose's phone number and asked to do a pre-talk story for *The Pitt News*. I distinctly remember the conversation, though I don't remember a single question I asked.

I'd roughed out a story on an Apple computer in *The Pitt News* offices before calling. I had some questions prepared. This'll be easy, I thought.

I made the call, explained who I was, and asked if he minded answering some questions. I remember a basic mounting frustration. The author of *The Albigen Papers*, *The Direct Mind Experience* and *Psychology of the Observer*, accomplished speaker and "Zen master," Rose was an interesting-sounding man. I would ask a leading question designed to give me some kind of usable quote—a certain class of response that I could jot down and plug into the story. Rose didn't cooperate. At some point I put down my pen and quit asking questions. After returning the phone receiver to its cradle, I just sat there. *Jesus. How can I use* this *stuff?* I started typing, trying to salvage some kind of usable quote for the article.

The first time I saw the man in person was at the William Pitt Union ballroom, a mirror-lined, crystal chandelier-hung large rectangular space in the elegant student union building (former Schenley Hotel) between Forbes and Fifth Avenues, bordering Bigelow Boulevard. I was there to cover his lecture for the paper. Sitting in a folding chair, waiting for the lecture to begin, I thought, *This'll be easy.* I'd covered things like this before. The time on the phone had been a fluke. This was concrete; easy to describe. Something was actually happening—easier to write about than someone's non-answers. I wrote in my reporter's notebook about the people, the setting, Rose's appearance. I figured I'd sit long enough to get a few quotes from Rose and the audience, maybe the first part of the Q&A, then dash up to the 4th floor to get my story in before tonight's deadline.

I sat through the long introduction someone gave—a very respectful testimonial. I looked at my watch. *Let's get on with it.* I was expecting a comprehendible narrative, a talk I could encapsulate and outline. I sat there with my pen poised over my paper for a long time. After a while, I began twirling my pen through my fingers. A sinking feeling settled in. *Uh-oh.* I sat through his talk. I don't remember a single detail of what he said. I just couldn't get a bite on it, couldn't summarize what he was saying in a neat package. I remember an overwhelmingly depressed feeling. Why would I have that reaction? I was under a self-imposed pressure to hurry up to the *Pitt News* offices above us to type in my story before the 9 o'clock deadline. It wasn't looking good.

Once the Q&A started, I looked at my watch again, resolving to get out of there once a single usable quote from the audience appeared. It seems I was doomed in this respect, too. After a while, I just left, certain I had no story. *And I didn't.* I went to the paper's office, having come up empty-handed once again. I wrote a story, something to the effect of "Richard Rose, Zen master, defies easy pigeonholing." Truer words…

I visited Rose's farm in the spring of '93 between TAT meetings—those four annual gatherings his organization held at his farmhouse in the hills above Moundsville in the northwest panhandle of West Virginia, 59 miles southwest of Pittsburgh. I felt leery of what looked like a cult of personality formed around this man. So I talked my way down there (initially, N.G. and B.G. were hesitant to respond to my curiosity about TAT and Rose and getting permission to visit the farm). I wandered the hills of Rose's 160-acre 'farm'—mostly wooded rolling hills and plunging ravines.

I attended the next TAT meeting—April, I think—where I was welcomed warmly and where I found myself surprised to be able to have meaningful conversations with seemingly sane people. I left after the weekend with a changed mind. *This is a valuable place*, I thought. I attended succeeding TAT meetings, developing friendships and growing an appreciation for Rose's perspective and life example.

That fall, I decided to go after the question that had been haunting me for the eight years since my father's drowning: *What is the meaning of life?* For the next three years, I was a "fanatical philosopher" as I deprecatingly refer to my former struggling self. For once, I was living to the beat of my own drum, completely and unapologetically.

In November 1997, after four months in a cabin (nearly three months of it spent in "isolation"), I moved away from the Rose farm where I had been helping keep up the place and maintain a presence that helped discourage vandals who explore uninhabited places. In 1998, I moved to the banks of the Mississippi River and entered graduate school at the University of Memphis. In 1999, I moved to Stuttgart, Germany to live with Andrée. In 2003, I returned to my hometown of Fowlerville, Michigan from Toulouse, France with my wife and 2 ½-year-old son, Guillaume. In 2004, I took my pregnant wife and son to a nursing home in Weirton, WV to visit Richard Rose, who was a resident in the Alzheimer's wing of a nursing facility there. It was the last time I'd see him alive. In 2005, I stood at the open casket during a memorial service for Rose in Wheeling, and a few hours later, with my family, stood at the border of his land, throwing handfuls of dirt into a hole where a headstone bearing his name now rests.

Andrée, Guillaume, Benjamin in his walker and I stood, long after everyone else filed away to walk up to the community building on the hill for his wake. We watched the grave diggers lower Rose's casket into the concrete liner, the placement of the vault lid, then the back filling with a portable digging machine. I sensed the men weren't used to people standing around watching the dirty work after the rich green fake grass was taken away, revealing piled up dirt. We threw handfuls into that hole, then turned to join the others. A beautiful hot sunny July morning. A heck of a day to be buried, I thought. When I drive by that spot on the way to a TAT meeting, I say, *Hey, Mr. Rose*. Maybe twice a year, on the meeting weekends, I park down the road and walk a long grass path to the grave and stand there under the trees for a few minutes. The following is something I wrote for the commemorative TAT Forum [online monthly publication] issue following Rose's death. A lot of folks wrote tributes. This was mine.

An Appropriate Gesture: My Tribute to Richard Rose, by David Weimer

When I met Richard Rose, I was surprised to meet myself in the form of an unfamiliar familiar old man. When I met Rose I was surprised to find that someone, anyone, had made their life a dedication to finding The Answer. I was chagrined at the time that I hadn't thought of it myself—taking my dreaming and thinking about life and turning it into a career, the only career that ever could matter.

I have my dad's dying to thank for meeting Richard Rose. If he hadn't drowned in Lake Superior in 1985, I wouldn't have spent two years in Germany, living and breathing the unblinking questions, *What is? What is? Why? Why? What?* I wouldn't have gone to North Florida after leaving the Army where my family had moved to make a new start, leaving painful memories back in Michigan. If I hadn't attended Lake City Community College, I wouldn't have met my first wife in the last semester and wouldn't have followed her to Pittsburgh to attend Pitt, where I was a campus reporter in the spring of '92 covering the first meeting of the Zen Study Group that semester. Later that year, I interviewed Rose on the phone for a story about his coming lecture on Zen.

I was in shock at the funeral of my father. I was eighteen. The guy lying there in the coffin wasn't Dad. When I stood before Rose's coffin twenty years later, I had the same sense of no one home anymore. Only this time, I found myself laughing. "Well you went and did it," I said. I addressed the body in the suit that vaguely resembled Richard Rose. At both funerals, I was saying goodbye to the same person.

Another TAT member told me that Richard Rose influenced him at least as much as their own father had. I nodded. My dad taught me how to work. But there is no one else who impacted me more than Rose. He was the right person at the right time. If I'd met him earlier I would have thought he was an interesting nut, maybe. Maybe not. I automatically related to this man who was two generations ahead of me and who had marched his life, unexpectedly, to a tune that I somehow recognized.

I heard bells when he spoke. He talked on a wavelength that I had thought only I was on. I didn't think anyone else pondered the unknowns of the universe like I did, staring at the starry winter sky countless times while growing up. Rose's life example inspired me. If he can do it, I can. I wish I had engaged in my own life quest for the Ultimate before meeting Rose. I hope that I would have come up with the notion if I'd never met him. I don't know. Rose said a person's yearning would result in their finding or running into a book or a teacher. I can't argue with that.

I had wanted a personal guru to advise me on what to do with my life, step by step. Rose wasn't interested in the job. He just didn't reinforce me like I wanted and needed. I reluctantly let drop my hopes of such a relationship. By default, I became self reliant. Around this time, I was sitting at the kitchen table in Rose's house in McMechen. "What specific advice can you give to me?" He answered without missing a beat. "Be celibate." It's not what I asked. I wanted *spiritual* advice. I drove back to Pittsburgh.

When I got home to our apartment, I sat in front of my desk and examined the unwanted souvenir that I'd brought back from West Virginia. I put it on the table with no great enthusiasm. Then I found myself thinking, *I'll try it. Even though I don't think there's anything to it. At least I'll know for myself.*

Instead of an unwanted bauble, I had received a multifaceted gift. I discovered that when I began to cultivate purity in all things, as the author Santanelli said in his book on hypnosis, I stopped scaring little children. Living a clean life, I no longer did things to be ashamed of and was free. The experience of celibacy allowed me to focus my energy and attention on a single goal. I might be a goat, but I'm not only a goat.

The second gift that I got from Rose was a frightening commitment. It gave me something to do with tension, and with my life. It was the career called My Search for the Meaning of Life. Somewhere, in the back of my mind, I'd heard the echo of him saying that a person has to make a personal commitment to achieve any goal they have in mind. I'll probably never forget when I did it. *Either commit to this thing or dump all the books in the trash and walk away from this stuff forever.* This is what I said in my head with my feet on a bookshelf of philosophy and mystic books, leaning back on my chair in the corner of our apartment where I thought every night as my wife watched TV in our bedroom with the cats.

I'd been a TAT member for a year and a member of the University of Pittsburgh Self Knowledge Symposium somewhat longer. I'd learned the shop talk and read the canon of required authors, including Rose, and was reading more each day. For some reason, it all came down to this solitary night in Oakland and a flash of *knowing* that I would be a hypocrite and worse if I spent another minute talking the talk without taking a first actual step. I think someone can spend years without being a real philosopher. When there's no life commitment, there's no life.

People are what they do. I have discovered this myself as well as many other things that I first heard a West Virginian say on recorded university lecture tapes. Only one tribute is possible for this man who is now cold and gone. If I have to attempt an appropriate gesture, I can live. I have been informed by him and his life. And beyond that, I feel paradoxically that it wouldn't matter if a single other soul ever learned that he had existed. The fact that such a man once upon a time lived his solitary shooting star arc in this infinite seeming tapestry of time is all that matters and all that ever will.

I hadn't planned on having to make an unbreakable commitment to myself to find the truth no matter what. The university group and TAT were fun and interesting. But in a single dark night I was faced with something ominous. Making a real, binding commitment. It felt like the stupidest thing in the world. Committing to finding the big answer. Who in the hell ever does? The alternative of being a hypocrite was, unfortunately, not an option. Between a rock and something worse, and to myself and to the All as my witness, I said, *Here goes nothing.* I was wrong.

Chapter 25 — In My Father's House, There are Many Rooms

This next short story puts you in a certain chair. I wrote it from inside my life on the University of Pittsburgh campus. I was 26.

Written for an intermediate fiction class dated 19 October 1993. I had forgotten I'd written it. How many things have you done or built and forgotten? My first-grade son came home yesterday with a construction paper and crayon creation called "Starry Night." Absolutely beautiful. I taped it on the top of my bookshelf just now. How many days of years do we *do* stuff? Like beautiful autumn leaves that fall in layers, compost and become part of the humus supporting living fresh green shoots. Piles of our sons' homework get taller and taller until my wife spirits them away somewhere. In our lives we leave a lot of footprints in the melting snow of time.

Regardez:

Doppelganger
by David W. Weimer

....panting, Wilderness Jack scans the inhospitable landscape for signs of the wolves. Raised by natives in this desolate Dakota Territory, he had been taught to live by his strength, cunning and courage. This man thrived where others often failed. He looked forward to confronting this pack; it would give him a chance to prove...

The college sophomore bent the upper left corner of a page to mark his place and stood as the Pittsburgh Area Transit (PAT) bus he was riding neared his stop. He leaned to counter the driver's hard braking and after the door whooshed open, took three steps down to the sidewalk, bending his tall frame to avoid hitting his head.

In fifteen seconds, the air had lost its diesel aftertaste and the wailing bus engine with its accompanying cloud of incompletely-burned fuel was faded into the normal traffic. Tristan unzipped his backpack and slipped *Arctic Trail* behind his class notebooks.

A breeze, an autumn sun and an hour to go before class... The young man could think of worse conditions to pass his time under. He could be running from a pack of wolves.

Tristan walked along Bigelow to Forbes Avenue, then cut across the Schenley parking lot in front of the Mary Schenley Fountain to sit in the shade of a giant sycamore. *A good place to eat lunch, and watch.*

Earlier in the semester, Tristan and Janice, whom he'd met at a lecture on hypnosis, were ambling down Thackeray after class when Tristan grabbed Janice's arm.

"Would you look at my doppelganger..." Tristan said, staring at a small group of students on the sidewalk in front of the teaching college.

"What?" Janice smiled. Her laugh was a second away.

"There," Tristan said, his voice lowering. "Behind the guy with the glasses. See that one in the orange sweatshirt? It's me."

Janice stared at the group. A few noticed her and raised their eyebrows. Tristan tugged on Janice's sleeve, steering her down the sidewalk.

"Would you *stop*?!" she said, the smile gone. "I didn't see anyone wearing orange... "

"He was right there," Tristan said.

Janice laughed uneasily. Tristan shrugged silently, letting the incident pass. They spent the rest of the afternoon flirting and talking about their classes.

Later, Tristan realized that Janice hadn't been any different from the others. He reluctantly admitted that he was the only person who could see his doppelganger.

The first time had been walking to his apartment from a convenience store with a loaf of bread. He had a craving for Velveeta and Wonder Bread grilled cheese. His mouth watered thinking about his feast, still a block away from his apartment. He looked casually across the street—then looked again. He stood with his mouth open, grilled cheese forgotten, as his own face stared with a knowing look out from the window of a 51C PAT bus accelerating away, headed downtown.

The second time was in the city theater. Tristan, James and James's girlfriend Kate were at the play, *I Stand Before you Naked*. A performer in the second act walked onto stage and looked into the audience—with *Tristan's own face*! Tristan quickly scanned James and his date for signs that they recognized him up there.

"Hey, take a look at that guy," he whispered. "Do you know him?"

"No. Why?" Their eyes spoke the truth.

"Never mind," Tristan said.

It had begun as an exciting and mysterious game, but now... After months of similar encounters, Tristan felt as though he were playing this game with an unknown opponent, and he didn't understand the rules. He wanted *answers*.

*

Sitting cross-legged with his back against the sycamore that stood with a row of others between the fountain and a memorial softball field built on the former outfield of Forbes Field—home of the Pittsburgh Pirates until 1971. A pink-footed pigeon strutted on the sidewalk in front of him, eyeing the remains of a Subway sandwich crumpled in its wrapper on the grass.

"Shoo." He waved a hand. The bird hopped back with dignity. Benches circling the fountain were peppered with students on break between classes in the early fall coolness. Tristan looked around often, waiting.

Half-listening to pieces from several conversations, he glimpsed his quarry crossing the road, heading to the fountain. Tristan gathered his trash and walked over to a squat green barrel near his double, who had just settled down, cross-legged on the lawn.

"We have to talk," his double told him before he could say anything, half-smiling and looking up with those strange-familiar eyes.

"I know," Tristan said. "What do *you* want to talk about?"

"The same thing; why no one else here notices that you're the same as me, or that I'm even here at all."

Tristan looked at the fountain, a sculpture of Poseidon, noticing the trickling sound of water and a ring of tortoises around the fountain's base. "OK. I'll skip Planetary Geology. Let's go."

His double stood and brushed grass from his pants. "This way," he said.

The two young men walked towards Forbes Quad, a complex of auditoriums, classrooms and offices, one not quite leading the other. They both pushed through a separate metal-and-glass door at the same time.

Just inside, Tristan's double stopped. His forehead was furrowed with concentration. He waited. He seemed confused and indecisive. After a moment, he gave a quick nod and walked quickly into the concourse, eventually turning abruptly right and leading Tristan through a set of double doors. It was a familiar setting; Tristan had taken a political rhetoric class in this very room. Fluorescents lit every corner of the empty classroom, creating a bright space free of shadows. Tristan's double walked down the sloped aisle to the front of the classroom. He approached the lectern and turned, appearing to study Tristan, who had remained at the top of the amphitheater, at the first row of empty seats.

"Have you looked into the mirror before?" the doppelganger asked him. He had backed up to the chalkboard, leaning with the eraser ledge at the small of his back.

Tristan spread his hands in a large gesture. "Sure." He headed down the aisle to close the space between them, then sat in the first row.

His double made a dismissive gesture. "When you see your reflection you're not seeing yourself. Your life could pass you by without your ever having seen what *others see* of you."

Tristan watched the second hand of the wall clock, not bothering to reply.

His double pushed off the blackboard and stood at attention. "Well go on, take a look."

Tristan got up and approached his double, then walked slowly around his likeness, inspecting from every position. He saw how *unfamiliar* this person facing him seemed. The feeling he always associated as *himself* was missing; It didn't *feel* like him, he thought, as he looked at the figure standing before him. It was almost like he was looking at himself inside-out.

Still, a strong intuition told him—this person was his exact duplicate.

Tristan took his double's former position, leaning against the chalkboard in the empty classroom. His double moved took the front row chair he had vacated.

"You are me," they said together. A jolt of fear moved through Tristan's chest.

"Or *you're* me," they said again, speaking with one voice.

Tristan felt dizzy. "Hey, wait! Yeah. Okay. Fine... What's going on? *You* act like you know something. Clue me in."

The other red-haired opened his mouth to speak, then stopped. He shook his head to himself. After a pause, he said, crossing his legs, "I remember that first time, when I was on the bus and you were at the gas station buying a Coke."

"Yeah. I remember, too."

Tristan's double nodded. "I think that if you want to know why we are *both* here, you should ask Him." The young man's legs were stretched out, crossed at the ankles. He pointed to the ceiling of the auditorium and looked up briefly. "*He's* responsible for this."

"Responsible? What? Who?" Tristan didn't like the turn of this conversation. A crawling sensation ran up the back of his neck.

His double sighed. "Let me put it like this: Right now, when I speak, someone is typing on a keyboard. Not only recording everything we say and do—and where we go—but everything we *think*." The doppelganger paused, studying Tristan's furrowed brow. "It's not easy, I know; but I have proof."

"Proof," Tristan muttered, looking around distractedly. His eyes wandered around the nearly empty room. He pushed away from the blackboard, took a halting step forward, his troubled gaze settling on the two sets of doors at the top of the auditorium. He couldn't look away. Which side? *Could* he choose? Left or right... What does this mean? He felt something moving in on his mind. *It was not right*... Left or right... Suddenly he was more afraid than he had ever been. With his backpack dangling forgotten in his hand, Tristan walked woodenly past his doppelganger and up the aisle.

Tristan's look-alike remained sitting, in the front row seat; he'd turned around to follow Tristan with his eyes as he walked away, up the aisle to the doors.

"You're walking into your oblivion, you know! Once you leave this place, you won't even exist! It will be the end of you! You *know* this!"

Heedless, Tristan pushed through the double doors and disappeared without a sound, head down, backpack dropping behind him to land on the floor. The pneumatic left-side door slowly pushed the abandoned backpack on the floor into the room as it reclosed with a final click.

The seated young man turned back around to face the blackboard and sunk down into his chair, hands folded.

"Great. Now I'm stuck with *you* again," he said to no one. "Why are you doing this to me?"

His wry, knowing smile was gone. The young double sniffed. He looked at a spot on the carpet between his feet—spilled *Coca-Cola*.

"*I'm scared, you asshole*," the copy—alone now—thought to himself. ...The words occurred in cadence with a faint sound of far-off typing.

The following are from writing-journal entries. 1995, I think. I was out of college, out of my first abortive post-graduating newspaper reporter job, and heavily into my serious metaphysical searching period. I was at our—Kathy and my—second-floor apartment at 4724 Maripoe Street between Bloomfield, Shadyside and North Oakland in Pittsburgh. Some of these entries are from our first apartment together at 411 Brownsville Road above the South Side. This was my university time, my running-a-student-philosophy-group time, and my spiritual seeking time. I would have things happen on the last, psychological, front in May 1996. The build-up, lead-up and immediate aftermath to that time are some of what I detect in the following writing-journal entries. I kept a daily journal as an accompaniment to my seeking-meaning quest. The last entry is from just after the fall—and I don't mean the season—in the midst of my divorce and accompanying life-changes—immediately after a week in the woods and my 'night of hell.' I think it *was* fall. I see a transition in this handful of entries from a period of time in my life when things had come to a head.

This is from 1994 or thereabout. Maybe I'm talking to Kathy's sister about her opinion on the meaning or purpose of life. The word-association stream-of-consciousness bit here, from 17 years ago, is interesting; what a younger me's mind put out—before kids, before living overseas with Andrée, before becoming a self-employed contractor—before so much...

I feel so stupid. Such a moron. Asking her sister about purposes in life and stuff. Who knows, who cares. Don't think about it, just go, don't stop. Sorry I asked. Never mind. Quit it end it stop.

Sure do feel dumb about what I asked her [Why? I wish I'd asked, in this writing].

That's part of it, she said. Living to reproduce. A matter of course. To have children and a family and to be a parent and grandparent... all part of living. That sounds so normal, logical, so right.

Super Bowl, morning paper, evening news, the weather, favorite shows on TV, going to the movies, putting gas in the car, paying bills, taxes, beer and pizza, calling family at Christmas and Thanksgiving, birthdays, big breakfast on Saturday morning, corn flakes, coffee, toast, bagel, grocery shopping, snow sledding, diapers, life insurance, check-ups, hospitals, convenience stores, malls, beef jerky, McDonalds, traveling, headaches, feeling angry, guilty, sad, happy, daydreaming, sleeping in, dreaming, going to the bathroom at home, restroom at restaurant, eating out occasionally, reading a book, telling the time, turning on a light in the morning, radios in cars, favorite music groups, cassettes, CDs, radio stations, eggs, milk, butter, lottery tickets, Sunday papers, pet dogs, zoos, recycling, Styrofoam, magazines, snow storms, rain, thunder-lightening, mowing the lawn, flowers, birds chirping, mosquito bites, flies, earth worms, fishing, barbeque, iced tea, Kool-Aid, Band-Aids, wrist watches, painted fingernails, pantyhose, alarm clocks, VCRs, video rental, Chinese food, exercise, football, basketball, hockey, baseball, horse racing, car racing, best seller, TV guide, cable TV, space shuttle, satellite, bright sun, moon at night, crickets, grasshoppers, deer hunting, rabbit, license plates, voting, cigarette butts, beer cans, Doritos, tooth decay, broken bones, cuts, scabs, toenails, haircuts, eyeglasses, contact lenses, baldness, wrinkles, hearing aids, bras, pants, shoes, dresses, coats, boots, gloves, hats, basketballs, quarters, spoons, lighters, matches, fireplaces, electricity, phone booths, vacuum cleaners, pencils, pens, antennae, tools, power saw, drill, hacksaw, crow bar, spare tire, concrete, asphalt, stop signs, stop lights, leaves, snow, wind, rain, bats, safety pins, vitamins, razor blades, tooth brushes, books, paperbacks, hardcover, posters, bookmarks, cardboard, plastic, wood paneling, nails, engine oil, semi truck trailers, blenders, coffee machines, coke machines, vending machines, tests, diplomas, classes, teachers, students, desks, chalkboards, glass windows, screen doors, light bulbs, famous, poor, rich, honor, coward, war, fighting, army, cannons, guns, bullets, shouting, boots, knives, stabbing, eat, sleep, bomb, weight bench, house plants, buttons, zippers, fans, sewing machines, filing cabinet, belt, underwear, neck ties, scarf, car keys, death, crying, laughing, shouting, breathing, hearing, listening, writing, telling, asking, answering, feeling, believing, remembering, wondering, silence, finishing.

Next, fatigued. **Must** *be 1994.*

I have to write. It is my function and destiny. I do it because I must.

Tired in body, more tired than I can say, and in these moments, fogged in mind, I still write about... what?

Let's keep it focused for a moment. Purpose. Mine. What?

To live. To learn by living, while living. To work and have a family and a marriage. This is to learn responsibility? To be the observer and, in doing a long-term commitment to a marriage and a job, learning. Unless I do something, speculation can only take me so far. I guess it is *doing* that matters because I will have experientially-based observation and wisdom and knowledge.

Here is something: feeling exhausted as I do, it is wonderful to watch Emerald scamper and play in her youthfulness. I am weary, and watching her live unafflicted in her powerful youth, it gives me a bit of pleasure. I can, now, imagine what old people feel when they sit and watch us running by. Grizelda and [I] are shuffling around here like two premature geriatrics.

The thing to be learned from this condition is: stripped bare of all that I take for granted—time, youthful energy—what is the meaning of <u>me</u>?

Keep asking.

How can I shake the numbing fatigue dragging at my eyelids and weighing so heavily on every surface of my body, like the gravity of a heavy heavy planet? Academic question. This thing, here, writing, is helping... ... ... something...

There is so much that...

If I can just...

If only...

I wish...

So, tomorrow. I will work on either that Ohgod story or do a useful character sketch, or dialogue, or description for a new, second story.

Meditation.

Setting the scene:

Here is January or February of 1995. I graduated from Pitt in December and had just quit the beat reporter job I'd lined up before graduating. I was overwhelmed. I don't know why. Maybe I didn't give myself enough time between things. Maybe I shouldn't do certain jobs. I was very uncomfortable and just walked away after one final long day. A person's core will react strongly when the wrong endeavor is undertaken. That's my excuse..

My first wife and I were probably living at Maripoe Street. Obviously, still at work for Captain Parkinson, who was attached to my FIST (FIre Support Team) section in the Pennsylvania National Guard at Hunt Armory. Before my coming apart the following year. Before our separation and divorce.

I'd seen Parkinson's 'work vehicle' after guard drill one Sunday. It looked like a giant chimney. He was a chimney sweep and when I asked him about his curious truck, he asked me if I was able to do some work; one of his guys had just quit. After quitting the reporter job, this was a happy stop-gap and stepping stone to my next job—framing carpenter.

This is looking through a peephole into that life back then. I worked, then stopped at a sledding hill on the way home, writing about it later at our apartment. This was before Kathy graduated with her bachelor's from Pitt after she'd transferred from Carnegie-Mellon. This was when life, our life together, was still somewhat routine and okay.

This exercise in writing is undertaken... because I made the schedule (vow) to write daily. "Good writing comes from practice, not chance..." as the quote goes.

Who woulda thunk it. I was wearing a tie every day and carrying my sort-of briefcase to work every day. In fact, tomorrow will be the one-week anniversary of my quitting the perfect writing job in order to "find myself." Or to find something. I wonder if, while at lunch tomorrow, I'll remember the afternoon of doubt that grew into a lonesome debate and ultimately, turned into the 12-hour day that ended my career as the *Advance Leader's* new ace beat reporter.

No matter. *This* job, the one I'm working now, is tiring. <u>Really</u> tiring. I am so physically beat. Literally beat! Amazing feeling. I quit the other job after a month because it took up too much of my mental energy and time. Now, *I'm a-working on the railroad, all the live long day*—and I'm not so sure which kind of energy I'd rather have left over at the end of the day— physical or mental. I'd like to keep both. If I remember correctly, before, when I was doing the reporter job, I was stressed and experiencing mental hardship... but I still had plenty of activity in my head at the end of the day.

At <u>this</u> manual labor job, so far, I leave the jobsite, and come home with my mind, the thinking-that-is-me, almost as still as a puddle after a rainstorm.

This could be good... Could be. As I remember the other job, my creative, intuitive self was subjugated, exhausted; so that when I came home, I felt hollow. Now, I come home exhausted physically. But there's this *feeling* that I have now. That self-knowledge, magic-in-the-air, gonna-see-things feeling is back. Only, I'm too wiped out to sit here now and think and write. I'm nodding off, literally, as I write and it's only 9:40 p.m. on a Wednesday in January, 1995.

I'm working for Nevins Parkinson, owner of "Smiling Chimney Sweeps," and there are four of us, including myself, working on a sub-contracting bit for the Tennis Roofing Company. We are re-pointing the brick work in the open bays at this former public school building. There is enough work for us for another two weeks. I'm outside all day now. I like it. I'm running a high-speed grinder (with diamond blades), and it's kicking my butt. I come home extremely tired. Man.

God. God, god god... I am falling literally falling asleep here, while typing this. My hands are the most tired. Oops, there I go again.

This is bizarre. It's like fading in and out of consciousness. Only there are snippets and bits of dreams and noises and sights. Even between these very words. Just here, then, another coma-attack. I AM TIRED.

Goodnight, then. I'll be going to get some rest. It's unreal, folks. Good night.

*

Boy-oh-boy. Fatigue in the extreme. It doesn't catch up on me until I close my eyes. If I lay down or sit in a chair or get in any way comfortable, the body powers down, and the next time I open my eyes, there is a weight on my body, from my aching *fingers* to my eyes, head, lower back, legs, and aching feet. There are layers to fatigue. There are levels, and I can sometimes feel myself slipping through them like taking a big book, an encyclopedia for example, and fanning through all the pages slowly.

Today is Tuesday, January 24, 1995. I am 27 years old. I am working for Nevins Parkinson (Smiling Chimney Sweeps) and am outside all day. It is snowing every day now, and the temperature is usually near 30 degrees.

This job is temporary. Was only projected to go two weeks or so. I work with Bill Phillips, Mitch and Nevins. We're at Hulton School (Wilkinsburg community center, Hulton house, or something like that). We are re-pointing the brick walls in two light wells, four stories deep, on either side of the central portion of this closed-down school. Re-pointing consists of grinding out the old mortar, creating new, fresh edges on the bricks, filling the spaces with new mortar, using thin tools to press the wet mortar into the cracks, and striking the joints— using another tool to press the mortar in more, and give it a concave appearance. There's more to it, always is, but that's all I say about the actual work for now.

We're the only ones on the roof now; the roofers left a while ago. There is from zero to more than a foot of snow drifted on the roof. Most of the day it snows, sometimes heavily, and there is a quietness and peace with the frozen precipitation. Today was a big grinding day, and we moved a large suspended scaffold to another section of the inner, longer, wall. The grinding is particularly bad for me because of the amount of mortar dust, grit, brick particles, chalk and general dirt that gets blown, sifted, projected and dropped into my eyes. There were three times today: Once, I looked up and a large quantity of mortar dust that had been resting somewhere along my forehead (maybe along the top edge of the goggles I was wearing) sifted down directly into both of my eyes. Like, literally, pouring a tablespoon of sand directly onto my eyeballs. God it hurt, God.

Then I got a particle, large and painful, in my left eye, which was in some way damaged or insulted yesterday (though not visibly or badly— no blood). This piece of something hurt more than I can say. I can catapult myself back easily, reliving the moment. It hurt, God it hurt. My left eye teared up and watered streams of tears. Ultimately, finally, luckily, it washed out. Third time, I looked up again and got the spoonfuls-in-the-eyes bit, although not as bad as the first time. Still, plenty painful.

I learned today what kind of person I am to others. Not a very nice one. It is depressing, knowing, seeing, what I am. How I step on people's feelings, how I am arrogant, self-centered. Really, the temptation is strong to become depressed. I think this realization of my nature is painful because it is a detriment to my ego. My ego, the part of me that would always look at me in the mirror from the most flattering angle, is not made stronger by a realization of my weaknesses or faults. I could work to counter the forces in me that I find painful. But then, I would be making my ego feel better— only. I could do nothing, continuing to be the same. On purpose. I don't think either of these things are good to do because of my [intention], that of peeling away the self, of finding out more and more, and of not playing games, ego-driven games. So I will keep in the forefront of my attention, for as long as I can or for as long as it is good to do so, the memory and knowledge of my "true colors."

[*I remember taking a lunch break in an unheated gymnasium in the former school we were working on. It was good to get out of the elements. I swung on the large rope hanging from the ceiling. A guy I was working with was there, too. In our interaction, this guy's reactions let me know he was bothered by something I said. I think I spouted something without thinking, seeing too late that it'd offended him. Something like that. I thought I was cool, and having a good time, and I realized how I'd tramped on someone else unthinkingly.*]

Oh, frabjous joy. It feels good to be home at this apartment. There are many things to be gleaned in daily living. Life, lived. Other people have value, too, remember and do not forget David. You aren't as great as you act. Try to remember, anyway.

It *did* feel very good this morning to work by myself. I felt at peace on the scaffold, grinding. Bill didn't show up today, so I quit waiting and started the job alone. I do prefer this. At least on this day, I did.

Nevins and I worked until four. After work, I stopped at Schenley Park on the way home. First, to the ice rink bathroom. I'd been drinking chicken broth all day, as well as a cup of coffee for lunch. I then parked on the street above the sledding hill. There was a family of five there: parents and three kids, youngish. I had my new plastic purple sled. It's pretty fast, when I finally got the hang of riding it, sitting and lying down. After only minutes, the kids, of all ages and shapes, though mostly in the ten-year-old and younger to slightly older range, came from here and there, carrying beat up plastic sleds, snow boards, plastic saucer sleds and inflatable and even two-runner sleds. A foursome of older males was there. I got along with the kids alright. The older ones, I could see, were cautious of me. [A group of dogs viewing another, solitary, dog.] They were aloof and askance, not talking to me much, though it got a little better as time went by. There were women up there—mothers, exclusively—and they weren't as interested in sledding. The men, boys and kids were interested in this activity.

I just got the idea to write a story about an encounter while sledding on this hill. Something interesting and meaningful and that will capture what I feel, nostalgia, when I go there (to that place on the land and in the land of my mind).

I had fun. I used my leg muscles a lot and bumped my left elbow hard on a jump, going head-first on my new sled after talking one of the guys into giving me a push. This hurt a lot. Partly because I hit it pretty hard, but mostly because it is the same elbow I smacked into the motor box on the lifter on the left side of the smaller scaffold at work.

Every day's a new day. I have had music in my mind all day it seems, one song after another, stuck and playing over and over. It's time to sign off and give this computer to Kath. She's got to rework a report for her literature class. This is an exciting time in my life. I am realizing that to live requires only intention. [*A friend reading this asked me what I'd meant by this. This is not my fresh epiphany insight into my life, today.*] Eyes open, David. Go in peace. End.

I'd kept a daily journal for years. Starting in 1990 or so at LCCC in Florida. From 1993 to 1999 I kept a daily journal as part of my 'spiritual practice.' I meditated, thought about stuff, read books, kept a dream journal and a daily journal. The following pieces are from a period of time, 1995-96, when we were living in the Maripoe Street apartment where I kept a writing-journal on my computer at home. The rest of my journals are written in spiral notebooks, and I was glad to rediscover these entries on a "floppy disc" because I could use them and wouldn't have to transcribe them!

The following was probably from 1998 in Memphis—another time in another city.

Tomorrow I will be at a place at a time with others. I will have had an influence on what occurs. It is so very hard to not take everything for granted—meetings with people, events witnessed, horrors heard, headaches...

The world is mine, I said once, in rapture. I was walking, moving rather, through the cool damp October night. It was 11 o'clock after a meeting on what? Do I remember? Yes, it was Heather's meeting on the paranormal, whatever that really is. 1996.

Miss American Pie is playing out of the little speakers of my Sharp portable radio, dust-covered, perched on a blue 5-gallon bucket near my outdoor-now-indoor weight bench. Emerald, "Emmie" comes over there, hind legs up on its edge, front pawing a clear space inside the covered litter box. Going inside, pee, cover, shake feet; she looks at me and hops away, not entirely comfortable with my presence but not unhappy either.

That is how my mind moved just now. Let's go back to that October evening of magic. Who's to say it will ever exist, anywhere, other than in my rapidly warping fading memory? I remember each step on the steep trail going into a wooded section of Schenley Park. The beautiful leaves underneath, that cushioned my steps damply, were dark and whispering to my white Reeboks. One of my favorite times is autumn because of the smell of fall leaves. A wealth of odors, that match, stride by stride, the incredible diversity in color, tone, shade, variation, contrast of changing leaves and foliage and trees in the fall. I soar when I take a moment, like when I stood on the edge of the woods where the golf course borders the narrow nature strand. I stood in awe.

The breeze blew from the open golf course a fresh moist air that cleaned my olfactory palate each time a waif blew near my head. I just had to stop and *live*. There is no way to put the emphasis I feel on that rare and simple statement. Stop and live. For a moment, all was forgotten, everything—the only thing that mattered was the here and these smells and the silence and my wispy sky and stars and coolness alone—and nothing else. How long did I stand there, on the edge of myself and the forest? I remember it was only a minute or less. It was all I needed. Filed for eternity, the experience and the breathing and the feeling were all, and enough...

End here, now. Will you listen to my pleas? Can you believe in me? Slipped into a dream-state there. Interesting things happen when you're tired. I was interested in clarity of mind; I oughta go to bed anyhow. Good night.

This one is from early 1994, from our Brownsville apartment—our (Kathy and my) first home living together. Don't worry; this goes forward by going backward...

I drank two beers last night and got wasted. I also keep waking up and thinking about the magic in my life I may be overlooking.

Ah— how to separate the magic from coincidence? Maybe the coincidental is really no coincidence, but magic—in the sense that I mean magic: the 'otherly' influences on our 'normal' plane is what I mean. It is the evidence around me that there is an 'other," another dimension to *being* that I sense myself longing for but never finding.

How now? I think it is possible that I am peering through this 'other-dimensional' magic without knowing it—thinking it is just coincidence or imagination. I don't want to begin deluding myself. Alcohol does funny things to me. It makes me not care, for one thing. A different state of mind, hard to talk about from outside of, the morning after. But alcohol makes you care about it. I never thought of it as addictive. Alcoholics, I always saw as people who drank way too much, not as people who were addicted. Strange, aeh... Anyway, like it was when I was quitting smoking, alcohol talks to you when you are most vulnerable. Actually, it isn't the alcohol, or it is, but it's easier saying it is, than saying, admitting, that I'm talking to myself. Talking myself into going to Lee's Bar just down the street for a six-pack of Iron City beer at twelve o'clock on Friday night, the same night that I sort of (you see, unconsciously blunting the edges there already —I had definitely decided to not drink that night) vowed to be alcohol-free.

Some could say I have no problem— I don't drink as much as others, after all, and it isn't affecting my performance at work or my class work... But it is. I am of the mind that anything I do, anything that I actually do to, or with, my body, anything that I think about doing, *all of it*, every bit of it, has an effect on me that is not inconsequential. *Everything* counts. Everything matters. Everything you do, think or actually do, has an effect. The way that I think about someone has an effect. So, drinking beer on weekends isn't "harmless fun." It is destroying my mind. Making me give in to the current and float belly-up, preparing for the reaper at the end of it all.

Let's have a story. Okay?

Idea: READING A BOOK (STEPPENWOLF), A FIRST-PERSON NARRATIVE, THE BOOK BEGINS TO INTERACT WITH THE READER'S THOUGHTS. THIS IS THE BEGINNING. IT ESCALATES TO A CLASSROOM; THIS PERSON IS TAKING A CLASS IN AMERICAN LITERATURE, READING BOOKS, BUT THE BOOK <u>HE</u> IS READING IS NOT ON THE BOOK LIST FOR THE CLASS.

IT GRADUALLY BECOMES APPARENT TO HIM THAT HE RECOGNIZES FEWER AND FEWER PEOPLE IN THE CLASS. THOSE HE REMEMBERED AND THOUGHT HE KNEW STOP SHOWING UP. OTHERS TOOK THEIR PLACES. HE WALKS INTO A CLASSROOM FILLED WITH PEOPLE HE DOESN'T KNOW. SHOW HIM PULLING THE SCHEDULE FROM HIS BACKPACK, LOOKING AT THE DOOR NUMBER, WATCH HIM CHECK THE DAY OF THE WEEK, THE DATE, THE TIME, AND HE SERIOUSLY QUESTIONS HIS GRASP ON REALITY, GOING IN TO THE CLASSROOM ANYWAY. "GOD IS NOWHERE." "GOD IS NOW HERE." BOTH WRITTEN IN BLOCK TEXT AT THE LOWER RIGHT CORNER OF THE CHALKBOARD.

NOW, THE *TEACHER* IS DIFFERENT. THE CLASS IS APPARENTLY STILL A LITERATURE CLASS, BUT HE KNOWS NO ONE AND THE DISCUSSION BEGINS TO TAKE A TURN. THE BOOK THAT HAD BEEN INTERACTING WITH HIS MIND, SCARING HIM... IT IS NOW THE *CLASS DISCUSSION* THAT IS INTERACTING WITH HIS THOUGHTS. HE THINKS SOMETHING, AND SOMEONE SAYS THAT THING, THE CLASS BECOMING AN EXTENSION OF HIS INTERNAL DIALOGUE. HE FEELS AT THIS POINT THAT HE HAS LOST IT. HE STANDS AND LEAVES THE CLASS. (WORK IN SOMEWHERE THE IDEA THAT, LIKE INTERSECTIONS OF RIVERS, CROSSROADS <u>ARE</u> SIMULTANEOUSLY TWO ROADS. A PERSON IN THE INTERSECTION IS STANDING ON BOTH

ROADS SIMULTANEOUSLY, LIVING TWO REALITIES. PUSH THIS FURTHER, PUSH...

Idea II. A girl. Thirteen and she hasn't had, or is on the verge of having, her first period. Show the social school situation, her being not included in it, feeling left out. She is reading a book of fiction. She becomes drawn into the world of the story because the person in the book is a girl in her exact situation. She finally seriously wonders: *Why are we so similar?* At which time, her thoughts and the thoughts of the book-girl merge. She wonders how such a thing can occur and the girl in the book, feeling left out, picks up a book and reads it straight through, all in a day; it's about a girl reading a book that answers her thoughts. Focus on the book girl, the reactions of the book girl, then jump to the girl outside, reading about the book girl reading about the girl with a book. Show that the first girl *was* the book girl, in reality. There was no first real girl. They were both real, both valid. Two mirrors facing each other, reflecting infinity. White space.

And. A ten-year-old boy walks into a library in a Catholic school, sneaks over to the Judy Bloom books, ones boys don't read because they invariably deal with girls' issues. Boys aren't even supposed to *like* reading. The boy picks up a book and begins to read about the girl reading about a girl with a book reading about a girl. He is captivated, reads half the book during recess, then hears noise in the hallway. He tucks the book in the back of his pants and leaves the library. He wonders whether the book will be missed. Maybe he'll keep it, but then he can't let anyone at home find it. Man, why not just leave it back there? Then jump ahead to show a boy reading about a boy that just read about the girls in the books. This telescopes out... And the boy, reading this larger book, thinks that the boy in the story could just leave the book on the shelf in the library and come back the next day at recess to finish it. The other boy, in the book, having become interested in the plot of the story as he has, hurries to read *his* book before recess ends.

A different reality

The following journal entries show a change in perspective I had recently gone through. This is from the time during our separation and before the final divorce. Three months after I spent an interesting week in the woods on the Rose farm in a tent followed by my 'night of hell.' After Kathy insisted she was serious about our divorce, I moved out of Oakland into a friend's second house on Suburban Avenue in the South Hills of Pittsburgh. The house was a former ashram, *where spiritual seekers, truth seeker guys, would live in the company of other similarly-obsessed people in a common setting that supported their life's aim—a contemporary ad-hoc monastery where one could read, study and meditate without outside distractions.*

*I lived on Suburban Avenue about four months. It feels like I was there a **lot** longer than that. Another guy was there. Paul worked at* Borders. *He was a fellow TAT member. This ashram had retired itself from being an active center some ten years earlier. There was a spare bedroom upstairs but a local friend of the owner had his audio equipment and other stuff piled in there up to the door. I was desperate for a place to stay and Bill, kind-hearted owner of the house, let me set up a cot in a corner of the enclosed back porch. In the 70s, it had been converted into an esoteric library and it held a fascinating range of books. I remember lying on my cot looking up at all those great titles.* I guess I'll have more time to read some of those now, *I thought with irony. I was grateful to have a place to sleep.*

8/1/96

Now that I hold pen in hand the muse that was rushing down steps like some kind of overflowing bath tub is a trickle, a damp floor, and nothing more. We fall in love with our cleverness, and pine away the hours away from her. And nothing more. I have been thinking about this lately, and other things.

If I spent all of my time recording all the significant insights and thoughts I notice each day—or hour—it seems that I'll have no time for anything but recording. Eventually I'd be immobile, noting this twitch or that itch and only that, and nothing more. Yet, there's a demand from within [right now] that says *I had better write this down*. I had better—this message goes not to deaf ears. Because I agree with it, and yet, prefer often, to stay in bed....

8/21/96

My emotions, the barometer of my being, are like the ceaseless waves crashing to shore on the ocean. Many are similar, then they gradually grow in size and intensity and then there are a few, or maybe one really, really big crasher wave and then things gradually decrease, or, stay the same—briefly—before starting some new, similar yet different, phase or cycle. Endless. Like clockwork. Always pounding the beach. Sometimes just the faintest hint of movement, just a mere lapping at the sand; always changing, always the same.

The beach is me. The sand is my feeble consciousness. I'm trying to build a sand structure of understanding that will withstand the forever waves—but this is impossible. Always, sooner or later, the ceaseless motion and repetition of the approaching and receding water wears my castle down to nothing—sand. Indistinguishable from the rest of the beach. There are scattered shells, flotsam and jetsam, but even this occasional bump or shape is worn away to nothing, to sand.

The sand is my feeble consciousness, that when I try to form it into a structured, ordered, fortress, fails. So then I look at this sea, and its motions. After frustration at fighting the ocean and losing, I look at this thing I have hated and have no energy to hate in my exhaustion at fighting it. I see it through eyes with no purpose, no plans to conquer.

It occurs to me, watching the waves roll over onto themselves to break against the sand, that there is a purpose to the sea and its movement. This thought is whispered, only. I watch the waves marching toward me. I am aware after a time that there is a rhythm. Nothing more. I don't plan or scheme—I only see that, there is something. I am removed from the thing, and still, there remains something there.

I am separate. The sea is the sea.

This is not the result of fighting or thinking, even. This is. When I stopped, paused long enough to look, understanding settled in.

Well.

Maybe I was wasting my energy, trying to fight my emotions. They just kept coming one after another, wave after wave. What could I do?

To fight was necessary. Otherwise I would never have hated. To hate is necessary, otherwise I would not have felt intense enough to keep fighting long past any reasonable stopping. To fail was necessary, so that I could finally **see**. To finally see was necessary, because now, I think, I can begin. This IS.

8/27/96

I've recently read a transcript of a talk Krishnamurti gave in 1944 [found on the shelves of my new library-home] where he recommends strongly that we DO write down each and every strong or weak impression on our consciousness; doing this, he says, slows down our whirlwind self and allows us to get a grip, a real first time grip, on our thought processes (or process). I think his suggestion is noteworthy and worth taking. A worthy experiment I will try.

Chapter 26 — Such a Simple Thing.

I took a ballroom dancing class with my first wife, Kathy in the Fall of '94, my last semester at Pitt. This was the last class that my wife and I took together; our first had been when we met. Maybe this class helped our divorce snowball roll a little faster...

Kathy and I met at LCCC in Florida where I was earning my A.A. We were in a writing class and I sat beside her. In this ballroom dancing class, I suspect Kathy felt self-conscious dancing in front of people. When we danced, she fought me. I felt loyal to her and danced with her every time until the instructors split us and everyone else. When we were all paired up with different partners, I found myself with a tall young woman who didn't fight! I was taken by surprise. It was unexpectedly strange and... heavenly. Until then, I'd assumed all women were the same, fighting the man taking the lead in a dance class.

I never learned the name of my perfect partner. As we danced over the course of several weeks, we came to speak to each other without words. It felt like we had been dancing forever. Looking back, I hope Kathy enjoyed her dancing that semester as much as I had. She probably did; I didn't see her fighting with the guy she danced with. Maybe she had a similar eye-opening experience. It may have been a relief for her, too.

I felt a flatness when I wrote this story told <u>only</u> in dialogue. I imagine two actors speaking these lines in a scene where they're dancing the waltz, with all of the pauses, silent conveyances, looks, and drama always contained in the interaction between two human beings. The mood I felt while writing this probably reflects something in my marriage at that time—or my sadness at its having ended. It could be from remembering the empty dark hallways walking to and from that night dancing class. There's a definite mood in this piece —for me. Most times, these feelings go unwritten by people, by <u>you</u>, but felt, oh yes, felt. I wanted to write something with only dialogue—no description of any kind. Here it is. Maybe you could find a partner to read through this with—just to hear what it sounds like. I think you'd be surprised. It's the difference between empty words in a silent script and actors on a stage performing in a play before an audience.

...Footprints in the mud.

While Dancing the Viennese Waltz

"You're not alone, you know."

"I'm sorry, what?"

"When you're so full of life you can't stand it, and no one knows—you can't tell them, I know; it's impossible to tell them. But you still try, of course. For me, it happens outside, when I'm alone, and its fall now, so I'm walking whenever I can and I smell those leaves crunching under my feet on dry days or damply carpeting my steps on the rainy ones."

"Why are you telling me this—?"

"When I walk to where I park my car, it's late at night after class or after a meeting, and I park it out there on purpose so that I can walk there— I stop in the middle of the woods, and I just stand there and breathe. The moon shines foggy through thin clouds; I can see some stars; it is quiet and cool and the leaves still fall, even in the dark. I feel... alive. In communion with everything—do you understand? You're not alone in this world."

"We should turn soon."

"Okay. There... Hey, we're getting better!"

"I used to dream—"

"I know."

"Well maybe you don't! *Listen*... It was when I was a little girl, and every night before I went to bed my father would dance with me to his records—Perry Como, Frank Sinatra, Nat King Cole, and I would stand on his feet and we would dance. When I was asleep I would dream about dancing in a glamorous ballroom. When I was by myself in my room I would play Mom's Streisand records, dance by myself and pretend..."

"I saw you dancing this morning."

"Mmm."

"I knew I had to talk to you. You can't tell me, I know, but watching you... I just knew."

"Would you... Just—"

"This isn't a pass. I'm married. This isn't easy. But God knows—I know you. I can't tell you how. But I've known you all my life, and even further back... I just wanted to let you know that I saw you, and the profoundness you feel in those moments is special. It feels like we're in a foreign country and everyone's speaking a language we use, with effort, but nobody speaks *our* language— you know? And when you see, when I recognize you— Whoops. Sorry."

"It's alright. Step, back and step— "

"Thanks. I'm not good at those turns. I wasn't paying attention. Anyway... I knew this would sound strange but I had to try to say... even if—"

"Every morning when I walk to class... Do you wake up early?"

"If I have to, but I feel it mostly at night, walking."

"How did you see me this morning?"

"I couldn't sleep. I was going to the Union for a bagel and some coffee."

"I don't need coffee. I wake at five or earlier. I can't *wait* to get up. There's so much magic in the earliest early hours. Everything is fine, before the day. I love the sunrise —that time between the long night and the day. It doesn't matter; I always get up as early as I can. I *greet* the morning."

"Yeah, like me and my nights—"

"— You're right. I think you're right. Just— hold on a minute—after this corner."

"Alright. One and, ready and—turn... there."

"That was good. Something in me feels time, and knows when to stop and just take it all in. Every day is new. Time isn't important. What *is* important is *timing*. Knowing when everything is lined up. I can't say what I—"

"—You don't have to. You think you're the only one?"

"Well, I thought there *had* to be someone else who felt what I did, but I didn't know. I don't think about it. Sometimes it seems like too much, like I should share this, but... Maybe it would be impossible, too, or maybe there'd be no point to it because someone who knows what I am offering would also *know* and not have to be told or shown. You know?"

"Well. I wanted to tell you that you weren't alone. I knew I had to let you know."

"Thank you, it feels good— you know... that someone..."

"You don't have—look out, here comes one of my famous turns. Ready and..."

"Better... much better. Music's about to end."

"I know. Seems fitting, doesn't it?"

"Yes."

Joseph Campbell, expert on world mythology, has described at length the "Hero's Journey." When I first heard him mention it on a PBS interview series called "The Power of Myth," I recognized instantly what he was talking about because I, too, had heard the distant call and one day, headed off in a different direction, leaving my familiar life of unfulfilment behind.

Campbell's description of The Hero's Journey or "Monomyth" is worth encountering. I recommend you search the internet or your local library (if it still exists by the time you read this) for more details and to read Campbell's own words. His book, The Hero with a Thousand Faces, *famously describes a basic pattern found in many narratives around the world.. A seeker of* anything *would benefit from exposure to Campbell's descriptions. Many YouTube videos feature Campbell speaking on his area of expertise— myth. I lifted the following summary from the internet.*

The words in this summary <u>are not mine</u>, but when I encountered them, I felt they were a good counterpoint to Campbell's quotes; there is something valuable and thought-provoking in each of the paired comments describing the "Hero's Journey." I hope <u>you</u> are provoked and inspired...

Departure

1) *The Call to Adventure*

The hero's normal world before the story begins. The hero starts off in a mundane situation of normality from which some information is received that acts as a call to head off into the unknown.

Campbell: "This first stage of the mythological journey—which we have designated the 'call to adventure'—signifies that destiny has summoned the hero and transferred his spiritual center of gravity from within the pale of his society to a zone unknown."

2) *Refusal of the Call/Reluctant Hero*

Often when the call is given, the future hero refuses to heed it. This may be from a sense of duty or obligation, fear, insecurity, a sense of inadequacy, or any of a range of reasons that work to hold the person in his or her current circumstances.

Campbell: "Refusal of the summons converts the adventure into its negative. Walled in boredom, hard work, or 'culture,' the subject loses the power of significant affirmative action and becomes a victim to be saved. His flowering world becomes a wasteland of dry stones and his life feels meaningless."

3) *Meeting Wise Mentor/Supernatural Aid*

Once the hero has committed to the quest, consciously or unconsciously, his or her guide and magical helper appears, or becomes known.

Campbell: "For those who have not refused the call, the first encounter of the hero journey is with a protective figure (often a little old crone or old man) who provides the adventurer with amulets against the dragon forces he is about to pass. What such a figure represents is the benign, protecting power of destiny."

4) The First Threshold

This is the point where the person actually crosses into the field of adventure, leaving the known limits of his or her world and venturing into an unknown and dangerous realm where the rules and limits are not known.

Campbell: "With the personifications of his destiny to guide and aid him, the hero goes forward in his adventure until he comes to the 'threshold guardian' at the entrance to the zone of magnified power. Such custodians bound the world in four directions—also up and down—standing for the limits of the hero's present sphere, or life horizon. Beyond them is darkness, the unknown and danger; just as beyond the parental watch is danger to the infant and beyond the protection of his society danger to the members of the tribe. The usual person is more than content, he is even proud, to remain within the indicated bounds, and popular belief gives him every reason to fear so much as the first step into the unexplored. The adventure is always and everywhere a passage beyond the veil of the known into the unknown...."

5) *Belly of The Whale*

The belly of the whale represents the final separation from the hero's known world and self. By entering this stage, the person shows willingness to undergo a metamorphosis.

Campbell: "The idea that the passage of the magical threshold is a transit into a sphere of rebirth is symbolized in the worldwide womb image of the belly of the whale. The hero, instead of conquering or conciliating the power of the threshold, is swallowed into the unknown and would appear to have died. This popular motif gives emphasis to the lesson that the passage of the threshold is a form of self-annihilation. Instead of passing outward, beyond the confines of the visible world, the hero goes inward, to be born again. The disappearance corresponds to the passing of a worshipper into a temple...."

INITIATION

6) *The Road of Trials/Tests, Allies and Enemies*

The road of trials is a series of tests, tasks, or ordeals that the person must undergo to begin the transformation. Often the person fails one or more of these tests, which often occur in 3s.

Campbell: "Once having traversed the threshold, the hero moves in a dream landscape of curiously fluid, ambiguous forms, where he must survive a succession of trials. This is a favorite phase of the myth-adventure. It has produced a world literature of miraculous tests and ordeals. The hero is covertly aided by the advice, amulets, and secret agents of the supernatural helper whom he met before his entrance into this region. Or it may be that he here discovers for the first time that there is a benign power everywhere supporting him in his superhuman passage. The original departure into the land of trials represented only the beginning of the long and really perilous path of initiatory conquests and moments of illumination. Dragons have now to be slain and surprising barriers passed—again, again, and again. Meanwhile there will be a multitude of preliminary victories, unretainable ecstasies and momentary glimpses of the wonderful land."

7) *The Meeting with the Goddess*

The meeting with the goddess represents the point in the adventure when the person experiences a love that has the power and significance of the all-powerful, all encompassing, unconditional love that a fortunate infant may experience with his or her mother. It is also known as the "hieros gamos", or sacred marriage, the union of opposites, and may take place entirely within the person. In other words, the person begins to see him or herself in a non-dualistic way. This is a very important step in the process and is often represented by the person finding the other person that he or she loves most completely. Although Campbell symbolizes this step as a meeting with a goddess, unconditional love and /or self unification does not have to be represented by a woman.

Campbell: "The ultimate adventure, when all the barriers and ogres have been overcome, is commonly represented as a mystical marriage of the triumphant hero-soul with the Queen Goddess of the World. This is the crisis at the nadir, the zenith, or at the uttermost edge of the earth, at the central point of the cosmos, in the tabernacle of the temple, or within the darkness of the deepest chamber of the heart. The meeting with the goddess (who is incarnate in every woman) is the final test of the talent of the hero to win the boon of love (charity: amor fati), which is life itself enjoyed as the encasement of eternity."

8) *Woman as Temptress*

At one level, this step is about those temptations that may lead the hero to abandon or stray from his or her quest, which as with the Meeting with the Goddess does not necessarily have to be represented by a woman. For Campbell, however, this step is about the revulsion that the usually male hero may feel about his own fleshy/earthy nature, and the subsequent attachment or projection of that revulsion to women. Woman is a metaphor for the physical or material temptations of life, since the hero-knight was often tempted by lust from his spiritual journey.

Campbell: "The crux of the curious difficulty lies in the fact that our conscious views of what life ought to be seldom correspond to what life really is. Generally we refuse to admit within ourselves, or within our friends, the fullness of that pushing, self-protective, malodorous, carnivorous, lecherous fever which is the very nature of the organic cell. Rather, we tend to perfume, whitewash, and reinterpret; meanwhile imagining that all the flies in the ointment, all the hairs in the soup, are the faults of some unpleasant someone else. But when it suddenly dawns on us, or is forced to our attention that everything we think or do is necessarily tainted with the odor of the flesh, then, not uncommonly, there is experienced a moment of revulsion: life, the acts of life, the organs of life, woman in particular as the great symbol of life, become intolerable to the pure, the pure, pure soul. The seeker of the life beyond life must press beyond (the woman), surpass the temptations of her call, and soar to the immaculate ether beyond."

9) *Atonement with the Father*

In this step the person must confront and be initiated by whatever holds the ultimate power in his or her life. In many myths and stories this is the father, or a father figure who has life and death power. This is the center point of the journey. All the previous steps have been moving in to this place, all that follow will move out from it. Although this step is most frequently symbolized by an encounter with a male entity, it does not have to be a male; just someone or thing with incredible power. For the transformation to take place, the person as he or she has been must be "killed" so that the new self can come into being. Sometime this killing is literal, and the earthly journey for that character is either over or moves into a different realm.

Campbell: "Atonement consists in no more than the abandonment of that self-generated double monster—the dragon thought to be God (superego) and the dragon thought to be Sin (repressed id). But this requires an abandonment of the attachment to ego itself, and that is what is difficult. One must have a faith that the father is merciful, and then a reliance on that mercy."

10) *Apotheosis*

To apotheosize is to deify. When someone dies a physical death, or dies to the self to live in spirit, he or she moves beyond the pairs of opposites to a state of divine knowledge, love, compassion and bliss. This is a god-like state; the person is in heaven and beyond all strife. A more mundane way of looking at this step is that it is a period of rest, peace and fulfillment before the hero begins the return.

Campbell: "Those who know, not only that the Everlasting lies in them, but that what they, and all things, really are is the Everlasting, dwell in the groves of the wish fulfilling trees, drink the brew of immortality, and listen everywhere to the unheard music of eternal concord."

11) *The Ultimate Boon*

The ultimate boon is the achievement of the goal of the quest. It is what the person went on the journey to get. All the previous steps serve to prepare and purify the person for this step, since in many myths the boon is something transcendent like the elixir of life itself, or a plant that supplies immortality, or the holy grail.

Campbell: "The gods and goddesses then are to be understood as embodiments and custodians of the elixir of Imperishable Being but not themselves the Ultimate in its primary state. What the hero seeks through his intercourse with them is therefore not finally themselves, but their grace, i.e., the power of their sustaining substance. This miraculous energy-substance and this alone is the Imperishable; the names and forms of the deities who everywhere embody, dispense, and represent it come and go. This is the miraculous energy of the thunderbolts of Zeus, Yahweh, and the Supreme Buddha, the fertility of the rain of Viracocha, the virtue announced by the bell rung in the Mass at the consecration, and the light of the ultimate illumination of the saint and sage. Its guardians dare release it only to the duly proven."

RETURN

12) *Refusal of the Return*

So why, when all has been achieved, the ambrosia has been drunk, and we have conversed with the gods, why come back to normal life with all its cares and woes?

Campbell: "When the hero-quest has been accomplished, through penetration to the source, or through the grace of some male or female, human or animal, personification, the adventurer still must return with his life-transmuting trophy. The full round, the norm of the monomyth, requires that the hero shall now begin the labor of bringing the runes of wisdom, the Golden Fleece, or his sleeping princess, back into the kingdom of humanity, where the boon may redound to the renewing of the community, the nation, the planet or the ten thousand worlds. But the responsibility has been frequently refused. Even the Buddha, after his triumph, doubted whether the message of realization could be communicated, and saints are reported to have died while in the supernal ecstasy. Numerous indeed are the heroes fabled to have taken up residence forever in the blessed isle of the unaging Goddess of Immortal Being."

13) *The Magic Flight*

Sometimes the hero must escape with the boon, if it is something that the gods have been jealously guarding. It can be just as adventurous and dangerous returning from the journey as it was to go on it.

Campbell: "If the hero in his triumph wins the blessing of the goddess or the god and is then explicitly commissioned to return to the world with some elixir for the restoration of society, the final stage of his adventure is supported by all the powers of his supernatural patron. On the other hand, if the trophy has been attained against the opposition of its guardian, or if the hero's wish to return to the world has been resented by the gods or demons, then the last stage of the mythological round becomes a lively, often comical, pursuit."

14) *Rescue from Without*

Just as the hero may need guides and assistants to set out on the quest, often times he or she must have powerful guides and rescuers to bring them back to everyday life, especially if the person has been wounded or weakened by the experience. Or perhaps the person doesn't realize that it is time to return, that they can return, or that others need their boon.

Campbell: "The hero may have to be brought back from his supernatural adventure by assistance from without. That is to say, the world may have to come and get him. For the bliss of the deep abode is not lightly abandoned in favor of the self-scattering of the wakened state. 'Who having cast off the world,' we read, 'would desire to return again? He would be only there.' And yet, in so far as one is alive, life will call. Society is jealous of those who remain away from it, and will come knocking at the door. If the hero. . . is unwilling, the disturber suffers an ugly shock; but on the other hand, if the summoned one is only delayed—sealed in by the beatitude of the state of perfect being (which resembles death)—an apparent rescue is effected, and the adventurer returns."

15) *The Crossing of the Return Threshold*

The trick in returning is to retain the wisdom gained on the quest, to integrate that wisdom into a human life, and then maybe figure out how to share the wisdom with the rest of the world. This is usually extremely difficult.

Campbell: "The returning hero, to complete his adventure, must survive the impact of the world. Many failures attest to the difficulties of this life-affirmative threshold. The first problem of the returning hero is to accept as real, after an experience of the soul-satisfying vision of fulfillment, the passing joys and sorrows, banalities and noisy obscenities of life. Why re-enter such a world? Why attempt to make plausible, or even interesting, to men and women consumed with passion, the experience of transcendental bliss? As dreams that were momentous by night may seem simply silly in the light of day, so the poet and the prophet can discover themselves playing the idiot before a jury of sober eyes. The easy thing is to commit the whole community to the devil and retire again into the heavenly rock dwelling, close the door, and make it fast. But if some spiritual obstetrician has drawn the shimenawa across the retreat, then the work of representing eternity in time, and perceiving in time eternity, cannot be avoided. The hero returns to the world of common day and must accept it as real."

16) *Master of the Two Worlds*

In myth, this step is usually represented by a transcendental hero like Jesus or Buddha. For a human hero, it may mean achieving a balance between the material and spiritual. The person has become comfortable and competent in both the inner and outer worlds.

Campbell: "Freedom to pass back and forth across the world division, from the perspective of the apparitions of time to that of the causal deep and back—not contaminating the principles of the one with those of the other, yet permitting the mind to know the one by virtue of the other—is the talent of the master. The Cosmic Dancer, declares Nietzsche, does not rest heavily in a single spot, but gaily, lightly, turns and leaps from one position to another. It is possible to speak from only one point at a time, but that does not invalidate the insights of the rest. The individual, through prolonged psychological disciplines, gives up completely all attachment to his personal limitations, idiosyncrasies, hopes and fears, no longer resists the self-annihilation that is prerequisite to rebirth in the realization of truth, and so becomes ripe, at last, for the great at-one-ment. His personal ambitions being totally dissolved, he no longer tries to live but willingly relaxes to whatever may come to pass in him; he becomes, that is to say, an anonymity."

17) *Freedom to Live*

Mastery leads to freedom from the fear of death, which in turn is the freedom to live. This is sometimes referred to as living in the moment, neither anticipating the future nor regretting the past.

Campbell: "The hero is the champion of things becoming, not of things become, because he is. 'Before Abraham was, I AM.' He does not mistake apparent changelessness in time for the permanence of Being, nor is he fearful of the next moment (or of the 'other thing'), as destroying the permanent with its change. 'Nothing retains its own form; but Nature, the greater renewer, ever makes up forms from forms. Be sure there's nothing [that] perishes in the whole universe; it does but vary and renew its form.' Thus the next moment is permitted to come to pass."

Just search online for "Joseph Campbell" and "Hero's Journey." That's what I did. I've quoted Campbell at length. His ideas and observations about the quest relate closely to what my life has been. I think this journey is important and Campbell's cross-cultural perspective is valuable to anyone considering a bold... departure... from the normal course of things in their life. Here, in a following story, are my little hero's first steps... I wrote "Carney" in '93 or so. I had already taken my own initial hesitant step on my own quest and followed the cadence of my own drum. This story is an echo on the breezes from that time.

This ship rests in the shallows of a desert island circa 1994. I could improve or possibly burry it—but both would work against what this book is trying to do—attempting to trace an outline of a moving target, me—a cave drawing, drawing itself—so that someone ten thousand years from now will puzzle over the scratched words, worn almost away, whispered-shouted on the wall, "David was here."

Carney

by David W. Weimer

The tree cast a shadow and grass waved in the breeze. The elf plucked one of the smoky smelling leaves from a branch and tucked it into the band of his hat. He jumped to hang from a low branch. He'd been barely fifty, a child really, the first time he saw a tree such as this.

Carney climbed to top branches where he used his legs to brace himself, hands free. He scanned the endless expanse of waving grass and sighed—the openness exhilarated and frightened him.

As a child, he used to scurry through intertwined vines and branches of the village to the elders Crèche to ask what lay beyond the land of the elves. Smoking wooden pipes, they would always change the subject.

He was an hour's hike away, once, when the council tracker caught him. It was his first of many attempts.

Carney smiled sadly. The confusion on his parent's faces when he was brought back, fighting the tracker's grip on his tunic, was something he'll always remember. He had told them, *there's too much out there*! His dreams were calling.

The elf moved down to the ground, his easy movements resulting from a lifetime in trees. He sat in the shade and took a swallow from his water jug. The continuous breeze, though not unbearably hot, wicked moisture from his body.

Carney was struck by the world he was entering. A vast sea. Back in the village, branches and vines were woven together to form a lattice-like canopy where his people spent their entire lives high above the ground. Now, just three days' walk from his village, the trees were far apart.

Carney arranged his pack and stepped into the grass. A far-off horizon beckoned darkly—*East*.

After pushing through the tall grass for most of the day, he rested near the bottom of a small hill. Walking for such long periods, an unaccustomed repetitive series of movements for his kind, was tiring. Newly used muscles were sore. He removed his soft boots and laid back. His feet felt good in the cool grass.

He slept. The sun crept further across the sky. When the grass cast a shadow over his sleeping form, Carney sat up and looked around. The air was still now, and the world was motionless.

Carney laced up one of his lightweight calf-high boots and was reaching for the other when he heard a swishing sound in the grass. It grew louder until it seemed as though a huge tree was falling. Instinctively, he ducked. A shadow passed over his head and something struck him behind the ear, knocking his hat off.

He lurched to his feet and drew his polished wooden dagger.

His fingers absently explored the lump behind his ear. On an impulse, Carney spun around.

A figure stood perfectly still. Its limbs were massive tree trunks and two arms hung to the ground, ending in monstrous three-fingered hands. The creature's knuckles rested on the stomped grass. Dark fur covered its giant body and a featureless head erupted from heavy sloped shoulders.

Carney gripped his dagger. "What do you want?" he asked.

The creature remained tree-like, rooted, unmoving.

The elf nervously eyed the surrounding grass land, while keeping the creature in sight. It stood three times his own height.

The sun was dropping lower now over a forest far, far in the distance.

A cool wind blew his hair into his eyes. His other boot—it was near the creature, along with his cloak and pack. He walked the ten feet to his things and picked them up in the lengthening shadow of the giant creature. He backed away, placed his dagger in his belt sheath and laced up his second boot. He secured his pack diagonally over his shoulders and addressed the creature again.

"Thank you for that much," he said, while backing away in the direction of the dark horizon. After fifty yards, he turned away and jogged eastward.

Carney continued walking long after dark, his excellent night vision allowing him to move confidently through the tall grass.

The night was getting cold and damp. He pulled his dagger, waded through the grass and cut handfuls from different places. He twisted grass into narrow strands, weaving quickly and automatically in the darkness. When he crawled into his grass sleeping crèche, he pulled his pack into the opening. He closed his eyes and was asleep almost immediately.

He found himself before a black wall and a row of statues. Each stone figure stood on a pedestal. They had no facial features. A familiar feeling grew as he drifted up and away, through a tunnel in the sky. Lights swirled around his head, then rushed away, leaving him in darkness. The gray dawn greeted his open eyes.

Carney emerged and stood slowly, looking around for the creature.

Later, while chewing a breakfast of dried fruit and bread as he walked, the elf felt he was being watched. He looked back and to the sides regularly. It could be his imagination. The morning wind picked up, waving the grass.

After some hours, Carney focused on his muscles and the rhythm of climbing rock. The tall grass had given way to patches of dark rock. The dark horizon grew steadily, reminding him of his dreams. He wasn't sure if he was dreaming now. Thoughts of home came unbidden: the warm greens and browns of his village.

He found a rock to shelter from the wind. He placed the grass crèche in a patch of dirt and ate. His supplies were low. Two more days, he thought.

***

Late in the third day, he came to a wall of rock. His water and food were gone that morning. The rock wall shot up higher than imagination, high up into the clouds.

The elf walked along the wall, searching. A change in the stone's appearance attracted his attention. A gust of wind blew swirling grit into his eyes. He reached out to steady himself— then stumbled and fell. The wall was gone!

Carney stood legs apart, blinking his watering eyes. The stone was a curious black in the smooth channel that led straight into the cliff. *This* was the place... The statues from his dream waited in a row ahead.

Carney swallowed dryly.

A shadow fell across him and the monster seized both of his biceps from behind in a powerful grip.

"Let go!" the elf yelled hoarsely. After he grew too fatigued to struggle, he panted, feeling a gentle touch *inside* his mind!

He turned to stare at the featureless fur-covered head.

The creature gave no indication it had communicated with him.

He sensed the *touch* again. Images from his past were pulled out through his mind in a blur: a child questioning elders, first attempts to leave their forest, a lifelong desire to explore...

He addressed the figure holding him. "*Why* are you doing this?"

A soft *touch*.

The elf felt radiating reassurance. The giant creature lifted Carney higher and moved toward a pedestal among the row of frozen figures. It stepped up onto the waiting platform.

Images flowed into his mind of great distances, bizarre scenes. "Yes," he said. "*Yes.*"

The creature held him on the pedestal. Carney sensed a prompting.

He nodded his answer.

The creature lifted Carney high. The elf felt himself grow lighter. Holding hands dissolved. He soared higher through an opening in the sky.

This is something I wrote for the TAT Forum. I don't think I ever actually submitted it. You can only truly understand someone who has done the same thing as you, been to their same place. I remembered this and decided not to send the piece. Most of the time, I only strain to explain. In this work, I include the following for posterity and for someone like me.

Circa 2004

Fowlerville, Michigan

I *do* believe in going after one's goal. When I was young, I was the same as I am now, only less experienced. I was a dreamer. I remember being in the woods, smoking my cigarette, walking in the leaves and *being*. There was no more profound a time for me. My whole life has been like that. Walking in wonder.

The only thing that has changed is that I have done what I was born to do. I've become my destiny. I've become myself. I live my life now, and do the things that I do, make the choices I make, and don't doubt for a second that I'm living the "right way." I don't doubt anymore. I don't mean that I'm content with *my* plan, *my* activities. I'm beyond *my*. I do what I can in the moment, but have let go of the reins, even though I still hold them. How can you give up, and yet remain involved? I have and do.

[Author's note: A friend asked me to take a stab at explaining that last part. I still feel a personal investment in my life's events. I fix my car when it breaks, I try to be a good parent to my boys and a better companion to my wife. I am obviously imperfect and try to be a better person in myself and for those around me. I make mistakes, wrong assumptions, lose patience with my kids and take my wife for granted at times.

My central focus isn't on "me" anymore, and his companion, "my." I've got a greater perspective, and inside of that perspective is this shadow guy, "my," and he's a one-dimensional character of minor importance. If a caterpillar turned into a butterfly, but still saw, looking down, himself crawling as a caterpillar, he'd know what it was like to crawl but he's not limited to the ground anymore. He's 'beyond' the ground.]

Wisdom. *Who* has it? To encounter a person who knows what is happening and to feel that certain *secure* feeling one gets from an anchor-like person. I wished, for a long while there, to encounter a personal guide who I could trust to lead me through the maze of my life. They never came. I got older. My ignorance remained unchanged; if anything, it increased. So by necessity, I became self-reliant. I somehow grew up. I believe *I've* become wise.

One thing I wish for now, more than anything, is to communicate with someone else who is *engaged* in the discussion. To see some light behind their eyes. To sense something relevant in the air. I find that I am 'wisest' in relation to other people when I am focused on a tangible aspect of life. I can sit in my chair, and reside in 'wiseness,' or I can say something, give my perspective on something relevant and real in someone else's life.

Life is but a dream... One of the profoundest things in a childhood song, "Row your Boat." Life is a dream. I go through this dream and it is just that.

There is one consolation. As solitary as we are, there is never the feeling of being alone when there is even just the vague memory of reading something someone once wrote who was *there*, too—someone who has been beyond their mortality. This consolation comes as a strong feeling of camaraderie.

We're all in this alone. I watched a documentary on an Alzheimer's unit and an old man with a blank expression wore a ball cap that said that. Ironic and true. I feel we are—at least *I* am—utterly alone. When we encounter *another* like ourselves, there is nothing like it. *We're both there*.

Chapter 27 — Our House.

In February 2000, I looked at the second pregnancy test in the bathroom of our Stuttgart apartment with a sinking sensation of doom. Andrée was pregnant. There was no escaping. No going back.

When I moved in the previous September, we knew we were moving in to be together for our lives. *I* knew that; I suspect Andrée was hopeful but worried about the future, perhaps. Ever since I looked into her eyes that first night in Switzerland during my ten-day visit in August and thought to myself silently, *Okay*, I had relaxed into my backwards fall off a cliff of domesticity [it's not a cliff <u>into</u> domesticity; it's a cliff <u>of</u> domesticity].

I'd been living as an ascetic going on four years. Even before my marriage to Kathy, my practice wife, in 1993, I was obsessively interested and engaged in my own quest—a search for the profound within. In Memphis, where I had been attending graduate school at the University of Memphis, I was living alone, immersed in a spiritual seeker's lifestyle—no addictions, engaging in self-inquiry, questioning myself, my motives and my world, keeping a daily journal, reading books of interest, living celibate and sublimating any building 'energy' into my intended purpose of understanding life —from a first person perspective—as completely as humanly possible.

When I visited Andrée, my longest and best girl-friend, in August 1999 between college semesters, I was presented with a choice. We rarely get a second choice, I thought. Here I was, face-to-face with someone. It was either let go and become a partner to this wonderful someone, or resist and say no, hanging on, clingingly, to my "spiritual" aspirations and ascetic lifestyle.

It felt I was going to jettison a whole lifestyle and pattern of living. I'd known Andrée for sixteen years; she was a part of my life and someone I accepted as part of me, my pattern, my existence. Here was a chance to join our lives. I felt I could be good for someone in this world—specifically, her. I also saw that to sacrifice the life I had been living wouldn't be any worse or better than any other sacrifice I could make—there's *always* a sacrifice. Something is always killed on the altar and thrown into the volcano. I pondered with my gaze in the far distance for a minute.

Letting my life as I knew it go, watching it flutter like a single sheet of music dropped from a great height with a wind blowing, I said to Andrée that night in Switzerland, "You never get a second chance; let's get married."

It was the right choice. Everything is the right choice. Even death. But this was right because I walked through this door before it closed—and the door <u>always</u> closes before we're ready to step through. This door between the unknown and known, that most everyone hesitates in front of, the door that will open again to a shove once it closes to reveal that *it never opens to the same place*. I assume that most hesitate at the boundary of their known world. They hesitate to walk into their destiny. The door swings closed and they spend the rest of their lives with that gnawing regret of having not having acted—yet when another door of fearful opportunity opens, they pause again, hesitate... What about practicing being a <u>forward walker</u>? I'm not talking about marriage; that's only one door. Don't settle for whatever you fall into, by default. Seek out your life and live without regret.

Back to our Stuttgart apartment and further developments...

When I walked out to meet Andrée in the hall (she'd said she couldn't bring herself to look at the test), I think that I had a big smile—a big, uncertain, willing, smile. We hugged and someone cried. I'd known that we would have children eventually. I felt we'd been given the one-in-a-million chance again of doing what we didn't do the last time. The door had opened and this time I walked forward. For me, 'thinking' and weighing things in instances like this is the activity of fearful hesitation; it's what my mind does when I'm afraid. It 'thinks' instead of jumping in. Maybe the water is full of sharks, so this pausing is probably good in some cases!

In the nine month lead-up to a very important date, I had the distinct feeling of dying. I felt like I was ending—David, with his preferences, opinions and reactions. The self-centered and self-serving guy. Comparatively, I seem to feel things profoundly which others appear to flow into and through without comment. Killing animals, watching water coming in to the shore on a beach, or being involved in beginning a family; I've watched others do these things seemingly indifferently while I stood, profoundly affected. I think I'm lucky to be made this way. I get to try to express in poems or essays what I feel. I'm talking about the way I seem to be made to feel and react to what I encounter in this world.

We got married in April 2000. This could have happened thirteen years earlier, when Andrée left France and I left Germany. When I left my American life and moved to Andrée in Stuttgart, in 1999, we'd had a 17-year engagement.

On our honeymoon, I experienced the increasing anxiety weight of *Oh god, the days are shorter and shorter until* <u>The Time</u>. We drove to Arizona from Tennesse. Andrée was a few months pregnant, and we only walked part of the way into the Grand Canyon.

Once back home in Stuttgart, the months melted. I remember a few weeks before the B-day, then a week before, then... Andrée was overdue. One day, two days... in a way, this was worse than the countdown. She was very uncomfortable with a pinched nerve in her shoulder at this time. Now, I can look back with sympathy for that poor scared couple. I wish I could lean back and whisper some reassuring things to them, but there's no such thing as reassurance before the first jump off a tall place. No substitution for becoming a parent.

October 15, 2000, Filderklinik in Filderstadt, Germany. Looking off the cafeteria balcony.

Having no more questions about my destiny or the meaning of life didn't make me indifferent or immune to living. When I stand on a cliff's edge, I feel fear in my belly. Anticipating unexplored life avenues results in the thought patterns I habitually have. I *can* do something new, because I'm comfortable. I'm also comfortable feeling fear. I've accepted it, along with every other emotion I have, as part of living here. I don't let them drive the car, but I don't tell them not to be. Those emotions are NOT at my center; they no longer rule my life. My center is occupied by a solid stillness. I can laugh while being afraid. People think someone with a clue walks around with their solemn arms crossed and an unfurrowed brow. Sure. When things are nice. Without responsibilities or cares for offspring. For me, I feel free to live my life pattern finally. It's okay. Be afraid. But *act* when it's necessary. I think I've finally just become my adult. Without a rite of passage, I think possibly a majority of people are just kids growing older, fatter and balder.

My lead-up anxiety might have been my version of sympathetic pregnancy. I think we resonate to the emotions of those we are in sympathy with. Maybe not the same emotion, but we are a tuning fork that vibrates when vibrations occur around it.

From Andrée's photo album: practice walking at Filderklinik. October 2000.

So there we were, finally, at the Filderklinik at Filderstadt, seven kilometers south of Stuttgart. A homeopathic hospital leaning towards natural medicine. In our earlier visits to different German hospitals in the region, this was the one that made Andrée feel the best. It felt good and the people seemed nice. Other hospitals had the more typical hard German quality that made Andrée's anxiety over hospitals soar.

I walked with her on the nice paths outside the hospital. Andrée was overdue and the doctors said to walk a lot, so we walked. I remember noticing the beautiful nature and feeling absolutely terrible with a morbid anxiety and kind of relentless depression. Maybe I was channeling or reacting to Andrée's emotions. I bet. It felt terrible. It *must* have been sympathetic resonance.

There followed fourteen hours of a typical horror story. Every woman tells of walking uphill both ways through blizzards on the way to giving birth. There was a threatened cesarean, induced labor, terrible pain, *Hilf Mir!* Andrée said to the maternity nurses as I stroked her hair. The spinal block was too late, and screaming was interspaced by exhausted silent minutes—all culminating with a relieved mother holding her precious baby on her belly and me, standing shocked and mortified at the deformed cone head the birthing staff had suction-cupped into this world. "Oh my God, oh my God…" I muttered, turning away from Andrée.

During this whole time, of course, only German was spoken. Doctors and Germans all learn English at school, but this was Germany, and we spoke German.

I went out in the hallway while they helped clean up Andrée after Guillaume's birth. I was devastated. A delivery nurse had come out of the room and I approached her. "*Bitte, Sagen Sie Mir,*" I asked. "*Wie ist mein Sohn?*"

I pantomimed, referring to the cone-like bulb I'd seen in place of my son's head immediately upon his birth. Once the nurse understood my concern, she patted my arm, laughing reassuringly and said this was completely normal when the doctors used a suction-like device attached to a rope to help pull the kid out. "*Wirklich?*" I asked. Yes, she nodded, patting me again.

My relief was indescribable. Once they allowed me back in, I embraced Andrée and Guillaume with joy. What a wonder. I, too, was born anew. Andrée was absolutely radiant. In our room afterwards, as she spoke to her mom in Rennes and then her father in Paris, I watched my wife. <u>Absolutely beautiful</u>.

We then received somewhat of a gift, although it didn't seem that way at the time. Guillaume aspirated some of the amniotic fluid during the protracted delivery and now had an infection in his lungs. Reluctant to administer antibiotics, the doctors opted to transfer him to ICU for observation. With an IV line in his soft head, a glowing red finger and multiple leads coming from his chest to monitoring machines, it sure felt less than wonderful. We had wanted Andrée to nurse our children and at the beginning, just like the over-due-date time, nature was holding back. So, until things flowed naturally, the hospital newborn care staff gave us *Stutenmilch* for Guillaume. Mare's milk. To this day, Guillaume's favorite animals are horses. He doesn't seem interested in riding them; he just likes them. I bet…

After 10 days in ICU, we got the go-ahead to take Guillaume home. What another anxiety time. We'd had the luxury of full-time help in caring for our son and had postponed the inevitable. Now we'd be responsible for him at home by ourselves! Every first-time parent goes through this, I suspect, although we had been given a ten day reprise. *Insane*, I thought at the time. *I have no idea at all what to do with this thing!* Obviously people have figured it out in the past—just as we eventually did. It seemed… wrong… to be given a living kid to take home with absolutely no expertise at all. I remember being in our apartment the first time—*us three*—hugging. I put Gui's crib on Andrée's side of the bed. We were home. We *were* a home.

Our Pittsburgh cats, Grizelda and Emerald were VERY concerned about this noise-making thing we'd brought home. Ears swiveling like active radar dishes on high alert. These were my children from my first marriage. When my practice wife had expressed her desire for kids right away, I said, "Well… how about a kitten?"

I'd asked Anne to send Griz and Emmie to us in the fall of 1999. The cats flew together in one crate to Frankfurt where we picked them up from surprisingly lax German veterinary customs. We took them to *their* new home. They'd already lived with me in three apartments and a house in Pittsburgh, in my mom's trailer near Cookeville, Tennessee and in Memphis. They settled in our place in Stuttgart. They always did. Their story of their lives is interesting all by itself.

The first night or two on our own were, of course, harrowing. I say 'us' but I wasn't living as Andrée. She was a super mother. I was the assistant. I warmed bottles of mare's milk, brought juice for my wife and helped change diapers. We started out using cloth diapers because I was environmentally-conscious and had a bad opinion of filling landfills with disposable diapers. After twice crouched, shaking out cloth diapers into the toilet, dropping the soiled things into a plastic bin to soak before washing (in our washing machine that we also wash our clothes in!), I had a sudden foresight of the future—of years of that. I would NOT do that. Someone had given us a package of disposable diapers as a gift. "Emergency diapers" I'd called them before. I broke into them and never looked back. We used the clean cloth diapers as dusters and dish rags. Thank God for those polluting throw-away diapers.

As part of Andrée's maternity care through the German health care system, Andrée had a *Hebamme* (midwife) visit a couple of times a week during the first month. It was a great thing to have someone say reassuringly to new parents, "You're doing fine." Usually family is around, right? Or at least friends who've had children. We were both *Ausländern*, foreigners, in Germany, so our family lived far, far away. Almost all of Andrée's friends were single without children.

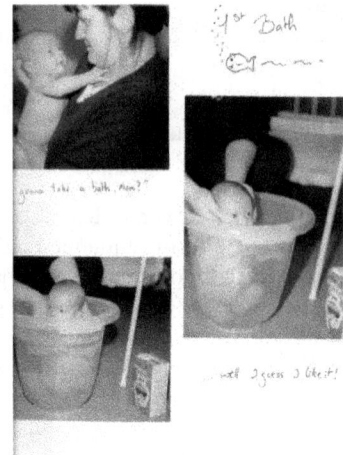

The homeopathic *Hebamme* told us not to bathe Guillaume for the first six weeks or so. She gave us natural oils to put on his skin, but she said bathing with soaps was too harsh for his skin. After four weeks or so, largish patches of skin peeled off his scalp. Something like a caul. "That's normal," said the *Hebamme*. Right. *He's going to get a bath*, I thought.

Gui's first bath was in a plastic transparent bucket. Great blackmail material for his teenage years. He didn't seem to mind at the time. He splashed around and seemed to take it as a matter of course.

Mommy with Guillaume during his first bath. Stuttgart apartment, November 2000.

So we had our first son. Andrée had a couple of months off from her software engineering job to stay at home. We became our little family. During Gui's birth and our 10-day stay at *Filderklinik's* ICU, I was working as an English teacher at different German companies and at the Amerikanische Sprachschule in the *Deutsch-Amerikanisches* Zentrum (DAZ) in Stuttgart. I'd go teach my classes, driving our Mercedes *Geländewagen* (SUV) or taking my bike and the U-Bahn or S-Bahn— mood dependent—then come back home.

Soon after Guillaume was born, I stopped teaching English. I'd had a 10-day intensive at the hospital that improved my spoken *Deutsch* exponentially. I didn't want to go back to learning nothing of this country's language so I determined to find a German job to continue this breath-of-fresh-air progress. I put a classified ad in the *Stuttgarter Zeitung*. One man answered: Herr Richard Lampert of *Lampert Et Sudrow, GmbH*, producer of designer office furniture. He loved things American and really loved France, where he had his Tischgestellen (table frames) and Tischplatten (table tops) made. I had a wonderful experience working for Lampert. I was *doing* something, and I felt myself a part of this society. No longer was I an outsider, moving as a separate visitor in train stations, parks, stores, city streets. I now walked with contentment and came home satisfied at having done something useful. *A job well done.* That's saying a lot. Incidentally—here I am in Flushing, Ohio, typing on a homemade table top (3/4" plywood covered by ¼" Masonite) supported by one of Herr Lampert's *Tischgestellen* metal table frames.

I took the S-Bahn to Benningen, north of Stuttgart, where I worked in Lampert's warehouse receiving and shipping tables and *Stehpult* sets (standing, architect-like tables)—talking on the phone in German, writing on packages, in notes, on boxes and to the company's secretary all in German; I spoke to workers from another company in another part of the warehouse, spoke with delivery truck drivers—again, all in German—and the practice paid off. I was functioning in this society. I had a young family and I felt good.

Guillaume was immersed in English and German. We pushed his *Kinderwagen* around our part of the city, through parks, while shopping.

Not long after Gui's arrival, we took a three-week vacation in the Haute Garonne region of France near Toulouse in the summer of 2001. We stayed in a circular bungalow at *L'Enclos à Donneville*, just a baguette's throw from the *Canal du Midi*. We'd taken our cats with us. Later, in the fall that year, we moved to *10 Domaine de la Chêneraie* in *Ramonville St Agne*, not far from Toulouse in time for Guillaume's first birthday.

Building our skate park in Saint-Lys, France. October-November 2002. Guillaume on Bobbie Car.

In Ramonville, we put Guillaume in a *halte garderie* (daycare) a few hours, a few days a week, so he could be with children of his age. He'd been hanging out exclusively with *les jeunes* (youth) French skate park enthusiasts. This reprieve also helped us schedule meetings with people where we didn't have to change a diaper in the middle of discussing our project. We'd been spending time with French mayors and adjutant mayors and teenagers and twenty-year-olds doing BMX, skateboard and inline at skate parks. Guillaume was like our cats in one sense; he thought he was one of us; he'd never spent time with anyone his own age.

We moved to America a few weeks before Christmas 2002 and found a decent single-wide trailer at 103 Lynn Drive in Alan's Mobile Home Park in Fowlerville, Michigan, the town where I graduated from high school. This is where we lived when Andrée was pregnant with Benjamin. Our "second time around" was as different as night and day. During Andrée's pregnancy, we ran a free portable summer skate park in a church parking lot in Fowlerville. Dealing with dozens of kids daily, Andrée shined. She was born to be with children.

Three-year-old Guillaume rode his Bobby car (the same one he'd scooted around in France as we built our skate park in Saint-Lys) on the

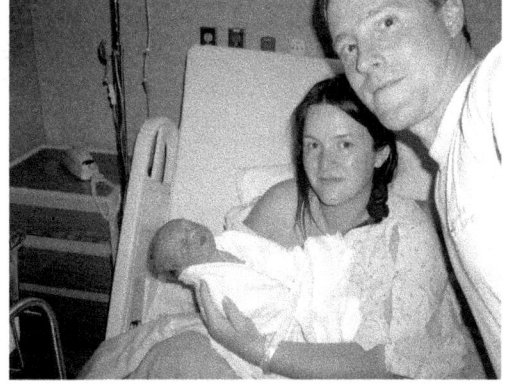

Beautiful mother, proud father & wonderful Benjamin. January 17, 2004 in Howell, Michigan.

ramps and rolling down the gradually-sloped parking lot. The American kids at the summer skate park treated Gui like their little brother.

Ben was born at St. Joseph Mercy Livingston Hospital in Howell, Michigan. I had grown up on a small farm outside of Howell and attended Catholic school in Howell until sixth grade, then middle school and ninth grade of high school. It was surreal to be back in the U.S., here, with Andrée. The doctor and nurses were very nice. It felt strange to be able to understand everybody effortlessly—it felt like cheating. They all spoke English. My mom lived in Rochester Hills at the time, an hour away, and came over for the important day to watch Guillaume. The experience of Ben's birth was unbelievable. Everyone was relaxed and everything went smoothly. Andrée was not traumatized by anxiety or labor pains and Ben arrived on time and without needing to be yanked into this world.

I smoked a cheap Swisher Sweet cigar in the cold January parking lot that night. I looked up at our third floor room, where Andrée, Guillaume and Ben were. Entirely different experience. We were more relaxed and a world away from the untried, scared couple we'd been the first time around on the other side of the Atlantic.

Watching the nurses clean and weigh Ben right after the birth, taking a photo with our delivery doctor—all of it I watched in detached wonder, profoundly aware of the contrast between this time and our first—and of the intervening years and experiences between the two births.

Robert Sass, 15, on the last day of our portable summer skate park, **Dream Extreme** *in Fowlerville, Michigan, 2004.*

Ben came home with us after a day. Guillaume being a big brother. The cats' less severe reaction—and our lives settled into its new rhythm.

Our second summer skate park at the church parking lot in Fowlerville was bigger and better than the first year. Local kids had anxiously anticipated this new installment—and with good reason. I'd found a

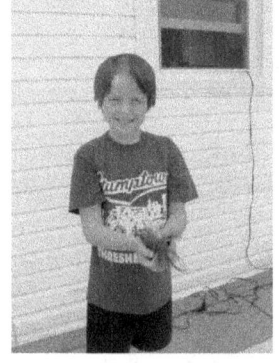

mini-half pipe to relocate and refurbish and place at the park. I constructed dirt trails with a Bobcat and doubled the number of 'modules' (ramps, etc.) for this skate park. We named our skate parks on the inauguration day of each one—after we'd built the ramps together and set them up for the first day of use. The first year's park was called "The Washout" and year two's incarnation was "DeX", short for Dream Extreme, the name of our association in France.

Gui, 8, with his own starting-of-the-summer crew cut.

I involved local kids in helping me build and work on the ramps. It was a real nice time. Ben took everything in stride, of course, accepting this setting as easily as I accept any new day. Our life circumstances; dozens and dozens of kids; the skate park atmosphere of zipping skateboards, weaving BMX bikes and scooters and skaters, of Band-Aids and scraped knees and knocked-out teeth; music on a sound system, brother and the summer sun and a mother and father. We were a family.

Ben, 5, after a first pass of his summer crew cut on our deck in Flushing.

Since that last summer skate park in 2004, we've moved to the Ohio Valley. Flushing, Ohio is about 25 miles west northwest of Wheeling, WV. We're in our first home. Benjamin is in second grade at Union Local Elementary and Guillaume is in fifth. They are growing up great kids. In the winter, they like to ride down hills on sleds in a train that crashes with their mom and other kids in a big laughing pile.

Last year, Guillaume played with animal figures and 'guys,' making up battles and adventures; this year it's Lego building—practicing his intended future career of designing and constructing new cities and renovating old ones. Ben has a scar on his left knee where he had 14 stitches; he is a creative soul like his mother. Last year he painted rainbows and monster trucks; this year it's K'nex creations and science experiments. Gui has a crooked front tooth and freckles. Andrée is a super mom. These are the best of times. I *know* it. The tragedies, crying times—sickness, health and crises—have been the weather of our lives. Most days are sunny, and I'm grateful, knowing the full range of things.. We have two young cats; Griz is buried and Emmie is gone. But it's the blush of spring again. Flowers are pushing up from the thawing dirt.

—DW 3/15/2011

This one is a journey that I took with the character. Possibly cathartic for you, too. I have a mood associated with this story; I did all the things that the kid in this piece does. Not in exactly this order. There was a dead cat. There is a grave. The cemetery is a real place in Fowlerville, and the train tracks and walking are from my middle school days in Howell. This is a patchwork of actual events and places from my life, put together with things that might have been. It was written in the winter of 1994.

The stories in this book are from my life and I had to write them until I got something right.

Just nodding
by David Weimer

The cat had died quickly.

Danny walked across his family's frost-covered lawn. His footprints followed him, dark on white frost, distinct, like after the first man on the moon. A wooden "For Sale" sign stood in front of the ditch along the road. Frozen dirt was piled around the square post. He gave the sign a kick when he walked by.

Swinging his embarrassingly-huge aluminum lunchbox in one mittened hand, with its thermos of powder-mix milk inside (that he normally poured out at the bus stop), the 12-year-old boy saw Smudge.

Every morning, for months, Danny had seen this cat on the way to the bus stop. Smudge was all black except for some white at the neck. Now Smudge was frozen stiff.

The boy hadn't known whether Smudge was male or female. He had thought maybe male. That's why he named him Smudge instead of something girl-sounding. Smudge was stuck on the hard part of the dirt road where wheels had pressed the dirt smooth. Opposite the Greene's split rail fence, the cat was stuck to the place on the road where cars, trucks, and tractors wore a smooth line. The blood froze the cat to the ground. Danny could see that Smudge was male.

The school bus would be approaching Pheasant Run soon.

Danny spotted a clump of saplings along the farm fence. He jumped into the ditch just off the road. It was waist high, and a thin layer of ice crackled under his feet. He snapped off a sapling, twisting it back and forth, and climbed back out of the ditch. He tried to push the cat off the road. Smudge was stuck good.

He pried and wiggled and finally got Smudge's back end worked loose. The cat was like driftwood from Lake Superior where his family went each summer— dry, light, old driftwood—with blood-matted fur.

In the fall, Danny had hunted squirrel with his dad for the first time. He shot two of them with his new .410 shotgun. He carried their oddly limp bodies to a broken section of fence on the edge of the woods and waited. And waited. He finally cut them open with his pocket knife. He tried to think about a cleaner way, but finally shoved his hand into the steaming, slippery, warm guts and pulled them out. He "field dressed" them. His dad didn't say anything when he walked up to his son; he just nodded as the boy proudly showed what he'd done. They headed to the house, walking side-by-side in the fall dusk.

Where the squirrels had been limp and hot, Smudge was stiff and frozen, and Danny had no plans to "field dress" the cat. He held up the cat's hind end with his foot and shoved the stick under where it was flattened, prying at the rest of the cat. Some fur stuck to the ground, and Smudge broke free.

A clear, frost-free blood shadow remained where the cat had lain. Danny threw the stick over the Greene's fence into a bristly, cleared corn field, and bent down to pick up Smudge. It occurred to him to throw Smudge into field along with the stick.

He knew that fox, raccoon, skunk, opossum, crow and other birds would get at the cat during the school day. Danny didn't have time to dig a hole before the bus came, so he took the cat to school.

The peanut butter and mayonnaise sandwich in wax paper and an apple went into his coat pocket. Celery and carrots went into the field. He knew the cat wouldn't fit in the lunchbox with his thermos, so he jumped into the ditch again, mud squishing under his feet now, and hid it at the base of the saplings, among some dried grass.

Danny picked up the cat by the tail and the scruff of the neck. It looked to be too big.

The bus was coming. He took a deep breath, then bent, forced, the cat's stiff limbs. The cat's crushed side was easiest; it folded there pretty good; it was the uninjured left side that gave him trouble. In the end, the cat fit—on its back with its heat tucked into the matted chest fur. Danny pushed in the fur that stuck out when the lid was almost closed. He picked up his book bag and held the lunchbox under his left arm. He ran.

The boy reached the *Pheasant Run* dirt road intersection in time to see his bus appear just over a rise. He got on and sat near the back of the bus. The lunchbox bounced under his arm as he looked out the rattling window.

***

"Waddya doin'?" Danny heard footsteps.

It was the woodshop teacher, Mr. Murley.

"Uh, the hinges on my lunchbox broke, and I remembered you had this tape."

"Humph..." The heavy-boned balding man lumbered over to Danny.

Danny had taped over handle and hinges, had wrapped it lengthwise and over the top, had completely covered every aluminum inch with wide silver gray duct tape.

"Usin' enough?"

"I wanted to make sure it wouldn't fall open."

"Maybe..." The man turned the lunchbox and peered at the shape from another angle. "Wacha got in there?"

"A cat," Danny said, and ripped a last yard-long piece of tape from the empty roll to wrap diagonally across the bundle. "A dead one."

The hall from the woodshop was one of the spokes that led to the "Commons," an area where kids gathered during lunch and between classes. Danny turned right and headed for the cafeteria. Ten minutes to homeroom.

Seventh- and eighth-graders milled in the halls, laughing, pushing; some talked with their heads close. Some leaned against walls, arms crossed—watching and commenting on everything that moved. They watched Danny hurry by with his bundle under one arm, a kid in too-short bell bottom jeans and a dumb-looking coat. "Dork," one boy said. Two others laughed.

The seats in the cafeteria were empty. The clatter of stainless steel utensils, pots and pans, the sound of water running in a large sink, women talking, and other sounds came from a door that stood open at the end. Danny went through where students slid their trays past glass-encased serving stations. Water steamed in the bottom of several empty warmers. He hurried and knocked at the open door.

"Excuse me," Danny said.

A fat man in a smock sat on a plastic pickle bucket, smoking. A skinny woman with black hair in a hairnet stood near a water fountain checking off items on a clipboard.

The woman looked up a moment then back down to her clipboard.

"Can I leave my lunchbox here until first lunch?" Danny held his bundle out.

"That depends," the fat man said, using a diet Pepsi can as an ashtray. He took a last drag and dropped a cigarette into the can. *Hiss.* "Do you pack a lunch *every* day?"

"Well, my mom makes me..."

The cook smirked.

The boy said, "This is my dad's old lunchbox. That's why I taped it— the hinges broke. Can I leave it here until lunch? Just 'til lunch...?"

The man stood, putting his Pepsi can on the pickle bucket. He waved for Danny to follow. "Don't leave it here all day," he said over his shoulder to the boy. "Or we'll throw it out."

"Okay, I won't."

The cook walked the boy to a stainless steel walk-in refrigerator. Cases of milk, cellophane-wrapped cheese stacked on metal shelves. Boxes of tomatoes in wood crates lined the metal floor. The man motioned to Danny, and the boy handed over his lunchbox.

"Your mom packs quite a lunch," the man said, hefting the tape-wrapped box.

"There's a big thermos of milk in there."

The man put the taped lunchbox shape on the shelf with cartons of orange juice.

"Like I said, don't leave it here after lunch, or it'll get tossed.

***

Danny didn't hear his homeroom teacher. When the bell rang, he walked automatically to his next class, Algebra. He sat in his front row seat. This was his favorite class, but...

Insulated, Smudge, and... Leave the road, maybe. Pulling....

The classroom went away. Other kids, the teacher writing on the chalkboard while asking questions—gone.

Danny pushed through the cafeteria doors and rushed into the room he'd met the cook in. Empty. He went to the kitchen and the walk-in refrigerator. Cooks paused in their work and watched him open the walk-in refrigerator door.

He searched the walk-in twice. Looked around again. Cold, he pushed the door open and looked around the warm kitchen, on metal counters, near a stack of plastic bun trays...

Danny rushed back out through double swinging doors. He stopped a thin man, arms heavy with trays. "Do you know where Hank is?"

The burdened man looked at Danny a moment. "Wait. I'll get him."

"Thank you."

The ropy-armed cook put the cafeteria trays on a counter, lifted the receiver of a phone on the wall, dialed, paused, talked, glanced at Danny, nodded, hung up.

He went back over to stall the nutty kid, but the kid was gone.

***

"Mr. Dobbs... Mr. Dobbs?"

The assistant principle covered the mouthpiece on the receiver. "Wait!"

Danny O'Riley waited. He *had* waited. Too long. He stared at the big cafeteria clock for sixty seconds.

The kids at Mannview Middle School didn't even have a nickname for the assistant principle responsible for discipline. His name alone was bad. Those who'd done two or three days in-school suspension or several hours after school in detention didn't call the man anything but "Mr. Dobbs."

In the school office, a secretary sat behind the counter desk. Her head barely poked above the wood top and Danny had waved and smiled as he walked by. "He's expecting me."

Mr. Dobbs was talking to his mom, Danny knew. He just *knew* it. But he wasn't scared. Not this time. Danny pushed the door open, stepped into the assistant principal's office and pulled the door closed.

"Mr. Dobbs."

The administrator looked up. "All right, then." He hung up the phone and folded his hands on his desk.

A thick piece of clear glass covered the desk, except for a narrow strip along the front. Under this glass were photos of the same two children, taken at different ages, from infants to ten-year-olds. The Dobbs twins, Andy and Sandy. A coffee cup filled with pencils, a brass name bar, *Jeffrey R. Dobbs, Assistant Principal*, and a picture frame of his family, turned toward visitors, lined in a row across the front of the desk.

"Son, just what do you think you are doing?"

"Give it to me!" Danny almost yelled.

"Excuse me?"

"It's *not* yours."

"Now look." The administrator's tone turned fatherly. He leaned back, his chair creaking, and clasped his hands behind his head. "Why don't you explain what's going on."

An invisible force field hummed between them. The boy's eyes distractedly took inventory of the office. A coat rack in the corner; a waste-can near the desk; two tan filing cabinets; three visitor chairs opposite the desk; a mirror on the wall to the left; diplomas and degrees and commendations on the wall. Fluorescent lights above.

Danny had not answered Mr. Dobbs. The silence stretched out.

The expression on the administrator's face shifted from condescending, to annoyed, to impatient. Danny watched the changes and waited. They always spoke first.

"Well?"

Danny stood unanswering.

"Sit down right now!" The assistant principal leaned his chair forward, put his hands on the desktop and began to stand.

"Son, do you have a hall pass?—"

Danny made a quick jump forward and grabbed the framed family portrait from the man's desk. He backed off and drew his right hand back to his left ear. He looked poised to throw a Frisbee a mile.

Dobbs stood slowly. *This kid is... Is he on some something? Remember that incident with Fred at Sandovan...* "Now son, just calm down."

"Give it back," Danny said. "Or I'll smash this on that wall!" The boy's voice shook.

"Well, I don't know—."

"You're a liar! I know you have it!

So... that taped-up lunchbox from the cafeteria?

"Just relax." The administrator held up his hand. "Let me call Miss Carmichael."

The assistant principal picked up the receiver, pressed one in a row of plastic buttons, asked someone to "bring in the package." Dobbs hung up. "It's all right. Everything's fine. Now why don't you sit down and tell me what's going on."

Danny shook his head quickly, cocking his arm higher, waiting, tense, ready to throw.

A quiet double knock on the office door. Danny backed up, keeping Mr. Dobbs in sight. A blond woman's head appeared. "Here's the 'thing' you — eeep!"

Danny threw the framed picture directly at the assistant principal and grabbed the lunchbox with both hands. The startled secretary backed into the school office and the man fumbled his family photograph in slow motion down to the floor, trapping it against his leg.

Danny ran out of the school office. He paused at the exit by the gymnasium, listening, then pushed the bar and quietly exited. The concrete block outside was cold against his back.

Danny's locker was in the hall spoke directly in the view of the school office. He couldn't go there. He walked along the outside of the building to the parking area entrance and went inside. He rushed through the warmer air to the lost-and-found outside the library and dug through the large wooden box. He found a pink sweater, and a yellow hooded sweatshirt. Two gloves, one brown and one black, fit. Then a black scarf and knit hat. The boy hurried back to the exit, slipped outside again where the wind blew cold November.

Danny followed the sidewalk to the Mannview Mohawks baseball field. The cigarette butt-filled dugout always smelled like urine. He ripped tape away from the top of the lunchbox, exposing the handle. He cut across left field and into another field of pale, dry grass, lunchbox in hand. Normally he'd go to the new high school under construction. Not today.

A stand of woods and a beaten dirt trail that ended at the corner of a parking lot behind First Baptist Church. Danny stood and looked at the cross on the back of the building. Each time he looked at it, it felt different. This time, he didn't think at all; he just stood. High school kids rode bikes on the trails and smoked in the woods behind the church in the summer when the leaves concealed them.

The boy left the church and cut through another lawn and walked under the great quiet trees of a public library. He looked at the heavy doors of his two-story safe-house-haven and felt a familiar, welcome loneliness. Many afterschool hours were spent in there. Danny cut through lots and between buildings and alleys downtown, past the post office and across Grand River Avenue.

On Mannview's Main Street, a quarter-mile past Howell Office Supply, was the lumber yard where forklifts, men in hard-hats and flatbed trucks moved constantly. A pine smell ever-present, like the fast food smell near an expressway exit. It was always there, depending on the wind.

Danny walked to a corner of the fence around the lumber yard, turned right, and walked the hundred feet or so to another corner. He took a short trail through some weeds to the train tracks.

To kids in Mannview, these were The Tracks. Two sets of tracks traveled heavily by freight trains. Three, four, five-engined trains moved from Detroit in the east and Grand Rapids to the west. Like those kids' bikes in the woods behind the church, these trains passed continually through Mannview on their way to other places. The tracks made a large crossing in Brighton, thirty miles west. Kids talked about hopping trains and how they found iron ore ingots and ball bearings, "steelies," between creosote-covered ties. Danny had a shoe box full of rusty railroad spikes under his bed, in the home that was for sale.

His feet were cold. The pink sweater and the yellow one were tight and warm, though. His nose and toes felt the weather. He unconsciously changed the lunchbox from hand to hand as each arm in turn got tired.

Danny was a natural at balancing on the rails. He could usually leap from one to the other without falling. He didn't feel like it today. And the weight of Smudge...

On a stretch where the trees and overgrowth crowded up to the gravel-lined railway, wires strung on miniature telephone poles crossed over a swampy area that froze in winter. It was just starting to get cold enough for the ice to stay most of the day.

On both sides of the built-up gravel, water reflected the gray bright sky and the trees. Thin ice clung at the edge of the water and to the brown grass in the water. A concrete passage for the water that went under the tracks broke its smoothness and Danny stopped. He put the lunchbox on the concrete ledge and skidded down to stand at the water's edge with his back against a concrete slab. The sun hit him in the eyes and a tree's shadow cut across his arms. He looked at himself in the water—a stranger wearing two sweaters, a scarf and a hat under a hood. The boy tipped his head back and looked up, feeling his head touch the lunchbox.

He straightened. His eyes drifted back to the reflection.

As far as he knew, his dad hadn't liked cats. Danny and his sisters' cats had to stay outside to "keep up with the mice."

Danny never saw his dad pet a cat. He never kicked them out of the way, either. When there were bones left over from dinner, his dad threw them to the cats over the fence on the way to feed the pigs. —*Get caught in a dog's throat*, he'd say—*cats'll eat 'em.*

Danny was the oldest, and a boy, and now he had to take care of his mom and sisters.

Leaning against the irrigation abutment, he caught a slow movement in the corner of his eye. A train. He looked at his reflection again. It was headed his way. He could see his dad. Or he could step up into a car and leave everything behind.

Danny pushed away from the concrete and climbed the bank. His cold feet were close to the vibrating tracks. The train's horn blasted.

The horn blasts. Fifty feet, and the rumbling diesel tone diminishes rapidly. The horn—again. He closes his eyes and the train, the massiveness of it, rushes by now, now two feet from his upturned face—the horn blowing — and a head leans out from the cab and looks back at him standing there; the diesel tone rises in pitch again— by his face… one, two, three, four. Four throbbing engines. The boy's eyes close, the vibrating, ground-shaking cars pass— his body in tune to the rumbling drumbeat that increases tempo. Rumble-space, rumble-space.

Danny sways with the lunchbox under his left arm. After the diesel engines have curved ahead, at a bend a few hundred yards ahead, he opens his eyes and is running, running—reaching—his heels hitting his backside. His brown-gloved hand grabs the cold metal handhold on the side of the swaying boxcar, his legs flying and a jarring final tripping leap, and then a miraculous foothold.

The lunchbox is held vice-like in the other, black-gloved, hand. He breathes an iron taste deep into his starving lungs, his arms linked through the handholds, his eyes streaming in the frigid wind. He blinks and rests his head against the swaying metal, watching everything retreat.

White letters, spray-stenciled onto the brown boxcar, blend into sound: MCMLX, MCMLX....

*

Behind: a scratching, ringing from the tracks and a shimmering muddy puddle that ripples not because of wind. Gradually—silence, and the wind, and silence where the boy had stood, and then nothing.

The boy jumped off before a long turn. The train had slowed down. Another trail led from the tracks behind the International House of Pancakes. Two vagrants watched the boy. A Mexican and another man, gray in appearance.

"Hey."

Danny walked, his head down.

"Wacha got there?"

The boy didn't answer. He held his lunchbox tightly in both arms.

He walked through a vacant lot, crowded with dilapidated signs. Tall brown grass among the signs. *Howard Johnson's; Arby's; Rax.* He made it to a narrow grass strip between the signs and IHOP.

Lllllllkkkkkkkkkkkkkkkkkkkkkkkkkkkkkkkkk

……and Danny boy was on the ground. The world tilted unexpectedly, not surprisingly, and faded.

The bums back by the tracks were drinking quarts of beer in paper bags. A small, concerned part of Danny faded as the world had faded.

*

The ground was hard on the boy's hip. His right ear burned where it rested on some pebbles. The sweater hood was half off. Danny groaned and patted the ground behind his back. He found the lunchbox and pulled it over his body, and pulled it up to his chest, hugging it tight. He pulled his knees up and curled up around the box.

Safety-Kote: a rubber sealing compound used to protect electrical outlets and components on outdoor advertisement signs. A gallon-can rested on its side by Danny. The sound of rush hour traffic on the street a hundred yards away was the first thing he heard. A spreading warmth, moving through his right side and ear after he sat up, was the first thing he felt. His first thought: …?.......?.......

Danny stood, holding the lunchbox in both arms. The warmth flowing through his side was a burning. Painful. The sun was near the horizon. It was after four o'clock. He limped across Grand River Avenue and walked along it as far as the *Best Western* (Dinner Buffet! $4.95! Crab legs! All you can eat!).

The burning in his side stopped and his whole body felt glowing. He couldn't feel his feet, but they carried him faithfully without faltering. Danny's mouth was open. Tears welled in his eyes and he was happy. He breathed deeply. The fog that had hung about his head for so long was gone and the coolness of clear emotions and honest sorrow was saving him.

***

Fall leaves crunched as the boy passed through the entrance of the cemetery. It was a grand, well-kept, treed, mowed, reverent, lonely, sad place. It rained a lot. It always seemed to rain a lot at the cemetery. Today it was cold and the leaves dry.

Near a green block building at the rear of the cemetery, Danny searched around for a shovel. He found a green metal fence post. Well, perfect. The U-shaped, corrugated, spade-bottomed, rust- and cobweb-covered length was a memory. His dad had showed him how to help and hold a post steady as he pounded them into the ground... had shown him how to handle pliers to wrap wire ties around barbed-wire and post. They had worked together putting up the fence on the family's small farm.

Danny put Smudge (still in the lunchbox) next to the dead flowers and plastic wreath. There was no headstone. The cemetery people told the family that they had to wait until the ground softened in the spring to dig and pour a proper concrete footer.

Now, the grave was marked by a dead strip of yellow sod.

Danny got to work using the fence post, the spaded end, to pry up the dead sod. He managed to flop it back in a single piece. His arms were tired, but his body had warmed. He had worked through the pain of his feet returning to life. He rested, then dug again.

He worked at that grave just like the squirrels his dad taught him how to skin in the basement.

The sod was set aside, flipped upside-down. Luckily, the dirt hadn't settled yet, though it was pretty hard at first. The boy hacked at the dirt, working around the hole from different sides, kneeling like a man with a set of post hole diggers. He set the post down to scoop out dirt with his miss-matched gloved hands.

How far down? the darkening day asked. *All the way*, the hole replied.

Danny stabbed at the earth until his hands began to slip, then he dropped the post to scoop more dirt, resting his arms and back. Again and again. After a long while, down in the hole, he hit the concrete vault lid. The boy threw double handfuls of loose dirt up and out of the hole. Dirt was inside his shirt and in his ears. He flung dirt back out behind him. The air was cold on his sweating back and arms. He stopped. In the hole, it was quiet. *Earth*. He breathed in deeply through his nose. He felt closer.

The boy slid down to sit cross-legged. He propped his head on his hands, breathing. He was home. Minutes passed.

"Hi Dad," Danny said.

Eventually he looked up, seeing stars overhead. He climbed out, got the lunchbox, and jumped back in—listening.

He pulled the duct tape off and let it fall in pieces. When he had torn it all away, he picked the lunchbox up and undid the two latches.

Smudge was on his back still. He looked like an old man asleep in a chair. The boy sniffed and carefully closed the lid. Everything was right. He imagined his father standing on the grass above him, watching, nodding.

Danny set the lunchbox down on the small patch of exposed concrete painted gold vault lid. The aluminum lunchbox sat there. The boy climbed up out of the hole and stood in the colder early night air. He grabbed a handful of dirt from the pile next to the hole and squeezed the dirt in his gloved hand.

Danny threw the dirt into the hole. It was the only thing to do. He kneeled down, scooped and pushed the dirt into the hole with his sweatered arms, hearing it first hit the aluminum lunchbox, carefully dropping it in to make sure the box didn't fall over. He used the metal fence post to pack in the dirt once the hole was mostly filled. He stomped all over the rebuilt mound. He flopped over the yellow sod. Tired, the boy threw the metal fence post behind the dark building then looked at the twinkling stars through bare tree limbs.

A station wagon, theirs, pulled in through the cemetery gates, slowly rolling towards him. He could see his sisters' faces in the front passenger side, where his mom *used* to sit when they traveled, by the dome light as his mom rushed to hug him.

∗∗∗

It's okay Mom."

"What were you?.."

"It's alright, Mom. It's alright."

Chapter 28 — Dream Extreme, *Southern France and* The One and Only Skate Park Project.

It's hard for me to write about this time. It was the best of times, and that's a fact. Well. This will unzip a compressed computer file I have chosen not to open for eight years.

I remember walking with Andrée in the summer in Stuttgart, pushing a sleeping Guillaume along the paths in *Rosensteinpark* or possibly the *Schlossgarten*. I remember it like it was now. We'd begun a conversation about our lives and what we should do while sitting on the *Balkon* of our second floor apartment. I felt it was an important question for us to bring up together, as we had linked our lives. Andrée seemed to have not considered the idea of consciously spending time on pondering our best fit in this life when I asked: *Pretending that money is not a factor—imagine you're financially secure forever—what would you want to do with your life?*

It's easier to ask some questions than it is to answer them without having already thought long and hard. She was reluctant or hesitant to answer. Maybe she didn't want to limit herself to one choice which might be lesser than another choice in the future. I abandoned my first question and asked, *What is it you like to do? What do you like to do more than anything else?* She replied, "I like to take care of people. I like to make people happy."

"Okay, let's make *that* your career!" I said. I introduced her to my idealistic credo: It's not really an option to live a life working or doing something unless it is centered on a passion, a thing that one did very well and derived great satisfaction and fulfillment from. Throughout the ten years before my questions, Andrée had existed in the cocoon of another notion: getting a stable job that provides ample income and allows for extensive vacations each year. That's a German thing, incidentally—ultimate security and world travelling.

Looking back, from now, I don't have as big a problem with the security-minded thinking as I did back then. As a self-employed handyman, living from job to job, with no security, I've been poorer and "stuck" in rural Michigan and Ohio for a number of years, trying to provide for my family—so I can't find quite as much fault with wanting to be financially worry-free and having just the *chance* to take a vacation. I wryly observe what my ideals do over time when confronted with the exigencies of life. I'm made more aware of another side of the coin.

Since that first time Andrée and I talked about life aims in Stuttgart, I've had to (surprise!) put my money where my idealistic mouth was and I admit it's *not* easy; I've acted, stepped forward into the unknown, with trepidation. Do what your passion is and the money will follow, I've said; do what is right for you, whatever it is, and everything will turn out fine. So very easy to tell someone—else. Determining to work for myself as a handyman painter was difficult. Anxiety over the future of my family. Taking the time off from my paying gig last winter to transition to writing for a profession. The actual *doing* of something ventured is a different order of experience than the armchair imaginings and commenting. Hiking the trail, swatting bugs, feeling the weight of the pack, and an earlier idea of walking the Appalachian Trail—are related but different. I *knew* this, as you do, but I didn't know it. Walking the talk. It has humbled me and made me less intolerant of people's hesitation when I offer them my encouragement to follow their passion or commit their life to seeking its meaning. It isn't easy to release one's grip on the floating dock and paddle toward a distant unseen shore. It is infinitely more rewarding and always lacks the chief feature of hesitation —regret. These are the only times I've really ever lived.

This was the beginning of an ongoing discussion between us, star-crossed lovers. That summer afternoon, pushing the sleeping Guillaume in a park, we continued talking about our future. A few hours before, I had stopped in this place and sat on a bench, thinking along the lines described. Andrée called on the cell phone in my pocket and I started to tell her about an idea for us to go to France and open a bed and breakfast Fantasy Island kind of enterprise where we would offer our German friends a tailor-made French theme vacation based on their preferences. We would organize a thrilling time, a relaxing time, a challenging time, an instructive time, a meditative time. We'd make all the reservations and arrangements. All they would have to do is step into their dream vacation. I thought this was a good way to use Andrée's talents and desire to make others happy. I envisioned us living doing just that. It felt perfect. I talked to her about this over the phone while pacing back and forth near some goldfish pools.

Then Andrée's voice said in my ear, *what about opening a skate park*? After a minute, I told her where I was and said come over so we could discuss it. It was there, on that afternoon, that we began a journey we didn't know we'd started. It had never been my intention to build or start a skate park. I was genuinely surprised by Andrée's suggestion.

The reason skate parks came up related directly to my obsession at the time. I had gotten into inline skating in Pittsburgh when I was separated from ex-wife Kathy. Skating saved me from riding public buses and was also my therapy; I'd skate for hours and hours in parking lots. After moving to Stuttgart, the *Landeshauptstadt* (capital) of the southwestern German state of Baden-Württemberg, I discovered glorious trails for skating throughout the region. Inline skating for fitness was a *big* deal there. I found myself happily skating everywhere. Since Andrée loved to explore and show me new things, we started skating together, pushing Guillaume in his *Kinderwagen*. Andrée was a real trooper in her Bauer skates. She was petrified of falling and yet she *did* actually skate with me, holding onto Gui's stroller with her death grip. We often skated at the end of the runways of the Stuttgart airport, watching the huge-bellied jets slowly float down from above to land. We skated on the trails of the Schlossgarten.

One day I noticed a skate park with ramps. And that was it. All over. Tentatively, I rolled up and down the radius of a small table-top ramp, losing my balance on the unexpectedly slippery-feeling curvature. *Crazy. People actually skate on these things?*

From then on, whenever it came time to pick a place to go on the weekends, I voiced my preference for a place near a public skate park. They were everywhere. A few in Stuttgart, including my favorite one downtown behind the *Deutsche Bundespost* (federal post office) building in a section of an underground tunnel that had been closed off and converted into a downward-sloping skate park with half-pipe, quarter-ramps and other modules. It was also a fantastic 400-foot long gallery for spray paint graffiti artists. During Andrée's pregnancy with Guillaume, and in the following months as a new parent, I would go once a week to this skate park, in all weather, early weekend mornings, when I was the only one, and I'd spend a few hours concentrating exclusively on those ramps.

I always had a trick or movement goal I was working on. I remember dropping into the half pipe backwards the first time. I'd taken a length of shoestring, tied it to the safety rail up top and stood with my left skate straddling the metal pipe between its second and third wheels at the lip of the drop-off. I leaned back, heart thumping, holding onto that thin string, feeling what I always feel when on the precipice of something dangerous and alluring. I told myself silently, *I've got to do this the first time* sometime—*the hell with it*—and pushed backward, rolling down into the half pipe. What a rush of adrenaline fear and thrill. I survived! I got back up there, right away, doing it again and again until I untied the string and put it in my pocket, then went off backward, dropping into the half pipe from above for real, unaided. What a feeling of accomplishment. What gratification. Going for something—through the fear barrier and beyond, to trial and error and breaking the sound barrier past the sonic boom of <u>first success</u>. The first attempt is the fear barrier. The first success is the graduation to the next plateau. Ever onward. Always further.

I loved skating, pushing limits, going after challenges. Often I would go back to our apartment and bring Andrée and Guillaume down to show them my newest trick—backwards into half pipe with three-sixty on the opposite side; handstand on lip of pipe transition into ramp; stopping on the rail; hang-time over the rail; hand grab; grind to one-eighty drop in…. It felt terrific showing Andrée what I was doing. God bless her, as they say. I don't know how she put up with me and my unbridled enthusiasm. *I* might have been bored stiff in her shoes, but she was a generously appreciative observer. I love her.

We visited all the skate parks within an hour or two's driving distance. I knew which were good and which were bad. *This* one had a great half-pipe but no sidewalk leading to it. *That* one had great access but the ramps were too small or spaced too closely together. *That other* one needs a garbage can and some lighting. I had a rating system, and I knew which ones I wanted to go to depending on which tricks or moves I was focusing on at the time—or depending on my mood.

Andrée went with me on all of those crazy expeditions. Sometimes we'd meet a friend and they'd walk together while I obsessively skated on ramps and rails, interacting with German skaters, BMXers and skateboarders.

When we were walking in the *Garten* that day, Andrée said, "Why don't we build a skate park in France?" I would build a great one, she said, that was perfect for practitioners like me, because I had an eye for the good features and knew what was lacking and knew exactly what I wanted.

"So what?" I told her. "Anyone can be picky." She replied that we could work together to make a park where someone thought of the people. She said how it was for her at these skate parks. And how it was for the families she saw bringing kids to the skate parks. She wanted to make it nice for them, too.

While we talked that day, I saw a world of possibility coalesce in my mind's eye. From doubtful to convinced and fully enthusiastic about this dream took two hours.

We had many more talks—in our apartment, on the balcony, walking in our neighborhood, in parks, along the river Neckar—until this dream fairly shined in the air in front of me. I could *see* it becoming real.

How would we get *there* from *here*? Simply put, we did. From living in Stuttgart, with Andrée very securely and successfully employed at Allianz, a large German insurance company, as a software test manager, to living in Southern France and hosting BMX, inline and skateboard enthusiasts in skate park planning meetings. My contribution was the certainty that it was better to go to France and try. We chose the Toulouse region in Southern France almost arbitrarily. I can't remember why we first went there. It was a brilliant stroke of luck. We spent a few weeks in the sleepy town next to Castanet-Tolosan on the Canal du Midi. What I saw our first day in downtown Toulouse was profoundly encouraging.

I pulled over to watch a few French guys on BMX bikes riding 'street.' I saw skateboards hanging from hands. I saw a group of aggressive inline skaters. All in the first hour we arrived. I *knew* this was the place.

We visited all the skate parks we could find. There were <u>so</u> many public skate parks. One private paying indoor park in Albi. Some great ones, some small with just a mini half-pipe and rail—yet they <u>all</u> were great because they showed me there was a passion for these 'extreme sports'. Somebody wanted them, so the skate parks were built. Andrée and friends we spoke to were immediately discouraged by discovering so many public skate parks. I see the instinctive turn of mind that causes a person react that way. I always felt like I was explaining something obvious to a slow-witted person again and again. "Don't you see?" I'd say. "There is a *market* here, to put in blunt business terms. The more skate parks we see, the more evidence there is that there are *practicants*! We aren't going to build another skate park; we're here to build a <u>home</u>. Encouragement. Training. The best equipment. Competitions. Support. *Home*. All the free public parks are doing our marketing work for us—they are luring in young people to practice skateboard, inline and BMX..." Even after explaining, I could see the dumb disbelief in people's faces. If only they were a skater, they'd know. They'd never heard of Camp Woodward (campwoodward.com) in Pennsylvania. I wanted to create *that* in Toulouse.

The public parks. Each park has its positive aspects. Each park has something or other that isn't optimal for the practitioners using them. Each park is devotedly visited by people passionate about their chosen sport—BMX, skateboard or inline. None of these parks is a *sanctuaire de l'extrême*. None is a sanctuary for the practitioners, built for the sole purpose of supporting and encouraging practitioners. To hold events, competitions, classes; to be the cutting edge of training and progression of the extreme sports. There was <u>no</u> Camp Woodward in France! It looks like Woodward is now looking to expand or translate into Europe now… Well, I was there first, because I saw the possibility. Of course, knowing a thing will work and being allowed to follow it through to completion are two remotely related things.

There are millions of practitioners and nothing in this area—yet, I told mayors and skate shop owners—nothing organized for and designed specifically to be HOME for the action extreme sports… Oh boy… I saw-knew it as clear as crystal. How often is one given the opportunity of finding a market for something that *only you* have the ready idea to create? It happens, but not every day. Bill Gates was there at the beginning of his thing. I recognized an amazing potential. I didn't imagine, or think, I *recognized*. You can believe that I know it.

Non-skaters or non-practitioners [what I mean by that is those people who did not practice BMX, inline, skateboard and other rolling "action sports"] looked at me with furrowed brows, suspicious of my sanity. Andrée, because she'd seen what I was talking about—she was there, after all, with me, at the skate parks, translating for me and talking to the youth; she saw (it was apparent for all to see) the passion that practitioners had for their sport, the nurturing and encouraging that was possible—she could hear, far off, the ringing of that bell of the truth I was going on about. We dreamed a very similar, complementary dream. The actual practitioners we met during that first three-week visit really responded to what I had been saying. No one else had spoken to them this way; that's my conceit and my guess. I would visit those skate parks with heartfelt abandon—and not on my shoes. I'd excitedly put on my aggressive skates, pads and helmet, and GO FOR IT.

I always looked for the next best trick I could do on the ramps or modules I found, impatient and laser-focused on my next effort. Watching someone else's best trick, or next best trick, encouraging them, and being inspired to go for my own next best trick, always pushing my limits. THIS is the common language I found among all practitioners of the "extreme sports" of inline, BMX, skateboard, luge, quad skates, urban *Parkour*, airbrush and spray paint art, and on and on, in both Germany and France. Utterly alone at a park, I was in heaven. With others there, though I had to wait my turn, I was encouraged to "up" my game; some of the wildest things I've done have been in the heightened atmosphere of one-upmanship.

I encounter this willingness go-for-it spirit in anyone doing their thing wholeheartedly. **_Any_** thing. It is utterly unimportant what they are doing—whether climbing Mount Everest, seeking an ultimate answer to one's existence, performing a double backflip on dirt freestyle BMX or designing a deck. There is something to pushing beyond the limits of one's personal atmosphere. I hope you find the top of your sky.

Chapter 29 —Coming Back Home

Picking up where I left off…

I wrote these seven words in this book at the end of February 2010. It was winter and I was at the end of my two-month 'book-writing' period. I'd hoped and planned for longer, but our family car, a 2000 Pontiac Montana, needed its transmission rebuilt. I didn't get that third month to work on this book. Just two. Actually, not even two months. More like a few weeks of actual work.

The best I can say is that I didn't work handyman painter jobs during that time. I created a writing blog, wrote some stories, wrote *something*—better than the past six years doing nothing in that realm. Now, nine months later, we've had our first snow of the new winter. As of this paragraph, it's Monday, November 8, 2010. It snowed heavily Saturday morning and the boys and I went sledding in the yard before breakfast. The snow was mostly melted by the time we were finished with Andrée's blueberry pancakes.

[Now, of course, it's Saturday, September 18, 2011. We just finished breakfast. It's a cool morning, perfect, sunny. Standing on our deck, looking down, I see our yard very nicely mowed. Life seems good. The boys have a train set sprawling on the living room floor and a Lego city in the dining room. Not much room to walk. Dog hair swirls like tumbleweed in all the corners. Andrée and the boys are downstairs trying a new game table they got yesterday in the two-family yard sale held at the Lancasters. The boys got some of the other family's stuff and the Lancaster boy, Charlie, bought some of the boys' contributions to the yard sale. I'm obviously typing here. In a little while, we're going to Wheeling where I hope we can ride on a sternwheel boat on the Ohio River. There's a Wheeling Heritage Port Sternwheel Festival this weekend.

I'm rushing through this book manuscript in my copyediting pass. Two years ago, in October, I made a commitment in front of people at the Self Inquiry Discussion Group (SIG) weekend retreat wrap-up around a campfire to write this book and transition to becoming a writer for a living. I want to present two pre-production copies of the book-in-the works to the folks there, and take advance orders for the book which I hope to print a first run of in December.

A lot has happened since the last time I wrote, father confessor. I'll have to leave it at that. We're all still on the ride, and things like working two summer months on a New York horse farm, visiting New York City, swimming in the Atlantic on the Jersey Shore, both boys starting fall soccer, Andrée commissioning a mural for the Wheeling library and me hopefully publishing my longtime book project this year—have kept us occupied.. There's more, of course.

I was just thinking about what I would do if I had a lot less time than I automatically assume. *Finish this book*, was my first response. What would it be, this book? The story of my life? It is, and stories take time. What if I didn't have the time to tell the whole story of my time living? What would I *want* to say? What would I need to say before going? What would be important? From that outlook, almost everything I've said so far is basically meaningless. From the standpoint of dying, nothing matters. This book is a picture of myself. What will I have said that I would want someone to remember after I'm gone? You'll have to pick something. Some of the things in here are good enough to keep, I think.

Back in France

This next section bookends one of the story lines of my life—my marriage, family and dream of living in France. We returned to France in June 2010. Five weeks in Andrée's country—the first time we'd been back since stepping into the cold Detroit air with two-year-old Guillaume. Time flies. Gui will be twelve this October.

If you and I were sitting together in my living room (or yours), and you asked, "So how was your trip to France?" I'd maybe pause and say something like, "It was really something," or, "The hardest part is being back here." Both are true, but how can I encapsulate an odyssey in a pithy sentence for a guest who doesn't have five weeks to get the real-time full-justice telling?

It *was* really something. Andrée and I talk about it occasionally and I gather she valued her time there, but I only know what I felt. I only feel what I do. It was the best and worst of times. Before going, I told Andrée I wouldn't care at all what we did; I'd be completely content to have made it back. Yes. While there, I didn't have a lot of strong "must see" preferences. In Paris, I wasn't dead-set on doing much of everything. I was glad to go along with whatever we came up with organically. I had preferences, but could easily drop them when Andrée suggested something or when circumstances precluded our being able to go on a boat ride on *la Seine* in Paris, for example—one of my fixations. I may not have cared what we did, but I *did* care very much about not spending any of our precious time there in a wasteful way: putting up with family squabbles, forcing my kids to whisper because *mamie* and then *papy* can't bear to hear their little voices… We'd put ourselves out on a limb to return and I had almost zero tolerance for anything I perceived as tainting our time there. Like achieving escape velocity and planetary orbit; I knew the value of the millions of pounds of fuel that got us there, so I wasn't about to put up with anything… stupid… Meaning—the stuff we ordinarily put up with in daily relating-to-our-fellow-humans.

We arranged to stay with Andrée's parents in order to save money on lodging. Two weeks with Nicole in Rennes, Bretagne; and ten days with Henry in l'Isle sur la Sorgue, Provence. Both taxed my nonexistent tolerance for needless suffering. Needing to restrain my six- and nine-year-olds continuously in order to not stress their *mamie*, who has lived alone unmarried after the divorce of Andrée's parents in 1986. Here we were in France, and I was growling at my kids to cater to the well-being of my mother-in-law's nerves. My kids are *not* poorly behaved; they're young boys. This wasn't tolerable. I refused to put up with it.

In Provence, it was the other side of that single same-sided coin. *Papy* was hyper-controlling of my boys. "Do this, put that here, give me this, don't do that," on and on into infinity. Though I didn't care what we did, I utterly refused being a prisoner for three-quarters of our 'vacation' in France. This was not the experience I wanted to take home with me to sustain me during the next separation drought until we make it across the ocean again.

First, in Rennes, after three days and four nights of incremental craziness, we found a *gîte* house to rent for a few weeks. Saint-Medard-Sur-Ille is a sleepy little village from our dreams. A *boulangerie* where we got our *baguettes* and *pain au chocolat* every day for breakfast and picnic lunches, an elementary school near the library, a *mairie* with a church. Everyone greeted us with open arms and friendship, giving us the keys to the town—literally. Our first day, the ladies at the *mairie* (courthouse) gave us the keys to the cathedral for us to look inside when we expressed interest in it. The library let Andrée and the boys check out French books for Gui and Ben to learn French even though we weren't "local" residents. A boy from the elementary school, Sylvain, befriended Andrée and our boys, playing soccer with Guillaume and Ben and accompanying us on walks and activities.

The *gîte* was my heaven. A picturesque water lily pond, replete with frogs and dragonflies. Benches under waving trees. An "English garden," Andrée said the French call it, surrounded the pond—shrubs and hedges, trees, green grass, a privacy wall—all for us, only us. Wow. The portrait on the cover of this book is done of a photo Andrée took of me there. The house, all one level, two hundred years old and renovated, with a small fireplace, dining table, two bedrooms two baths, a deck to eat breakfast or lunch on in the sun—all surrounded by pastures with curious grazing cattle and ponds. We had our own private world! I was so grateful to Nicole. If she hadn't been bothered by our staying there, we would have remained in her dark, close, plain second floor apartment in an uninspired block of Rennes.

Past the *gîte's* pea-gravel drive was a 19th century canal where barges were once pulled by draft animals. Today, boats make their way sedately along the wonderful waterway, changing levels in the various *ecluses* (locks) that raise and lower the boats to different levels of the canal. This was Shangri-la, and reminiscent of our *Canal du Midi* days near Toulouse.

Guillaume taking pictures of flowers and the boys frog fishing at our paradise, la maison blanche and its private grounds, near Saint-Medard-Sur-Ille in Brittany.

The first thing I demanded we do after being dropped off by our taxi with all our worldly possessions, was to have a family scream and yelling minute. We could open our lungs and our feelings. I led our little troupe in a noise-making session. <u>This</u> is what I had been dreaming of every year for the past eight summers away. *Thank you, Nicole.* I meant it with all my heart. I warmly thanked her often, in those following weeks.

Later, arriving in L'Isle sur la Sorgue in the south of France, it was with a big slam that I was introduced to a militantly-obsessively controlled environment. Andrée's dad controlled our every move and everything we initiated was quashed or disapprovingly frowned upon. I couldn't take this very long, but we were stuck. I got us away for a couple of nights to an overly-expensive hotel in town that we wouldn't have chosen—but it was that *freedom*, again, from squeezing-tight restrictions. Immense freedom. On the days we were prisoners at her dad's house, we got away for as much of the day as much as possible. I wanted to give my boys a good taste of France. I wanted my wife and I to hold each other and smile, knowing we made it.

So: unwanted, unanticipated times. The reality of any situation is always different from imaginings before arriving on the new scene. This was definitely not a one-dimensional journey. We got our money's worth, I'll say that. There is an overall feeling that is impossible to put into words. I'll have to write a 'poem' to try to show what I felt then and now.

> *Lying in bed in France, I breathe in and look at the ceilings over me and whisper silently, Am I really here?*
>
> *Walking in a park to a fountain, sitting with my youngest son, we take off our socks and put our feet in the cold water on the hot sunny day. I'm dreaming.*
>
> *Drinking good inexpensive wine, eating fresh baguettes with salted butter and camembert, feet propped up, sitting on the deck in plastic lawn furniture, flowers over there. The sound of frogs. Air moving in my hair, sun glasses on and I know I'm in heaven. We're here, and I distantly know it wasn't always so and yet, this feels like forever. This moment, right now, forever.*

"How was it?" people often asked when we returned. I was not accommodating. How could I answer them? Nothing would be worthy. The more complete an experience is, I think the less we are able to even point in its vague direction, let alone accurately convey the experience. Yet, when I get a step beyond my reluctance to talk about our return trip, it would be a Mandelbrot Set, an infinitely unfolding fractal. I might focus on an experience we had with jellyfish on the beach in Normandy, or standing under giant swooping wind turbines in the lush French countryside. Maybe I'd start out talking about the people we met and ate with, and give an example of a full daily schedule there. I'd surely mention our changing lodging. But then I'd zero in on… something particular—our first swim all together in the Atlantic on *this* side (France)—finally. How it was a very windy brisk cold overcast day, but we were in Bretagne (Brittany) at last. The descriptions would continue, unfolding a view of a world of experiences we'd… experienced… those five weeks.

Brittany History

The area known to the Romans as Armorica (from the Celtic term for 'costal area') was said to be renamed Brittany ("Little Britain") after the people who migrated there from Britain, particularly from Cornwall, in the 5th or 6th centuries A.D.

Breton is a Celtic language considered endangered, and is spoken mainly in Brittany [Breizh] today by about 200,000 people).

We were on the wide beach at Saint Malo, where Andrée lived for weeks with her family every summer in her grandmother's seaside house. I thought back to Andrée's letters, with her drawing of the coast, showing me where this city was in relation to Rennes. This day, the wind was blowing steadily at what I guessed was 30 miles-an-hour. The sand blasted my calves, feeling like needles. I was wearing three layers under a windbreaker and shivered. The wind wicked the heat right out of me. "I don't know about you, but I'm swimming!" I yelled to my family over the wind. We were a hundred yards to the low tide water line where two-foot breakers marched in. Sea salt in the air. The ocean. Guys in wetsuits kite surfing to the left and right of us. No one was crazy enough to actually swim today. But we were here! Finally!

The year before, we'd spent a week at Cape Henlopen State Park in Delaware, on the American side of the Atlantic because we couldn't afford to visit France, but we wanted to *feel* like we were getting closer to returning. I told my boys *that* June, kneeling with my arms around them in the shallows, "Next year, we'll be waaaay way over there, in France, on a beach, looking back *this* way, to where we are right now, and we'll all yell, 'We made it!'"

Here we are. People travel all over, all the time. Sure. But this was a gift. I used to live here, but now I don't take it for granted.. I took off my windbreaker, long-sleeve shirt and two t-shirts, took off my shoes and socks and stood on the cold wet sand in my swim shorts. *Here goes*! I hoped my heart wouldn't stop when I got in the water. I stepped in the shallow waves, followed by first Benjamin and then Guillaume. The wind pushed us hard and it was cold. Feeling crazy, I dove under the frigid waves after a whoop. I came up and shouted, "Vive la France!" I tasted the salt water running down my face. I held the boys hands. We yelled that "Long live France" phrase three times. A coming-home ceremony.

Going under the water was not bad; each time, it became more bearable. The wind was worse, of course, although it was "warmer" than when we first arrived. Guillaume stayed with me as Ben ran shivering back to Mom, who held all of our clothes. She wrapped him in a towel and helped him into sweaters, windbreaker and hat. After a while, first Gui and then I followed suit, running. We retreated to the boardwalk wall and reoccupied our wind shelter behind a stone staircase. In an online version of this book, I would include a short clip of this moment, reminiscent of summiteers video recording on the summit of Mount Everest:

> *Andrée hangs our windbreakers from the hand railing of stone steps coming down to the beach and the wind blows them, popping and snapping, horizontally. Andrée records a short video in the shelter from the blowing sand focusing on Ben and Gui playing, making trails and castles in the sand next to the sloping stone wall.*

When I do something, and time passes, I have a feeling, a smell, a taste of what it was like. Sometimes that 'memory', for want of another word, is so strong and present that it seems only minutes since I was there. *Those* are the ones. Yes. I have a lot. I'm grateful. The birth of my sons; hunting in northern Michigan; swimming in Lake Superior; riding my bike in Stuttgart from the hillside where we lived down to *Stadtmitte* to get a video of *The X Files* from *The English Shop*; my time at universities—all there, all golden.

The following, dated February 20, 2009, is about a nostalgic tendency of mine.

I remember everything

By David W. Weimer

Seeing my boys in the distance on the rope swings under the tree, turning my eyes to look back down at the hole I was digging.

I remember the times that I didn't tell you I loved you.

I remember not hugging you.

I remember forgetting what was important.

I remember my anger at my oldest son for not doing something the way that I wanted. I remember spanking my youngest son; I don't remember why. But I'll remember his shocked crying. I remember that moment that I realized this was my burden.

I remember great, reaching friends of my childhood—those trees–and wondering, among these friends, what my life would be. Hopeful, expectant, sad, full of wonder; these were my conditions. At twenty, feeling aimless, drifting in place while time kept going by—I remember waiting for fame.

I remember Dad, Mom, Pat, Anne, and Daisy, Lucky, Sabbath. My childhood is still back there, still and waiting.

I remember times that I worried. And both of my weddings. I remember checking the mailbox for my French pen-pal's letters when we were young. I remember, a world of years later, the night of my second son's birth. I smoked a cigar in the January parking lot, looking up past the snow at the lighted window where my newest relative waited, warm, with my pen-pal-now wife.

Sometimes I turn from the sad things. Later, if I want, I can come back and feel a nostalgia. Some things are in there, in me, unsaid, even though I remember them as sharp as anything. Staring into a fire under a night sky is the only kind of time when talking might work, because we can hear each other sometimes when the flames dance silently.

I've forgotten most of the people from my past. And most of the people that I've met. I remember effortlessly my way through cobbled streets and public gardens in Stuttgart. I remember where my clothes were, my bed, my shoes. These places are part of my self that I walk around with. My morning shower, drinking coffee from small cups, listening to music, staring into the distance from the edge of a hillside vineyard in the fall. Looking at the moon.

I remember leaving for work, knowing I'd forgotten something; remembering only, in a flash, when I was miles away. All of these times are fading into one another. It's all a single moment like a mountain.

I remember believing I was a much better person [than I likely was]. I remember, later, when I accepted that I'm getting worse. Getting slower, weaker, less capable of handling multiple tasks. I'm forgiving others more and more every day.

I was not good enough to be a husband or a father. I remember having no choice but to be good enough for those who called me these things. I'm still not good enough. But I've accepted this, too, and do my best anyway.

I remember running, running, running. I remember turning and facing—an attacker, the dark, a vicious animal, an illness. I remember becoming something other than myself. It was a surprise.

We're all the same, I discovered. I dropped hate. I had no choice.

I resolved to be a better person in this life and lost track of that resolution. I remember doing this. I remember good times, no pain, no worries, no discomfort, no problem. When I was content. That memory is thin away and far off, but still comforting.

I hope you will forgive me. When we knew each other... I hope I was a good companion some time, or, just once, for you.

The nausea, chills, sweating of my most recent stomach virus. These things drift away as my health returns. I am surprised by this health. It seems a solitary miracle every time.

I remember a cold room in the hot Memphis July, sitting with older people than me, waiting for our next turn for the nurse to remove gauze, for the doctor to cut away a larger rind of skin, again, from around an exposed wound or crater on our face, back, neck and hand. I remember the scalpel as a shadow in the corner of my left eye, then feeling the pulling and numbed heavy pressure of cutting.

Adventures in space, in magic lands, with mystery, turmoil, war and discovery—I turned away, always away from my day to day and turned pages and pages immersed in another place and time. I remember reading long past sleep.

I remember my eternal first day at Army basic training, absorbing the dread. Maybe it was a collective shocked silent moan of the recruits surrounding me that echoed in my head. Maybe it was only me.

I remember my first love; my first son's birth; my first punch; first car; first squirrels gutted hunting alone; first heartbreak, first foreign language, first turbulent marriage, first skydive.

I remember everything. I feel, still, the warmth of idealism, its afterglow of dreaming and hoping. It's there—behind my eyes a grand slide show. I'm interested and patient and prepared to watch for a long time. I'm the perfect audience. I'm no longer immortal.

Do audiences and shows always merge? What if I die? Will I remember this past or will I merge into it, forgetting, finally, that 'out there' even exists?

I remember feeling the overwhelming need to explain something. The irresistible compulsion to convey an idea. Now, I feel the grip of that compulsion easing from around my neck.

Flash—moments, time spent, treasured then and now, of inline skating in Germany, France, and later, in the U.S. Reliving days of hours fixing myself on a skill or trick on ramps, steps, table tops, rails. Working on parts of me, on courage; fearing, trying, exalting at having really gone for it *once*. And a soaring overarching confidence as I became progressively more proficient, comfortable, relaxed in my skill.

The more I remember, the more there is.

How far down do *I* go? Do I touch something else? Or is that something else *me*? My own father's memory thread was cut short in the summer of his year. I have entered this time of myself. His buried life rests below my well, and it, too, was deep—as deep as mine is now—I am sure.

Billions of fathers and sons have come and gone. Certainly trillions of all the kinds on our planet since its beginning. Does this approach the trillions of similar pairs of stars, staggered in their order of arrival, living, having lived and to-be-lived in their eternal, singular, impermanent lives, separate yet related, burning in this universe? What *is* this universe?

Something beckons from inside of me at such speculation. From further down than I can go—before remembering myself. Before remembering everything about me. Deeper than me. Beyond me. Infinitely empty. A dream to me, it says. *It's all a dream to me.*

France is *here*. *Right now*. I made a presentation at the Wheeling philosophy meeting about our France trip at the request of one of the regulars, who ironically wasn't there on the night I made the digital video projector presentation of photos and short videos from our trip. After an hour and a half, people were at the end of their patience. That's when I noticed it. Maybe they'd reached that point earlier. I was looking at the projected images and talking. I prefaced the presentation with a comment about my dad's home movies inflicted on visitors. Here I was, carrying on the family tradition.

At the end of that evening, I had a sinking feeling that nobody got anything out of seeing and hearing what I had to show of our France visit. I believe it's true. If you go through something or visit a place, you're the only one who appreciates what you say as you describe it. There are exceptions. The first and most automatic exception is the person who has been where you have been, done what you have done. For them, there is a recognition and a shared familiarity. The second exception is the person who has a pre-existing interest in your subject. Someone who's always dreamed of going to France will be glad to look at the images and hear the descriptions; they'll be looking through the lens of their desire and hunger to go there.

This book, and a lot of what I've said, will be of no interest to probably most people. My hope for you is that you fall into one of the two categories. You're a dreamer, an idealist, a thinker, an aficionado of touching moments in life—and you recognize my tracks in the blowing sand; you're a relative, or you're drawn to stories like mine because you've wanted to marry your pen-pal sweetheart, live abroad, learn languages, dedicate yourself to finding the meaning of life, and notice things that catch your attention.

Paris. I wrote my name at the top of *la Tour Eiffel* twice. At 19 and 43. At 33, I drank hot chocolate on top with my fiancée, sheltering in the café from the blowing December rain and wrote a postcard to a friend in Pennsylvania. Last year in Provence, I ate lunch with my wife and boys in the 700-year-old ruins of the Bishop of Cavaillon's castle high above the village of Fontaine de Vaucluse, looking down, down, at the river *la Sorgue* flowing from its source just beyond *there*, from melting snow coming to this hot southern region out from under the French alps. The blazing sun accompanied by an occasional warm wind. Gui and Ben, eating salted butter, cheese and ham *baguette* sandwiches prepared by Andrée; my wife and I sharing wine from plastic cups.

I'm driving, this minute, through Paris, trying to find Andrée's aunt's apartment. Andrée is very nervous whenever we're in big city traffic. I tell her don't worry. When we were in Paris last time, to go to the American consulate for paperwork to get Andrée's "green card," I was proud to drive in the rond-point around the *Arc de Triomphe* at night, beeping the horn of our VW station wagon. I *always* wanted to do that… Climbing on the roof with Andrée on the way up to the dome of Sacré-Coeur Basilica in Montmartre in Paris for the first time; a young, engaged couple on our way from Stuttgart, Germany to visit her dad in Paris to ask for her hand in marriage. Climbing on top of Montmartre again last June… Looking out over Paris from the dome—the quiet nostalgia I felt, being in the same place again, climbing those worn stone steps—with my wife of ten years now—and two boys, six and nine.

Ben, 6, and Gui, 9, on a rock ridge at the top of castle ruins in Fontaine de Vaucluse on June 30th, 2010.

I wondered then, before we made it, whether I'd be allowed to do it again, and who I'd be with then. Some of the astronauts on the moon may have looked at the earth above them and thought the same kind of thought— honored to be there and hopeful to return…

It would be nice to include little video clips from our times there. The picture at the right, for example, is captured in live action by a 40 second video where you hear the wind and Andrée narrates a panorama including the river below, water wheel and castle ruins.

For now, look at this photo. You'll have to supply the shimmering heat, the water, way, way down below, the lush green panorama, outdoor odors and warm wind, the taste of wine, baguette sandwiches and olives…

I sit here, typing, and I am there. What do I want to remember next? Like choosing another amazing sample from a box of chocolates. Ah—sitting on a chair in the warm sun on a cool morning on the deck at our *gite*. Yes. Go on without me; I'll be awhile. The sun on my face. I close my eyes and feel it through my eyelids and one side—letting it bake into my head. The boys are frog fishing over there now with cane poles and string with at the pond with their mom. I'll join them in a little while...

Chapter 30 —Being *Back*...

It's *being* back…

I'm writing at my Masonite-topped corner desk in the living room. Andrée is watching Dancing with the Stars and the boys have been building and "flying" their Lego creations around the house. Gui is going over a spelling list for a spelling bee he's trying to enter. He takes after his mom; he's an automatic speller with an effortless memory. Monday, November 15th, 2010. Just finished a day of primer painting, calking and scraping at a house I'm painting. Yesterday I was at a TAT meeting. The last one, it turns out, that will be held in November on the Richard Rose farm in West Virginia. All good things end—or do they? Almost forty years of metaphysical and philosophic meetings at that place. The TAT Foundation, which Rose founded, will continue quarterly meeting in PA and eastern West Virginia, probably growing, possibly establishing a permanent center somewhere else eventually.

So *we're* back, of course, but since I'm writing this, I'll say "I." Like the memory of a toothache, I remember our first week back. It did not bother me to come back home. I didn't mind at all as we spent our last night at a hotel in Nantes before flying back to Montreal. Suddenly, though, I found myself at home vacuuming cat hairs and mowing waist-high hay in our bowl-shaped nearly-one-acre lawn. In the back of my mind—actually the whole of it—I was not glad to *be* here. *Being* here.. I wanted "being here" *there*. Being there had felt like forever, like we had always been and always would be. I hadn't really believed we would make it back until I looked down and noticed my feet walking on the sidewalk or trail below swinging arms, hearing a conversation in French behind us. The bad and the good happened in a timeless procession of forever days. I just watched the newest *Alice in Wonderland* remake with Johnny Depp and thought, "Yeah… like *that*." A place where everything happened magically, surprisingly, and time doesn't apply.

I look at *this* place with different eyes, now. It's good to be here in our life again, but I don't hold onto it. This "life" includes my lawn mowers and weed-wacker, front yard and work van, tree house and garden. *All* of that can go, and it would be alright. There's another world I'd prefer. When it comes up, I naturally tell people I prefer living in France. They act surprised. I say we're going to retire over there and I'm not going to wait until I'm sixty. Next year wouldn't be too soon. Why? I feel at home there. I used to think it would be too disruptive a move for the kids with school and establishing a home all over again. I know that's not true. Everything would be fine. Kids adjust and so do we; we organize our laundry and kitchen pantry and life can go on… anywhere. The only thing in the way is us.

I'm an astronaut on an EVA (Extra-Vehicular Activity) floating serenely outside the capsule with no attaching lines. I go through life here, working, going to the bank, attending weekly philosophy meetings, putting gas in my van and reading books and I know I can do that anywhere, anywhere at all.

A hundred years from now? It's easy to imagine a hundred years *ago*, seeing old photos from the turn of the century or from World War I. Those old-fashioned faces in their black and white seriousness or frivolity. They were living in their modern world, just we are now. It's amazing. From 4-g phones and old fashioned "modern day" texting, way back to living with no televisions or internet—all in the span of a lifetime.

Charlie Duke, from *In the Shadow of the Moon*, a 2007 documentary featuring the astronauts who'd walked on the moon during the Apollo program said, "My father was born shortly after the Wright Brothers. He could barely believe that I went to the Moon. But my son, Tom, was five. And he didn't think it was any big deal."

Will there be another hundred years? What if time ceases to exist? Does it exist? What if we do something terrible to ourselves and our little soap bubble world floating in the immensity of space? A plague? A war? What if something terrible happens to us, like the ill-fated dinosaurs? A meteor? None of us are going to survive this…

I'm re-reading Douglas Adams' *The Hitchhiker's Guide to the Galaxy* in the bathroom. What I have is a giant tome of five of his novels I got for a few dollars at the Paradox Book Store in Wheeling. Adams died at 49 in 2001; for him, there *will be* no hundred years more. In this, his first novel in the collected work, the Earth is a computer named *Deep Thought*, created to calculate "the Answer to the Ultimate Question of Life, the Universe, and Everything." The answer was eventually discovered: 42. Unfortunately, the 'computer" had worked for so long on coming up with the answer that the original question had been somehow… forgotten. Deep Thought then predicted another more powerful computer would be made and designed to back-calculate the original question for this answer, 42. What if Deep Thought's answer to everything was 49, the age at which Adams died? It would have meant as little as 42—to him.

At a certain point in *Hitchhiker's Guide*, the earth is destroyed to make way for a hyperspatial express route, five minutes before Deep Thought's 10-million-year program would spit out the answer to everything. I wish I could be clearer on the plot progression, but I started (re)reading *Restaurant at the End of the Universe*, Adams' second novel, since I'd already read—and forgotten—*Hitchhiker's Guide* and the other four of his "trilogy in five parts" before.

When the Earth goes, where do *we* go? If we're lucky, we catch a space cab just before the big explosion. But what if *we* go before the Earth? I've heard there's a Native American tribe, the Algonquin, that had no word for time.

Some of our specific words relating to that thing we imagine and call time: minutes, seconds, hours, days, weeks, months, years, decades, centuries, lifetimes… Oops—that last one isn't really in the same class as the others. Too subjective. You're as old as you feel, the saying goes. No doubt. Some people refuse to celebrate birthdays because they see them as a conspiracy to chain them to the paradigm of getting older and dutifully dying as close to the watermark four score and twenty years (100-years-old) as a person can get. I know a yodeling singer/songwriter from Brooklyn living in Wheeling now who states with seeming certainty that he's going to live to be 150. For him, there isn't a hundred years from now; there's only eighty more, then nothing. He's in his 70s, so he's going to miss the hundred mark by a score.

Maybe the *universe* doesn't care about our word, "time". Maybe we merely come and go, in a dance of motion—blooming and fading, dying, reemerging and living—an endless Mandelbrot set of existence that we sticks-in-the-mud try to pin down like the butterfly we've captured to be shown to others as a "thing apart." Apart from me? You? From other "things"? What if the rest of the universe thinks that everything *is* everything? What if we are a part of a neuron cluster in the great brain named by us "universe"? A cluster of neurons stuck in a loop of reoccurring nightmares where creatures try, and seem to succeed, in catching time?

Richard Rose, that West Virginia guru, said that when he closed his eyes, the sun disappeared. This sounds simplistic and ridiculous at first.

We humans make sense of our reality with our minds-senses. If we *see it*, it exists. If we don't, it doesn't, can't, exist. This is depending on ourselves as a kind of infallible truth-teller. How can this be? When we only see, hear, feel, taste and smell a small fraction of what is seeable, feel-able, taste-able and smell-able? Can we taste space? Are we space to space? (un-taste-able to one another because of an utter difference in condition of being) What about another world, with another atmosphere? Do autistic people live in another world? Undoubtedly. Which of our worlds is "right"? We imagine and assume so much. I know this can go on to apparent absurdity, but this is the territory that a serious philosopher—a lover of wisdom—eventually will find himself or herself encountering at some point. Questioning our very selves and everything we rest on and within. Why don't we talk to the air? Question it? Do fish ever consider the water they're swimming in? Can they even notice it? What about our thinking? It is our mental water—very comfortable and apparently known. But can we ever know anything else, as long as we're in our fishbowl?

When 'ordinary' people—by that, I mean part-time philosophers—get to a point like this, they generally become nihilists and declare that "all is relative," the exact nature of the universe is unknowable (un-pin-able) and that God is, in fact, dead. They possibly become more sure (or unsure) of this position as time goes on and repeat it as often as possible for the rest of their lives. But do they know this? You know: the old question— did people a thousand years ago believe that the world was flat or know it was flat? I bet that some of them knew it deep in their assuming. Just as people nowadays "know" beyond any creeping uncertainty that there is no answer, no permanence, and no all-encompassing comprehension of everything to ever be experienced first-hand. They've bricked up a grand entrance. A friend who read this said to me, "I went through a long phase of believing nothing was certain. Then I started wondering how I could be certain of that."

Another category of folks consists of full-time believers who've also diligently and incrementally worked toward a total commitment state of certitude. Maybe they had a wobbly moment along the way, but they've grown sure and now feel more stable than ever on their feet. They *are* right, of course. Most others are sadly wrong and misguided. *These* people, though, are not plagued by doubt any more and will be able to live their lives inside a feeling of great personal purpose they share with some others. They'll try to encourage as many lost souls as possible to share in this revelation, and pray for the ones who won't see their errors. They'll possibly die secure. Hopefully. I'm guessing, as everyone must do who is looking at something from a distance instead of thinking from inside of it.

Douglas Adams seemed to take pleasure in highlighting and ridiculing people's pet beliefs, obsessions and attachments. He seemed to take nothing seriously, but probably took everything extremely seriously. I feel a refreshing lack of judgment in his writing; he considers all with equanimity. All are fools. Some are wise. I don't know what his personal life was like. I don't know if he was content. I don't know what his view of the universe was... Or *can* you?

Can you know an animal by its footprints? Can you know me by mine? Where do my words come from? From an essential me, a mercurial me, the 'me' of the moment? From some annoyed, saddened, gladdened, or maddened aspect of me? Probably yes to all. A running animal leaves tracks spaced far apart. A confused animal leaves circles of footprints spiraling and weaving. A hurt animal pauses often, leaving spots of blood in the snow or on fallen leaves... The same animal leaving... different prints. So can we know something of a *total* person, the *essential* person by looking at their tracks on a page? Is a composite-person asking you these questions? A multiple-personality self? A fundamental I-ness? Essential my-ness? I *feel* something essential. I even detect it, permeating into my personality. I feel this person speaking now has a *voice*...

I feel a lot more than the words I use, and I know you do, too. A portrait of words is convenient because it doesn't need to make sense in all its particulars to convey something of its totality.

It could be like a mirror. I look in the mirror—most often not too closely—but only see an opposite-person as daily companion, never the actual me, because I can't step outside of "me" to look directly at me. In the mirror, my hair is parted on *this* side, but it's really parted on *that*, as everybody else "knows." My scar, here, is really on the other side. So, with this book, a reader of my words will see what my mindless servant feet have done—obeying vague, arbitrary commands sent from the "head office"—but they'll never "know" what it feels like to be me. They'll *feel* it. Will they be "right"? Yes, of course they will be right; there's <u>no way</u> they could be right about what it feels to be me. But you know, *it happens*.

We're all a book. Most get thrown into the hole unwritten. Big, thick books of years and years of memories and experiences—down with the ship, no survivors. I watched my dad's parents die like this, their books largely unopened. One day, driving back from the hospital where my grandmother lie dying, my grandfather Harry, a stern man of few reflective words, made a passing comment about some fields we were driving by in the fall dusk. "I worked those fields," he said. I'd assumed out loud that it was with the tractor I knew he'd used for years. "No!" he scornfully growl-barked. "With mules; later with the Farmall."

I heard those hours and hours of solitary hours spent under sun and rain and days and days in his voice, his tone, his look out the car window. But he said nothing of it. Years later, recovering in a nursing home after having broken his femur in a fall, nearing his ninetieth birthday and years after his wife's eventual death, he repeated to me, as if it were a particularly revealing revelation, "I never thought I would end up here. I never thought it'd be like this."

I think that when the end of our lives comes or is nearing (nearing the last stop on the train line), we're possibly too occupied in the business at hand to be 'reflective' about ourselves and our lives. So, the book gets chucked into the hole with us, to land on our folded hands, unopened. We're all a book—beginning middle and end—and most are never read.

So there's my partial motivation for this book. If I'm allowed, by my destiny or fate, I have plans for other books: a collection of short stories, a first novel attempt, books written on themes. I don't count on being able to do them; I don't count on being able to do *this* one, but I'm keeping at it while I can. The Titanic is going down (they all are), and I'm making the effort of painting on this canvas: "Study of an Animal Leaving Tracks."

A picture can be put together of this animal talking in its head to you. Could an omnipotent, all-knowing God know me? No! says 'I'. Not without living in my shoes every second. Maybe God does this. Maybe we *are* God. An image: a God-finger pointing down at the inconsequential moon named David, who squeaks in its orbit, "I believe! I am unique!" But that ever-loving pointing finger is not the moon, remember? From the other side of this mirror, can this moon, desperate for uniqueness, know itself? Can the forest see itself, in spite of its total identification with forest-ness? "I" can't see myself objectively and another can't know me completely. Sounds like we're all in this alone. Sounds like I need a therapist.

I need a therapist not identified with the things I think are important. And yet... this specialist can't be a valid authority on me and myself until he thinks with my thoughts, and walks in my shoes. Otherwise, he'll be an outsider interpreting me and my actions through his <u>own</u> set of self-based understandings. Totally valid for oneself, sure. Thinking with another's thoughts... That would be method acting: walking and talking a part. There's no "acting" them; there's being what you "are." Screen and stage actors get awards for losing themselves in a role, becoming indistinguishable from another person by thinking with that person's thoughts and patterns.

I read things by other authors that move me profoundly. My reading their considered mind-products (words), somehow affects me, changes me, and creates a reactive mood in me. Through this mood, I feel things I've never felt, consider things never considered, and *pick up on their pattern*... I guess there's hope for understanding. Understanding enough.

Can God walk and talk my part and simultaneously be an impartial witness of this animal leaving its confused and hurried, slow and deliberate tracks in the snow? Maybe he does just that. Maybe God *is* the universe. Maybe what people call God is the totality of everything. In a hundred years I won't be here. I'll be gone like I never was—a faded echo will remain, if that. And these pseudo-speculations will be old tracks leading nowhere, not quite brushed out yet. Or, maybe they were obliterated five minutes later by a necessary road construction project. Where does my understanding of this coming-and-going life leave me *now*?

The type of thinking associated with these words is what drove me to look for some solid answer to life while I was here, alive. I wanted to *know* what the real overview was. I'd experienced various over-moods that I could look at my life through; they shifted kaleidoscopically with currents of my perceptions and ponderings, but they weren't a final, stable perspective. I sensed such a view existed. I sensed that there *was* a final solid perspective, one which would "answer" everything—or *be* the answer to everything. From that cannon shot of my dad's death, to the rumblings of the avalanche that calved away from the cliffs of myself, I found myself asking, "*What? What?...* I wanted to know the meaning of life. I doubt that many people who hear this know what I mean. Maybe <u>everyone</u> who hears this knows exactly what I mean, but decides to go with the flow. For those who are driven like I was, *they'll* know... enough.

So what *is* the meaning of life? Who ever finds the answer? Who ever dedicates themselves to the search for this answer that is often felt but never found? For these questions, I would answer, "*Me*" and "*me.*" In the beginning, I totally disregarded people who were sure, who *knew* that there was no answer (they knew the world was flat) because I *felt the pull* of something greater, my own sureness that there was something big residing in the place where this question leaned. I didn't have the answer, but I *knew* I could feel... something.

Chapter 31 —Starting Over Again for the First Time

I am leaning towards a hoped-for life condition for myself and family. I would like to live in France. We can go over there with nothing, stay with family and depend on the kindness of strangers at first, fighting it out of the mud *that* way, but I'd rather not. Not again. I'm not twenty, and my willingness to start over from scratch is….low.

Though not important on a cosmic or planetary scale, I'll say my life events are important to me. This book is a recording of happenings, as well as various products of my mind. Returning to the States at twenty after leaving the active Army, I had to 'decide' what to do with my life and rejoined the remnant of my family then living Lake City, Florida. My dad had died and my sister had moved out to be with her then-boyfriend now-husband of many years. I got my first apartment and first post-military job. After two years, I was laid off and enrolled in a community college because the greatness I'd been awaiting hadn't come yet.

[What is a decision? I don't know if I can comprehend the totality of that concept. I doubt my ability to sketch an image of it with words. What is a feeling of "fate" or "destiny"? What do we call the part of us that holds out, waiting for something "better"? Who is doing the weighing of advantages and disadvantages? What part can look into the future and play out a certain line of possibility? Who is the "decider" and what is motivating them? Is this the survivor, reproducer, goal-achiever, lover? At different ages, I've found different characters seem to inhabit this office in my own private White House. A 'decision', whatever that really is, has resulted in whole new scenes for me, whole different jobs and surroundings at turning points in my life.]

Moving to Pittsburgh to attend Pitt—that was a 'starting over' at 25. A new city, no job yet, enrolled in a four-year university.

Moving into a friend's (B.K.'s) two-story former ashram house in the South Hills of Pittsburgh when my first wife divorced me. It was a blow to my life-as-planned at 29. A 'plan' had coalesced as we lived our shared lives—moving to Tennessee where I would get my master's and teach writing at a community college and she would… I forgot what.

[People constantly remind me I haven't mentioned much in this book about the facet and years of my life with my first wife. They're right. If you feel that I've teased you by hinting at things but withholding the details, I apologize. I don't want to write about that part of my life because I am living in another world, with another person, with children of our own and a home of our own. I don't want to exhume an old, dead life. Maybe I can write short stories that embody lessons learned or times experienced 'back then.' For now, I'm going to leave that shovel and pickaxe in the tool shed…]

Moving to Memphis at 31 felt like a decidedly new chapter. After three months in a remote cabin on Richard Rose's farm [*not to be confused with my week in the woods and one endless night of hell in a cabin at 29*], I moved to that Mississippi River town with no place to stay, no job, no formed plans except to *find* a job and place to live before the spring semester, when my classes at graduate school in the English Department of the University of Memphis start. I stayed at a veterans' home for recovering addicts the first night, then three weeks in a tent at Graceland KOA, where I saw Elvis' private jet, the *Lisa Marie*, whenever I'd unzip the tent flap each morning to go shower before work as a painter at the FedEx headquarters.

Moving to Stuttgart, Germany, to live with Andrée—having disenrolled from classes in grad school and buying a one-way ticket to Europe. At 32, that was a definite change. I'd no idea what that would entail. It didn't *feel* as drastic as other changes because there was a roof over my head and a feeling of security—Andrée'd be there to help me. It turned out to be one of the biggest changes in my life, of course. Starting a whole new life plan—because we were going to get married and because I'd left my American life with no intention of going back.

Moving to Ramonville Saint Agne, in Southern France near Toulouse. *That* was a big change. Going there with my fledgling family—wife, oldest son and two cats, along with a mountain of furniture and possessions—to an uncertain future and to live an idealistic dream of creating *Le sanctuaire de l'extreme* for action sports practitioners. 34-years-old.

Returning to the States after selling and rebuilding our demonstration skate park permanently in Saint Lys, a small town north of Toulouse, saying goodbye and <u>*Sorry*</u> to all the members of our association, *Dream Extreme*, and everyone we'd come to know and love. That was a big, big move that was <u>really</u> starting over from scratch with nothing. Living in my best friend's basement for a few weeks before finding a single-wide mobile home to live in. What to do now? was a question that I'd grown used to finding a way of answering by bringing my best to the game, day by day. 35-years-old.

2005. Moving to the Wheeling area after a couple of good years running summer skate parks in Fowlerville, Michigan for that area's young, excited, earnest children. We were searching for a place to raise our sons, where we wouldn't have to move from for awhile. We headed east. Starting new, again. No friends to rely on this time. No family. No job. I was going to get a job writing for the Wheeling paper. I got it. Then I quit the same day. Thus began the dread-full quest for *any* kind of work. I was on my way down to a warehouse on the river in Martins Ferry for a press gang call when an aquaintence called and asked whether or not I had some time on my hands to paint his house. "And how," was all I could say.

I'll always be grateful. This was my first step on my current career trail as self-employed handyman painter. That friend, N.G., also introduced me to Richard Rose when I was 25. I owe this friend a debt of gratitude twice over. I was 38 when I started working for myself. I'm 44 now [and counting].

Big step, that one. I felt unemployable. Between all my 'starting over' points, I worked more than thirty different jobs and was growing weary of beginning anew. That's more than thirty first days on the job. More than thirty learning-new-computer-systems, new machines, new rules, new routines, and on and on—each one a world. I couldn't keep putting on the happy-to-learn-what-you-have-to-teach-me-sir act. My last job for someone else was at Precise Finishing Systems in Howell, Michigan. Each solitary second on the job I tiredly treaded water in the overwhelming feeling of dread and certainty I was wasting my life.

I didn't doubt this sense. I questioned where it came from, certainly. It was my destiny calling. It felt inevitable. I *yearned*, more than anything, to be able to feel contented with my job. It was the best job I'd ever had, after all! Nice people; I was good at the work and it was suited to me; I had a steady income, security, etc. But I was simply staring into the distance all day, every day. A friend recently asked whether my "thoughts and feelings were fooling me." What can I say? Sure? It was my reaction to perhaps my whole lifetime. Many things factor into a person's appraisal of things—which can all boil down to one thing. A woman who'd given birth a dozen times; a soldier who'd seen death upon death and experienced terror upon terror. Ask if their feelings and thoughts are "fooling them" when they walk away from a job. I don't have the answer to my friend's question. I'd given up digging that particular hole—of analyzing my motivations and reasons for every act. I'm past that? Yes. I'm lazy, that way.

I'm in my seventh year as boss-of-one and employee-of-many. I'm proud. I don't feel the daily dread, so I've got that going for me. My life is… even.

Still, I have a vision and view of the life I feel would be optimal—one I was always meant to have. It goes like this:

I'll think and feel and write. Write opinion pieces, edit a periodical, write poetry. I'll work on books. Always work on a book. A collection of stories, a novel.

Andrée will work as an artist, painting works and murals and entering exhibits and selling prints of her original work on her website, **frenchfineart.wordpress.com**. We'll live in the States and in France—Brittany or Normandy and New York State or California. I can attend TAT meetings when I'm on this side of the ocean. We'll home school our boys until they're done with school. They'll be truly bi-lingual, living in both societies.

I'll publish books, Andrée will paint, create and sell artwork. The boys will grow up in France and be able to attend universities in Europe. *That's* what I want.

I simply want to spend more of my time staring at water. That's what I was made to do. This past January and February I did that every day. I'd trudge through the thigh-deep snow in my snow pants and stare at the snow swirling across the frozen pond in our village park. The snow would blow and the trees sigh and groan and I would be at home, again, for the first time since I was a boy. This was the ending I was made for.

Thanksgiving 2010. It's in the past now. How different was it from 1710? The year 10? 2010 B.C.? I'm grateful. I take being alive for granted most of the time.. Andrée's in her studio painting a watercolor memorial portrait of a man in our village who died a couple days ago. He and his wife had had a string of what most would call bad luck. First something bad happened, then something else bad happened, then their furnace broke, then the woman hit a deer with her car and then the man died of a heart attack. So, I'm reminded of… the verities of life. Calamity, windfall, shock, acceptance, peace and calm, catastrophe and death. These are truths. Storms and sun.

Andrée and I just argued the way only married couples can argue. It's a routine thing that comes around with unwelcome regularity. We've been married eleven years. We've known each other for twenty-eight years, although this 'knowing' doesn't count; being together is what counts; it's when you are in each other's lives daily, weekly, yearly—and it *is* better and worse.

It would be great to have mandated clubs that meet for sharing and supporting those a little under their current level. The Ten-Year Club, the Twenty-Year Club. Like the VFW (Veterans of Foreign Wars). The misery that loves company can then commiserate. There would be an outreach (or downreach) program where Forty- and Fifty-Year clubbers would visit the Ten- and Twenty Year-ers, offering the benefit of their hard-won wisdom and experience. Maybe marriage could last more persistently as an institution if there were a formal support structure for this crazy fundamental arrangement we humans call marriage. *What do geese, who mate for life, call it?*

I just talked to my brother and his kids at their church in Reykjavik where they're preparing for their Thanksgiving banquet. I used Skype and got to see and hear them for the first time in some months, I'd say. Pat took us on a tour of renovations he's in the middle of, through the hangar-like structure that houses his "Christian missionary in Iceland" church.

I then spoke to Mom and Anne and her kids in Tennessee on Skype. It was good seeing all of them in their environment. Anne was peeling potatoes, her daughter Samantha was taking photos, Glen, her son, was outside helping his dad rake leaves. We carry on the same tradition of calling at Christmas and Thanksgiving that my parents had while I was growing up.

They don't have Thanksgiving in Europe, so there won't be a call to France for *that*, but Andrée's dad periodically calls—during the morning here—using Skype. Its nice seeing into their living room I remember being in—what feels like yesterday, in l'Isle sur la Sorgue. Andrée's mom is devotedly no-tech, but her brother Eric has a computer at home so we can send photos or share uploaded videos of us with Andrée's nephew and niece, my boys' cousins, Maxime and Maude. Andrée's sister, Isabelle in Saint Malo has three wonderful daughters who we occasionally contact on Skype; they don't have a webcam, so we can't see them, but we can hear them and they can see us and seem to enjoy seeing into our living room in Flushing.

This is not a paid product placement for Skype (though it could be—hint, hint). It's to show that although we live near Wheeling, and far, far away from family, we are able, thanks to this blooming technology, to see loved ones we never could have in years past. We can look through a window into a part of their lives—living rooms, kitchens, porches. I grew up without the internet and with prohibitively expensive international phone calling. Now we have email, video phoning and unlimited calling to France with our internet telephone service. What will the future bring? Teleportation? The funny thing is how outdated this brief depiction of technical capability will be to each successive generation of people who come across these words. I'm assuming this memoir will survive on shelves to be read by a descendant some day.

The way things are going, I'm not so sure books will exist. Everything is going hand-held device. All will be Kindle readers and digital format mp3 file downloads, streaming and cloud computing. The matrix. Nothing will exist on shelves but…

So what will Thanksgiving 2011 bring? What about 2051? Where will the meteor hit? One thing I am sure of: never-ending-seeming process.

There is progression to a dripping faucet. It starts out as a newly-installed, shiny, working object in a new kitchen. After years of use, the rubber washers, springs and O-rings wear out and the faucet handle moves looser. In time, a water drop hangs from the faucet end, dropping off whenever someone bumps the sink or closes a door. With time, the drop falls with slow regularity. I recently replaced the rubber seats and springs in a neighbor's kitchen faucet that had been dripping twice a second.

These neighbor friends had been collecting the dripping water to water their plants outdoors. The dripping noise had become increasingly annoying. What if they left one day, never to return? The water would have continued to leak until building up mineral deposits inside the cartridges constricted the places that the water could flow; the drip became a dribble that would have run down the underside of the faucet and caused an encrusted line to form down the stainless steel sink to the drain. There, this line—calcium, iron and other dissolved minerals—would take on a green-black tinge as mold and slime established itself in this miniature river valley. Dust would have continually settled on the electrostatically-attractive damp surface of this slowing river, adding substrate for more mold cultures. Decades would pass (assuming the furnace still ran in winter and the copper water lines didn't freeze and burst). The roof would begin leaking where shingles blow off in a wind storm. Birds and wasps move into first the soffit and fascia, and then the attic, and then in corners in closets. From the garage, there would be an ingress into the house where woodpeckers or rats had chewed a hole through the drywall. Rotting rafters, sagging and moldy drywall ceiling, spreading damp circles on the floor. A century would bring this house down on itself in places; the house itself would slump, settling lower every fall, growing smaller each spring as trees, hedges, tall weeds and vines grow over, obscuring and blurring the edges of this once-new structure.

This house was brand-new once. A painter carefully cut with his brush around the window casement trim; carpet layers put the final touches on their job; roofers put the last blob of asphalt sealant on the last shingle of the ridge. People mowed the grass weekly and friends and family rang the doorbell the first time. This place had a birth and a process continues. This place is one speck on a continuum—as are, apparently, every one of us.

Chapter 32 —Final Message in a Bottle

No man is an island, said John Donne during his time on this world in the modern-day 1600s London. We're also, each of us, utterly alone, as I now fondly tell people whenever appropriate. Think: *Who is in your shoes?* No one. Most books are buried. By books I mean people, of course, and their lives and experiences. I wanted to write this recording of myself while I could, this minute, typing. Who knows what the next minute will bring in this ever-changing windmill dripping faucet called life. *Everyone say this:* "*My…life… My… Life…*"

For my children to get a feeling about how I felt about things and how I thought. Yes. For other wonderers, other seekers of wisdom and answers who may be reassured and encouraged that a similar soul existed. Yes. For me. Sure. Tomorrow may never come… When it comes to details in this reality we loosely call life, this constant flow of events like weather, we can know trends and probabilities—only after they've occurred. Like statistics. *This* number of people typically lose their job during this month. *This* number retires each fall. *This* number buys a new car.

This is what I have to say this morning [again, now, too, two years ago—and the clock is ticking, relentlessly…]. In a hundred years, or a hundred thousand, something might feel different from *this* moment, as I breathe in and out. The cave artists in Lascaux, in southwestern France, 17,000 years ago, breathed in and out, too. I can imagine watching them paint. The artists, 30,000 years ago, who left the Upper Paleolithic cave paintings in Altamira Cave, near Cantabria, Spain, breathed in and out, cut their fingers, stubbed toes, laughed. I focus on these artists from the foggy modern-day stone age past because they were saying: *This is life; this is my life, my experience of living. These animals are part of my life.*

The following is excerpted from an email correspondence with M.L., a guy two decades younger than I am, living on the East Coast. He'd finished his email to me with, "What do you think about all of this? Any suggestions would be much appreciated." I'll pick up from my 'suggestion' section of my reply.

Sunday, November 28, 2010

Hi M.,

….I think you might benefit from hearing from a number of different people. I think there's a triangulation effect, as I'm sure you know, from hearing from a number of different points of view. Each person, other than you, is standing in their own unique position. They're on their own life path, in whatever position they are on. Some perhaps older than you, some after traumas, some after years of effort and some who have transcended aspects of themselves that had previously held them up. Of course, I'm preaching to a member of the choir because I sense or suspect that you are already doing this—getting other's perspectives.

The thing is, I don't know or recognize many people whose paths and lives I can relate to. By "relate to," I mean: recognize as being very similar to myself and my 'way.' Who is right? The person that echoes my own thinking! So, my way is the way I relate to the world; the way I have approached and dealt with obstacles in my life; the way I have hoped and yearned for things—and the way I view the world and its happenings now.

It's good for you, I suspect, that I don't have a whole list of people I 'relate' to. If I trotted out a whole list of people I could 'relate to,' you'd just be getting a lot of things that sounded the same, and what's the point of that? Except… maybe it would feel like a kind of validation; that this perspective or opinion is "right."

What I'm talking about is separate from the final or satisfactory conclusion that [some fortunate] people arrive at. Separate but intertwined. One guy is angry, an extrovert, an introvert, sad primarily, happy, and on and on. Everyone is different. Their 'ways' reflect this difference. But the end of all their ways, and lives, might be very, very similar (with different words, taken from each of their private dictionaries in their heads, all pointing at something they've all felt).

One guy, Shawn Nevins, who I don't resemble or relate to much at all in terms of similarities in background, personality type and so on, is very similar in terms of outlook and perspective. The voice he writes with and the answers he gives to questions I hear people posing are things I recognize; I feel I would have said nearly the same things.

This is what drew me to Rose, I think. I recognized in his words something I'd always felt or known as he said them. I heard a bell when he talked. So there's the birds-of-a-feather-flock-together thing, perhaps. Certain birds relate to certain birds.

So maybe check out what some others [have to] say on your comments or life situation. [Even from *different* 'birds'] The following people are those who I think might have something valuable to say to you. Translated: they are the people I feel match something in you and I like where they're coming from, perspective-wise. This isn't logical; it's intuitional. They're all different, of course, but maybe you'll get something from hearing a spectrum of replies to your stuff.

So, try emailing Shawn Nevins. I'd suggest specific questions. You already talk to A. M., I assume. I think his view would be good, especially on specific questions. Tell him what you said, and ask for his suggestions, comments or advice. M. W.'s perspective might be valuable. I think he would give your comments the benefit of his perspective and life experience. In some ways, you remind me of P. C., so you might see what his take would be on your thing. I think M. C. might have a good perspective for you. He doesn't do email anymore, I believe. H. M. would probably have his phone number. From what I hear, he is very willing to talk to anyone on the phone. H. is a good person too, for that matter, to bounce ideas off. Ask her [for] specific advice, comments, and answers.

[I was suggesting that "M.L." approach others I know in the TAT Foundation whose thinking patterns vary but who all share a similar quality—all people serious about their thing. I believe you

have to use other people; compare notes with them, see what they have to say about your subject. We delude ourselves pretty readily (it's the royal 'we' I'm using) and encountering others' opinions—comparing our own ideas to those of others—helps shake us up a bit; we see our ideas or positions as a thing apart, where formerly, we saw through these things and weren't even aware that we had the glasses on....]

I relate to Ramana Maharshi and Nisargadatta. At least, to what I've read that is attributed to these guys. *I Am That*, by Nisargadatta (Q&A) and a collection of Q&A with Ramana Maharshi [*Be as You Are: The Teachings of Sri Ramana Maharshi*]. I like Marcus Aurelius, the 1st century Roman Emperor, author of *Meditations*. I like Peace Pilgrim, a woman who walked her talk, literally. If you Google search Peace Pilgrim, you can get a copy of her book, *Peace Pilgrim: Her Life and Works in Her Own Words* from the foundation that makes them available. They'll ship one to you for free, although they rely on donations. The Q&A section at the end of her book [is] great. I like *The Essential Rumi*, a collection of poetry from the 13th century Persian Sufi mystic. There's a lot of freeing things in there.

I'm a big fan of Hermann Hesse's. All of his books and stories. *The Poet*, a short story and his little book Siddhartha, are good ones that ring a chord with me. I got a lot out of the Carlos Castaneda books, starting with *The Teachings of Don Juan*. [The notion of being a warrior, a steer-er of one's own ship.] I like Willa Cather's work. Everything I've read by her is good. *Paul's Case* is a short story that resonated. Probably because I know Pittsburgh, where the story takes place, but something else, too. *Beyond Mind, Beyond Death* is a surprising collection of *TAT Forum* (http://tatfoundation.org/forum.htm) essays and poetry. Surprisingly good. If you haven't read it, I highly recommend it. And lastly, Shawn Nevins' talk, *Is My Hair on Fire Yet?*, in the *What is Spiritual Action?* DVD box set of the April 2006 TAT meeting. Highly, highly recommend this—for you. Just watched it recently again with the M&M group in Wheeling. His talk is worth the time, but <u>especially</u> the Q&A. Couldn't get much better.

All of the stuff here is probably obtainable in a good library. Except for the TAT stuff, of course....

Now, on to your comments.

My world has been getting pretty interesting lately. I recently took a job working with mentally handicapped kids my age which has kept me pretty busy. It also has the added benefit of making me feel like I'm giving something back, or doing something for someone else besides myself.

Well, you're dabbling in wisdom beyond your years (or mine or anyone's). I think there's a great deal to 'learn' from doing what you're doing. To learn about yourself and others. And to become something else.

Like I say that being a parent and a husband in the family scenario is 'completing' me in a way that nothing else could, I think that the activity you are engaged in calls forth latent aspects of "you" that could never have come to the surface no matter how much speculation or introspection you did, because, before you step up to the plate you have never swung the bat at a ball before. We have potential (to fight, to love, to share) that remains only that, potential, until we actually do these things—and we can only do them when they are the appropriate response to some action done in close proximity to us. Someone hits us so we hit back. Someone needs help, so we offer it. And so on.

Obviously there still is a selfish aspect to it, but it feels good to see that I'm helping others, it's been something that has been missing from my life. As for the spiritual search I feel like things are finally starting to happen. I've been spending a lot of time looking at my direct experience and many questions have started to come up about who or what I am with a lot of force.

I assume the "selfish aspect" you're referring to is the self-knowledge or progress on the spiritual path [aspect]. I can really relate to your saying that helping others had been missing from your life. That's what I meant by family life 'completing' me. I'm in a position to do things like "help" on a daily basis.

I'm glad to hear about the "questions coming up with a lot of force." You have the potential of actually being a giant walking question mark. That is a true seeker who has <u>become the path</u>. This only means a seeker of truth who has stepped beyond idle speculation or latent potential. It's living wholly efficiently. Do you make use of 90 percent of the energy in a gallon of gas or only 20 percent? Do you walk and embody all of your potential in this direction or just a fraction? You know, Rose's "Law of Proportional Returns." [It is] when you walk your questions, live them, that… movement occurs, I believe.

Most of these questions are very simple but they come up with a lot of doubt as to what I believe. It seems that before I was so sure of what was what, even though I've read that certain aspects of experience should be questioned I never really believed that what I thought could be wrong.

Yes. Paradigm shifts. Seeing your old paradigm as a thing apart. Apart from your current or new position of standing. This is revealing and educational as hell—as it relates to simple existence and questions about all those unquestioned and accepted beliefs and assumptions that previously felt so solid, so reliable. At a certain point, I had nothing solid whatsoever. Only myself, floating in space, wondering with earnest intensity, what the hell was *really* going on.

Now much more doubt in what I believe has been coming up. These questions seem to center around the Douglas Harding experiments. It's kind of funny though, I read some of his stuff and couldn't really relate to it… I thought something that simple couldn't do it. But all of the sudden one day I noticed that absence of my own head for a moment or two and it became blatantly obvious that I had been imagining this head that I considered to be me behind my direct experience all these years as a reference point.

I didn't relate too much to some of Harding's words that I'd read either, although I have a pull to read Harding's *The Little Book of Life and Death*. [It's] the title. However, I liked watching the man in person, getting a feel for his perspective (in a [recorded lecture] a friend gave me). I don't know what he's got, but I've seen friends (Nevins, A.M.) seem to benefit from exposure to Harding and his ideas and experiments. If the absence of one's own head can be brought about by [his thought] experiments, then... Wow! That would be as good as a drug-induced introduction to something beyond the limited self with all of its attachments to accepted beliefs and assumed reality-attributes. What I mean is this bypasses a LOT of work that a normal, stupid seeker would need to do in order to arrive at this [same] point.

I remember almost three days of no mind or 'broken brain,' as I thought of it. No presence of the reflexive, reactive 'me.' It [was] utter silence, absolute motionlessness. I woke into another world where nothing moved and no sounds existed. *I* didn't exist. It came after an immense amount of tension or stress. If you can experience a similarly different experience from your normal one by doing an experiment, then wow. I don't know what ultimate value, for you, that would have, but it's <u>got</u> to have some benefit! Something different *must* be good. New data, right?

Instead of questioning with effort, new questions seem to arise the more I just look at what I'm seeing.

That's what I mean by being a walking question mark. To become a seeker is <u>not</u> to ask questions but is to <u>be</u> a question. You become one with the activity. I think there is a LOT here, in your "questioning with effort" reference. It implies will, of course. Of forcing or straining at an activity. So. What the 'LOT' I'm referring to is, is what lies underneath your particular and specific activity (of straining).

Who wants to do the questioning? **What** lies beneath or behind the "want"? What is the motivating thing? **Which** aspect or facet of the person you find yourself being is the "Who"? The activity, "questioning"—what specific guise does this activity take? It is very revealing to see what the tracks of the animal called M. look like. Looking at the "questioning" activity, what are the characteristics of this action, in-an-of-[itself]? They will be direct reflections of the assumptions and leanings of whatever aspect or agent (some facet of 'yourself') [that is] responsible for them.

I used my curiosity (like a flashlight)—once it finally occurred to me to do so—on myself. Where previously I would have strong reactions and opinions about things, now I suddenly looked at all of the products of 'myself' with the motive or underlying intention to understand what is there. To comprehend. This I called 'learning the geography' of myself. Just knowing the territory. Knowing one's hometown completely, with all the alleys and boulevards, all the names of the streets and businesses—[knowing myself] as well as a competent taxi driver in London is required to know their own intricate city.

The more I question these things the less I seem to know what is really going on, who I am, or what things are. Sometimes my experience becomes almost dream like and a lot more wonder has come into my life about what anything is at all.

Uh oh. I recognize this. Well, welcome to your club (no one exists here but you, I mean). Similarly, I remember when I was fascinated with perception. Literally seeing, hearing—all of that. I remember walking across the Birmingham Bridge to the South Side in Pittsburgh, looking down at the light dancing on the water. I remember looking at a marble floor at work at LRDC in Oakland. For a second, I was able to let go or drop my 'knowing' of what I was seeing.

Suddenly the world was dancing and shimmering a foot in front of my eyes. I felt they must be angels. The marble floor was deep; I could reach down into it forever. Around that time, I learned the trick of the eyes that you have to do to see the *Magic Eye* images [computer-generated three-dimensional holographic pictures that one must focus both eyes at different depths to "see"]. I would look at any regular pattern (floor tiles, wallpaper, etc.) and see depth that wasn't there in my 'normal' seeing. I suddenly saw that the reality I had so comfortably known, didn't exist. I walked in[to] a new open world of possibility.

My old 'known' world was a boxed-in, limited view fraught with assumptions and accepted-without-question explanations. But there was an immense thing 'out there' or 'in here' now that took my breath away. Quantum mechanics talks about probability; that nothing is certain—except this or that percentage of probability that something will occur (or be) here or there. String theory talks about vibrating energy and everything touching everything in this universe. Yes.

I guess all this opened up possibilities in my awareness. I suddenly let things be (where before I would quickly, reflexively 'define' them to myself). So I became more open, where previously I 'knew' things. This is my reaction to your comments about dream-like experience and wonder. Later, in Memphis, I focused on my dreams very intently for a while, and the 'normal' world dissolved and became flat, and the dreaming world became 'real', full and meaningful.

Experience. That's what this stuff is, though. I believe from my own... perspective, that there is something drastically more real than me. Something permanent exists—and it's not related to my experiences or me. It IS. And that's different. But I think the sense of wonder I felt, similar to a newborn's, was probably very important. Without that, I don't think much would have been possible. Before, I was too sure, too cemented into the belief in my explained-world. "Become as a child again to enter..." That's another true quote thing from the Bible.

The thing that upsets me is that when I attempt to put effort into this type of questioning it never seems to lead anywhere. It seems like these questions and this direct seeing happen spontaneously at times when I don't expect it to come.

Again, what kind of effort, specifically? **Who** is doing or directing that this effort be done? I'm not asking a rhetorical TAT-like question here. I'm being literal. Not holier-than-thou. What about wondering what the hell is going on here? And going where *that* question leads? I'm sure you already tend to do this, but this can be the royal road. Your way. Sometimes we have to, or maybe should, go after exactly what is being presented to us in our lives. Koans, they're called, these *seemingly* unanswerable questions. Rose said that life throws them at us by the handful; we don't have to go to a monastery and get one from a master. Our master, called our own life, is showering us with these koans (or, variations on a theme —our theme..). So.

One thing I realized is if I keep quiet then this headless seeing is more likely to come in. When I drive or when I can sit alone or in silence I try, that's one thing that seems to happen.

Again, I'd wonder what is going on. Really, I'd want to know the <u>why</u> underneath the statement above. If I understood the 'why,' I'd understand everything relating to the phenomenon. If you understood any one word in the dictionary (whether the one in your head or one on shelves or online), you'd understand every other word in the world/paradigm/dictionary. Because... well, you should be able to see why that statement *might* be true (it's not really true until you've verified it personally).

What do you know for sure?

[To understand completely any one word means you would have to understand its context; that means all the words relating to it, and what those mean, and on until the whole "universe" of words is gotten.

'Knowing my own geography' is like that. Why am I angry now? What do I mean by angry? What is angry compared to something else on a spectrum? *Why* is this spectrum? What is "now," compared to time, or circumstances, in general? Why do I have reactions at specific times I call 'now'? Once I understand the interrelated-ness of my reactions and those of others, I step back and ask, "Why is this the situation for us? Would an alien culture be exactly the same? What advantages, evolutionary-wise, do feelings of anger or happiness give me? Is there a God? What reason would God have for creating me, this questioning person? Why couldn't I be made perfect? Was God lonely? What do I mean by "God"? What I've accepted from others? What about me? What would God be for me?

This is what I did with myself. I didn't sit here with my head spinning with all the questions at once. I'd ponder each one at length and depth. It was better than being ignorant and continuing to resent misunderstood happenings in my sphere of awareness. It helped—me. I don't know if it did a single thing to bring about the extinguishing event I call my 'night of hell.' This kind of investigation and the corresponding epiphanies, insights and realizations certainly have no relation whatsoever to the 'other-than' condition resulting from obliteration. Nothing has any relation to that. What else could I do? Wallow in ignorance? I'd been doing that for years. I had to start where I was, with what I had; I was in my shoes, and I had my mind. I'll tentatively accept that this is the case, I thought. Now back to my letter to M.L.]

But my trying to bring the questions up myself usually yields very little.

Again, here's your own private "M. L. life koan," gift-wrapped and presented to <u>you</u>, the only inhabitant here in your life. Figure this one out, and you'll have one giant AH HA about your life. You'd see the grand pattern and your place in it and understand how it all fits together and why. That would be a *satori*. Like Rose's algebra example. Don't take my word. It's what I think.

Another added benefit of all this seeing is that silence is starting to come in where there was once incessant mental chatter. These periods are pretty short lived but very enjoyable.

I am hopeful for you. I wish you all the silence you can get. You deserve it. We all do. It's our right. Our gift from our existence. If we could just remember to *stop*, even ten minutes a day (in my case). Eternity is in the present moment, a guy said a couple of weeks ago in a Wheeling M&M meeting. Yeah. I've literally felt that. Not guessed, not thought or speculated. "Retreat to the present," I called it. Probably told you already. In a stressful time of my self-employed life I found this happening, of necessity.

This feeling of eternity in the present moment, however, is <u>not</u> the solid thing at the center of me. But maybe it's the closest that David, the reaction pattern person, can get. It feels a lot more peaceful than normal activity, and it bleeds over into the 'normal activity' after a while, I found. The solid thing at the center of me underlies my personality. It IS, and my personality tends to be (I'm purposely saying 'my personality' instead of the more accurate 'the personality' because I think speaking of oneself in the third person can sound pretentious--and probably is).

The silence, or peace my personality can experience in the present moment is nice but it's not *That*. *That*—the underlying solid-ness, which can become more... *pronounced* in [my personality during] a moment of silence or in rapport with someone close-enough—is something else altogether. I should just delete all of this, M., but for whatever reason I won't. I suspect this will be nothing but confusing, but what the hell.

> *[I wanted to make the point that the profoundest feeling of present moment-ness is not the same as that solid stillness at the center of me. A profound feeling of present moment-ness is the best that "I" can do; what results or what* Is *when "I'm" completely gone—is something else <u>altogether</u>. It is not orders of magnitude greater or lesser than the personality/ego/I; it is altogether other-than any of that or this. There I go again, trying so hard to show you, dear reader. You* know *what I mean.]*

M., I want to thank you for giving me the opportunity to react to your email comments. It's good exercise and I might get better with practice. I probably do better with specific questions. I can give you my automatic reactions to things you say. Sometimes I can get out of the way, or, more accurately said, I can allow truthful or appropriate reactions to come up without being in the way. How about trying throwing specific questions in my direction?

Well, I wish you well. Good to hear from you!

Dave

This young man had emailed me with comments about what he'd been up to recently and asked for my reactions or recommendations. We'd only met once in person; we spoke for maybe 30 seconds. He's a new member of the TAT Foundation. In a recent email, he said "Happy Thanksgiving" and I replied in kind, asking what had been happening in his world lately.

I gave someone my honest reaction to something. I responded. Sure, if given the chance I would edit what I said, trying to get it said better. But in this case, in this book, I'm putting my reactions to people out there—and here—pimples and all. Taking plaster casts of drying tracks in the mud before the next storm washes them away.

I do this in daily life—give people my best reaction. As soon as I write that, I get guilty flashes of numerous times when my sons interrupted me when I was busy—when I didn't give them my best. When I said, "Uh huh," distractedly, or "Not now!" How long will my sons continue to come to me to show me something or to ask me something? Parents of older kids have told me that this gradually stops happening until puberty and then, wham! The door is closed. Ho, ho, ho. Oh no.

I try to, hope to, respond to someone in kind, bringing my own outlook to the scene. At the bank, we exchange comments about the weather, and who prefers what temperature range. With a customer, we talk about their paint job or renovation, and I give my professionally-based comments.

When I get an email, I respond. What I'm getting at is I don't have the inner machinations that go into a well-considered reply. I find it easier to not lie. I consider the subject matter, not the political context. If a woman at the bank asks me about what I think about the purpose of life, I'll give her my honest answer—not one crafted or considered for some other reason—but it'll be aimed at <u>her</u>.

Last week, at the M&M Philosophy meeting in Wheeling, a guy about ten years older than I am spoke philosophically about his view of life upon seeing his dad take his last breath in a hospital bed. Today, my youngest son Ben (who's working on a Christmas book of crayon coloring for me that he's writing, illustrating and stapling together) told me that when he grows up, he wants to be "almost exactly like" me.

This guy at the M&M meeting, Mike, said that upon watching his dad take his last breath, he thought that one day he, too, would take his last breath, which caused him to wonder what life was all about, and I replied, "Yeah. Exactly. That's what drove *me*. I was a dreamer, a wonderer, but my dad's death was a catalyst and suddenly all I was able do was ask, 'What? What? What is going on here?'"

To Ben, when he said that he wanted to be almost exactly like me, I said I hoped he would grow up to become better than me because it would make me feel like I was a good parent.

When Ben seemed to think this reply was not preferable, I said, "If *you* had a son who grew up not quite as good as you, not quite as strong or smart, you might feel sad because, you know, you want the <u>best</u> for *your* boy! Right? So, I want the *best* for you! I want you to be *better* than I am. That would make me happy." A big grin now replaced my then-six-year-old's uncertain frown. He knew that I loved him, and this was enough. He was saying he held me in high regard—that he loved me —when he said he wanted to be almost exactly like me one day.

This book is my message in a bottle—a big bottle. It's for anyone who reads it. I don't expect *you* to be endlessly fascinated by my life (I used to, until in fourth grade at St. Joseph's Catholic school in Howell, I had the sad realization that no one was as captivated by the details of my opinions as I was). In fact, based on past interactions, I expect many to be what is referred to as "bored" by my strung-together mind-products. I'm betting there *are* some who relate to my point of view. If you relate to some of what I've said, I am grateful to be on *this* side of our relationship coin.

Be you descendent, stranger or a friend; for having read this far, I say, "Well met."

Covered bridge at the Flushing exit off I-70 where I like to spend ten minutes whenever I can.

I wanted to write a multi-media book, download-able on line, that you could copy or excerpt from. A thing with hypertext links, video clips, photos, audio clips, prose, poems, essays, correspondence, short stories and more. If there are E-books, the next logical step would be multi-media books. In Douglas Adams' book, *Hitchhiker's Guide to the Galaxy*, his character, Arthur Dent, consults whenever seeking diversion or explanation. That book is *worlds-wide-web-enabled* to continuously incorporate constant updates to its contents. In fact, that imaginary book of Adams' was so voluminous that the only way it could be accessed was through a virtual reader; this is the form the *Guide* takes—a web-enabled connected reader. Adams' literal guide to the galaxy took up as much volume as a medium-size city.

Maybe I'll have this book continuously updated and built into the headstone at my grave… Naaah. Still, a Wi-Fi broadcaster in the headstone would have a 200-meter zone people could repose within —along with their portable devices—to access the streamed content… Maybe just a name with a start and end date is more accurate and appropriate, in the grand scheme of things.

The hopefully longer-lived singer songwriter friend from another generation, Yodeling Dick Brooks, a.k.a. Richard Bruce Morriale, has a wonderful song, "My Never Ending Song." When I listen to it, I have the feeling of something that just continues on, pleasantly forever. I think it's a ten-minute song. It's soothing and wonderful and I could listen to it constantly. It has some reincarnation themes in it, as well as his Methuselah notions of living nearly two centuries. There's also a feeling of leaving something behind, some momento, when he finally *does* go—if only that song. Future virtual editions of *this* book will include an audio clip of Dick's song.

October 2010: Ben, 6, cutting his Jack-O-Lantern by himself for the first time.

Portrait of a Seeker: Born to Wonder, has finally materialized out of dream-space —or at least out of one dream-place into another. Like any good or bad idea, things tend to fade or exist only within a mood until I actually *do something* to make it "tangible." For seven years I've walked around with this half-forgotten, persistent notion in the back of my head where it hid in a corner to avoid the blanketing dust of forgetfulness. Now that my footprints have been left in the dust, I can leave the chamber and venture out into new territories. Anything's possible.

Once a start is made, habitual force and inertia—Newton's First Law of Motion—says, "The tendency of an object in motion is to remain in motion, or an object at rest, to remain at rest, unless acted upon by a force." With this in mind, it is likely I will continue to do something, footprint-wise, until I am stopped or acted upon.

I'll never be as good an author as I'll be by my twentieth book, but I'll never get to number twenty until I've written the nineteen previous, less-than-perfect volumes. I hope I'm around—and you're around too—for that twentieth work. Short stories, novels, opinion pieces, collections of poetry and essays are on the way. I'm grateful to have had your company on this first leg of my literary journey. I feel like I have a new friend. Good luck in your life. I hope you find all that you want. Meet you at the finish line.

David W. Weimer
Flushing, Ohio.
2011

From a handout for a talk I gave at the Wheeling Island Holistic Center a few years ago called, "On Becoming a Modern Mystic." A friend reading this suggested that I add "Doing an isolation and helping others" to the list.

"On Becoming a Modern Mystic"

or

21 Things That I Wish I Had Told Myself When I Was Younger:

This isn't for other people. I'm no authority on others' lives; they've got to become that on their own. They might find this useful, however. If I could have talked to an earlier version of myself and that self had asked me for pointers, here is what I would have said:

Dave, once you notice that finding an answer to your life is more important than anything else, make a personal commitment to achieve this thing and go for it. Make it your life's career.

Start where you are, with what you have. No need to say, "I don't know where to begin." No one does. Start. You won't regret it.

1. **Become honest**. Start with "small" things. This isn't vague. Be honest with yourself and others. How can you become the Truth when you're telling lies?

2. **Go to bookstores**, online book sources and libraries. Keep your eyes and ears open for book recommendations. Read intuitively. If a book doesn't do it for you, close it without looking back but *check them all out*, especially the ones that you don't think will help you.

3. **Listen** to those people that you don't automatically agree with. Try.

4. **Walk into fearful opportunities**. You know hesitation and its fruits; this is familiar territory. Take one step forward when you feel fear. You'll enter a new world where acting on hunches and intuition is the major mode.

5. **Question** your actions, decisions and reactions. Why are you doing what you're doing? Be very honest (see #1).

6. **Check out groups** and anything else that is remotely related to your search, quest, and purpose in life (examples: yoga, meditation, study groups, prayer groups, esoteric philosophic groups, religious groups, astrology, divination, psychology, etc.). You are an explorer in search of an answer. Look under every rock.

7. **Adopt a <u>daily</u> meditation practice**. Sit, run or walk. Do what seems right. Be consistent and persistent. You've admitted to yourself that this is a worthwhile pursuit.

8. **Don't** do <u>anything</u> that you don't want to do (that someone tells you to do). Do what *you* think is best for yourself; it's your boat, not theirs. Don't do what a spiritual seeker "should do."

9. **Keep a journal** like a mountain climber who records daily climbing activities in the tent after each day. Thoughts can be captured and examined by writing them down. <u>You</u> are the most available subject matter at hand in this quest for enlightenment, truth or ultimate answers. Writing is working through things.

10. **Keep a dream journal**. What do you have to work with in this most subjective endeavor? Study these definitive products of your mind.

11. **Conserve all of your personal energy** for this most important task at hand. Free from all other addictions and obsessions, every bit of energy and attention can be poured into a desired direction towards an answer. Practice celibacy; free yourself from alcohol, tobacco, drugs, and television programs. These are some places where you may spend tremendous amounts of time and energy doing nothing getting nowhere.

12. **Strain** in the direction of your yearning with all of your might.

13. Go on spiritual retreats. Go on any retreat.

14. **Try** fasting with a spiritual purpose or profound intention in mind.

15. **Spend time around those** that you have a common interest with. Compare notes with these others who are on their own personal path toward an ultimate answer.

16. **Hunt** for gurus, masters and authorities on this most important subject. Nail them with the most important questions that you have.

Don't' be intimidated. No one is more important in your life than you. It is your sacred right to find your life's meaning. Ask, "What do you know?" Genuine teachers will meet you readily and honestly on your level of inquiry. False ones will play games and play God.

17. Learn to pray for help.

18. **Learn to continue walking** or climbing when there is no guidance from others. When you die, the only thing that you'll have is what you've discovered or become in your lifetime. Other people's words and books—all books, all people—will dissolve, leaving you with only yourself. You can be afraid or uncertain at times, and still do your best with this sacred life. Be your own captain. Steer your boat.

19. **Look into** hypnotism. Be hypnotized. Learn to hypnotize other people. Try fire walking. Try skydiving. Challenge yourself.

20. **Give yourself the authority to stand up and do your best** in your life. Give yourself the authority to make your own decisions about things.

21. **Live in another country**. Learn the language. Go native.

Finally:

Two 'lost' named chapters from this book—both places I intended to go in this narrative. Much has been left out, remaining behind, by the side of my road.

I want to leave these two chapter headings here, like headstones where I will faithfully replace withered flowers. I will remember they once were.

Lest we forget—and we do (I do), each day in our onrushing, unfolding, ever-melting snow people lives.

- Two companion cats missed now and fading fast, like these magic marker words in Guillaume's nine-year-old hand, written on Grizelda's cross under the pear tree near our garden that I push the mower around in the summer and that is currently weathering a third winter:

Grizelda's Grave
Age 18, liked milk
and very friendly.
We will miss you Griz
Dad, Mom, Guillaume, Ben

- The world-within-a-world of our time living in France creating *The One and Only Skate Park Project* and *l'association Dream Extreme*. Encountering our hundreds of like-minded friends, being on live French television, featured in magazines and in newspapers, creating idealism, excitement, friendships and skate park dreams. I cracked the door, but never let you in.

Chapter 33—Eighteen-year Unwritten Arc

Grizelda and Emerald:

World-Traveling Cats:

From Then to Now.

As you read this, I reach over and feel Griz's side—her laying on a couch beside me. Emerald is over there, in the dining room, on her chair under the table.

CHAPTER *34—What We Actually Did and Where We Are Now.*

Skate Park Together Dreams:
Andrée and I carry this story inside our hearts and heads.
—what we actually did over there
France; where we went and where we are.

Previously-Designated Chapter 11

Eons surround us,
unnoticed.
Time walks uphill
steadily.
Steady as rain.

Photos

5011 Jewell Road house, circa 1975. Photo taken with Brownie box camera mom gave to me.

Me and my jeep, in Germany, backed into a ditch. 1986.

7 Apr 2000, from Montmartre, top of "Sacre Coeur," while visiting Henri Lepérou, to ask for Andrée's hand in marriage.

Me, 8, with peaches from our tree in front of Howell back porch, circa 1975.

Andrée, Nov. '99, Paris, to make our rings and to ask her father.

School photo. 15- or 16-years-old.

Landing at Petersburg Airport, Ohio, 1993. First tandem skydive.

Last grade before St. Joseph Catholic School & move to Howell family farm. (3rd row up, 3rd from right).

Taken at 18, in Bravo Btry., 1/32 FA, Fliegerhorst Kaserne, Germany.

Me with Daisy at Howell house, circa 1976.

Eleven-years-old. Showing dogs.

1991, Jungle Warfare training, Panama.

July 2006, at Dad's grave in Fowlerville, Michigan cemetery with Gui, 6, and Ben, 3.

Andrée, Gui, me and St Lys mayor of sports, St Lys Skate Park inauguration, Nov 22, 2002.

June, 2009. Crew cuts on the back deck of our Flushing house. Preparing to go to the ocean at Cape Henlopen State Park, Delaware, for one week instead of France (we'd make it over there the following June).

Howell tree house from my childhood.

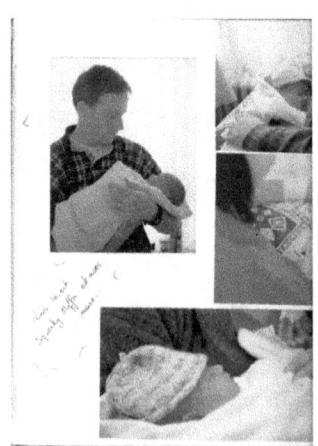

From Andrée's photo album. Gui's birth.

Scary sky one day during our Nov. 15-22 2002 construction of St. Lys skate park.

The boss builders: Me, Franck Floutier & Fabien Koudoyor, St. Lys skate park construction, Nov 2002.

Me and Guillaume on Gino's tractor. Last day taking Gino's barn down Oct. 25, 2003

Fowlerville High School Jazz Band, 16-yrs-old. (right, front)

Andrée & Gui, 1, on our apartment Balkon in Stuttgart.

Me on yearling Satin and Anne on Frosty, Fowlerville home, circa 1984.

Mom and Dad on back porch in Howell, circa 1976. I think they were fighting.

Me, at the skate park I built in St. Lys, France. Enjoying inauguration day. Doing a basic 360 from a kicker over the table. Nov. 2002.

Spring 2001 visit with Guillaume to Andrée's dad and stepmother, Henri and Yvette Lepérou in Paris.

Lifting Andrée's veil, Wedding Ceremony, April 21, 2000 at The Beechwood, Sparta, TN

Gui and Ben, Jan. 2009 at Flushing home.

Woods during 3 months of isolation on Rose's farm, circa August 1997.

Winter 1986 "Field Problem." Near Hanau, Germany.

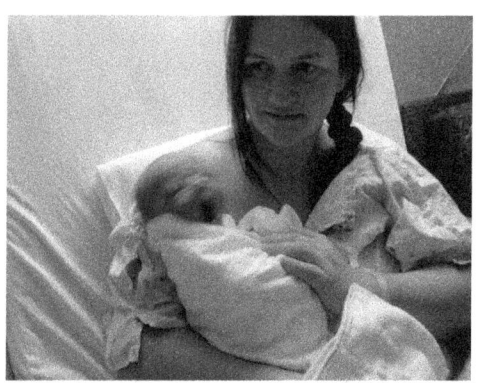

The most beautiful woman in the world, Andrée, with Ben just born (moving). January 17, 2004, Howell, Michigan.

New Years by ourselves on the TAT farm above Moundsville, WV.

Andrée in airport to return to Stuttgart from first USA trip together as engaged couple, Jan. 2000.

Born to Wonder   555

Dad and sons on quad at Dave Soehnlen's farm in Navarre, Ohio. Circa Oct. 2006.

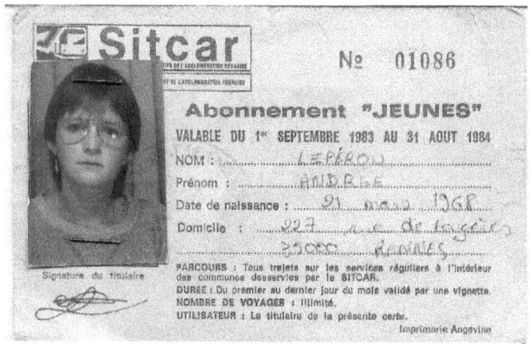

Andrée, 1983, who sent me that first letter from Rennes, France…

At my covered bridge in Belmont County, Ohio. Circa 2006.

21 Nov. 1999. Trip to Paris to make wedding rings.

Le Tour Eiffel. Oct. 16, 2002. Visit to American Consulate in Paris for Andrée's immigration to the U.S.

Gui, April 22, 2005.

Circa 2005. Revisiting the church near Stahlstown, PA where I was married, in 1993, and Andrée wanted to jump up and shout, "Stop! I'm the one!"

Happy. 7 Apr 2000, on top of La Basilique du Sacré Coeur de Montmartre.

Gui and Ben on TAT farm near campfire place.

At the White House, Spring 2010, on a D.C. day trip to renew Andrée's French passport.

Ben, 3. Moving into first house! May 2007.

Me and Ben. Aug. 3, 2006. St. Clairsville, Ohio.

L'arc de Triomphe from La Tour Eiffel at dusk, 21 Nov 99.

Our reflection, shop window in Ludwigsburg, near Stuttgart, Jan 2000.

Recommended Reading

Thousands of books have deeply inspired and encouraged me. I escaped through words into worlds almost as soon as I entered this one, straining to teach myself to read the nighttime stories my parents read to me at three or four. In my quest for completeness and understanding (and often, escape), I am grateful to the authors of works that I immersed and still immerse myself in. Most of the following are what I would call <u>inspirational</u>, however, as opposed to pure escape. At different times, I've needed different books.

The works on this list inspired me to become my highest good, and encouraged me to continue to reach for something more, by their ringing a bell of recognition inside me. Some have a mood I feel is conducive to "inner work," a nostalgia like a siren song, beckoning. Others, from <u>my</u> adolescence and childhood, took the place of an empathic mentor, reassuring me that I could align myself with something more significant than shallow external accomplishments. For you, cherished reader: <u>you</u> may glimpse a more nuanced portrait of <u>me</u> by contemplating the books and works I have responded to...

I'm hopeful you will find inspiration and encouragement in the following authors' work—just like I did. If someone asks, "How does reading fantasy and science fiction help me become?" I would talk to them a bit, trying to get a feel for where they were coming from, and then suggest books and authors I felt they might get something out of. Everyone is different; this is my list—I hope you find something in it for you.

*Where I say, '**and anything else**' about an author's work, I mean any other example of their work would easily convey "that special quality" about them I responded to. The titles I chose to list are the titles I currently have on my shelves. These are 'highly recommended.'*

*Saying, '**and <u>everything</u> else**' about an author's work means that I hold <u>all</u> of their work to be equally profound and capable of inspiring the very highest—in another reader like me... These are my 'highest recommendations.'*

My list constantly changes. Some highly recommended used to be highest. I'm sure your list changes with time, too, as you do.

No list can be complete until I die. I'll continue to encounter writing that I feel is top notch and which I relate to. In my life, I have dived into many genres of writing—science fiction, fantasy, mystery, westerns, mythology, classics, self-help, historical fiction, biographies, philosophy, metaphysics, spiritual, speculative fiction, literature and on and on. Each genre was rich and full and deep; the authors I found were lifesavers and truthsayers who whispered, "This... this... this." I'm sure I've read tens of tens of thousands of books and stories. I've re-read some of them multiple times. My mainstays, science fiction and fantasy, began with the captivating tales by Edgar Rice Burroughs and E.E. "Doc" Smith. I've always been drawn to fantastic, magical, hopefully beautiful worlds.

The following list is what I would give to you if I was going away forever (which I am) and was forced to scribble on a scrap of paper what I could remember having treasured…

David's Book List

The complete *Hyperion* series, by Dan Simmons.
Beyond Mind, Beyond Death, TAT Foundation Press.
Ender's Game, by Orson Scott Card.
Be As You Are: The Teachings of Sri Ramana Maharshi, David Godman, Editor.
The Essential Rumi, Coleman Barks, Editor.
The Honorable Schoolboy, and everything else, by John le Carré.
The Chronicles of Amber, and anything else, by Roger Zelazny.
Love Not Human, and anything else, by Gordon R. Dixon.
The White Dragon, and anything else about that world, by Anne McCaffrey.
Stranger in a Strange Land, and anything else, by Robert A. Heinlein.
All Creatures Great and Small, and everything else, by James Herriot.
Octagon Magic, and anything else, by Andre Norton.
The Fires of Paratime, and everything else, by L.E. Modesitt, Jr.
The Varieties of Religious Experience, by William James.
The Albigen Papers, Carillon, the audio recordings of university lectures and anything else, by Richard Rose.
The Golden Apples of the Sun, and anything else, by Ray Bradbury.
Star Trek episodes, and everything else, by James Blish.
The Hobbit, and *The Lord of the Rings*, by J.R.R. Tolkien.
The Poet, and everything else, by Hermann Hesse.
All the poetry and prose by Shawn Nevins.
Winesburg, Ohio, by Sherwood Anderson.
The Sun also Rises, and all the short stories, by Ernest Hemingway.
Moby Dick, by Herman Melville.
The Indispensable Calvin and Hobbes, and everything else, by Bill Watterson.
The Teachings of Don Juan, and all the related books, by Carlos Castaneda.
The Dragons of Eden, by Carl Sagan.

Children of Infinity, Roger Elwood, Editor.

The Turning Place, by Jean E. Karl.

The Song of the Lark, and <u>everything</u> else, by Willa Cather.

Drawing of the Dark, by Tim Powers.

A Wrinkle in Time, and everything else, by Madeleine L'Engle.

The Adventures of Huckleberry Finn, by Mark Twain.

Meditations, by Marcus Aurelius.

Discoveries: Fifty Stories of the Quest, Second Edition, Schecter & Semeiks, Editors.

Emergence: Labeled Autistic, and anything else, by Temple Grandin.

The Chronicles of Narnia, by C.S. Lewis.

The Justice Cycle, by Virginia Hamilton.

Foundation Series, and anything else, by Isaac Asimov

The Other Side of the Sky, and anything else, by Arthur C. Clarke.

The Canterbury Tales, by Geoffrey Chaucer.

<u>Any</u> play by Shakespeare.

"Lance Missiles"

Smells trigger an instant association for me. Diesel fumes transport me to a composite twelve-year immersion in Army culture and, at the same time, to one hot-and-sunny-turned-stormy frightening-in-retrospect ocean excursion afternoon on my uncle's sailboat off the coast of Fort Lauderdale. The following block of technical-sounding text takes me back to my two-year stint as a nineteen and twenty-year-old castaway in Germany; it's a nostalgic package bookmarked by this reminder. It has earned its "squatter's right" to remain here, in perpetuity.

If I hadn't told you this, you might have interpreted the missile paragraph as merely random, explanation-less as the word, "mayonnaise" in white font on the bright red back cover of Richard Brautigan's Trout Fishing in America. *Every leaving by every being seems "random" or explanation-less to others. When* you *feel it from the inside, nothing left by any being is meaningless. Everything comes from something. I think it was an undergraduate writing professor who told a class of us about someone asking Brautigan why he had put the word "mayonnaise" on the back of his book. Brautigan replied, "I always wanted to do that."*

I've got his book on my desk right now, next to my left arm while I'm typing this. I tried to find that account but gave up after five minutes. A three-ring binder hard copy of this manuscript is open in front of me, my arms resting on the pages, and I'm typing on the keyboard up there, just in front of the nice flat screen gently-used Dell computer monitor a kind-hearted friend, Shawn, from Alabama, sent me in a box last winter. I'm leaning back in the office chair Andrée got me for Christmas before I took two months off to start writing this book. Brautigan's book is backside-up, bright red back cover and the word mayonnaise on it. Brautigan, born in 1935, was an iconoclastic American writer who became famous and wrote several books and then became less famous and killed himself in Bolinas, California when he was forty-nine, the same age that Douglas Adams made his own unexpected departure.

"Tactical neutron bombs," is from an online source about the tactical nuclear artillery Lance *missile. I was a member of a Lance missile battalion while stationed at the U.S. Army base, Fliegerhorst Kaserne, from 1985-1987. I had the paragraph below at the end of my book's Word file throughout months of writing and compiling. I, of course, had considered writing about my time in the Army in Germany. As I returned to the manuscript of this book, time and again, day after day, I typed my new words in the blank space above that paragraph. It's been a goad for me to write further, covering things not yet covered, and a nostalgic reminder of those unsung yet forever felt Dark Ages of my ancient youthful past.*

Yearly qualifying launches at the NATO base in Crete, Greece.

Tactical neutron bombs. ENHANCED RADIATION WARHEAD, a specialized type of small thermonuclear weapon that produces minimal blast and heat but which releases large amounts of lethal radiation. The neutron bomb delivers blast and heat effects that are confined to an area of only a few hundred yards in radius. But within a somewhat larger area it throws off a massive wave of neutron and gamma radiation, which can penetrate armor or several feet of earth. This radiation is extremely destructive to living tissue. Because of its short-range destructiveness and the absence of long-range effect, the neutron bomb would be highly effective against tank and infantry formations on the battlefield but would not endanger cities or other population centers only a few miles away. It can be carried in a Lance missile or delivered by an 8-inch (200-millimeter) howitzer, or possibly by attack aircraft.

Model of the launch vehicles used in my unit

The End

Acknowledgements:

For my parents, Bill and Mary Jo Weimer, who had their shot at raising a family: I half-realize how fortunate I was to be born into your lives. Occasionally I fully appreciate it before slipping back into acceptance. *You* created a world that I could live in and take for granted and brag about and visit repeatedly in my adulthood. You gave me my foundation and springboard. I don't often call; I am living. My life whispers a profound "Thank you" I can never express.

Anne and Pat, dearest sister and brother—it was great growing up with you.

My sons, Guillaume and Benjamin, constantly remind me of the most important thing. I pray that I am able to hear them, and hear them and hear them each time they excitedly ask me to look at a bridge made of glued-together popsicle sticks or if I can throw a football with them.

My thanks to Andrée, a formidable person I'm fortunate to attach myself to with the words: "My wife." The word formidable means "wonderful" in French. She is. And she's formidable. She doesn't need my words to be wonderful. She's my number one supporter, standing in front of me in that line. She read my book before anyone else and painted the portrait of me for its cover; she is unfailingly encouraging and appreciative of my writing. She is wonderful and I have no idea what I did to deserve her.

Mike, our old new dog. Cats, Snowball and Rainbow, and their predecessors, Grizelda and Emerald. Lucky and Satin, my horses. My first dog, Daisy. Companions all—accepting my affection and tantrums equally.

To my friends: Yes, you're after these animals (you're not lesser, only different). Gino Costantini, best friend from teenage years to now. Peers on my path in life today and in my past—I bow, and remain bowed.

Now for those who have helped me make this book: *Your willingness to extend a helping hand is a constant source of wonder for me. Help is rarer than a snowflake in a furnace. Thank you.*

Michael Luce, bright-eyed and euphoric, troubled and unhappy, brave and anxious. First of my "test audience" readers to cross the finish line of reading *Portrait's* first draft. The kindest of my initial readers and an inspiring reminder to me that there <u>are</u> people who can emerge from the curl on a monster wave—against all odds.

Agustine Monge, Jr., critical, meticulous, persistent and prodding. Number two across the line. Still smarting from his comments, I am still more grateful for his efforts than I can convey.

Eric Clark, restrained (barely), demonstrative, taciturn, surprising ally in this book-writing effort. Critical help. Third across the finish line—a gold-colored bronze. Proofreader extraordinaire. *Merci, mon ami.*

Shawn Pethel, driven, kind, blunt, intelligent friend on the path. SOLID *is* real—for me. Hopefully one day for you, too.

Leonore Rodrigues, thanks for taking a stab.

Jeff Crilley, thanks.

Finally, **Richard Rose**: Thank you.

Index

A New Story..................................336
A Story With No People (told by God)..................................400
A terminal condition..................150
A.M.
	correspondence....60, 93, 105, 411
All of Me..75
An Appropriate Gesture\..................
	My Tribute to Richard Rose...429
Andrée and Me..........................342
Another.......................................151
Awhile...259
back in the States again..............243
Bob...
	correspondence.....................325
Carney..461
Coming Back Home...................503
D
	correspondence...............190, 209
Dad's Letter..................................58
Doppelganger.............................433
dream journal.............................267
Eons surround us.......................548
Extremes....................................176
Final Message............................528
going after one's goal.................465
Going South, by the Way............87
Group work................................423
Groups..422
I knew that there was something really wrong..............................373
I remember everything..............508
I wrote this on the S-Bahn.........275
If I had to say only one more thing..................................272
In the Valley of the Shadow of Death..................................179
Journal entries...........................283
Journal entry - August 4, 1996....257

Journal entry – December 7, 1996
....262
Just nodding...............................475
Just turns away..........................180
King Bacchus...............................99
M..
	correspondence.....................528
Micrographic surgery.................135
Mike...
	correspondence.....................229
Mike C...
	correspondence.....................201
Muteland............................176, 177
My Book List..............................563
My Own Private Tsunami, 2004..292
No Safety Net............................311
Ohgod..375
On Becoming a Modern Mystic..541
On Human Achievement...........259
Our House..................................468
Our Wedding Story....................181
Paul...
	correspondence.....................183
Point of Departure.......................78
Relativity Speaking....................119
Report..246
Run in the head.........................138
seizure on Suburban Ave..........254
sensory-deprivation tank...........251
Seven days in May......................46
Shane..
	correspondence........197, 202, 206
Shawn...
	correspondence..............223, 331
Starting Over Again, for the First Time..................................522
Strawman, starman...................142
Taking on...................................145
Ten Altogether...........................361
The Art of Breathing..................140

The One and Only Skate Park
    Project..................................300
The Truth......................................194
Three Months in Isolation............155
Tony..
    correspondence........................320
Two Ships....................................414
What happened?...........................355

what would you want to do with
    your life?..................................497
While Dancing the Viennese Waltz
   453
wild dogs.....................................287
writing-journal entries.................437
younger brother, Pat.........................
    correspondence........................114

www.ingramcontent.com/pod-product-compliance
Lightning Source LLC
Chambersburg PA
CBHW080526170426
43195CB00016B/2484